THE
TOP 100
DEVOTIONAL
COLLECTION

To my favorite
niece! Diana.
God Bless You Always:
Lovingly yours
Auntie Deb

THE
TOP 100
DEVOTIONAL
COLLECTION

The Top 100 Women of the Bible
The Top 100 Men of the Bible
The Top 100 Miracles of the Bible
The Top 100 Names of God
The Top 100 Women of the Christian Faith

BARBOUR
PUBLISHING

Print ISBN 978-1-62836-648-8

eBook Editions:
Adobe Digital Edition (.epub) 978-1-63058-085-8
Kindle and MobiPocket Edition (.prc) 978-1-63058-086-5

Bible translations used in each book of this collection are indicated beginning on page 503.

Published by Barbour Books, an imprint of Barbour Publishing, Inc., P.O. Box 719, Uhrichsville, Ohio 44683,
www.barbourbooks.com

Our mission is to publish and distribute inspirational products offering exceptional value and biblical encouragement to the masses.

Printed in the United States of America.

CONTENTS

THE TOP
100
WOMEN
OF THE BIBLE

INTRODUCTION

Read some Bible commentaries and you may see only minor references to events involving women. But the prophetesses, wives, sisters, and mothers of the Bible are strong, active, and often powerfully faithful. These people made a difference in the world, and without them, how much smaller our faith—and the biblical record—would be.

Read the scriptures, and you'll find women portrayed in politics and in the home, in the temple and in the workplace. No corner of human activity goes unreported by the Word. And nowhere does God denigrate women or their importance to the spread of the Gospel. Indeed, women are honored and blessed for their faithfulness to God.

In this book, *The Top 100 Women of the Bible*, you'll find women of all sorts. Some are strong and faith filled; others are weak or wicked. A handful hold positions of worldly importance, while others—simple peasants, really—have changed the world even more than their seemingly more powerful sisters. In these stories you'll admire one woman's faith, while wondering what another was thinking in the path she pursued. But each woman inspires, warns, or leads us. And her example can turn us away from sin or draw us closer to God.

As you read, draw from the lives of these women. Learn from them how to live faithfully in a fallen world. And as you turn to the scriptures that describe them, delight also in the Bible that brings them to you. For there, lived out before your eyes and placed in your hands to read again and again, is a record of what it means to be a faithful Christian.

God has a special place in His heart for women, as you'll discover from the ones who fill the pages of His Book.

ABIGAIL

His name was Nabal and his wife's name was Abigail.
She was an intelligent and beautiful woman,
but her husband, a Calebite,
was surly and mean in his dealings.

1 SAMUEL 25:3

Here is one of the Bible's great mismatched couples. Since it was the custom of the day to arrange marriages, Abigail had probably been wed to Nabal for his wealth, not for any meeting of the hearts. While she was a faithful and savvy woman, he was not only named "Fool" (the meaning of *Nabal*), his actions showed he was one.

Though women of that day generally had much less respect and authority than men, the Bible speaks highly of Abigail while recording only the mean-spiritedness and wrongheadedness of her husband. The two were certainly spiritually incompatible. While Abigail had faith, her husband had no time for God—certainly his attitudes and actions were not those of a faithful believer. Still, though theirs could not have been an easy relationship, resentment didn't crush Abigail's spirit. Instead, she used her many personal gifts and graces to bring the best to her household.

At the festive sheep-shearing time, the surly and greedy Nabal intentionally offended King David. Recognizing the danger, one of the wealthy landowner's servants knew whom to approach: he reported the situation to Nabal's wise wife. Immediately, Abigail understood the foolishness of turning down a polite request for support from the displaced David. Though the newly anointed king was fighting Saul for the throne, his warriors had protected Nabal's fields and clearly deserved some recompense. Food for his band of men did not seem an unreasonable request. Nabal had much, and the common custom of the day would have demanded that he share with those who had protected him and his household from harm.

Instead of wasting time arguing with her husband, Abigail prepared food for David's men and set off to approach their leader to make peace. She mounted her donkey not a moment too soon. On the road to David's camp, she met the warrior-king and his men, headed in her direction and intent on exacting retribution.

Abigail knew her husband's attitude had risked all his holdings and placed her in a difficult position—yet her dependence lay not on her spouse, but with God. Understanding that David was doing God's work and required her support, she provided it. That simple intervention and her humble words and attitude before Israel's anointed-but-on-the-run king prevented unnecessary bloodshed.

David immediately appreciated Abigail's faith and good qualities and praised God for her quick actions. If Nabal did not know how to recognize his wife's value, the king did. He turned aside his wrath because of this faithful woman's generous response.

While Abigail worked out a peace plan, her husband partied. She returned to find him drunk, so not until the next day did she explain how she'd spent her day. Hearing what his wife had done, the brutish Nabal literally had a fit—perhaps experiencing a stroke. A few days later, he died.

David saw Nabal's death as God's justice and immediately sought Abigail's hand in marriage. In a moment, faithful Abigail moved from a fool's wife to a king's bride.

In Abigail we see many examples of faithfulness. When difficult relationships become part of our lives, we can follow her example. Will bitterness and resentment overwhelm our faith? Or, like her, can we trust God will make use even of our hardest situations? Do we do the good that falls our way, knowing that God's wisdom will bring benefit to ourselves and others?

Though matched with an unbelieving spouse, Abigail remained faithful to her Lord. Like her, do we resist allowing unsatisfactory relationships to stall us out in our faith and continue on, trusting our God?

Humility clothed Abigail's strength. No radical, angry woman, she paved the way for all women of strength to walk humbly before their God and make peace in broken relationships. God alone brings tranquility to broken lives. Abigail experienced that, and so can we. And, like Abigail, we may find that when we've passed through the troubles, God gives us a better life than we ever expected.

ABIHAIL

Rehoboam married Mahalath, who was the daughter of David's son Jerimoth and of Abihail, the daughter of Jesse's son Eliab.
2 Chronicles 11:18

Abihail, whose name means "father is strength," was the daughter of Jesse's first son, Eliab, which means "God is father." She certainly had an impressive lineage, since her uncle David and his son Solomon became Israel's greatest kings. And Abihail married one of David's sons, possibly by a concubine.

Abihail's daughter Mahalath married a king, Rehoboam. But this mother's heart must have been saddened to watch the kingdom fall apart in her son-in-law's hands. Doubtless Mahalath also suffered as his wife, since Rehoboam had eighteen wives and sixty concubines. It couldn't have been a satisfying marriage.

Abihail proves that even a "premier family" background can't guarantee a trouble-free life. The Bible doesn't describe her sorrows, but we may easily read between the lines and understand that lineage isn't everything.

Today, it still doesn't matter if you hail from a family of great stature or a very humble one—troubles will come your way. Only God, the strongest Father, can protect His children and bring them through each storm. He is powerful enough to help us withstand each problem in life and bring us through safely.

ABIJAH

Hezekiah was twenty-five years old when he became king,
and he reigned in Jerusalem twenty-nine years.
His mother's name was Abijah daughter of Zechariah.
2 CHRONICLES 29:1

There are not many references to Abijah in scripture, but a very important one commends her son, the king of Judah: "Hezekiah trusted in the LORD, the God of Israel. There was no one like him among all the kings of Judah, either before him or after him" (2 Kings 18:5). Abijah's husband, Ahaz, surely never influenced his son to trust in God, for he increasingly worshipped the pagan gods and even closed Jerusalem's temple. If either of Hezekiah's parents positively influenced his faith, it would have been Abijah.

No matter what a child has experienced, one faithful parent can have a powerful influence for God. While her husband gave himself over to pagan gods, Abijah's quiet faith may have turned her son to the Lord. It is no different today. God still raises up the children of faithful mothers. The unfaithfulness of a father can even become a clear warning and sad contrast to a mother's faith.

No matter what challenges a mother faces, Father God always remains with her if she trusts in Him and prays faithfully for her child. Though a human father may fail, our Lord never will.

ABISHAG

Then they searched throughout Israel
for a beautiful girl and found Abishag,
a Shunammite, and brought her to the king.
1 KINGS 1:3

Abishag had an unusual job: keeping the old and infirm King David warm. And not just by covering him with blankets—the comely Abishag was expected to crawl into bed with the king. David's servants said to him, "Let her lie in thy bosom, that my lord the king may get heat" (1 Kings 1:2 KJV). That's exactly what happened, as Abishag "ministered" to David in a nonsexual way.

We have no biblical record of Abishag's feelings toward her job. Perhaps she was pleased to be chosen as the great king's personal body warmer. Maybe she found lying in bed with a dying seventy-year-old man distasteful. Possibly, her feelings shifted from day to day.

Our feelings toward our own responsibilities—at home, at church, at the office, wherever—can vary widely. But whatever we've been called to do, we should do to the best of our abilities. As the apostle Paul wrote to the church in Corinth, "Now it is required that those who have been given a trust must prove faithful" (1 Corinthians 4:2).

Dream job or nightmare, know that God has called you to this particular time and place. Do your best—and, if appropriate, pray for the chance to move on.

ACSAH

And Caleb said, "I will give my daughter Acsah in marriage
to the man who attacks and captures Kiriath Sepher."
Othniel son of Kenaz, Caleb's younger brother, took it;
so Caleb gave his daughter Acsah to him in marriage.
JUDGES 1:12–13

Caleb's declaration seems strange to us. How could he almost raffle off his daughter to the man who was successful in battle? But in Israel a victory in battle could pay off the bride price, which was owed to the father before the marriage. So maybe the man who really wanted her got her through his bravery.

And the man who won Acsah would have been a good choice as a husband. Othniel became the first major judge of Israel, the leader who freed the nation from subjection to Cushan-Rishathaim, king of Aram (see Judges 3:8–9).

As part of her dowry, Acsah received dry land in the Negev. So she told her husband to ask Caleb for another field, one that had springs. When Othniel didn't do it, Acsah took on the task herself and got the land. Surely Caleb was a loving father, being generous with his daughter.

What did Acsah think about this marriage? We don't know. Sometimes brides were asked for their consent, or perhaps Caleb saw this as a way to give her the man she wanted without asking money from his brother. Either way, what a method for finding a good man! No woman today would think of it.

Like Acsah, we may find romance in unexpected places. Let's remember to let God do the choosing for us—and no matter what the time or situation, we will be blessed. After all, look at the husband Acsah got.

ADAH

Lamech married two women,
one named Adah and the other Zillah.
GENESIS 4:19

Lamech, a man of Cain's line, became the first polygamist in Hebrew history, marrying both Adah and Zillah. Though it might have seemed fun for him, what a wreck it made of women's lives for centuries. For though he was the first to do it, he was hardly the last Hebrew to think more wives were better. From his example came a long history of marital confusion, conflict, and disobedience to God.

The Bible describes Adah and Zillah's children but does not tell us how their mothers got along. Yet if Hebrew family history is any example, they probably didn't have a smooth life. For God intentionally commanded that one man should marry one woman (see Genesis 2:23–24). Those who disobey God pay a price, so marital harmony probably wasn't a part of this tenthold.

Lamech's rebelliousness didn't limit itself to marriage. He took vengeance by killing a man who wounded him. Like Cain, he overreacted and failed to seek God's counsels.

From Adah's story we learn the importance of following God's laws. What must it have been like to live with this angry man? And how could Adah share her husband with Zillah, yet understand God's complete commitment to those who love Him?

This quick picture of Adah's life teaches us to let God control our marital choices. In Him, we'll experience the warm, loving relationship we're looking for. Apart from Him, we may feel only pain.

AHINOAM

Abigail. . .went with David's messengers and became his wife.
David had also married Ahinoam of Jezreel,
and they both were his wives.
1 SAMUEL 25:42–43

Nearly every time the Bible mentions Ahinoam, David's other wife, Abigail, appears, too. Though Ahinoam was first married to David, the wealthy Abigail seems to overshadow her. Ahinoam didn't even come from an impressive city, for Jezreel was only a town in the hill country of Judah. Since her name means "gracious," perhaps Ahinoam never made trouble—but she had to feel slighted.

With David and Abigail, she traveled to find protection among the Philistines so Saul could not destroy her husband. While David went to war at the Philistine king Achish's side, the Amalekites raided his home at Ziklag, capturing Ahinoam and Abigail. David returned early to rescue the women. What a joyous moment it must have been for Ahinoam to see her husband and his troops, for she might otherwise have become a slave.

After Saul died, David became king of Judah, and Ahinoam bore his son Amnon. Amnon would grow up to dishonor his half sister Tamar, but Ahinoam may never have known that—since she's not mentioned in the story, she may no longer have been living.

Ahinoam has only a small part in biblical history, though she was the wife of a king. She may have been quiet and faithful, getting less press than David's other wives. Like Ahinoam, can we take a backseat? Or would we become resentful, needing front-page attention to be satisfied?

ANNA

There was also a prophetess, Anna,
the daughter of Phanuel, of the tribe of Asher.
She was very old; she had lived with her husband
seven years after her marriage, and then was a widow until she was eighty-four.
She never left the temple but worshiped night and day, fasting and praying.
Coming up to them at that very moment,
she gave thanks to God and spoke about the child to all who were
looking forward to the redemption of Jerusalem.
LUKE 2:36–38

This is all we know of Anna—you've just read the whole biblical account of her. But it is enough to give a thumbnail sketch of her character and devotion to God.

Her name means "gracious," and grace seems to have permeated her life. She married, but after her husband died, she dedicated the rest of her life to God. Hers was a service of many years; at eighty-four, this widow was still constantly in the temple. She may have lived within the temple confines or perhaps lived nearby and simply spent most of her time "at church." Certainly her fellow Jews would have honored her for remaining single and dedicating her life in devotion to her Lord.

As a prophetess, Anna held a position of honor. Clearly, God spoke to her as she remained in the temple, worshipping, fasting, and praying. Is it any wonder that when the Messiah first entered the temple, she walked in on Him and His parents? Surely God led her there, to be blessed by the sight of the One she had long hoped for. Immediately recognizing Jesus, she thanked her heavenly Father and spread the news to others.

Like Anna, do we need to remain single and live in the church? Hardly. But whether we are married or single, we need to ask if we share her single-hearted devotion to God. Are our spirits so tuned to His voice that we hear and obey His call in our lives? When His Spirit whispers to us, is that still, small voice drowned out by the cares of the world, or are we so attuned to Him that we can obey at a moment's notice?

When we share Anna's ability to obey, we'll discover how gracious God has been to us. His spiritual blessings will spill over into our lives and others', too.

ATHALIAH

When Athaliah the mother of Ahaziah saw that her son was dead,
she proceeded to destroy the whole royal family
of the house of Judah.
2 CHRONICLES 22:10

Athaliah, daughter of Israel's wicked king Ahab, is one of the bad babes of the Bible. Instead of being a godly mother, scripture tells us she encouraged her son Ahaziah to do wrong (see 2 Chronicles 22:3). After becoming king of Judah, Ahaziah joined his uncle Joram, king of Israel, in a battle against Hazael, king of Aram. Following the battle, the warrior Jehu, who had already killed many of Ahaziah's heirs, wiped out Judah's king, too.

When Athaliah heard the news, she immediately sought to kill off all her grandchildren so she could gain the throne. Once she did that, her claim would be reasonably uncontested. This power-hungry woman literally sacrificed her family on the altar of her own ambition.

Had she been successful, the line of the Messiah would have been destroyed. So God placed a faithful woman, Jehosheba, near Ahaziah's son Joash. This half sister of the dead king saved her nephew and his nurse, hiding them in a bedroom. For six years the child king remained in hiding at the temple while his grandmother ruled (see 2 Kings 11:2–4).

In the seventh year of Athaliah's rule, the priest Jehoiada introduced Joash to the Israelite war commanders. They covenanted with Joash and protected him while Jehoiada anointed him king. Hearing the noise of her grandson's coronation, Athaliah called out, "Treason!" but the troops ignored her objections and obeyed the priest. Removing her from the temple, they took her life in Jerusalem's Horse Gate.

Athaliah's actions are shocking. Few of us would sacrifice our children or grandchildren to gain power. But sometimes our fast-paced, twenty-first-century existence causes us to shortchange our family of time and attention. If our jobs always come first, we travel incessantly, or we place our children too often in the hands of others, perhaps we've begun to make the same mistake as this wicked queen. We don't have to serve a pagan god or want to rule a nation in order to get our priorities mixed up.

If we fail, we aren't bad babes in the mold of an Athaliah—but we do need to repent, confess our wrongdoing, and find a way to make changes. Maybe that means reorganizing our time, refusing a promotion, or working a part-time job. Whatever it takes, let's not sacrifice our families to get ahead. Because, in the end, we won't be ahead at all—either with our loved ones or with the God we serve.

BATHSHEBA

One evening David got up from his bed and walked around on
the roof of the palace. From the roof he saw a woman bathing.
The woman was very beautiful, and David sent someone to find out about her.
The man said, "Isn't this Bathsheba, the daughter of Eliam
and the wife of Uriah the Hittite?"
2 SAMUEL 11:2–3

Bathsheba must have been a real looker—a king was unable to resist her when he got a look at her from the roof of his palace. David sent messengers to bring the Hittite's wife to him, and then David slept with her.

Scripture never seems to ask how Bathsheba felt about this. Was she offended at being commandeered by a king, or was she flattered that he had noticed her? Whatever her response, she didn't have any say in her situation.

Then, to her horror, Bathsheba discovered she was pregnant. In Jewish law, the punishment for adultery was death for both the man and woman. Fear must have struck this beauty's heart. Even if she thought to pass the child off as her husband's, Uriah had been away at war and surely would know the child was not his. So she told David, and the king came up with a solution. He called Uriah back to Jerusalem, assuming Bathsheba could entice him into a romantic interlude—and the problem would be solved.

But the king, who had fallen into this sin when he should have been on the battlefield, did not count on the uprightness of this foreigner who had taken the Jewish faith to heart. Coming to the king as ordered, Uriah refused to so much as cross his own threshold. When others were camping out, readying for war, he would not sleep with his wife in Jerusalem. David made him drunk, but he still would not go home. Seeing no other alternative, and perhaps feeling growing guilt over his own sins, the king changed plans, commanding that Uriah should be placed in the heat of battle and left defenseless. The plan worked: Uriah died.

Bathsheba lost her husband at the connivance of her lover. Perhaps she initially felt relief at getting out of a very tight situation. But if her husband treated her tenderly, as Nathan's accusation of David in 2 Samuel 12:3 implies, she must at least have felt some emotional conflict.

When Bathsheba's short period of mourning ended, David made her his wife. In a few months, she gave him a son. Though the Bible never blames Bathsheba for the sin between herself and the king, she shared in his grief when God punished David by taking the life of their child. But God quickly blessed her with another son, Solomon, who was loved by God and would become one of Israel's greatest kings. She also had three more children (see 1 Chronicles 3:5).

Years later, Bathsheba stood up for her son's right to become king of Israel when his older brother Adonijah sought to grab the throne from the aging David (see 1 Kings 1:5–21). At her request, David kept his promise to make Solomon king (see verse 29).

Still, Bathsheba must have been more kindhearted than politically savvy, for when Adonijah asked to marry Abishag, who'd been David's nurse in his old age, Bathsheba pled his case to Solomon. Solomon deeply loved his mother, if the great respect he treated her with is any sign (see 1 Kings 2:19). But he immediately saw that his brother was again threatening his throne, denied her mission, and had his brother killed.

Bathsheba's story is that of the second chance. Her life was turned upside down by a king's desire, and she was seduced into sin with him. But she didn't stay there. God gave her another chance as David's wife, and the rest of the biblical account shows her as a caring mother and concerned wife. No one accused her of further sin, and she lived blamelessly.

When God gives us second chances, we can follow in Bathsheba's footsteps. As long as we are alive, we are on a mission for Him. Will we make ours as successful as hers? Remember this: Bathsheba is one of only four women mentioned in the lineage of Jesus (see Matthew 1:6).

BILHAH

Laban gave his servant girl Bilhah
to his daughter Rachel as her maidservant.
GENESIS 29:29

Had Bilhah known what this change in her life would mean, perhaps she would have run the other way. For serving Rachel meant more than looking after her and running her errands. When Rachel did not have children, she decided her husband, Jacob, should follow a custom of the day and take Bilhah as a concubine. According to the custom, Rachel would adopt Bilhah's children as her own. But instead of establishing a happy family, Rachel began a competition with her sister, Leah, Jacob's other wife, who had borne him four children. Eventually their face-off saddled Jacob with twelve sons and a far-from-peaceful household, disrupted by two wives and two concubines, Bilhah and Zilpah. Though God used Bilhah to raise up some of Jacob's sons, who would eventually become leaders of the twelve tribes of Israel, her role was not a thoroughly pleasant one.

God established marriage as between one man and one woman (see Genesis 2:24) to reflect His covenant. Ignore that, and your family life, like Jacob's, can become as confused as the plot of a modern-day soap opera. But God blesses marriages that reflect His covenant love. Faithful love ends soap-opera lives and establishes a firm family that can serve God well. Would that describe your family? If not, what can you change?

CANDACE

So he started out, and on his way
he met an Ethiopian eunuch, an important official
in charge of all the treasury of Candace,
queen of the Ethiopians.
This man had gone to Jerusalem to worship.
ACTS 8:27

In the first century, unlike today, *Candace* was not a name, but a title. It belonged to the queen mother of the ruler of an area the Greeks called Meroe, around the upper reaches of the Nile River. The people of that nation felt the king was so holy he was good for nothing temporal, so Candace carried out many of his earthly responsibilities. As a trade center, her country was very wealthy, so her powerful official in charge of the treasury would have had the ability to travel to the Holy City for worship.

From this trip, he brought back more than Candace would have expected— the news of the Messiah struck the Ethiopian eunuch's heart quickly, and he accepted Christ. According to tradition, the woman he served also accepted Christ.

We never know, when we share our faith, what important person may be touched by our words. Though our friends might be humble, we may connect with a powerful man or woman who needs to come to faith. With a single witness, like Philip, God's Word may reach a person of influence. Speak up!

CHLOE

My brothers, some from Chloe's household
have informed me that there are quarrels among you.
1 CORINTHIANS 1:11

We don't really know anything more about Chloe or her household than this verse reveals, but she was probably an important woman, since she's named as the head of her household. And we know a lot about her church from Paul's letters to the Corinthians.

Chloe didn't belong to a perfect congregation—division, not unity, was the hallmark of the Corinthian church. Everyone wanted to choose a leader to follow: Paul, Apollos, Peter (Cephas), or Christ. No one seemed to be in charge.

Obviously some faithful believer from Chloe's household, perhaps even Chloe herself, became troubled by the quarrels that divided the Corinthian church. A report got back to Paul that these foolish arguments had separated believers. When he heard, he confronted the young Corinthian Christians, even generally naming the source of his information. Because Paul received this report, he was able to save the church from an implosion.

Should we find ourselves in her situation, Chloe gives us an example. *Do we drop a word in a church leader's ear or keep it to ourselves?* we wonder. God provides us with the wisdom for each problem we face. By speaking now, we could defuse a serious problem later.

COZBI

And the name of the Midianite woman
who was put to death was Cozbi daughter of Zur,
a tribal chief of a Midianite family.
NUMBERS 25:15

Her name means "deceitful," and deceit had helped her seduce the Israelite leader Zimri. But it doesn't seem Zimri was slow in following her, and he wasn't the only one of his people who fell. Many followed the Moabite and Midianite women into sexual sin while worshipping their idols.

God's anger burned brightly against His people, and retribution followed. He commanded Moses to kill the leaders and show off their bodies to His people. Meanwhile a plague broke out among the Israelites, perhaps to give them a picture of the deadliness of their sin.

At that moment, in front of everyone, Zimri led Cozbi, the daughter of a

Midianite chief, into a tent—the sort of place for prostitutes. While the rest of Israel repented of their sins, Zimri marched right by the whole assembly of Israel, ready to continue his wrongdoing.

Aaron's grandson, Phinehas, quickly took care of the problem by running a spear through the couple's bodies, taking their lives. With the deaths of this willfully disobedient pair, the plague on Israel stopped—but not before twenty-four thousand people died.

Cozbi shows us that sin doesn't pay. God may be patient with us, but He does not wink at disobedience. If we boldly continue in sin, it will eventually bring terrible judgment. Worse yet, our wrongs may affect many innocent lives as well as our own. Are we willing to take that risk?

DAMARIS

A few men became followers of Paul and believed.
Among them was Dionysius, a member of the Areopagus,
also a woman named Damaris, and a number of others.
ACTS 17:34

Luke mentions some men who accepted Christ as their Savior when they heard Paul's message in Athens; then suddenly he drops in the name of a woman: Damaris. Perhaps, as John Chrysostom, a fourth-century archbishop of Constantinople, thought, she was the wife of Dionysius. Others suggest she was an important, educated woman, perhaps from another country. But in an age when women rarely got much mention, she must have had some stature to be listed immediately after a member of Athens' ruling council. Indeed, for her to be present at the meeting where Paul spoke would indicate she had some unusual importance.

The next time someone tells you women aren't important in the Bible, remind them of Damaris, Priscilla, and the Marys of the Gospels. People may write women off as being unimportant, but God never does. He includes them at every point in His story of redemption.

You, too, are important to God. Whether or not you're ever mentioned in a book or known worldwide, God cares for you. His Son died for you to draw you to His side. No one for whom Jesus died is unimportant or forgotten.

THE DAUGHTER OF PHARAOH

Then Pharaoh's daughter went down to the Nile to bathe,
and her attendants were walking along the river bank.
She saw the basket among the reeds
and sent her slave girl to get it.
She opened it and saw the baby.
He was crying, and she felt sorry for him.
"This is one of the Hebrew babies," she said.

EXODUS 2:5–6

Being important doesn't mean everyone knows you. Though this woman was the daughter of Egypt's powerful ruler, the Bible never records her name or even that of her father. All we know of Pharaoh's daughter is her position and the fact that she had a kind spirit, for when she saw the baby Moses floating in a basket, her heart opened to him. The woman knew he was one of the Hebrews whom Pharaoh had commanded to be killed, yet this woman disobeyed her father and bravely saved the baby, who ironically became the prophet God used to free the Hebrews from Egypt's grasp.

In time, the princess adopted Moses, opening doors of education and power to the young Hebrew. Because of the training he received in Egypt's court, he was probably in a better position to rule over the rebellious Hebrews. As an educated man, he would be able to record the first five books of the Bible for all people to read through the ages.

Though we don't know that she ever came to faith, the princess played an important role in God's plan. Without her, the tiny baby would not have had the advantages he needed. But God placed the right woman in the right place at the right time, and He moved her heart to help young Moses. Her name may have disappeared, but her good work hasn't.

We're probably all familiar with someone who doesn't know God but performs many good deeds. An unsaved family member may help us out and enable us to fulfill God's will in our lives. Do we recognize that this, too, comes from God? God may use many different people to accomplish His goal, but He does not abuse them. He never forces them to have faith in Him.

Many daughters of Pharaoh live in our midst, unconsciously guided by their Creator to do His will. Yet they have no spiritual connection to Him. Do we reach out to them, hoping to help them understand His role in their lives? We can rejoice when they come to know Him, too.

DEBORAH, REBEKAH'S NURSE

Now Deborah, Rebekah's nurse, died and was buried under the oak
below Bethel. So it was named Allon Bacuth.
GENESIS 35:8

Did you know the name of Rebekah's nurse? Genesis 24:59 told us she accompanied her charge to their new home with Jacob, but it did not mention the nurse's name. Now, at Deborah's death, we finally can put a name with a position.

Deborah spent plenty of years with her mistress. Perhaps Rebekah appreciated Deborah's kindness to her when she was tiny. Rebekah would have still needed her nurse as she grew, because Genesis 29:29 makes it obvious the bride had no maid. For a while after Rebekah's marriage there were no children to change in the middle of the night, but Deborah helped her charge settle into a new way of life. When children did come, Rebekah desperately needed the nurse, since she had twins. Deborah was always there to dandle a crying child or wrap him in a blanket.

Many of us have received help with our children from a friend, teacher, or youth-group worker. Do we appreciate the effort that goes into caring for children? Like Deborah, many give tender care to youngsters who are not theirs. Will it be a thankless task or one that receives appreciation? Rebekah appreciated her nurse: The name of that oak under which Deborah was buried became Allon Bacuth: "oak of weeping."

DEBORAH THE PROPHET

Deborah, a prophetess, the wife of Lappidoth,
was leading Israel at that time.
She held court under the Palm of Deborah
between Ramah and Bethel in the hill country of Ephraim,
and the Israelites came to her to have their disputes decided.
JUDGES 4:4–5

God doesn't explain Himself. Suddenly, in a time when Israel has become unfaithful to the Lord, the scripture proclaims the position of Deborah, the only female to rule Israel during the years of the judges—that era between Joshua's death and Saul's accession as king. Deborah was not just a minor judge; she was an authoritative woman who decided disputes between men and held the power common to all Israel's judges. Nor was this a piece-of-cake leadership for Deborah. Israel had been subjugated by the Canaanite ruler Jabin of Hazor, yet the Israelites never brought an army against him until this woman was in charge.

Deborah became the answer to the prayer for help her people sent up to God as they saw the Canaanite commander Sisera heading their direction followed by nine hundred chariots.

God had chosen an unusual leader in Deborah, a very strong-minded woman who was also very close to Him. (Just read her interaction with her military commander, Barak, in Judges 4:6–9, and you'll see she was used to being obeyed.) As a prophetess, Deborah would have heard and communicated God's will to His people. Though she is not the only prophetess in the Bible, she alone ruled Israel. Not only that, she effectively led her country during wartime, when many people might have chosen a man for the job. After all, she couldn't command an army, could she? In a way, she showed the doubters that she could.

God had given her authority, and Deborah obeyed His will implicitly. Maybe you've known a powerful woman like her. An in-charge kind of person, this judge rallied her leaders and the people against the Canaanites. Barak, chosen by God as the country's military commander, seems shy and retiring compared to the confident prophetess. God spoke to her, and she told Barak all He had commanded. Deborah did not make decisions based on her own desires, but on God's direction for His people. And she showed greater faith than her commander. She was probably a "God says it, I've heard it, that settles it" kind of believer, because she did not understand why Barak balked at going to war when God told him to. Barak flatly refused to go to battle without Deborah. That may have been fueled in part by an understanding that following her was following God, but doubt also played its role. Because of Barak's hesitancy, God commanded that a woman would take the life of Sisera.

Deborah accompanied the ten thousand troops who attacked Sisera's forces and gave them the order to go into battle on God's chosen day. When Barak and his men obeyed, God caused the Canaanites to flee before them. But this was something other than Barak's happiest moment. Deborah's prophecy of Sisera's death was fulfilled when Jael, a woman, killed Sisera in her tent, after all the Canaanite troops had been destroyed.

Judges 5 records Deborah's wonderful song celebrating the victory. Together with Barak, she gave the credit to God. From her verses we get a clear picture of how sad life had been under the Canaanites. She described herself as "a mother in Israel," but she had also been something of a mother *to* Israel, encouraging, warning, and setting the pace for a whole nation. She praised Jael for killing the enemy with a tent peg and hammer. Through Jael, God ended the fighting and gave Israel a complete victory.

Need a picture of a confident, powerful woman who was also humble and faithful? Look to Deborah. Being an unlikely leader didn't stop her in her tracks, and it doesn't need to stop a Christian woman today, either. She can be a successful mother, leader, and wife, if she's obeying God every day.

DELILAH

Some time later, he fell in love with a woman
in the Valley of Sorek whose name was Delilah.
JUDGES 16:4

Say her name, and most Christians get an immediate picture of a sultry woman and desire gone wrong.

The physically powerful Israelite judge Samson fell for this beautiful and desirable Philistine. As wise as he must have been, Samson had one fatal flaw: He never chose well when it came to women—those foreign temptresses forbidden by God's Law always seemed to claim his attention. His marriage to a Philistine woman had ended disastrously, yet here he was, becoming romantic with Delilah. Maybe he thought it was okay as long as they didn't marry, but he should have read God's Law a bit more carefully.

No sooner had Samson fallen for this bad babe than the rulers of her nation asked Delilah to do some spying for them. The Israelite was so strong that they couldn't capture him, and they had a series of grudges against him. So they asked Delilah to find out what made her lover so powerful. Once they had his secret, the rulers planned to make him a slave.

Maybe it was the money that made this bad girl decide Samson was expendable. Eleven hundred shekels from each of five rulers was no small amount of cash in that day. Delilah must have decided that all she needed was money, not love, and in her greed, she betrayed Samson completely.

At the same time, you have to wonder what Samson was thinking. Perhaps he enjoyed playing romantic games, but didn't he get the least bit suspicious when his beloved asked how his strength could be subdued? Didn't he figure that she was a Philistine and that others could be putting her up to something? He'd had a very similar experience with his wife, before their marriage fell apart, so you'd think he had to have had an inkling, especially when he gave Delilah three false answers. You wonder how many times God had to show Samson the same lesson for him to learn.

But when Samson should have left off dallying with Delilah, he kept coming around—giving her the opportunity to nag him endlessly. "You don't love me," she complained, and evidently he couldn't bear to see her unhappy. Eventually she wore him down, and he admitted that his vow as a Nazirite—and the long hair that was part of it—gave him his strength. Cut his hair, he said, and he'd be as weak as any other man.

The Philistines took complete advantage of this information. Delilah got Samson to sleep in her lap, and a man came in to shave his head. Awakened, Samson soon stood powerless, and the Philistines made him a sightless slave. But these temporary victors forgot that hair grows again! And grow it did.

Inside their temple, the Philistine rulers and an assembly gathered to rejoice at the capture of Israel's strong man. In the midst of their reveling, the crowd called Samson out to perform for them.

"Now the temple was crowded with men and women; all the rulers of the Philistines were there, and on the roof were about three thousand men and women watching Samson perform" (Judges 16:27). Adorned with a new head of hair and imbued with renewed strength, Samson stood before them, prayed for strength, pushed against the pillars with all his might, and brought down the pagan temple, killing himself and everyone in it.

Who knows if Delilah was also there amid the crowd? Though she didn't seem like the religious kind, perhaps she had taken that opportunity to rejoice at the effectiveness of her sexual powers.

Look at Delilah, and you get a clear picture of how *not* to live. Need an example of what loose living will get you? She's the poster child for it. The pain she caused someone who loved her ran so deep that Samson didn't mind sacrificing his life, if he could destroy the pagan temple he'd been taken to. Samson had been used by an immoral woman who evidently felt no guilt at betraying him.

Delilah backs up God's Word, which commands a faithful husband-and-wife lifestyle. Romance is not a game, but a lifelong commitment. And any sexual activity outside marriage leads to heartbreak. Maybe yours won't come as quickly as Samson's did, and you may not die, but you can count on some pain when you don't live God's way.

Just ask Delilah—if you can find her under all that rubble, that is.

DIANA

So that not only this our craft is in danger to be set at nought;
but also that the temple of the great goddess
Diana should be despised,
and her magnificence should be destroyed,
whom all Asia and the world worshippeth.
ACTS 19:27 KJV

Diana, also known as Artemis of the Ephesians, isn't, strictly speaking, a woman. She was a pagan fertility goddess who got the apostle Paul and his disciples into a lot of trouble. When Paul's ministry to Asia took off, Ephesian craftsman Demetrius the silversmith saw his nice little business of creating Diana idols going down the drain. So he called a guild meeting and got the backing of his fellow silversmiths to take action.

If they didn't act, the magnificent temple of Diana would suffer, the silversmith warned. Today that temple is known as one of the seven wonders of the ancient world. In Demetrius's day, thousands of pilgrims flooded Ephesus to worship there, but he knew they wouldn't if the pilgrims became Christians. So Demetrius and his coworkers started a riot. Only the intervention of the city clerk saved Paul and his men, and Paul wisely moved on to Macedonia.

Diana led a lot of people into idolatry and away from the gospel. But her magnificence and her following only lasted a short time. After all, no one worships her today. Are you putting your faith in something that won't last long or in the God who created the universe and will never fail you? Don't follow a Diana when you can draw close to the eternal Lord.

DINAH

Now Dinah, the daughter Leah had borne to Jacob,
went out to visit the women of the land.
GENESIS 34:1

In this simple sentence begins one of the saddest events of the book of Genesis. Dinah, a young and thoughtless girl, comes to a new country and unwisely goes out to seek friendship with the pagan women there. On the way, she is raped by Shechem, son of Hamor the Canaanite who was ruler of the city that shares his son's name. Afterward, when young Shechem belatedly decides to marry Dinah, he unknowingly brings disaster on his people.

Hamor, pushed on by his son, approaches Jacob to arrange a marriage. It was a common practice of that day, and the heartbroken Jacob listens. But before he makes a decision, Jacob's furious sons intervene. How can they give their sister to an unbelieving man? Surely Jacob must have struggled with this idea, since his father had commanded him not to marry a Canaanite—but what could he do that would benefit his daughter? Though Jacob is unaware of it, his sons come up with a wicked suggestion: If the Canaanites will accept circumcision, Jacob's sons inform Hamor and Shechem, they will accept the marriage. But there's more to their offer than meets the eye.

Hamor agrees, but not because he's had a sudden conversion experience—he's interested in getting his hands on Jacob's wealth, the large herd of sheep in his possession. But the ruler has not reckoned with the brothers' anger. The siblings plot to kill the male Shechemites while they are still in pain from the surgery. Three days after the circumcision rite, Simeon and Levi, Dinah's full brothers, begin the attack on the city. All the male Shechemites are killed, and the Israelites loot the city. In order to keep his family safe, an angry Jacob moves his family out of the area.

Double sorrow was Dinah's: her rape and her brothers' precipitate actions. Scripture gives us no clue about her life after this event, but it was surely changed forever. Dinah's life shows us that sometimes even simple, foolish decisions impact us powerfully. We need to be careful how we walk and with whom we associate.

DORCAS

*In Joppa there was a disciple named Tabitha
(which, when translated, is Dorcas),
who was always doing good and helping the poor.*
ACTS 9:36

This faithful woman lived in the seaport city of Joppa, outside today's city of Tel Aviv. *Dorcas* was actually a Greek translation of her Aramean name, *Tabitha*, which means "gazelle." Scripture doesn't tell us if her frame matched her name, but it does say she leapt to do good works for others.

While Peter was visiting nearby, Dorcas died. Her fellow Christians readied her for burial and sent a message to the apostle, who hurried to them. The sorrowing believers showed him examples of Dorcas's generosity. After clearing the room, the apostle raised Dorcas from the dead. What a day that must have been for Dorcas, the other Christians, and even for those who heard about the miracle and came to faith in Christ.

Do our lives testify to our faith as clearly as Dorcas's did? Living, dying, or being resurrected, she glorified her Lord. If we died, would our fellow Christians want to have us back as a powerful Christian testimony?

DRUSILLA

*Several days later Felix came with his wife Drusilla,
who was a Jewess. He sent for Paul and listened to him
as he spoke about faith in Christ Jesus.*
ACTS 24:24

Drusilla may have been a Jewess, but she wasn't a very faithful one. Felix was not her first husband—after only a year of marriage, she had left her husband Azizus, king of Emesa, to go with Felix.

Perhaps this lack of faith isn't surprising, considering her background. Drusilla was a great-granddaughter of Herod the Great and daughter of Herod Agrippa I. Ruthlessness, not belief, was a hallmark of her family.

When the Jewish leaders brought Paul to Felix, demanding that he be punished for troublemaking, Paul took the opportunity to witness to Felix and his wife. They never came to faith, perhaps because they had another agenda—Felix was hoping for a bribe, not seeking the truth. Perhaps his wife had the same attitude.

It does not matter if we come from a long line of faithless people. Each of us has an opportunity to accept Christ through a personal witness, a book, or the testimony of a preacher. Will we remain in a godless past or reach out to Jesus through faith? It's our choice alone.

ELISHEBA

Aaron married Elisheba,
daughter of Amminadab and sister of Nahshon,
and she bore him Nadab and Abihu,
Eleazar and Ithamar.
Exodus 6:23

Aaron's wife doesn't get a lot of press in the Bible. Her brother Nahshon gets more mention as a leader of the tribe of Judah, but Elisheba would have been well known to the Israelites, as wife of their high priest.

Elisheba had a wonderful husband, but her children were another matter. Leviticus 10:1–2 describes the death of her first two sons, Nadab and Abihu. Instead of following God's directions in worship, they pridefully made an unauthorized incense offering. As punishment, God consumed them with fire. Some scholars suspect that Nadab and Abihu had been drunk at the time, a condition that led them to take such unholy actions. The scholars' reasoning comes from the fact that soon after this incident, God warned Aaron and his sons not to drink before worship (see Leviticus 10:9).

Not every woman of God has children who make her proud. Every child is different, and while one may delight a mother, another may bring much sorrow. Christian mothers may faithfully witness to their children yet be unable to turn them away from wrongdoing.

But, as in the case of Elisheba, God may also provide a believing mother with a great blessing. Eleazar, Elisheba's third son, honored his parents' faith, following in his father's footsteps. He became the head of the Levites and then high priest in Aaron's place.

ELIZABETH

But they had no children, because Elizabeth was barren;
and they were both well along in years.
LUKE 1:7

The godly Zechariah and his wife, Elizabeth, both from the priestly line, were aging people who seemed unable to have children. What a shock, then, for Zechariah to receive a visit from an angel who told him he and Elizabeth would have a son, John.

Is it any wonder Zechariah doubted? But saying the equivalent of "Oh no, you must be wrong" to an angel? What was he thinking? God showed a sense of humor, making the expectant father unable to speak until the birth of the promised child—perhaps so he wouldn't say any other silly things.

Some time later, Mary visited Elizabeth. Mary's relative immediately knew this young woman would bear the Messiah and praised her Lord for it. What a time of fellowship this must have been for these women who bore children with missions unlike any others in the world.

When Elizabeth had her son, the relatives assumed the couple would follow custom by naming him after his father, Zechariah. But the angel had declared his name would be John, and that's what Elizabeth called the boy. The family questioned the father. As soon as he wrote, "His name is John," Zechariah's mouth was opened and he praised the Lord. From that moment on, all could see that John was somehow special. They wondered what the Lord would do with his life.

Elizabeth must have been amazed at the turn life took for her. Long accustomed to being thought barren, she was suddenly given a special child who would serve God in an unusual way. How blessed she must have felt!

When life takes unexpected turns for us, will we be a doubting Zechariah or a faithful Elizabeth? Trusting God takes a lot of faith when our lives are suddenly turned upside down. We have two choices: We can simply allow God to control whatever happens, or we can spend time worrying about the future.

Since we can't change the future—and God has it all under control anyway—we may as well follow Elizabeth's example. We, too, may find God has given us unexpected blessings.

ESTHER

Mordecai had a cousin named Hadassah, whom he had
brought up because she had neither father nor mother.
This girl, who was also known as Esther,
was lovely in form and features,
and Mordecai had taken her as his own daughter
when her father and mother died.

ESTHER 2:7

Displeased with his queen, Vashti, King Xerxes of Persia put her aside to seek out another. After a nationwide search, his eye lit on a woman who had been exiled to his land. But Esther never told the king about her Jewish family background.

Perhaps Xerxes' find-a-queen contest was fun. With many other girls, Esther was brought to the court and given beauty treatments. Maids waited on her. Then came the night when Esther was sent to the king as his concubine. Though He is never mentioned in this book of the Bible, God certainly guided Esther's life—for of all the women, she was most attractive to this far-from-virtuous king. Xerxes made her queen.

In time, Esther's cousin, Mordecai, uncovered an assassination plot against the king. But instead of honoring the Jew, the king raised his courtier Haman to the highest position among the nobles. When Mordecai refused to bow down to Haman, the king's favorite hatched a plot to rid himself of Mordecai and the Jewish people. Haman got the king's unwitting approval to wipe out his queen's race.

Mordecai revealed Haman's plan to Esther and told her to go to the king. Since anyone who approached the king without invitation could be put to death—and Esther had not been called for a month—the queen feared for her life.

Mordecai warned her, "Do not think that because you are in the king's house you alone of all the Jews will escape. For if you remain silent at this time, relief and deliverance for the Jews will arise from another place, but you and your father's family will perish. And who knows but that you have come to royal position for such a time as this?" (Esther 4:13–14). Esther promised to go, if her cousin would fast and pray for her.

Esther went before the king, who spared her life and offered to do anything she wanted. She asked only that he and Haman attend two banquets—one that day and the other on the morrow. Though thrilled to be so honored, Haman's attitude soured when he saw Mordecai again. A furious Haman ordered a gallows built for his enemy.

That night, an insomniac Xerxes had the record of his reign read to him—and discovered that Mordecai had never been rewarded for his faithfulness. In an amusing turn of God's plan, the king asked Haman what should be done to someone the king wished to honor. Haman, assuming that person was himself, suggested a kingly robe and a royal horse be brought, and that a nobleman lead the honored man through the city, declaring why the king was honoring him. What a shock to Haman when he was the nobleman commanded to honor Mordecai that way! But Haman had to obey.

When Haman attended the queen's second banquet, Esther revealed the plot to the shocked Xerxes. The king commanded his courtier be immediately hanged on the gallows built for Mordecai—and ordered Mordecai to write a new law protecting the Jews. So for one day, the Jews were able to fight off their enemies. They killed every one, leaving their people safe and instituting the holiday of Purim.

God's name is absent from Esther's book, but His hand on her life is apparent. And so it will be with us: when we face trials, we can also trust He is working out something positive on our behalf.

Though becoming a king's concubine may not have seemed good, God watched over Esther so that she became queen. Even our most traumatic moments are in God's hands. When we trust Him, nothing can go terribly wrong.

Obedient Esther acted on God's will, heeded her cousin's wise counsel, and was safe. Likewise, God protects us, especially when our faithfulness puts us in danger. If He can stay the hand of a powerful ruler, what will He not do for us?

EUNICE

I have been reminded of your sincere faith, which first lived in your grandmother Lois and in your mother Eunice and, I am persuaded, now lives in you also.
2 TIMOTHY 1:5

For Timothy, faith was a family affair.

His mother was a believing Jewess (see Acts 16:1), and his grandmother also believed. According to the references Paul makes to this young man's family, Timothy had received an important spiritual inheritance, though his father, a Greek, had evidently never come to faith. These two female relatives show how important a woman's witness can be to her children and grandchildren. Despite certain influences of unbelief, a son or grandson can learn from a faithful life lived out before him.

Today, many single moms wonder how they can influence their sons for Christ. They need not fear. God can work in a family where even just one member is yielded to him. Obedience, prayer, and the blessings God provides to His faithful people are a powerful influence on a young life. When doubts seemed to trouble Timothy, Paul did not hesitate to remind his young friend of his family history. Clearly, the apostle knew what a powerful influence a mom can be.

EUODIA

I plead with Euodia and I plead with Syntyche
to agree with each other in the Lord. Yes,
and I ask you, loyal yokefellow, help these women
who have contended at my side in the cause of the gospel.
PHILIPPIANS 4:2–3

These verses show us that though these two women had "contended at [his] side in the cause of the gospel," Paul felt their contention with each other endangered their church. Certainly their interpersonal problem was serious enough to deserve a mention in his letter to the Philippians.

But don't be mistaken: these weren't heretics or women of small faith. Even sincere, hardworking Christians can allow contention to separate them. Paul pled with their fellow congregants to help Euodia and Syntyche find a solution to their difference of opinion.

Not much has changed in the years since Paul's ministry ended. Christians still have heated debates, whether they're over what color to paint the church or how to witness for Christ. Paul warned another church, "Do not let the sun go down while you are still angry" (Ephesians 4:26).

Anger will come, but it need not remain and damage one's faith, the church, and the Christian witness in the world. All of us need to quickly talk to each other and end the anger. If we need help, it's as close as wise counselors in our congregation.

EVE

Adam named his wife Eve, because she would become
the mother of all the living.
GENESIS 3:20

The first woman had it made. Specially created by God for her husband, she never had to worry about arguments over who was going to do the dishes or how to spend the family money—there were no such things in Eden. She lived and worked in a beautiful God-planted garden and got to speak to God personally every day. Nothing was wrong with Eve's life.

But one day, a serpent whispered in Eve's ear, tempting her to eat fruit from the one off-limits tree in their beautiful backyard. That crafty snake told Eve that God was holding out on her—if she ate that luscious produce, she'd know good and evil. Though she had no clue what that meant, it sounded interesting to Eve.

Had she been able to see where this was heading, Eve would have stopped that critter in his tracks. But knowing evil looked so good from her perfect place. So not only did she eat the forbidden fruit; she passed it on to Adam, too. The results of her choice, though, weren't quite what she expected. It wasn't as if she suddenly had God's power to know all things—instead, evil entered all human lives through her one bad choice.

Now, when God came into their garden, the couple disappeared. He had to seek out the embarrassed pair who suddenly understood the impact of a bad choice. How guilty they must have felt! But how could they hide from the Lord of the universe? He cornered them, and the blame game began: Adam blamed Eve; Eve blamed the snake.

All offenders, from the snake on up to Adam, received a curse intimately related to their situation. For Eve, it was pain in childbirth and being ruled by her husband—you might say the "battle of the sexes" started here. For Adam, the curse meant having to work hard to make the land yield a crop. For both, eternal life was now a thing of the past. After God banished Adam and Eve from their lovely garden, He placed a flaming sword to guard their access to the tree of life.

Once outside of Eden, Eve had two sons, first Cain and then Abel. Following the pain of childbirth, she rejoiced at the gifts God had given her—two sons—but sin was already affecting her entire family. The pain of childbirth was just the beginning of her anguish.

As adults, both her sons came to God with an offering. Abel brought the best of his flock, while Cain brought his produce. God approved of Abel's offering, while turning aside Cain's. From Genesis 4:7 it's obvious that God's approval has more to do with Cain's heart than the quality of his physical offering. But the firstborn became terribly angry and, as children will, took it out on his sibling. He killed the approved one, Abel.

What sorrow Eve must have felt. Doubtless, all the promise she felt at Cain's birth was dimmed. She had lost her younger son, and God had condemned her older one to wander the earth. Yet God renewed his promise by giving Eve a third son, Seth. Of course, no child can take the place of another, but Eve again felt God's love and comfort. And through Seth came the line of salvation, in Noah and his family.

We know no more of Eve's family life than this, but all women can relate to her failings, hurts, and hopes. Just as she is the first woman, from whom all others spring, Eve's life speaks to all of us. Our doubts, sins, and experiences parallel hers. Like her, we may make hasty choices that separate us from God. But like her, we discover that though we desert God, He will not give up on us. He is always calling us back to the garden of His love.

GOMER

When the LORD began to speak through Hosea, the LORD said to him,
"Go, take to yourself an adulterous wife
and children of unfaithfulness,
because the land is guilty of the vilest adultery
in departing from the LORD."
So he married Gomer daughter of Diblaim,
and she conceived and bore him a son.
HOSEA 1:2–3

Talk about taking your work home with you! That's what the prophet Hosea did when he married a faithless woman, Gomer. But God had a plan: He wanted to show Israel just what their unfaithfulness to Him looked like. So He gave His people a practical view of it by having the prophet marry a woman who would seek out other men and bear illegitimate children.

Gomer's second and third children were probably those of her lovers, not her husband. Each child had a name with a meaning. The name of her first son, Jezreel, means "God scatters," a warning to Israel about what was to come. The first daughter was named Lo-Ruhamah or "not loved." And Lo-Ammi, the last son, has a name that means "not my people." Sometime following their birth, Gomer left her husband to live as a prostitute. Her actions picture the increasing distance between God and His people. Just as Gomer's sin separated the prophet and his wife, Israel's worship of pagan gods parted the Lord and His people.

Eventually both Gomer and the Israelites were brought to an impasse. After all her wild living, Gomer ended up a slave. But God commanded the prophet to love her again, so His people who were also about to be enslaved would comprehend how much He loved them. Obedient Hosea bought Gomer back, just as Jesus bought us out of our sin. With great tenderness the prophet returned his wife to her home and commanded her to be faithful.

We cannot know if Gomer appreciated her husband's compassion. Israel did not immediately repent, and perhaps Gomer didn't either. But her fall and reinstatement give today's Christian a clear picture of how much God loves His erring people and the extent to which He will go to reclaim their love. He does not hold grudges, but calls the wrongdoer to make an about-face and come to Him again.

Have you failed God? He will never fail you. Turn in repentance, and draw near to the One who has never disappointed His beloved. No matter what you've done, He offers forgiveness. Just ask—He's been waiting for you all along.

HAGAR

Now Sarai, Abram's wife,
had borne him no children. . . .
So. . .Sarai his wife took her Egyptian maidservant
Hagar and gave her to her husband to be his wife.
GENESIS 16:1, 3

Perhaps Sarai meant well, but when she tried to generate God's promised child by giving her slave to her husband, she created a relational mess for everyone involved.

Poor Hagar had nothing to say in the situation, and Abram simply went along with his wife's desires. But the plan went miserably awry. As Abram's second wife, Hagar's position became worse, not better. Once she conceived, she despised Sarai and brought trouble down on herself.

Though Sarai had caused the dissension in the family, she blamed Abram for the situation. Abram, who truly loved Sarai and probably simply sought peace in his own tent, left the solution to the problem up to Sarai. She decided to mistreat her slave, so the pregnant Hagar finally fled. Over the desert, she headed for her home in Egypt, though she had little chance of completing the journey.

In the desert, the angel of the Lord appeared to Hagar and turned her back from the dangerous trip, promising she would have a son and that her descendants would be "too numerous to count" (Genesis 16:9). He also prophesied division between Hagar's son, Ishmael, and the child of promise, Isaac.

Fourteen years would pass before Isaac was born, and the division between Sarah, as God had now named her, and Hagar grew even wider. When Ishmael mocked young Isaac, Sarah insisted that her husband, now called Abraham, send the youth away. This time, Abraham went to God, who told him to do as Sarah wished. And once again, God promised that Ishmael would father a nation.

Hagar left with her son. They traveled until they were exhausted, and death from thirst seemed imminent. But God intervened yet again to provide well water. And God continued to watch over Ishmael, who became the father of the Arabs.

The mistreated Hagar seemed deserted as she twice headed off into the desert. But even though she made mistakes and the people around her mistreated her, God never ignored her. At key points, He protected and guided her and her son.

So it can be for us. Life may turn us on our ears, but nothing we experience is beyond God's wisdom or control. With Him, we are always safe, comforted, and protected. He will never leave or forsake us.

HANNAH

[Elkanah] had two wives;
one was called Hannah and the other Peninnah.
Peninnah had children, but Hannah had none.

1 SAMUEL 1:2

Did all the women in the Bible pick on those who couldn't have children? No, not really. But from the biblical record, it seems to have happened often enough. Perhaps God was showing His people why polygamy isn't part of His plan.

Though Hannah's husband, Elkanah, loved her deeply, that only seemed to make her situation worse. Elkanah's second wife, the jealous Peninnah, kept picking at the childless favorite until Hannah completely despaired and would not eat.

When they made their annual visit to the tabernacle, Hannah poured out her heart to God. Though she had probably prayed often before this, now she made a special promise: if God would give her a son, she would give the child back to Him to serve Him. She wanted her son to take the Nazirite vow—a sign of special dedication to God—as Samson had.

Even during her heartfelt prayer, more pain came Hannah's way. Eli, the priest, confronted Hannah, accusing her of being drunk. She had to explain that it was her deep need, not wine, that had made her pray silently, yet with her lips moving. The chastened priest believed Hannah and sent her on her way, blessing her. Then Hannah felt peace in her heart as her face shone and she ate once again.

Soon, Hannah received the answer to her prayer. She conceived, and in time had a son, whom she named Samuel—which means "heard of God." The next year, when her husband wanted her to visit the tabernacle again, she promised to give Samuel to the Lord's service, but not until he was weaned. Since there was no way to keep milk in that era, children were usually weaned around three years old. So Samuel would have had those early years of influence by a godly family, especially his mother. Though Samuel was very young, Hannah must have had a powerful impact upon him, for he became one of Israel's greatest prophets. He led Israel, spiritually, through the important age of the founding of the monarchy.

Hannah kept her promises to her husband and to God. Once Samuel was weaned, she brought him and a generous offering to the tabernacle. After the offering was made, she gave her son to Eli to raise and train in the priesthood.

This amazing woman must have felt sorrow at leaving her child, yet the words from her lips were all praise for the Lord who had brought the situation to pass. She glorified Him for His deliverance, feeling as if she had won the battle with the arrogant Peninnah. Her prayer showed deep devotion to God and trust that He was in charge of all that happens on the earth. Perhaps that was why she could leave Samuel with Eli, though his own sons had fallen into wickedness and would be with young Samuel in the tabernacle. She trusted that God would fulfill all she wanted for her son.

Though her contact with Samuel was limited to the annual visit, Hannah faithfully showed him her love, providing him with a gift from home—a robe, which he would have worn every day and remembered her by.

Eli prayed for Hannah and her husband, and they had five more children. The barren woman became fully blessed, because she trusted in God and committed all of her life—even her relationship with her miracle child—to Him.

Isn't Hannah a woman you'd like to meet in heaven? Can't you relate to her on many levels? Her pain has been yours, even if you haven't had trouble conceiving, because relationships are so often complex and hurtful. Like her, you've had to give some treasured things up to God and trust that He would bless you for your sacrifice. You've taken risks for Him and hoped you'd never regret them.

This wonderful mother who almost wasn't one is a beautiful picture for every godly woman today.

HEPHZIBAH

Manasseh was twelve years old when he became king,
and he reigned in Jerusalem fifty-five years.
His mother's name was Hephzibah.
2 KINGS 21:1

"My delight in her" was what Hephzibah's name meant, and though she may have been delightful, her son Manasseh certainly wasn't. Though his father, Hezekiah, sought God and followed him, the boy went the opposite direction, until his name became a byword for evil.

Manasseh returned Israel to pagan worship that was worse than that of the godless nations that previously inhabited the land (see 2 Chronicles 33:9). Only when the Assyrians captured him and brought him to Babylon did the king repent. Though he returned to Jerusalem and reestablished faith in Yahweh, he never successfully wiped out pagan worship practices.

Scripture does not tell us how Hephzibah felt about her son. Perhaps she encouraged him in his wrong practices. Or maybe she wept for his unfaithfulness—and her faithful prayers led to her son's eventual return to God. Either way, her story reminds us that no child is so far away that God cannot reach him. Bringing the lost to Himself is God's plan, even for our own straying children.

HERODIAS

For Herod himself had given orders to have John arrested,
and he had him bound and put in prison.
He did this because of Herodias, his brother Philip's wife,
whom he had married.

MARK 6:17

As another of the bad babes of the Bible, Herodias had a checkered career when it came to marriage. She'd married her uncle, Herod Philip—but when his brother Herod Antipas visited the couple in Rome, he enticed Herodias to leave her husband and marry him. Herod Antipas's position as tetrarch of Galilee and Perea was near that of a king, so she furthered her own career by going with him. Seemingly, scripture's condemnation of such a relationship (see Leviticus 18:16) did not matter.

But when John the Baptist told Herod the marriage was unlawful, Herodias's marital situation suddenly became very important. It wasn't that Herodias wanted to do right—she just wanted to get rid of a critic. But Herod did not (see Mark 6:19–20).

So the manipulative Herodias had her daughter by her first husband—not identified in scripture but known to history as Salome—dance erotically for Herod. Pleased, Herod offered the girl whatever she wanted. What she requested was what her mother wanted—John the Baptist's head.

When people say that how you use your sexuality doesn't matter or that divorce is really okay, remember Herodias. Faithful living before God is built day by day, piece by piece. When we are faithful in the most basic things—like our marriage commitments—we build a good life.

HULDAH

Hilkiah and those the king had sent with him went to speak to the
prophetess Huldah, who was the wife of Shallum son of
Tokhath, the son of Hasrah, keeper of the wardrobe.
She lived in Jerusalem, in the Second District.

2 CHRONICLES 34:22

When a prophetess spoke, she had to speak the truth—all the time (see Deuteronomy 18:20). And this prophetess did just that, no matter what message God gave her.

As Judah's King Josiah refurbished the temple, his men discovered the Book of the Law. These commands of God had been overlooked for years, when the people of the land had completely fallen into pagan practices.

Confused, the king sent to Huldah to ask what he should do, and she did not withhold the truth. Huldah prophesied that the faithless nation would suffer disaster. But because Josiah had humbly turned to God, it would not occur in his lifetime.

Huldah must have felt compassion for the faithful king whose people would suffer God's wrath. That didn't change the truth, though, and she spoke the bad news faithfully. But can't you almost hear the gentleness in her voice as she describes God's mercy on the king?

Like Huldah, we need to speak the truth—never harshly but always faithfully. Sometimes we need to bear bad news, but we must also remind people of God's mercy. We may not be prophets, but God can use us to speak to others. Are we faithfully portraying His message?

JAEL

Sisera, however, fled on foot to the tent of Jael, the wife of Heber the Kenite, because there were friendly relations between Jabin king of Hazor and the clan of Heber the Kenite.
JUDGES 4:17

As Israel's commander Barak led his men into battle against the Canaanites, a mysterious woman took a hand in the history of God's people.

The Israelites won the battle. Fleeing on foot, the Canaanite leader Sisera unwittingly leapt from the frying pan into the fire. Jael's husband was a Midianite and had good relations with the Canaanites, so Sisera figured he had found a safe haven when he came to their camp. Perhaps being hidden by a woman seemed particularly safe. Who would barge into her private tent to play "general, general, who's got the general?"

Though Jael hid Sisera in her tent, gave him a drink, and covered him, she had a big surprise for the man. Canaan's commander asked this woman to lie about seeing him, but her only lie was to him. For the bloodthirsty Jael violated her people's laws of hospitality, which required her to protect a guest. Instead, once Sisera fell soundly asleep, Jael used a mallet to drive a tent peg through Sisera's temple.

Interestingly, scripture does not portray Jael as one of the bad babes. Deborah's song of praise pictures her as a heroine (see Judges 5:24–27). Though scripture provides no commentary on Jael's personal morality, Deborah's words approve the salvation she brought to a nation. Surely we must assume God somehow worked in this woman.

Why did Jael suddenly become so vicious? We can only guess. But through her, God fulfilled Deborah's prophecy to the doubting general Barak in Judges 4:9: God handed Sisera over to a woman.

We may ponder Jael's thoughts and actions and wonder what God says through her. But when we look at the larger picture, we can be certain God was in control, protecting His people. Whether Jael was an Israelite who married an unbeliever or whether she was a stranger to God, she became part of His plan.

Just as God acted for Israel's good in the Old Testament, He does so for us today, too. No matter how strange or dangerous our own position, we can be sure God has not left us alone. As we obey Him, He may even use a Jael to bring blessing into our lives. Whenever we entirely trust ourselves to His hands, we are safe.

JAIRUS'S DAUGHTER

Then a man named Jairus, a ruler of the synagogue, came and fell at Jesus' feet, pleading with him to come to his house because his only daughter, a girl of about twelve, was dying.
LUKE 8:41–42

A distraught father approached Jesus, begging him to save the life of his young daughter. Though we don't know the girl's name, we can tell how much Jairus loved her. For though he was a leader in his synagogue and Jesus was a controversial figure, this father set aside fear for his position to seek help for his dying daughter.

Jesus agreed to help and turned toward Jairus's house. But at that moment, a woman who had suffered from bleeding all the years Jairus's daughter had lived approached Jesus. She had faith that a simple touch of Jesus' clothing could heal her.

How horrified Jairus must have been when Jesus stopped to heal the woman. Didn't Jesus know Jairus's little girl, the apple of his eye, lay breathing her last breaths? What a stressful few minutes it must have been for the synagogue ruler. But worse was to come. News arrived that his daughter was dead, the messengers advising Jairus not to "bother" Jesus (see Luke 8:49).

But for Jesus it was no bother. He simply encouraged the synagogue ruler to believe and moved on. When they reached the house, Jesus immediately calmed the wailing family members and ignored their mockery when He told them she was "asleep" (Luke 8:52). Then He took the girl's hand and called her to get up. She immediately obeyed, amazing her parents.

What would it have been like to be one of the few people Jesus raised from death? This young girl must always have been special. For the rest of her life, others would have pointed her out because of this event. What importance must she have placed on her own life, knowing God had brought her back from death.

Scripture never says how long or how faithfully this woman lived. Nor does it say how much she appreciated her father's actions on her behalf. But we can assume she never forgot the blessing Jesus gave.

Do we understand how importantly God views each of us? We probably won't be raised physically from the dead—but He has raised us from spiritual death to life in Him. What amazing value our lives must have, if the King of kings died just for us. What more do we need to understand how important we are to Him?

Like this nameless girl, we have been touched by Jesus. Let's live for Him!

JEMIMAH

The first daughter he named Jemimah,
the second Keziah and the third Keren-Happuch.
Nowhere in all the land were there found women
as beautiful as Job's daughters, and their father granted them
an inheritance along with their brothers.
JOB 42:14–15

Her name meant "daylight," and after the long, hard night of suffering her father had, is it any wonder he found joy in her? For Jemimah was the first daughter born after God ended Job's suffering and blessed his life even more than before. Though no child could replace the ones he'd lost, he must have found new delight in Jemimah and her sisters Keziah and Keren-Happuch, along with their seven unnamed brothers.

Since scripture rarely cares much for physical beauty, we can, perhaps, assume that Jemimah also had a spiritual beauty that reflected her father's faith. For how could she have failed to pick up on the joy her father found with God? Job had experienced the Lord's greatness, which must have affected all that he said about God and His blessings.

Whether or not God replaces something we have lost, He can bring us new joy. No matter what our past, we can always delight in the new life He offers day by day.

JEPHTHAH'S DAUGHTER

*When Jephthah returned to his home in Mizpah, who should come out
to meet him but his daughter, dancing to the sound of tambourines!
She was an only child. Except for her he had neither son nor daughter.
When he saw her, he tore his clothes and cried, "Oh! My daughter!
You have made me miserable and wretched, because I have
made a vow to the LORD that I cannot break."*

JUDGES 11:34–35

Jephthah made an ill-considered promise to God, one that took the form of a
bargain: You bring me home as a victor, and I will make a sacrifice of the first
thing that crosses my threshold to greet me.

What was I thinking? he must have asked himself when his daughter danced
across the threshold, rejoicing at his return. That thoughtless promise had to be
fulfilled at the loss of his only child. His brave daughter agreed to follow through
on her father's promise, if for two months she could grieve with her friends in
the mountains.

Though the Bible says Jephthah "did to her as he had vowed," interpretations differ as to whether the girl was killed or perhaps given to God in some
other fashion—perhaps as a temple servant who would never marry. Either
way, Jephthah never delighted in grandchildren. But his story is a cautionary
one. Let us all beware what we promise God, and may we never try to bribe
Him with our obedience.

JEZEBEL

*While Jezebel was killing off the LORD's prophets,
Obadiah had taken a hundred prophets
and hidden them in two caves, fifty in each,
and had supplied them with food and water.*

1 KINGS 18:4

If the child Jezebel had gone to school, her report card might have read "Does
not play well with others." She is one of the Bible's *really* bad babes, a manipulative woman who just had to have her own way. Ever wonder what a completely
conscienceless person looks like? Here she is.

This Sidonian princess married Ahab, king of Israel, and spread the corrupting influence of her pagan gods to the chosen people of the one true God.
In the end, Ahab did more to provoke the Lord than all the other kings of Israel
who'd gone before him (see 1 Kings 16:33).

Perhaps Jezebel didn't want to hear how bad she was, because she decided to kill off as many of God's prophets as she could (see 1 Kings 18:4). But she didn't catch Elijah. In time, God sent Elijah to the king, to confront Ahab about the pagan priests and prophets imported by Jezebel. The prophet commanded the king to bring the pagan leaders to Mount Carmel, where Elijah proposed a duel between himself and Baal's prophets. They would seek to discover who was more powerful—Baal or God—as the two sides would begin a sacrifice and call on their respective deities to light the fire.

No matter what the Baal worshippers did, their sacrifice would not ignite. Taunting them, Elijah made the challenge harder on himself—and God. He had the Israelites cover his wood with water, jars and jars of it. Then, instead of making a spectacle, he simply prayed. And God's fire fell from heaven, igniting the sacrifice. After that, Israel knew who was really God.

When Jezebel heard what had happened, she wanted to kill Elijah, too. He had to flee, but God protected him from the wicked rulers.

Sometime later, Ahab tried to get a vineyard owner, Naboth, to sell his land to make room for a kingly garden. Naboth rightly refused to give up his inheritance from God. When Jezebel found her husband sulking, she promised to get the land for him—by setting up Naboth. On a day of fasting, she arranged to have two men accuse the honorable Naboth of cursing God and the king. The punishment? Stoning to death. Such an end Naboth suffered, all so Jezebel could get his land for her husband.

Then God sent Elijah to the queen with a message: He confronted her with a murder accusation and promised that where Naboth had died, she would die, too. Worse yet, dogs would eat her body. But not immediately.

When Ahab died in battle against the king of Aram, Jezebel manipulated her sons, Ahaziah and Joram, who also became kings of Israel. So she remained powerful for about ten years. Her sons were wicked rulers, much like their father.

But Elijah's prophecy did not go unfulfilled. In time, God raised up Jehu to kill off Ahab's line. Jehu killed Joram, who had succeeded to the throne after his brother died from injuries from a fall. Then Jehu, the new king, fulfilled God's prophecy concerning Jezebel—he had her thrown down from her window, where her blood spattered the wall and she was trampled by horses. When servants went to bury her, there was very little left. The men who reported back to the king merely told him of Elijah's prophecy.

"Crime doesn't pay" might be the moral behind Jezebel's life. Her defiance of God got her nowhere. And when she turned to a criminal act, God prepared punishment for her. Though many years passed between Elijah's spoken words and Jezebel's death, God never forgot.

God doesn't forget our deeds, either. When we obey Him, He protects us, as He did Elijah. When we do wrong, we reap a bitter reward.

Are you frustrated by the wicked and powerful? Let's remember we have not read the end of their story. Like Jezebel, they may be storing up disaster for themselves.

JOANNA

Jesus traveled about from one town and village to another,
proclaiming the good news of the kingdom of God.
The Twelve were with him, and also some women who had been cured
of evil spirits and diseases: Mary (called Magdalene) from whom
seven demons had come out; Joanna the wife of Cuza,
the manager of Herod's household; Susanna; and many others.
These women were helping to support them out of their own means.
LUKE 8:1–3

We're left with many questions about Joanna. This passage and Luke 24:10 tell us all we know of her. Though scripture doesn't recount her personal history, we know she was important to Jesus' earthly ministry, since her generous giving helped make it happen.

Some commentators assume Joanna was a widow, since she freely followed Jesus. Cuza would have held an important position in Herod Antipas's household, watching over all the tetrarch's household affairs. If Cuza was still alive, he must have been sympathetic to the Gospel, to allow his wife such freedom. Perhaps he was thankful Jesus had healed his wife.

Whatever her marital situation, Joanna provides an excellent example of generous giving. Because she and the other women faithfully continued in this support role, the Gospel went out to the world. Do we think our financial support is small or unimportant? Take another look at Joanna and be thankful for the opportunities we have to give.

JOB'S WIFE

His wife said to him,
"Are you still holding on to your integrity?
Curse God and die!"
JOB 2:9

Not exactly the "supportive wife" was Job's mate. The cruelness of these words has forever branded her as an unfeeling woman who could not bear her husband's suffering or trust that God would bring good out of it.

But let's not join Mrs. Job in her insensitivity. Before her stood a man suffering with all of his anatomy—even his breath stank. Her future, along with his, seemed to have landed in a cesspit. She had lost all her children and her hope for future security. Her husband's wealth seemed lost to them. Grief burdened her soul.

Since sudden death was seen as punishment for cursing God, Job's wife encouraged him to blaspheme the Lord and end the pain quickly. As she sought a quick way out, Satan used Job's most intimate family member as a tempter. Fortunately, even through his pain, Job understood that taking her advice would only make things worse. He decided his life lay firmly in God's hand—and he would leave it there. Job would not try to manipulate God.

When Job's suffering ends, God blesses him again, making him richer than ever before. The Lord even gives Job ten more children (see Job 42:13). How like God to turn a heart from sorrow to joy, through trust in Him!

Since Job's wife is not directly mentioned again, some have assumed Job's post-trial children to be by another wife. But if Job's first wife was still with him, joy may have filled her heart at her husband's recovery. And God may have blessed her, too, with the thrill of those new lives.

From Job's wife we learn what *not* to do spiritually. Trials and troubles, whether irritating or overwhelming, come to all. From great trials, however, even greater faith may grow—if we don't give in to Mrs. Job's despair.

Look at the wonderful experience Job ultimately had with God. Though his suffering and the incessant blathering of his friends fill most of the book that bears his name, in the end Job understood the priceless depths of God's greatness.

As we deeply trust in God, we follow in Job's footsteps. Clinging to the Lord, we discover nothing can separate us from Him. Holding on to our integrity, we discover God's instead.

JOCHEBED

The name of Amram's wife was Jochebed,
a descendant of Levi, who was born to the Levites in Egypt.
To Amram she bore Aaron, Moses and their sister Miriam.
NUMBERS 26:59

Scripture only mentions her by name twice, but through her children we have a clear picture of the kind of mother Jochebed was. Moses became the Old Testament's premier prophet, while Aaron supported him as high priest and Miriam became a prophetess. What a godly influence Jochebed must have been from her children's earliest days.

When Pharaoh declared that all the male Hebrew babies should be killed, Jochebed decided to save Moses. Hiding him as long as possible, she then placed the baby in a rush basket in the Nile River and allowed his sister to hide and watch over him.

How much faith it must have taken for Jochebed to float her son on the river and await his salvation! What fear she must have felt as her baby lay there!

But God's plan was better than Jochebed's wildest dreams: He sent an Egyptian princess to find the boy; Miriam, standing nearby, got to bring her mother to the princess, who made Jochebed the baby's nurse. So the faithful Hebrew mother raised her own child—and obviously trained him in faith. Where else would Moses have gotten his knowledge of the Lord? Certainly not from the pagan priests who filled the Egyptian court.

Jochebed did a good job, too. Moses never forgot her faith lessons, and years later stood up for his enslaved people. When, as a newly called prophet of God, Moses resisted the call, the Lord even provided him with a mouthpiece in his brother, Aaron. Together these boys would do their mama proud, proclaiming God's truth to a whole nation. The books of the Bible penned through Moses begin the Bible's history and tell of God's claims on the lives of believers.

In time, Miriam, too, would join her brothers in a key place of praise and leadership (see Exodus 15:21; Micah 6:4).

When modern society tells you motherhood isn't important, remember Jochebed and her children. The children you tenderly nurture today could tomorrow lead others to Christ through their faithful words and actions. When a woman immerses herself in God, her influence extends around her like ripples in a pool—and who better to be touched by that faith than her children?

JUDITH

When Esau was forty years old,
he married Judith daughter of Beeri the Hittite,
and also Basemath daughter of Elon the Hittite.
They were a source of grief to Isaac and Rebekah.
GENESIS 26:34–35

Esau married late, but the forty years he'd lived didn't bring him wisdom. He wed two women, both of a pagan people. And these marriages must have caused a lot of family strife, since his parents refused to allow their second son, Jacob, to marry a Canaanite (see Genesis 27:46–28:1).

The Canaanite fertility religion, which encouraged prostitution, probably deeply offended Isaac and Rebekah. It certainly wasn't what they had in mind for their eldest son, and perhaps they saw it leading him to disobey God. Since scripture never mentions Judith again, the grief she caused her in-laws is our entire legacy of her.

We, too, may attract the dislike of a prospective in-law. Not everyone will like us—perhaps we'll be criticized because we come from a different ethnicity or because we aren't "important" enough.

But when the critics complain, let it be because we are faithful Christians, not women who lead others astray. Let the slings and arrows fly, but not because we have dishonored God. He's the One we need to please, with our marriages and our lives.

JULIA

Greet Philologus, Julia, Nereus and his sister,
and Olympas and all the saints with them.
ROMANS 16:15

We may not know much about Julia, but the very fact that Paul greeted her indicates she was a faithful believer. Will future generations know as much about us? Will they understand that God applauded us for our faith, as He did Julia, even if we never get public mention?

This unknown woman was probably a slave or a former slave who had won her freedom. During the first century, many masters freed slaves—so many that Rome actually taxed masters who did so. But a Roman slave might have had a more secure life than a freedwoman. At least she would know she had a place to live and food to keep her alive. Though a freed person had more liberty, security was the price she paid for those greater legal rights.

If Julia was a slave, perhaps her freedom in Christ comforted her. If a freedwoman, perhaps her security lay in Him. But whatever her condition, she remained true to her Savior.

May we pass this truth on to future generations, too: it pays to be faithful to the One who saved us, no matter what our situation may be.

KETURAH

Abraham took another wife, whose name was Keturah.
She bore him Zimran, Jokshan, Medan,
Midian, Ishbak and Shuah.
GENESIS 25:1–2

Keturah probably wasn't really a "wife"—1 Chronicles 1:32 calls her a concubine. Scholars disagree on when she entered Abraham's life—some think there was an early wedding, while others say it happened after Sarah's death. A third group says there was no wedding at all.

Whatever her legal status, scripture is clear that Keturah's many children had nothing to do with God's promise. Though God turned these boys into many nations, they never held the place of Isaac.

So before his death, Abraham gave gifts to these six sons and sent them away. Faithful Abraham did not seem concerned about the anguish that might create for Keturah or her children. But it had to have created a distressing situation for everyone.

Like others in the Bible, Keturah and her sons discovered that being out of the center of God's plan can be emotionally painful. We've seen it when friends or family members become romantically involved with non-Christians—or very unfaithful ones. We've seen it when children walk away from faith and into trouble.

Relationships that are not in line with God's will generate a lot of hurt, so they all need to be centered in Jesus. Leaning on Him won't keep us from every problem—but it helps to know He's always right at our side.

LEAH

And Jacob did so.
He finished the week with Leah,
and then Laban gave him his daughter Rachel to be his wife.
GENESIS 29:28

It's hard not to feel sorry for Leah, marrying a man who loved her sister. Her father tricked Jacob, who'd worked seven years for the right to marry his beautiful daughter Rachel. But Laban put his older and plainer daughter, Leah, into Jacob's bed on the wedding night.

How much did Leah know of this plan? Wouldn't she have understood the sorrow that plot would bring to her sister's heart? Was she afraid of her father, an innocent victim of his conniving, or an eager part of the plan? We don't know. But the situation Laban instigated made his daughters' family life incredibly complex and agonizing.

To "solve" this marital problem, Laban suggested that Jacob marry Rachel, in exchange for an additional seven years of work. Both daughters must have felt manipulated by their father, who clearly wanted to keep a good worker at the expense of his own children's happiness.

Jacob loved Rachel, and everyone in the camp must have known it. But God had compassion on the unloved Leah and gave her children, while withholding babies from Rachel. Though Rachel received her husband's love, God gave two very special things to Leah—Israel's priestly line came from her third son, Levi, and the Messiah's ancestry from her fourth son, Judah.

Unfortunately, Leah believed that having babies was the way to win her husband's heart—and Rachel became so jealous of her sister's fertility that she started a personal version of "can you top this?" that made everyone in the family miserable. Rachel told Jacob to take her maid, Bilhah, as a concubine, to bear sons in her place. Leah immediately retaliated by giving her maid, Zilpah, to Jacob, too. Bilhah had two sons, and Rachel felt she had won. Then Zilpah bore Gad and Asher, and Leah rejoiced.

One day, Leah's first son, Reuben, found some mandrake roots, which were superstitiously believed to affect fertility. Desperate Rachel begged her sister for them, and the depth of Leah's pain is clear in her mournful answer: "Wasn't it enough that you took away my husband? Will you take my son's mandrakes too?" (Genesis 30:15).

In return for the mandrakes, Rachel offered Leah the chance to sleep with their husband. Leah agreed, and again became pregnant. She had two more children before God gave Rachel her first son, Joseph.

When God told Jacob to return to his homeland, Leah and Rachel didn't object—probably because Laban hadn't been such a wonderful father. They slipped off, with all the flocks Jacob had received from his father-in-law, while Laban was away.

Only once more would Leah see her father, when he followed the fleeing family—not from concern for his children but to seek out some missing idols. He didn't even try to lay claim to his daughters or their children, though he finally created a covenant between himself and his son-in-law that considered his children's welfare.

Later, when Jacob faced his cheated brother, Esau, whose anger he feared, he made it clear which wife was most important: Leah was placed nearer to danger than Rachel. How that must have pained Leah! But more pain was coming. On the trip to Jacob's home, Leah's daughter, Dinah, was raped by a local prince. It seemed as if anguish was Leah's lot.

Leah may have been the most unloved woman of the Bible. Through no fault of her own, she never had her husband's affection—only his children. Nor did her conniving father care for her. But Leah shows us what God can do, even with a hurting heart. Though she didn't have anything approximating a perfect life, God blessed her in ways that escaped the more-loved Rachel.

God can also take our less-than-perfect lives and make them perfect in Him. We may never get all the human love and attention we'd like to have, but He'll always draw us near His side. And isn't that where we really want to be anyway?

LOIS

I have been reminded of your sincere faith,
which first lived in your grandmother Lois
and in your mother Eunice and,
I am persuaded, now lives in you also.
2 TIMOTHY 1:5

When she first believed, Lois probably never thought she was starting a spiritual legacy. But she passed her faith on to her daughter, Eunice. As they went about their daily lives, these two women powerfully impacted the man whom the apostle Paul would see as a surrogate son and a partner in spreading the Gospel. To young Timothy, Paul passed on an important ministry that has touched believers around the world.

Ever feel as if you're "only a mother"? Yours is an important role that influences lives. Someday you may be a grandmother, too. How many young people could be touched by your faithful example, years in the making? Lois probably never thought her faith legacy would be reported twenty centuries later. But Paul's letters to her grandson still guide Christians today.

LO-RUHAMAH

Gomer conceived again and gave birth to a daughter.
Then the LORD said to Hosea, "Call her Lo-Ruhamah, for I will no
longer show love to the house of Israel, that I should at all forgive them."
HOSEA 1:6

Imagine being named "not loved." How devastating it must have been for this child to know that God was using her as an example to her people—an example of the results of their sin. God had set the nation aside because of its unbelief, and Lo-Ruhamah's mother, Gomer, had acted out on that lack of faith. Her daughter probably wasn't even Hosea's child.

No matter how well Hosea treated her, that knowledge must have marred this child's life. But just as God wooed His people back to Himself, perhaps He called Lo-Ruhamah to Himself. For even when God declares their sin to His people, it is only to separate them from the wrong and bring them into relationship with Him.

As God called His ancient people away from their transgressions and into His love, He calls us. Are we trapped in sin? He will cleanse us from it. Do we crave love? He provides all we need. None of us must remain unloved. We need only to seek Jesus with all our hearts—and we will find Him.

LOT'S WIFE

But Lot's wife looked back, and she became a pillar of salt.
GENESIS 19:26

Angels rescued Lot's family from the destruction that fell on the city of Sodom. The city was so evil that God saved only Abraham's nephew and his immediate family. Physically pulling Lot's family from Sodom, the heavenly beings warned the humans not to look back.

What a temptation it must have been to look over a shoulder and see the horrifying events. Didn't each person wonder what had happened to the friends and family members there—especially the daughters' fiancés who would not come with them? But only Lot's wife gave in to the temptation. And she lost her life, turning into a pillar of salt.

On top of all the mayhem and destruction, how awful that must have been for Lot's family. But it showed them—and us today—that disobedience of God's express commands comes at a very high cost. We may never become salt monoliths, but how does sin impact our lives?

Can we look back at damage sin has caused? Or sin confessed that still calls our names? Or wrong choices we've repented of that still haunt us? God doesn't want that backward glance to destroy us. We live in Him today—so let's peer forward at the goals He's set before us.

LYDIA

One of those listening was a woman named Lydia,
a dealer in purple cloth from the city of Thyatira,
who was a worshiper of God.
The Lord opened her heart to respond to Paul's message.
When she and the members of her household were baptized,
she invited us to her home.
"If you consider me a believer in the Lord," she said,
"come and stay at my house." And she persuaded us.
ACTS 16:14–15

The first person to be baptized on European soil was Lydia, a prosperous merchant. A "seller of purple," she sold either purple dye or the fabric it tinted. You might call Lydia a first-century businesswoman.

But she wasn't just about business. Lydia listened carefully to Paul, and God opened her heart in faith to receive Jesus as Savior. Quickly, she acted on her faith and invited Paul, Silas, and Timothy to her home. Later, after Paul and Silas were briefly imprisoned on flimsy charges, she did not fail to welcome them to come again to her home.

What an example of immediate, purposeful faith Lydia is for us. Do we move forward in the right direction or hold back, waiting until we see if our choices will be popular? Lydia set her sights on doing God's will and carried on. Do we?

MAHLAH

Now Zelophehad. . .had no sons but only daughters,
whose names were Mahlah, Noah, Hoglah, Milcah and Tirzah.
They went to Eleazar the priest, Joshua son of Nun, and the leaders and said,
"The LORD commanded Moses to give us an inheritance among our brothers."
So Joshua gave them an inheritance along with the brothers
of their father, according to the LORD's command.
JOSHUA 17:3–4

You might say the leaders of Israel appreciated women's rights. At least, following Moses' former decision (see Numbers 27:1–7), they confirmed the rights of women to inherit when there were no sons who could. How much safer Mahlah and her sisters must have felt, knowing they would never be left poverty-stricken.

But Numbers 36 tells us more of these women. The men of their clan became worried that their lands would pass into other tribes of Israel, once the women married. So God commanded that these ladies marry within their own tribe.

But think about it: Hadn't God already planned their weddings, even from the moment He told Moses they could inherit? Every detail of a believer's life is thought out beforehand by our glorious Lord. All things work together for good—and for God, when we walk faithfully in our Master's way.

MARTHA

As Jesus and his disciples were on their way, he came to a village
where a woman named Martha opened her home to him.
LUKE 10:38

Martha was a warmhearted woman. We know that because she invited Jesus and His disciples to visit, even though that would be a lot of trouble. After all, feeding such a crowd on short notice wasn't the easiest thing in the days before refrigerators, microwaves, and gas or electric ovens.

It didn't matter that she and her family were probably well-to-do. That just meant Martha had to organize her staff, perhaps bring on some temporary help, and get everyone to work quickly at the last minute to feed over a dozen houseguests. But that major challenge didn't stop Martha from being generous.

Perhaps the honor of having Jesus in her home made Martha want to excel in her entertaining. It had to be a real Martha Stewart event in His honor. But while she worried if the centerpiece would be just perfect, directed the servants, and debated with herself if she'd have enough food, she missed out on an important event: Jesus was teaching in her own home, and she didn't hear a word.

Finally, irked that her sister, Mary, wasn't helping, Martha asked Jesus to intercede and make Mary lend a hand. What a shock it must have been when the Master took her sister's side! The kingdom of God was more important than a single meal, as Jesus gently told Martha.

Despite Jesus' rebuke, this dinner helped cement a strong relationship between the family and Jesus, for when Martha and Mary's brother, Lazarus, fell ill, they sent directly for Him with the message, "The one you love is sick" (John 11:3). Martha and her sister obviously expected that, at the news, Jesus would come running to heal their brother. After all, hadn't He done that for many in Israel? Though they waited, Jesus did not come—and time ran out for Lazarus.

John 11:5 tells us that Jesus loved the family, yet he intentionally waited, knowing the wonderful miracle He would perform in a few days. For Martha and Mary, those days were agony. Four days after their brother's death, Jesus appeared.

"'Lord,' Martha said to Jesus, 'if you had been here, my brother would not have died. But I know that even now God will give you whatever you ask'" (John 11:21–22). Such freedom of speaking shows that Martha's relationship to Jesus had remained close, in spite of His earlier rebuke. Despite the awful situation, as her brother's body began to decay, Martha's faith that Jesus could still help her remained strong.

Jesus responded vaguely, speaking about the resurrection. Martha had no doubt that her brother would be with God at the last day, but she was more interested in this day than the last one.

Jesus encouraged her to have faith, and her response, "Yes, Lord. . .I believe that you are the Christ, the Son of God, who was to come into the world" (John 11:27), shows her understanding of who He was—and is.

But what a huge shock it still must have been when Jesus raised her brother from the dead. Rejoicing mingled with amazement. Jesus had done just what she'd asked, and as a result, He'd performed a miracle that would set all Israel on its ear!

Many of us can see ourselves in Martha. We have a great desire to serve God, and we open ourselves to service—then get bogged down in the little things that don't mean much to ministry. With this well-meaning woman, God shows us where the important things are—in our relationship with Christ, not the busyness of doing things for Him.

Obviously Martha learned her lesson. When her brother became ill, she focused on the important things. And her relationship with Jesus had become one of deep trust. She did not fear asking Him for the one thing she really needed—the return of her brother to earthly life. And Jesus gave her just that.

Are we afraid to ask Him for what we really need? Perhaps that's the only thing He's waiting for. It's a technique Martha would recommend.

MARY MAGDALENE

Jesus traveled about from one town and village to another,
proclaiming the good news of the kingdom of God.
The Twelve were with him, and also some
women who had been cured of evil spirits
and diseases: Mary (called Magdalene)
from whom seven demons had come out. . .
LUKE 8:1–2

How embarrassed and even angry Mary of Magdala might feel if she were with us today. She suffers from a terrible reputation, even though scripture gives us no reason to believe it.

All we know of her background is that, once Mary Magdalene had been healed of a horrible demon infestation, she followed Jesus faithfully, helping support the ministry out of her own money (see verse 3). But somehow, perhaps because of her unusual demon possession or because of the story that comes shortly before the mention of her name, people have erroneously connected her to Luke 7:36–50, which tells of the prostitute who washed Jesus' feet with perfume.

Until Jesus came along, how this woman suffered, in torment from evil spirits that probably influenced her body, mind, and spirit. Though she may have been somewhat well-to-do (since she could afford to support Jesus' ministry), what did that money mean if no one could heal her? How welcome the relief of Jesus' touch on her life. She had great reason to feel deep devotion toward her Savior.

Since Mary's name appears at the head of lists of the women she associates with, perhaps she had more stature than the others. Whatever her position in society, she has an important role in scripture. She was there, among a small coterie of women, when Jesus was crucified (see Matthew 27:56). She was the first to see the resurrected Jesus, and since John tells the women's story from her point of view, the disciple must have relied heavily on her recounting of events when he wrote his Gospel (see John 20:1–18). And the other women mentioned in Matthew 28:1, Mark 16:1, and Luke 24:10 certainly backed up her description of the events.

On that Sunday after Jesus' death, while the male disciples were still in bed or perhaps hiding from the Roman authorities, the women went to the grave site to prepare the body. Now that the Sabbath was ended, they could complete Friday's hurriedly performed task (see Mark 16:1).

What a surprise awaited them at the tomb: There was no body! Though the women had followed Him faithfully and listened to His preaching, this was beyond their expectations. At the command of the angels they met at the tomb, the women ran to get the disciples Peter and John, who could hardly believe their tale—but came to see for themselves.

Once the disciples had left, the most amazing thing happened. Two angels appeared to Mary Magdalene, sitting where Jesus had been laid. They asked why she cried, and she replied that someone had taken her Lord away. Turning, she saw, but did not recognize, Jesus Himself. When He asked why she cried and what she looked for, she demanded to know where Jesus' body had been taken. But as soon as He spoke her name, Mary recognized Him. Jesus sent her to the disciples again, bearing the joyful news.

Appreciative of the work Jesus had done in her life, Mary spent the rest of her life in His service. Whether she followed Him during His ministry or ran to tell the confused disciples of her experience, Mary always had Jesus at the center of her existence. While others slept, she wanted to care for His body. Is it any wonder that Jesus appeared first to this faithful woman?

Do we constantly seek Jesus in our lives, too? Or does He live on a back shelf, to be trotted out when we feel we have time for Him? Like Mary, we are blessed when we make Him the focus of our being. As we are increasingly obedient, we'll be amazed at the way He uses us to minister to others.

MARY OF BETHANY

And after she had said this,
she went back and called her sister Mary aside.
"The Teacher is here," she said, "and is asking for you."
When Mary heard this, she got up quickly and went to him.
JOHN 11:28–29

Mary is the sister who chose "what is better" (Luke 10:42). While her sister, Martha, saw to making a special dinner, Mary relaxed at Jesus' feet and listened to Him speak. While Martha saw to bodies being fed, Mary's soul received sustenance. Though a meal would be consumed in an hour, Mary's food lasted for eternity.

Martha was a faithful woman, but Mary may just have had that extra devotion that sets some people apart. While others easily became distracted, she only had eyes for Jesus.

Scholars suspect that Martha was a widow, with a house in which her younger siblings lived with her. It would be natural, then, for her to see to the arrangements for dinner. One could understand, though, if she had given directions to her servants, then returned to Jesus to hear His words. But foolish household cares distracted the older sister while the younger one made a wiser choice.

The next time we meet these sisters, their brother has died. Though Jesus loved Lazarus deeply, He did not respond to a call for help from Mary and Martha until Lazarus had been in the grave for four days. As Lazarus lay dying, how the sisters must have wished for Jesus' presence. When He came, they both said mournfully, "Lord, if you had been here, my brother would not have died" (see John 11:21, 32).

But it wasn't that Jesus was insensitive to the women and their brother. When Mary spoke, He was troubled. He understood the pain of death in human lives, and on His way to the tomb, the Savior wept.

What joy must have filled Mary's heart to have her brother returned to life by Jesus. Though decay had started to destroy Lazarus, Mary's Savior restored every cell in her brother's body and returned his spirit to it.

Because many believed in Him that day, the jealous Jewish leaders plotted to take Jesus' life. And in the way the Spirit often works, Mary was later inspired to do something to help people understand that the Savior came to die.

Six days before the Passover, as Jesus passed through Bethany on his way to Jerusalem, Mary did something extraordinary that is recorded in three Gospels (Matthew 26:6–13; Mark 14:3–9; John 12:1–8). While He dined at the home of Simon the Leper, Mary came to Him with a fine alabaster jar containing pure nard, a very expensive perfume. As was the custom in that day, she anointed Christ with the perfume, pouring it over his head and feet.

In doing this, Mary had taken the task of a servant. Buying a costly perfume, waiting on Jesus herself, and wiping His feet with her hair all showed her humility. In Mary's day, a woman of her position would not unbind her hair in public. But she was so caught up in her devotion that even that did not seem too much. She was totally empowered by love.

When Judas tried to pour cold water on the beautiful act, complaining that the money spent on the perfume could have done much to help the poor, Jesus stood up for Mary and connected her service to His coming death.

Every Christian woman asks herself if she's a Mary or a Martha. The truth is probably somewhere in the middle. It wasn't that Martha didn't love Jesus. She just needed a course correction when she got caught up in less important things. Sometimes we do that, too. But Mary reminds us that a clean house and chef-quality food are less important than our relationships, especially our relationship with Jesus.

Are we settling for the good things of this world and ignoring more valuable spiritual matters? If we're not building our relationship with Jesus, perhaps we've turned into Marthas who need to walk on Mary's side for a while.

MARY, MOTHER OF JESUS

But the angel said to her,
"Do not be afraid, Mary, you have found favor with God.
You will be with child and give birth to a son,
and you are to give him the name Jesus."
LUKE 1:30–31

Mary is surely the best-known woman of the Bible. She got to do something no one else could—bear and raise God's Son, Jesus.

This young peasant girl was engaged to Joseph when an angel appeared to say she would bear the Messiah. Shocked, but still showing faith, she asked, "How will this be. . .since I am a virgin?" (Luke 1:34). Though the angel's news must have troubled her, she quickly responded, "I am the Lord's servant. . . . May it be to me as you have said" (Luke 1:38).

What questions surely filled her mind. How would she explain this to Joseph? What would the neighbors think? How would her life change?

But Mary's heart was true to God, and she accepted His glorious mission— the most intimate mission a woman could have. Her sacrifice of body and soul is unparalleled in human history.

God immediately gave Mary encouragement through her cousin Elizabeth, who was pregnant with John the Baptist. When Elizabeth confirmed what the angel had said, Mary praised God for His great blessing. Indeed, God blessed every aspect of her life as He worked out all things for the mother of His child—from the explanation to Joseph through the birth and all the troubles that followed. All her life, Mary clung to the truths of those days, which would guide her faith.

What work and delight it must have been to raise the Savior! But we know little of this time. The only mention of Jesus' early days, following His birth and circumcision, comes in Luke 2:41–52, when Mary and Joseph lost the twelve-year-old at the temple. The couple didn't always understand this divine Son, but they raised Him faithfully.

Mary became part of Christ's first miracle at the wedding in Cana, for she pointed out the need and told the servants to follow His commands. But from that point on, God's Son pursued His holy mission, and Mary is rarely mentioned. We can guess the anguish she must have felt as she heard of the religious leaders' disapproval of Jesus. What this peasant woman understood, at least in part, these powerful men had no inkling of: God's Son stood before them.

As Jesus' ministry grew, Mary and her other children went to Him to make Him rest from it (see Matthew 12:46–50; Mark 3:31–35; Luke 8:19–21). Jesus' choice to hold fast to God's will for Him, rather than clinging to family ties, must have concerned His mother.

At the foot of the cross, Mary appears again. At His first visit to the temple, the prophet Simeon had prophesied that a sword would pierce Mary's soul (see Luke 2:35). Watching Jesus' death undoubtedly wounded her like nothing else could, for she had given Him His earthly birth. But even from the cross, Jesus watched over Mary and placed her in the care of His disciple John. She went to live with him.

Mary's final appearance is found in Acts 1:14, in the upper room with the disciples and her other sons. Though she surely had many questions along the way, and though Jesus' half brothers must have wondered at much that He did, in our last glimpse of Mary and her family, they are united in the church.

Mary had no easy life. She was not born into wealth, as one might have expected of the woman chosen to bear God's child. Her reputation was destroyed by the unusual circumstances of her first child's birth. But through it all, she pondered the revelation she had been given and continued to trust in God. And He never forsook her.

What a wonderful example Mary is to us. Do we give ourselves completely to our Lord—body, soul, and spirit? Or do we hold back when He asks something that seems "unreasonable"? Mary didn't. Though she obviously had her doubts, she remained true to God's calling for her life. Mary stood firm during pain, doubt, and fear. Will we do less?

MICHAL

Now Saul's daughter Michal was in love with David,
and when they told Saul about it, he was pleased.
1 SAMUEL 18:20

While David was still pretty much a nobody, Michal fell in love with him. Because of David's successes, her father, King Saul, had given him a high position in the army. But when this new commander won victory and the people's acclaim, the king became jealous. To bind David to himself, Saul offered marriage to his eldest daughter, Merab. But Saul didn't keep the promise, and she married another man.

Now, hearing that Michal loved David, the crafty Saul decided to use her to entrap the popular young man. He sent David out to battle after telling his prospective son-in-law that the price of the marriage was to be one hundred foreskins from Philistine warriors. Saul figured the Philistines could take care of this thorn in his side by killing David off.

But God defended David, who came home with twice the number of foreskins required. Saul had no choice but to marry off Michal to David. Realizing that God was favoring David, King Saul feared his son-in-law even more—so he again plotted the younger man's death. But Saul made a mistake in telling his son Jonathan of the plan. Jonathan loved David and warned him.

In the grip of an evil spirit, Saul tried to kill David himself, flinging a spear in his direction while his son-in-law played the harp. Following David's escape, Saul sent men to watch his house.

Michal warned David that her father would kill him the next day and helped her husband escape through a window. Then she placed an idol in his bed, covering it to make it look like the sleeping David. When Saul's men came after her husband, she lied, saying David was ill. Cornered in her deceit by her angry father, Michal again lied, saying she let David go so he wouldn't kill her.

Saul continued to harass David and had Michal married to another man, Paltiel, son of Laish (see 1 Samuel 25:44). Scripture doesn't say whether Michal objected to the change in husband. As long as Saul was powerful, she remained Paltiel's wife. But David gained strength, and when Abner, Saul's commander-in-chief, went over to his side, David demanded that Abner bring him Michal. Though her second husband came weeping behind her, she was forcefully carried to David. Had her love for David died or was she just tired of being a political pawn? The Bible never tells us.

Having Saul's daughter as his wife secured his political position, and David became king of all Israel. But perhaps his high-handed attitude had damaged the relationship with Michal. When he came into Jerusalem, bringing the ark of the covenant back, David danced before it. Michal watched from a window, not rejoicing at the return of the ark, but despising her husband. When he returned to the palace, she met him on the doorstep, criticizing his supposedly undignified actions. Offended, David told her he was celebrating before God and would be even more undignified, if that was what it meant to worship the Lord. We can surmise that the virile David had nothing to do with Michal after that, for she never had children.

Michal had a sad life. Her father and David used her to gain their own ends. Obviously she wasn't Suzie Sunshine either, since she lied easily to her father and had an idol handy to slip into David's bed. But we can't blame her for disliking her treatment as a pawn in the political game.

Michal's personal woes stemmed from her confused marital status. Let us remember that God takes marriage very seriously: it pictures His relationship with us and cannot be put on and taken off at will. Those who forget that may find their relationships unnecessarily tangled. Lifelong faithfulness to a loving husband pays a real bonus in later success.

MIRIAM

Then Miriam the prophetess, Aaron's sister, took a tambourine in her hand,
and all the women followed her, with tambourines and dancing.
EXODUS 15:20

Though she had an important task, Miriam is not named in the scriptures' first reference to her. Exodus 2:3–4 simply tells us that Jochebed placed her son Moses in a basket and allowed her daughter to watch over him.

Can there be any doubt that Jochebed had carefully instructed her daughter in what to do? But it was still a hard task. As young Miriam guarded her brother, did she begin to get bored, or did fear keep her on edge? How long did it take for the princess to find Moses? Yet Miriam waited. This brave child took on the job her mother assigned her and did it to perfection.

Once her brother had been found, Miriam, who'd watched from a distance, came forward and asked the Egyptian princess if she'd like her to find a nurse for the child. Could the princess have expected anyone but the boy's mother? Yet even though she knew the babe had to be a Hebrew, the princess did not use that information against Miriam or her mother. Brave though she'd been, how grateful Miriam must have been that there was no trouble and that her younger brother would be safe.

Many years later, we briefly meet Miriam as a worship leader, following the Hebrews' successful crossing of the Red Sea. And Exodus 15:20 describes Miriam as a prophetess. Though her brothers held the positions of foremost prophet and priest, she had an important role, too, in her people's faith life. God had given her a great gift to use for their benefit.

But when God gave seventy elders the gift of prophecy, Miriam and her brother Aaron became jealous of Moses' special relationship with God. Perhaps they felt their positions had been lessened. So, like many people, they picked an argument on a minor point—Moses' marriage to a Cushite. Whether this was Zipporah or a second wife is unclear, but the situation caused trouble for their brother. Still, the meek Moses did not react in anger—God did. Before Moses, He confronted Miriam and Aaron with their sin. Why, He asked, weren't they afraid to do this to Moses, before whom He spoke face-to-face? Then suddenly, God left them.

As the brothers turned and looked at Miriam, they must have been amazed and terrified. She stood before them as a leper, her skin white. Immediately, Aaron repented and asked that Moses bring her healing. So Moses called out to God. The Lord commanded that for a week Miriam should be confined outside the camp as one who was unclean. Since Miriam was brought back into the camp, we know she had been healed both physically and spiritually. For no one with leprosy would have been allowed back in the community, and God's healings always affect the spirit as well as the body.

Since she was the one punished, Miriam probably started this trouble—but it must not have been her usual sort of action, if the love with which her brothers immediately responded tells us anything. Aaron confessed their mutual sin and sought her healing. Moses quickly turned to God, showering his own forgiveness on his sister. Perhaps the prophet remembered that as a child, without her help, he might not have lived.

Miriam died in Kadesh, according to Numbers 20:1, and was buried there.

She was a God-gifted leader who held an important position in her nation and must have strongly led her people in belief—though she was far from perfect. God gave Miriam a place of authority, and she misused it for a short time. Her punishment was also short-term, so she must have learned her lesson.

If we are in positions of leadership, we also may fail. Let us not judge Miriam, but learn from her mistake. Many years of faithfulness do not armor us against sin. Every day the evil one tempts us. Only constant watchfulness keeps him from our door. Yet when we draw close to Jesus, we can live faithfully for Him.

A MOTHER REWARDED BY SOLOMON

Now two prostitutes came to the king and stood before him.
One of them said, "My lord, this woman and I live in the same house.
I had a baby while she was there with me.
The third day after my child was born,
this woman also had a baby. We were alone;
there was no one in the house but the two of us.
During the night this woman's son died because she lay on him."

1 KINGS 3:16–19

These women hadn't chosen wisely in their profession, and they weren't the kind of folks faithful Jews wanted to be around. But somehow their case landed in the king's court, perhaps because it was such a difficult decision. In a short time, each of the women had birthed a child. But one morning one babe was dead, and both women claimed theirs was the living child.

In God's wisdom Solomon called for a sword and offered to solve the problem by dividing the single baby between them. One mother cried out to give the child to the other, so the king awarded her the child. Such love identified the loving mother, who deserved to have a child in her care. But along with Solomon's court, she undoubtedly was stunned at the king's ability to discern the truth.

Have you ever been surprised at the way God's truth works in your life? When things seem at their lowest, He quietly intervenes, and life is changed. Suddenly that thorny problem is solved by a knowledge beyond anything you possess.

NAAMAN'S SERVANT GIRL

Now bands from Aram had gone out
and had taken captive a young girl from Israel,
and she served Naaman's wife. She said to her mistress,
"If only my master would see the prophet who is in Samaria!
He would cure him of his leprosy."
2 KINGS 5:2–3

This nameless servant had been torn from her home and all that was familiar by a marauding band of Arameans. Now she was the servant of the commander in chief of the army.

But no one had torn her from her faith. Perhaps her master and mistress were kind to her, for when she saw the man's hurt, she had a good idea: Naaman should go to Elisha the prophet and seek healing.

Desperate, Naaman decided to take her advice. He got an introductory letter from the king of Aram, written to Israel's king, and carried with him a small fortune in gifts. When he received the letter, King Joram of Israel feared the Arameans were actually trying to provoke a war. But Elisha demanded to have the man sent to him. By his actions the prophet would prove the power of God to this foreigner.

Proud Naaman went to Elisha, expecting to be treated like an important person. But the prophet thought humility would better serve this powerful man. So he did not meet him but sent a message: Wash seven times in the Jordan River.

At first, Naaman refused, angered that the prophet had not treated him as he would have expected. Naaman was even insulted that the rivers in his own land were not deemed good enough. It took some humble people—his servants—to convince Naaman that he risked remaining a leper, when he could be made whole. Once the commander obeyed Elisha, he was healed entirely, both physically and spiritually. Naaman returned and confessed his faith to Elisha, wanting to follow God in his own land.

Though the servant girl had lost her home and freedom, she remained a witness for God. Through her simple suggestion a leader of the Arameans came to the Lord. Who knows what kind of witness he became?

Are we witnesses in the simple things of everyday life? Or are our mouths closed by doubt and fear? Like the unimportant servant girl, we need to do God's will wherever we are. Let's not be deterred by our place in life, our enemies, or anything else. God uses the most unexpected people to serve Him well.

NAOMI

Then Naomi said to her two daughters-in-law,
"Go back, each of you, to your mother's home.
May the LORD show kindness to you, as you have shown to your dead and to me.
May the LORD grant that each of you will find rest in the home of another
husband." Then she kissed them and they wept aloud.
RUTH 1:8–9

Naomi had fallen on hard times—in a strange land. Famine had caused her and her family to move to Moab. Then her husband and sons died, leaving her with only two daughters-in-law. How could three women make it in a world where women didn't exactly have career options?

Naomi selflessly decided to send the younger women back to their own homeland, where they were more likely to find new husbands. You might say she encouraged them in the best career choice for women of that day.

One of the women, Orpah, took Naomi's suggestion. Perhaps she did find a fine husband, but scripture doesn't say. As she walked out of Naomi's life, she exited the biblical record.

But Ruth clung to Naomi and refused to leave. Maybe she had seen something in her husband's faith that she didn't want to lose. Perhaps she believed in God and felt bound to her mother-in-law. Whatever the reason, the two returned to Naomi's homeland at Bethlehem. When her friends recognized her, Naomi told them not to call her by her name, which means "pleasant," but to call her *Mara*, which translates as "bitter." Grief had overwhelmed Naomi's gentle heart to the point that she felt afflicted by God.

Instead of following their traditional right and leaning on a man of Naomi's extended family, the destitute women fended for themselves. During harvest-time, the law commanded landowners not to take in every bit of the crop (see Leviticus 23:22). They were to leave some grain at the edges to provide for the poor and the alien. So poor and alien Ruth volunteered to gather barley for herself and her mother-in-law.

But God had a better plan. In one of those divine "coincidences," Ruth found herself gleaning the fields of Boaz, a wealthy man distantly related to Naomi's husband. Boaz had heard reports of Ruth's industry and her care for her mother-in-law, so he commanded his workers to leave her a little extra grain and look after her the whole day. Boaz made it his job to protect this foreign woman who understood the requirements of God's servant.

That evening, as Ruth told Naomi about her day, the older woman recognized Boaz as one of their kinsman-redeemers—a man who could be called on to rescue them in need. As the harvest ended, Naomi decided to help romance out a bit by placing Ruth in Boaz's path.

Naomi sent her daughter-in-law to Boaz during the threshing time with a plan: Ruth was to tell Boaz of his responsibility to help them. And help them this generous man did. After looking into their legal situation, he took responsibility for the women, though he was not their closest kinsman-redeemer. Perhaps because he admired so, he married Ruth and also provided for Naomi.

Following the command of Deuteronomy 25:5–6, Ruth's first child, Obed, became the heir to Ruth's first husband. So Naomi's sorrow turned to joy, and she was not left destitute in her old age. God provided for her through another generation.

Though Naomi had hard times, God looked after her. Ruth may have seemed an unlikely supporter, but she was faithful—and, through God's blessing, provided well for both of them.

Over time, have things so changed that our Lord no longer cares for His people? No! He never promises lives of ease, just that He will take care of us. Though our life roads may take unexpected turns, we cannot go anywhere that He cannot reach us.

We may feel discouraged, but we must not give up. Who knows when a Ruth or Boaz will enter our lives and do wonderful things for us? There will always be a kinsman-redeemer. God never forgets any of His children—He saves every one.

NOAH'S WIFE

And Noah and his sons and his wife and his sons' wives
entered the ark to escape the waters of the flood.
GENESIS 7:7

God came to Noah with a mission of salvation: Build an ark, bring in the animals and your family, and be saved.

You have to wonder how Mrs. Noah heard about her husband's future plans. Over breakfast one morning did he say, "Oh, by the way, God says I should build an ark, because there's going to be a flood"? Maybe his wife wondered what practical experience her husband had that would make him good at boat-building. And what was a flood anyway?

Did Noah's neighbors make fun of him for his ark-building project? Maybe so—but as far as we know, his wife never discouraged him from continuing. Perhaps she trusted her husband because she'd seen evidence of the wisdom his faith brought him. Maybe she walked closely with God, too.

Whether or not she'd chosen it, Mrs. Noah became part of Noah's salvation mission. She had to live on the ark for many months, smelling the terrible odors the animals put off and trying to keep "house" in impossible circumstances. There must have been times when she wondered how she got into this—and what was going to become of her family. Stress-free living certainly wasn't part of the ark experience.

Yet the day came when God commanded everyone to come out of the ark. Noah prepared a sacrifice, and God promised such destruction would never again happen. He blessed the members of Noah's family and commanded them to multiply and cover the earth. What joy must have filled the earth as the animals headed off to their favorite watering holes, caves, and other spots.

Sometimes, like Mrs. Noah, we end up part of a mission that doesn't have our names on it. When a husband takes on a role in church leadership, it impacts his wife, too. When a church decides to open a new ministry, we may find ourselves drafted into an unexpected position. How do we respond? Are we good-natured supporters, or do we start whining and complaining? Complaints never glorify God, but willing service—like Mrs. Noah's—always will.

ORPAH

At this they wept again.
Then Orpah kissed her mother-in-law good-by,
but Ruth clung to her.
RUTH 1:14

Orpah will always be known as the woman who left her mother-in-law when times were hard. But to do Orpah justice, she made what she thought was the best decision in the midst of a heartbreaking situation.

After Naomi's husband and two sons died, her daughters-in-law, Orpah and Ruth, began to accompany Naomi on her journey back to Israel. But when they set out on the road that would lead them back to the land of Judah, Naomi began to have second thoughts. She told her daughters-in-law, "Go back, each of you, to your mother's home. . . . May the LORD grant that each of you will find rest in the home of another husband" (Ruth 1:8–9). After all, Orpah and Ruth were not Israelites, and Naomi didn't know what would happen when she returned to her own land. The two younger women probably had a more secure future in their own country of Moab, where they could marry more easily.

After weighing her options, Orpah took her mother-in-law's advice. She may or may not have been selfish when she made that choice—scripture doesn't tell us. Orpah simply took the logical, time-honored path for a widow and sought remarriage in her own land. Any person of her day would have seen the sense of her decision. But unknowingly, in aiming for security, Orpah lost out on a lot.

Of course, it wasn't certain Orpah would find a husband when she returned home. Perhaps she did, but scripture never says. Did she ultimately raise a fine family and enjoy marital bliss? It could have happened. But no matter how wonderful her later life may have been, it could not begin to compare to that of Naomi's faithful daughter-in-law, Ruth. Though she was not an Israelite, Ruth ended up marrying a wonderful man—and became one of the forebears of the Messiah. Her faithfulness earned her an unmatched place in Jesus' genealogy.

Sometimes the logical solution to a problem isn't God's solution. He may ask us to risk all by doing what seems illogical. As we begin to walk down that path, doubts may assail us. Let's remember, though, that while stepping out in faith may appear risky, it's only because we're looking at it from a human point of view. Anyone who follows God is surrounded by His powerful hands. What can harm a Christian who places complete trust in her Lord?

Orpah went for worldly security. Ruth sought God's security. While one looked at today's world, the other obeyed God and received a special place in eternity. Who made the better choice?

PENINNAH

Whenever the day came for Elkanah to sacrifice,
he would give portions of the meat to his wife
Peninnah and to all her sons and daughters.
But to Hannah he gave a double portion because he loved her,
and the LORD had closed her womb.
1 SAMUEL 1:4–5

Peninnah was the "other woman" in Elkanah and Hannah's marriage. But instead of meeting secretly with Peninnah, Elkanah had brought her home as a second wife. Not that he really loved her—he probably just wanted her to have the children that Hannah could not seem to bear.

Though Elkanah loved Hannah best, she had to see this other woman every day and know she shared her husband. And Peninnah had to know she'd never be as treasured as Hannah. Though Peninnah had the blessing of Elkanah's children, she didn't really have his love.

Elkanah did right by his second wife, giving her what was required, but he wasn't as generous to her as he was to Hannah. Knowing she'd always be second best, Peninnah responded in one of those odd ways people react when they feel unloved: she tried to irritate her competition at every opportunity.

Of course, that wasn't going to make her beloved by Elkanah, who certainly would have wished for peace. And it clearly didn't make a friend of Hannah. But can we blame her for not wanting to share her husband? How trapped she must have felt in a marriage with no hope. Though Peninnah had the children and spent her life caring for them, she would always feel second best, underrated, and empty.

What woman could feel happy in such a situation? Since His children's happiness is important to God, from the very start He designed marriage as a one-man, one-woman relationship (see Genesis 2:24). The patriarchs who tried to change that plan paid the price for their sin. Scripture never gives an example of a happily married threesome.

This kind of marriage didn't work in Elkanah's day, and it won't work in ours, either. That's why God calls us all to be faithful to one spouse—in both body and spirit. Sometimes that takes a huge quantity of patience. But, as Elkanah found, waiting might just prove the best path. Because, after a while, God allowed Hannah to have children, too. Imagine the grief this family could have avoided if the husband had trusted God and waited for children in the Lord's timing!

Let's resist the temptation to redesign marriage. God knows just how we are made and provides for our needs. Finding satisfaction in marriage brings a peace multiple relationships can never provide.

PERSIS

Greet Tryphena and Tryphosa, those women who work hard in the Lord.
Greet my dear friend Persis, another woman who has
worked very hard in the Lord.
ROMANS 16:12

We don't often think of Paul as having a dear woman friend. Timothy, Silas, and other guys might have been close to him, but we barely think of the apostle's relationship with women. Perhaps we even think he didn't much like them.

But when Paul listed the hard workers in the Roman church, he added Persis's name and words of high praise. Though his male disciples made great efforts, where does he give them such an accolade?

We don't know what Persis did to build the Roman church. Did she tirelessly bear witness to her friends? Suffer deeply under persecution? Teach the young people of the congregation? Paul doesn't say. We know nothing of her trials and tribulations. A few words simply tell us of her hard work.

Today, when we work diligently in the Lord, do we do it for attention and affirmation? Or would we be pleased if no one knew what role we play in forwarding God's kingdom?

In eternity we'll meet many believers who built God's church. Are they any less important because no one praised them? God's rewards in heaven will not shortchange anyone—even giving a cup of cold water will receive its reward. Are we content to wait for ours?

PETER'S MOTHER-IN-LAW

Jesus left the synagogue and went to the home of Simon.
Now Simon's mother-in-law was suffering from a high fever, and
they asked Jesus to help her. So he bent over her and rebuked the fever,
and it left her. She got up at once and began to wait on them.
LUKE 4:38–39

In the days before antibiotics and other highly effective medications, a deadly illness was often foreshadowed by a high fever. So when his mother-in-law was afflicted with a fever, it's no wonder that Simon, whom Jesus later named Peter, called on the Master.

The disciples had seen Jesus' miracles of healing. But now Simon's trust in the Master led him to invite Jesus into his own home, to heal a family member. Jesus, in command of all illnesses, rebuked the fever, which immediately left this woman who is known only by her relationship to Simon. She must have quickly felt the change, since she got up right away to wait on Jesus and four of His disciples—James and John, and Simon and his brother Andrew (see Mark 1:29). That instantaneous restoration of health impacted many lives through these few verses.

We have seen Jesus do many miracles—if not bodily healings, healed hearts and spirits through His gentle touch. Does this encourage us to serve immediately and faithfully? Peter's mother-in-law had the right idea: serving Jesus is our praise for all He's done for us.

PHOEBE

I commend to you our sister Phoebe, a servant of the church in Cenchrea.
I ask you to receive her in the Lord in a way worthy of the saints and
to give her any help she may need from you, for she has been
a great help to many people, including me.
ROMANS 16:1–2

Since it was not uncommon in Paul's day for a writer to introduce the bearer of a message to the ones receiving it, Phoebe may well have delivered his letter to the Romans. She had traveled to Rome from Cenchrea, a seaport near Corinth, perhaps on some business of her own.

The word *servant* indicates she was a deaconess, and a generous one, too, to judge by Paul's approval of her. She had not taken on the job to further her own position in the church. She was active, aiding those who came within her orbit. Though that may have included the women of the Cenchrean church, even leaders like Paul benefited from her ministry.

Are we like Phoebe, giving generously of our time and energy to the church? Or do we prefer to let others take on the work? God is not looking for those who simply accept Him and sit back in an easy chair. Helping others is a great service to Him, as Paul attests. Will we receive such kudos from Jesus when we meet Him in eternity?

PILATE'S WIFE

While Pilate was sitting on the judge's seat, his wife sent him this message:
"Don't have anything to do with that innocent man,
for I have suffered a great deal today in a dream because of him."
MATTHEW 27:19

Though she may not have been a believer, God used Pilate's wife to warn the Roman governor that he was about to make a grave error in trying Jesus. Early in the morning, as Pilate was about to start the trial, her message came to him.

Though Pilate had doubts about Jesus' guilt, he seems to have ignored the message from home. Even his wife's concern that testified to the Messiah's innocence, a sort of last-ditch effort to get through to the governor, was pushed aside by the issues of the moment. Pilate unjustly condemned Jesus to die.

Maybe the governor's wife wasn't surprised that he disregarded her dream, but she had bravely tried to do the right thing. Perhaps that helped her live with the results of the trial.

Can we bravely stand up for the truth, even when no one seems likely to listen? If so, we follow in this woman's footsteps. Though others may ignore us, we will have been a voice for God. Are we willing to speak out?

POTIPHAR'S WIFE

Now Joseph was well-built and handsome, and after a while
his master's wife took notice of Joseph and said, "Come to bed with me!". . .
And though she spoke to Joseph day after day, he refused
to go to bed with her or even be with her.
GENESIS 39:6–7, 10

No shy and retiring woman had Potiphar married. She ordered slaves to do her will, even if that was to join her in bed. She always got what she desired—and now she wanted Joseph.

She was probably someone who saw sex as recreation. In a rather boring life, she could fill her hours with men. And, with Joseph in charge and Potiphar caring for nothing but his own food, perhaps her husband was careless of his wife.

Feeling unloved, she would take any man she could get. Why not the handsome slave Joseph, who was easily within reach?

But Joseph was different. He preferred to obey God, and perhaps he remembered the time his sister, Dinah, was raped—and all the horror and the trouble that had caused. As a follower of God, Joseph honored marriage. And, in practical terms, he probably wanted to avoid the trouble he'd find if his master discovered such a dalliance.

Potiphar's wife meant to be the downfall of Joseph. When he refused her, she accused him of rape. But, ultimately and ironically, her actions eventually brought Joseph into the second position in all Egypt. He gained authority only slightly less than Pharaoh's.

Though this slave suffered for his stance, God blessed Joseph in a way no one could have imagined. We have no record that he used that authority against his accuser or her husband. Joseph eventually understood that God had been behind it all.

Nothing more is said of Potiphar's wife. If she continued in this lifestyle, she was undoubtedly unhappy. After this, her husband may have watched her more carefully. Or perhaps he gave up on her entirely.

This unnamed woman warns us that sex is not a game. Joseph could have given in to her demands because, as a slave, he could suffer for disobedience to his mistress. But he stood his ground and, because of it, God gave him great responsibility. Those who can be trusted in their sexual life can be trusted in high office, too.

Would anyone have wanted Potiphar's wife in a position of great authority?

PRISCILLA

Greet Priscilla and Aquila, my fellow workers in Christ Jesus.
They risked their lives for me. Not only I but all the churches
of the Gentiles are grateful to them.
ROMANS 16:3–4

The Bible never speaks of Priscilla (who is also called Prisca) without mentioning Aquila, and vice versa. They are a matched set, like pepper and salt shakers. But the salt they spread was the Good News.

How did Priscilla and Aquila risk their lives for Paul? We don't know. But we have some details about their stalwart leadership in the early church. Acts 18 tells of their meeting with the apostle and some of the work they did within the church. But it does not speak of a conversion, so this Jewish couple may already have believed when they met the apostle.

Except for one instance, Priscilla's name appears first, causing some scholars to think she might have had more worldly stature than her husband. Whoever the world thought was more important, Priscilla and Aquila took on every mission together.

From Corinth, where they had met Paul, this couple from Asia Minor went to Ephesus with him. First Corinthians 16:19 shows they stayed there and established a church in their home. The apostle left that church in their capable hands.

When Apollos came through the city, preaching something less than the entire gospel, Priscilla and Aquila took him in and taught him about the resurrection and the Holy Spirit's baptism. They must have been successful in their schooling, since the church in Ephesus supported Apollos when he moved on to Achaia, giving him a letter of introduction to the believers there. They never would have sent a false teacher to another church.

In Acts and the epistles, we get only tantalizing glimpses of this couple's lives. But they appear to have been a real marital team, working together to further the Gospel. Paul calls them "fellow workers," so doubtless they spread the Good News in their city and anywhere else they traveled. In each place where he mentions them, he speaks highly of Priscilla and Aquila and their work.

If you're married, are you and your husband a spiritual team? If you're not married, do you want to marry someone you can partner with in the faith? Priscilla and Aquila show every believer how wonderful such a collaboration can be. What is stronger than two people joined in Christ, working to further His kingdom? Nothing.

THE PROVERBS 31 WOMAN

A wife of noble character who can find? She is worth far more than rubies.
Her husband has full confidence in her and lacks nothing of value.
She brings him good, not harm, all the days of her life.
She selects wool and flax and works with eager hands.
She is like the merchant ships, bringing her food from afar.
She gets up while it is still dark; she provides food
for her family and portions for her servant girls. . . .
She sets about her work vigorously; her arms are strong for her tasks.
PROVERBS 31:10–15, 17

What an intimidating woman this is. She makes today's career woman look absolutely lazy! Yet we haven't even gotten to the end of her description.

Okay, maybe she isn't one real woman. She's a picture of what the faithful believer can do when empowered by God. A good wife might not accomplish all these things in the same day, either. (Let her sleep in occasionally—she's going to need it, with all those tasks ahead.) Maybe she won't even do them all in the same year. But she gives us a lifelong picture of what it means to be a Christian woman.

Read to the end of Proverbs 31, and you'll know where God says to put your efforts. You'll also learn that He has nothing against a woman who runs a business, juggles many tasks, and still loves her family.

Who is this woman? It could be you.

THE QUEEN OF SHEBA

When the queen of Sheba heard about the fame of Solomon
and his relation to the name of the LORD,
she came to test him with hard questions.
1 KINGS 10:1

News of Solomon's wisdom had penetrated a country in southwest Arabia, known for its trade with India and great wealth (see Psalm 72:15; Isaiah 60:6). Sheba's queen probably wanted to confer with Solomon on trade issues, but perhaps news of his acumen made her visit in person, rather than sending a representative. Since she brought many expensive gifts, she obviously wanted to impress Israel's king.

Even the best Sheba had to offer fell short of Solomon's court, for the queen was overwhelmed. When she praised him, the queen touched on the reason for his blessings of goods and mind: "Because of the LORD's eternal love for Israel, he has made you king to maintain justice and righteousness" (1 Kings 10:9).

Where does true wisdom come from? Not from education or position or anything else of human origin. This probably pagan queen got it right: God alone can give a mind that understands so much.

Though we may never rival Solomon's understanding, God will give us wisdom, too. Like Sheba's queen, we simply need to seek it.

RACHEL

Leah had weak eyes, but Rachel was lovely in form, and beautiful.
Jacob was in love with Rachel and said,
"I'll work for you seven years
in return for your younger daughter Rachel."
GENESIS 29:17–18

Jacob did what Mama wanted—he looked for a woman of his own people to marry. At his father's bidding, he traveled to his uncle Laban's home and sought out one of Laban's daughters as his wife.

At a well near Laban's home, Jacob met Rachel the shepherdess and watered her sheep. Surely he wanted to impress this beautiful woman! And he did just that. Rachel went home to her father and told him about his sister's son.

Within a month, Jacob was deeply in love. To secure his bride, he promised to work for Laban for seven years, "but they seemed like only a few days to him because of his love for her" (Genesis 29:20).

At the end of those years, they had a wedding celebration. But that first night Laban duped his nephew by bringing his daughter Leah to the new son-in-law's bed. Jacob didn't discover the deception until morning. Angry at Laban, he still demanded the woman he loved.

Rachel's father promised her to Jacob as a second wife, setting up a terrible situation for all involved. Rachel undoubtedly felt used by her father's duplicity and betrayed by her sister. After all, for seven years everyone had known of Jacob's love for her. And then there was the embarrassment of it all. Those emotions would overwhelm Rachel her whole life.

But Jacob still loved Rachel best. As they started their married life, she must have felt the promise of their love, only to have it denied as babies failed to appear. Jacob and Rachel's great passion did not bear the fruit that seemed so necessary to a woman's happiness.

Instead, Leah had the children. And the more children she had, the more Leah hoped her husband would love her. But after four sons, nothing had changed in her emotional life. Jacob still loved Rachel, and Leah, too, felt betrayed.

Following in Sarai's footsteps, the loved but angry and jealous Rachel gave her maid, Bilhah, to Jacob to have children in her place. Rachel named Bilhah's second son Naphtali, meaning "my struggle." Rachel proclaimed, "I have had a great struggle with my sister, and I have won" (Genesis 30:8). Obviously family harmony didn't live in these tents.

Leah, seeing that Bilhah was having children, did the same as Rachel, giving her maid, Zilpah, to Jacob. So two more children were born into this unhappy family. Then Leah had three more children, including Jacob's only daughter. Finally God remembered Rachel, and she bore Joseph, who would one day be second only to Pharaoh.

Jacob wanted to return to his homeland. For a while, Laban convinced him to stay by offering Jacob whatever he wanted. Once Jacob had developed a large flock, though, he fled, with the goodwill of his wives. There was nothing to bind them to their home. Laban followed, searching for the household gods Rachel had hidden in her tent. He didn't find them, as Rachel was sitting on them, saying she couldn't stand during her monthly "custom of women" (Genesis 31:35 KJV). After Laban, the deceiving father, had himself been deceived, Jacob and his family went on their way.

Jacob settled in Bethel, where Rachel had a second son. But shortly after his birth, she died. Though she asked that he be named Ben-Oni, "son of my trouble," Jacob called him the more positive Benjamin, "son of my right hand."

Rachel and her sister mothered the sons who began Israel's twelve tribes. Though the lives of Rachel and Leah were much less than smooth, God kept His promise to make a large nation of Israel.

Like these two women, we may experience hardship due to others' decisions. But God is always in control, planning things we have yet to see. If Rachel had known she'd have two sons, would she have started the baby competition with her sister? Maybe if she'd waited, she would have had four more sons to make up those twelve tribes. We'll never know.

But we do know we can always trust our Lord. No one derails His plans.

RAHAB

Then Joshua son of Nun secretly sent two spies from Shittim.
"Go, look over the land," he said, "especially Jericho."
So they went and entered the house of a prostitute
named Rahab and stayed there.
JOSHUA 2:1

Innkeeper or prostitute? Scholars have pondered which Rahab was, since the word used here for "prostitute" could be translated either way. It's probable this woman of Jericho both ran an inn and offered the guests a second service on the side.

Whatever her sexual morality, Rahab had no trouble lying about Joshua's men when Jericho's king asked her to bring out the two Israelite spies he'd heard of. Well prepared, Rahab had already hidden the Israelites on her roof, under drying stalks of flax. Instead of directing the king's officers upstairs, she told them the men had left the city before the gates had closed for the night. So the king's men set off on a wild-goose chase.

Had Rahab already heard such wonderful things about the Lord that she began to realize how empty a life of prostitution had become? Since she knew quite a lot about Joshua and his people—and was willing to put her life on the line for them—she must have come to belief before the two men knocked on her door.

Rahab was brave, willing to help these spies, and faithful in carrying out their directions. Though she must have feared the damage Joshua and his people could cause, she threw in her lot with the strange men. All she asked was that her family be spared. The men agreed quickly, so using a rope, she lowered them out of her window. Perhaps the spies had chosen her house with this in mind, for it sat upon the city wall, a convenient place for two men who wanted to leave surreptitiously. They quickly obeyed Rahab's directions to "head for the hills."

Before they left, the spies made Rahab promise not to tell anyone where they were heading. In return, they would be faithful to their promise and save her family. But she would have to gather her entire family together and hang a scarlet cord out the window she'd use for their escape.

Once the king's men stopped looking for them, the two spies returned to Joshua and told him what Rahab had reported: the people were terrified of the Israelites' coming. She was right, for as soon as the Israelites crossed the Jordan, the Canaanites lost their nerve. Jericho shut its gates, and no one went in or out.

Once "the walls came tumbling down" by God's power, Joshua sent the two spies to make good on their promise and save Rahab and her family. After their rescue, they were placed in an encampment outside Israel's camp. Since the newcomers had been involved in a pagan religion, Israel needed to be sure they'd turned away from their past before allowing them into the camp.

Rahab became one of the few women mentioned in Jesus' lineage (see Matthew 1:5). She may not have had a perfect background, but she was a changed woman. When this former prostitute showed her faith, it was so all could see. Hebrews 11, the faith chapter, lists her among many of the Bible's great saints (see verse 31). James 2:25 tells us that Rahab was justified by her actions.

Faith is not only a matter of mental assent or a powerful spiritual experience. Our actions show where our hearts are. And Rahab's heart was surely with God.

Do we show our faith as clearly as this former prostitute? Will our actions show whose side we are on in the battle between Christianity and unbelief? Like Rahab, we need to be brave, willing, and faithful in doing His will. We never know when God may send someone to our door!

REBEKAH

Isaac brought her into the tent of his mother Sarah, and he married Rebekah.
So she became his wife, and he loved her;
and Isaac was comforted after his mother's death.
GENESIS 24:67

How wonderful is the romance between Isaac and Rebekah. He loved her so much that he was his only wife. In an age of polygamy, their love must have stood out from their neighbors'.

Even before they met, God worked to bring their love into being. Abraham sent his chief servant on a trip. This caring father feared the influence of the pagan Canaanites and wanted the best in marriage for his son. So a servant traveled to Abraham's own homeland to find a wife for Isaac.

Trudging across the desert with camels bearing gifts, the man approached the town of Nahor. There he found the beautiful and generous Rebekah who both gave him a drink and offered to water the camels. When he discovered her father was Abraham's brother, the faithful servant worshipped God. *This* was the right woman!

Rebekah invited the man to the house of her father, Bethuel. There it was quickly decided Rebekah should be Isaac's wife. Along with her nurse, Rebekah traveled to meet her new husband.

Even if Isaac didn't experience love at first sight, it didn't take long for him to fall for this beautiful woman. He brought her to his mother's tent, married her, and loved her. As was the case for so many Bible women, there would be no quick conception and birthing. But after Isaac prayed, God finally gave Rebekah not one child, but twins.

The phrase "easy pregnancy" was not part of Rebekah's vocabulary for those nine months. The children struggled within her, and God told her she had two nations in her womb. One would be stronger than the other, and the older would serve the younger.

Rebekah delivered two sons. The first was red and hairy, so he was called Esau, which means "hairy." The second child grasped this brother's heel, so they named him Jacob, or "grasps the heel." Esau became a hunter, while Jacob turned into a homebody. Though Isaac loved his first son, Rebekah loved Jacob best. One day, the hungry Esau sold his birthright as eldest son to Isaac for a red lentil stew.

When famine touched their country, Isaac moved to the land of the Philistines. Because Rebekah was so beautiful, he feared the men of that land would kill him to get her—so Isaac called her his sister. When King Abimelech discovered the deception, he issued a stern reprimand—and then protected Isaac. Later, King Abimelech said to Isaac, "Move away from us; you have become too powerful for us" (Genesis 26:16).

So Isaac left, eventually settling in Beersheba. Esau, meanwhile, married two Hittite women, bringing sorrow to the family.

When Isaac became old and blind, he wanted to bless Esau as his firstborn, but Rebekah conspired with Jacob to gain that blessing for the younger son instead. Ignoring God's promise that her favorite son would have the place of importance, she helped Jacob deceive her blind husband. Rebekah prepared a goat dinner, and Jacob brought it to his father, pretending to be Esau. Jacob received the blessing, but at a great price. He had to flee Esau's anger and never saw his mother again.

We don't know what Rebekah was thinking when she cooked up this plot. Did her trust in God fail? Maybe—or maybe she thought she was helping God's will along. Either way, it certainly wasn't her most successful meal.

A woman of faith is not judged on a onetime act but on her whole life record. Rebekah, beautiful and generous in her youth, becomes a conniving woman who will do anything to see her favorite son benefit.

God calls us to be consistently faithful, to run the whole race well. When we are young, with the world before us, we may think we can do nothing wrong. But it takes character and deep faith to build a consistent testimony for a lifetime. The hard times and doubts come, but those who remember God's promises and cling to them never fail.

God walks beside us, just as He walked with Rebekah. If she had sought His will before cooking a goat dinner, things could have been so very different.

RHODA

Peter knocked at the outer entrance,
and a servant girl named Rhoda came to answer the door.
When she recognized Peter's voice, she was so overjoyed
she ran back without opening it and exclaimed,
"Peter is at the door!"
ACTS 12:13–14

What joy lit up Rhoda's face when she saw the apostle Peter standing on her mistress's doorstep. Peter, who only minutes before had been locked in a Roman jail! Delighted at his release, Rhoda darted off to tell Mary, John Mark's mother. But she had forgotten to open the door, so Peter patiently kept knocking.

When Rhoda reported the news to the Christians gathered in Mary's home, she didn't get the expected response. "You're crazy!" they essentially replied. When she wouldn't give up, they decided it must be his angel. Only when they saw for themselves would they believe this simple servant's testimony. Peter came inside and told the story of his miraculous release by an angel, urged them to tell others of his release, and then departed.

Though many of higher rank doubted her testimony, lowly Rhoda stood firm. Even getting them to check it out for themselves was difficult, but her persistence succeeded. Do we need the same persistence in our own faith? Doubters may come to belief, if only we stand firm.

RUTH

But Ruth replied, "Don't urge me to leave you or to turn back from you.
Where you go I will go, and where you stay I will stay.
Your people will be my people and your God my God."
RUTH 1:16

She wasn't Jewish but belonged to a pagan people. She had nothing in this world to gain and everything to lose—yet Ruth clung to her mother-in-law and refused to return to her homeland when Naomi left for her own land of Israel.

Ruth, her sister-in-law Orpah, and Naomi had seen their husbands die. Now, with no one to care for them and no career by which to earn a living, things looked very bleak. Yet when Orpah left, Ruth remained steadfast. If she was going to face hard times, it would not be alone.

Perhaps Ruth's husband and his family had been such excellent witnesses to their faith that Ruth didn't want to miss this God they worshipped. From her actions in the book that bears her name, it's likely she was already a believer. Or maybe she simply loved Naomi enough not to walk away. But Ruth was a woman of character who followed her mother-in-law into dire circumstances—and saved them both from utter destitution.

Together, the women traveled to Bethlehem, where Naomi declared her affliction to her onetime neighbors. But the life that looked so dire was not to end in tragedy, for her faithful relatives would come to her aid.

First among them was Ruth, who quickly went to work picking up the leftovers from the barley harvest. God commanded landowners to leave some grain for the poor, and Ruth was not too humble to join others in gathering what she could to support herself and Naomi. As God (not luck) would have it, she ended up gathering the grain in the fields of Boaz, who was related to Naomi's husband, Elimelech.

The industrious woman stood out to Boaz, and he commanded his servants to watch over her, making certain she had enough grain. He told Ruth to stay close to his servant girls for protection. He even told her to share his workers' food and water.

Humbled, Ruth wondered why he would be so generous. Boaz replied that he had heard what she had done for Naomi. But this wealthy landowner, who was a close enough relative to be a kinsman-redeemer, was about to do even more for the women.

A kinsman-redeemer was responsible for protecting family members in need. In Naomi's case, her nearest relative could not act. So Naomi told Ruth to go to the threshing floor and lie at Boaz's feet, a way of asking him to marry her. Touched by Ruth's willingness to marry an older man, and reminded that he was a close enough relative to be the kinsman-redeemer, Boaz took on that role. He took care of the legalities and announced that he would marry Ruth. Having received the elders' blessing on his proposal to a Moabite who had been so faithful to Naomi, he followed through on his promise.

Boaz and Ruth's son, Obed, would care for Naomi in her old age—but more than that, he would become the grandfather of King David. Even greater, he became part of the lineage of the Messiah.

Ruth's is the story of an unbelieving woman who came to faith, a poor woman who was richly blessed, a woman who was redeemed by one who pictures what the Savior does for all who come to Him in faith. Ruth was liberated from physical and spiritual need.

The Lord who rescued Ruth still rescues us today. Are we in need physically, spiritually, or emotionally? God will bless us, if only we have the character to cling to Him. Do we have doubts about our future? He has not forgotten us. Though we may gather grain for a while, He will not leave us empty. For Jesus, our Kinsman-Redeemer, married us when we came to Him. He will never leave us or forsake us.

SALOME, JAMES AND JOHN'S MOTHER

Then the mother of Zebedee's sons came to Jesus
with her sons and, kneeling down, asked a favor of him.
"What is it you want?" he asked.
She said, "Grant that one of these two sons of mine
may sit at your right and the other at your left in your kingdom."
MATTHEW 20:20–21

By combining Mark 15:40 and Matthew 27:56, we know the name of Zebedee's wife. Her husband and sons, James and John, worked what must have been a fairly extensive family fishing business, since Zebedee had hired men working for him (see Mark 1:20) and Simon was in a partnership with them, too (see Luke 5:10).

Salome had a fairly comfortable life. And with two fine sons, what more did she need?

When James and John suddenly left their nets and followed Jesus, it must have been a surprise to Salome and her husband. But it probably wasn't a bone of contention in the family. She may have been proud of her sons' standing with the Master.

Obviously Salome wanted her wonderful sons to "get ahead" not only on earth, but in eternity. That's why she asked for key places for them in His kingdom. But Jesus couldn't promise that. She must have been humbled by His denial, but it did not damage her faith—she's one of the women at both Christ's crucifixion and resurrection (see Mark 15:40; 16:1).

Salome had a good life with some unexpected bends in the road. She could have become angry when her sons left the family business, but obviously she supported them. Nor did anger ruin her faith when Jesus redirected her desires away from greatness for her children.

Like Salome, we need to accept the changes God makes in our lives and obey His will. Then we may find great joy in the life God designs for us—His plan may be marvelous beyond our expectations.

SALOME THE DANCER

On Herod's birthday the daughter of Herodias danced for them and pleased Herod so much that he promised with an oath to give her whatever she asked.
MATTHEW 14:6–7

Josephus, not scripture, records her name, but the Bible tells of her heinous act. At the request of her mother, Salome asked for the death of John the Baptist; Mama Herodias had an ax to grind with John, who had publicly condemned her marriage to Herod.

On her stepfather's birthday, Salome performed an erotic dance before him and his guests. Pleased, Herod offered her whatever she wanted. Who knows what young Salome might have asked for herself—it was her mother's idea to request John the Baptist's head on a platter. The king didn't like the idea, but since he'd promised and she'd requested in public, he felt he had to make good. So John literally lost his head.

Though her request may have pleased her mother, this gruesome gift was not otherwise of much use to Salome. And certainly the guests did not appreciate having their dinner so discomposed.

From Salome we learn to ask wisely for the things we want. What we desire may change someone else's life—hers ended John's existence. Salome would hardly be remembered if she hadn't done this evil thing. Do we want to be remembered for our worst request?

SAMSON'S MOTHER

Manoah. . .had a wife who was sterile and remained childless.
The angel of the LORD appeared to her and said,
"You are sterile and childless, but you are going to conceive and have a son.
Now see to it that you drink no wine or other fermented drink
and that you do not eat anything unclean, because you will conceive
and give birth to a son. No razor may be used on his head,
because the boy is to be a Nazirite, set apart to God from birth,
and he will begin the deliverance of Israel from the hands of the Philistines."
JUDGES 13:2–5

This unnamed woman is not the only one in scripture who waited long to have a child and then had an important son. Samson's mother, though, received the extra command not to drink anything fermented or eat anything unclean. For Samson was to be a Nazirite.

He would take a special vow of dedication to God (see Numbers 6:1–21), which the angel outlined to his mother. Though many people made a Nazirite vow that lasted only awhile, Samson was dedicated to God from the time of his conception, because this boy would begin the deliverance of Israel from the Philistines.

Samson's mother understood the favor God had shown in sending the angel to her and then to her husband. Dedicated to God, this couple must have raised Samson with God's promise constantly in mind, if Manoah's concern for the child's upbringing is any indication (see Judges 13:8–14).

As Samson grew, God blessed him, and one day His Spirit stirred the young man, empowering him for his mission. If only Samson had continued as he began. For though he became Israel's judge, he did not remain separated to God—at least not in his romantic life. He married a Philistine, against his parents' desire, and when his marriage failed, he became entangled with Delilah, who led him into sin and ultimately to his death.

Though his mother must have grieved over Samson's moral failures, God was still faithful. Even in these unlikely situations, Samson began the deliverance of Israel. Though enslaved to the Philistines, Samson destroyed his enemies' temple and killed many of them, too.

Do you know a Christian mother who has painfully watched children turn from the Lord of their childhood, making her wonder what she might have done wrong along the way? In our sin-filled world, no parent is perfect—and neither is any child. But God can work all things to good, despite the sorrow of wrong choices on both sides. His plan can never be destroyed, even by an unruly child or a less-than-perfect mother.

SAPPHIRA

Now a man named Ananias,
together with his wife Sapphira, also sold a piece of property.
With his wife's full knowledge he kept back part of the money for himself,
but brought the rest and put it at the apostles' feet.
ACTS 5:1–2

You can't fool God. But Ananias and Sapphira had to learn that lesson the hard way. The *really* hard way.

In a time when the church was persecuted, many believers, like Barnabas (see Acts 4:36–37), gave generously, from the heart. But Ananias and Sapphira's greedy hearts combined their desire for money with a wish to be well thought of in the church. Since they balked at losing all their investment, together they hatched a shortcut plot to sell some property and give money to the church—just not *all* the money.

When Ananias told the church of his gift, Peter, prompted by the Holy Spirit, confronted the deceiver with his lie. It wasn't that Peter objected to his not giving all the money to the congregation—what angered Peter was Ananias's lie that he *had* given all the money, when he had actually kept back a portion. This lie, the apostle pointed out, was aimed not toward men but at God.

As Peter's words hit his ears, the deceitful man died. The young men of the church came forward and immediately took care of Ananias's burial.

Three hours later, the unwitting Sapphira came in. Peter asked the price she and her husband had gotten for the land. From her mouth popped the fraud she and Ananias had agreed on. Peter demanded, "How could you agree to test the Spirit of the Lord? Look! The feet of the men who buried your husband are at the door, and they will carry you out also" (Acts 5:9).

Sapphira also died on the spot, and the congregation buried her next to her husband. As a result of this couple's example, the whole church feared doing wrong.

We don't want to follow in Sapphira's footsteps, but in the path of the Christians who learned from her lesson. Sapphira wanted to *look* good but not *be* good. Like that early church, we need to fear and avoid wrongdoing. Because even if we lie and don't expire immediately, a little part of us does die—our spirits diminish a bit every time we do wrong.

Sure, we can receive forgiveness, but how much better never to sin. Then we become good witnesses to our Savior, and new life—not death—begins.

SARAH

"I will bless her and will surely give you a son by her.
I will bless her so that she will be the mother of nations;
kings of peoples will come from her."
GENESIS 17:16

God promised to raise up a great nation from a couple who had yet to have any children and pledged to give them the whole land of Canaan as an everlasting possession. As crazy as that may have sounded, the husband, Abram, and his wife, Sarai, believed God and, with their retinue, set out for Canaan, God's promised land.

After they'd been there awhile, famine came—and Abram and Sarai moved to Egypt. Fearing the Egyptians would kill him to gain his beautiful wife, Abram asked Sarai to allow him to call her his sister. It was partially true—she was his father's daughter by another mother—but Abram failed to mention that she was also his wife.

After noticing Sarai's stunning beauty, Pharaoh took her into his palace. In response, God afflicted the Egyptian ruler and his household with diseases. When Pharaoh discovered the reason, he took Abram to task and tossed him and his wife out of Egypt.

Abram returned to Canaan, where God again promised him land, to be inherited by many offspring. But Sarai, who was at least sixty-five, had yet to have a single child.

As time went on, Abram began to wonder, "So where is this child, Lord?" Would a servant become his heir? Again God promised a child and made a covenant with Abram.

It's not hard to imagine the doubts that filled the couple's thoughts. Time was wasting. Their best years for reproduction had passed, and no child was in sight. So Sarai decided to generate a child by her slave, Hagar. The babe would be considered Sarai's, and maybe God's promise would be fulfilled. Too bad she didn't check with God before making that choice, for she was bringing great anguish to their family life.

Once Hagar was pregnant, it must have struck Sarai that she herself was at fault for her and Abram's inability to have children. Abram's reproductive parts were clearly working. When Hagar conceived, she despised her mistress. In return, Sarai treated the servant so badly that Hagar fled. Only God's intervention returned her to the camp.

After the birth of Ishmael, Hagar's son, God confirmed his covenant with Abram and renamed him Abraham. Sarai would be called Sarah. Again God promised that Sarah would have a son, and his would be the covenant line. A year before the birth, three mysterious men appeared and promised

Abraham that Sarah would have a son. Sarah, listening in her tent, laughed at the idea.

Before his son Isaac was born, Abraham proved he hadn't learned one lesson. He returned to the Negev and again claimed Sarah was only his sister. And again, a king—this time of Gerar—took her. But God protected His people, coming in a dream to warn Abimelech of his unintentional wrongdoing. So Sarah was again returned to her husband, along with many gifts to cover the offense.

Finally, in their old age, Sarah and Abraham had Isaac. But now Hagar and her son became jealous, so Sarah demanded that they leave. God told Abraham to follow his wife's desire. The line He'd promised was from Isaac, not Ishmael, though he, too, would become a great nation.

Then came a great test of faith. God commanded Abraham to sacrifice this son of promise. Scripture doesn't mention Sarah when it tells of this event. Perhaps she didn't find out until after the fact, when her son was saved. But we can easily imagine her emotions in the situation: fear, doubt, and questioning were replaced by the certainty of God's salvation.

Sarah lived to be 127 years old. When she died, Abraham asked the Hittites for a tomb for her, and they offered him the best available. He bought a choice spot near Mamre for his much-loved wife.

She was not perfect, but her God was. Even after Sarah made a tragic error of judgment and tried to have a son in the wrong way, God confirmed His promises. And she is commended by Him in 1 Peter 3:6, so we can assume she was a woman of real faith who, under real stress, had a moral failure.

Like Sarah, we do not have to be perfect for God to love us. He has chosen to do that, and He will not change.

SHIPHRAH

The king of Egypt said to the Hebrew midwives,
whose names were Shiphrah and Puah,
"When you help the Hebrew women in childbirth
and observe them on the delivery stool,
if it is a boy, kill him; but if it is a girl, let her live."
EXODUS 1:15–16

Two midwives seem unlikely folks to engage in civil disobedience, but that's just what brave Shiphrah and her coworker, Puah, did when Pharaoh demanded they kill the Hebrew boys. Because they feared God more than Egypt's ruler, they let the children live—and told the ruler that the women gave birth before they got to them. Did the two women feel guilt over their lie and confess it to

God? He did bless them for their stand, despite this wrongdoing.

Since two women could never have helped birth all the Hebrew children, these two were probably in charge of all the Hebrew midwives. They had an important responsibility, but even more, they understood their responsibility to God. When they had to disobey someone, they looked to the good of their souls before their high positions. So God rewarded "them [with] families of their own" (Exodus 1:21).

Are there some things in our own lives that are worth standing up for, no matter what the cost? Losing a job or an important community position might be better than offending God. Will we stand with Shiphrah or Pharaoh?

THE SHUNAMMITE WOMAN

One day Elisha went to Shunem.
And a well-to-do woman was there,
who urged him to stay for a meal.
So whenever he came by, he stopped there to eat.
2 KINGS 4:8

Her hospitality might seem a small thing, but because she gave generously to the prophet, the Shunammite woman saw amazing things happen in her life.

Her ministry began when she gave Elisha a meal. Soon he stopped by whenever he traveled her way. So the woman decided to provide a room for the prophet to stay in.

This hospitality obviously meant a lot to Elisha, who wanted to give her something in return. When he asked her, this humble but prosperous woman admitted to no need. But the prophet's servant, Gehazi, pointed out that she had no child. So the prophet promised that in a year, God would give her a son.

Perhaps she had given up hope of having a child by her older husband, or maybe there had been miscarriages. But she objected, "No, my lord. . . . Don't mislead your servant, O man of God!" (2 Kings 4:16). Perhaps previous disappointments filled her heart with doubt. But in a year, as the prophet promised, she held a boy in her arms.

One day, when the boy went to join his father and the reapers, his head began to hurt. The servants returned the boy to his mother, who held him on her lap until he died.

This faithful woman, without even telling her husband of their child's death, asked him for a donkey and traveled to see Elisha. Elisha immediately sent Gehazi before him, but nothing the servant did raised the boy. So Elisha came, prayed, and stretched himself on the boy, who immediately revived.

Sometime later, the prophet warned the woman to move to avoid a famine in her land. So she and her family left for Philistia. When they returned, the husband was no longer living, so the Shunammite went to the king to beg for her house and land back. As she came to him, Gehazi had just finished telling the king of her story. She immediately received everything back, even the income her land had produced during the seven years she'd been gone.

God blesses his faithful servants, even when their service may seem small. Like the Shunammite, we may provide some minor but essential service that has helped move the Gospel into others' hearts. Will God forget our faithfulness and fail to repay? Never! Look at the great blessings the Shunammite reaped for her hospitality.

SYNTYCHE

I plead with Euodia and I plead with Syntyche
to agree with each other in the Lord.
Yes, and I ask you, loyal yokefellow,
help these women who have contended
at my side in the cause of the gospel,
along with Clement and the rest of my fellow workers,
whose names are in the book of life.
PHILIPPIANS 4:2–3

Maybe Syntyche got into an argument with Euodia about how they should help the poor of Philippi, or perhaps she thought the church kitchen should be painted a different color. It didn't have to be a large issue that started their disagreement, but it clearly affected the whole congregation.

Faithful Christians don't always agree. Sometimes their personal preferences don't align perfectly, and that can cause stress and contention. It doesn't mean that either has given up the faith. But all believers need to "agree to disagree in love," as John Wesley said. Their personal preferences should not cause damage to the Gospel.

When you have a difference of opinion with another believer in your congregation, do you deal with it in love, or does it become an opportunity to battle each other? You don't have to love everything your brother or sister does—just agree with that person that in Christ you will work together for His kingdom, not your own aims.

THE SYROPHOENICIAN WOMAN

In fact, as soon as she heard about him,
a woman whose little daughter was possessed
by an evil spirit came and fell at his feet.
The woman was a Greek, born in Syrian Phoenicia.
She begged Jesus to drive the demon out of her daughter.
MARK 7:25–26

Though Jesus was trying to get away from the crowds, one desperate Gentile woman followed Him, fell at His feet, and begged for help. Disappointingly, Jesus replied, "I was sent only to the lost sheep of Israel" (Matthew 15:24). Yet still she persisted in asking for His help for her much-loved child.

But Jesus objected, saying, "It is not right to take the children's bread and toss it to their dogs" (Mark 7:27).

She could have become angry at being compared to a dog, for dogs were not favored in Jewish society. Instead, this humble woman agreed, but pointed out that she wasn't asking much—even dogs eat the crumbs from the master's table. Not only did this mother's faith and determination win the daughter's healing, but she became a preview of the message of salvation Paul would carry to the Gentiles.

When we face faith challenges, do we stand as firm as this unnamed woman? Though success seems doubtful, do we trust in God rather than our own abilities? If so, in the end, we will enjoy God's blessing, too.

TAMAR, JUDAH'S DAUGHTER-IN-LAW

Judah then said to his daughter-in-law Tamar,
"Live as a widow in your father's house until my son Shelah grows up."
For he thought, "He may die too, just like his brothers."
So Tamar went to live in her father's house.
GENESIS 38:11

Tamar's father-in-law, Judah, thought she was a curse against his sons. She had married his two oldest sons, successively, for the custom of the day was for a second son to give his older brother's widow a child as heir. Both of Judah's sons were wicked, though, so God saw to it that they died. Tamar, however, got the blame.

When it came to marrying his third son to Tamar, Judah balked. Instead he sent her back to her family and only *promised* Shelah to her. Time went by, and the marriage never took place. So Tamar hatched a plan.

Pretending to be a prostitute, Tamar wooed the un-suspecting Judah. Since her face was covered, he never recognized her as his daughter-in-law. As a pledge of payment for services that were about to be rendered, Tamar requested Judah leave his seal, its cord, and his staff in her possession. Judah gave them to her and slept with her.

Their liaison resulted in pregnancy. Three months later, still completely unaware of his own role in the situation, Judah was told that his daughter-in-law was with child. He demanded Tamar be burned to death for prostitution. That's when she showed him the belongings he had left with the "prostitute."

Once he knew he was the father, Judah admitted he had wronged Tamar and that her cause was righteous. Out of this union, God gave Tamar twin boys.

God had compassion on Tamar and gave her the children who would provide for her, since her father-in-law had not done so. Though her methods were wrong, her cause was not—and God gave her aid.

We, too, can count on God's help when we seek it righteously. But, unlike Tamar, let's not forget to obey His laws, too.

TAMAR, DAVID'S DAUGHTER

In the course of time, Amnon son of David fell in love with Tamar,
the beautiful sister of Absalom son of David.
Amnon became frustrated to the point of illness
on account of his sister Tamar,
for she was a virgin, and it seemed impossible
for him to do anything to her.
2 Samuel 13:1–2

What Amnon called love was pure lust. It took only the whisper of a false counselor for the young man to begin a plot that led to his destruction.

At that counselor's advice, he pretended to be sick. Then Amnon asked his father to have Tamar come to his place and prepare food for him. So she came and baked bread—though bread wasn't what Tamar's half brother was really interested in. He got her alone and asked her to sleep with him.

Horrified, the virtuous Tamar tried to warn him of his desire's danger. But when he couldn't persuade her, Amnon raped her. Immediately his guilt turned to anger, and he tossed her out of his house. Distraught, Tamar put ashes on her head and tore her robes, indicating what had happened to her. Then she headed for her brother Absalom's house, where she found comfort and support.

Since King David did nothing about the wrong done to his daughter, in time her brother Absalom took matters into his own hands. Two years after the event, he plotted Amnon's death. Not long after, he conspired to gain the throne.

Have you ever been in Tamar's situation, innocently walking into trouble, which exploded in your face, bringing great damage with it? As Christians, we must live innocently but not expect wicked people to do the same. Guarding ourselves against sin, we also need to guard against sinners.

TRYPHENA

Greet Tryphena and Tryphosa, those women who work hard in the Lord.
ROMANS 16:12

There are plenty of Tryphenas and Tryphosas in the church today—women who work hard to spread the Gospel, care for the hurting, and help others grow in Christ. Paul didn't denigrate or ignore the women who supported his ministry across the map. He knew he could not work effectively without them and remembered some of them in the greetings of his epistles. Who knows what great things came from their daily ministries—work that may have seemed unimportant at the time.

Is there a Tryphena in your church? Help and encourage her. Learn from her willingness to serve, and spend time with her so you can absorb some of the things that have made her a successful Christian.

Scripture gives us little more than Tryphena's name and the apostle's commendation. But with this verse we see how important our service to God is, even to the most important leader. This "unimportant" woman received a reward on earth and even greater ones in heaven, just like today's faithful women will be approved by Jesus in eternity.

VASHTI

On the seventh day, when King Xerxes was in high spirits from wine,
he commanded the seven eunuchs who served him. . .to bring before him
Queen Vashti, wearing her royal crown, in order to display her beauty
to the people and nobles, for she was lovely to look at.
But when the attendants delivered the king's command,
Queen Vashti refused to come.
Then the king became furious and burned with anger.
ESTHER 1:10–12

Any modest woman can understand why Queen Vashti preferred not to appear before the king and his courtiers—they'd just enjoyed a seven-day drinking party. But refusing the king's wish was a dangerous act, for it made Xerxes look as if he had no control over his own wife, let alone his country. Instead of showing off his lovely queen, the king was made to feel small. And kings of large empires don't like feeling small—especially when their wives generate the feeling.

Xerxes' counselors were immediately called. After a quick huddle, they gave their paranoid opinion: All the women in the kingdom, following the example of the queen, would soon refuse to obey their husbands. This had to be stopped immediately! Vashti should be stripped of her rank and never again be allowed to see the king.

Maybe this opinion reflected their own relationships with their wives more than the truth. Or maybe, as guests of the party, they'd been whooping it up a bit too much and were at less than their wisest. But the king took their advice, and Vashti was no longer queen.

The Bible doesn't tell us exactly why Vashti took this dangerous step. Perhaps she didn't want to be shown off at the party, or maybe she had another reason for not appearing. Whatever the cause, this action pushed her off her throne and out of the history books, at least for a while.

Because of Vashti's stand, Esther became queen—and the beautiful young Jewess was in a position to save her people when Haman wanted to kill them. God used Vashti's disobedience to protect His own people, who were enslaved by this powerful ruler.

Ironically, Vashti didn't entirely drop out of history. When her son Artaxerxes became king, she again held power as queen mother.

God's power worked even in the life of this pagan queen. She lost her throne, and Esther saved her people. But in the end, justice came to Vashti, too.

God is in control of all our lives, even when that seems unlikely. When we face hopeless situations, when we seem to be punished for our faith, and when we suffer for no apparent reason, God has not deserted us. We may not see His purpose or justice until the end, but we can be certain He will prevail—just as He did for both Esther and Vashti.

THE WIDOW OF ZAREPHATH

Then the word of the LORD came to [Elijah]:
"Go at once to Zarephath of Sidon and stay there.
I have commanded a widow in that place
to supply you with food."
1 KINGS 17:8–9

When the prophet Elijah prophesied a famine over Israel, he didn't mean the food shortage would affect only the wicked King Ahab. Even the prophet didn't have much to eat, so God fed him by sending ravens with food. (Though it was effective, it doesn't seem like the most appetizing method of delivery.)

But once the prophet's water source dried up, God directed Elijah to Zarephath, a Gentile city. It was home to Israel's enemies and a poor woman who was making a last meal for herself and her son.

The widow didn't have a secret store of food and water, just a great need. And at first she must have doubted the wisdom of sharing what little she had. But her small sacrifice gave great benefit. Amazingly, her only sustenance—an almost empty jar of flour and a bit of oil with which to bake—would not disappear until God sent the rains again.

Awhile later, the woman's son became ill and died. Emotionally wounded, this mother reacted against the man she saw as causing the problem. The woman said to Elijah, "What do you have against me, man of God? Did you come to remind me of my sin and kill my son?" (1 Kings 17:18).

Elijah took the boy, laid him on his bed, and passionately cried out to God to restore his life. God responded, and the boy lived. The mother responded with belief in Elijah as a man of God and in the truth of his message.

God could have continued Elijah's previous arrangements, with the prophet camped out in a gorge, being fed by ravens. God even could have provided a new source of water when the first one dried up. Instead, He sent His prophet to a poor woman of an enemy nation, one who seemed unlikely to be able to help. Of course, the aid she provided was really from God, not her—but God graciously allowed this woman of no stature to become part of His plan of salvation.

God reached out to a woman who had nothing to offer and used her to accomplish much. He loves the weak ones and wants to draw them to Himself. The strong and powerful may easily resist His Word, but the weak and those of no stature seek that one last meal that brings salvation. Let us not despise these spiritually poor people.

THE WIDOW WHO GAVE TWO MITES

As he looked up, Jesus saw the rich
putting their gifts into the temple treasury.
He also saw a poor widow put in two very small copper coins.
"I tell you the truth," he said, "this poor widow has put in more than all the others.
All these people gave their gifts out of their wealth;
but she out of her poverty put in all she had to live on."
LUKE 21:1–4

In just a few words, we get a picture of two kinds of people: the wealthy and perhaps somewhat generous givers who could put bags of money in the temple vaults, and a woman who gave much more.

Jesus had just warned his disciples of the love the religious leaders had for places of honor and the gain they made from defenseless widows. At that moment, a generous woman walked into the treasury and dropped in her tiny offering. How could her almost valueless coins compare to the greater gifts? While the rich gave of their extra money, she had deposited all her income into the "Bank of God."

What a sacrifice that must have been. Can you imagine her thinking beforehand: *I need to give something, but this is all I have. How will I have enough food? What if I have a crisis?* Whatever her worries might have been, the woman put her complete trust in God and dropped the coins into the temple chest. Maybe she gave the two mites, instead of one, because the single mite would not even have bought her a loaf of bread.

Can we have any doubt that God blessed her richly for this incredibly generous giving?

This humble woman gives us a painful example. If we look at ourselves honestly, we probably have to admit that we're more like the rich men bringing their offerings than the woman who "put in all she had to live on." We may plan our giving, working it into our budgets, but she gave her whole budget. She gave 100 percent, while many faithful Christians today squawk at giving a small portion of their income.

We cannot give too much to God. He's not demanding destitution for us, but calling us to give our all—spiritually and physically—into His keeping. He who owns the cattle on a thousand hills will never let us fail, if only we trust in Him.

THE WITCH OF ENDOR

Saul then said to his attendants,
"Find me a woman who is a medium, so I may go and inquire of her."
"There is one in Endor," they said.
1 SAMUEL 28:7

Saul wasn't the first hypocritical politician, and he surely wasn't the last. And the witch of Endor wasn't the first woman who knew she was making a living illegally. A fine pair of duplicitous people they were.

As the Philistines massed to attack Israel, Saul asked God about his situation, but heaven seemed to have closed up to him. No response came, no matter what Saul tried. Desperate with fear, Saul took matters into his own hands.

Though he had tossed the spiritists and mediums out of Israel, Saul asked his attendants where to find one. They knew—and we have to wonder how, if they were faithful Jews. Whatever the case, once Saul knew her location, he visited to ask her to call up Samuel for him.

Either the medium wasn't so smart or her spirit was sleeping on the job, because not until she saw Samuel did she recognize Saul and his deception. But the king commanded her to proceed.

"I see a spirit coming up out of the ground," the medium reported.

"What does he look like?" asked Saul.

"An old man wearing a robe is coming up," she replied (see 1 Samuel 28:13–14). After that incredibly definitive description, Saul was convinced it was Samuel.

Throughout his life, Saul hadn't listened much to Samuel—but suddenly, he was all ears. Explaining his situation, Saul waited for the prophet's advice.

The response could not have been worse. Samuel stated that the Lord had become Saul's enemy and was keeping a promise to take the kingdom from Saul's hands. The Philistines would win the upcoming battle, and Saul and his sons would die.

Devastated by this news—information that God had compassionately kept from him—Saul was overcome with fear to the point of physical weakness. The witch tried to get him to eat and go on his way, but it took much coaxing before he agreed to have dinner and head out. Demoralized, Saul lost the battle and his life, as predicted.

Scholars differ on their interpretation of this story. Was the image conjured up by the witch of Endor really Samuel? Perhaps not. The father of lies could have deceived the king. The awful news the apparition gave would certainly have pleased Satan. Or perhaps God permitted the prophet to give this last, damning prophecy.

Looking to the scriptures, we see that God's Word forbids all sorts of witchcraft (see Deuteronomy 18:9–12). If God wasn't upset with Saul before he visited a witch, certainly they would be at loggerheads after the appointment. A real trust in God and occult attempts to peer into the future are not good bedfellows.

Some people like to dabble in the occult—or at least turn a blind eye to it—ignoring the dangers God warns of. This witch didn't wear a dark, pointy hat or make pets of spiders; she was more dangerous than any Halloween costume. Her craft totally demoralized the king and probably contributed to his fall.

When God does not tell us something, He has a reason for it. Don't go seeking hidden knowledge—just trust Him.

THE WOMAN ACCUSED OF ADULTERY

The teachers of the law and the Pharisees
brought in a woman caught in adultery.
They made her stand before the group and said to Jesus,
"Teacher, this woman was caught in the act of adultery."
JOHN 8:3–4

After being snatched up in the midst of an adulterous act, this woman was forced to stand before Jesus, pilloried before her accusers and the rest of the gapers around her. How painful that moment must have been! Fear, doubt, guilt, and hatred for her accusers must have flooded her aching soul.

But as far as the condemning leaders were concerned, the point of this event wasn't to bring her to justice. They wanted to corner Jesus. If He told them to stone her, as the Law of Moses commanded, He could be prosecuted for defying Roman law. If He said to let her go, He would defy God's Law. They thought they had trapped him perfectly.

But they were wrong.

One of the first clues that these men were not interested in justice was that the man with whom the woman committed adultery did not appear before Jesus. According to the law, both offenders were to be stoned. Yet only the woman stood before Jesus for judgment. Who was the man, and where had he gone?

Jesus, well aware of the craftiness of His enemies, responded perfectly. He began writing on the ground while they threw questions at Him. Straightening up, He said, "If any one of you is without sin, let him be the first to throw a stone at her" (John 8:7). Then He returned to His writing.

Aware of their own imperfections, the older ones began to slip away; then the younger lost their nerve and followed, until no man stood before the adulteress.

"Woman," questioned Jesus, "where are they? Has no one condemned you?"

She replied, "No one, sir."

"Then neither do I condemn you," Jesus stated. "Go now and leave your life of sin" (see John 8:10–11).

Relief must have flooded this woman's soul! Not only had her accusers disappeared, but Jesus had forgiven her—and given her life new direction. Perhaps at that very moment, salvation poured into her spirit. If she was wise, she never made that mistake again and began to live for her Lord instead.

We've walked in this woman's shoes, haven't we? As we've done wrong, we've worried that others might find out. Perhaps our sins might not have been "big ones" like adultery, but we've felt the fear of public opinion against us, even when no one knew what we did. Inside, we've wondered if life could ever be the same if our wrongdoing went public.

Or maybe we've had others publicly accuse us—and hated them for their venom as they announced our sins to one and all. Whatever the case, we've all experienced painful wrongs and wished we had a way out of them.

Jesus is that way out. He doesn't tell us we never sinned. He doesn't excuse us, but He takes the wrong on Himself, pays the price for it, and commands us to live for Him. And in His power, we can do that—though not perfectly. Daily we come to Him for forgiveness, and daily we receive it.

Just like the woman caught in the act of adultery.

THE WOMAN AT THE WELL

When a Samaritan woman came to draw water,
Jesus said to her, "Will you give me a drink?" . . .
The Samaritan woman said to him,
"You are a Jew and I am a Samaritan woman.
How can you ask me for a drink?"
(For Jews do not associate with Samaritans.)
JOHN 4:7–9

When this woman walked to the well, she couldn't imagine the barriers about to fall. The division between her people and Jesus' people was just the first of the walls about to disintegrate.

She was a member of a people who had been resettled in the land, moved there by the king of Assyria after he conquered Samaria in 722 BC. They had been taught and partially accepted the faith of Israel, but retained their old pagan religions, too (see 2 Kings 17:24–41). Such syncretism was abhorrent to faithful Jews, so they avoided these Samaritans, whom they considered unclean.

Traveling from Judea to Galilee, Jesus and His followers had to pass through Samaria—unless they wanted to take a long detour. They chose the shorter road, and Jesus sat by a Samaritan well while His disciples went off to buy food.

When the woman approached the well, Jesus asked her for a drink. She responded with surprise and mockery, used to the idea that no Jew would accept water from her—any faithful Jew would have considered himself ceremonially unclean if he touched a cup she had handled.

Apparently this was a woman who had thought over spiritual things, even if she didn't have them right. So Jesus led her into a deeper discussion, mentioning the "living water" He could give her.

At first she took Him literally, thinking He meant the water within the well, and deriding Him for offering her water He could not reach. Did He think He was greater than Jacob, whose well this was? Christ persisted, telling her plainly that He spoke of eternal life—but she still didn't quite catch His point. Her interest remained with Samaritan religious history, not really a vital faith.

But, intrigued at the thought of parting with her heavy water jar, she asked for Jesus' water. Since the water He spoke of was eternal life, He confronted her numerous sins. In opposition to Jewish law, this woman had had five husbands and had not married the sixth man she then lived with. Even in today's loose culture, she might have raised a few eyebrows among those who knew her sexual history.

Perhaps in an effort to avoid Jesus' uncomfortable truth, the woman turned the discussion to His ability to know things she had never told Him—and then started a diversionary topic about the proper place to worship. Jesus answered her question, pointed her toward the spiritual nature of real worship, and declared Himself the Messiah. At some point, all the barriers of religion and nationality fell, and she believed in Jesus.

When the disciples returned, the woman took her opportunity to tell all her neighbors, even the ones who criticized her immorality. "He told me everything I ever did" (John 4:39) was her testimony. The Samaritans invited Jesus to stay for a couple of days, and in that time many were converted.

When we read this story, how do we see ourselves? Are we the wounded woman at the well, with a long history of sin behind us? If so, we can take heart in the forgiveness of the Savior, who confronts our sins, calls us to Himself, and forgives us.

Or are we the one witnessing to the lost? Like Jesus, we have heard many objections and need to cut through unimportant diversions and quickly get to the real message. Few of the people we speak to will readily accept our witness. Like Jesus, we need to patiently and lovingly deal with the important issues and turn each person's thoughts to real faith.

Either way, when the barriers fall, we will worship God "in spirit and in truth" (John 4:24).

THE WOMAN OF TEKOA

When the woman from Tekoa went to the king,
she fell with her face to the ground to pay him honor,
and she said, "Help me, O king!"

2 SAMUEL 14:4

If we were giving an acting award to women of the Bible, it would have to go to the woman from Tekoa. With her thespian abilities, she tried to bring peace to a nation.

King David had banished his rebellious son, Absalom, but this father's heart still ached for his errant child. So Joab, David's nephew and commander of his army, called on the wise woman of Tekoa to go to the king. She asked the king's help and, following Joab's script, described a family situation very similar to that between David's sons Amnon and Absalom—one son had killed the other, she reported, and her clan demanded that the killer be put to death. The king promised to intervene.

Then she confronted David with his own family situation, for he had not brought Absalom back from banishment. "God does not take away life; instead he devises ways so that a banished person may not remain estranged from him" (2 Samuel 14:14), she reasoned, calling on the king to do likewise.

Immediately, David recognized Joab's hand in this, and the woman admitted it. The king called for Absalom's return, but he would not see his son for two years.

This nameless woman wanted to bring peace to her nation. Though the peace she sought was a long time coming—and did not last long—that wasn't her fault, because Absalom foolishly rebelled against his father.

We, too, sometimes need to seek peace in our own families and communities. Are we willing to work with others to help them understand the need for forgiveness? Can we gently help them see how their own mistaken choices have led to painful situations, and give them hope for change? If so, we've become peacemakers, and God will bless us.

THE WOMAN WHO ANOINTED JESUS' FEET

Then he turned toward the woman and said to Simon,
"Do you see this woman? I came into your house.
You did not give me any water for my feet,
but she wet my feet with her tears and wiped them with her hair.
You did not give me a kiss, but this woman,
from the time I entered, has not stopped kissing my feet.
You did not put oil on my head, but she has poured perfume on my feet."
LUKE 7:44–46

The scene is a party at Simon the Pharisee's house. All the correct people must have been there: friends and acquaintances who prided themselves on their holy living, and maybe even a few really important men of faith. But one uninvited guest found her way in, carrying a jar of perfume. She slipped up to Jesus and, in the weeping of repentance, began to anoint His feet, first with her tears, then with the perfume.

Simon, who thought Jesus was just a prophet, immediately began to question His claims. After all, if Jesus had God's wisdom, couldn't He tell what everyone in Galilee already knew—that this woman was a terrible sinner? But before the Pharisee could speak, Jesus confronted his thoughts by telling a story of two men. They were both indebted to a moneylender—one owed five hundred denarii, about five hundred days' wages, while the other owed only fifty. Which one, Jesus questioned, would love him more when the moneylender forgave the debt?

The religious man, an able student though doubtful of Jesus' point, answered quickly that he supposed it would be the one with the bigger debt.

Jesus turned Simon's attention to the sinful woman. He gently rebuked Simon for not providing the hospitality customary to a guest: water to bathe His dusty feet. But that failure had made the way for this repentant sinner, who washed Jesus' feet with her tears and anointed them with the perfume. And she had not stopped with these signs of love, but kissed His feet, too. Because she was forgiven for many sins, Jesus told the proud religionist, she loved much. The clear implication was that since Simon's sins were so few (at least in his own eyes), he loved little.

Turning to the woman, Jesus said, "Your sins are forgiven" (Luke 7:48), causing an immediate whispering among the honorable guests. Who was this man who claimed to forgive sins? They knew only God could do that—and wondered what Jesus was claiming for Himself.

To complete the lesson, Jesus told the woman, "Your faith has saved you; go in peace" (Luke 7:50).

Scripture does not specifically say what sins this woman committed. But many scholars have concluded she was a prostitute. What an ending she brought to a very proper party! Guests probably talked about the event for days, if not weeks, and wondered about Jesus, the man who forgave her.

For Jesus, it was clear: it isn't how much faith you carry into a relationship with Him, it's how much forgiveness you receive when you place your sins at His feet.

What was true for this sinful woman is true for us, too. Are we, like Simon, sitting pridefully on our faith, thinking our own good works lead to salvation? If so, look out! Our good works are like filthy rags to our perfect Lord (see Isaiah 64:6). They will never get us to heaven.

But if, like this woman, we come to Jesus aware of the awfulness of our sins, asking Him to forgive them, our lives are made new in a way Simon, the proud Pharisee, may have never known.

Who are we like in this story? Simon and his guests? Or the forgiven woman?

THE WOMAN WHO TOUCHED
JESUS' CLOAK

As Jesus was on his way, the crowds almost crushed him.
And a woman was there who had been
subject to bleeding for twelve years, but no one could heal her.
She came up behind him and touched the edge of his cloak,
and immediately her bleeding stopped.
LUKE 8:42–44

Many women must have touched, brushed against, or otherwise had contact with Jesus' garments. But scripture records only one being healed by such a touch. The difference? Her faith told her that just a touch would lead to her healing—and it did.

For twelve years this woman had suffered from bleeding of some sort—we know no more of her medical condition, but that is enough. The emotional and physical need had ravaged her. Not only had her body endured misery, but because she had been "unclean" according to the Law, she had been an outcast spiritually, too. She could not approach the temple, no matter how deep her faith. And other Jews would have kept her at a distance, to avoid contamination. Hers must have been a lonely life. Mark 5:26 tells us she had gone to many doctors, spending all her money in her search for healing.

In a last effort, she came to Jesus. Reports had told her of His ability to heal. But this time things were different from her doctors' visits. She had nothing to offer Him but her unclean, impoverished self. No money, no importance, no hope.

Jesus was on His way to heal someone else, the daughter of a synagogue leader, when the woman touched His clothing. Poor, humble, and diseased, perhaps she thought she didn't deserve as much as a moment of the Savior's time. Or maybe she expected an outcry against her condition, for faithful Jews did all they could to avoid contact with the unclean.

As her fingers briefly latched onto the cloth, her body responded to Jesus' power. Suddenly, the bleeding stopped.

Just then, Jesus turned, asking, "Who touched me?" (Mark 5:31). Though His disciples doubted His words, pointing out that He was surrounded by a crowd, Jesus insisted someone had grasped Him with purpose. Of course, in His divinity, He must have known which person had held the cloak between her fingers—but He wanted her to come forward with her testimony.

Fearfully, perhaps thinking He would criticize her for wrongly taking advantage of Him, the woman fell at Jesus' feet. But the Lord didn't react with disgust or try to keep her at a distance. To Him, she was as important as the synagogue leader's child, and because of her need and her faith, she was deserving of His time and attention.

Then, before the entire crowd, the woman who had hoped to go unknown declared the truth of her healing.

Jesus replied mildly, "Daughter, your faith has healed you. Go in peace" (Mark 5:34).

What a thrill! What all the doctors could not accomplish, one touch of Jesus' cloak had done. Faith sprang up like a fountain in her heart as she rejoiced in her healing.

Like this woman, each of us needs Jesus' powerful touch. It may be a physical illness, or it may be spiritual. Like the woman, we desperately need healing. We come to Jesus poor and hopeless, seeking Him as the only possibility for healing.

What do you need to bring to Jesus? Approach Him with your need in both hands, and you will find Him right beside you.

ZILPAH

And Laban gave unto his daughter Leah
Zilpah his maid for an handmaid.
GENESIS 29:24 KJV

Upon her marriage, Laban gave his eldest daughter, Leah, a servant of her own. Perhaps Zilpah looked forward to this new place that would give her more importance.

But instead of happiness, a good deal of sorrow was headed her way. Jacob, Leah's husband, hadn't wanted to marry Leah. So he ended up marrying Leah's sister, Rachel, too. The sisters quickly began a battle of the babies to see who could give Jacob the most children. When Leah thought her childbearing days were over, she gave Zilpah to her husband as a concubine.

How did Zilpah feel about all this? We don't know. But we do know she felt blessed to have her first child, naming him Gad (meaning "good fortune" or "a troop"). It seems her outlook was positive, even though life wasn't perfect.

Zilpah obviously delighted in her children, since she named her second son Asher, which means "happy." But the marital relations in the camp brought a good deal of sorrow and contention, too.

And when Jacob returned to his homeland, it wasn't his beloved Rachel he put out in front of their caravan, in harm's way. It was Zilpah and Rachel's maid, Bilhah, also Jacob's concubine. These women were not loved for themselves—Jacob loved Rachel. The other three were primarily desired for the children they bore, who would start the twelve tribes of Israel.

Like Zilpah, none of us have perfect lives. But do we focus on the less than perfect or thank God for the many blessings He sends our way? We can choose to live in God's joy or in complaining. Which will make us happier?

ZIPPORAH

And Moses was content to dwell with the man:
and he gave Moses Zipporah his daughter.
EXODUS 2:21 KJV

You'd think that a powerful leader like Moses would have married a woman strong in faith, wouldn't you? Well, you'd be wrong.

Moses married Zipporah, the daughter of a Midianite priest named Reuel (or Jethro). The Bible never tells us what gods she worshipped, but it also doesn't show her as a believer. In fact, her only action recorded in scripture is the circumcision of one of her sons. This somewhat obscure passage says that God, angered at Moses' disobedience, was prepared to kill him. Zipporah concluded it was because Moses had not circumcised one of their sons and unhappily did the job herself.

A family disagreement on the subject—Midianite tradition called for the rite when the child was older—had probably caused Moses' lapse. Certainly his wife's attitude following the circumcision was not a pleasant one, so the issue may have been a bone of contention for some time.

Zipporah is last mentioned, briefly, in Exodus 18:2, when Jethro returns her and their sons to Moses. Scholars believe Moses may have left his family in Jethro's safekeeping while he made the dangerous trip to Egypt.

Zipporah did God's will only when her husband's life was threatened—when push came to shove, so to speak. Do we do the same? Will we wait until we face serious trouble before we obey, or will we consistently obey our Lord?

If you've read this entire book, you know what the answer should be. Go live the adventure of faith!

THE TOP
100
MEN
OF THE BIBLE

To the memory of F. Scott Petersen,
a faithful expositor and teacher of God's Word,
who now walks with his Savior among the great men of the Bible.

INTRODUCTION

Because there are many fascinating and important men in the Bible, choosing the top one hundred is somewhat subjective. Maybe this isn't the be-all-and-end-all of choices, but here are one hundred men of the Bible, most men of courage and faith, some scoundrels. Many are admirable men, flaws and all. A few were never believers or pretended to be, but their actions, leadership, or spiritual insensitivity affected many people. This collection of saints and sinners had a profound impact on Christian history and faith.

Among the one hundred, you'll find many different characters and personalities. Some you'll greet as brothers or friends, whereas others will exact a shiver of revulsion. When you read of a believing brother's trials, you may feel they speak to your own situation, or the victories found here may remind you of some of your own.

Learn from these men, be inspired by them, and avoid their mistakes. Scripture has recorded their lives to help us. May they challenge your faith and help it grow.

AARON

Then the LORD's anger burned against Moses and he said,
"What about your brother, Aaron the Levite?
I know he can speak well. He is already on his way to meet you,
and his heart will be glad when he sees you."
EXODUS 4:14

You could almost envy someone with a right-hand man like Aaron: a brother who would stand by you, no matter what. Called by God, Aaron became high priest to his younger brother Moses' greater role of prophet, and together they led Israel out of slavery in Egypt and toward the Promised Land.

From the time God called them, Aaron and Moses usually appear together through the biblical story. If Moses had been a different kind of guy, he might have sought the limelight for himself alone, but he feared speaking out for God. So Aaron joined him in ministry, and together they fostered Israel's exodus.

But brotherly love has its limitations. At times, Aaron must have deeply felt his role as second fiddle. His few failures took place when he was not in close contact with Moses. The first one happened following the Exodus, while Moses lingered on Mount Sinai, receiving God's Law. The Israelites became dissatisfied. *Where did Moses go?* they wondered. *Maybe he has deserted us.* The crowds clamored noisily for a new god. Perhaps Aaron feared the people, or maybe his own doubts influenced him. But he became a goldsmith, made a bright, shiny calf, and declared it to be their new god.

Seeing the idolatry, God sent Moses back to confront His faithless nation. Momentarily cowed (pardon the pun), Aaron blamed the people. But he must have repented of his sin, because shortly afterward, God reconsecrated His failed priest along with His new tabernacle.

We're told of only one other time when Aaron failed—and failed hugely. He and his sister, Miriam, became angry when Moses married a Cushite woman. Jealously, they tried to increase their own importance. God responded rapidly by afflicting Miriam with leprosy. But mercifully, He did not make the high priest unclean, and Aaron got the point.

Despite Aaron's two outstanding flops, his many years of faithful service to God and Moses far outweigh his failures. If he were our employee, we might be inclined to sideline him, but God called Aaron for a purpose and did not give up. Instead, He turned the priest again to faith and used him to establish Israel's priestly line.

Have we failed? It's no time to despair. As long as we're breathing, God has a purpose for us—to glorify Him forever.

ABEL

Abel brought fat portions from some of the firstborn of his flock.
The LORD looked with favor on Abel and his offering,
but on Cain and his offering he did not look with favor.
So Cain was very angry, and his face was downcast.
GENESIS 4:4–5

You might be tempted to think, from the story of Abel and his brother, Cain, that "nice guys finish last." But if that's what you think, then you've been misled.

Abel, second son of Adam and Eve, was the family "good boy." He may have consistently done what his parents asked. Certainly he loved God deeply, for when it came time to make an offering, he brought his heavenly Father the best he had. And God smiled on him.

Cain, the elder son, may have thought, *Mom has always loved you best—and Dad does, too. Now even God is taking your side.* Quickly, brotherly competition overcame brotherly love. Feeling unloved and unaccepted because God knew that his sacrifice wasn't from the heart, Cain took out his aggression on his brother. Soon, he committed the first murder in history, and he was condemned to wander the earth for the rest of his days.

Abel didn't have a long life, but judging from the joy that accompanied his sacrifice to God, it was a successful one. Jesus commended Abel as a righteous man (see Matthew 23:35). Though Cain lived on for many more barren years after killing his brother, who will say those days and months of life were better?

If finishing last means joy in eternity, maybe being last is the first thing we should aim for.

ABRAM/ABRAHAM

The LORD had said to Abram,
"Leave your country, your people and your father's household and go to the land
I will show you. I will make you into a great nation and I will bless you;
I will make your name great, and you will be a blessing."
GENESIS 12:1–2

Abram was a man with an immense promise: if he followed God out into the unknown, he and his descendants would be blessed. With that promise, God began to turn the childless Abram, whose name means "exalted father," into Abraham, "father of a multitude of nations."

So Abram headed for Canaan with his family. The Canaanites would have been shocked to know that God had promised their real estate to this newcomer.

But Abram didn't stay long enough to put down tent pegs. He soon traveled on to Egypt to avoid a famine. There, to protect himself, Abram conveniently didn't tell Pharaoh that his lovely "sister," Sarai, was really his wife. Pharaoh brought her into his household with romantic purposes in mind. But when God confronted him with his near sin, Egypt's ruler tossed Abram out of the land.

Over time, no heir was born. So when God appeared to Abram saying, "Do not be afraid, Abram. I am your shield, your very great reward" (Genesis 15:1), Abram admitted his doubts. In polite language, he asked why he had no son. God made a covenant with Abram that he would receive both an heir (in fact, heirs too numerous to count) and a land for their possession.

But when the new covenant still didn't provide a baby, Sarai decided to help God out. As was the custom of the day, she gave Abram her servant, Hagar, as a concubine, hoping that Hagar would conceive and bear a child whom Sarai could call her own. Abram unwisely went along with the plan. But instead of improving the situation, Sarai's plan created tension within the family life and planted the seeds of enmity between the Jews (the descendants of Abraham through Isaac) and the Arab nations that would come from Hagar's son, Ishmael.

When Abram reached ninety-nine years old, God renewed His promise and changed Abram's name to Abraham and Sarai's name to Sarah, meaning "princess." As a sign of their covenant, God instituted the rite of circumcision. But despite the many good things that God gave to Abraham and Sarah, the blessing of a child still evaded them.

Abraham moved to the Negev Desert and took up residence in the territory controlled by a king named Abimelech. Again Abraham introduced his wife as his sister. And again God intervened when King Abimelech, like Pharaoh before him, took Sarah into his house. Unlike Pharaoh, Abimelech gave Abraham money and offered him and Sarah a place to live. Eventually, Sarah bore Abraham a son, Isaac. But the camp still was not peaceful as Hagar and Sarah contended for their sons' positions. Finally, Sarah tossed Hagar and Ishmael out, and God told Abraham to allow it.

You can imagine Abraham's surprise when God commanded him to sacrifice Isaac, the son of promise. Quickly, and seemingly without argument, Abraham set out for the region of Moriah with Isaac and a bundle of wood for burning the sacrifice. Not until Abraham had laid Isaac on the altar did an angel stay his hand. God provided a ram instead, and with great relief Abraham removed his son from atop the wood.

When Sarah died, Abraham married again. But the children of that marriage did not change God's promise for Isaac and his descendants. Abraham arranged for Isaac's marriage to Rebekah, and then he died at the age of 175.

Though scripture clearly reports Abraham's imperfections, "Abraham believed God, and it was credited to him as righteousness" (Romans 4:3). Through the patriarch's long life, we see an increasing love for God and a willingness to obey Him.

God promised much to Abraham. Some of it was a long time coming, but it came. Every promise was fulfilled. Are we willing to wait for God's blessings, growing in faith along the way? Or are we like Sarah, in such a rush that we will risk our own future? Let's walk like faithful Abraham, trusting God.

ADAM

So the man gave names to all the livestock,
the birds of the air and all the beasts of the field.
But for Adam no suitable helper was found.
GENESIS 2:20

Imagine being the first man ever. No one had ever done this manly thing before. One day, Adam felt God's breath in his nostrils and sort of woke up, alive for his first day. Adam lived in a God-planted garden, with animals he got to name—from springboks to hoopoes to butterflies. And God didn't even complain about any name Adam chose! But living in the Garden of Eden was still lonely. Unlike the animals, Adam didn't have a mate. So God put the first man to sleep and created a woman from his rib. *Wow* (or words to that effect), Adam must have thought. *Look what God made just for me!* He evidently recognized the connection between this new creature, this woman, and God's surgery on him, because he responded, "This is now bone of my bones and flesh of my flesh; she shall be called 'woman,' for she was taken out of man" (Genesis 2:23).

Adam and Eve lived in perfect peace with each other. Not a marital disagreement disjointed their days. They were, as you might say, joined at the rib. They were living in paradise. What could go wrong?

A lot.

Adam should have put his (bare) foot down when Eve offered him some fruit that looked suspiciously as if it had come from the one tree in the garden from which God had forbidden them. If he'd known about sin, Adam might have pointed out that God's thinking was perfect, not Eve's, and they'd better follow it. But innocent Adam knew nothing about marital discord, so he took a bite.

Suddenly, the only two humans on the planet realized they were naked. Someone (like God) might see them! So they made up clothes of fig leaves (ouch!) to cover their sin. When God came walking in the garden that evening, the couple hid from Him. For the first time, they feared their Creator. Though Adam told God he was afraid because he was naked, his sin condition, not his skin condition, was the problem.

Eve immediately came forward to blame the serpent who had tempted her to eat the fruit, so God justly cursed the snake. But Adam and Eve didn't escape punishment. Eve received pain in childbirth and a desire for her husband. He got the pain of sweating to till an earth filled with weeds. Life became drastically different from the ease and comfort they'd known in the garden.

God drove the couple out of the garden so they would not eat from the tree of life. An angel with a fiery sword guarded the entrance.

In their new land, the couple had two children, Cain and Abel. But like their parents, the boys sinned, and Cain became the first murderer when he became jealous of his brother and took his life. Not only did Adam and Eve lose Abel, but God also punished Cain by making him wander the earth. Eventually, he married, but Adam and Eve probably never knew their grandchildren through Cain.

Perhaps at least in part to comfort them, God gave Adam and Eve another child, Seth. Through Seth, God began the covenant line that would lead to Noah and beyond. Adam lived for 930 years, enough time to see many of these successive generations come to adulthood.

Unlike Adam, we don't have to blaze new territory. All of us have had some man we can look up to—a father, grandfather, or friend who has shown us the way. And we know the dangers of sin, perhaps because we've fallen into its trap more than once. Adam's failure in the garden left us with a sin-filled nature that entraps us all too often.

But Adam's fall was not the final word. "For as in Adam all die, even so in Christ shall all be made alive" (1 Corinthians 15:22 KJV). What we in our weakness could not do for ourselves, Jesus did at the cross. In Him, we have new life—life for eternity.

AHAB

Ahab. . .did more to provoke the LORD, the God of Israel,
to anger than did all the kings of Israel before him.
1 KINGS 16:33

This report of scripture on Ahab's life says a lot. Because it's not as if the kings of Israel before Ahab had been a chorus of choirboys. They'd irritated God plenty. Ahab was just extraordinarily good at being bad.

Scripture doesn't detail many of Ahab's sins. But Ahab married a wicked Sidonian princess named Jezebel, who drew him and his country deeply into Baal worship. That's where the evil seems to have started.

During a drought, God commanded Elijah to appear before Ahab. Here's how the king greeted God's prophet: "Is that you, you troubler of Israel?" (1 Kings 18:17). Their relationship wasn't about to get better, for Elijah instigated a showdown between Baal and the Lord—and Jezebel's god didn't win. Elijah finished off the priests of Baal, and the drought ended along with the showdown. But by that time, both the king and queen deeply hated Elijah.

Then Ben-hadad, king of Syria, gathered thirty-two other kings and sent an imperious message to Ahab, claiming his household. Though Ahab sent back a conciliatory message, it wasn't enough for Syria's ruler: he wanted it all. But Israel's elders encouraged their weak-willed king to stand firm.

God used the wicked king to defend His people. He promised to give Ben-hadad's huge army into Ahab's hand, then provided Israel with specific war strategies. When Israel's attack began, Ben-hadad was drunk, and the other kings did not effectively defend themselves. Syria's king barely escaped with his life.

The following spring, Ben-hadad returned. He claimed that the Israelites had won the first round because their God was a God of the hills. So God was about to show that He ruled the plains, too. Ben-hadad chose his spot, and God proved His point. In a single day, Israel killed 100,000 Syrian warriors, and the 27,000 who escaped to the city of Aphek died when the wall fell on them. But Ben-hadad was still alive, and he sued for peace. The price Syria offered seemed good to Ahab, so Ben-hadad went free. But a prophet came to Ahab and told him that his life would replace the life of Ben-hadad, whom God had desired to destroy.

When the sullen Ahab traveled to Samaria, his eyes fell on a nice vineyard that he wanted to own. But its owner, Naboth, aware that the vineyard was his patrimony, given by God, would not sell or trade. While Israel's king sulked in his room, Jezebel plotted to get the land. By paying off some men to give false testimony about the righteous Naboth, she had him killed for blasphemy.

As Israel's ruler rejoiced in his new acquisition, Elijah arrived to report that the Lord knew the truth and that dogs would lick Ahab's blood in the place where Naboth had died. The wicked king repented, for a time. But three years later, when the king of Judah enticed him into battle against Syria, Ahab listened to false prophets, who advised him to go to war. Cowardly Ahab disguised himself, but during the fight he was hit by an archer and died after hours of suffering. His body was carried to Samaria, and the blood that had gathered in his chariot was licked up by dogs, just as God had promised.

People may think that being wicked is exciting or powerful. Ahab shows us otherwise. He was a coward who was ruled by his wife. Though he won a few battles, it was not because of his own strength.

Want real strength? Serve God alone.

ANANIAS, HUSBAND OF SAPPHIRA

Now a man named Ananias, together with his wife Sapphira,
also sold a piece of property. With his wife's full knowledge
he kept back part of the money for himself, but brought
the rest and put it at the apostles' feet.
ACTS 5:1–2

Had he been a wiser man, Ananias could have been known as generous, too. If he'd simply given whatever he and Sapphira chose and not claimed it was the full price of the property, his brethren might have praised him. But one seemingly small lie, which sought to make him seem less self-serving than he really was, turned the name Ananias into a Christian byword for greed.

When the apostle Peter confronted him with his wrongdoing against God, Ananias died. It probably wasn't just the shock of being found out—his was a godly judgment that kept other early Christians honest. When Sapphira died in the same manner, the people had no doubts about God's opinion of the couple's deeds.

Unlike Ananias and his wife, we may not die when we do wrong. But our deceptions hurt us nevertheless. God may not respond as quickly as He did with Ananias, but He does not ignore our sin. Will it take a lightning bolt from heaven to command our obedience, or just a word to our hearts from our Savior?

ANDREW

The first thing Andrew did was to find his brother Simon and tell him,
"We have found the Messiah" (that is, the Christ).
JOHN 1:41

How eager are you to tell others about Jesus? Instead of delighting in the prospect of such work, many of us struggle with what could be called "analysis paralysis." We worry about the best way to do it and never broadcast the message that Andrew spoke so simply.

Perhaps Andrew had a God-given predisposition to seek the Lord, but he had something even more important: a God-given mentor. The apostle John tells us that Andrew was a disciple of John the Baptist. For how long? Evidently it was long enough for the prophet to make quite an impression on this young man of Galilee.

We can only imagine what Andrew learned from John the Baptist. Perhaps he was among those who heard John take the Pharisees to task, saying, "[You] brood of vipers!" (Matthew 3:7 NKJV). We can be sure that Andrew heard the prophet's heralding of the coming Messiah. It was in the very forefront of all that John taught—and he declared it *emphatically*! He may have had a Greek name, but Andrew was more than Jewish enough to know about the Messiah. No doubt he knew about Him well before he met John.

Then came a day when Andrew heard his mentor say, "Behold the Lamb of God!" Scripture says, "The two disciples heard him speak, and they followed Jesus. Then Jesus turned, and seeing them following, said to them, 'What do you seek?' They said to Him, 'Rabbi' (which is to say, when translated, Teacher), 'where are You staying?' He said to them, 'Come and see.' They came and saw where He was staying, and remained with Him that day" (John 1:37–39 NKJV).

What was this first meeting like, and what did Jesus say? Whatever happened, it had a profound impact on Andrew, because not long after, he declared to his brother Simon, "We have found the Messiah." Andrew had discovered his true Mentor—and much more than that! Convinced of who Jesus was, Andrew brought his own brother to meet Him. Though Jesus Himself could have easily arranged the meeting, He allowed Andrew the privilege of introducing his elder brother to the Messiah.

Like Andrew, all of us bring others face-to-face with Jesus, but only in direct proportion to our conviction that we have found our own personal Lord and Savior. Is our conviction as firm as Andrew's?

APOLLOS

Meanwhile a Jew named Apollos, a native of Alexandria, came to Ephesus. He was a learned man, with a thorough knowledge of the Scriptures.
ACTS 18:24

Though Apollos knew the Old Testament scriptures well, something was missing. He'd been taught about Jesus but only knew the baptism of John. This eloquent man had yet to be acquainted with the workings of the Holy Spirit. So two leaders of the Ephesian church, a couple named Priscilla and Aquila, brought Apollos up to date on the work God was doing and the impact the Spirit had on Christians.

The golden-tongued preacher must have listened carefully and obeyed God's will, for when he moved on to Achaia, the Ephesian church leaders wrote a note of introduction to the believers there. We know that Apollos's improved ministry was influential in the Corinthian church, because some of its quarrelsome members claimed to follow him instead of Paul.

Like Apollos, are we able to admit that we don't have all the truth grasped in our hands? When another Christian points out a flaw in our thinking, can we humbly listen, compare that correction to scripture, and perhaps change course? Being able to do so may enable us to touch more lives for Jesus.

BALAAM

When the donkey saw the angel of the LORD,
she lay down under Balaam,
and he was angry and beat her with his staff.
NUMBERS 22:27

Imagine being a prophet who's dumber than a donkey. That's Balaam's reputation in scripture. And it was well earned by a man who wasn't quite faithful to God.

Following the Exodus, as the Israelites entered Moab, fearful King Balak hired Balaam, a Midianite prophet, to curse the invading nation. God ordered the prophet to go to the king but only speak His words, for He knew that Balaam was less than wholeheartedly faithful.

As Balaam headed toward Moab, God became angry (perhaps because the prophet was already thinking of ways to evade His command) and sent an angel to block his path. Balaam couldn't see the angel, but his donkey could. Three times, Balaam's donkey tried to avoid the heavenly being. Each time, the prophet struck the beast. Then God allowed them to have a conversation, and the donkey pointed out the angel. When Balaam saw it, he recognized his sin and offered to return home. Again he was warned to report God's truth.

Three times, Balak had the prophet offer sacrifices, hoping to get him to curse Israel, but each time Balaam obeyed God and blessed the nation. But on the sly, the false prophet suggested that Moab lead the Israelites astray by encouraging them to worship Baal (see Numbers 31:16). His plan worked. So when Israel attacked Moab's allies, the Midianites, Balaam was put to the sword.

Balaam was partly faithful to God. But when it served his own purposes, disobedience was still an option. Are we, like him, only willing to listen to the commands we like to hear, or do we follow God completely?

BARNABAS

*Joseph, a Levite from Cyprus, whom the apostles
called Barnabas (which means Son of Encouragement),
sold a field he owned and brought the money
and put it at the apostles' feet.*

ACTS 4:36–37

From the moment he appears in scripture, it's obvious that Barnabas is an admirable man. Scripture describes him as "a good man, full of the Holy Spirit and faith" (Acts 11:24). First-century Christians didn't call this church leader "Son of Encouragement" for nothing; look at his ministry, and you'll understand how he got his nickname.

Saul, the former persecutor of the church who became known as Paul, benefited from Barnabas's warmheartedness. When everyone else in the church worried about whether Saul's conversion was genuine, Barnabas collected the new convert and brought him to the apostles. The Son of Encouragement must also have been a risk taker for his Lord, because if he had been wrong about Saul, Barnabas would have been bringing enemy number one into the church.

Next, the church leaders in Jerusalem sent Barnabas to Antioch to check out some fellow Cypriots who were preaching to the Greeks (unlike other Christian preachers at the time who were preaching only to the Jews). Barnabas approved of what he found in Antioch, as many Greeks were being converted, and he later brought Paul to Antioch. For a year the two taught the new converts, leaving only briefly to take a relief collection to Jerusalem. After they returned, God sent them out on their first missionary journey, to Galatia.

During this adventurous journey, they were driven out of Antioch of Pisidia, fled from Iconium, healed a man at Lystra, and were declared gods there. But Paul was stoned in Lystra, so they kept moving, returning eventually to Antioch. There they confronted Judaizers, who demanded that the Christian community be circumcised.

Sent on, they traveled to Jerusalem to report on their mission. There they again faced Judaizers and, with Peter's support, convinced the church leaders not to require Gentile circumcision.

Finally, Paul and Barnabas went their separate ways after a disagreement about having John Mark as a companion on their missions. John Mark had left the first missionary journey midstream, and Barnabas evidently forgave him, but Paul was not ready to have him back. So Barnabas and John Mark went to Cyprus together—and Barnabas's faith in his young companion was fulfilled, because John Mark went on to become the writer of the Gospel of Mark.

Barnabas was exactly what the early church needed—a wise, patient leader. Wouldn't we like a handful of them in each of our own churches? Even more, wouldn't we like to be one of them? From Barnabas, we learn what it means to encourage others in faith and leadership. Like him, do we trust in God's plan, no matter what we face? Do we put faith in His working it out through the imperfect people we deal with daily?

BARTIMAEUS

Then they came to Jericho. As Jesus and his disciples,
together with a large crowd, were leaving the city,
a blind man, Bartimaeus (that is, the Son of Timaeus),
was sitting by the roadside begging. When he heard that
it was Jesus of Nazareth, he began to shout,
"Jesus, Son of David, have mercy on me!"
MARK 10:46–47

As Jesus and His disciples left Jericho, a large crowd surrounded them. Someone whispered in the ear of a blind beggar sitting on the side of the road that Jesus was passing by. Destitute Bartimaeus probably wasn't anyone's image of an ideal disciple, but from his cry to the Savior, "Son of David" (a messianic title), we know that he knew who Jesus was and wanted Him for his Master.

Despite being discouraged by Jesus' followers, Bartimaeus persisted, crying out even more loudly. Amazingly, Jesus called the beggar to Himself. Bartimaeus jumped up, dashed to the Savior, and begged for his sight. Jesus swiftly healed him, commending him for his faith, and the man rushed to follow his Lord.

Are we persistent, or can others turn us aside from crying out to the Master for our needs? If what we seek is God's will, we can follow the beggar's example and unrelentingly call on Jesus. Will He fail to answer us?

BOAZ

So [Ruth] went out and began to glean in the fields behind the harvesters.
As it turned out, she found herself working in a field belonging to Boaz,
who was from the clan of Elimelech.
RUTH 2:3

The young Moabite woman named Ruth must have been the talk of the town when she came to Bethlehem with her mother-in-law, Naomi. Boaz must have heard of the foreign woman's care for her in-law even before Ruth began gleaning his field. Then one of his men told him of Ruth's modest and unassuming behavior. So this kindhearted man watched out for her, telling her to stay near his women for protection and to drink from the vessels his men filled with water. He even ordered his men to give her extra grain.

Confronted about his concern for her, he replied to Ruth, "May the LORD repay you for what you have done. May you be richly rewarded by the LORD, the God of Israel, under whose wings you have come to take refuge" (Ruth 2:12). Perhaps Boaz was unaware that he himself would be part of the reward.

At home that evening, Naomi informed Ruth that Boaz was one of their kinsman-redeemers—a close relative of her husband, Elimelech—who could come to the widow's aid by marrying her. But instead of desiring Boaz for herself, Naomi put her daughter-in-law in Boaz's path, sending her to the threshing floor to essentially make a marriage proposal to the kinsman-redeemer by sleeping at his feet.

In the morning, Boaz met with the closest kinsman-redeemer in the family. When the man turned down the opportunity to act on his claim, Boaz bought Elimelech's land and promised to marry Ruth.

For his faithfulness, Boaz gained not only a wonderful young wife, but also a place in history, for he became the great-grandfather of King David and has a place in the lineage of the Messiah.

Boaz took a risk, marrying a foreigner who might not have remained faithful to the Lord. But he listened with his heart and spirit and willingly paid a price to bring her into his home. How willing are we to risk ourselves to do God's will when He calls us to do so? How kind are our hearts when we encounter others in need?

CAIAPHAS

During the high priesthood of Annas and Caiaphas,
the word of God came to John son of Zechariah in the desert.
LUKE 3:2

Chronologically, this is the first mention of the ungodly high priest who held authority during Jesus' ministry. Caiaphas had gotten the position when the Romans deposed his father-in-law, Annas. Because some Jews still viewed Annas as the high priest, maybe Caiaphas always felt as if Annas were looking over his shoulder. Certainly the Romans were: they wanted to keep a tight lid on the rebellious Jews, or they'd all lose their jobs.

Maybe that explains why Caiaphas acted more like a political leader than a religious one. He worried more about what people thought than about what was right. So when Jesus came along, it wasn't hard for him to make some really bad decisions.

When Jesus raised Lazarus from the dead, Israel's religious leaders, the Sanhedrin, got really concerned. This might lead to rebellion. The Romans would blame it all on them and replace them with leaders who could keep the peace. They envisioned themselves losing power, as Annas had.

Caiaphas offered a solution—kill Jesus. There was only one problem: under Roman law, the Jews couldn't kill anyone. So these selfish leaders held a kangaroo court in which Caiaphas accepted any testimony that would rid them of the Galilean. Then he passed Jesus on to the Roman authorities, who were also concerned about keeping the Jews quiet and thus found it expedient for Jesus to die.

After Jesus' death, His apostles still pestered the high priest by preaching the good news. Twice, Caiaphas arrested some of the apostles but found himself unable to do more than warn them not to preach. We hear no more of him in scripture after the early chapters of the book of Acts.

Caiaphas was a church leader gone wrong. His faith never informed his actions, so it's hard to believe he was anything but an unbeliever. Would we have people say that of us, or will we commit to acting out our faith in love and trust in God?

CALEB

[Caleb said,] "But I wholly followed the LORD my God."
JOSHUA 14:8 NKJV

Imagine having to wait forty years for the realization of your dream. That's how long it took for Caleb, Joshua's comrade-in-arms, to obtain Mount Hebron in the land of Canaan. Quite likely, Caleb first discovered his heart's desire while spying out the land of Canaan with Joshua and the ten others whom Moses dispatched for that purpose. He was then forty-five years old.

Caleb and Joshua's fellow spies issued a disheartening report about the land, and Israel tragically succumbed to their fear, to their own disgrace and demise. Caleb proclaimed that he (and Joshua) had followed the Lord wholeheartedly. Together the two faithful men delivered a favorable, determined report that almost led to their being stoned, were it not for the intervention of God Himself (see Numbers 14). So began a miserable wandering in the desert for forty long years; one year for each day the spies were in the land of Canaan. Everyone Joshua and Caleb knew fell in that desert wasteland.

Then came the day when Canaan was finally apportioned among the twelve tribes of Israel. While Judah was receiving its portion, Caleb boldly stepped forward and told Joshua, "You know the word which the LORD said to Moses the man of God concerning you and me in Kadesh Barnea. . . . Now therefore, give me this mountain" (Joshua 14:6, 12 NKJV). Caleb hadn't given up on his dream, and he was prepared to fight for it if he had to. He said, "And now, here I am this day, eighty-five years old. As yet I am as strong this day as on the day that Moses sent me; just as my strength was then, so now is my strength for war, both for going out and for coming in" (Joshua 14:10–11 NKJV).

There was no hesitation on Joshua's part. Evidently, Caleb had shared his desire to possess Mount Hebron with Moses, and Moses had agreed. Joshua obviously knew about this and gladly gave Mount Hebron to his dear friend.

It has been said that while Caleb's feet were treading the desert, his heart was atop the heights of Mount Hebron. God has a dream in mind for each of us, just as He did for Caleb. It might not require us to wait forty years for its fulfillment; it does require that we follow the Lord our God wholeheartedly and commit to our part as He enables us and leads us to the realization of our dreams.

THE CENTURION WITH A PARALYZED SERVANT

The centurion sent friends to [Jesus], saying to Him,
"Lord, do not trouble Yourself, for I am not worthy that You should enter
under my roof. Therefore I did not even think myself worthy to come to You.
But say the word, and my servant will be healed."
LUKE 7:6–7 NKJV

Although he was not Jewish, the centurion loved the Jewish people and even built them a synagogue. The Jewish elders begged Jesus earnestly to come and heal the Gentile's servant, who was dear to him and gravely ill. Such regard for a Roman centurion was extraordinary!

Jesus proceeded at once with them. He wasn't far from the centurion's home when he met some friends of the centurion, who passed along this message: "Lord, do not trouble Yourself, for I am not worthy that You should enter under my roof. Therefore I did not even think myself worthy to come to You. But say the word, and my servant will be healed. For I also am a man placed under authority, having soldiers under me. And I say to one, 'Go,' and he goes; and to another, 'Come,' and he comes; and to my servant, 'Do this,' and he does it" (Luke 7:6–8 NKJV).

Most folks wanted Jesus to prove Himself. Not this man. He simply said, "Just say the word." He knew enough about Jesus to believe that if Jesus spoke words of healing, even from afar, it would be done. Perhaps this is why Jesus said, "I say to you, I have not found such great faith, not even in Israel!" (Luke 7:9 NKJV).

It has been said that the greatest challenge any Christian faces is to believe in the trustworthiness of God's Word. How much do we trust?

CORNELIUS THE CENTURION

The angel answered [Cornelius],
"Your prayers and gifts to the poor have come up
as a memorial offering before God."
ACTS 10:4

Gentile! The word isn't usually used as a compliment. In the time of Jesus, Jews weren't to associate with Gentiles. During the very earliest days, the church consisted of Jews only, beginning as a sect of Judaism.

Converts to Judaism were obviously Gentiles. Scripture tells us that Cornelius was one of these, although his conversion might not have encompassed all the rituals. Male Gentiles who did not undergo circumcision were referred to as "God fearers."

Even so, Cornelius exhibited genuine faith in the God of Abraham, Isaac, and Jacob, and a fervor for prayer and almsgiving. In time, a heavenly messenger appeared to him and told him that his prayers and alms had come up for a memorial before God. He was instructed to send for the apostle Peter. Meanwhile, God gave Peter a vision in which he was told not to call anything unclean that God had made clean. This opened the way for Peter to visit Cornelius and baptize him and his entire household—the first Gentile converts to Christianity!

Could it be that God chose a military commander as the first Gentile convert to Christianity because the man was accustomed to giving respect? For all his authority, note the respect Cornelius showed Peter. How well do we follow Cornelius's example toward godly messengers in our day?

DANIEL

Then Daniel answered, and said before the king,
"Let your gifts be for yourself, and give your rewards
to another; yet I will read the writing to the king,
and make known to him the interpretation."
DANIEL 5:17 NKJV

The event in this verse didn't happen during the first part of Daniel's life. His character-defining moment came when he was a thoroughly experienced man who had completed decades of service as prime minister to the king of Babylon. But in a life marked by devotion to duty, above all, the prophet showed his devotion to the God of his native Israel.

Daniel's worldly success began in a way that he probably never would have dreamed. As part of the fortunes of conquest, Daniel found himself taken captive and forced to march to the distant heathen land of Babylon. No doubt this was a wrenching experience for the devout young man. Suddenly, he found himself immersed in a culture foreign to all that he knew, a culture steeped in paganism. If that weren't enough, Daniel was chosen to serve the king of Babylon, to be taught the language and writings of the Chaldeans, and to take a Babylonian name (Daniel 1:3–7). Can we possibly appreciate how utterly repulsive all this was to Daniel? Yet he had no choice, nor did his companions, Hananiah, Azariah, and Mishael. Escape was impossible, and the penalty for any such attempt would have been severe. Eventually, Daniel developed an allegiance to King Nebuchadnezzar. What this king spoke was law without question.

Despite his situation, through God's enabling, Daniel managed to develop an agreeable disposition without compromising his obedience to the Lord. He built a reputation of the highest integrity, discharging his duties diligently and honestly.

God also blessed Daniel with a particular ability to see beyond immediate reality and interpret dreams. At least twice, Daniel interpreted dreams for Nebuchadnezzar. On one of these occasions, Daniel saved not only the lives of the wise men of Chaldea, but his own life, too (see Daniel 2). Apparently, the keen wisdom God gave the prophet made him the most respected and influential of all the wise men in Babylon. Yet Daniel never let his ability go to his head. The more deference he showed, the higher his stature rose in the kingdom. Daniel's life was undergirded by faithful prayer and meditation upon the Law God gave to Moses.

Then came the scene in the great banquet hall of King Belshazzar. The handwriting is on the wall. The king's knees are knocking. What does it mean? Who will interpret it? The queen knows exactly whom to call. "O king, live forever! Do not let your thoughts trouble you, nor let your countenance change. There is a man in your kingdom in whom is the Spirit of the Holy God. And in the days of your father, light and understanding and wisdom, like the wisdom of the gods, were found in him; and King Nebuchadnezzar your father—your father the king—made him chief of the magicians, astrologers, Chaldeans, and soothsayers. Inasmuch as an excellent spirit, knowledge, understanding, interpreting dreams, solving riddles, and explaining enigmas were found in this Daniel, whom the king named Belteshazzar, now let Daniel be called, and he will give the interpretation" (Daniel 5:10–12 NKJV).

Daniel's whole character seems to converge in this moment. The summation of all that he is as a man shows through in the few words he speaks to Belshazzar. The king has promised gifts and the highest recognition to anyone who can answer the riddle. Daniel is not after a reward but boldly makes clear the revelation of God, whom the king has defied by his desecration of sacred vessels from the temple in Jerusalem. Not only is Daniel correct in his interpretation, but he is fearless in exposing the king's wickedness and his fate. The rewards of the king pale in comparison to God's rewards.

Although he never returned to Judah or Jerusalem, this man of God shone as a great light in pagan Babylon. Not many of us will rise to the stature of a Daniel, but he himself would tell us that unswerving devotion to God and not worldly fame is what counts most in our walk with the Creator.

DAVID

He raised up unto them David to be their king;
to whom also he gave testimony, and said,
I have found David the son of Jesse, a man after
mine own heart, which shall fulfil all my will.
ACTS 13:22 KJV

Even before David came to power as king of Israel, he had God's full confidence. David started out well. The former shepherd boy began by serving King Saul and fought Goliath, bringing honor to God and destruction to the Philistines. Saul made David a military commander, hoping he would be killed, but the people loved the new commander's battlefield success.

Jealous Saul tried to kill David, so the young warrior fled and ended up hiding in a cave. But not alone. His family and many whom Saul had treated badly joined him—about four hundred men. As civil war began, Saul must have realized he had trained his own enemy! Yet throughout the battles, David never harmed God's anointed king.

Finally, fearing for his life, David became a mercenary for Philistia but avoided fighting Israel. Instead, he made certain that no one lived to tell the Philistine king, Achish, that David was battling the other peoples of the land when he was supposed to be attacking Israel.

While David retrieved two of his wives, who had been kidnapped by the Amalekites, the Philistines fought the Israelites. Badly wounded, Saul killed himself, and three of his sons died in combat.

David was anointed king over Judah, but Ish-bosheth, Saul's only surviving son, became king of Israel. When two of his own men killed Ish-bosheth, David received Israel's crown.

In Jerusalem, David's faithful walk became much less consistent. The new king, who already had three wives, built a beautiful home, took many more wives and concubines, and went out to battle and defeated the Philistines. Then David brought the ark of the covenant to his capital city, in hopes that it would bring blessing. But while his army defeated the Ammonites and Syrians, David remained in Jerusalem, where he was attracted by a beautiful married

THE TOP 100 MEN OF THE BIBLE   125

woman, Bathsheba. He fell quickly into sin with her, and when she discovered she was pregnant, David plotted to have her husband, Uriah, die. His plot was successful, and he quickly married the widow.

Greatly displeased, God rebuked David through the voice of the prophet Nathan. The prophet reminded David of God's care for him throughout his life and declared that because of his sin, David's house would not have peace.

Nathan's prophecy was fulfilled among David's children, as God had promised. His illegitimate child by Bathsheba died. His daughter Tamar was raped by her half brother, Amnon. Tamar's full brother, Absalom, then murdered Amnon and started a conspiracy to take the throne from his father, who had to flee from Jerusalem. Only when Absalom was killed could his grieving father return to his throne.

Again David sinned, taking a census of his people. Perhaps having learned from his tryst with Bathsheba, he immediately confessed to God. God gave him three choices of punishment. The humbled king decided to receive his punishment from the hand of God, so David had to fight a pestilence rather than another nation. Mercifully, God did not send David the third choice: three years of famine. When David built an altar to God to avert the plague, God ended it.

As David's life dwindled, his son Adonijah attempted to grab the throne, which was intended for Solomon. Only the intervention of Nathan and Bathsheba saved Solomon's inheritance. David ended the issue by declaring Solomon his heir and having him anointed as king.

When we read of David's life, we begin to understand that our lives are not made up of compartments. We cannot keep our work life in one box and family life in another. When David sinned in his personal life, it affected his rule. When he was faithful, everyone benefited. Our lives need that consistency that glorifies God.

Though David had some major life failures, God made him one of the most powerful kings in Israel and brought the Messiah from his line. Though any man fails, God does not desert him—that is true for us as it was for David.

THE DEMONIAC OF GADARA

*Then they came to Jesus, and saw the one
who had been demon-possessed and had the legion,
sitting and clothed and in his right mind.*
MARK 5:15 NKJV

Is there a more desperate biblical figure than the out-of-control, demon-possessed man of Gadara? Infiltrated by a horde of demons, who called themselves "Legion"

(Mark 5:9), he had been reduced to a humiliating state and separated from home and friends. It's likely that this unhappy fellow had toyed with sin until it had a stranglehold on him.

It has been said that whenever Jesus confronted demons, they did what even the religious leaders of the day refused to do: they acknowledged Him to be the Son of God. It was no different in this case.

From the start, Jesus was in control of the entire situation, demons and all. Imagine the freedom the man felt when the demons left him! Once the man's sanity was restored, Jesus and the apostles clothed him. He begged to go with Jesus, but the Master sent him home to share the message of his healing (see Mark 5:19).

This man keenly knew what he had been saved from. If Jesus has saved us, do we comprehend what we have been saved from, and does it drive us to share our faith with others?

ELI

Year after year this man went up from his town to worship and sacrifice to the LORD Almighty at Shiloh, where Hophni and Phinehas, the two sons of Eli, were priests of the LORD.
1 SAMUEL 1:3

The household of a less-than-faithful priest, whose sons scripture describes as "worthless men" (1 Samuel 2:12 ESV), seems an unlikely place for the budding prophet Samuel to grow up.

Eli wouldn't have gotten the Father of the Year award. His sons bullied worshippers to do wrong, and they became involved with religious prostitutes. Their father must have received many complaints. When he finally took his sons to task, clearly it was too little, too late. God blamed Eli, who had failed to stop the boys' sin when they were young. God promised that the two sons would die young and on the same day.

But God not only raised up a new priest to take Hophni's and Phinehas's places; He graciously let Eli rear his replacement—Samuel, who was faithful to God.

This gentle, caring man had put his sons' wills before the Father's, with disastrous results. Will we learn from him? Or will we nurture our children but fail to correct them? If so, like Eli, we may find them overwhelming our households with sin. Are we raising "worthless men" or children who will glorify God?

ELIJAH

So [Elijah] said, "I have been very zealous for the LORD God of hosts;
for the children of Israel have forsaken Your covenant, torn down Your altars,
and killed Your prophets with the sword. I alone am left;
and they seek to take my life."
1 KINGS 19:10 NKJV

Of all God's prophets, none is more striking than Elijah, the prophet of fire! Like all the other prophets, he appeared at a critical juncture in biblical history. The prophets' chief function was to challenge the people of Judah and Israel to repent of their sins and return to the Lord after they had plunged headlong into apostasy. Often, prophets were directed by God to challenge the people in dramatic ways, such as Isaiah's walking naked in public (see Isaiah 20) or Jeremiah's smashing a clay pot (see Jeremiah 19). These spectacles were definitely attention getters, and they were effective to a certain extent.

In scripture, Elijah seemingly appears from out of nowhere, as was frequently the case with prophets. God sent him to testify against the northern kingdom of Israel and its evil king, Ahab. From the time of Jeroboam, Israel's first king, the northern kingdom had been on a continual descent into iniquity. Ahab and his malevolent wife, Jezebel, represented the very worst in all Israel. Elijah was sent by God to apply the "dive brakes" and lead the kingdom out of its downward plunge toward hell.

Prophets were not "nice guys," nor were they intended to be. They were deadly serious in their preaching and gave no quarter to those who opposed their message, which was literally a matter of life and death. This was certainly so with Elijah. Consider his courage and boldness as he confronted an entire nation and their king, thinking himself the only one left capable of taking a stand. Such strength would not have been possible or properly applied were it not for God's enabling and leading.

In his very first prophecy, Elijah stated emphatically to Ahab, "As the LORD God of Israel lives, before whom I stand, there shall not be dew nor rain these years, except at my word" (1 Kings 17:1 NKJV). The words "before whom I stand" can also be interpreted as "in whose presence I stand." Elijah had intimacy with God, an intimacy that came by diligently seeking the God of Abraham, Isaac, and Jacob. Evidently, the more Elijah focused on seeking God, the closer he was drawn to Him and the more zealous he grew toward Him.

This is what Elijah carried with him to the heights of Mount Carmel. This drove him to display matchless faith in contrast to the heathen priests of Baal. "You had better work a little harder, boys," he railed against them. "Perhaps your god has gone on a trip and can't hear you." Not the words of a tepid, halfhearted soul. The victory wrought by God that day atop Mount

Carmel was a triumph of His power at work through the witness of the one man He steeled for the task.

But Elijah was no superhero. It's comforting to know that he was a man "with a nature like ours" (James 5:17 NKJV) and not some superhuman. Still, God caused an outpouring of miracles to occur through Elijah as He did through Moses. When the time of his departure from this world came, Elijah was carried alive into heaven in a chariot of fire. The prophet Malachi tells us that Elijah will return "before the coming of the great and dreadful day of the LORD" (Malachi 4:5 NKJV). Is it any wonder that he alone accompanied Moses at the meeting with Jesus on the Mount of Transfiguration (see Matthew 17:1–13)?

None of us may be called to stand as boldly as Elijah did; nor are we likely to be swept up in a chariot of fire. Nevertheless, each of us has been given what Augustine called a "God-sized hole" in our hearts. If we pursue God as the primary objective of our lives, God will fill that void with His holy presence. Then He will enable us to zealously follow in the footsteps of Elijah by fitting us for the works He has prepared for us beforehand to accomplish (see Ephesians 2:10).

ELISHA

Elisha said, "Please let a double
portion of your spirit be upon me."
2 KINGS 2:9 NKJV

What a moment in biblical history! Both Elijah and Elisha are about to be engulfed in a spectacular supernatural event: Elijah's departure from this planet. Elijah, caring to the very last, asks his disciple if there is anything he can do for him before he departs. As if he's always known what to ask for, Elisha asks his master for a double portion of his spirit. "You have asked a hard thing," says Elijah. "Nevertheless, if you see me when I am taken from you, it shall be so for you" (2 Kings 2:10 NKJV).

Suddenly, a chariot of fire and horses of fire appeared and carried Elijah away, body and soul, into heaven. What an incredible event this must have been. Yet it was over as quickly as it happened. Elijah's mantle now lay at Elisha's feet. Elijah had cast this same garment over Elisha when he first came upon him as he was plowing his father's field. The prophet of fire had passed the torch to his successor.

Elisha, dazed by what he'd just witnessed, stooped down and picked up the mantle. He took it not as some relic to be worshipped, but rather as an emblem of the legacy Elijah had left him and the solemn responsibility he had conferred upon him. Elisha hadn't asked for wealth or prestige. He'd asked to be amply fitted for service to God. Taking up Elijah's mantle, he carried on his master's work, serving as a father to his fellow prophets and confronting the same enemies Elijah had. His work was twice as long as Elijah's, with twice as many miracles, and so much more would be required of him. Can there be any doubt that the Holy Spirit led Elisha to ask for what he did?

Elisha returned to the Jordan and struck it with Elijah's mantle. He simultaneously invoked the God of Elijah by saying, "Where is the LORD God of Elijah?" (2 Kings 2:14 NKJV). The waters parted, and Elisha walked across to the other side. When his fellow prophets saw him, they knew the spirit of Elijah rested on Elisha (2 Kings 2:15 NKJV). It's interesting that the first miracle Elisha performed was the very last performed by his master.

In the Bible, miracles came intermittently, in clusters, most notably during the ministries of Moses, Elijah, Elisha, and Jesus. The power to perform miracles was conferred by God to authenticate the call He had given each one of them. Miracles also demonstrated a mighty movement of God's hand at these junctures in biblical history.

Elisha dealt with the rebellious house of Jeroboam and the northern kingdom of Israel. Thus, some of the miracles he performed were meant to confront and punish, as in the case of the scoffing youths recorded in 2 Kings 2:23–25. What at first seems like an overreaction is, upon further investigation, justified. The youths lived in Bethel, the site of one of the two calf idols Jeroboam had made. It's said the locals didn't like being rebuked for the idol's presence, so the youths were simply acting out on their parents' disdain for Elisha and God; hence, the dramatic bear attack.

In most of the miracles he performed, Elisha demonstrated God's concern for ordinary people and the nation. A stunning example of this would be the story of the Syrian force that came to capture Elisha in Dothan (see 2 Kings 6:8–23). Here we see God's mercy in reassuring Elisha's servant, but also in sparing the Syrians whom He had blinded. Elisha led them right to the king of Israel but protected them from his wrath. Elisha understood that God's intent is to draw others to Himself either by His discipline or by His mercy.

Elisha had learned well from his master and predecessor and thus carried high and nobly the torch passed to him. His example could be summed up in the words of John L. Mason, who counseled that we're to follow no man (or woman) any closer than that person follows Jesus.

ENOCH

After he begot Methuselah,
Enoch walked with God three hundred years,
and had sons and daughters.
GENESIS 5:22 NKJV

What does it mean to walk with God? We have no better example than the biblical figure of Enoch. Though little is written about Enoch in scripture, much can be inferred about his life and character.

In a day when we're told that character isn't all that important, let's remember that by our character we make visible the kingdom of God. For those of us who claim the title *Christian*, making God's kingdom visible is our life's purpose.

Enoch also lived at a time when character wasn't valued very much. In fact, humanity was on a slippery slope toward hell. Cain's descendants were becoming more and more corrupt. Their ungodliness caused a gross degeneration of the human race. Before long, their corruption had even begun to contaminate the godly descendants of Seth, Adam and Eve's third child. Eventually, God could no longer bear such widespread iniquity and passed judgment in the form of a great flood. Enoch's great-grandson Noah and his family were the only ones who escaped that awful event.

Scripture tells us that after Enoch fathered his son Methuselah, he walked with God. Presumably, up until Methuselah's birth, Enoch lived no differently than other men of his time. He might not have been so vile as others, but he only walked *after* God instead of walking *with* Him. Bible commentator Matthew Henry writes that walking with God is "to make God's Word our rule and His glory our end in all our actions." Scripture doesn't tell us what caused this change in Enoch's walk, but it was probably something extraordinary. Perhaps the repulsiveness of humanity's increasing degeneration drove him nearer to God. Sanctification is a series of steps from grace to grace.

The epistle of Jude tells us that Enoch prophesied against those of his generation and predicted a dire outcome for them. Undoubtedly, this cast him in a bad light with the world of his time. Without trying to be self-righteous, Enoch may have become as repugnant to the world as it had become to him. His profound love for God may very well have been what caused his departure, body and soul, from this earth. Scripture says, "And Enoch walked with God; and he was not, for God took him" (Genesis 5:24 NKJV). Matthew Henry beautifully comments, "God showed how men should have left the world if they had not sinned, not by death, but by translation."

Are we walking so close to God that unbelievers recognize it? Their disfavor matters nothing if we're gaining God's favor instead.

EZEKIEL

*The word of the LORD came expressly to Ezekiel the priest,
the son of Buzi, in the land of the Chaldeans by the River Chebar;
and the hand of the LORD was upon him there.*
 EZEKIEL 1:3 NKJV

Life can be anything but easy—and Ezekiel knew it, because he lived in one of Judah's most difficult times. The Assyrians had begun losing power to the rising Babylonian Empire, and Judah was stretched between the warring factions until Babylon conquered Jerusalem in 597 BC. That year, many Jews were exiled to Babylon, among them this son of a priest. In the new land, Ezekiel received the call to be a prophet.

Ezekiel's message wasn't a cheerful one. Unlike Jerusalem's false prophets, he told his exiled people that their time away from home would not be short—they'd better settle in. Jerusalem and the idolaters who remained there would be destroyed, and God's presence would leave the temple.

Over and over, Ezekiel confronted the people with their sin and promised that judgment would follow. You can imagine that he wasn't the most popular man in town. Those who stand up to false prophets never get a lot of kudos, especially when they continually repeat the same cheerless message. Ezekiel's countrymen didn't like the message and often didn't listen to it.

But just about the time the people of Judah were thoroughly tired of Ezekiel's message, God gave him another one. He spoke about the sins of Judah's neighbors and painted a picture of dry bones (all the Israelites) that would come back to Israel and serve God faithfully. Ezekiel saw a rebuilt temple and God's glory returned to it. God's people would again own the land.

For twenty years, Ezekiel's ministry focused on sin and judgment. He probably got tired of it himself, but he faithfully repeated God's message until God chose to reveal His future plans. God had not deserted His people, though they were tempted to think so. In the right moment, Ezekiel reminded them of that fact.

When life does not seem easy and we don't have a cheerful message for others, are we still faithful? Or are we so caught up in the need for happiness that we can't accept the pain that life sometimes brings? Like Ezekiel, we need to speak clearly for our Lord and trust that He will bring the good news we've been seeking day by day.

EZRA

Ezra went up from Babylon; and he was a ready scribe
in the law of Moses, which the LORD God of Israel had given:
and the king granted him all his request, according to
the hand of the LORD his God upon him.

EZRA 7:6 KJV

When King Darius I commanded Ezra to return to Jerusalem and oversee the rebuilding of the temple, he wasn't offering the scribe-priest a cushy job. Ezra may have had all the money and protection he needed from the powerful Persian ruler, but plenty of trouble lay ahead.

A first wave of temple rebuilders had returned to Jerusalem when King Cyrus commanded the temple to be rebuilt in 538 BC. But succeeding kings had seen the rebuilding project as a threat and had stopped it. Much work lay ahead for Ezra.

When Ezra gathered his band of Israelites and priests and had a prayer service to ask for God's protection on the journey, he needed all the prayer he could get. Months later, as he entered Jerusalem, he landed himself in big trouble. Though the Israelites living in Babylon hadn't had an easy life, at least they had been mindful of their background and God's commands. Those remaining in Jerusalem had become lax, to say the least.

Before Ezra had time to get his new home in order, the reports were already in. The Israelite officials told the new guy in town that many Jews, even priests, had intermarried with the local pagan peoples. They expected Ezra to do something about the influence this had had on their nation. Not exactly the way to gain popularity in your homeland, was it? But Ezra didn't worry about that. He immediately turned to God in prayer, confessing the sins of his people and asking for forgiveness.

Graciously, God heard the priest's prayer and sent revival to His people. Those who had married apart from His Law put away their foreign spouses and returned to Him. Forgiveness covered the land.

When we face sudden, seemingly overwhelming troubles, do we worry about others' opinions, seek the counsel of the powerful, or begin by turning to God in prayer, believing He will act? Whether or not God responds immediately, His help is the first thing we need to seek. For when His grace intervenes, whatever its timing may be, our problems are solved.

GIDEON

So [Gideon] said to Him, "O my Lord, how can I save Israel?
Indeed my clan is the weakest in Manasseh, and I
am the least in my father's house."
JUDGES 6:15 NKJV

The biblical period recorded in the book of Judges is perhaps the saddest in all of scripture. It stands in stark contrast to the triumphant book of Joshua. We're told that after the death of Joshua, another generation arose that did not know the Lord or what He had done for Israel. Instead, every man did what was right in his own eyes. Add to this that Israel disobeyed God and had not eliminated the heathen people of Canaan, and you have a recipe for disaster.

In Gideon's days, all Israel was besieged by raiding parties of Midianites and Amalekites, who stole across the Jordan River to plunder food and whatever else they could get their hands on. The Israelites hid their produce from these raiders in dens and caves in the mountains. In such a setting, Gideon had a heavenly encounter. While covertly threshing wheat in his father's winepress, he was suddenly greeted by an angel: "The LORD is with you, you mighty man of valor!" (Judges 6:12 NKJV).

Stunned, Gideon managed to ask why Israel had fallen victim to misfortune. When the angel told him that he would be the one to liberate Israel from its oppressors, Gideon was unnerved. Confessing the lowliness of his father's clan, he also begged for a sign to confirm the angel's words. Accordingly, God built faith in Gideon by miraculously causing his offering to burn; He answered his requests for a wet or dry fleece; and then He allowed Gideon to hear the misgivings of his enemies (see Judges 6:19–22, 36–40; 7:8–14). What a comfort to know that God Almighty stoops paternally to strengthen us in our weakness.

God also performed a masterful "screening process" for Gideon's soldierly band, reducing their number to a mere three hundred men. He graciously informed Gideon as to why He did this (see Judges 7:2). Then, with his meager force armed only with trumpets, pitchers, and torches, Gideon, strengthened and guided by God, created deadly chaos in the enemy's camp, which led to a complete rout and total victory.

Time and time again in scripture, the children of Israel are told, "The battle is not yours; it is God's" (see Exodus 14:13–14; 2 Kings 6:8–16; 19:32–34; and 2 Chronicles 20:15, 17). Those words are just as true for us today as they were for Moses, Elisha, Hezekiah, Jehoshaphat, and Gideon. Can we respond with the same faith as these men?

GOLIATH

A champion named Goliath, who was from Gath,
came out of the Philistine camp.
He was over nine feet tall.
1 SAMUEL 17:4

When the Israelites saw the massive Goliath and his impressive armor, their mouths must have gaped. It's not hard to understand why no one wanted to fight the huge Philistine champion. Who could win against a man with Goliath's battle experience and mighty weapons?

Only one Israelite believed he had a chance of winning. David, a shepherd boy who had defeated wild animals with his slingshot, saw Goliath as a wild man—one who had the nerve to defy God. The youth didn't think much about his opponent's size or armor; he was too busy thinking about his own powerful God.

David's confrontation with the giant made Goliath an example of "the bigger they are, the harder they fall." As David trusted God, his slingshot aimed accurately. A stone hit Goliath squarely in his forehead, and the huge fellow collapsed, dead. Quickly, David grabbed Goliath's giant sword and cut off the giant's head while the rest of the Philistines ran for their lives.

We may never have gone into battle, but we've faced our own giants. Do we throw in the towel, or do we follow in David's footsteps and trust God?

THE GOOD SAMARITAN

"But a Samaritan, as he traveled, came where the man was;
and when he saw him, he took pity on him."
LUKE 10:33

Scripture doesn't actually use the word *good* to describe this Samaritan. And he wasn't an actual person, just a man Jesus created in a parable. But his story has had a powerful impact on people since the day our Lord told this tale.

The Good Samaritan came into being when a lawyer, trying to find some wiggle room when Jesus told him to love his neighbor, asked, "Who is my neighbor?" By the end of Jesus' response, the legal beagle probably wished he hadn't asked the question, for the Lord's answer has challenged everyone who has ever heard the story. It doesn't allow anyone to escape the harsh truth about the difficulty of loving others.

Jesus told of a man who traveled from Jerusalem to Jericho, a dangerous route along which robbers had easy access to their victims. The innocent traveler was attacked, beaten, and left for dead. As he lay in the road, others passed him without helping. First, a priest walked by, probably on the very far edge of the other side of the road. *What if the man is dead?* he probably asked himself. *If I touch him, I won't be able to do my priestly duty.* Or maybe the religious leader was just too busy or didn't want to take responsibility for a stranger.

Next, a Levite, one who acted as a priest's assistant, came along, and he, too, avoided contaminating himself with the man in need. He probably shared the same concerns as the priest.

Left to these "religious" folk, the man in the road might have died. That's why God sent a Samaritan along. To the Israelites, Samaritans were particularly unsavory characters. After the Assyrians conquered Israel and deported much of the population, the conquerors repopulated the country with other peoples. The Samaritans' forebears were Jews who had intermarried with these pagans. Not only did this race have mixed blood, but they had also combined their faith in Yahweh, the God of Israel, with pagan religious practices. So the Samaritans were hated by the Jews on the basis of both their background and their beliefs.

But this "unholy" outlander had a heart of gold. When he saw the injured man, compassion filled his heart. He medicated and bandaged the hurting traveler, placed him on his donkey, and carried him to the closest inn. There he paid the bill and promised the innkeeper more money for caring for the stranger.

Following this brief tale, which never tells us what ultimately happened to the traveler, Jesus asked the lawyer which of the three passersby was a neighbor to the hurting man. Perhaps constrained by his distaste from pronouncing the hated name *Samaritan*, the lawyer answered, "The one who had mercy on him."

"Go and do likewise," Jesus commanded.

The Samaritan's tale challenges us not to become so caught up in the legalities of faith that our hearts turn cold. Like the religious leaders who passed by on the wrong side, it's easy for us to get wrapped up in our own lives and ignore those in need. But Christian faith requires that we not only tell people about Jesus, but live out the kind of faith that makes Him real to others.

Are we up to the Good Samaritan's challenge? Only if Jesus fills our hearts each day!

HEROD

*After Jesus was born in Bethlehem in Judea, during the time of King Herod, Magi
from the east came to Jerusalem and asked, "Where is the one who has been born
king of the Jews? We saw his star in the east and have come to worship him."
When King Herod heard this he was disturbed.*

MATTHEW 2:1–3

When Herod the Great wasn't happy, nobody else was either. Unhappy with his
sons, he murdered a few—even his favorites. As Emperor Augustus declared, it
was better to be Herod's pig than his son.

This paranoid king exterminated anyone who threatened his authority. That's
why, when he heard about Jesus' birth, he killed all the young boys in Bethlehem.
But while he tore people down, Herod was known for his building projects—he
began work on rebuilding the temple and erected pagan altars and many public
buildings.

When Herod died, three of his sons inherited his lands. Herod Antipas,
who governed Galilee and Perea, became involved in the Jewish dispute that led
to Jesus' death.

Herod the Great spent his life worrying about losing power. Do we
also worry about the things of this world at the expense of eternity? No one
remembers Herod's building projects, but even well-read non-Christians can tell
you he murdered his sons and innocent children.

HEZEKIAH

*Hezekiah trusted in the LORD, the God of Israel.
There was no one like him among all the kings of Judah,
either before him or after him.*

2 KINGS 18:5

Scripture never tells us how a son of wicked King Ahab of Judah became a faithful believer. But at age twenty-five, Hezekiah came to power, removed the pagan
places of worship from his land, and destroyed false objects of worship.

Scripture praises Hezekiah highly for his faithfulness. His walk was a
consistent one, unlike those of many other rulers of his age. God blessed him
for this, making him successful in his rebellion against the king of Assyria and
in battle with the Philistines. But in the fourteenth year of Hezekiah's reign,
King Sennacherib of Assyria captured Judah's fortified cities and sent his military
counselor to talk Hezekiah into admitting defeat. Though Hezekiah gave the
powerful king a huge tribute, it was not enough. Sennacherib wanted Hezekiah

out of office. So an Assyrian military commander came with a message and even tried to sway the men of Jerusalem with dark warnings of what would happen if they held out against his master.

Judah's king knew where to go in times of trouble. He immediately dressed in sackcloth, indicating his spiritual humility, and sent two men straight to the prophet Isaiah. The prophet offered the king encouraging news: Sennacherib would hear a rumor that would send him quickly home. When Sennacherib's commander returned, he denigrated the power of Hezekiah's God. Judah's king turned to God in prayer, placing all his fears before the Lord. Again Isaiah prophesied that Jerusalem would not be hurt.

That night, 185,000 men in the Assyrian camp died at the hand of the angel of the Lord. Sennacherib returned to his home and was killed there by two of his sons.

Then, scripture tells us, Hezekiah became deathly ill. Isaiah warned him to prepare for death, but the king prayed again, and God gave him fifteen more years of life and promised to protect his city.

The king of Babylon sent envoys to Hezekiah, who proudly showed off his wealth to them. Perhaps Judah's king wanted to impress the Babylonians, but instead he gave them other ideas. After the envoys returned home, Isaiah prophesied that all Hezekiah had shown them would be taken to Babylon in a coming exile. The king was simply thankful it would not happen in his lifetime.

When Hezekiah faced problems, he didn't worry. He became a prayer warrior. Do we do likewise, placing our cares firmly in the hands of the Almighty, trusting He will save us? Then we, too, are faithful Hezekiahs, who may hear God's praise for our lives.

HOSEA

When the LORD began to speak through Hosea,
the LORD said to him, "Go, take to yourself an adulterous
wife and children of unfaithfulness, because the land is
guilty of the vilest adultery in departing from the LORD."
HOSEA 1:2

Could God really have commanded His prophet to marry a prostitute? Scholars disagree. Some say it really happened, while others maintain that Hosea had a vision so real that it was as if it had really occurred. But scripture recounts the story as fact.

In the northern kingdom of Israel, Baal worship had been combined with worship of God. Hosea lived in the midst of this syncretism, with people who added pagan practices on top of a biblical faith and didn't seem to think that

God would mind. The book of Hosea depicts these events as a family split by marital infidelity.

Daily, Hosea stood in the middle of the division between real faith and paganism. In his own family life, he lived on the fault line of unbelief and real faith. Scholars who believe the story is literal conjecture that Hosea's first child was his own, but the following two were the result of his wife's unfaithfulness. This wasn't an ideal marriage by any means. But it's God's honest picture of what His relationship with Israel was really like.

Hosea tenderly describes God's love and the pain His people's unfaithfulness brought Him. Even as, through the prophet, God promised judgment, He wooed His beloved ones back with a promise of mercy.

God commanded Hosea to love Gomer, a woman who did not love him in return. When she left him, he was sent by God to bring her back into his life. Though his wife had run to a lover, Hosea bought her out of slavery and gently directed her to remain faithful to him. Like Gomer, Israel had been drawn away by the sinful attractions of neighboring countries. To most of Israel, the fertility god Baal looked more pleasing than the Lord. But the Israelites were running themselves toward destruction. Their kings sold out to the pagan kings of Assyria, looking there for protection instead of to God. Israel had sown the wind and would reap the whirlwind (see Hosea 8:7). Yet the Lord warned them of the coming danger and called them back to Himself.

Though God repeatedly chastised His people, He did not end the book of Hosea in judgment, but by again calling His unrepentant people back to Himself.

Have you ever doubted that God really loves you? Read the book of Hosea. Could anyone on earth forgive you that much, want you that much, and be that patient with you? Maybe you'll never love anyone that way, under your own power, but God can empower you with His unending love.

THE IMMORAL MAN OF CORINTH

It is actually reported that there is sexual immorality
among you, and of a kind that does not occur even
among pagans: A man has his father's wife.
1 CORINTHIANS 5:1

We often assume that most Christians won't engage in the "big sins." Sure, we all struggle with something, but sexual immorality of the sort Paul describes here shocks us as much as it did the fertility-god-worshipping Greeks.

All sorts of sinful behavior may go on, even within the church. But it usually happens behind closed doors; and when it's unearthed, woe to the sinner! Yet in Corinth, the whole congregation knew that one man was having sexual encounters with "his father's wife," believed by many Bible teachers to be the man's stepmother—but no one intervened to rebuke the sinner. So Paul came down hard on the whole church.

These relatively new Christians deserved the rebuke. Everyone in Corinth was no doubt gossiping, "Did you hear what's going on over there in the First Corinthian Church? They enjoy incest!" The congregation's witness had been damaged. So Paul insisted that the Corinthians toss out the man who had sinned in order to make things right.

It may seem hard on the sinner to toss him out summarily, but if we're wise, we won't condone sin in our churches or in our lives. Better to toss one man out than to have others caught up in the same sin. A repentant sinner can always return, but ignoring sin will ruin Christians and their churches.

ISAAC

"Your wife Sarah will bear you a son, and you will
call him Isaac. I will establish my covenant with him
as an everlasting covenant for his descendants after him."
GENESIS 17:19

If good things are worth waiting for, Isaac must have been wonderful. His parents received the promise of his birth twenty-five years before his birthday. When they heard his first cry, how excited Abraham and Sarah must have been! Here, after all these years, was their covenant child of promise.

To protect him, the couple made Isaac's jealous half brother, Ishmael, and his mother, Hagar, leave their camp so that nothing would threaten God's gift. Sarah had tried to lend God a helping hand and had given her maid to Abraham to have a child for her. Now Ishmael was a terrible problem and had to be gotten rid of.

Then God asked Abraham to sacrifice Isaac on an altar. As father and son drew near to the place of sacrifice, Isaac realized that they lacked an animal to place on the altar. God would provide it, Abraham promised. Yet suddenly, Isaac found himself on top of the altar, and his father had a knife in his hand. How both must have rejoiced when they heard the bleat of that ram in the thicket and knew that God had provided. Perhaps Isaac wiped his brow with relief. No doubt the word *salvation* had new meaning for him.

We next hear of Isaac when Abraham arranged a marriage for his forty-year-old son, sending a servant back to his homeland to seek a bride. The servant returned with a dream girl, Abraham's grandniece Rebekah, and Isaac loved her.

But when the babies didn't come, Isaac prayed for a child. That must have been some prayer, for God gave the couple twins—Esau and Jacob. Esau was his father's darling, but the favored son easily sold his birthright to Jacob. Then Rebekah plotted with Jacob to gain Isaac's blessing, which would give Jacob authority over the family. Jacob's successful bid for power forced him to flee Esau's wrath. Many years would pass before he returned and made peace with his brother. But at least he was there when his aged father died.

God's faithfulness shines through Isaac's life. God promised Abraham a son, and though he was a long time coming, Isaac was born, and he trusted in the Lord. The incident in which he almost became a sacrifice did not separate Isaac from God. No turn of life broke his faith. Isaac held fast to the Lord.

Can others say the same of us?

ISAIAH

The vision concerning Judah and Jerusalem
that Isaiah son of Amoz saw during the reigns
of Uzziah, Jotham, Ahaz and Hezekiah,
kings of Judah.
ISAIAH 1:1

The four kings who heard Isaiah's prophetic messages may have been hearing God's word to them from a relative. Some scholars believe that Isaiah was the nephew of Judah's King Amaziah. Yet the prophet didn't hold back. He offered a straightforward and less-than-pleasing message: Judah had rebelled against God and offended Him at every turn.

Isaiah worked in an age of political instability. He took up his prophetic mantle in 739 BC, the year King Uzziah died. During the monarchies of Uzziah and Jotham, the militaristic Assyrian Empire had ignored the tiny countries to its southeast. But during Ahaz's reign, a succession of Assyrian kings expanded their empire in the direction of Judah.

Israel and Syria begged Judah to join them in repelling the encroaching nation. They didn't take Ahaz's refusal well and fought him. As other nations opportunistically attacked Judah and Ahaz's power began to crumble, he called on Assyria to support him. It did. Israel was vanquished by the Assyrians in 722 BC, and Judah became a vassal state.

Still, things did not go well for Ahaz. Assyria intended to have Judah under its own control, not his. Instead of turning to God, Ahaz followed the Assyrians into open idolatry. He closed the temple and removed its valuable objects.

When Isaiah prophesied to Ahaz, his messages combined encouragement with predictions of future destruction for Judah's opponents. Yet Ahaz ignored the prophet and became a thoroughgoing pagan. He was so bad that when he died, his people would not bury him with Judah's other kings.

Though Isaiah's book records many messages that God spoke through him, and we know the history of the kings, scripture does not tell us much about the prophet himself. His glorious prophecies, filled with information about the coming Messiah and a deep understanding of God's nature, indicate that he was a man of extremely deep faith.

Yet only a few chapters in 2 Kings show the prophet in action. In 701 BC, under King Hezekiah, Judah rebelled against Assyria. King Sennacherib, determined to take command over the nation, conquered Judah's outlying fortresses and sent a messenger to Jerusalem with an ultimatum: Give up.

Faced with the threat of annihilation, faithful Hezekiah called upon the Lord and sent his men for Isaiah. The prophet promised that Sennacherib would return to his own country, leaving Judah whole, and that Sennacherib would be killed in his homeland. Quickly, Hezekiah received a message that confirmed the first part of that promise.

Relieved and thankful, Hezekiah praised God for the deliverance, and God heard the king's prayer. That night, He took the lives of 185,000 Assyrian soldiers, and the rest of the army fled for home. There Sennacherib's sons killed him.

Hezekiah must have been a powerful man of prayer, for scripture tells us of a time when he was ill. Isaiah broke the bad news: the king would not recover. But Hezekiah wept before God, and the Lord extended his life by fifteen years. Isaiah reported that good news and God's promise to protect Jerusalem from the king of Assyria. As a sign, the prophet moved a shadow back ten steps.

When the king of Babylon sent envoys to Hezekiah, he showed off all his treasures. In the final prophecy ascribed to Isaiah, he had the sad job of telling Hezekiah that all he'd shown off would be carried away to Babylon. But it would happen during the reign of one of his sons, not while faithful Hezekiah was still alive.

According to tradition, and possibly alluded to in scripture (see Hebrews 11:37), Isaiah was eventually put to death by being sawn in two.

Isaiah's messages are filled with colorful imagery, a vital understanding of God, and a clear vision of the Lord's plan for His people. The prophet drew close to God and gained an awesome depth of understanding from his faithful walk with Him. In a dangerous time, he spoke clearly and honestly to a people who did not want to hear him.

Wouldn't we all like to be faithful like Isaiah?

JACOB

Jacob said to his father, "I am Esau your firstborn.
I have done as you told me. Please sit up and eat some
of my game so that you may give me your blessing."
GENESIS 27:19

Before Jacob and Esau were born, God promised that the older twin would serve the younger—a backward situation in that culture and time. But God didn't stop there. He continued blessing Jacob, the younger son, over his disobedient older brother, even though the chosen Jacob often lived a less-than-perfect life.

As the twins grew, Jacob became the home-loving son, while brother Esau turned into an outdoorsman. Though Jacob was his mama Rebekah's favorite, his father, Isaac, favored Esau. One day, when Isaac was old, weak, and nearly blind, he asked Esau to hunt some game and make him a meal. In return, he'd bless his most-loved son, ignoring God's promise.

Rebekah overheard the conversation, warned Jacob, and came up with a plot. Jacob would pretend to be his brother. Having his mother make up a goat stew and covering himself in goat hair worked: Isaac gave him dominion over Esau.

But now Jacob had to deal with his brother—a very angry man who was ready to commit murder. For Jacob's safety, Rebekah convinced Isaac to send her favorite son on a visit to Uncle Laban, to find a bride. During the journey, Jacob had a dream in which God promised to bless him.

But the deceiver was about to receive a taste of his own medicine. No sooner had he neared Laban's neighborhood than Jacob met his cousin Rachel and fell head-over-heels in love with her. He promised his uncle that he would work seven years for his bride. But Laban's older, less beautiful daughter, Leah, needed to marry first. So on the wedding night, crafty Laban slipped the wrong woman into Jacob's tent. By morning, the young man could do nothing but admit that he had a wife he didn't want and negotiate a new deal to get Rachel.

So Jacob began a life that denied God's plan. To gain Rachel, he worked another seven years for his uncle. Meanwhile, Leah began bearing him children—while Rachel remained barren—and a competition started between the sisters. Desperate to provide a son for Jacob, Rachel gave him her maid to bear children for her. Then Leah gave her maid to Jacob as well. Before long, Jacob had more women than he could handle, and they kept adding to the family. By the end, Jacob had twelve sons and a daughter. Conflict must have filled the camp until Jacob felt like leaving. Instead, he set himself up to gain a large herd of livestock, making a deal with Laban that he twisted to his own advantage. Yet despite his conniving nature, Jacob was blessed by God.

Then Jacob took his family and moved toward his homeland. And God renamed him Israel.

Israel's reunion with Esau was surprisingly uneventful. But at Shechem, his daughter, Dinah, was raped by the son of the ruler. Two of Israel's sons, Simeon and Levi, all but started a war over the issue, so Israel and his family and flocks moved on to Bethel. There God gave Israel His covenant promise, and he built an altar.

Just about the time that Israel might have felt things were settling down, his older sons sold off his favorite son, Joseph, Rachel's firstborn, and sorrow filled the camp. For years, Israel didn't know what really happened, until a drought came and he sent his sons into Egypt for provisions. There they discovered that the brother they thought was dead was now the second most powerful man in Egypt.

At Joseph's request, Israel and his family traveled to Egypt, where Joseph could care for them. Israel blessed his sons before he died in Egypt and made them promise to return his body to their homeland. Joseph had his father's body embalmed and returned to his homeland to fulfill that promise.

Though Jacob had seasons in which he obeyed God less than perfectly, God never changed in His purpose or commitment. He never abandoned Israel. Though we may find ourselves in baffling situations that turn out in ways we never expected, God will never give up on us, either, as we seek His will.

JAMES, BROTHER OF JESUS

"Isn't this the carpenter? Isn't this Mary's son
and the brother of James, Joseph, Judas and Simon?
Aren't his sisters here with us?" And they took offense at him.
MARK 6:3

When the truth that Jesus was more than an ordinary man suddenly hit the people of Nazareth, they were astounded. How could He be more than an everyday fellow? After all, wasn't He just like His brother James? An admirable person maybe, but nothing more.

The truth is, at first James didn't believe in his half brother's claims either. Perhaps he couldn't get away from His teaching, but that didn't mean he had to agree with Jesus.

But a change came over James. In the book of Acts, he appears as a church leader: he spoke for the Jerusalem council that heard Paul's objections to circumcision for the Gentiles, and Paul reported to that council on his missionary experience when he returned to Jerusalem.

James probably wrote the biblical book that bears his name, which is filled with guidance for living an effective Christian life. Within the early church, he was known as James the Just because of his upright character. He was martyred in AD 62, after being thrown down from the temple.

As we've come to know Jesus and have seen His power, have we had a change of heart like the one James had, from unbelief to faith?

JAMES, SON OF ZEBEDEE

James son of Zebedee and his brother John
(to them he gave the name Boanerges, which means Sons of Thunder).
MARK 3:17

While James and his brother, John, quietly mended their fishing nets, Jesus called them to become fishers of men. These two hotheads—"Sons of Thunder," Jesus called them—didn't stop to think; they simply jumped out of the boat and ran to the Master. But it was the best quick decision they'd ever made. The two went from being part of a family business to becoming key members in the family of God.

James and John became part of the inner circle of Jesus' most trusted disciples. James was there when Jesus healed Simon Peter's mother and when He quietly raised Jairus's daughter from the dead. Only Peter, James, and John witnessed the second event. There must have been a special trust between these men and their Lord.

The same three disciples saw Jesus' clothing turn bright white and heard Him speak to Elijah and Moses on the Mount of Transfiguration. Stunned by this preview of Jesus' eternal glory, the three hardly knew what to make of it. But they trustingly kept the secret when Jesus commanded them to.

As Jesus headed to Jerusalem for the final time, He stopped in a less-than-welcoming Samaritan village. When James and his brother discovered the town's attitude, they suggested a fine Christian response: "Let's command fire to come down and wipe out these folks." Jesus, of course, rebuked these two, who still had a long way to walk in their faith.

In Jerusalem, the brothers' mother, Salome, had a request: she wanted Jesus to give her sons places right beside Him in His kingdom. Perhaps she had overheard her sons discussing one of the Twelve's favorite topics: Who was greatest among them? Wasn't this the ultimate in seeing her sons succeed in their work?

When Jesus responded by asking whether they could drink the cup He was about to drink, James and John confidently asserted they could. No doubters, these two, in their own powers.

Finally, in the Garden of Gethsemane, the three trusted disciples heard Jesus' prayers as He prepared for His great sacrifice. Yet James's name is missing from the accounts of the Crucifixion. Though we're told that John and Salome stood by watching, neither James nor Peter is mentioned. We next hear of James in Acts 12:2, when Herod Agrippa puts him to death by the sword.

Confident and brash, perhaps James doesn't seem perfect apostle material. But God called him, and he followed determinedly, despite his failings. God uses all personalities, the brash and the timid, to do His work, if only we'll follow Him.

JEREMIAH

The words of Jeremiah the son of Hilkiah,
of the priests who were in Anathoth in the land of Benjamin,
to whom the word of the LORD came in the days
of Josiah the son of Amon, king of Judah.
JEREMIAH 1:1–2 NKJV

Jeremiah is known as Judah's "weeping prophet," and he had a lot to cry about, as you'll see if you read his prophecies and the book of Lamentations. He spoke to people who refused to listen to his message—God's last-ditch effort to reach the nation of Judah before destruction fell upon them. Called to his ministry while still young, Jeremiah never married; instead, he single-mindedly conveyed God's call to repentance for more than forty years.

Assyria, which had conquered Israel, was the first to fall to the Chaldeans of Babylon. The conflict between these two superpowers left Judah to prosper under good King Josiah. When Josiah died in battle against Assyria's allies, the Egyptians, Jeremiah lamented the loss of the king. Egypt transported Josiah's son Jehoahaz and made his brother Jehoiakim king.

In 612 BC, the Babylonians conquered Assyria and began building an empire. Jeremiah started warning his rebellious people of their dangerous future. Babylonian King Nebuchadnezzar invaded, and Jehoiakim became his vassal. But three years later, he rebelled. Following a tumultuous eleven-year rule, wicked Jehoiakim died, and his young son, Jehoiachin, took his throne. In just over three months, Nebuchadnezzar replaced Jehoiachin with the evil Zedekiah.

Life must have become nearly unbearable for Jeremiah as the new king, the officers of the priests, and the people were all unfaithful. Zedekiah rebelled against Nebuchadnezzar, who retaliated by attacking Jerusalem. After the Babylonians suddenly withdrew, Jeremiah was called a traitor to his people and imprisoned until a eunuch in the king's household came to his aid.

Nebuchadnezzar retaliated for Judah's rebellion by burning both the city and the temple of Jerusalem and killing all of Zedekiah's sons and nobles. The king's life was spared, but his eyes were put out and he was taken captive to Babylon. Jeremiah, too, was delivered from death, and he was eventually taken to Egypt when his people fled there against his advice. He most likely died while in Egypt.

Though he struggled greatly and was deeply hurt by both kings and common people, Jeremiah remained ever faithful to his unchanging God. His situation did not set the agenda for belief or action. Instead, his faith determined all he believed and did. When our lives are troubled, do we follow in Jeremiah's faithful footsteps?

JESUS

Jesus said to them, "My food is to do the will of
Him who sent Me, and to finish His work."
JOHN 4:34 NKJV

Where do we start in talking about Jesus? After all, didn't the apostle John say that if everything Jesus did was written down, the world couldn't contain all the books about Him?

What better place to begin than with what He Himself considered foundational. Numerous times throughout the Gospels, Jesus refers to "Him who sent Me." Keenly aware of the mission He had been sent to accomplish, Jesus was also wholeheartedly committed to the One who had sent Him.

To accomplish His Father's will, Jesus had to vindicate His Father's glory, which Satan had hopelessly tried to usurp. Yes, Jesus came to atone for sin, but His greatest objective was to perfectly glorify His Father. Jesus was determined to show the entire universe that, contrary to Satan's claims, God the Father was still holy, just, and righteous. The achievement of this objective culminated in Jesus' crucifixion, death, and resurrection.

Do we have the slightest inkling what it took for Jesus to live with such precision? Among other things, He had to perfectly fulfill the entire Law that God had given to Moses—and He was the only One who ever did. Aside from that, He had to fulfill all the messianic prophecies. John the Baptist was aghast to see Jesus coming forward to be baptized. "I need to be baptized by You, and are You coming to me?" he said. But Jesus replied, "Permit it to be so now, for thus it is fitting for us to fulfill all righteousness" (Matthew 3:14–15 NKJV). Jesus didn't have to be baptized, because He'd never sinned. Still, He went ahead with the rite in order to qualify as *the* Sin Bearer.

Surely, Satan did everything he could to trip Jesus up. Just after Jesus' baptism, scripture says He was led away by the Holy Spirit into the desert. While there, Jesus fasted for forty days, after which He was hungry. Satan seized upon this opportunity to tempt Jesus. Three times, the evil one tried by appealing to need, greed, and ego—all basic human drives. Yet for each temptation Jesus had but one weapon—the Word of God. He would not be hindered from accomplishing the Father's will, no matter what Satan hurled at Him.

A large part of Jesus' accomplishment of the Father's will had to do with His selecting and cultivating twelve ordinary men to be His apostles. This was a real test for Jesus. Unlike Him, all of them had faults and weaknesses, and one of them would actually betray Him. If that weren't enough, Jesus had only three short years in which to prepare these men to become His leading ambassadors. If ever we're tempted to feel as if we don't measure up in Jesus' eyes, we need look no further than the apostles for perspective. Here was a group of imperfect men, all too often seeking their own will instead of God's. Even so, Jesus patiently bore with them and never once gave up on them, even on that fateful night at Gethsemane when they all abandoned Him.

Gethsemane was Jesus' next to worst test. His worst was when the Father turned His back on Him as He hung on the cross. Jesus became sin on that cross, sinking lower than any human being ever had or ever will. The Father, repelled by sin, could not bear to look upon His Son. Driven to despair, Jesus cried out, "My God, My God, why have You forsaken Me?" (Matthew 27:46 NKJV). Then came the triumph of all triumphs. Jesus knew He had carried out the Father's will to the very last and said, "It is finished!" More beautiful words of liberation could not be spoken.

Jesus' weapon against Satan is our weapon as well. Let us never forget that God's Word is all we need to seek, know, and do for His will to become our own. It is also all we need to repel the fiery darts that Satan hurls at us.

JOB

In the land of Uz there lived a man whose name was Job.
This man was blameless and upright;
he feared God and shunned evil.
JOB 1:1

Why do bad things happen to great believers? Job wondered. He'd spent his life trying to follow God, making the right sacrifices, putting his spiritual life first. But one day, everything seemed to fall apart. Job went from owning thousands of livestock and having a happy family to losing it all. Oxen, donkeys, sheep, and camels were stolen or killed. Before the messengers who brought the news could finish their tales, another came to tell Job that all his children had died when the house had been destroyed by a terrible wind.

Yet Job worshipped God.

Sores erupted on his whole body. Still, he held firmly to his integrity, though his less-than-supportive wife suggested that he curse God and die.

Three of Job's friends came to comfort him. For a week they sat, mouths closed. What could they say to a faithful man who had suffered so deeply? When they finally started talking, Job probably wished he could gag them. Perplexed by his troubles, they quickly came to the conclusion that Job had sinned. Why else would God punish him? Job contended with them as they yammered on and on about the impossibility of his innocence. As Job speaks, we get a clear picture of the physical, spiritual, and emotional pain that dogged him.

Just when the three might have been winding down, Elihu, a young man, joined in the abuse. Though he glorifies God, like the other less-than-comforting comforters, he also ends up condemning Job.

Finally, God intervenes and answers Job in a strange way. He does not explain that the events came about because He was showing Satan Job's faithfulness. Instead, the Lord gives Job a glorious picture of His power and authority. Job is silenced. As God continues, Job admits his own ignorance and repents.

God rebukes the comfortless comforters. He orders them to make a sacrifice of repentance and promises that Job will pray for them.

God gave Job back all that he had lost—new flocks and a new family. But the best part of this new life was probably Job's new, deeper relationship with the Lord. He could trust Him, no matter what came into his life, for God was infinitely greater than he'd imagined.

When we face trials, will we remember the God who revealed Himself to Job and place our entire future in His hands?

JOEL

The word of the LORD that came to Joel son of Pethuel.
JOEL 1:1

We really don't know a lot about Joel, or even about his book of the Bible, beyond the evidence it gives about itself.

Because Joel does not mention his country or king, we cannot date his book with precision. He is largely concerned with Jerusalem, so he was probably from Judah, but scholars have differed on the time in which he lived. Joel uses language typical of all the prophets, so using linguistic methods to date his book has not proved successful.

Joel reports the desolation of the land by locusts and invaders. Desperation fills the people, and the prophet calls for repentance. Then he pictures the day of the Lord, both in the immediate sense, as his people are attacked, and the long-term vision in which the Lord will judge all nations. One day, as pagan nations are judged, God's people will be restored. In either case, Joel encourages God's people to trust in Him as their refuge. His book ends with the words "The LORD dwells in Zion" (Joel 3:21).

Whether disaster or blessing overcomes us, do we believe that God remains on His throne and rules our lives?

JOHN THE APOSTLE

When [Jesus] had gone a little farther, he saw James son of Zebedee
and his brother John in a boat, preparing their nets.
Without delay he called them, and they left their father Zebedee
in the boat with the hired men and followed him.

MARK 1:19–20

When Jesus called John to be His disciple, He had to have a lot of imagination about His new follower, who probably had more of a reputation for his temper than his holiness. John and his older brother, James, came from a family that owned their own fishing business. Things must have gone well for Zebedee, because he employed not only James and John, but also some hired hands.

Perhaps success is why the sons of Zebedee were used to having things their own way: they certainly had commanding personalities. When the disciples met a man who was driving demons out in the Master's name, John planned to stop him in his tracks. After all, the stranger wasn't one of *them*. Later, when a small village didn't take kindly to having Jesus and His twelve disciples take shelter with them, James and John wanted to call down fire on these people. The brothers' fiery tempers earned them a nickname from Jesus: *Boanerges*, which means "Sons of Thunder."

Despite his short fuse, John became Jesus' dearest disciple. Jesus called him, along with James and Peter, to witness key events such as the healings of Peter's mother and Jairus's daughter, the Transfiguration, and Jesus' prayer in the Garden of Gethsemane. Scholars also generally believe that "the disciple Jesus loved," who is referred to in John's Gospel and experiences some of the most crucial moments in that book, is John himself.

John's Gospel and epistles show an intense, passionate love relationship with God. Along with Peter and James, John experiences some of scripture's most intimate spiritual moments with the Savior. And the biblical books that bear his name show a deep, tender understanding of the Master. His Gospel relates incidents that do not appear in the other Gospels. But as he neared the end of his life, John had become humble. In his Gospel, he never tells of his own call by Jesus or overemphasizes his own role in the spread of the Good News.

Yet clearly the humble disciple had a key place in the Gospel mission: Because John knew Caiaphas, the high priest, he and Peter got to view and report on Jesus' trial. At the Crucifixion, Jesus gave His mother into John's care. And Mary Magdalene came to John and Peter to report the disappearance of Jesus' body.

As the church grew, John stood by his friend Peter when Peter healed a beggar in the temple gate. Together, the friends were arrested by the authorities and firmly declared their intention to continue spreading God's message of His Son.

John's epistles to the church do not name him as their writer. The early church fathers record his relationship to these letters. First John encourages believers and gives them the tools to fight against the heresy of Gnosticism. His practical advice must have been a real boon to the church in a turbulent age. The following two smaller books are personal letters that give us insight into the Christian life in his era and into the relationships John had with others.

John's most stunning book is his prophecy of the last times, Revelation. As the nascent church struggled to exist, John envisioned a glorious future in which Jesus will rule eternally, victorious over sin and earthly tyrants.

With his church, John suffered persecution. Near the end of his life, he was exiled to the island of Patmos, where he wrote Revelation, but tradition has it that he returned to his ministry in Ephesus and died of old age. He is the only apostle not to have been martyred.

Because John was willing to follow his Lord faithfully, God took a firebrand and made him into a humble apostle. Not every firebrand does the same, but God seems to use a fair number of them. Struggle with your temper? Don't forget what God can do. Give Him authority, and He can turn you sweet with love for Him.

JOHN THE BAPTIST

[John said,] "He must increase, but I must decrease."
JOHN 3:30 NKJV

When John the Baptist arrived on the scene, four hundred years of prophetic silence came to a crashing end. From out of nowhere, this electric figure hastened upon the scene, full of energy and conviction. No knight in shining armor astride a mighty steed, but a rough, desert-hewn figure in coarse clothing, wielding the very Word of God. The Messiah's herald had finally come like a whirlwind out of the desert, "in the spirit and power of Elijah" (Luke 1:17 NKJV).

To be in the company of John the Baptist was to live in a charged air of immanency concerning this Anointed One of God called the Messiah. In centuries long past, the prophets had predicted His coming. The angel of the Lord had even given the prophet Daniel a timeline pinpointing the Messiah's arrival (see Daniel 9:20–27). If the Messiah did not come within that timeline, He would not come at all!

In light of this, John's message to the people of Israel was urgent and uncompromising. "Repent, for the kingdom of heaven is at hand! . . . Even now the ax is laid to the root of the trees. Therefore every tree which does not bear good fruit is cut down and thrown into the fire" (Matthew 3:2, 10 NKJV). This John proclaimed to all, whether they listened or not. To underscore his words,

John controversially adapted an existing ritual—baptism. Baptism was the norm for converts to Judaism, but those who were already Jews? God imposed a new requirement for cleansing, and the people came willingly to be baptized. Even Jesus subjected Himself to this requirement, "to fulfill all righteousness" (Matthew 3:15 NKJV). So serious was John about this matter that, when he saw Pharisees and Sadducees approaching to be baptized, he exploded, "Brood of vipers! Who warned you to flee from the wrath to come? Therefore bear fruits worthy of repentance, and do not think to say to yourselves, 'We have Abraham as our father.' For I say to you that God is able to raise up children to Abraham from these stones" (Matthew 3:7–9 NKJV). With these words, John destroyed all self-importance forever!

John the Baptist had a mission, and he clearly understood it. Asked by the priests and Levites who he was, he answered, "I am 'The voice of one crying in the wilderness: "Make straight the way of the LORD," ' as the prophet Isaiah said" (John 1:23 NKJV). Pressed further about his baptizing, John said, "I baptize with water, but there stands One among you whom you do not know. It is He who, coming after me, is preferred before me, whose sandal strap I am not worthy to loose" (John 1:26–27 NKJV). "I indeed baptize you with water unto repentance, but He who is coming after me is mightier than I, whose sandals I am not worthy to carry. He will baptize you with the Holy Spirit and fire" (Matthew 3:11 NKJV).

By virtue of the Holy Spirit, John understood he was but the forerunner of One far greater than he, and he was content with that. He also understood his limitations and knew that the One coming after him was vested with powers and abilities far beyond his own. John was preparing the people for and pointing them to Jesus. While languishing in Herod's prison, he sent his disciples to Jesus to hear from His own mouth that neither they nor John need look for anyone else but Him.

Prior to his arrest, John humbly acknowledged that it was time for him to step aside to allow Jesus to take center stage. "Therefore this joy of mine is fulfilled. He must increase, but I must decrease" (John 3:29–30 NKJV).

In this day of "Me first!" it would seem that very few men are content to play second fiddle. Those who want the spotlight will usually do anything they can to get it. Not so with John the Baptist. He understood who Jesus was. Not until we ourselves understand who Jesus really is will we be able to step aside like John and let Jesus reign in our lives.

JONAH

But Jonah arose to flee to Tarshish from the presence of the LORD.
JONAH 1:3 NKJV

Well now, here is a man who didn't need to be taught prejudice. For Jonah, it was only natural to hate the wicked city-state called Nineveh.

Ironically, the name Nineveh means "agreeable dwelling." The city itself is believed to have been a marvel. Scripture refers to it as "that great city" (Jonah 1:2 NKJV). It was surrounded by high walls and numerous watchtowers. In Jonah's day, Nineveh's earthly defenses were unparalleled. Inside the city, there was an array of buildings and palaces, the decor of which would rival that of any other great city of its time. Nineveh's commerce and industry were thriving and without comparison.

Yet for all its splendor and magnificence, Nineveh was an abomination in the eyes of God. He told Jonah, "Arise, go to Nineveh, that great city, and cry out against it; for their wickedness has come up before Me" (Jonah 1:2 NKJV). Wait a minute! A Hebrew prophet being sent to preach to a heathen city, and the archenemy of Israel to boot? Unheard of!

What sort of wickedness could have aroused God's wrath? For one thing, Nineveh was a center of excess where common, ordinary, everyday folks didn't matter. Drunkenness and sexual immorality of the vilest sort were rampant. Most any sort of crime or vice prospered within its walls. Sound familiar?

If this weren't enough, the Assyrians weren't known for their compassion toward conquered people. If anything, they were ruthless and barbaric in their treatment, as evidenced by the mounds of skulls that served as "monuments" to their conquests. Aside from all this, they didn't care much for either Judah or Israel. In fact, they would have much preferred to make both kingdoms a vast tract of rubble.

No wonder Jonah wasn't too keen on going to Nineveh. It's quite likely that Jonah himself could have been a victim of Assyrian cruelty as a result of one of their military ventures into Israel. That would have only reinforced his hatred for Nineveh and cemented his decision to disobey God.

When God finally did get the prophet's attention, after turning him into fish bait, Jonah resolutely set out for Nineveh. Getting the Ninevites' attention wasn't any great trouble for Jonah, for he was a sight—and smell—to behold! He drew crowds in Nineveh, but they no doubt kept him at arm's length, holding their noses. Word reached the king about this conversation piece who was proclaiming a dire message of unalterable doom. Then to Jonah's amazement and disgust, all the people of Nineveh, as well as all their animals, donned sackcloth and ashes, and the people prayed for God to relent.

Jonah knew God's mercy. He said, "For I know that You are a gracious and merciful God, slow to anger and abundant in lovingkindness, One who relents from doing harm" (Jonah 4:2 NKJV). Even so, Jonah wished that Nineveh had perished in perdition.

Where or what are the Ninevehs in our lives? Are they cities or places we can't stand, the very mention of whose names makes us bristle? Are they perhaps sports teams we just love to hate? Who might the Ninevites be in our lives? Are they folks with a particular philosophy or bent that is diametrically opposed to ours? Are they folks whose language or skin color is different from ours? We all have our prejudices, don't we? And though we don't like to admit it, deep down, we all have our hatreds, too. With most of the world consisting of unbelievers, it's quite likely that those we dislike or hate do not even know Jesus, and in many cases couldn't care less about Him. Are we content to let 'em all literally go to hell? That's pretty much the way Jonah felt until God got through his hard crust. What will it take for God to break through our hard-heartedness where the lost are concerned?

JONATHAN

And Jonathan had David reaffirm his oath out of love for him,
because he loved him as he loved himself.
1 SAMUEL 20:17

Mention the name Jonathan, and David's name immediately pops to mind, too. For theirs was the most powerful man-to-man friendship recorded in scripture.

But life didn't always go smoothly for these friends. Though Jonathan was King Saul's eldest son, he could not control his father's actions against David. As the young commander who had killed Goliath for denigrating God became ever more popular, Saul became increasingly jealous—even to the point of madness.

Jonathan, a brave warrior who had single-handedly attacked the Philistines, felt such love for David that jealousy had no place in their relationship. Though he knew God was planning to replace Saul as king, Jonathan never became angry with David, who would take the throne. Being the heir to Saul's kingdom was less important than doing God's will. If God wanted his friend to rule, Jonathan would follow.

Their friendship began at first sight, and Jonathan made a covenant with his new friend. But their relationship was quickly strained as the people of Israel praised their new commander. Jealous Saul tried to kill David, first with his own hand, which held a spear, then by sending him into battle against the Philistines to earn the bride price for Saul's daughter Michal. When the Philistines didn't do the job for him, Saul tried to get Jonathan to kill David. Instead, the prince warned his friend and tried to convince Saul that David had only brought him good. For a while, the king seemed to agree, but again an evil spirit came on him and caused him to attack David. Michal helped her husband escape.

Jonathan kept in touch with his friend, much to his father's dissatisfaction. Saul began throwing spears at Jonathan, too. Knowing his father would kill David, Jonathan warned him with a prearranged sign.

Jonathan died in battle against the Philistines, along with his father and two of his brothers. David lamented their deaths but began a fight with Jonathan's brother Ish-bosheth for the throne God had promised him. After gaining the throne, David kept his covenant with Jonathan and treated Jonathan's son Mephibosheth kindly.

Jonathan's faithful character caused him to sacrifice much for his friend. Do we also look out for our friends' best interests, or are we too busy feeling jealous about their accomplishments?

JOSEPH OF ARIMATHEA

Now when evening had come,
there came a rich man from Arimathea, named Joseph,
who himself had also become a disciple of Jesus.
MATTHEW 27:57 NKJV

You're a high official within your country's governing body. You have a reputation and wealth to safeguard, not to mention the welfare of your own family. You've also been secretly keeping company with a very controversial figure. Being found out could mean your ruin. That's what Joseph of Arimathea was up against when he walked into Pontius Pilate's office to request the body of Jesus. Joseph did even more than that, though. He and Nicodemus, a fellow colleague from the Jewish Sanhedrin, took Jesus down from the cross and laid Him to rest in a tomb that Joseph owned. This took some courage. And because of the form of execution, it also took a certain amount of "stomach." Jesus' body was not a pretty sight at that point. This burial was not for the faint of heart.

Joseph risked everything that day. He may very well have been confronted by other colleagues who cast aspersions on his deed. Some may also have had nothing more to do with him from that day onward. Nonetheless, by his daring that first Good Friday, Joseph personified the word *nobility*.

What would we have done if we had been in his place?

JOSEPH, FOSTER FATHER OF JESUS

When [Joseph] arose, he took the young Child and
His mother by night and departed for Egypt.
MATTHEW 2:14 NKJV

Joseph had already been through trials that would have undone other, lesser men. He'd had to face the fact that his bride-to-be was already pregnant—and not by him! An angelic messenger told him to go ahead with his betrothal anyway, because Mary had conceived by the Holy Spirit. Then Joseph and his pregnant bride were forced to take an arduous journey to Bethlehem so he could register in the city of his ancestry for tax purposes. Upon arrival, they discovered that all the lodgings were sold out. Joseph and his wife had to camp out in a smelly stable. If that weren't enough, Mary went into labor and had her baby right then and there.

After the couple was visited by a strange retinue of wise men from the East, another angelic messenger told Joseph to make haste and flee—to Egypt! Talk about dedication. This man had it in spades. We never hear him grumble or complain. We don't hear much else about him beyond the flight to Egypt. Yet Joseph isn't merely a footnote in the New Testament. It was quiet, unassuming, obedient men like him whom God used masterfully to unfold His wondrous plan of salvation.

God is still filling His quiver with such men today.

JOSEPH, SON OF JACOB

So Pharaoh said to Joseph,
"I hereby put you in charge of the whole land of Egypt."
GENESIS 41:41

Joseph's birthday must have been one of the happiest days in the lives of Jacob and his favorite wife, Rachel. But it wasn't the happiest day in the lives of everyone in their camp. For Jacob loved this son best of all, and his sons by his other wives didn't appreciate it.

A typical youngster, when Joseph got an opportunity to tattle on his older brothers, he took advantage of it. And when he had dreams that showed he was more important than they, he couldn't help but brag. So his siblings retaliated when Dad was nowhere nearby. As his ten half brothers watched over the family flocks, Joseph came by to check up on them. The brothers tossed Dad's favorite in a cistern for a while, then sold him into slavery when some Midianite traders happened by. The ten took the many-colored coat Jacob had given Joseph, dipped it in goat's blood, and reported that Joseph was dead, killed by a wild animal.

While Joseph discovered the hardships of slavery, Jacob mourned the loss of his son. Joseph had been carried to Egypt and sold into the household of Potiphar, Pharaoh's captain of the guard. Despite his lack of freedom, Joseph clung to his faith and served his new master well, for God blessed him. That blessing drew the attention of Potiphar, who promoted Joseph to take charge of his household. Although still a slave, Joseph was becoming upwardly mobile.

And even though Potiphar's wife lusted after Joseph, the faithful slave refused her repeatedly. Finally, she cornered Joseph and demanded that he sleep with her. Recognizing his dangerous situation, Joseph tore away from her, leaving his clothes in her hand.

Not to be disgraced, this unfaithful wife accused Joseph of attempting to seduce her. Enraged, Potiphar tossed Joseph into prison. But even there, Joseph prospered. He ended up in charge of all the prisoners. It wasn't the typical path to success, but Joseph was climbing the corporate ladder more quickly than he could know. It just didn't look like it at the moment.

After a while, two important prisoners were incarcerated: Pharaoh's cupbearer and baker. Joseph attended them. One night, each had a dream and wanted it interpreted, so Joseph obliged them. The cupbearer got good news: he would soon be released. But Joseph foresaw the death of the baker. And that's just what happened.

Though Joseph had asked the cupbearer to remember him, court life must have caught the fellow up. Not until two years later, when Pharaoh had a couple of bad dreams, did the cupbearer remember Joseph. Then the Hebrew slave was brought before Egypt's ruler. Joseph reported that the dreams Pharaoh had were dual warnings of a famine to come. He advised Pharaoh to plan ahead by gathering food in the good years that would precede lean ones. Immediately, Pharaoh appointed Joseph to oversee the project and set him over all Egypt. For seven years, he collected the country's grain.

Then the famine came, and people of all nations flocked to Egypt to buy grain. One day, Joseph's half brothers showed up. Untrusting, Joseph tested his siblings. He accused them of spying and held them in custody. After three days, he freed all but Simeon and required that they bring his younger brother, Benjamin, to him before he'd return Simeon to them.

Only when their food was very low would the brothers be able to convince Jacob to allow them to return to Egypt with Benjamin. In Egypt, Joseph again tested the ten, arranging to have Benjamin accused of stealing. But this time, instead of leaving their brother to slavery, the ten begged for his freedom.

Certain of his brothers' change of heart, Joseph revealed himself to them and arranged to bring the whole family into Egypt.

Joseph began as a thoughtless youth, but slavery and the dependence on

God that it required brought him great wisdom that led to worldly success. When we suffer far less than slavery, do we use it as an opportunity to gain God's wisdom? What worked for Joseph will work for us, too.

JOSHUA

Moses said to Joshua, "Choose some of our men and go out to fight the Amalekites.
Tomorrow I will stand on top of the hill with the staff of God in my hands."
EXODUS 17:9

As Joshua led the Israelites in battle against the Amalekites, victory depended not on his battle plan, but on the hand of Moses. For when the prophet raised his hand, Israel prevailed. As the day wore on, some Israelite leaders held up weary Moses' hands, and Joshua led his people to victory. That battle, in which we first meet Joshua, shows us the hallmarks of his life: he became a strong fighting man of deep faith.

From youth, Joshua was Moses' right-hand man. Only Joshua accompanied Moses to Mount Sinai to receive the Ten Commandments. Moses' trusted assistant also spent much time in the Tent of Meeting, where the prophet spoke face-to-face with God. As the Israelites came to Canaan, Moses sent Joshua to spy out the new land. Of the twelve men on the mission, only Joshua and Caleb came back with a report based on faith instead of fear—and only those two men would come into the Promised Land when God allowed Israel to return to Canaan after their forty-year adventure in the desert.

As he neared death, Moses commissioned Joshua as his successor, and he must have known he had big shoes to fill. How humbling to know that he would complete the job Moses had started: bringing the Israelites into their new land.

Following Moses' death, God warned Joshua he'd need to be strong. He wasn't kidding. There was a lot of work ahead—and many battles. The job would demand all of Joshua's experience and faith.

Israel's first battle, at Jericho, was an amazing event. For six days, the warriors silently circumnavigated the city, accompanied only by the sound of the priests' ram's-horn trumpets. The people of Jericho must have found this God-designed attack pattern strange. On the seventh day, after they'd circled the city seven times, the Israelites let out a huge shout, and the walls of the city fell. Then Israel destroyed the metropolis, except for faithful Rahab, who had assisted the Israelite spies before the battle.

Israel as a whole had yet to learn a lesson that Joshua thoroughly understood: when they obeyed God, they would be successful, but when they sinned, they would fail. So they had to attack Ai twice in order to subdue it. When Joshua led them against the king of Jerusalem at Gibeon, the obedient warriors succeeded. God gave the king of Jerusalem and four other Amorite kings into the Israelites' hands. This was only the beginning of Joshua's lifelong conquest that still did not complete the task at hand.

God promised an aging Joshua that He would finish the conquest. He commanded Joshua to divide all the Promised Land between the tribes. After setting forth each tribe's property, Joshua shared God's promise of conquest with his people. Then he commanded them to obey God and His laws. "You shall cling to the LORD your God just as you have done to this day," he admonished them (Joshua 23:8 ESV). Otherwise, God would not drive out the nations from their land, and pagan nations would become a snare to Israel. Reminding them of God's covenant, Joshua called them to serve God alone and to put away foreign gods.

Joshua died at age 110 and was buried on his own land.

Have you heard that faith is for weaklings? Then look at Joshua, who combined deep trust in God with a strong warrior's arm. Given a challenging task, he spent his life accomplishing it. But even all the faith and experience at his command could not bring Israel's land under complete control. Ultimately, Joshua had to trust God for its completion.

Our lives may not be a continual battle, but we still relate to Joshua's war of faith. For we, too, rarely live in total peace. When God calls us to fight for Him, let's remind ourselves of faithful Joshua and look to our Lord for all the strength we need.

JOSIAH

Josiah was eight years old when he became king,
and he reigned in Jerusalem thirty-one years. . . .
He did what was right in the eyes of the LORD.
2 KINGS 22:1–2

Josiah followed two unusually wicked kings—his grandfather, Manasseh, and his father, Amon. These two did all they could to destroy the spiritual life of Judah. But at age sixteen, Josiah began to seek God, and four years later he began to eliminate the pagan influences in Judah by destroying idols and their altars.

In the eighteenth year of the good king's reign, when Josiah ordered repairs on the temple, the high priest discovered Moses' Book of the Law. He immediately sent it to the king, who had it read to him. When Josiah discovered how far he and his people had strayed from God, he tore his robes in anguish.

He consulted the prophetess Huldah, who foresaw disaster but not during

Josiah's life. Josiah had the book read to the people and reinstituted the celebration of Passover. But when Josiah went to battle against Pharaoh Neco, he was badly wounded by the Egyptian archers and died in Jerusalem.

We remember Josiah for his attitude about God's Word. He recognized its importance, made sure that people knew what it said, and encouraged others to obey its commands. His attitude affected a nation.

Will we be known for loving and obeying the scriptures, or are we too busy obeying the call of something else?

JUDAS ISCARIOT

The evening meal was being served, and the devil had already
prompted Judas Iscariot, son of Simon, to betray Jesus.
JOHN 13:2

Here's a man we love to hate. But he puzzles us, too, for Judas Iscariot walked daily with Jesus during His incarnation. Judas saw the miracles, heard the preaching, and had fellowship with Jesus and the other eleven disciples who were closest to Him. Yet this wayward disciple turned Jesus in to His enemies.

How could Judas do that? we wonder. He walked with Jesus, yet he led soldiers into the Master's presence. Judas had already offered Jesus up to the chief priests.

Did money get in the way of Judas's commitment to Jesus? After all, he was the keeper of the money donated to Jesus to provide for His little band of disciples. John records that Judas used to dip into the till for his own wants.

Perhaps money had its lure, but would that alone make Judas take this rash step? Probably not. It seems there would be more to gain from pilfering the disciples' purse than what he received from the priests for his betrayal.

In many ways, this disciple will always remain a mystery to us. Scripture doesn't divulge Judas's thoughts. Obviously he had some wrongheaded idea about who Jesus was and what He came to accomplish, but how did Satan tempt him? We may never know.

Judas brought the soldiers and Jewish officials to a private place where Jesus often met with the Twelve. He betrayed the Master with a kiss. What was he thinking? But the news that Jesus was condemned to death came as a surprise to him. What private world was Judas living in, to think the priests meant Jesus no harm?

When he discovered what he had done, after throwing the blood money into the temple, Judas hanged himself in sorrow.

In a once-and-for-all act, Judas betrayed the Son, leading to the end of His earthly life. But while we question Judas's motives, are we aware that we aren't all that different from him? How easily we, too, fall into wrongheaded thinking and walk in ways that cannot glorify the Son. Despite the fact that we, too, have walked with Jesus, we easily fail.

Have we heard Jesus' call? Then let us remain vigilant so Satan's charms will not delude us. May our private worlds be centered on the Son, instead of on temptations that lead us astray.

KORAH

Korah son of Izhar, the son of Kohath, the son of Levi, and certain Reubenites—Dathan and Abiram, sons of Eliab, and On son of Peleth—became insolent and rose up against Moses. With them were 250 Israelite men, well-known community leaders who had been appointed members of the council.
NUMBERS 16:1–2

Moses and Aaron had a congregational rebellion on their hands. Factions within the worship community became jealous of Moses and his brother and tried to grab authority, accusing them of a misuse of power.

Kohath wanted to be a priest, even though his line of Levites had other duties in the tabernacle. The Reubenites were angry because Moses had led them not into the Promised Land but into the desert again. Neither group asked God's opinion of their ideas.

Moses, far from intimidated, called on Korah and his followers to appear before God with their incense-filled censers at the ready. God would decide who was holy and who wasn't.

The next day, Korah gathered Moses' opponents among the Levites. But first the prophet went to the tents of the Reubenites, who had refused to appear at the Tent of Meeting. At their own tent doors, Moses confronted the rebels. There God split apart the earth beneath them, and it swallowed up their households and their men. Then fire came up and burned up the 250 men who were offering the incense.

Makes you think twice about starting a church rebellion, doesn't it?

LAZARUS

Now a man named Lazarus was sick. He was from Bethany,
the village of Mary and her sister Martha. . . . So the sisters sent word to Jesus,
"Lord, the one you love is sick."
JOHN 11:1, 3

When faithful Mary and Martha faced a crisis in their brother's health, they knew where to turn. Sending a message to Jesus, they requested Lazarus's healing. Then the sisters waited, in nail-biting fear, for the Master to appear. As the hours went on, they must have wondered what had happened. Had their messenger failed them? Was he hurt or killed? And as life receded, Lazarus might have questioned whether Jesus could have betrayed him.

Jesus got the message, but He waited two days before returning to Bethany to heal His friend. When He arrived, mourning for Lazarus was in full force. The distraught sisters were clearly puzzled that Jesus had not come sooner. Lazarus had lain in the tomb for four days.

As Jesus commanded that the stone be rolled away, a stunned Martha pointed out that the corpse by now would be stinky. She had to wonder what Jesus was thinking.

Loudly, Jesus prayed to the Father and called Lazarus to come out of the tomb. And his sisters, in amazement, saw their sibling walk out of the grave, with linen still wrapped around him and a cloth over his face. Suddenly, mourning turned into delighted rejoicing—Lazarus had returned to life.

The celebration didn't end there. People came from all over to hear of the man who'd returned from the grave. The report of this almost unbelievable event spread by a super-fast grapevine through the countryside. And many of the curious came to faith because of Lazarus's reporting skills.

When the chief priests heard of the event and the people's reaction, they plotted to kill both Jesus and Lazarus to hide the truth. They were successful with Jesus, but did Lazarus live? Scripture doesn't tell us how long Lazarus remained in this life after his resurrection. Was it years? We'll never know this side of heaven. But no matter if he lived weeks or years, his new life was a faith-filled success.

We know that Jesus still brings the dead back to life—many of us have closed the tomb door on sin and have experienced the joyous new life that only Jesus offers. And that's just a down payment on the future, when all believers will live eternally in Him.

LOT

*[Abram] took. . .his nephew Lot, all the possessions they had accumulated
and the people they had acquired in Haran, and they set out
for the land of Canaan, and they arrived there.*
GENESIS 12:5

Lot was raised by his grandfather Terah and then went to Canaan with his uncle Abram. But after a while their grazing land could not support both men's vast herds, so Abram let Lot choose where he wanted to live and moved his herd in another direction.

Lot chose the Jordan Valley and headed to a spot near Sodom. Perhaps this righteous man was somehow attracted by the sinful city. He eventually moved in and became a captive when the kings of Elam and Sodom fought. Abram had to rescue him.

Later, Lot offered hospitality to a couple of angels and tried to protect them from the wicked men of his city, who demanded sex with them. But Lot ended up being the rescued one, as the angels hustled him out of the soon-to-be-destroyed metropolis. On his way to safety, Lot saw his wife disobey the angels' command not to look back, and he saw her turned to salt.

The rest of the family sought shelter in a cave. His despairing daughters tricked Lot into incest so they would have children. Their sons became two of Israel's enemies.

Ever wonder what it's like to have one foot in the world and the other in God's kingdom? Then look at Lot. Being somewhat worldly didn't bring him the benefits he expected. Instead, both Abram and God had to intervene to keep him from harm.

Does sin attract us? Beware! We, too, may need that rescuing angel.

LUKE

Our dear friend Luke, the doctor, and Demas send greetings.
COLOSSIANS 4:14

Luke was both a doctor and an excellent historian. But this well-educated man didn't spend time on his own public-relations campaign—he never even mentions himself as the author of the two biblical books that are credited to him: the Gospel that bears his name and the book of Acts.

Luke didn't meet Jesus personally. So when he wanted to describe Jesus' ministry, he did historical research. He left us with information that none of the other Gospel writers reported. Six miracles and nineteen parables appear only in his Gospel. We also read Mary's story of Jesus' birth and of the angels' visitation to the shepherds who witnessed His coming.

Luke's history has proven to be accurate. The map he draws of Paul's missionary journeys shows us the larger scope of life during the Roman Empire. The places and names are correct, and he appreciates differences in culture and language. In fact, this master of the word not only wrote excellent Greek; he properly reflected the use of other languages, too.

In Luke, we see a brilliant man totally dedicated to his mission for God. We know nothing of his job as a doctor, but as a Christian, he shines. Any believer would do well to walk in Dr. Luke's footsteps, no matter what the profession.

THE LUNATIC'S FATHER

Immediately the father of the child cried out and said with tears,
"Lord, I believe; help my unbelief!"
MARK 9:24 NKJV

How many of us in our lives have spoken these words? Because of our fallenness, each of us is tied to this world. We are accustomed to harsh realities that so often seem overwhelming. They challenge our faith and make it difficult at times to believe God can help us.

This caring father was at his wit's end in seeking relief for his son, whom he watched being terribly afflicted by a demon. Imagine what it was like for him to repeatedly pull his child out of flames and out of water. We get the sense that his own sanity hung by a slender thread.

Then Jesus appears on the scene. He tells the father that if he can believe, all things are possible. The father, beside himself with desperation, probably screamed, "I do believe; help my unbelief!" For all his misfortune, here was an honest man. Jesus didn't take him to task for his lack of faith. Instead, He met the father and his son at their point of need and healed the boy right then and there.

No matter what our circumstances, Jesus is master of them all.

MALACHI

The oracle of the word of the LORD to Israel through Malachi.
MALACHI 1:1 NASB

The author of the last book of the Old Testament is a bit of an unknown quantity—we know very little indeed about him. Malachi was probably born in Judah and prophesied in Jerusalem. His book seems to have been written around 465 to 430 BC. Some scholars have even concluded that because his name means "my messenger," it was a title and not a proper name.

Ezra and Nehemiah would have been contemporaries of this minor prophet who spoke to the people in a time of adversity. Though they had returned to their homeland, the Israelites found life harder than they'd expected. God didn't appear to be helping them, so they started having serious doubts about Him. Their lives certainly proved their lack of faith, as they married into pagan families and ignored God's commands.

Though we don't have a lot of information about who Malachi was, it doesn't matter. The prophet had a revelation of God and His call to His people. Malachi called these hurting people back to obedience to their King and Creator.

Like Malachi, even if no one remembers the details of our lives, wouldn't we like others to benefit from our faithfulness? May God's message become our legacy to the future, even when our personal stories fade out.

MANASSEH

Manasseh was twelve years old when he began to reign,
and he reigned fifty-five years in Jerusalem. And he
did what was evil in the sight of the LORD.
2 CHRONICLES 33:1–2 ESV

Though his father, Hezekiah, was a good man, Manasseh turned in the opposite direction. Second Chronicles reports that Manasseh burned his sons as offerings to pagan gods, became involved in occult practices, and "did much evil in the sight of the LORD" (33:6 ESV). He even set up an idol in the temple.

Manasseh led Judah to become worse than the Amorites, whom Israel had routed from Canaan. When Israel didn't respond to God's call to change, He got their attention another way. Assyria attacked Judah, captured their king, and dragged him to Babylon.

That got the king's attention! Manasseh called on God, who heard his pitiful cries, and the unfaithful king repented and returned to his throne. Manasseh removed the pagan altars from the city and restored the worship of the Lord. But he could not totally eradicate pagan practices in Israel.

Though Manasseh repented, he learned what many Christians have discovered: the influence of past sins doesn't entirely disappear. New believers must become witnesses to alter the influence that those past sins have on others' lives.

THE MAN BORN BLIND

As [Jesus] passed by, He saw a man blind from birth.
And His disciples asked Him, "Rabbi, who sinned,
this man or his parents, that he would be born blind?"
JOHN 9:1–2 NASB

In an age that knew very little science, Jews commonly believed that illness was caused by sin. Why would a good God inflict pain and suffering on one of His people?

The disciples were looking for a quick, easy answer that laid the blame on someone. If the parents had sinned, there was reason for God to have given them a blind child, and the disciples could go home happy. But why would God do this to an innocent child? Inquiring believers needed an answer.

Jesus made it clear that sin and illness do not necessarily equate. God had a purpose for this illness—it would bring glory to God as the Savior performed a healing.

While the disciples talked, the man must have waited hopefully. If he was not to blame, why shouldn't Jesus heal him? Hadn't He done such miracles before? Suddenly, Jesus' hand touched his eyes, spreading a combination of mud and saliva over them. Not the most pleasant way to be healed, but the man wasn't about to argue. At Jesus' direction, he rushed to wash in the pool of Siloam.

The blind man came back seeing. What delight to look on his neighbors' faces, to enjoy the world God had made, and to know that he would never again have to beg.

As he went, people started asking questions. Was this really the beggar, or just someone who looked like him? The man admitted the truth of his healing. But when he looked for Jesus, He was gone.

Instead, he came before the Pharisees, who were not pleased at this event and questioned him sternly about Jesus. Knowing no more, the man declared Him a prophet. So the unbelieving Pharisees questioned the man's parents. Fearful of being put out of the synagogue, they turned the issue back to their son's testimony. Again the rulers questioned the son, who did not budge. Did they want to become Jesus' disciples, he asked, since they were so interested?

So the rulers cast the man out of the synagogue. Then Jesus came to him. With answers to a few quick questions, the man understood and worshipped Him.

We have asked the disciples' questions when a child is hurt or ill or a devoted disciple is not healed. Can we accept that all will work out to God's glory, even if no earthly healing occurs? We may not have our answers on earth, but in heaven all will be clear.

MARK

Now Barnabas was determined to take with them John called Mark.
ACTS 15:37 NKJV

Whether he's called John, his Hebrew name, or Mark, his Greek name, this is the man who wrote the second Gospel, which reports the apostle Peter's outlook on Jesus' ministry.

Mark's mother was a believer who had a prayer meeting in her house. After Peter was freed from prison, he went there. The apostle seems to have been close to the family, because he refers to Mark as his son. Another of Mark's faithful family members, his cousin Barnabas, took Mark on a missionary journey with the apostle Paul. But at Perga, Mark left the missionary work, returning to Jerusalem. Paul didn't appreciate Mark's lack of stick-to-itiveness, and when a second missionary journey was in the offing, he refused Barnabas's suggestion that they give Mark another chance.

The disagreement became so fierce that it caused a rift between the two missionaries. Paul and Barnabas split up and spread the Gospel separately. But by the end of his life, Paul had forgiven the errant missionary and let Mark again join him. The apostle even asked Timothy to bring Mark from Ephesus because he was "useful."

From useless to useful, Mark's life is a picture of a believer who grows in faith and consistency. He who draws near to God again, as Mark did, may become a valuable tool in the Lord's hand.

MATTHEW

As Jesus passed on from there, He saw a man named
Matthew sitting at the tax office. And He said to him,
"Follow Me." So he arose and followed Him.
MATTHEW 9:9 NKJV

One day, Jesus passed by a tax gatherer in Capernaum and called out, "Follow Me." And Levi, later called Matthew, dropped everything to dart after the Master.

Something powerful was at work with this man, who left behind wealth to spend his time on the road with Jesus. But Levi was delighted to make the change and threw a big feast for all his friends to introduce them to his new friend. To mark his new life, he even changed his name to Matthew, which means "a gift of God." The former tax collector must have felt this new life, with its spiritual freedom, had indeed been God's gift to him.

Later, Jesus selected Matthew as one of the Twelve—His closest disciples, who would go on to be apostles. Though scripture tells us no more of Matthew's mission, his Gospel speaks for itself. A book written in the last half of the first century, it reveals Jesus as Messiah to his fellow Jews.

Matthew depicts the joy of leaving sin behind to follow Jesus. No earthly wealth can bind us when we accept our Savior's love.

MELCHIZEDEK

Then Melchizedek king of Salem brought out
bread and wine. He was priest of God Most High,
and he blessed Abram, saying, "Blessed be Abram
by God Most High, Creator of heaven and earth."
GENESIS 14:18–19

How little we know of this mystery man, who appears briefly in Genesis and receives more explanation in the New Testament than in the Old Testament.

Melchizedek emerged when Abram returned from rescuing Lot from the clutches of the king of Elam. This king of Salem (or "king of peace") came to Abram, carrying a banquet with him. He blessed Abram, using words that indicated he was speaking not of a Canaanite deity, but of the Lord God. And Abram responded by giving Melchizedek a tenth of the plunder he'd gained from the king of Elam and his allies.

If there was any question about whom this king-priest referred to, Hebrews 7 clears it up. The New Testament passage compares Salem's ruler with the Son of God—priest and king and superior to the Levite priesthood.

If nothing else, Melchizedek keeps us and our theology humble. We wonder just where this king came from and how he relates to Jesus. Is he Jesus, or just a picture of Him? Let's remember not to be too secure in our private interpretations. God doesn't tell us everything about Himself—or about mystery men like Melchizedek.

METHUSELAH

So all the days of Methuselah were nine hundred and sixty-nine years; and he died.
GENESIS 5:27 NKJV

You don't have to be a biblical scholar to have used the phrase "as old as Methuselah." He's become a byword for living an incredibly long life. He makes the centenarians of our age look positively youthful.

But Methuselah wasn't the only one in his family who did something unusual. His father, Enoch, "walked with God, and he was not, for God took him" (Genesis 5:24 ESV). First his father went to God without dying; then Methuselah lived such a long life that it probably seemed to his neighbors that he would never die. He finally passed on at the age of 969.

But scripture doesn't tell us any more about Methuselah's life. Was he a strong believer? Perhaps his faith contributed to his long life. But if he wasn't, perhaps the years dragged on seemingly unendingly.

How many years we live matters less than the way we live them. Are we endlessly seeking useless ways to fill idle hours? Or do we serve God with each moment? If we seek our Lord's will for each part of our day, whether we live a few years or many, we'll be blessed—and we'll be glad when we meet Jesus again.

MICAH

The word of the LORD that came to Micah of Moresheth during the reigns of Jotham, Ahaz and Hezekiah, kings of Judah— the vision he saw concerning Samaria and Jerusalem.
MICAH 1:1

Micah's name asked a question: "Who is like Yahweh?" But his name alone did not lead the people of Judah to understand God's greatness. Along with the prophet Isaiah, Micah confronted both Israel and Judah about their faithlessness. As we read the record of this minor prophet's preaching, we see that he didn't paint a pretty picture. More often than not, he spoke of judgment, though God's mercy and a promise of restoration also appear in his book.

Micah preached during the reigns of Jotham, Ahaz, and Hezekiah, kings of Judah during a difficult time. Assyria attacked and captured Israel, but God defended Judah when the Assyrian king Sennacherib attacked Jerusalem. Yet Jerusalem was not completely safe: eventually, it would fall before Babylon, the pagan nation that replaced Assyrian power in the land.

Micah clearly prophesies the future Messiah and the peace that will flourish under His reign. Micah didn't speak the words his people wanted to hear, but he offered a hope that generations have treasured. The peace of the Messiah touches our lives, along with the hope of His eternal rule. How are we sharing that message with other hopeless hearts?

MORDECAI

Mordecai had a cousin named Hadassah, whom he had brought up because she had neither father nor mother. This girl, who was also known as Esther, was lovely in form and features, and Mordecai had taken her as his own daughter when her father and mother died.
ESTHER 2:7

Kindhearted Mordecai took in his cousin when her parents died, and he treated her like a daughter.

When Esther went, with many other beautiful young women, to compete for the position of queen, Mordecai may already have been a Persian official, because he already lived in the citadel. No doubt his family had been part of the Jewish nobility, exiled to Persia with the rest of the Judean upper class.

When Esther went to the king, wise Mordecai had warned her not to broadcast her Jewish heritage. Perhaps because she did this, God used her to bring about the salvation of His people.

After Esther became queen, Mordecai caught wind of a plot to harm King Ahasuerus. The honest official warned the queen, who passed word on to her husband. The plotters were hanged and a record made of Mordecai's actions. But before he could be rewarded, Mordecai got into trouble with the wicked politician Haman.

The king had placed Haman in the highest political position, but when everyone else bowed down to him and paid homage, Mordecai refused. Scholars suggest that Haman, who is called an Agagite, supported King Agag, leader of the Amalekites and enemy of the Jews. In response, Haman overreacted and planned to kill both Mordecai and all his people. This powerful court official went to the king and bribed him to kill all the Jews in the Persian Empire. The king went along with the idea and had an edict written accordingly.

When Mordecai heard the news, he grieved publicly and reported the situation to Esther, even providing her with a copy of the edict. Esther doubted the wisdom of going to see the king. Unless he wanted to see her, she could be killed just for coming into his presence. Mordecai warned that cowardice would not save her, and who knew but that she had been put in her position "for such a time as this" (Esther 4:14)?

The queen went to her husband and was well received. She invited the king and Haman to two banquets. Before going to the second feast, Ahasuerus discovered that Mordecai had never been rewarded for foiling the plot against him. At Haman's suggestion, Esther's cousin was paraded through the streets and honored for his act. But when he discovered it was Mordecai who was to be so honored, not himself, the shock grieved Haman to his core.

At the second banquet, Esther revealed her own nationality and Haman's plot. Furious, Ahasuerus had Haman killed on the same gallows his henchmen had prepared to kill Mordecai. Then the king requested that Mordecai draft a decree to protect the Jews from Haman's edict. According to Persian law, the king could not retract his original edict, but a new law allowed Jews to fight back against anyone who attacked them.

All Haman's lands became Mordecai's, and he was greatly honored by the king and raised to a high position. The Jews rejoiced, and on the day Haman had slated for their destruction, they destroyed all who came against them. The celebration of Purim was instituted to honor this day when God had protected His people.

Though God is not mentioned in the book of Esther, His presence is easy to see. He used the queen and her cousin to save His people from harm.

Mordecai courageously responded to God's call. Had he refused to act, or had Esther failed to confront the king, He would have found another way, but God often chooses to use His people to bring about great moments of salvation. It is a joy to those who obey and a blessing to those who receive the salvation. Will we be ready to respond if God calls us to do His will?

MOSES

There the LORD showed him the whole land. . . . "I have let you see it with your eyes, but you will not cross over into it." And Moses the servant of the LORD died there in Moab, as the LORD had said.
DEUTERONOMY 34:1, 4–5

As Moses stood looking at the Promised Land, he also saw God's provision for His people. Because of their disobedience, they had wandered for forty years in the wilderness, but now the Israelites were headed into the Promised Land flowing with milk and honey.

Moses knew what God's care meant in his life. Hadn't the Lord watched over him when his mother placed him in a basket and set him afloat on the Nile River? Without God's intervention, would he have been picked up by a softhearted Egyptian princess? Would he have grown up in the court and learned how to deal with Pharaoh? God even gave Moses his brother, Aaron, to speak for him and lead the people's spiritual lives, and his sister, Miriam, to act as a prophetess.

After killing a man in defense of his people, Moses spent many years in the desert, herding sheep—perhaps a great background for someone who would lead a stubborn and rebellious people. For God called Moses to lead His people from Egypt to the Promised Land of Canaan.

When the Israelites first heard of Moses' plan to lead them to freedom, they were probably enthusiastic. But the battle between Pharaoh and the prophet became long, dark, and dangerous as one plague after another hit the land. Still, God protected His people, gave them a celebration of the event in Passover, and led them to freedom.

As they set off, the trouble didn't stop. Egyptian warriors followed them and herded the slaves up against the Red Sea. Miraculously, God made a way for them to cross the sea and covered the pursuing army with water. Still, the people weren't satisfied. Before they walked through the sea, they were already complaining, "Why, Moses, did you take us out of our nice, cushy slavery? Are you going to let us die here?"

Dealing with periodic rebellion became part of Moses' job description, and he heard complaints about the food (or lack of food), the water, and every other part of the journey to their new land. Even when Moses went apart to receive God's Law, the irrepressible Israelites got into trouble, making a golden idol to worship. Yet neither God nor Moses gave up. God renewed His covenant with His people, and Moses led them on.

When God brought them to the Promised Land, the worst was yet to come. Moses sent twelve spies to check out the situation in Canaan. Ten came back saying, "We can never win over these people; they're too strong for us," as if they, not God, were in charge of the battle plan. Only two faithful men, Caleb and Joshua, encouraged the people to rely on God and take the land for themselves.

For forty years, the Israelites wandered around in circles, doing laps in the desert as punishment for their faithlessness. God provided manna to eat, laws to guide their spiritual lives, and much forgiveness. But until the original generation died, except for the two faithful spies, He would not lead them to the Promised Land again.

Not even Moses got to cross the border. He viewed it from afar, knowing God's promise would be fulfilled. But Moses died on Mount Nebo, just short of Canaan, and was buried in Moab.

The greatest prophet in Israel's history transmitted God's Law to the nation and took part in God's provision for His people, from salvation from Egypt to salvation of their souls. When pagan nations threatened, God protected them. When a harsh environment endangered them, God bestowed food and guided them in the right path.

Like Moses, do we, too, look back on our lives and see God's provision? When we see His great works, are we thankful, or do we simply seek another benefit? Let's appreciate all God has done for us, unlike those faithless Israelites who perished in the desert.

NAAMAN

So Naaman said, ". . .Yet in this thing may the
LORD pardon your servant: when my master goes into
the temple of Rimmon to worship there, and he leans on my hand,
and I bow down in the temple of Rimmon—when
I bow down in the temple of Rimmon, may the LORD
please pardon your servant in this thing."
2 KINGS 5:17–18 NKJV

Naaman was an able and valiant military commander for the king of Syria. He was also a leper. In ancient times, leprosy was an incurable, dread disease that disfigured the body.

Happily for Naaman, a young Israelite woman captured by Syrian raiders was serving in his home. This young woman believed the prophet Elisha could cure Naaman and said as much to her mistress. When Naaman was told, he went off to see Elisha.

When Naaman arrived at Elisha's house, the prophet sent out a servant to tell him to bathe in the Jordan seven times. This wasn't good enough for Naaman, who was expecting much more. Leaving in a purple rage, he finally relented, when persuaded by his aides, and heeded the prophet's counsel. Dunking seven times in the Jordan, he was cured of his leprosy. Overwhelmed by his cure, Naaman vowed to worship no god but the God of Israel.

Then we're told that Naaman asked for pardon whenever he would accompany his master into the pagan house of Rimmon and bow with him. At first, this request appears to cast doubt on the genuineness of Naaman's conversion. Instead of lowering the boom on him, Elisha told him to go in peace. Elisha trusted God to work out the matter in Naaman's heart.

If we commit to walk with God, we cannot hold on to any sin. Only God can enable us to make that kind of commitment, as He likely did for Naaman.

NATHAN

*Then the LORD sent Nathan to David. And he
came to him, and said to him: "There were two
men in one city, one rich and the other poor."*
2 SAMUEL 12:1 NKJV

The prophet Nathan is best known as a storyteller who came to King David with a tale that made the ruler understand his sin.

This wasn't the first time Nathan had brought David bad news. The godly king had wanted to build a temple for the Lord. Recognizing David's spiritual fervor, Nathan directed him to start. But God told the prophet to halt the building plans, for they were not His plan. Humble David accepted Nathan's redirection.

Maybe that gave Nathan the courage to confront David after the king had taken Bathsheba for himself, despite the rights of her husband, Uriah. David, the rich man in Nathan's story, took advantage of poor Uriah, who had only one lamb. When David recognized the point of story, he repented of his sin in setting Uriah up to be killed and taking Bathsheba for himself.

No bad feelings destroyed the relationship between prophet and king. At the end of David's life, Nathan worked to warn the king that another son was deposing the heir, Solomon.

Nathan was a brave man who followed God's directions. Though offending the king would have been dangerous, the prophet cared more for God than for man—even a very powerful man.

Do we?

NATHANAEL

*Jesus saw Nathanael coming toward Him, and said of him,
"Behold, an Israelite indeed, in whom is no deceit!"*
JOHN 1:47 NKJV

Nathanael is a bit player in scripture who stands out in our minds. His story appears in a single paragraph, but we don't forget him.

This forthright man, approached by Philip with the news that Jesus was Messiah, didn't immediately pray the sinner's prayer. But Jesus did not condemn him for responding, "Can anything good come out of Nazareth?" (John 1:46 NKJV). On meeting this less-than-tactful man, Jesus declared him to be without deceit. Nathanael still had questions for Jesus. But the news that He'd seen him under the fig tree was proof enough. This plain-spoken man called Him Messiah.

Jesus promised that Nathanael would see much more than this simple miracle. Jesus told him that he would see heaven open.

Like Nathanael, who is also called Bartholomew in the lists of the Twelve, we need to study the scriptures. Nowhere had the Old Testament referred to the Messiah as coming from Nazareth. So Nathanael had honest doubts. He came to Jesus seeking to know the truth.

Are we honest seekers, or do we come to God with an agenda? How will our Bible study be different if we only seek to discover the truth God has for us today?

NEBUCHADNEZZAR

In the second year of the reign of Nebuchadnezzar,
Nebuchadnezzar had dreams; his spirit was troubled,
and his sleep left him.
DANIEL 2:1 ESV

Nebuchadnezzar, king of Babylon, ruled the most powerful nation in the world. But conquering the world didn't solve his problems, though he commanded an army that brought fear into the hearts of its enemies. So the king became a very angry person.

In 605 BC, Nebuchadnezzar conquered Judah and took the finest young men of that nation back to Babylon. Among them were Daniel and his companions, Shadrach, Meshach, and Abednego, who proved themselves wise beyond the king's expectation, better than all his pagan magicians.

One night when the king had counted hundreds of sheep but still couldn't sleep because of his bad dreams, he commanded his magicians to tell him what was wrong.

"Tell us your dream," the men requested. But the king, tired of lies and prevarication, adamantly refused. They must tell him the dream and its interpretation or he would kill them.

"No one," the magicians insisted, "can do that. Only the gods can interpret this dream." So the king prepared to carry out his threat.

When the captain of the guard sought to kill him, Daniel insisted on making an appointment with the king. Before they met, God gave Daniel a vision concerning the king's dream. When Daniel revealed the nightmare and its meaning, Nebuchadnezzar worshipped the Lord, and the magicians were spared.

However, this power-hungry king hadn't gained humility or true faith. Nebuchadnezzar set up an idol and expected everyone to worship him. So Daniel's three friends spent time in a fiery furnace and were saved only by God. Again the king worshipped the Lord, but again he didn't quite understand.

Finally, Nebuchadnezzar had a bad dream of a tall, beautiful tree that was lopped down to a stump. When the king's magicians couldn't interpret the dream, Daniel told the king it meant his own humiliation until he accepted God's authority. A year later, as the king boasted of his own power, Daniel's prophecy came true. Nebuchadnezzar was driven out from mankind and chomped on grass, like an ox, living in the wild. When the fallen king recognized God's power, he received his reason back and praised the Lord.

Spiritually empty, Nebuchadnezzar tried to fill the vacuum with his own greatness. This useless spiritual tactic never worked for him, and it won't work for us, either. Only God can fill the immense vacuum in our hearts that is just His size.

NEHEMIAH

The words of Nehemiah son of Hacaliah: In the month of Kislev. . .Hanani,
one of my brothers, came from Judah with some other men,
and I questioned them about the Jewish remnant
that survived the exile, and also about Jerusalem.
NEHEMIAH 1:1–2

Though Nehemiah held a prestigious position in the Babylonian court, he wasn't happy. As long as his people in Jerusalem lived in danger, this exiled Jew's heart remained with them. Hanani had reported that Jerusalem's walls were broken and the gates destroyed, and Nehemiah knew that meant invaders could easily destroy what was left of Judah's capital city. Nehemiah immediately mourned, wept, and prayed.

While Nehemiah waited on King Artaxerxes I, his sorrow became apparent. Powerful kings weren't used to their cupbearers looking as if they were about to dilute the wine with tears. But when Artaxerxes heard of Nehemiah's problem, he supported his desire to help Judah. In a few minutes, Nehemiah had permission to go to his homeland, provision for his journey, and authorization to get building materials.

Three days after he arrived in Jerusalem, Nehemiah quietly made a nighttime inspection of the walls he'd heard so much about. Then he informed the city officials that they needed to rebuild. What could they say but yes?

Meanwhile, other voices screamed, "No!" The leaders of the surrounding nations liked having Judah weak and helpless. So local leaders of neighboring lands, Sanballat, Tobiah, and Geshem, accused Nehemiah of rebellion. The city building project began with guards surrounding Jerusalem and prayers being lifted up for God's protection. Even the workers wore swords.

Once the wall and gates were rebuilt, Governor Nehemiah reformed

Jerusalem's politics and brought his people back to faith. But when he left to report to Artaxerxes and came back to discover that the job was far from completed, he faithfully continued the necessary work.

When we're taking on a project for God, do we expect all the wheels to run smoothly, the gas to be cheap, and our fellow travelers to support us? It doesn't always work that way. Nehemiah had opposition from within his own people and from outsiders. When he wanted to build, he had to hand his laborers swords. Resistance sometimes indicates we're doing just what God wants—and what Satan detests. So let's work faithfully, even when unbelievers argue. We're working for God, not the enemy!

NICODEMUS

Nicodemus answered and said to Him, "How can these things be?"
JOHN 3:9 NKJV

The Sanhedrin was Israel's supreme council and court of justice in the first century. Its members, leading figures and more often than not men of means, had reputations to consider. Perhaps that's why one of them, Nicodemus, came to Jesus by night. By now, Jesus' fame had spread far and wide throughout Israel. Many regarded Him as a great prophet "mighty in deed and word" (Luke 24:19 NKJV). But the Jewish leaders didn't exactly approve of this new prophet.

Nicodemus had obviously thought a lot about Jesus, as evidenced by his words: "Rabbi, we know that You are a teacher come from God; for no one can do these signs that You do unless God is with him" (John 3:2 NKJV). Nicodemus took Jesus seriously.

Yet Jesus responded jarringly. "Most assuredly, I say to you, unless one is born again, he cannot see the kingdom of God" (John 3:3 NKJV). To Nicodemus, it must have seemed a strange and incredible statement. You can imagine his face contorting in puzzlement as he began struggling to comprehend what he had just heard. "Stay with me, Nicodemus; there's more," you can almost hear Jesus respond. He continued, "Most assuredly, I say to you, unless one is born of water and the Spirit, he cannot enter the kingdom of God. That which is born of the flesh is flesh, and that which is born of the Spirit is spirit. Do not marvel that I said to you, 'You must be born again.' The wind blows where it wishes, and you hear the sound of it, but cannot tell where it comes from and where it goes. So is everyone who is born of the Spirit" (John 3:5–8 NKJV).

Nicodemus, by now totally befuddled, replied, "How can these things be?"

With that question and Jesus' subsequent answer, Nicodemus was brought to a heavenly plane of understanding. The evidence of his comprehension? Nicodemus stood up in defense of Jesus (see John 7:50–52) and joined Joseph of Arimathea in burying Jesus' body (see John 19:39), two actions fraught with risk for a Jewish leader.

We can fault Nicodemus for using the cover of darkness to meet with Jesus, but darkness or not, he met with Jesus. Furthermore, he was serious about his inquiries into Jesus' teaching, though at first he couldn't quite grasp what Jesus told him. How seriously do we take Jesus? Is He nothing more than a distant figure of history, or is He as alive to us as anyone living can be? Only the Holy Spirit, blowing on the embers in our hearts, can fan them into the same flame of conviction that Nicodemus had.

NOAH

Thus Noah did; according to all that God commanded him, so he did.
Genesis 6:22 nkjv

Cataclysm: Webster's defines this word as "a momentous and violent event marked by overwhelming upheaval and demolition." In our all-too-distracted lives, do we have any idea the number of cataclysms God has spared us from on this planet? Should a tenuous section of one of the Canary Islands give way and fall into the Atlantic, it would generate a monstrous tidal wave that would destroy the entire East Coast of the United States as well as many other parts of the Atlantic. For those who live on the Indian Ocean, the prospect of a tsunami became a terrifying reality on December 26, 2004. For all our technology, we are still vulnerable!

Not long after God created humankind, His forbearance ran out, and He decided to bring a cataclysm upon the earth. He selected a man named Noah to undertake the world's first shipbuilding project, but not until after He told Noah what He planned to do.

Noah was a descendant of Seth, Adam and Eve's third child. The children in this line sought God faithfully at first. One of them was a man by the name of Enoch, whom God translated alive into heaven body and soul. Noah was Enoch's great-grandson. The descendants of Cain, on the other hand, were unfaithful to God and thus became corrupt. In time, the corruption of Cain's descendants had spread so malevolently as to also contaminate Seth's line. The cancer of sin spread virulently on the earth and became deeply ingrained in humans. In short, in the eyes of God, humanity was too far gone.

What an awful time it was to be alive back then. Society (if you could call it that) ran wild with every kind of crime and vice imaginable, and did so with impunity! It was a world not fit for man or beast. It was in such a world that Noah lived.

Aside from his building of the ark, scripture doesn't tell us much else about

Noah. Still, we wonder how any man or woman could have survived spiritually in such a society. We can only imagine the kind of pressures Noah faced, the allurements and enticements of a world that had become hell on earth. Apart from God's saving grace, could any human have survived? Only by God's grace was blameless Noah able to resist the downward pull of all the evil surrounding him and rise above it.

Undoubtedly, he had to contend with heaps of ridicule toward his God-given nautical project. Perhaps the area in which he lived was far from any sizable body of water. That would have made his project all the more ludicrous. Still, in unquestioning obedience, Noah kept building. It is also quite likely that he became an evangelist—perhaps the first one since the Creation! Knowing what was to befall those he knew must have propelled him to sound a clarion alarm, whether or not anyone would listen. Surely those who mocked ceased their mocking and paused in wonder when they witnessed a vast, orderly train of animals streaming toward the ark, all led by an invisible hand.

Then came the day when God ushered Noah and his family aboard and sealed them within the ark. It was all over but the waiting. The ridicule reached a crescendo. Can you imagine the jeering and taunts and laughter of those outside? Seven days later, the laughter changed to cries of horror. In a moment, relatives, neighbors, friends, and acquaintances were all swept away by the deluge. There was nothing Noah or his family could do about it. What a fearful death! Only Noah and his family were spared. And with this event, the world got a picture of God's salvation. A piece of the world floated safely atop the oceans until He brought them onto dry land again.

Noah went against a mighty tide of sin. Until spared, he paid a dear price for it, and so must we as ambassadors and apologists for Jesus. Like Noah, our faithfulness to God's Word will be contrary to everything the world stands for. But every time we see a rainbow, it reminds us of His faithfulness!

PAUL

Continue in your faith, established and firm,
not moved from the hope held out in the gospel.
This is the gospel that you heard and that has been proclaimed
to every creature under heaven, and of which
I, Paul, have become a servant.
COLOSSIANS 1:23

A zealous Jew and a Pharisee, well educated as a pupil of Gamaliel, Saul of Tarsus probably could have quoted the Old Testament better than many Christians of his day. But until Jesus laid him flat on the road to Damascus, religion was a matter of rules and regulations to Saul. Getting knocked down and blinded during his road trip got this Pharisee's attention. Understanding how spiritually sightless he'd been, he accepted Jesus as Messiah.

As soon as he started preaching his newfound faith, persecution became Saul's lot. He had to escape from Damascus to avoid death. For the next three years, he lived in Arabia.

Returning to Jerusalem, Saul faced a new kind of persecution. Christian leaders doubted his conversion. Was this some new ploy to infiltrate their community? But Barnabas supported Saul. Finally, the former persecutor of Christians was accepted into the church and began preaching.

The Holy Spirit chose Barnabas and Saul for a missionary journey, and they sailed for Cyprus. Scripture first records that here Saul was called by his Roman name, Paul. The missionaries started preaching to the Jews, but opposition in the synagogues grew. At Lystra, Paul was stoned by Jews from Antioch and Iconium and left for dead. Clearly Paul's real mission would be to the Gentiles.

Before long, Christians began asking, "Should new converts have to follow Jewish practices like circumcision?" Paul and Barnabas debated the issue in Antioch, then went to Jerusalem, where the council of leaders agreed that Gentile circumcision was unnecessary.

After the two missionaries reported back to Antioch, Barnabas wanted to return to the new churches they'd founded. But he and Paul seriously disagreed about whether to take Barnabas's cousin John Mark with them. John Mark had dropped out of their previous mission, and now Paul didn't want him along. So the companions split up, and each took another man along to begin a fresh mission.

Paul's new road was not an easy one. He got more beatings than kudos, and even the believers he spoke to often gave him grief. Paul continued the plan he and Barnabas had begun, going into a town, preaching to those who would listen, and establishing a church of converts. When Paul was traveling, he wrote letters addressing the most crucial issues in the churches he'd founded. These became the biblical epistles to the churches of Greece, Rome, and Asia Minor. Periodically, Paul returned to these young churches to encourage them in their faith and to address doctrinal issues.

As he went, Paul also developed new leaders, taking men like Titus and Timothy along to learn the ropes. Then they, too, trained the people in the growing congregations.

Eventually, the turmoil that followed the apostle's message caught up with him in Jerusalem, where a group of Jews accused him of wrong teaching and defilement of the temple. Though the charges were spurious, Paul ended up appealing to Roman law and being sent to Rome. He lost his life as a martyr in Emperor Nero's persecutions.

Paul was a highly dedicated Christian, a servant of Christ. Whether he was being threatened by a shipwreck on his way to Rome or standing before a cantankerous ruler, he stood firm for Jesus. So it's not surprising that Paul's epistles describe a brass-tacks religion. There's a lot of practical help here for struggling new Christians or mature believers who need to address a problem in their congregations or personal lives. Paul recognized that faith is a matter of what you do, as well as what you think and believe.

Are we inspired by Paul's demanding view of faith? Or do we discount it as something no modern-day believer could accomplish? On our own, we could never reach the world for Jesus. But empowered by His Spirit, we feel inspiration, not confrontation, as we look at the life of His servant Paul.

PETER

When Simon Peter saw it, he fell down at Jesus' knees, saying,
"Depart from me, for I am a sinful man, O Lord!"
LUKE 5:8 NKJV

He might seem the least likely man to become an apostle of Jesus. Rough-hewn, hardworking, and relatively uneducated, Simon, son of Jonah, was a no-nonsense kind of man. He may have been a bit coarse and vulgar, too. As a fisherman, he had his good business days and not-so-good days.

Simon was in a business partnership with Zebedee, father of James and John, whom Jesus would also call to apostleship. Jesus had referred to them as "Sons of Thunder," perhaps implying their father had a fiery temper. Were that so, it's possible that Simon and Zebedee had their quarrels, some of which were probably high volume/low prosperity.

Then came the day that Simon's younger brother Andrew told him that he'd met the long-awaited Messiah. We have to wonder what Simon thought about his brother's news and how he reacted when he first met Jesus. Top that with Jesus' immediately giving Simon the name Peter (or "Rock").

Next, a momentous event occurred. After using Peter's fishing boat as a waterborne pulpit, Jesus tells Peter to put out from the shore and cast his net over the side for a catch. Having had one of his not-so-good days, Peter is reluctant at first but then agrees to Jesus' request. In no time Peter hauls in perhaps his greatest catch ever. Sensing something supernatural is taking place, Peter falls at Jesus' knees, begging Him, "Depart from me, for I am a sinful man, O Lord!" (Luke 5:8 NKJV).

We wonder what made Peter say what he did, but more important, what was it about Jesus that made him say it? Clearly, Peter didn't let his sinfulness keep him from following Jesus to become a fisher of men.

Another momentous event occurred in the synagogue at Capernaum. Jesus said, "Whoever eats My flesh and drinks My blood has eternal life, and I will raise him up at the last day. For My flesh is food indeed, and My blood is drink indeed" (John 6:54–55 NKJV). Nothing like this had been heard before in any synagogue. Those listening recoiled in horror. People muttered, "How can this Man give us His flesh to eat?" (John 6:52 NKJV). Sadly, many chose to leave Jesus right then and there.

Jesus turned to His apostles and asked if they wanted to leave, too. Peter replied at once, "To whom shall we go?" and then added, "You have the words of eternal life. Also we have come to believe and know that You are the Christ, the Son of the living God" (John 6:68–69 NKJV). Peter had an understanding of who Jesus was, though it was far from complete.

Finally, on the night before Jesus' death, He gathered with His disciples for His last Passover meal. During the meal, Jesus foretold how all of the disciples would abandon Him later that evening. As always, stalwart Peter proclaimed that he would never leave Jesus, even if everyone else did. If he had to die with Jesus, he would not deny him (see Matthew 26:31–35).

Jesus replied, "Will you lay down your life for My sake? Most assuredly, I say to you, the rooster shall not crow till you have denied Me three times" (John 13:38 NKJV). If that came close to breaking Peter's heart, what Jesus said next probably made it skip a beat. "Simon, Simon! Indeed, Satan has asked for you, that he may sift you as wheat. But I have prayed for you, that your faith should not fail; and when you have returned to Me, strengthen your brethren" (Luke 22:31–32 NKJV). The prospect was both chilling and encouraging. Oh yes, Satan would sift, and sift he did, but Jesus would triumph in the life of Peter.

Peter went from an impulsive, headstrong follower to a Spirit-filled leader. God took a raw lump of coal and refined it for His purposes. He will do the same with each of us if we put aside our own pride and ego.

PHARAOH

"When Pharaoh does not listen to you, then I will lay My hand on Egypt
and bring out My hosts, My people the sons of Israel,
from the land of Egypt by great judgments."
EXODUS 7:4 NASB

The ancient Egyptians believed that their pharaoh was a god; and if anyone let that idea go to his head, it was the pharaoh who ruled during the age of Moses.

Though we know all about his authority and the events recorded in scripture, one thing we don't know is this ruler's name. The Bible calls him simply "Pharaoh," yet because the history of that era is so vague, we don't know for certain which Egyptian pharaoh went head-to-head with God and His prophet Moses.

What we do know is that this was a major contention. Moses and his brother, Aaron, confronted Pharaoh, asking him to free the enslaved Hebrews. As God had forewarned Moses, Pharaoh would have none of it. When Aaron threw down his rod and it turned into a snake, the Egyptian magicians did the same, only to have their snakes eaten by Aaron's.

When Pharaoh did not heed Moses' request, God, who had hardened the Egyptian ruler's heart, gave Pharaoh ten attention-getting plagues: turning water to blood; overrunning the land with frogs; covering the earth with gnats; filling Egyptian homes and ruining the land with flies; killing livestock; afflicting man and beast with boils; killing animals, plants, and people with hail; destroying with locusts what few crops were left; and covering the entire land with darkness. When none of these plagues worked, God finally took the life of the firstborn of every Egyptian animal and human.

Pharaoh might have gotten high marks for stubbornness, but his attitude ruined his country before he thrust the Hebrews out of Egypt. Yet even then he made an unwise decision and sent his army in pursuit of the former slaves in an attempt to return them to his kingdom, but it was too late. As God's people miraculously crossed the Red Sea, the Egyptian army followed and was destroyed in the waters.

Stubbornness has its uses, but only when combined with godly wisdom. Pharaoh ran aground when he defied God and was willing to go to any lengths to get his own way. Will we learn from him before we, too, head down our own path, ignoring the call of God?

PHILEMON

Paul, a prisoner of Christ Jesus, and Timothy our brother,
to Philemon our beloved friend and fellow laborer.
PHILEMON 1:1 NKJV

Faithful Philemon must have felt honored to receive a personal message from the apostle Paul. But the topic of Paul's note wasn't such a pleasant one, and perhaps Philemon would have preferred not to share its contents with his house church. Philemon's slave Onesimus had run away from his master, and Paul expected the wealthy slave owner to be justly angry when he discovered that Onesimus was with Paul in Rome.

Yet Onesimus had become a Christian under Paul's ministry. And for Paul, the once-useless slave now lived up to the meaning of his name: "useful." The apostle would rather have kept Onesimus with him, but he sent the slave back with a request that Philemon treat him as a brother in Christ. Some scholars think the apostle might even have been encouraging Philemon to free him and return him to Paul.

Philemon had a hard time viewing slaves as people, but Paul impressed upon him the need to do so. Are there some "less important" or less-than-lovable people in our lives? God calls us to be gentle Philemons, especially toward our brothers in Christ. They're no less important to God than this first-century slave was.

PHILIP THE APOSTLE

The next day Jesus decided to leave for Galilee.
Finding Philip, he said to him, "Follow me." Philip, like Andrew
and Peter, was from the town of Bethsaida.
JOHN 1:43–44

With His usual brief "Follow Me," Jesus called Peter's fellow townsman to discipleship. And the newly commissioned Philip didn't sit on the good news. The next day, he shared it with Nathanael: "We have found the one Moses wrote about in the Law" (John 1:45). When Nathanael doubted, Philip didn't argue; he just invited his friend to check out Jesus.

Again we see Philip at the feeding of the five thousand, when he asks Jesus, "Where can we buy bread to feed these people?" (John 6:5 THE MESSAGE). Philip recognizes the problem but cannot solve it.

Philip's real skill was leading people to Jesus, as he did with some Greeks who asked to see Him. When Jesus began getting into deep theology, at the end of His ministry, Philip, confused, asked to see the Father. He may not have been a heavyweight theologian, but Philip still had an important mission—bringing others to Jesus. Whereas some might have felt intimidated, he became excited. It didn't matter whether he had all the answers; this disciple just wanted people to know his friend and Savior.

Do we share Philip's zeal for making Jesus known?

PHILIP THE EVANGELIST

Then Philip went down to the city of Samaria and preached Christ to them.
ACTS 8:5 NKJV

One of seven deacons chosen for their good reputations and willingness to serve, Philip was part of the first church growth experience. Even as Saul's persecution of Christianity grew, the number of believers expanded.

Because they were tossed out of Jerusalem, Christians started preaching wherever they went. In Samaria, Philip had so much evangelistic success that Peter and John were sent to expand the mission. Receiving word from an angel,

Philip headed on toward Gaza. In the desert, he ran into an Ethiopian eunuch who was reading from the book of Isaiah.

"Do you understand what you're reading?" Philip asked the man, who invited the evangelist to explain it to him. What a wonderful opportunity to preach Jesus to a wide-open heart. As soon as they found water, the eunuch asked to be baptized. Philip completed the rite and then was carried away by the Spirit, leaving a praise-filled eunuch behind him.

The last time scripture mentions Philip, Paul stops by his home in Caesarea. Philip not only reached others with the Gospel, but his family believed, too. He had four believing daughters who prophesied.

Wherever he went, Philip brought along his message. Do we do the same? Or do we only talk about Jesus when we're at church?

PONTIUS PILATE

"What shall I do, then, with Jesus who is called Christ?" Pilate asked.
MATTHEW 27:22

These words, thundering down to us through the corridors of time, were spoken by a man caught up in the pomp and circumstance of his own office as governor of a troublesome outlying Roman province. Here we have a striking confrontation between the quintessential autocrat and God incarnate!

Pontius Pilate was what we would call a "company man." He knew (or thought he knew) which side his bread was buttered on. His allegiance was to Rome, not to the ideology of an occupied people. No doubt he knew of their heritage, including the God whom they worshipped and to whom their temple was dedicated. While all of this might have made him wonder, there can also be no doubt that he valued Roman power and prestige over the religion of Israel. Perhaps he thought, *If their God is so great, how did He allow them to fall under our heel of iron?*

Then he met their Messiah face-to-face. At Passover, a boisterous crowd gathered outside the Praetorium, Pilate's headquarters in Jerusalem. The mob, replete with the Jewish leaders of the day, brought a man with them. He stood out from the rest of the crowd, His bearing noble yet besieged. They accused him with trumped-up charges, such as "perverting the nation, and forbidding [people] to pay taxes to Caesar" (Luke 23:2 NKJV), a charge obviously designed to get Pilate's attention.

As Pilate sized up the accused, he must have sensed that no ordinary man stood before him. This is evident by the train of interaction that follows between Pilate and Jesus and the crowd. Pilate seemingly did not suffer trifles lightly. "You take Him and judge Him according to your law" (John 18:31 NKJV), said the governor to the crowd. "Don't bother me with petty crimes you are capable of handling," was the implication.

But the crowd was not so easily dismissed. Before long, Pilate realized that the people were clamoring for nothing less than Jesus' blood. Then began an interrogation by Pilate to assess Jesus' guilt, one that would lead Pilate to understand what was really going on. Scripture says, "For he knew that they had handed Him over because of envy" (Matthew 27:18 NKJV). Pilate, who had the power either to release Jesus or to crucify him (see John 19:10), found himself trying to save a man who otherwise would have meant nothing to him. What prompted Pilate to act this way? Was it Jesus' admission that He was a king and that His kingdom was not of this world? Was it the crowd's accusation that Jesus had declared Himself to be the very Son of God? Was it his wife's urging to "have nothing to do with that just Man" (Matthew 27:19 NKJV)?

In any event, the mob finally cried out, "If you release this Man, you are no friend of Caesar; everyone who makes himself out to be a king opposes Caesar" (John 19:12 NASB). Here were words that Pilate clearly understood, and they must have rattled him. Things were beginning to get out of hand, and Pilate, ever the shrewd administrator, sensed the situation was only a few steps away from becoming a full-fledged riot. Not exactly the stuff a Roman governor wanted to be known for—and certainly not with these people who were already fed up with Roman domination.

If Pilate was a risk taker, he was at his limit. Like Julius Caesar before him, he had arrived at the banks of his own Rubicon—without even realizing it. Would he refrain, or would he cross? Tragically, Pilate swallowed the mob's raging words and "surrendered Jesus to their will" (Luke 23:25).

Where do we stand when the going gets rough, when our allegiance to Jesus is tested? Since that fateful day in Jerusalem, many martyrs throughout the centuries have answered Pilate's question with their own lives. Most of us will never face execution. But scorn, ridicule, and perhaps even persecution will come. Then we will not be able to avoid the question, "What shall I do, then, with Jesus who is called Christ?" (Matthew 27:22).

THE PRODIGAL SON

Jesus continued: "There was a man who had two sons.
The younger one said to his father, 'Father, give me my share of the estate.'
So he divided his property between them."
LUKE 15:11–12

This character in one of Jesus' parables may not have been a real person, but he's very true to life. You probably know someone like him—or maybe your life before you met Jesus was not unlike this young man's.

As the prodigal son grabbed his inheritance, packed his bags, and set out to see the world, life looked good. Like many young men, he wanted to test his ability to do what he pleased. High living appealed to him, and when he got to a foreign land, he quickly engaged in just about every sin available.

But money spent on loose living is a bad investment. In time, the prodigal found himself penniless. The moment he clinked his last two coins together, all his so-called friends disappeared. Now that he couldn't buy the wine, women, and song, the prodigal wasn't worth their time.

As life often has it, just as the money disappeared, a severe famine arose. Now the boy had two troubles. How would he feed himself? No one was looking to hire an experienced wastrel. Maybe his reputation went before him, because the boy ended up tending pigs. Caring for an unclean animal would have been abhorrent to a good Jew. The lad was as low as he could go, both spiritually and physically.

Just as this vagabond was contemplating how good pig pods would taste, an idea struck him: *My father's servants eat better than this!* So he planned to return to his father, not as a favored son, but as an abject servant. After composing a nice, humble speech designed to persuade his father to let him become a servant, he set out on the road home.

How surprised this sinner must have felt when, while he was still traveling homeward, his father ran up and embraced him. While the son had been wasting his time and money in a foreign land, his father had been on the lookout. He'd foreseen what would happen and wanted to intervene in his son's hard life as soon as possible. All he'd looked for was repentance in the boy's heart.

Before the prodigal could spit out more than his admission of sin, his father sent servants to get a robe, shoes, and a ring symbolic of authority. He ordered a celebration feast, too.

Naturally, someone had to pour cold water on the festivities. The upright elder brother came back just in time to learn what had happened. When he found out that his brother was back, anger darkened his face. He sat outside and sulked. A servant must have let the father know about his elder son, for he came out to lovingly invite him to the celebration. Immediately, the son who up to then had done no wrong let his father know just how shortchanged he felt. He'd never had so much as a young goat for a feast with his friends, and here the sinner got the fatted calf cooked for dinner. Was that fair?

The father reminded the son that everything he had was his—indeed, the good son had not spent his inheritance, and the younger son wouldn't have a bit of what was left. But how could this tender father fail to celebrate when his lost son returned?

The story ends there. We don't know if the younger son worked hard to build his own financial future, or if the elder brother forgave him. What we do know is that the father, who is a picture of God, loved both sons enough to forgive them completely.

When you read the story, are you the prodigal or the upright elder brother?

Are you aware of your sin or of your own goodness? Whether you sin with ease and remorsefully turn back to God in repentance, or you tend to think too much of your own righteousness and hard-heartedly expect others to pay, forgiveness is yours. All you need to do is turn to the Father in love. He forgives both wastrels and critics.

THE PUBLICAN

Two men went up into the temple to pray;
the one a Pharisee, and the other a publican.
LUKE 18:10 KJV

Contrast a first-century Pharisee and a publican (or tax collector). One, an upstanding member of the community, prays frequently and seeks to obey the law. The other works for the Romans, who oppress his people, and rarely sets foot in the temple.

The highly religious Pharisee felt he had an edge on those who engaged in obvious sins like adultery or extortion. As he bragged to God of his own goodness, he denigrated the tax collector, who obviously couldn't meet that holiness standard.

The humble publican hardly raised his eyes as he worshipped in the temple. What was he doing there, laden with all his sins? He understood his own lack of worth, and sin bore him down so heavily that he barely whispered his need for mercy into God's ear. The publican compared himself to God, not another human, and he came up far short.

As Jesus told this parable and praised the humble publican, He shocked His righteous audience. After all, they were used to thinking highly of their own attempts to please God, and wasn't obedience a good thing? But no person lives sinlessly. Every believer humbly needs to recognize the temptation to sin that sits constantly at the heart's door.

THE RICH FOOL

"But God said to him, 'Fool! This night your soul will be required of you;
then whose will those things be which you have provided?' "
LUKE 12:20 NKJV

Andrew Carnegie believed "the man who dies thus rich dies disgraced." In Luke 12:13–21, it appears we have a man who didn't quite subscribe to that philosophy.

Quite possibly, this fellow wasn't even miserly; he may have been quite generous to others as God blessed him. But he still became all too comfortable, all too self-satisfied, all too self-absorbed. He may have hit a point in his life when he no longer cared much about giving. He had all he needed and then some. Why bother? He was preoccupied with how he would store all his excess.

We're told that God had something to say to this man. It began with, "Fool!" Having another person call you a fool is one thing. Having God call you a fool is quite another.

Why was God so harsh? For one thing, this man was "goods-centered" instead of God-centered. It isn't wicked to be rich, but it is wicked to be selfish. This man never thought to ask the One responsible for all his blessings what he should do with his wealth. He failed to acknowledge that only God can fill the void within us. He also failed to prepare for eternity. He clearly had only this life in view.

Jesus warns us, "So is he who lays up treasure for himself, and is not rich toward God" (Luke 12:21 NKJV). Are we taking Him seriously?

THE RICH YOUNG MAN

So [Jesus] said to [the rich young man],
"Why do you call Me good? No one is good but One, that is, God."
MATTHEW 19:17 NKJV

You're a young and wealthy man with a position of prestige. You've heard about this new Rabbi who is rapidly becoming known for His teaching and His healing. You want to meet Him, so you seek Him out. When you find Him, you pose what seems like an innocent question. Wanting to impress Him, you begin with, "Good Teacher." Number one mistake! You're surprised when Jesus says, "Why do you call Me good? No one is good but One, that is, God" (Matthew 19:17 NKJV). Little do you know that Jesus has just revealed to you the primary obstacle to faith in God. You're trusting in your own goodness to get you through heaven's gates.

"Oh," you say, "I've kept all the commandments since I was a tot." Have you? You must have been sleeping in synagogue the day Psalm 14:3 was read. It says, "There is no one who does good, not even one."

Full of yourself, you ask Jesus what more you could possibly do. "Sell everything you own and follow Me," He says.

"Oh no," you say, "not that. I couldn't." Couldn't you? Do you walk away sad because you have great possessions; or do they have you?

SAMSON

And it came to pass, when [Delilah] pestered [Samson] daily with
her words and pressed him, so that his soul was vexed to death,
that he told her all his heart.
JUDGES 16:16–17 NKJV

He was a man of incomparable strength, dedicated to the Lord from birth as a Nazirite. Almost single-handedly, he valiantly waged war against the Philistines. No one could touch Samson or bring him down—no one, that is, except himself and his own weakness.

The angel of the Lord had appeared to Samson's barren mother and told her she would give birth to a son. He also gave her special prenatal instructions, because her son would be set apart for special service to the Lord.

Samson was born during a time in the history of Israel when "everyone did what was right in his own eyes" (Judges 17:6 NKJV). For forty years prior to Samson's birth, the children of Israel had sinned greatly against God. As a result, God allowed the dreaded Philistines to dominate them.

It wasn't long before Samson's feats of physical strength gained him a reputation among his own people and the Philistines. He became a real thorn in the Philistines' side. As he wreaked havoc among them time and again, they became obsessed with doing away with this mighty Hebrew upstart. They went looking for flaws in Samson, and sure enough, they found some.

Samson's physical strength made him and others vulnerable. Impressed with his own might, Samson became rather self-centered. Oftentimes this flaw was detrimental to those closest to him (see Judges 15). Worst of all was his bent toward sexual immorality. This flaw led to his downfall. Samson liked women, and no doubt they liked him, too, given his reputation. Because unlawful intermingling had occurred between the Israelites and the Philistines, Samson had a much wider (and deadlier!) field to play. Sure enough, he set his sights on a Philistine beauty named Delilah. Evidently, she bewitched him. When Samson's Philistine foes found out about this affair, they hatched a plot. Money talks, and they paid Delilah well for her services. "Tell me the secret of your strength," she purred demurely. Ever thought about how superficial the web of a seductress is? Delilah, trained in the art of seductive nagging, spun her web skillfully. Finally, the mighty man from the tribe of Dan had had enough. He bared his most cherished secret, and the rest is history. His enemies enslaved him and blinded him—but he killed more Philistines in his death than in his life (Judges 16:30).

Samson fell for one of the subtlest and oldest traps ever. We have no strength but God's to keep our sexual drive from going into overdrive and entrapping us!

SAMUEL

So in the course of time Hannah conceived and gave birth to a son.
She named him Samuel, saying, "Because I asked the LORD for him."
1 SAMUEL 1:20

Samuel's name means "heard of God." But this prophet didn't just hear of God; he did God's will in a time of great civil unrest.

Samuel's mother knew that God had heard her request for a child, so she dedicated her child to Him. Because of this dedication, the boy grew up in the household of Eli the priest. Because Eli's own sons were unfaithful, God spoke to Samuel instead and made him a prophet.

Young Samuel saw the Philistines constantly battling his nation, and Israel was always on the losing end. So Samuel called Israel to renounce idol worship, and they did. For the first time in years, Israel won a battle over the attacking Philistines.

As God's prophet and judge, Samuel played a key role in building the nation of Israel. For many years, he ruled over the nation as their judge. But when he was old and his sons did not follow his good leadership example, the people asked Samuel to give them a king, as the other nations around them had. God warned that they'd have problems with kings, but He gave them Saul to rule over them, and Samuel anointed him.

Though King Saul started out well, before long he became caught up in his own power and he turned from God. While Samuel, his spiritual adviser, grieved the infidelity of the king, God had the prophet anoint David as king in Saul's place.

But David had to fight for his throne. Once again, strife destroyed the peace of Israel. Before David had consolidated his power, Saul died, and "all Israel. . . mourned for him" (1 Samuel 25:1 ESV). By the time of Samuel's death, the Israelites had again begun to worship idols.

Samuel is a fine example of a man who remained faithful, though he did not live in an ideal world. Although his own connection with God was clear, the people whose lives he directed were less than faithful. Though King Saul's rule seemed so promising, the leader designed to replace the elderly Samuel failed miserably.

But no matter who battled around him, Samuel remained true to the Lord. The prophet's message never changed. Neither did his devotion to the One who was primary in his life.

When we face times of strife and stress, do we blame God and immediately turn from Him, or like Samuel, do we trust that God will guide us through? Samuel may not have seen David take the throne, but because God is faithful, he knew it would happen.

SAUL, KING OF ISRAEL

He had a son named Saul, an impressive young
man without equal among the Israelites—
a head taller than any of the others.

1 SAMUEL 9:2

Saul is the Bible's promising politician gone bad. When Saul came to Israel's throne, he didn't have a lot to recommend him. Sure, he was good-looking and tall, and his dad was wealthy, but what leadership experience did he have? Yet all Israel, fed up with the corrupt rule of the prophet Samuel's sons and constantly battling numerous enemies, looked forward to having him in charge. Hope filled the air in Israel when Saul went hunting down some missing donkeys and ended up being anointed king by the prophet Samuel.

At first, it was obvious that God's Spirit was on the new king. Saul became an effective warrior for his beleaguered nation. But as time went on, his subjects found him less successful spiritually than militarily. Saul began by defeating the Ammonites, but when the Philistines attacked, Saul became impatient for battle and took it upon himself to perform the sacrifice that Samuel had promised to make. As neither priest nor prophet, Saul did not have this right. So when Samuel came, he warned Saul that God sought a man after His own heart to be king—and that man was not Saul.

Meanwhile, Saul's son Jonathan began a foray that led to the Philistines' defeat. But a foolish vow his father made almost cost Jonathan his life. Only the rebellion of the army, in Jonathan's defense, brought Saul to his senses.

Warfare continued as Saul defeated more of Israel's enemies. God commanded the king to attack the Amalekites and destroy all the people and their livestock. But Saul disobeyed, keeping their king alive, along with the best of the Amalekites' cattle. Samuel confronted the king with his disobedience. After a halfhearted admission of guilt, Saul saw his partial obedience as a good thing and could not understand the prophet's concern. Then this brave warrior-king became a coward as he blamed his own actions on the people.

Saul had rejected God, Samuel announced, so God had rejected him as king. If Saul thought he'd had opposition from Israel's enemies, he was about to face a new, internal conflict that would be even worse. For God sent Samuel to anoint the shepherd David as king in Saul's place.

Deserted by God's Spirit, Saul became prone to depression. To ease his suffering, Saul's attendants suggested they hire a harpist to soothe the king's disease. And whom did they choose but David, the man God had anointed king in Saul's place. David not only sang to the king; he became the people's favorite war commander. When his subjects praised David's deeds, Saul became jealous, and as his madness increased, he attempted to take the life of the shepherd turned warrior. Then, to trap David, Saul gave him his daughter Michal as his wife—a relationship that turned out badly for everyone involved.

Saul's son Jonathan favored David, creating tense moments within the royal family. Finally, Jonathan helped his friend escape. From then on, Saul and David's disagreements took place on the battlefield. But even when Saul could have been at his mercy, David spared God's anointed.

As the Philistines again gathered against Israel, Saul sought a word from God on the battle's outcome. When no response came, the king looked to the witch of Endor for an answer. She called up a spirit that Saul believed was Samuel, but the king probably would have preferred not to hear his news: Saul would lose the battle.

That prediction came true. In defeat, Saul took his own life, and the Philistines made a grisly show of his body—and those of his sons killed in battle—on the walls of the city of Beth Shan.

Though Saul's son Ish-bosheth ruled briefly in Israel, eventually David became king of both Judah and Israel.

Saul reminds us that starting well is not enough. Lifelong consistency of belief is what God calls us to. Every day, we need to serve Him well.

SILAS

About midnight Paul and Silas were praying and singing hymns. . . .
Suddenly there was such a violent earthquake that. . .
all the prison doors flew open.
ACTS 16:25–26

The apostle Paul's companion after the split with Barnabas, Silas crossed much of the Mediterranean world with him. Their mission began when Paul and Barnabas came to Jerusalem to discuss what the church expected of the Gentiles, and the Jerusalem council decided that Silas should return to Antioch with them.

Shortly afterward, Paul set out with Silas for a tour through Syria and Cilicia. Later, Paul received a call to Macedonia, and Silas was one of the band of men who accompanied him.

In Philippi, they met an irritating slave girl with a demonic spirit that predicted the future. Paul cleansed her of that possession, and as a result, he and Silas were beaten and tossed into the jail, then put in the stocks. Together they praised God and remained in prison to preach to the jailer.

Silas went to a lot of trouble to serve God, crossing land and sea with Paul, and got little public commendation. Do we need attention to feel we're important Christians, or will we be faithful like Silas?

SIMEON

[Simeon] took Him up in his arms and blessed God and said:
"Lord, now You are letting Your servant depart in peace,
according to Your word; for my eyes have seen Your salvation."
LUKE 2:28–30 NKJV

Throughout the ages, the children of Israel anticipated the coming of One called the Messiah. The Old Testament is full of references to Him; the prophets spoke at length about Him. The Virgin Mary had the singular privilege of bearing Him.

A heavenly messenger informed a man named Simeon that he would not see death until he saw the Messiah. We're not told very much about this aged man. Scripture says that he was righteous and devout and looking forward to the Messiah's arrival. Then came the day when, led by the Holy Spirit, Simeon entered the temple in Jerusalem to find a couple with a baby. It was the moment of moments for Simeon. Here was the Messiah at last!

Imagine a joy that makes you perfectly resigned to depart this life. That's what Simeon felt as he took the baby reverently up in his arms. God led Simeon to recognize the Messiah and to proclaim words about this child that astonished all who heard, but most of all his parents. "This Child is destined for the fall and rising of many in Israel, and for a sign which will be spoken against," prophesied Simeon (Luke 2:34 NKJV).

Time has borne out Simeon's prophecy. Who do you say this child was?

SIMON OF CYRENE

They found a man of Cyrene, Simon by name.
Him they compelled to bear His cross.
MATTHEW 27:32 NKJV

We have more questions than answers about this man Simon, who appears briefly in Jesus' life, at a moment of pain, as the Lord was forced to carry the cross to Golgotha.

Simon, who had two sons, Alexander and Rufus, hailed from a large city in what would be modern-day Libya. Many Jews had settled in Cyrene, so perhaps he'd traveled with a group to Jerusalem for the Passover. But here he stands alone. Once we've looked at these bare facts, reported in a single verse in each synoptic Gospel, we have scripture's whole record.

Simon was simply an innocent bystander, dragged into the Crucifixion story by Roman soldiers who plucked him out of a crowd and made him carry the thirty- to forty-pound cross. The duty they called him to was thoroughly unpleasant and unexpected.

Was Simon a Christian? We don't know. But he reminds us that no matter what happens to us, God is still in control. Before time began, God designed His plan of salvation; and though Simon's part was a surprise to him, it wasn't a surprise to God.

If God pulled us out of a crowd to do His will, would we be ready to feel the cross's splinters in our hands?

SOLOMON

Then David comforted Bathsheba his wife,
and went in to her and lay with her.
So she bore a son, and he called his name Solomon.
Now the LORD loved him.
2 SAMUEL 12:24 NKJV

"Give me the whole world but not God, and I'll still be miserable," warns Solomon's worldly and sophisticated but empty life.

But it wasn't always that way. From the day of Solomon's birth, God loved him. Despite the sexual sin his parents had fallen into, God had forgiven and blessed David and Bathsheba with this son. And David and his wife weren't the only ones: "The LORD loved him" is a wonderful testimony to the start of a great relationship between God and Prince Solomon.

Just before David died, many of his sons tried to grab the throne. But the king fulfilled an old promise he'd made to Bathsheba and had Solomon crowned as his heir. As a last gift, David provided detailed guidelines that would help his son rule well. Feeling honored, the new king started out, in the flush of youth, with many good intentions.

Shortly after Solomon's ascension to the throne, God asked him what he wanted. Given carte blanche, the king requested wisdom with which to rule the people. Pleased by this unselfish choice, God promised Solomon wisdom—and much more. Empowered by the Spirit, Solomon made wise choices for his people and penned the books of Proverbs, Song of Solomon, and Ecclesiastes. And the Lord added prosperity to the king's many other blessings.

Solomon's glorious reign expanded Israel's power and instituted beautiful building projects. After he made an alliance with Pharaoh and married his daughter, Solomon built both a new temple and a palace. An alliance with Hiram, king of Tyre, gave Solomon access to wonderful building materials and the craftsmen to make use of them. Within seven years, the first temple was completed, and the workmen began a thirteen-year palace-building project.

At the highest point in his career, Solomon dedicated the new temple. He began with a wonderful worship service and called the people to believe steadfastly in their Lord. A huge, impressive sacrifice followed, and celebration broke out among the Israelites. God promised that the obedience of Solomon and his heirs would establish his throne forever. But if they turned from God, Israel would be cut off from the land, and God would reject the temple.

Solomon's fame and fortune spread. The Queen of Sheba conferred with him, and his riches surpassed those of every other ruler. But to make alliances that expanded his power, Solomon married seven hundred wives and took three hundred concubines, actions that flew in the face of God's commands concerning marriage.

For years, Solomon remained faithful. At first, he seemed untouched by his wives' various religions, but as time passed, he began building altars to their gods so they could worship their pagan deities. Then he began to feel the attraction of these gods himself and worshipped them. The results of his unfaithfulness appear in Ecclesiastes, which pictures a cynical, doubtful ruler who has seen the world and discovered its emptiness.

This partial commitment angered God. So He raised up enemies against Israel, and Solomon's nation was attacked from within and without. After forty years of rule, Solomon died, and his son Rehoboam assumed his embattled throne.

Solomon grew up in a believing household, and God blessed him, but when the wealthy, successful king failed to flee from sin, a promising spiritual relationship slipped into compromise.

Can we relate to Solomon's story? We, too, have been given much, but it's still easy to find ourselves making something other than God central to our lives. Though we've served Him for many years, we can never relax our vigilance. Satan stands at the door, ready to slide back in and attack.

When we're young and enthusiastic, it's easy to think that our spiritual success is a piece of cake. But faith in God requires that we look toward the long haul. When life is difficult and a spiritual desert faces us, will we be as strong? Only God's Spirit gives us the determination and dedication we need.

STEPHEN

Now Stephen, a man full of God's grace and power,
did great wonders and miraculous signs among the people.
ACTS 6:8

Stephen, blessed by God, had a powerful message. But not everyone liked his words. The Synagogue of the Freedmen objected to his Christian testimony, not because they thought it didn't make sense, but because they could not refute it.

So, like many faithful believers, Stephen found himself in hot water with his opponents, who dragged him before the Sanhedrin. The synagogue attendees found a few immoral men willing to accuse Stephen of blasphemy against God and the Law. When questioned, Stephen presented the Jewish rulers with a wonderful testimony based on the Law of God. But that didn't make them any happier, for he accused them of resisting God. Finally, Stephen saw a vision of Jesus and proclaimed that He stood at God's right hand.

At this, his enemies covered their ears and dragged him out to stone him. The dying Stephen asked for forgiveness for his attackers.

Stephen's testimony is a shining example of faith. Don't we all wish we'd respond as powerfully in the face of persecution? The Holy Spirit empowered Stephen, and He strengthens us, too. But we cannot wait until persecution arises to seek God. Daily we need to draw near Him and seek His filling. Then, when a moment of attack comes, we will be ready.

THOMAS

And Thomas answered and said unto him,
My Lord and my God.
JOHN 20:28 KJV

Thomas was a man who liked to see things plainly and clearly. When anything began to look muddy, he confronted it directly. But his attitudes haven't made him an admired Bible character, because we prefer to read about people who trust and never question: "God said it; I believe it; that settles it."

Thomas was a believer. When Jesus was headed into danger, going back to Bethany to raise Lazarus, Thomas willingly accompanied his Master to an expected death. It was a plain thing he could understand and face bravely. But when Jesus began talking vaguely about going to prepare a place for His disciples, Thomas wanted more facts: How would they know the way to Jesus? No pie-in-the-sky religion for this disciple.

Thomas is best known for not being with the other disciples when Jesus made a post-Resurrection appearance. Again Thomas doubted what he could not see, until Jesus stood before him. Then "doubting Thomas" immediately went to the other extreme, accepting Jesus as the living Lord.

Like Thomas, we often prefer hard facts to hard faith. But, like him, are we willing to accept Jesus' statement that those who do not see are blessed? Are we ready to become one of the unseeing believers?

TIMOTHY

*For this reason I am sending to you Timothy, my son whom I love, who is faithful
in the Lord. He will remind you of my way of life in Christ Jesus,
which agrees with what I teach everywhere in every church.*
1 CORINTHIANS 4:17

As a young man, Timothy received high praise from the exacting apostle Paul.
So close did he and the apostle become that the peripatetic Paul thought of
Timothy as a son, brought him on numerous journeys with him, and sent him
as an envoy, too.

Young Timothy didn't come from the "perfect Christian home." His Jewish
mother, Eunice, became a Christian, but the little we know of his father suggests
he was an unbelieving Greek. However, his grandmother Lois also believed, so
spiritually, Timothy had at least two family members in his corner.

Timothy joined Paul on his second and third missionary journeys and part
of the fourth. When they were not together, Paul wrote the two biblical books
that bear the young pastor's name. The advice he offered has encouraged many
church leaders.

Though Timothy seemed to be somewhat timid, in God's hand he became
an example to all leaders. Despite our limitations and failures, are we willing to
let God shape our lives as He will?

TITUS

Paul. . .to Titus, my true child in a common faith.
TITUS 1:1, 4 ESV

Along with Timothy, Titus, a Greek, joined Paul on the second and third missionary journeys and part of the fourth. Despite church contentions about
Gentiles, Paul supported Titus and refused to make him be circumcised.

Paul must have trusted Titus deeply, for he sent him on special missions that
would have taken tact and an ability to relate to people. First, he sent Titus to the
Corinthians, bearing a very sensitive letter. Paul had the unhappy task of correcting
the Corinthians, who had fallen into sin. So he needed a man who would treat them
both firmly and tenderly. The mission went well, the Corinthians repented, and after
reporting back to Paul, Titus returned to Corinth with another minister, possibly
Luke, to encourage the church.

Finally, Paul sent Titus to Crete to appoint elders in the church. While
Titus was there, Paul penned the letter that bears Titus's name, a brief epistle
that pictures what a church should look like.

Could we be trusted with a delicate mission for God? Let's study to be sensitive to others, considerate of their needs, and concerned for their spiritual walk. Then, like Titus, we may be used by God in just such a situation.

URIAH

David sent someone to find out about her.
The man said, "Isn't this Bathsheba, the daughter
of Eliam and the wife of Uriah the Hittite?"
2 SAMUEL 11:3

Uriah the Hittite was not an Israelite, yet he proved more upright than the Jewish king he served. This foreigner was part of David's royal guard, carefully picked men who were much more than common soldiers (see 2 Samuel 23:18–39). But while Uriah was on a military campaign, King David glimpsed Uriah's lovely wife, Bathsheba, as she bathed on her roof, and he lusted for her. He brought her to his palace, slept with her, and returned her home. Then she discovered she was pregnant.

David wanted to make it appear that the child was Uriah's, but though his dedicated soldier returned to Jerusalem at David's command, he would not give in to the comforts of home when his comrades were on the battlefront. So David placed Uriah in the heat of battle, and he was killed. After he died, the king married Bathsheba.

Uriah, a foreigner who served the Lord by protecting the king, had a focus on fidelity that escaped his master. The most unlikely person may serve God faithfully, while a much-honored one fails. Remember, God is no respecter of persons, and even the humblest may do His will.

Do we recognize the importance of humble belief over social standing? Are we looking to the things of God's kingdom or to earthly importance?

THE WIDOW OF NAIN'S SON

And when He came near the gate of the city, behold,
a dead man was being carried out, the only son of his mother;
and she was a widow. And a large crowd from the city was with her.
LUKE 7:12 NKJV

As her son was carried out of the city gate, the widow stared destitution in the face. She had no career opportunities to speak of, and she was an older woman.

She had plenty of support on the day of her son's burial, but who would care for her from then on?

Jesus saw the situation and had compassion. "Do not weep," he told the grieving mother. He touched the young man's coffin and told him to rise. Immediately, the boy sat up and began to speak. Jesus reunited mother and son as the crowd glorified God and praised Jesus as a prophet.

If the crowds were amazed, how much more the son must have felt. Reunited with his needy mother, he must have wondered why Jesus had chosen him for resurrection, of all the people who had died that day.

We, too, have been raised to new life. "Why did Jesus choose me instead of another?" we may ask ourselves. Like the widow's son, we can only make the most of the days that God has given us. God's choice is always wise.

ZACCHAEUS

Now behold, there was a man named Zacchaeus
who was a chief tax collector, and he was rich.
LUKE 19:2 NKJV

"Zacchaeus was a wee little man, a wee little man was he," many of us sang as children. As we grew, this wee man stayed in our hearts, the sign of a disadvantaged fellow who had plenty of money. For not only was Zacchaeus small; he also had a small life, ostracized by other Jews, who resented his work for the occupying Romans. Who among us cannot relate to this underdog who won't be kept down?

When Jesus came to town, the little man determined to see Him and climbed a tree (maybe that's why we liked him so much when we were children). Jesus saw Zacchaeus, called to him, and invited Himself to his home. No host could have been happier. Zacchaeus quickly repented and promised to make restitution for more than the amount of money of which he'd defrauded people. Salvation came to the unpopular tax collector—suddenly he was friends with Jesus.

We, too, began as Zacchaeus did, separated from God and out of touch with humanity. Called by Jesus, we leaped to believe and, perhaps more slowly than the tax collector, changed our lives. We became friends with Jesus, and joy filled our lives. Are we living in that joy today?

ZACHARIAS, FATHER OF JOHN THE BAPTIST

And Zacharias said to the angel, "How shall I know this?
For I am an old man, and my wife is well advanced in years."
LUKE 1:18 NKJV

"Is anything too hard for the LORD?" asks God in Genesis 18:14. These words were spoken by God to Abram's wife, Sarai, who laughed at the thought of having a baby in her old age.

Centuries later, Zacharias and his wife, Elizabeth, were on in years. Elizabeth was barren and already beyond the point of having children. You can imagine, then, how surprised Zacharias was when told by the archangel Gabriel that Elizabeth would bear them a son. Wouldn't the supernatural appearance of an angel be enough to underscore the certainty of what Zacharias had been told? But no, Zacharias wanted proof. Gabriel gave him more than proof. He made him unable to speak. Not until his son, John, was born would he regain his ability to speak, and then he had nothing to say but glory to God!

Is anything too hard for the Lord? Zacharias would answer with an emphatic "No!" He had witnessed the undeniable power of God—a God who keeps His word. Do we need an angel to appear in order for us to take God's word seriously?

ZECHARIAH THE PROPHET

In the eighth month of the second year of Darius,
the word of the LORD came to Zechariah the son of Berechiah,
the son of Iddo the prophet, saying, "The LORD
has been very angry with your fathers."
ZECHARIAH 1:1–2 NKJV

It was business as usual in Israel: The people were following the bad example of their forefathers. But neither the prophet Zechariah nor the Lord wanted it to stay that way. That's why God again spoke to His people. He not only told them that their fathers were wrong; He also called them to repent.

A postexilic prophet-priest and a contemporary of Haggai and Zerubbabel, Zechariah held out hope to the people of Jerusalem during the later part of the era of the rebuilding of the temple. For some years, progress on the building project had faltered. Then it stopped altogether. Now the people needed encouragement to build again.

Zechariah's message looks forward to the future and includes numerous messianic references. The prophet looks toward the work God will do in his own generation and beyond that to the coming salvation of God.

Like the people of Zechariah's age, we, too, falter and face terrible trials. Are we fainting? God did not desert Zechariah's people, and He will not forget us either. Look to the future with hope!

THE TOP
100
MIRACLES
OF THE BIBLE

INTRODUCTION

What is a miracle? We tend to use the word rather loosely, to describe anything from our getting across a busy street safely to the birth of a child. Strictly speaking, miracles are not simply wonderful things that happen, like the birth of a baby, though through such events we may begin to understand God's miraculous work of creation. Real miracles are events that break the laws of nature and require God's direct action.

Miracles do not appear in every book of the Bible. They tend to come in clumps, mostly during the Creation and during the lives of Moses, Elijah, Elisha, and Jesus, and again during the apostles' ministries in the book of Acts.

Nor does scripture describe miracles with one word. They are variously called "signs," "wonders," "mighty works," or "works." These words describe what the miracle does, the purpose God has for working it. A sign evidences God's presence. From it, observers clearly understand that He, and not a human, is taking action. Wonders cause those who see them to be awed by what God has done. And mighty works show God's power and authority in this world.

In these pages, when I speak of a man working a miracle, of course I do not mean he did it on his own. All true miracles come from God and are empowered by Him. Man can do many things, but he cannot make a miracle happen. Those involved in biblical miracles are God's servants, and His power flows through them when the amazing events take place. A real servant of God would never say otherwise.

While most miracles are positive, some, like the plagues inflicted upon Egypt, are examples of God's judgment. God uses miracles to protect and encourage His people, but He also uses them to show both believers and unbelievers the error of their ways and the authority that is His. Often miracles so influence those who see them that they recognize their sin and turn to the Lord in faith. But that is not a universal response.

Likewise, some miracles are focused on an individual while others address a broad number of people—frequently the whole Jewish nation. Elisha and Jesus performed many miracles that affected one person: an intimate healing that seemed to influence only that individual. But events like the parting of the Red Sea or the feeding of the five thousand touched a multitude. The scope of miracles clearly shows that God cares about those things in our lives that we deal with personally and those that influence our society or our world. Yet the biblical miracle we consider unimportant may have changed one person's life and made him touch his world effectively for the Lord. Rarely do we see that side of the story in scripture—only in eternity will we know the full impact a single miracle had.

Several Gospels frequently tell the same miracle stories. In order to make this book more readable, I have rarely identified the parallel Gospel passages.

Most details of the story that do not appear in the quoted passage should be in the other Gospels. Careful students may want to check a study Bible to identify the parallel passages and read all the information scripture provides about each miracle.

It has been popular with unbelievers through the centuries to deny or denigrate miracles. Doubters have tried to bring the scriptures down to their own level by implying that of course such things could never have happened. The biblical writers, they would claim, made up or expanded on the original events. These doubters' earthbound view of God appears nowhere in scripture for a good reason: to believe in miracles requires faith, and those without faith will never understand the events portrayed in the Old and New Testaments. Those who try to eradicate miracles from the scripture lose all faith's joy, for they are left with little more than moral rules to live by.

CREATION'S BEGINNING

In the beginning God created the heavens and the earth.
Now the earth was formless and empty, darkness was over the surface of the deep,
and the Spirit of God was hovering over the waters.

GENESIS 1:1–2

Of all the miracles of the Bible, this may be the most stunning. It certainly counts as a miracle—something far beyond what humanity could do, a disruption of the natural order. What natural order existed before God created heaven and earth? Nothingness.

Scripture's account starts with the rather matter-of-fact description "In the beginning God created the heaven and the earth" (Genesis 1:1 KJV). Those few words tell us a lot about God and His work in Creation while cloaking our planet's beginnings in a great mystery. Creation didn't just happen. Some authorless Big Bang didn't simply explode on the universe. But out of a seemingly blank emptiness, life appeared. All that existed, prior to this event, was God, a fact scripture takes for granted.

God didn't take old matter and refashion it. He required not so much as a molecule to start with. In a specific moment, out of a great emptiness, life took form as He "call[ed] into existence the things that [did] not exist" (Romans 4:17 ESV). In a flash God ignited the new creation. The word translated "God" is the Hebrew word *elohim*, the majestic plural that indicates the whole Trinity is at work in this moment. In case we miss it, Genesis 1:2 tells us the life-giving Spirit hovered over the waters. Nor does the New Testament leave us in doubt that Jesus took part in the event (see John 1:1, 3, 10; Colossians 1:15–17).

The few words that begin Creation's story provide us with important information. This is a planned event, begun by an infinitely powerful Being who was able to organize everything from the smallest details to the whole massive grand plan. Instead of leaving us hanging, believing life always existed or has no rhyme or reason, God gives us a view of how life began.

When did this event happen? Scripture doesn't define it by as-yet-uncreated years. That indefinite timetable may irritate our desire for scientific understanding, but how else can a work that began before time be described? God's Word accurately details the main events that took place under His hand.

Genesis 1 doesn't give us the roiling, chaotic description of the new world that some scientists offer, because it's not the totally out-of-control event they imagine. God managed everything, no matter how unorganized it seemed. Creation might not have been a neat period, but it was not about to fly off on an unexpected course, either. As scripture shows us, creative order prevailed as God orchestrated each event.

How do we know it happened this way? Scripture does not refer us to scientific treatises or hard-and-fast proof. "By faith," it declares, "we understand that the worlds were framed by the word of God" (Hebrews 11:3 NKJV). The Old Testament is not interested in scientific theories any more than it was in the pagan creation stories of its day. Just as the multiple deities of the Greeks and other nations could not impact God's account of His doings, colorful scientific theories need not disrupt our faith. Chance did not begin this world or the universes beyond it: God did.

The ancient Hebrews may have had it over us in understanding God's message. We tend to see the Creation story in scientific terms. But in a world that knew nothing of black holes, quarks, and other scientific mysteries, they turned to spiritual mysteries instead. As we seek hard-and-fast "realities," perhaps we miss out on the spiritual realities that overwhelm the best scientific research mankind can do.

But here begin the greatest spiritual realities of this world. God graciously created a world just for humans, a stage on which the salvation drama would be acted out. The playhouse is prepared; the first actors will be placed in it. Life has begun!

TURNING ON THE LIGHT

And God said, "Let there be light," and there was light.
God saw that the light was good, and He separated the light from the darkness.
God called the light "day," and the darkness he called "night."
And there was evening, and there was morning—the first day.
GENESIS 1:3–5

God speaks, and over the formless earth appears light, a symbol of both Himself and the salvation that is yet to take place for mankind. Where did the light come from? Some scholars maintain it was a light emanating from God, while others correlate this passage to verse 14 and the creation of the heavenly bodies. Whichever is true, God used His words to create light and then separated it from darkness, creating the first day and night. Looking at the newborn light, God pronounced it good.

We may balk at knowing only that God's speech initiated the creative power, directed by His own will. But scripture focuses not on the how of Creation but the who of the Creator. From His mind leapt this element of Creation that will forever describe Himself. With this concrete picture, we begin to understand our Lord. He "turns on the light" in our own souls, and darkness separates itself from us, though in this life it never entirely disappears. With the daylight turned on in our hearts, we can serve Him day and night.

SEPARATING THE WATERS

And God said, "Let there be an expanse between the waters to separate water
from water." So God made the expanse and separated the water under the expanse
from the water above it. And it was so. God called the expanse "sky."
And there was evening, and there was morning—the second day.
GENESIS 1:6–8

On the second day, God began a serious reorganization of His formless creation. A brand-new sky, along with its cloud-bound waters, separated from earthly waters below. This was only the beginning of a vast creation project. God started at the top of the earthly realm.

Describing God's glory, David portrayed this day of creation as such: "He stretches out the heavens like a tent" (Psalm 104:2). Rain-bearing clouds rose above the earth's firmament for the first time. Below lay the mere beginnings of oceans, seas, and rivers.

When we look upward, what does the sky remind us of? Will fluffy clouds, a clear sky, or signs of a storm coming remind us of God's glory and the miracle He commanded on that second day? Let's remind ourselves that our planet was once a huge void: light and darkness, sky, oceans, and rivers all washed together. From this, God created an expanse that warns us of coming storms, sends us rain, or simply delights us on a balmy summer day.

Isn't our Creator glorious?

SOMETHING TO STAND ON

And God said, "Let the water under the sky be gathered to one place,
and let dry ground appear." And it was so. God called the dry ground "land,"
and the gathered waters he called "seas."
And God saw that it was good.
GENESIS 1:9–10

This is an especially important miracle for those of us who walk on earth, for had God not gathered the sea in one place and raised the land above it, there would have been no place for human or animal life. Even birds might have gotten rather wing weary, never having a place to alight, and what would they have eaten, with no bountiful earth to sustain them?

Instead of creating one large oceanographic planet, on creation's third day God sank the oceans, rivers, and even streams into the earth. Land rose up, in mountains, jagged shores, and barely-above-sea-level flats. Though this vegetationless land had yet to look like the world we recognize, God's orderly creation had begun to develop, and the world became a place to stand on for all the life yet to come.

Have you thanked God today for having a place to stand? Whether He created large masses of land or small, delicate islands, He was thinking of you and the other creatures that would put their feet there someday.

THE PLANT KINGDOM

Then God said, "Let the earth bring forth grass, the herb that yields seed,
and the fruit tree that yields fruit according to its kind,
whose seed is in itself, on the earth"; and it was so.
GENESIS 1:11 NKJV

As the third day continued, God covered the land with all kinds of vegetation, grass, and trees. Annual and perennial flowers and vegetables appeared; the limbs of massive oaks and slender beeches crisscrossed the sky. And for the first time, God gave part of creation the ability to continue His creative process: all the plants bore seeds. That reproduction must have begun immediately to support the new world. Each plant contained a genetic code, so it would reproduce in keeping with its own variety. Trees would not bring forth grass, nor flowers produce grain.

While the immovable foundations of the earth would always be fixed, plant growth, which provided food for man and beast and a home for the birds of the air, would vary every year. God's ongoing provision for all the earth was established in a way that required dependence on Him. And the ancient peoples appreciated this as their harvests came in well one year and were pitiful the next. Vegetation had the ability to remind people of the Creator and His call on their lives.

Do we, too, remember that call?

LET THERE BE LIGHTS

And God said, "Let there be lights in the expanse of the sky
to separate the day from the night, and let them serve as signs to mark seasons
and days and years, and let them be lights in the expanse of the sky
to give light on the earth." And it was so.
GENESIS 1:14–15

Imagine yourself, early on the fourth day, standing on the earth as God created the moon and stars. The velvety dark mantle above the earth would suddenly have shown soft pinpricks of light as far-flung universes came into being. Then the sun would have risen with its brighter light, warming the vegetation beneath and providing it with the ability to grow.

But the most amazing miracle would have been that the sun was placed in a perfect position that allowed life to exist and thrive. Had it been closer, Earth would have overheated and been unable to sustain plants, animals, and humans. Farther away, and it would have been too cold to sustain this delicate balance of existence we take for granted.

Before Moses' era, paganism overtook most of the earth, and the sun and moon became deities to many people. So God does not even name them when He transmits this part of the Word. Scripture simply tells us the sun, moon, and stars were made to define human lives, separating day and night and identifying the seasons. This would have been particularly important to ancient believers, as the Jews told time through a lunar calendar.

Yet God specifically prohibited His people from following their neighbors and worshipping or fearing the heavenly bodies (see Deuteronomy 4:19; Isaiah 40:26). The sun and moon and stars were meant to encourage worship of the Lord God, not to be used as pagan gods or a focus of occult practices.

The heavenly creation described in Genesis 1:14–19 is to provide light for the earth and act as a timekeeper for mankind. These bodies in no way rule the earth, for that is God's job. Though they are not the light of God, the sun, moon, and stars illuminate our way in a purely earthly manner. In eternity there will be no need for them, as the New Jerusalem will be lit by God's glory (see Revelation 21:23).

So let's enjoy the lights' beauty here on earth, when daylight begins to touch the dark sky with delicate color or slips into night with an incredible range of blues, rising from the horizon in ever-darkening hues. God has given the stars and planets to delight us as we worship Him faithfully. So let's rejoice in the miracle of this day of creation as we worship the Creator.

ABUNDANT LIFE

Then God said, "Let the waters abound with an abundance of living creatures,
and let birds fly above the earth across the face of the firmament of the heavens."
So God created great sea creatures and every living thing that moves,
with which the waters abounded, according to their kind, and
every winged bird according to its kind. And God saw that it was good.
GENESIS 1:20–21 NKJV

The waters God had created lay empty, except perhaps for seaweed and other vegetation. No seagulls flew across the ocean surface, no seabirds dive-bombed from toothlike rocks. Fish never broke the ocean waves.

Again God spoke, and these waters teemed with new life: whales and fish and even sharks. Through the sky above, the birds darted, and all had a purpose in God's plan. God gave all the creatures the ability to reproduce, just as He had done for the plants. He blessed them all, commanding them to multiply and fill the seas and sky.

As we read of God's inventive creation on the fifth day, are we reminded that it is ours to care for and enjoy? Let us treasure the gift given in this miracle of creation. It's part of the abundant life He offers.

CREATURES GREAT AND SMALL

And God said, "Let the land produce living creatures according to
their kinds: livestock, creatures that move along the ground,
and wild animals, each according to its kind."
GENESIS 1:24

When He'd filled the seas and skies with creatures, God didn't stop. Before Him lay the land—empty except for vegetation and birds nesting in the trees. Nothing roamed the land. So God began to fill His landscape with all kinds of creatures. Cows and horses; carnivorous tigers and lions and bears; gentle deer and antelope; and snakes, lizards, and other creeping creatures were placed in their proper habitats. On savannahs, on mountains, and in wetlands, animals designed for each environment appeared.

Think about the amazing detail involved in this creation. Creatures from intriguing polar bears and penguins, who inhabit the frigid ends of the earth, to ordinary tree-climbing squirrels and earthbound chipmunks were designed specially for the places in which they'd live.

But God had another consideration in the creation of the animals. He made some animals clean and others unclean. For fallen man they became a picture of holiness—Jews were to avoid eating the unclean animals. And God would give mankind stewardship over all the creatures He'd created, from elephant to skink.

God teaches us much about His world through the creatures He put in it. We're awed by the details of His Creation and challenged to care for it well. What lessons have you learned from the animals God made?

MADE IN THE IMAGE

Then God said, "Let us make man in our image, in our likeness,
and let them rule over the fish of the sea and the birds of the air, over the livestock,
over all the earth, and over all the creatures that move along the ground."
So God created man in his own image, in the image of God he created him;
male and female he created them. God blessed them and said to them,
"Be fruitful and increase in number; fill the earth and subdue it."
GENESIS 1:26–28

As whales breeched in the ocean; parrots, kingfishers, and sparrows flew in the skies; and buffalo stampeded on the plains, God perfected His Creation. Though you might doubt it looking at the world today, as He created man He was about to come to the pinnacle of His creative process. After the Father, Son, and Holy Spirit considered together the form this creation should take, Adam was made in the Creator's image.

This new creation was made not in a physical likeness of God, but with a soul, to have communion with Him. Theologians have debated just what being made in God's image entails, but at the very least this first man had attributes the animals lacked. He had a larger ability to think and communicate, and he had a soul. Of all the beings on earth, he was the most like God, while still only a distant reflection of His nature.

God also made humans in male and female forms, though Eve's creation account is detailed after Adam's. Before Eve was brought into being, God gave Adam dominion over the entire world. He was to rule over the animals, birds, and sea creatures. No creature had more authority than he, though many had more physical strength. This somewhat puny being was to have command over powerful elephants and alligators. Together, Adam and Eve were commanded to fill and subdue the earth. As part of their God-given task, they too were to be fruitful and multiply, for God was just beginning to fill the earth with all the good things He had created.

What must this couple have thought, standing, newly created, in a garden filled with beautiful plants, the noise of the animals and birds ringing in their ears? As they looked at the bright, untouched Creation, did they feel the weight of God's trust on them? Did they understand the importance of the command He had given them? Everything in the garden was new, including the couple in charge of it.

God had made Adam and Eve and declared them good. Doubtless they were up to the task. At this point, it never would have occurred to the only humans in the world to do wrong by the plants and animals or to disobey God. The ideas of wrong and disobedience had yet to be thought of. Theirs was a perfect world, in tune with God.

When they took up their new mission, did Adam talk to the animals while Eve picked fruit for breakfast? Whatever they did, it was the start of a wonderful existence in which the humans used each moment to glorify their Creator.

Are you awed when you think about the creation of the first man and woman? Have you thought about what it meant to God to create the height of His Creation? How does that make you feel about the fact that God made you, too?

Because man is made in the image of God, Christians have a high view of the value of other people. How should this make a difference in your life?

A BEAUTIFUL CREATION

So Adam gave names to all cattle, to the birds of the air,
and to every beast of the field. But for Adam there was not found
a helper comparable to him. And the LORD God caused
a deep sleep to fall on Adam, and he slept; and He took one of his ribs,
and closed up the flesh in its place. Then the rib which the LORD God had taken
from man He made into a woman, and He brought her to the man.
And Adam said: "This is now bone of my bones and flesh of my flesh;
she shall be called Woman, because she was taken out of Man."
Therefore a man shall leave his father and mother
and be joined to his wife, and they shall become one flesh.
And they were both naked, the man and his wife, and were not ashamed.
GENESIS 2:20–25 NKJV

After God introduces the subject of the creation of man, scripture gives us the details of Eve's introduction to the world. Once Adam, who got to find a name for each creature, had finished this first task (can you imagine what Eve thought when she heard of Adam's creativity in this direction? "So tell me, why did you name it a hippopotamus?"), it became apparent just one thing was missing: a mate for Adam. So God knocked out the first man, delved into his side, took one of his ribs, and made a wife for him. Eve must have been some beautiful woman, considering the poem Adam immediately created as he named her woman.

This couple was just perfect for each other. The goodness of God's creation extended to their relationship. No divisions, no doubts about each other, no "battle of the sexes" existed in the Garden of Eden. From the very first, scripture also makes it clear that monogamy is God's design, for the two are designed to be one flesh—not merely connected, but related in the most intimate way. They were completely intimate, with no shame dividing them. Nor did anything come between them and their Creator.

But this picture of marital harmony was not to last long, for even if Adam and Eve had not thought of disobeying God, Satan had. The crafty fallen angel, taking on the form of a snake, started asking Eve a question—one designed to separate her from God. His ploy of raising doubts in her mind worked, and little by little, his temptation began to appeal to her. Instead of saying, "Let's ask Adam what he thinks," Eve made a selfish choice. Once her interest in the only forbidden fruit in the garden peaked, she picked some and fed it to her husband, too.

In a moment, the miracle of the pinnacle of creation became deeply marred, and sin entered the once-idyllic world. Adam and Eve immediately started sewing leaf loincloths, because they knew they were naked. When God came for a stroll in the Garden, the damage to their relationship became apparent. The couple ran from Him for the first time. Separation between God and His creation had begun. And God gave each of the offenders an appropriate punishment. For Adam and Eve, it meant leaving their beautiful garden and living with the sin that broke their intimacy with their Lord.

God made Eve as a wonderful gift for Adam, and Adam appreciated her. But since the fall, marital relationships have become much more challenging. How does the relationship described in the Garden of Eden compare with marriage today? What can people do to appreciate the miracle God did for Adam and bring something of that kind of relationship to their own lives?

Adam and Eve's story not only tells of the blessings God gives but shows the huge change sin makes in our lives. The blessings of a miracle are not indestructible in this fallen world. Let's be careful with the miracles that have touched our lives.

BURNED BUT UNCONSUMED

Now Moses kept the flock of Jethro his father in law, the priest of Midian: and he led the flock to the backside of the desert, and came to the mountain of God, even to Horeb. And the angel of the LORD appeared unto him in a flame of fire out of the midst of a bush: and he looked, and, behold, the bush burned with fire, and the bush was not consumed. And Moses said, I will now turn aside, and see this great sight, why the bush is not burnt.
EXODUS 3:1–3 KJV

By the time Moses was confronted by a burning bush, he was a man with a history. Adopted by Pharaoh's daughter, he had a cushy life, until he began to understand how the Egyptians abused his own people, the Hebrews. To protect one of his people, Moses killed a man and had to run for his life. Following his escape, he met the daughters of Jethro, married one of them, and became part of the family business. That's how he ended up at the back side of the desert, herding sheep.

On what was probably a fairly ordinary day, Moses led his sheep out to graze. As they moved through the barren landscape, the shepherd looked up and saw an amazing thing: a burning bush that was not consumed by the fire. Curious, Moses went to inspect the plant and was confronted by something even less likely: the angel of the Lord appeared in the bush, and God spoke to him!

God told the stunned shepherd to remove his sandals, for he stood on holy ground. Hiding his face in fear, Moses received the astonishing news that God had a plan for him: Moses would return to Egypt to lead God's people from their oppression and into a new land.

If the bush had seemed spectacular, this news was even more so. God would work through a shepherd to bring about a world-changing plan. For the first time, a nation would escape slavery in the powerful Egyptian empire. It's not surprising Moses had his doubts about this plan.

Just as the bush was burned but unconsumed, Moses would be. He had much to face from the people he led: doubt, criticism, and rebellion were his lot from them. But because of God's power in him, the prophet was not destroyed by their attitudes.

We, too, need not be consumed by the world, if we trust in the Lord alone and seek to serve Him. Do we?

WHAT'S IN YOUR HAND?

And the LORD said unto him, What is that in thine hand?
And he said, A rod. And he said, Cast it on the ground. And he cast it on the
ground, and it became a serpent; and Moses fled from before it. And the LORD said
unto Moses, Put forth thine hand, and take it by the tail. And he put forth
his hand, and caught it, and it became a rod in his hand.
EXODUS 4:2–4 KJV

If anyone wonders if God has a sense of humor, show them this miracle. God turned Moses' staff into a snake, and the prophet, perhaps not realizing that God was in control even of the slithery creatures, ran away from it. Could the Lord have kept from chuckling?

Worry got Moses into this reptilian situation. The Lord had commanded His prophet to go to Egypt and confront Pharaoh, but Moses feared no one would believe his message. As God showed Moses how to prove the truth of His word, the prophet leapt away from the fast-moving snake, more afraid of the serpent than any of the Egyptians would ever be. Yet when, at God's command, Moses gingerly picked up the snake, he again held his staff. The former shepherd probably took a good second look at the rod that had been his support for many years.

The snake was more for Moses' and his people's benefit than the Egyptians', who didn't believe it meant anything, even when Moses' snake ate up their own. But knowing that he could prove himself probably meant a lot to the prophet, and when Pharaoh requested a miracle, he was prepared. This miracle also gave Moses' fellow Israelites a clue that what he said was really from God. And the reason God ordained Moses to do this miracle was so that His people would know Him.

At least it should have given Pharaoh one idea about Moses, for a cobra had long adorned the crown of Egypt. With his snake that ate the Egyptian reptiles, Moses was about to become a serious threat to Pharaoh's rule.

God doesn't always prove Himself in miraculous physical ways, as He did in this instance. But He often uses the things that are right in our hands to show His faithfulness to us. With them, we can always be ready to show forth God's truth to those who doubt. In His hand, the common becomes uncommon, and amazing events can happen.

Do you doubt God's ability to work in your life? Ask yourself if the shepherd Moses ever thought he'd be leading a horde of two or three million people out of Egypt and toward the Promised Land.

AN UNPLEASANT MIRACLE

Again, the LORD said to him, "Put your hand inside your cloak."
And he put his hand inside his cloak, and when he took it out, behold, his hand
was leprous like snow. Then God said, "Put your hand back inside your cloak."
So he put his hand back inside his cloak, and when he took it out,
behold, it was restored like the rest of his flesh.
EXODUS 4:6–7 ESV

God not only gave Moses the ability to turn his staff into a snake; He had a backup plan, a less pleasant miracle. Leprosy was a much-feared disease in this age, and anyone who could heal it would be a wonder-worker indeed. His God would be one to look up to and worship faithfully.

God commanded that anyone with leprosy was unclean—separated from his fellowman so the illness would not spread. Such a man was also a picture of spiritual unbelief or failure. Anyone who could work this miracle would be someone to follow and respect, for surely this would be God's representative.

Does God have to make us fear Him before we obey? Will only the unpleasant get our attention? Then He will use such a method. But He would rather woo us, calling us into obedience with a gentle voice. Are we listening?

BLOOD EVERYWHERE!

The LORD said to Moses, "Tell Aaron, 'Take your staff and stretch out your hand over the waters of Egypt—over the streams and canals, over the ponds and all the reservoirs'—and they will turn to blood. Blood will be everywhere in Egypt, even in the wooden buckets and stone jars." Moses and Aaron did just as the LORD had commanded. He raised his staff in the presence of Pharaoh and his officials and struck the water of the Nile, and all the water was changed into blood. The fish in the Nile died, and the river smelled so bad that the Egyptians could not drink its water. Blood was everywhere in Egypt.

EXODUS 7:19–21

The prophet and his brother, Aaron, appeared before Pharaoh numerous times. First they politely requested that the Egyptian king allow the Israelites to hold a religious feast in the wilderness. Pharaoh didn't have to think for a minute before he said no to that one; he didn't respect the Lord and didn't like the idea of losing his slaves. Instead Egypt's ruler punished all the Israelites, increasing their workload by requiring them to make bricks without the strengthening element of straw.

At God's command, the brothers returned to Pharaoh's court to confront him. Aaron's staff turning into a snake didn't get the Egyptians' attention, so God commanded that Moses return a third time to the Pharaoh to initiate the first of ten plagues Egypt would experience at God's hand.

You couldn't say that God hadn't been patient with Pharaoh, but Egypt's ruler had a hard heart when it came to hearing the message.

Since Pharaoh was unlikely to let Moses and his brother into the court, God sent them to the Nile River to confront Pharaoh. The first plague struck at Egypt's lifeblood: the Nile River. This civilization depended on the overflowing river to water its crops, and one of the nation's numerous deities, the god Hapi, was associated with the river and the provision of life for the Egyptians.

When God told Moses to turn the Nile to blood, He struck both a political and religious blow. By disproving the power of Egypt's gods, He showed the powerlessness of their religion and the ruler who was considered one of the gods.

As Aaron lifted and dropped his staff to touch the Nile River, Egyptian life entered a crisis. The water in the entire Nile and in every water-holding wood and stone vessel turned to blood. The fish that once swam in the Nile now lay dead on top of it. The river stank, and no one could drink from it. Everyone had to dig wells along the river for potable water.

In response, the Egyptian magicians turned water into blood—a rather ineffective reaction, since turning blood into water would have been more useful. Some scholars think blood filled the Nile for seven days. Yet because his magicians had turned a small amount of water into blood, or at least made it look like blood, Pharaoh remained unmoved.

Certainly the God whom Moses and Aaron worshipped didn't appeal to Egypt's king. Hard-hearted Pharaoh trusted his foolish magicians. After all, why should Egypt's leader give up believing he was a god because a shepherd claimed he had a better God?

Like many people today, Pharaoh was comfortable in his unbelief. The world seemed to revolve around him, and he liked it that way. There was little room in his life for real truth that confronted his false reality.

When we witness to people who refuse to believe, let's understand that they are caught in Pharaoh's trap. Only God can release them from the hardness of their own hearts. Before we seek to bring the Word to them, we'd be wise to spend time in prayer that seeks to open hearts to Him.

OVERFROGGED

Then the LORD said to Moses, "Tell Aaron, 'Stretch out your hand
with your staff over the streams and canals and ponds,
and make frogs come up on the land of Egypt.' "
So Aaron stretched out his hand over the waters of Egypt,
and the frogs came up and covered the land.
But the magicians did the same things by their secret arts;
they also made frogs come up on the land of Egypt.
EXODUS 8:5–7

A week after Aaron's rod had turned the Nile to blood, he and his brother were back on Pharaoh's doorstep, repeating God's demand to let His people go. But the king refused, so out of the streams, canals, and ponds erupted a super-abundance of frogs: frogs in his palace, frogs in his bed, frogs in the houses of his officials and his people. Frogs filled the ovens and kneading troughs, making food production a disaster. Almost every part of daily life must have been affected by this second plague. Along with all those frogs, the king must have heard a lot of complaining, probably from his family, his court officials, and the mobs who wanted to know how he planned to solve this problem.

It must not have taken long for the king to weary of this overabundance of amphibians. And for once, the fact that his magicians had added a few frogs to the mix didn't deter him from wanting to lose all those critters. He called Moses and Aaron to him and begged them to pray for him. Pharaoh was desperate for an end to the crisis.

Moses promised that the next day the frogs would again inhabit only their normal habitat. His goal was to show the king that the Lord was God. When God did what Moses asked, perhaps the king almost wished he hadn't requested the solution. For now he had dead frogs in his palace, in his people's homes, in courtyards and fields. All Egypt stank of dead frogs. But once they were piled up out of reach of his nasal passages, Pharaoh again hardened his heart.

Pharaoh probably didn't see the eruption of frogs into his life as a miracle, but he could certainly appreciate their sudden removal. But once the frogs were dead, maybe it didn't seem like such a big thing. We can relate to Pharaoh's about-face, can't we? For we, too, have begged God for relief from a problem, only to forget all He's done for us when our pain is relieved.

Do we forget God's graces too easily? Is He truly Lord of our lives?

THOSE PESKY GNATS

Then the LORD said to Moses,
"Tell Aaron, 'Stretch out your staff and strike the dust of the ground,'
and throughout the land of Egypt the dust will become gnats."
EXODUS 8:16

If you've ever been at a gnat-infested picnic, you know the trouble Egypt was in when the Lord commanded that Aaron's staff should inflict a third plague on Egypt. As Aaron's staff hit the ground, gnats as numerous as the dust rose up to annoy both humans and beasts. Small as they were, they were highly irritating. Where could anyone get away from them?

With this plague the Egyptian magicians were foiled. They could not make gnats. Maybe the people of Egypt were glad; after all, who needed any more of the annoying creatures? Nor could the magicians stop the infestation. Finally, they were forced to admit God had done this. But proud Pharaoh was not convinced.

Insidious as the bugs were, they should have given Pharaoh a message that God was determined to get through to him. We've seen this determination in our own lives, when God has wanted us to understand that the life we've been living is not what He wants. He will continually redirect us until we finally listen.

Is God redirecting us today?

FLYING IN GOD'S FACE

"If you do not let my people go, I will send swarms of flies on you and your officials, on your people and into your houses. The houses of the Egyptians will be full of flies, and even the ground where they are."

Again Moses appeared at the riverside when Pharaoh was preparing for an agreeable sail. But the news the prophet bore wasn't pleasant. Since gnats didn't have an impact on Pharaoh, God was going to send something larger: swarms of flies, so many they would ruin the land. But to make it clear to the king whose God He was, the Hebrews, living in the land of Goshen, would remain unaffected by the purely Egyptian plague.

When the annoyance became too much, Pharaoh called Moses and his brother back. This time he wanted to negotiate with God. He offered to let the Hebrews sacrifice inside Egypt. When Moses refused, the king offered to let them go into the wilderness, but less than the three days God had stipulated. Moses agreed to plead with God but warned the king not to cheat again.

Again, Pharaoh gave the predictable response.

God is not One to be bargained with, as Pharaoh would discover. Just as he could not turn God from His purpose, neither can we. Do we try to cheat with Him?

CATTLE PROD

"If you refuse to let them go and continue to hold them back, the hand of the LORD will bring a terrible plague on your livestock in the field—on your horses and donkeys and camels and on your cattle and sheep and goats. But the LORD will make a distinction between the livestock of Israel and that of Egypt, so that no animal belonging to the Israelites will die."

EXODUS 9:2–4

Streams and rivers of blood, frogs, gnats, and flies: none of these plagues deterred Pharaoh. So God announced that in one day He would send a fifth, terrible plague that affected the animals of the land. Again, the Israelites' animals would remain untouched by the affliction.

Though Pharaoh had enough warning to stop the deaths, he remained adamant, and the cattle fell throughout the land. What a health problem that must have caused! And it certainly would have seriously damaged Egypt's economy.

As Egypt's ruler remained hard-hearted before God's prodding, the Lord

THE TOP 100 MIRACLES OF THE BIBLE   221

began to touch his nation's economy. Where formerly the vegetation had been harmed, now the country's ability to produce milk and meat had been killed off. Small farmers and wealthy landowners alike saw their futures destroyed as their most valuable animals died.

Standing adamant against God is never profitable. Without His blessing, we harm both our livelihoods and our spiritual well-being.

THE FEEL OF SIN

So they took soot from a furnace and stood before Pharaoh.
Moses tossed it into the air, and festering boils broke out on men and animals.
The magicians could not stand before Moses because of the boils
that were on them and on all the Egyptians.
EXODUS 9:10–11

In the sixth plague, God commanded Moses to do a strange thing. Picking up soot from a furnace, he tossed it into the air, and painful, debilitating boils broke out on man and the few beasts left in Egypt. Just about every living thing must have been in agony. Neither could Pharaoh's court stand before it, as the men the king depended on for spiritual counsel failed him. Still, probably covered himself with the painful, pus-filled eruptions, Pharaoh stood firm in his hard-heartedness.

Anyone who consistently stands against God will suffer increasing pain, spiritual or physical. Here God made Pharaoh and his people feel the pain of sin in their own bodies. There was no way to escape or forget about God's message.

Not all physical problems come from sin, but illness is certainly something we need to discuss with God. Have we brought it on ourselves by our bad habits or bad attitude? Do we need to seek Him and ask for clean hearts, as well as clean bodies?

NO HAIL OF REPENTANCE

When Moses stretched out his staff toward the sky, the LORD sent
thunder and hail, and lightning flashed down to the ground.
So the LORD rained hail on the land of Egypt; hail fell and lightning
flashed back and forth. It was the worst storm in all
the land of Egypt since it had become a nation.
EXODUS 9:23–25

Again God warned Pharaoh of destruction to come, and again the Egyptian ruler ignored Him. So at God's command, heavy, damaging hail fell throughout

Egypt, except on His people, the Israelites. It fell on people, animals, and fields, in the worst storm that nation had ever experienced.

As if the fields hadn't had a hard enough time under the plagues, now everything grown in the land was destroyed, even the trees.

Finally Pharaoh seemed to repent and turn to God, but Moses could tell this was not true repentance. Still, Moses prayed that the hail would stop, and it did. As soon as his land was no longer damaged by the storm, Pharaoh again hardened his heart.

Real repentance does not come and go. One who turns to the Lord in faith will not quickly decide it was all a mistake or return to former hard-heartedness. Sure, we all make mistakes, but a heart touched by God will always show.

STUBBORN IN DEFEAT

And the LORD said to Moses, "Stretch out your hand over Egypt so that locusts will swarm over the land and devour everything growing in the fields, everything left by the hail." So Moses stretched out his staff over Egypt, and the LORD made an east wind blow across the land all that day and all that night. By morning the wind had brought the locusts; they invaded all Egypt and settled down in every area of the country in great numbers. Never before had there been such a plague of locusts, nor will there ever be again. They covered all the ground until it was black. They devoured all that was left after the hail— everything growing in the fields and the fruit on the trees.

EXODUS 10:12–15

When Moses again appeared at his doorstep, Pharaoh had to know it wasn't with good news. Sure enough, Moses came with another warning: Let my people go to worship, or you will be inundated with locusts.

After Moses left, Pharaoh had a discussion with his officials, who counseled him to let the Israelites go worship. Did he realize Egypt was ruined? they asked.

So Pharaoh unbent a little, called back the prophet and his brother, and said he'd allow the Israelites to worship. But there was one catch: only the men could go. And of course God would not settle for that! So again Egypt received a plague. An east wind blew over the land and brought with it locusts by the ton. They covered all the land and ate what few green things remained. If the counselors of Pharaoh thought they were ruined before, this was even worse. What few farmers had survived the former plagues were now ruined, too.

Quickly, Pharaoh called back Moses and Aaron and asked them to stop the plague. But again, once the plague was gone, it was as if Egypt's king had forgotten it ever happened.

Pharaoh was a proud man but not one who learned quickly. He seemed unable to realize that a ploy that had not worked before would not work a second time. And he had promised to free the Israelites more than once.

Are we like Pharaoh? When God tells us to do one thing, do we repeatedly try to head in another direction? What are we thinking when we act that way? Does God change His mind or forget what went before? Pharaoh was stubborn in defeat, and it did not work. Neither will it benefit us. Let's obey God the first time instead.

DARKNESS FALLS ON EGYPT

Then the LORD said to Moses, "Stretch out your hand toward the sky
so that darkness will spread over Egypt—darkness that can be felt."
So Moses stretched out his hand toward the sky, and total darkness
covered all Egypt for three days. No one could see anyone else or
leave his place for three days. Yet all the Israelites
had light in the places where they lived.
EXODUS 10:21–23

Without warning Pharaoh, the Lord commanded Moses to begin the ninth plague, and the prophet stretched a hand toward the sky. Darkness spread throughout the land of Egypt. But it was not the normal darkness of night, but one the people could feel. It was so thick no one could see anyone else, and even the lamps that lit Egyptian homes could not break through it.

The Egyptians would have understood the meaning of this plague, for they worshipped Ra, the sun god. But for three days they could not celebrate the sunrise. God was showing the people that He was more powerful than their pagan deity. So it's not surprising that the Hebrew people still had light.

An irritated Pharaoh called Moses to him and commanded the Hebrews to go worship God, but again he tried to hold on to the slaves, insisting that they leave their flocks behind. Moses pointed out that they could not make sacrifices without the animals. The king's heart hardened again.

Pharaoh commanded Moses never to darken his door again, on pain of death. The prohibition seems to have been fine with the prophet. By now the two men were probably tired of seeing each other in this spiritual and political deadlock.

Those who are blinded by unbelief live in darkness as black as the ninth plague. As Christians who enjoy the benefits of the Light, we often wonder why people will not turn to Him. Their darkness is not the ordinary middle-of-the-night sort, but one that so thoroughly covers the eyes that they have no inkling of the Light.

What lifts this darkness? Only repentance and faith in Jesus. We can discuss faith with unbelievers until we turn blue in the face, but until they trust in Him, they cannot fully understand.

DEATH OF THE FIRSTBORN

*At midnight the LORD struck down all the firstborn in Egypt, from the
firstborn of Pharaoh, who sat on the throne, to the firstborn of the prisoner,
who was in the dungeon, and the firstborn of all the livestock as well.
Pharaoh and all his officials and all the Egyptians got up during the night, and
there was loud wailing in Egypt, for there was not a house without someone dead.
During the night Pharaoh summoned Moses and Aaron and said,
"Up! Leave my people, you and the Israelites!
Go, worship the LORD as you have requested."*
EXODUS 12:29–31

Without warning to anyone but the Hebrews, God acted. Moses and all his people had received God's directions for celebrating the Passover. Every household would put lamb's blood on the doorposts and lintel. The lamb would be roasted for dinner, and they would eat it with unleavened bread and bitter herbs. All the people were to be dressed for travel and ready to leave as soon as the order came. As they hurriedly obeyed all God's directions, the Israelites must have had a sense of intense excitement running through their community. God was going to do something spectacular!

The death of the firstborn Egyptian in each family came as a shock to Egypt's leaders. In the middle of the night, Pharaoh lost his son, but the plague did not end there, nor did the ruler immediately declare that God's people could leave. Every Egyptian household, even the humblest, lost the oldest child, and none remained unaffected. Even the livestock lost their firstborn. The wailing in Egypt must have been awful to hear. But the Hebrews, off east in Goshen, wouldn't have heard it.

Finally, after this sudden affliction, Pharaoh understood he was vanquished and called back the man he'd declared he'd never see alive. When Moses came, the ruler agreed to let all the Hebrews, with every one of their flocks and herds, go. It was a terrible comedown for the leader of a world power.

Egypt's populace couldn't see the backs of the Israelites quickly enough. The people of this wealthy land gave the former slaves gold, silver, and clothing, hoping they'd leave before every Egyptian died. That's how God prepared His people for their long journey.

The Israelites, standing ready, grabbed their unleavened dough and carried it with them. They hurried off before Pharaoh could change his mind.

While the Egyptians had been punished through the ten plagues, God had blessed His own people. They had remained untouched by the plague horrors, and now they received physical benefits from the people who had enslaved them. The Egyptian goods would provide for God's people as they traveled through the desert. And they would need all of it, since their trip would be one of many years.

Because of their rebellion against Him, God inflicted great pain on the Egyptians. Though He'd made it clear He was more powerful than their own gods, they preferred to stick with their familiar deities and live in sin. So they brought their troubles on themselves.

But the unwitting Israelites did not take this warning God placed before them, either. On the trip into the Promised Land, they began to doubt the Lord who delivered them. As they faced hardship, they doubted His care for them. For their rebellion against God, they spent forty years in the wilderness between Egypt and the Promised Land.

Are we tempted to doubt? Let's remember both the Egyptians and Israelites and take heart again. Trusting God will never be a bad choice.

BONDAGE ENDED

Then Moses stretched out his hand over the sea;
and the LORD caused the sea to go back by a strong east wind all that night,
and made the sea into dry land, and the waters were divided.
So the children of Israel went into the midst of the sea on the dry ground,
and the waters were a wall to them on their right hand and on their left.
EXODUS 14:21–22 NKJV

After the tenth and final plague, when Pharaoh allowed them to leave Egypt, the Israelites hurried off into the desert. But instead of worshipping God by making burnt offerings, they worshipped with their feet—obedient to God, they set off to the Promised Land and freedom from bondage!

Pharaoh heard his slaves were not returning, called out his chariot force, and headed after them. It could hardly have been a surprise to him that they did as he'd expected them to do and headed for the hills.

The Israelites looked up and saw the Egyptian forces following them, and terror filled their hearts. First they cried out to God and then began to blame Moses for leading them into the desert to die. "Weren't there enough graves in Egypt?" they demanded. "Why did you bring us here when we told you to leave us alone?" Their hindsight wasn't exactly twenty-twenty, was it? They'd been happy enough to leave Egypt.

God, knowing they might run back to Pharaoh's land in such circumstances, had backed them up against the Red Sea. They had nowhere to go, so Moses ordered them to stand firm in God, who would deliver them. "The Lord will fight for you," he promised.

God directed Moses and his people to move forward as the prophet held out his hand over the sea, and He promised that the waters would divide before them. The angel of the Lord, who had gone before them, turned and stood behind God's people, and the cloud of God's presence joined him as a rear guard.

Moses stretched out one hand, and through the night the sea was driven back by a strong east wind. The waters separated into two walls, and dry land appeared between them. The Israelites and all their animals walked between the two walls of water, dry-shod.

After the Israelites entered the sea, the Egyptians dashed after them. At the end of this long night, God threw the opponents of His people into confusion. Their chariot wheels began to fall off their vehicles, and their destruction was imminent. By now the Egyptians were experienced enough to know why this was happening. "Let's get away," they cried. "God is fighting for the Israelites" (see 14:25). They knew the Lord's power and feared Him but still would not bow the knee to this mighty One who had outdone their own idols.

God commanded Moses to raise his hand again, and the water closed over the Egyptian warriors. They were swept off into the sea, and none survived. According to Moses' praise song after this event, Pharaoh lost the best of his officers (see 15:4).

But all the Israelites had passed safely through the sea. As Moses had prophesied, they would never again see any of those Egyptians. On dry land again, Israel had a praise party, worshipping the Lord who had saved them from their enslavers.

Moses had commanded his people to stand firm and watch God fight for them, and they had seen Him do just that as the waters enveloped their pursuers. God has not stopped fighting for His people. He still protects them from their enemies and watches their backs.

If the Israelites could trust Him when their backs were to the sea, can we do any less? No matter what we face today, if we've trusted in Him, we are His children. He will never fail us. What enemy need we fear?

MOSES MALIGNED

And the people thirsted there for water, and the people complained
against Moses, and said, "Why is it you have brought us up out of Egypt,
to kill us and our children and our livestock with thirst?"
So Moses cried out to the LORD, saying,
"What shall I do with this people?
They are almost ready to stone me!"
And the LORD said to Moses, "Go on before the people,
and take with you some of the elders of Israel.
Also take in your hand your rod with which you struck the river,
and go. Behold, I will stand before you there on the rock in Horeb;
and you shall strike the rock, and water will
come out of it, that the people may drink."
EXODUS 17:3–6 NKJV

As the Israelites traveled toward their new home, they became distinctly crabby. It wasn't the easiest journey, and at times it must have seemed to Moses that every one of the millions of people he was escorting had something to say about the difficulties of the trip. It didn't matter that God turned bitter water sweet at Marah or sent manna and quail to feed His hungry people. The Israelites, looking back at their lives in Egypt, wanted something better. Every time they faced a challenge, they acted as if they were about to die.

Moses feared his own people would take his life. They'd given him an ultimatum: Either he gave them water, or they would stone him as a traitor! So the prophet consulted with God. The Lord told Moses to take with him some elders and the staff with which he'd struck the Nile. God promised to stand before him at Horeb. As the prophet struck the rock, water would flow out.

The people wanted a judgment, and God gave them one, with their elders as witnesses. But the judgment was not on His prophet. God stood before the people and protected Moses, who had done His will faithfully, despite the Israelites' grumbling.

If we seek to criticize one of God's faithful leaders, we'd best beware. For God does not take such actions lightly. When we follow a leader who walks closely with God, it's better to appreciate him than grumble. Was God planning on letting His people die of thirst in the desert on their way to the Promised Land? That's unthinkable—except to those complaining Israelites. Had they trusted, they would have both received water and refrained from maligning Moses.

Are we grumbling Israelites?

THE LOST REBELLION

Now it came to pass, as he finished speaking all these words, that the ground split
apart under them, and the earth opened its mouth and swallowed them up,
with their households and all the men with Korah, with all their goods.
So they and all those with them went down alive into the pit;
the earth closed over them, and they perished from among the assembly.
NUMBERS 16:31–33 NKJV

On what probably seemed an ordinary day as he went about his work as a prophet, Moses suddenly faced rebellion in the ranks of the Israelites.

The prophet had simply commanded them to wear tassels on their robes to remind them to be holy to God. In response, two groups of malcontents forged an agreement and rose up against him. Dathan, Abiram, and On of the Reubenites might not have been a surprise, but Korah was a Levite, one of Moses and Aaron's tribe, a man who served in the tabernacle. With these four stood 250 congregational leaders.

It was hardly a disagreement over tassels. The insurgents claimed all the people in the congregation were holy—a manifestly ridiculous statement, assuming that every one of millions of people was without sin. More than likely, these proud rebels felt guilty about their own sins and sought to cover them up with noisy complaints. Then they accused Moses and Aaron of exalting themselves above the rest of Israel.

Moses didn't argue—he reproved Korah for his dissatisfaction with his temple role, then simply allowed God to judge. He called everyone to come to the tabernacle the next day, but the rebellious Reubenites refused the invitation.

The following day, the rest assembled, censers in hand, at the Tent of Meeting. God warned Aaron and Moses to step away from the rebels, and the two men quickly fell before God in prayer. In response to their plea for their people, the Lord told them to warn the innocent ones to stay far from the errant Reubenites who stood at the openings of their tents watching the events before them.

Moses described the terms of God's judgment: the Lord would destroy those who had sinned by swallowing them up in the earth. Immediately the ground split and gobbled up Korah and the rebel Reubenites. Fire destroyed their 250 supporters. All the rest of Israel fled, fearing God's wrath on themselves.

Here, God gives us a concrete picture of what He thinks of rebellion against Him. For rebellion against His appointed, faithful leaders can also be rebellion against the Lord they serve.

Have we been tempted to rebel against God by attacking His devoted followers, especially those leading in His name? Maybe we'd best watch the ground beneath us!

SPARE THE ROD?

And Moses spake unto the children of Israel,
and every one of their princes gave him a rod apiece,
for each prince one, according to their fathers' houses,
even twelve rods: and the rod of Aaron was among their rods.
And Moses laid up the rods before the LORD in the tabernacle of witness.
And it came to pass, that on the morrow Moses went into the tabernacle of witness;
and, behold, the rod of Aaron for the house of Levi was budded,
and brought forth buds, and bloomed blossoms, and yielded almonds.
NUMBERS 17:6–8 KJV

Korah's rebellion didn't end the Israelites' dissatisfaction with their leaders. Again they rebelled, and Moses' intercession saved their lives from a plague, but not before 14,700 died.

God chose to end the rebellion with a miracle that showed everyone whom He wanted in control. At God's command, the leaders of each one of the twelve tribes of Israel gave his staff to Moses. In case there was any question, scripture records that as high priest, Aaron's staff stood for the tribe of Levi. Each rod had the name of its owner written on it, and they were laid before the ark in the holiest part of the tabernacle.

The next day, of all the staves, only Aaron's had budded, bloomed, and fruited with almonds. There was no question about whose rod it was, since his name was right there for all to see.

With this concrete proof, the Israelites could have assurance that they were following the right man. God did not spare the rod when it came to letting His people know they had displeased Him. Through a miracle, He set them on the right path again, though, unhappily, it did not completely quell the complaints of His people.

God does not spare the rod when His people fail Him. Sometimes He punishes them, as He did when the plague appeared. But He had a choice: He could wipe out all the rebels, and only a small band of people would reach the Promised Land, or He could show compassion and turn at least some hearts. God chose to be compassionate.

Do we willingly turn to God's will, or does He need to take out a rod and show us what He means? If we demand proof of Him, let's remember that God could spare the rod and send us a death-dealing illness. Do we really want to take that risk?

Doesn't obedience sound a lot more pleasant now?

SNAKE ON A POLE

Therefore the people came to Moses, and said, We have sinned,
for we have spoken against the LORD, *and against thee;*
pray unto the LORD, *that he take away the serpents from us.*
And Moses prayed for the people. And the LORD *said unto Moses,*
Make thee a fiery serpent, and set it upon a pole: and it shall come to pass,
that every one that is bitten, when he looketh upon it, shall live.
And Moses made a serpent of brass, and put it upon a pole, and it came to pass,
that if a serpent had bitten any man, when he beheld the serpent of brass, he lived.

NUMBERS 21:7–9 KJV

The Israelites had a nationwide attitude problem. No matter what Moses and Aaron said or what miracle God showed them, they were determined that life was miserable and they had to have things their way. Now Aaron was dead, and ignoring the fact that God had just given them victory over the king of Arad, again they began to grumble.

"Why did you bring us into the wilderness?" they whined at Moses in their familiar chorus. "We're tired of manna today, manna tomorrow, and manna for who knows how long." They even called the manna "worthless."

Had they forgotten their hunger in the desert, when they first began the trip to the Promised Land? These determinedly sinful people seemingly forgot how painful their slavery had been and looked back longingly to Egypt. Did they remember how difficult it had been to make strawless bricks?

So began a real whinefest, for they not only complained about Moses, but having lost the convenient target of Aaron, they complained about the Lord, too. Did they simply like complaining because it gave them an opportunity to hear their own voices? Well, no one else wanted to hear it—especially not God. What were they thinking, to expect that He would put up with their petty complaints? Past experience should have made them wiser. God didn't ignore their whining and complaining. Instead He sent a fearsome affliction: fiery, poisonous serpents that bit the people. Many Israelites died.

Now they remembered their previous experiences, and the remaining sinners knew where to go when they were in trouble. The suddenly penitent people knocked on the flap of Moses' tent, seeking salvation. They asked Moses to pray, and the prophet immediately responded to their need.

God heard the prayers of His prophet and provided a way for their physical salvation: He commanded Moses to make a snake and set it on a pole, and those who were bitten could look at it and live. This miracle turned around the effect of the fearsome plague of snakes and showed forth God's abundant compassion on His failure-prone people.

Obediently, Moses fashioned a bronze serpent and set it on a pole. Those who looked upon it would not die, even though they had been bitten. How many Israelites would have been foolish enough to refuse that sight? Only those so steeped in sin and so foolish that they had no fear of God or the poisonous snakes.

It's not hard to understand why theologians see Jesus in this Old Testament image. For we, too, look upward to a kind of pole for our salvation. In the cross is our only hope, since none of us has failed to bellyache when we did not like the direction in which God has sent us. Or, if we've avoided that sin, we've looked back to our own Egypt, the site of our previous sin-filled life. None of us fails to be affected by moral and spiritual failure, so all of us need to look to the cross for our salvation. It will not stop sin from biting us, but it will bring us to the gracious Father, through the sacrifice of His only Son.

THE RED SEA REVISITED

*The priests who carried the ark of the covenant of the LORD
stood firm on dry ground in the middle of the Jordan,
while all Israel passed by until the whole nation
had completed the crossing on dry ground.*
JOSHUA 3:17

It took Israel two tries to cross the Jordan River. Forty years earlier spies had doubted that Israel could conquer, and that doubt had condemned a generation to wander in the desert for forty years. This time the men sent into Jericho gave a good report. So Israel prepared to enter Canaan.

None of the people who stood on the bank of the river had been there before. But the new generation joyfully consecrated themselves to enter the new land. Ready for success, they trusted God.

The priests carried the ark of the covenant forward, into the flow of the river, and the stream of water stopped, just as it had at the Red Sea when Moses led Israel out of Egypt. When everyone reached the other side, dry-shod, God commanded that they leave a memorial of twelve stones in the river.

Like the second-generation Israelites, do we have memorials to the work God has done in our lives? Do we remain mindful of His blessings and power? Let's not make God turn us away from blessings because we've doubted. We don't want to miss out on the best things He has planned for our lives!

TUMBLING WALLS

On the seventh day they rose early, at the dawn of day,
and marched around the city in the same manner seven times. . . .
And at the seventh time, when the priests had blown the trumpets,
Joshua said to the people, "Shout, for the LORD has given you the city."
So the people shouted, and the trumpets were blown.
As soon as the people heard the sound of the trumpet,
the people shouted a great shout, and the wall fell down flat.
JOSHUA 6:15–16, 20 ESV

When God commanded the Israelites to head for Jericho, it must have been an intimidating prospect. This was the oldest walled city in the world, a strategically placed trade metropolis. The Lord had an admirable battle plan when He directed the attack of these walls that defended the Palestinian hill country. But when the Israelites first set eyes on Jericho, they could have feared that success was likely to come at a high price. Yet they took heart in the fact that God promised that the city was already theirs, for He had given it into their hands.

With God in command of this expedition, it was about to be a battle unlike any other. When Israel headed for the city, the people of Jericho shut themselves behind the walls and probably hoped that the Israelite army would pass them by. As God's army camped outside their walls, the city dwellers must have become terribly confused. For the newcomers did not attack. Instead, an army of silent Israelites surrounded seven priests with their constantly blaring ram's horn trumpets and marched around the city once a day for six days. Each time, following their walk around Jericho, the men returned to their camp. By the end of the third day, everyone inside the walls must have been jittery. What could this mean?

On the seventh day, when nerves on both sides may have been tight, God commanded His army to march around the city seven times. The Israelites rose early to get at the job. Can you see the people standing on Jericho's walls, counting? One, two, three, four. . .

After the Israelites had silently circumnavigated the city six times and were ending their final round, Joshua told his men to shout, for God had given them the city. As they shouted, the walls of the city fell down flat. So the Israelites went into the city and captured it.

God had commanded Joshua that everything in the city was to be destroyed—all the people and animals. The only human exception was Rahab's family. Since this woman of Jericho had hidden the Israelite spies who scoped out the situation in her city, God preserved her and her household. And all the valuable vessels in the city were gathered to be made part of the Lord's treasury.

Though archaeologists have disagreed over the dating of the destruction of the Old Testament city of Jericho, there is clear evidence that it was completely destroyed. Actually, there were two walls around the city, one six feet thick and an inner one, twelve feet thick. In a 1930 archaeological report, the outer wall is described as having fallen down the slope of the hill. The inner wall remained standing only near the citadel. The rest of the city had been destroyed by fire, and some evidence shows this occurred suddenly.

If we spend much time arguing about archaeological issues that may never be proved either way, will we miss the point of this story? God performed this miracle in order to bring His people into the Promised Land. He devised a battle plan that took few if any Israelite lives and eradicated a pagan people whose pagan practices could have quickly destroyed the faith of His own people.

But God did not simply tumble down walls then forget about His people in the following centuries. The walls He destroys today may not be physical ones, but He still removes dangers that lure believers from truth and keep them from fulfilling His mission.

What wall has tumbled down before you?

SUN AND MOON DAY

Then Joshua spoke to the LORD in the day when the LORD
delivered up the Amorites before the children of Israel,
and he said in the sight of Israel:
"Sun, stand still over Gibeon; and Moon, in the Valley of Aijalon."
So the sun stood still, and the moon stopped,
till the people had revenge upon their enemies. . . .
So the sun stood still in the midst of heaven, and did not hasten
to go down for about a whole day. And there has been no day like that,
before it or after it, that the LORD heeded the voice of a man;
for the LORD fought for Israel.
JOSHUA 10:12–14 NKJV

When Adoni-zedek, king of Jerusalem, heard that Israel had captured the city of Ai and that the great city of Gibeon, only six miles from his city, had made peace with the invaders, he was filled with fear. What would this strange people, who had quickly conquered other cities in Canaan, do to his city? Better to attack one of Israel's friends and fight on our own terms than wait for these Israeli invaders to come to us, he must have thought. After all, look what happened to Jericho.

So Jerusalem's king sent a message to the other Amorite kings of the city-states of southern Canaan and invited them to unite with him on a military campaign against Gibeon. Five kings banded together to take on a single peaceful city: Hoham, king of Hebron; Piram, king of Jarmuth; Japhia, king of Lachish; and Debir, king of Eglon, joined their armies to Adoni-zedek's and headed for Gibeon.

One day Gibeon peacefully sat in the sun; the next they saw an army on the horizon. Before they closed their gates, Gibeon's citizens sent a message to Joshua, encamped with his people in Gilgal. Their short missive could be translated in a single word: "Help!"

Though Gibeon had tricked Israel into making the treaty with them, Joshua did not fail the city. God promised that the gathered armies would not stand before his army, so Israel's leader confidently headed out with his warriors. After marching all night, traveling about twenty miles uphill, the Israeli army attacked the Amorites. Struck by the Lord with a sense of panic, the Canaanite attackers fled before Joshua's troops. Israel got a new burst of energy and chased the enemy for miles, cutting soldiers down as they ran. As the Amorites dashed away from Beth Horon, God took a hand and rained large hailstones down on the enemy. More men died at God's hand of judgment than at the hands of His people.

As the day waned, in an unusual prayer, Joshua asked God to make the sun and moon stand still while Israel avenged itself on their enemies. Some scholars believe it was a request for a longer day in which to finish the battle.

God's people were victorious and extended their control of Canaan through this battle. Only a remnant of the warriors escaped into fortified cities. As Israel chased the Amorites, their terrified kings hid in a cave. Joshua decreed his men should block the five rulers in their safe place until the battle was finished. Following the end of the engagement, Joshua killed all five as a sign of the Lord's judgment on Israel's enemies.

As a by-product of the battle with the Amorite kings, Makkedah, one of the cities in the path of the running battle, was also conquered by Israel and completely destroyed. Six kings conquered in one day has to be some kind of record! One that could only be accomplished with God's power.

Scripture comments that there was never a day like that one, when God listened to the voice of man. And it's true that God does not often stop the sun and moon in their courses. But He does listen to prayer every day. So if we face attackers from five different places, we need not fear. God answers prayer—sometimes in amazing ways. But we do need to pray.

ONE WEAK SPOT

Behold, a young lion roared against [Samson].
And the Spirit of the LORD came mightily upon him,
and he rent him as he would have rent a kid, and he had nothing in his hand. . . .
And the Spirit of the LORD came upon him, and he went down to Ashkelon,
and slew thirty men of them, and took their spoil.
JUDGES 14:5–6, 19 KJV

No wine or strong drink should have passed Nazirite Samson's lips, so an alcohol-abuse problem probably had nothing to do with his sudden desire to show off his muscles. Scripture tells us the power of God's Spirit gave him a strength that must have amazed the elders of his day and made the young men pick up their weights and pray that God would so bless them. But no one was as powerful as the Bible's strongman. When the men of Gaza wanted to kill him, Samson took a midnight stroll, grabbed the city gates, and carried them off to Hebron (see 16:3).

But the strongman had one weak spot: women. He could never keep a secret from one. When Samson became entangled with the beautiful Delilah, Israel's Philistine overlords came to her and demanded that she seduce Samson and discover the secret of his strength. They'd pay her well. She nagged at her lover, and three times he lied to her. Finally, he dropped his guard and told her that if she shaved his head, he would become weak. When Delilah had a man shave him, Samson lost his power—probably more because he'd repeatedly contravened his Nazirite vows than because he lost his hair.

The Philistines blinded Samson and made him a slave, but when his hair grew, he regained his strength. During a pagan Philistine festival, the Philistines demanded that Samson entertain them. Following his performance, the Israelite did his best act: he pushed down two of the weight-bearing pillars in the temple, destroying the building and all the people in it.

Samson proves that even the strongest man has weaknesses. Though he had astonishing physical prowess, Samson's moral and spiritual powers were slowly depleted as he broke the vows that set him apart to be holy to the Lord. Let's take Samson's example to heart and keep ourselves daily devoted to God. For Samson's failings did not happen quickly: he slowly slipped into error as he forgot his vows and the commandments God had given His people.

WAKE-UP CALL

"I will call upon the LORD to send thunder and rain. And you will realize what an evil thing you did in the eyes of the LORD when you asked for a king."
Then Samuel called upon the LORD, and that same day the LORD sent thunder and rain. So all the people stood in awe of the LORD and of Samuel.

1 SAMUEL 12:17–18

In his last address to his people, Samuel pled with his rebellious people, who had denied God by asking for a king, to be faithful to their Lord. If they obeyed King Saul and did right, all would be well, he promised.

To prove that his words were not simply idle chatter and that God was Lord, the prophet told Israel to watch. Then he called on God to send thunder and rain. Though it was the dry season, the thunder crashed and the rain plummeted from the skies. Impressed and understanding their own sinfulness and God's power, the Israelites suddenly feared they might die.

It wasn't as if Samuel had never before told the people about sin. They'd heard his words but never accepted them, but his miracle finally stopped them in their tracks and made them realize what they'd done.

Has God spoken to us of sin, and we've tried to ignore it? Does He have to jounce us out of our complacency with a notification that He's still in control?

RAINMAKER

Now Elijah the Tishbite, from Tishbe in Gilead, said to Ahab,
"As the LORD, the God of Israel, lives, whom I serve, there will be neither dew nor rain in the next few years except at my word."

1 KINGS 17:1

Israel's King Ahab was one in a long line of disobedient kings. But his forebears couldn't hold a candle to this evil ruler. Through the influence of his wife, Jezebel, he served the pagan god Baal and fell into exceedingly wicked ways.

So the Lord sent the prophet Elijah to the king with a message: Unless Elijah gave the word, no rain or even dew would fall on the nation. Then God had the prophet hide by a brook east of the Jordan. When that stream dried up, God sent the prophet away from Israel, to Zarephath in Sidon.

After three years of drought, God sent Elijah back to parched Israel and her king. Elijah had a showdown with the priests of Baal that proved their god Baal impotent. After the pagan priests were killed, Elijah prayed for rain, and it poured down on Israel, proving the Lord, not Baal, controlled the weather—and everything else, too.

Over and over, God uses His control of this world to show forth His power. Are we open to that message? Or will it take a three-year drought to get our attention?

SOME OIL AND FLOUR

The widow answered, "In the name of the living LORD your God,
I swear that I don't have any bread. All I have is a handful of flour
and a little olive oil. I'm on my way home now with these few sticks to cook
what I have for my son and me. After that, we will starve to death."
Elijah said, "Everything will be fine. Do what you said. Go home and fix
something for you and your son. But first, please make a small piece of bread and
bring it to me. The LORD God of Israel has promised that your jar of flour won't
run out and your bottle of oil won't dry up before he sends rain for the crops."
1 KINGS 17:12–14 CEV

Elijah hadn't been living well while he hid from Ahab in the Kerith Ravine, though he had water and food, since ravens miraculously delivered his meals. But the stream that provided the water dried up, and the prophet had to move on.

God told the thirsty prophet to head for Zarepheth of Sidon, a small seaside town. It seemed an odd place for God to send him. After all, the Phoenicians were Gentiles who worshipped Baal, the pagan god whose worship had infiltrated Israel. And Queen Jezebel, who had brought such worship into Israel, hated Elijah. Though there seemed to be no sense in the place God had sent His prophet, in going there, Elijah became the first prophet to reach out to the Gentiles.

Not only did God send His prophet into Baal country; He sent him to a very poor widow. For widows of that age, poverty was common. They had no career paths open to them, and unless a family member took care of them, they could easily end up destitute. That's the situation this woman found herself in. She was gathering firewood, about to make a last meal for herself and her son. There was nothing more in the cupboard, and she did not expect to have anything in the future.

So when Elijah asked for some water and food, the woman willingly went for his drink but was not enthusiastic about sharing the little food she had. She explained her situation to the prophet, who told her it would be all right: her flour and oil would not run out before the rain came.

Perhaps this woman had no faith in the Lord God, but with deference she referred to Him as "the living LORD your God" (17:12 CEV). She trustingly followed the prophet's directions, and everything happened as Elijah promised. For many days, they had enough to eat, even if it wasn't a perfectly balanced diet.

God provided for the widow, her son, and the prophet when her own god failed her. He even provided for these three while His own people suffered from the drought. Surely she must have thought about the power of a God who did this. Perhaps she even came to know Him because of it.

Had the people of Israel known where Elijah was, they probably would have thrown a fit. Why was he living in this pagan village instead of providing them with the water they needed? They might have been dumbfounded at the idea that this unbeliever was cared for while they struggled so. But God had a twofold purpose: the Israelites would learn of their own sinfulness while He saved the life of this poor widow.

God does not see people the way we do. To us, the well-to-do, powerful, or highly spiritual folk seem important. We can imagine God doing wonderful things for them. But so often, God chooses to bless the quietly faithful or totally unworldly person we'd pass by in a minute.

Sometimes we stand amazed when good things happen to unbelievers and wonder why the faithful Christian is passed over. We need to understand that God has His own purposes. He's working out a wider plan that may bring salvation to a hurting soul. Let's not judge too quickly. Instead, let's trust in the Lord who rules this earth and can touch any heart in it.

TENDER LOVE

Then [Elijah] cried out to the LORD and said, "O LORD my God,
have You also brought tragedy on the widow with whom I lodge,
by killing her son?" And he stretched himself out on the child three times,
and cried out to the LORD and said, "O LORD my God, I pray, let this
child's soul come back to him." Then the LORD heard the voice of Elijah;
and the soul of the child came back to him, and he revived.
1 KINGS 17:20–22 NKJV

One day, the widow with whom Elijah was lodging in Zarephath came to him, lamenting. Was he trying to make her aware of her own sin, she asked, by taking the life of her only son? For the boy, her only hope in old age, had become terribly ill and now was not breathing. The grieving mother had begun to wonder if she'd done wrong in taking in the prophet who stood before her.

Elijah didn't stop to ask why she hadn't consulted him earlier. He picked up her son, took him to his own room, and laid him on the bed. Stretching out on the boy, he prayed fervently, crying out to God, almost repeating the widow's words to him. He pointed out to God the benefit this woman had been to him, opening her home to him.

Obviously, in the time he'd been there, Elijah had come to care for this little family. The fact that they were Sidonians, not Israelites, did not matter. The widow had taken Elijah in though she and her son were in desperate straits, and he valued her for her deep-pocketed kindness.

The Lord heard the prophet's prayer, and the boy miraculously regained his life—the first time such a thing had ever happened. Elijah picked up the boy and returned him to his mother. What joy must have filled them when they saw the work God had done.

The widow, convinced that Elijah was just what he said he was, declared: "Now by this I know that you are a man of God, and that the word of the LORD in your mouth is the truth" (17:24 NKJV). Can one doubt that by this point she had come to faith?

God's compassion on the widow is such a touching story. But is He any less tender to His people today? Those who call on Him in pain will know His gentle love.

WAVERING FAITH?

"O LORD, God of Abraham, Isaac, and Israel, let it be known this day that you are God in Israel, and that I am your servant, and that I have done all these things at your word. Answer me, O LORD, answer me, that this people may know that you, O LORD, are God, and that you have turned their hearts back."
Then the fire of the LORD fell and consumed the burnt offering
and the wood and the stones and the dust,
and licked up the water that was in the trench.
1 KINGS 18:36–38 ESV

As Elijah entered Israel and met the king, Ahab greeted him with the words, "Is it you, you troubler of Israel?" (18:17 ESV). Nice to have been greeted so warmly, wasn't it, when he controlled the rain flow over the nation! Three years of drought surely hadn't improved Ahab's disposition or gotten God's message through to him.

Elijah told the king to bring together all the pagan priests and prophets whom Jezebel supported at Israel's expense. Perhaps because he wanted to end the drought, the king obeyed. They met Elijah and all Israel's people on Mount Carmel. There Elijah confronted the Israelites about their idolatry and proposed a simple showdown: The priests of Baal would make one offering, and Elijah would make another. The one whose sacrifice was consumed by fire would be the better deity.

The people liked that idea. So the priests of Baal prepared their offering and called on Baal for half a day. At noon, Elijah mocked their god and the stories their religion told of this anthropomorphic deity. Desperate, worshippers began mutilating themselves to try to get Baal's attention, but of course it did not work. Now it was Elijah's turn.

After calling his people to himself, Elijah took twelve stones, symbolic of each of Israel's tribes, and rebuilt the Lord's altar, which had been destroyed by the idolaters. The prophet made a trench around the altar that would have held about fourteen quarts of seeds. Then he set the wood on the altar and cut up the sacrificial bull. He had some men fill four jars with water and pour it over the offering and wood. They did this three times, until water ran around the altar and filled the trench.

Then Elijah prayed: "O LORD, God of Abraham, Isaac, and Israel, let it be known this day that you are God in Israel, and that I am your servant, and that I have done all these things at your word. Answer me, O LORD, answer me, that this people may know that you, O LORD, are God, and that you have turned their hearts back" (verses 36–37 ESV). No ranting and raving, no cutting himself. Just a simple prayer.

The fire of the Lord fell and miraculously consumed the offering, the water, the wood, stones, and dust, and licked up the water in the trench. The Baal worshipers had no chance to imply that there'd been any funny business going on.

When they saw this sign of wonder, the people fell on their faces and started repeating, "The Lord, he is God" over and over (verse 39). They'd gotten the point. While their faith was strong, Elijah commanded them to grab Baal's priests. They did, and all the pagan priests were slaughtered in the Kishon Valley (verse 40).

Elijah prophesied that a heavy rain was coming and went to the top of the mountain to pray that God would end this curse on His people. After repeated checks on the sky, his servant reported a small cloud on the horizon. Shortly dark clouds appeared, and the rain poured down. God's drought was at an end.

"How long will you waver?" Elijah asked his people when he confronted them about their idolatry (see verse 21). They had gone back and forth between pagan beliefs and knowledge of the Lord. Now the prophet showed them clearly who to believe in.

Are we tempted to waver? Let's remember the power God showed on that day and turn back to Him. He strengthens His people when they trust in Him.

JUDGMENT BY FIRE

The captain went up to Elijah, who was sitting on the top of a hill,
and said to him, "Man of God, the king says, 'Come down!'"
Elijah answered the captain, "If I am a man of God, may fire come down
from heaven and consume you and your fifty men!" Then fire fell
from heaven and consumed the captain and his men.
2 KINGS 1:9–10

Israel's King Ahaziah succeeded his father, Ahab, and walked in his wicked footsteps. When Ahaziah injured himself in an accident, he sent to inquire of

Baal-Zebub, Ekron's god, if he would be healed.

God sent Elijah to the king's messengers to ask if Israel had no God and to tell them the king would die. When the men returned to Ahaziah, the king sent a captain and fifty men to the prophet to call him to himself. But Elijah called down fire from heaven, and all fifty-one were consumed. The stubborn king sent another company of men to the prophet, and they met the same end (verses 10–12).

The third captain was wiser and begged Elijah to have compassion. So God allowed Elijah to go to the king. Not that it changed the message. Elijah repeated what he'd said before, and the king died (verses 13–17).

Sometimes we ignore the tenderheartedness of God. Do we know that we can hurt Him when we go elsewhere with our troubles? What problem should we bring to Him today?

TAKING UP THE MANTLE

Elijah took his cloak, rolled it up and struck the water with it.
The water divided to the right and to the left,
and the two of them crossed over on dry ground. . . .
[Elisha] picked up the cloak that had fallen
from Elijah and went back and stood on the bank of the Jordan.
Then he took the cloak that had fallen from him and struck the water with it.
"Where now is the LORD, the God of Elijah?" he asked.
When he struck the water, it divided to the right
and to the left, and he crossed over.
2 KINGS 2:8, 13–14

Elijah wasn't telling him about it, but his disciple Elisha knew God planned to take his master to heaven, and he wasn't going to miss that. He followed Elijah the whole day. When they went to cross the Jordan, Elijah rolled up his cloak like a staff and struck the water with it. Like Joshua, the prophet and his disciple saw the Jordan divide, and they walked through on dry ground.

On the other side of the Jordan, chariots of fire appeared, and Elijah went to God on a whirlwind. Then the sorrowing disciple took up Elijah's cloak and repeated his miracle, proving himself Elijah's successor.

Want to know if people are what they claim? Look at their lives. What they do proves who they are, just as Elisha's miracle showed others that God had given him His power.

SPRING RENEWAL

Then he went out to the spring and threw the salt into it, saying,
"This is what the LORD says: 'I have healed this water.
Never again will it cause death or make the land unproductive.' "
And the water has remained wholesome to this day,
according to the word Elisha had spoken.
2 KINGS 2:21–22

After Elisha took on the mantle of his teacher, the men of Jericho came to him with a problem: their water was bad. The new prophet asked for a bowl of salt. He took it to their spring, tossed in the salt, and the water was purified.

Much of Elisha's ministry focuses on compassionate, personal miracles, so it's appropriate that it should begin so. Obviously, salt alone would not have made their water more potable, but it was also a sign of God's covenant with His people. The Lord improved the water that sustained their lives.

When God does good things for us, do we recognize that He's keeping covenant with us? Are we keeping up our part of the covenant, too?

NAME-CALLING PUNISHMENT

From there Elisha went up to Bethel. As he was walking along the road,
some youths came out of the town and jeered at him. "Go on up, you baldhead!"
they said. "Go on up, you baldhead!" He turned around, looked at them
and called down a curse on them in the name of the LORD.
Then two bears came out of the woods and mauled forty-two of the youths.
2 KINGS 2:23–24

Judgment follows compassion as Elisha curses a horde of youths who jeer at him in Bethel. This city had become the center of idolatry under Jeroboam. Obviously, this crowd of youngsters had picked up all the worst religious habits of their elders. Since forty-two were mauled, it was a large group that defamed the prophet, and perhaps the mauling critters stopped them from taking more belligerent action.

It wasn't gentle, innocent children who mocked the prophet. Their punishment may seem sharp, but their lack of faith and respect for God earned it for them, not mere name-calling.

Do we treat God and His servants with respect? Or do we need to look to the woods and see if a bruin is heading our way?

OVERFLOWING BLESSING

Elisha said, "Go around and ask all your neighbors for empty jars.
Don't ask for just a few. Then go inside and shut the door behind you and
your sons. Pour oil into all the jars, and as each is filled, put it to one side."
She left him and afterward shut the door behind her and her sons.
They brought the jars to her and she kept pouring.

2 KINGS 4:3–5

Can't you see this woman and her sons running to every neighbor, borrowing crocks, bottles, and bowls? No vessel in the area avoided spending time in her house. Every corner of her home held a bowl or jar.

With the smidgen of oil she had in the house, she began pouring, and the bowls began to fill. As she moved from one vessel to the next, so must her amazement have grown. Her sons kept bringing her more bowls, and the oil kept flowing.

When they ran out of bowls, the oil stopped. But by then this widow had run out of worries. Instead of having her two sons sold as slaves to make good her dead husband's debt, she had oil to sell. Elisha told her there would be enough left over to take care of her family.

When God gives, He does so generously, providing His people's needs— even ours.

BLESSING GONE WRONG?

When Elisha reached the house, there was the boy lying dead on his couch.
He went in, shut the door on the two of them and prayed to the LORD.
Then he got on the bed and lay upon the boy, mouth to mouth,
eyes to eyes, hands to hands. As he stretched himself out upon him,
the boy's body grew warm. Elisha turned away and walked back and forth
in the room and then got on the bed and stretched out upon him once more.
The boy sneezed seven times and opened his eyes.

2 KINGS 4:32–35

The wealthy Shunammite woman was one of those people for whom good works is a way of life. She surely knew how to use her money wisely and began by feeding Elisha whenever he came to town. Then she suggested to her husband that they build a little room on their roof for the man. Just to make it more convenient, you know. Now Elisha had a place to spend the night, too.

The prophet had probably stopped by a number of times before he decided to do something for her. But like many selfless people, asked what she needed, she replied, "I'm just fine."

So Elisha got to choose a special gift for her: he conferred with his servant, Gehazi, who pointed out she had no child. So the prophet promised the barren woman the joy of having her own child. She doubted, asking him not to lie to her. But the next spring, she bore a son.

For a few years, all was fine as the child grew. But one morning, at harvest-time, as he visited his father in the fields, the boy's head pained him. The father had his men carry his son home, and the boy sat on his mother's lap, being comforted, until he died at noon.

The sorrowful mom laid her son on the prophet's bed, in the room they'd built for him. Shutting the door behind her, she went out to seek the prophet. Not even her husband knew what had happened.

The Shunammite hurried to Mount Carmel. Before she got to Elisha, the prophet sent Gehazi out to see if all was well. The prophet didn't need a spyglass to know something was up, and it wasn't good. But she would not tell her troubles to any but Elisha. She came to him and grabbed his feet, a sign of respect. Then she started talking. Hadn't he given her a son on his own, without her asking for him? Hadn't she asked him not to deceive her? She was probably thinking it would have been easier never to have had a child than to lose this much-loved boy. How would her heart ever heal?

Elisha tried healing the boy at a distance, sending his servant to the boy with his own staff. Gehazi was to hurry to the Shunammite's home, without speaking to anyone, and lay the staff on the boy's face. But the child remained inert. So the prophet went into the home himself.

Then Elisha did as Elijah had done with the son of the woman of Zarephath. He lay on him, stretching out on the boy, who began to become warm. The prophet walked around a bit, then repeated his previous actions. Suddenly the child sneezed seven times, and what a blessed sound it must have been to his mother. Elisha called his servant and told him to bring her to him. When she saw that her son lived, she fell at the prophet's feet in thanks.

Can we trust God with our most treasured possessions, even our family? It takes a lot of faith, and this unnamed woman had it. Trustingly, she went to the prophet when her life seemed dark, perhaps hoping that, like Elijah, he could bring her son to life. Whether or not she expected this, she trusted God instead of turning her back on Him.

Do we have such faith? Can we turn to Him in our darkest hours? Remember, God often gives us surprising benefits when we trust fully in Him.

MORE THAN ENOUGH

Then a man. . .brought the man of God bread of the firstfruits,
twenty loaves of barley bread, and newly ripened grain in his knapsack.
And he said, "Give it to the people, that they may eat."
But his servant said, "What? Shall I set this before one hundred men?"
He said again, "Give it to the people, that they may eat;
for thus says the LORD: 'They shall eat and have some left over.' "
2 KINGS 4:42–43 NKJV

Famine had struck Gilgal. So when a man came to Elisha with his firstfruits offering, it was a momentous occasion. "Give the holy offering to the hungry people," Elisha commanded, handing his servant a terrible problem. *How can I choose who should get one of these small loaves?* Gehazi wondered. And even so, would those who got one have enough? Not likely! When he confronted him, the prophet commanded his servant to obey and pass the loaves around. There would be more than enough.

We don't know how, but the small loaves not only filled one hundred men—there was some left over, too. Does it sound like another miracle you know well?

God knows our needs and cares and sends us help in the right time. Does it seem too little too late? Let Him multiply, and it will be more than enough.

A CHANGED MAN

Now Naaman was commander of the army of the king of Aram.
He was a great man in the sight of his master and highly regarded,
because through him the LORD had given victory to Aram.
He was a valiant soldier, but he had leprosy. . . . So he went down
and dipped himself in the Jordan seven times, as the man of God had told him,
and his flesh was restored and became clean like that of a young boy.
2 KINGS 5:1, 14

A powerful soldier, Naaman, was laid low by a skin disease, though it probably was not the same one we call leprosy today. In Israel, such an outward affliction was seen as being a sign of sin. It's not surprising, therefore, that when Naaman's wife's servant, a captured Israelite, heard of her master's trouble, she suggested that he travel to her homeland to see the prophet Elisha.

Full of hope, the commander went to his king, asking permission to leave his post for a time. Because he valued his soldier, King Ben-Hadad of Aram (Syria) put all his authority in train to help him. But instead of sending him to a prophet, Ben-Hadad sent Naaman to a king: Jehoram of Israel. Perhaps this was wise, as there had been minor border conflicts between his nation and Israel, though officially the two countries were at peace.

Naaman set out, carrying silver, gold, and plenty of clothes, along with a letter introducing him to Israel's king. Jehoram must have been something of a drama king, for when he read the letter, he immediately went into his theatrical act. First he tore his clothes (we can all only hope it wasn't his best duds). "Who am I to heal anyone of leprosy?" he demanded. Then he had an idea: "Aha! The king of Aram is looking to start a quarrel with me!" Nothing like assuming the worst in any situation: the king figured he was facing a potential war.

When the prophet Elisha heard the news, he took it calmly and sent to the king, suggesting that he send Naaman along to him. He'd show him what Israel's prophet could do. So the king sent Naaman back north, to the prophet's house in Samaria.

Naaman and his impressive retinue pulled up at the prophet's home. But they didn't get greeted the way they expected. Instead of being graciously received by the prophet, a messenger appeared before them and told the leper to go down to the Jordan River and wash in it seven times.

The important warrior felt rage course through his body. He'd expected something a lot more impressive than a mere message. And weren't the rivers of his native land better than the muddy Jordan? he asked. He stomped away in a huff.

Naaman couldn't see the futility of his attitude, but his servants could. Wouldn't it be worth anything to be rid of his disease? So what if he had to wash in the Jordan instead of another river? They convinced the man to do as the prophet said. So Naaman went to the Jordan, dipped himself in it seven times, and was healed. Could the prophet have required anything more simple?

After his healing, Naaman recognized the Lord as God and dedicated himself to His service. He was truly a changed man. He even offered Elisha a gift. Perhaps mindful of the warrior's earlier attitude, the prophet would not even let him imagine he'd purchased his healing.

Maybe the commonplace attitude that sin caused leprosy was not so far off. Naaman certainly had some attitude problems. Wrapped up in himself, he almost missed out on being healed. In addition to having the skin problem, the warrior was self-important. The attitude showed itself in his hot-tempered rejection of the help he needed.

Do we almost miss God's greatest blessings because we're so caught up in ourselves that we can't even see them coming? Let's remember the example of Naaman, turn, and serve the Lord completely.

WHITE AS SNOW

"Naaman's leprosy will cling to you and to your descendants forever."
Then Gehazi went from Elisha's presence and
he was leprous, as white as snow.
2 KINGS 5:27

After the healed commander Naaman left Elisha, the prophet's servant decided his master had been too easy on the Gentile. Elisha had flatly turned down the offer of a gift. But Gehazi decided he'd like to have something, so he followed the Aramean and told him that two prophets had come to visit, and Elisha needed a talent of silver and two festal garments.

The unsuspecting soldier gave him the money and the garments without question. Then he sent two of his own men back with Gehazi. When the three arrived at Elisha's house, the servant grabbed his booty and hurried Naaman's servants away.

Didn't Gehazi work for a prophet? How could he think he'd keep his wrongdoing from a man who could see through him? As soon as he saw his servant, the prophet asked where he'd been.

"Nowhere," the servant answered.

Elisha told him what he'd been doing and announced that Naaman's leprosy would cling to him and his descendants forever. Gehazi left, white as snow from the disease.

Greed may not make us leprous, at least not on the surface, but it will damage our hearts and spirits as certainly as leprosy ruined Gehazi's skin. Are we careful to be honest?

FLOATING METAL

But as one was felling a beam, the axe head fell into the water:
and he cried, and said, Alas, master! for it was borrowed.
And the man of God said, Where fell it? And he shewed him the place.
And he cut down a stick, and cast it in thither; and the iron did swim.
2 KINGS 6:5–6 KJV

Israel's prophets' school was involved in a building project, adding more space to their communal home. They went down to the Jordan to fell some trees to build the addition.

One of the men dropped his ax head into the water and cried out to Elisha, for an ax was a valuable and hard-to-find item, and the man had borrowed this one. These were not wealthy men, and its replacement would have been a problem. Not only that, but the work could not go on as effectively without the tool.

So the prophet tossed a stick into the water to recover the iron ax head. Under normal circumstances, it would never happen this way, but by God's power the metal floated, and the man was able to recover the valuable tool.

Is our need great? We can count on God for help, though the way seems impossible. We know where to turn when troubles would stop us in our tracks. Let's turn to the One who can even make metal float.

CAPTURED!

Behold, the mountain was full of horses and chariots of fire round about Elisha. And when they came down to him, Elisha prayed unto the LORD, and said, Smite this people, I pray thee, with blindness. And he smote them with blindness according to the word of Elisha.
2 KINGS 6:17–18 KJV

Israel was at war, and one of their best intelligence officers was the prophet Elisha. He would warn Israel's king not to send his army to certain places, because their enemies would be there. It was driving the king of Aram crazy! At first he thought there was a traitor in his ranks, until one of his officers explained that the prophet had been his downfall. So Aram's king ordered that Elisha should be captured. When intelligence reported the prophet was in Dothan, a strong force of men with chariots went to surround the city.

Elisha's new servant saw the men and their machines and warned the prophet. Despairingly, he asked what they should do.

"Fear not," Elisha answered. "For they that be with us are more than they that be with them" (6:16 KJV). Then he prayed for God to open his servant's eyes, and the man saw hills full of horses and chariots surrounding his master. God's army protected His prophet.

When the opposing army began to attack, Elisha had a battle plan: he prayed, asking God to blind his attackers. God responded. Then Elisha slipped into the ranks of the blind men and told them to follow him. He led them to his fortress hometown, Samaria, where they regained their sight.

When Israel's king heard of this, he asked if he should strike down the formerly blind soldiers. But Elisha declared that just as a king would not strike down those he'd already captured, Israel should allow these men to live. After providing a great feast for the captives, the king sent them home to Aram.

Because of the prophet's compassion, the raids that had plagued Israel for so long ended.

Elisha was a particularly effective peacemaker, and he never fought a battle, killed a man, or met with a king's representative. All his opponents suffered was temporary blindness.

When we face enemies, or even just troublesome people, are we constantly set on battle? Or are we open to a firm but gentler solution? Sometimes kindness has a powerful impact on others, when warfare would only antagonize and destroy. God provides the wisdom that will help us know when to use each. Are we listening to Him?

SECOND CHANCE

So it was, as they were burying a man,
that suddenly they spied a band of raiders;
and they put the man in the tomb of Elisha;
and when the man was let down
and touched the bones of Elisha,
he revived and stood on his feet.
2 KINGS 13:21 NKJV

Following a fifty-year ministry, Elisha died and was buried.

Every spring, Moabite raiders dropped in on Israel to pick up a few things they weren't entitled to. The Israelites were not particularly successful at fighting back. In fact, they were better at running than defending themselves. So when raiders happened by a grave site, the men who were burying another man there simply dropped the body into Elisha's tomb for safekeeping.

How amazed the grave diggers must have been when their friend revived and stood up, perfectly healthy because his defunct body had touched the prophet's. How many other hopeful Israelites brought dead bodies to touch the prophet in the days that followed?

Scripture doesn't tell us why this man was revived or what happened to him. What did he make of his second opportunity at earthly life?

God may not bring us back from death, but He gives us second chances, too. What do we do with them?

MISPLACED TRUST?

And it came to pass on a certain night that the angel of the LORD went out,
and killed in the camp of the Assyrians one hundred and eighty-five thousand;
and when people arose early in the morning, there were the corpses—all dead.
So Sennacherib king of Assyria departed and went away, returned home,
and remained at Nineveh. Now it came to pass, as he was worshiping
in the temple of Nisroch his god, that his sons Adrammelech and Sharezer
struck him down with the sword; and they escaped into the land of Ararat.
Then Esarhaddon his son reigned in his place.

2 KINGS 19:35–37 NKJV

Assyria had attacked and conquered Israel and now was looking in Judah's direction. Before the battle for Jerusalem began, Assyrian king Sennacherib sent his supreme commander, his chief officer, and his field commander to Israel to intimidate the small nation. Hadn't they seen what he'd done to the nations around them? the field commander, their spokesman, asked. How could Israel hold out? Why not give up now, make a bargain with Sennacherib, and join Assyria in battle against other nations? The commander made certain the people of Jerusalem heard these words as he spoke to Hezekiah's representatives. "Hezekiah and the Lord cannot protect you," was the gist of his message.

When King Hezekiah received reports of that message, he tore his clothes, sent for two of his best men and the top priests, and had them dress in sackcloth, a sign of mourning and repentance. Then he sent these trusted men to Isaiah the prophet, to ask him to pray for the nation. According to Assyrian records, Sennacherib had already taken forty-six fortified Judean cities when his eye fell on the nation's capital, Jerusalem.

Isaiah replied to his king with comforting words: They should not fear. The Lord had heard the terrible blasphemies spoken by the Assyrian official, who had dared to compare other nations' idols with the Lord. God would take care of everything, the prophet assured Hezekiah. King Sennacherib would hear a certain bad report and return to his own country. There he would die by the sword.

Hezekiah received a second message from Assyria, denigrating God. The faithful king went to the temple and began to pray, glorifying God and asking for deliverance. Later, he got a message from Isaiah, confirming and expanding upon the original promise. Assyria would be destroyed. But Hezekiah received a promise that though two harvests would be affected by the Assyrian attack, by the third, Israel would be planting as usual. Jerusalem would be saved by God, who would defend it without a battle.

That very night, the angel of the Lord quietly went into the Assyrian camp and put to death 185,000 men. The next morning, when the dead bodies were discovered, Sennacherib quickly decided to remove his troops from Judah. He returned to his capital, Nineveh, and never bothered Judah again.

Isaiah's prophecy of the Assyrian king's death came true, too. Years later, when he was worshipping his pagan god, two of his sons came and cut him down with a sword. Another son succeeded him as king.

Hezekiah was an admirable man who stood firm for his Lord. Even a second attempt to scare him into compromise did not work—he turned again to God in worship instead of wasting his time in fear.

The God we trust in is as reliable today as He was in Hezekiah's time. He will fight our battles for us, and often, when we trust Him in remarkable circumstances, He will respond in an unexpected way. The problem we expected may never come to pass. The difficult issue will be resolved with no action on our part. Or the enemy will simply return home, never to bother us again.

Hezekiah's trust was not misplaced. Neither will ours be.

THE POWER OF PRAYER

Hezekiah turned his face to the wall and prayed to the LORD,
"Remember, O LORD, how I have walked before you faithfully
and with wholehearted devotion and have done what is good in your eyes."
And Hezekiah wept bitterly.
2 KINGS 20:2–3

Hezekiah was very ill when Isaiah visited him and told the king to put his house in order and prepare to die. Hearing this, the ruler did not give up but prayed to his Lord instead, reminding Him how devotedly he had served Him. Hezekiah cried bitterly.

Before Isaiah could walk out of the palace, God's word directed him to return to the king with a new message: God heard his prayer and would graciously heal him. Hezekiah would have fifteen years more of life on this earth. Only two things were required of the king: he had to go to the temple in three days, and he had to be treated with a fig poultice. The king had no trouble doing either.

Hezekiah must have been mighty in prayer and a truly faithful believer, for God did not contend with his estimate of his own faithfulness, and He did as the king asked.

Will our prayers be equally powerful because we have lived as faithful Christians? When we have believed with all our lives, we open ourselves to answered prayer.

TEN STEPS BACK

*Hezekiah had asked Isaiah, "What will be the sign that the L*ORD *will heal me*
*and that I will go up to the temple of the L*ORD *on the third day from now?"*
*Isaiah answered, "This is the L*ORD*'s sign to you that the L*ORD *will do what he has*
promised: Shall the shadow go forward ten steps, or shall it go back ten steps?"
"It is a simple matter for the shadow to go forward ten steps," said Hezekiah.
*"Rather, have it go back ten steps." Then the prophet Isaiah called upon the L*ORD*,*
*and the L*ORD *made the shadow go back the ten steps*
it had gone down on the stairway of Ahaz.
2 KINGS 20:8–11

After God promised to heal King Hezekiah, the surprised ruler asked for a sign that the healing would occur. Because he was faithful, God complied. Isaiah promised that a shadow would move on the steps of Ahaz. But he left it up to the king as to which direction it would move. Hezekiah requested that the shadow do the harder move, going back ten steps, and God did as he requested.

God gave Hezekiah the sign he requested only because he was faithful. Have we so trusted Him that He can show us such grace, knowing we are not asking out of doubt?

HUMILITY AND TRUST

And, behold, there came a leper and worshipped him, saying,
Lord, if thou wilt, thou canst make me clean.
And Jesus put forth his hand, and touched him, saying,
I will; be thou clean.
And immediately his leprosy was cleansed.
MATTHEW 8:2–3 KJV

After preaching the Sermon on the Mount, Jesus turned back toward Capernaum. As He headed toward the city, a leper came near, but perhaps not too near, since those who had leprosy were considered unclean and had to stay away from the "clean" people. Though this man was unable to go to the temple and suffered physical and spiritual separation from his people, he came humbly, not angrily, to Jesus. Kneeling before Him in a worshipful attitude, he made his request with deference, leaving the ending up to the Savior.

The man's humility must have pleased the Master. He healed him in a moment, told him to offer the sacrifices required by the Law, and enjoined him not to tell anyone about what had happened. Can we doubt the former leper joyously obeyed?

When we face dire straits, can we react in similar humility and trust? Or are we so concerned about our need that we forget the power of our Lord and the respect He deserves?

IS SEEING BELIEVING?

The centurion answered and said, Lord, I am not worthy that thou shouldest come
under my roof: but speak the word only, and my servant shall be healed.
For I am a man under authority, having soldiers under me:
and I say to this man, Go, and he goeth; and to another,
Come, and he cometh; and to my servant, Do this, and he doeth it.
When Jesus heard it, he marvelled, and said to them that followed,
Verily I say unto you, I have not found so great faith, no, not in Israel.
MATTHEW 8:8–10 KJV

Romans would have considered themselves the master race in Jesus' era. They had conquered most of the known world that surrounded the Mediterranean Sea and some areas beyond it. Many probably wouldn't have cared much about a servant's illness, much less a Jewish teacher, even one who could heal. What problem couldn't the power of Rome solve?

But this man, a leader of a hundred soldiers, was a real leader. He cared enough for his paralyzed servant to humble himself and go before Jesus. As a Gentile, his claim on the Lord was tenuous, to say the least. So some of Jesus' fellow Jews went to tell the Master that this God-fearing soldier had helped them build a synagogue (see Luke 7:2–5).

But this man did not need such a testimony. His own attitude was self-explanatory. He wouldn't even call Jesus into his home, because he felt guilty, knowing it would make the Master ceremonially unclean. Looking to his military background, he gave Jesus an idea: heal the servant from a distance. If the Lord said it was done, the soldier could trust it would happen.

Jesus marveled at the man's faith, for even in Israel He'd not seen such trust. He healed the servant immediately.

Are we like the Israelites, who needed to see everything right before them, or can we trust like the faithful centurion? Though he came from another land, his trust was obviously in the Lord. What God said, he believed.

If we really believe, seeing is not all there is to believing.

IF ONLY WE ASK

And when Jesus was come into Peter's house,
he saw his wife's mother laid, and sick of a fever.
And he touched her hand, and the fever left her:
and she arose, and ministered unto them.
MATTHEW 8:14–15 KJV

Jesus not only healed the masses of people who came to Him with serious ill-nesses; when He came to Peter's house and discovered Peter's mother-in-law suffering from a fever, He went to her, took her hand, and gently helped her up. The fever left her body.

Perhaps, knowing Jesus would be coming, she had lain in bed worrying about the preparations she could not make. For as soon as she felt healthy again, she rose to minister to Jesus and His men.

Is there an illness, either spiritual or physical, that is too small to gain Jesus' attention? Isn't He aware of all that goes on in this universe? Is there anything we can hide from Him? Let's bring all our cares before our Lord's throne and share any need that comes our way. Just as He lifted up Peter's mother-in-law, He can lift us up, too, if only we ask.

HE IS LORD!

Then he got into the boat and his disciples followed him.
Without warning, a furious storm came up on the lake, so that the waves swept
over the boat. But Jesus was sleeping. The disciples went and woke him, saying,
"Lord, save us! We're going to drown!" He replied, "You of little faith, why
are you so afraid?" Then he got up and rebuked the winds and the waves,
and it was completely calm. The men were amazed and asked,
"What kind of man is this? Even the winds and the waves obey him!"
MATTHEW 8:23–27

Since childhood, this has been one of our favorite dramas: the disciples battling the waves while Jesus sleeps and the wonderful miracle that follows. In a few short verses we get a vivid picture. The master storytellers of scripture give us a brief, vibrant vignette of Jesus and His authority over the world.

Some of the men in the boat, probably the ones sailing it, were extremely familiar with the Sea of Galilee. Fishermen Peter and Andrew, John and James had doubtless sailed on this body of water since childhood. They understood the vagaries of its winds. For this sea lies between two ranges of hills and is about 700 feet below sea level, so the winds filling the sails of the first-century small fishing boats that plied this sea were erratic. Cool Mediterranean winds met the warm air in the sea's basin, and strong winds and sudden storms often resulted.

This was hardly the first sudden storm the fishermen had run into. They'd honed their sailing skills here. They'd sailed with a boat piled with a full catch and with one empty except for a few men. They made their livings from the sea's bountiful schools of fish.

Now these sailors probably called out sharply to one another as they sought to keep their boat under control: "Grab this line." "Do that." "Head into that wave, or we'll be swamped." The rest of the disciples probably huddled down, trying to stay out of their way and waiting to see what would happen. In a small, open vessel, at the best of times it would have been a very wet ride.

Perhaps some of the "landlubbers" first cried out to Jesus as the small vessel tipped first to one side then to the other and rose and fell on the churning waves. Water entered the boat. Fear filled their hearts, and their trust in the sailors waned. The fishermen were probably too busy looking to their boat to give thought to aught else. Or maybe Peter had shouted a command to the others to wake Jesus before they all drowned.

The fearful disciples had seen Jesus do miraculous healings, and in this dire situation, they turned to their exhausted Master, who slept on a pillow in the stern (see Mark 4:38). "Lord, save us! We're going to drown!" they cried.

Jesus awoke and took command, but first He reminded His disciples of their lack of faith. With Him there, what had they to fear? Realistically, would God really have ended this earthly mission by letting His Son's chosen men drown? Then He rebuked the winds and waves, and all was quiet.

The disciples had gotten what they asked for, yet they sat in the steady boat, stunned. Terrified, they asked each other who this was, who could do such a miracle.

We may never set foot in a sailing vessel, but our lives are also filled with storms: emotional, physical, and spiritual. Like the disciples, we turn to Jesus for our answers. But are we surprised when He answers us in powerful ways? He is God. It was the only conclusion the disciples could come to as they watched the sun sparkle on a sea that lapped gently at the sides of the boat. It's the only conclusion we can come to, based on the scriptural evidence and our own experiences with Him.

HOLD ON!

When Jesus arrived at the official's home, he saw the noisy crowd
and heard the funeral music. "Get out!" he told them.
"The girl isn't dead; she's only asleep." But the crowd laughed at him.
After the crowd was put outside, however, Jesus went in
and took the girl by the hand, and she stood up!
The report of this miracle swept through the entire countryside.
MATTHEW 9:23–26 NLT

As soon as Jesus stepped off the boat that sailed the water He'd just stilled, a crowd began to surround Him. Through it pushed a man on a mission. Mark 5:22 tells us his name was Jairus, and he was the synagogue leader—a man who either performed administrative duties for his congregation or held this as an honorary title. Whichever it was, he was an important man. He came to Jesus trusting that He could heal his only daughter. Jesus headed toward Jairus's home. But before he could take many steps, a hurting woman stopped Him with her need.

Hurry, hurry, hurry, Jairus must have been thinking. While Jesus spoke a few words to the woman, men of his own household came to tell Jairus his daughter was dead. How the fond father's face and heart must have fallen. But Jesus told him not to fear, just believe. Taking with them only His closest disciples, Peter, James, and John, Jesus and Jairus headed for the synagogue leader's home.

By the time Jesus reached that house, the flute players for the funeral had already been hired. The Lord told them and the wailing and crying crowd surrounding them to go home, for the child was simply asleep. They laughed at Him.

Inside, with the parents and His few disciples in attendance, Jesus took the child by one hand and said, "Little girl, I say to you, get up!" (Mark 5:41). She stood up and walked around, astonishing her parents and the disciples. After warning them not to tell anyone about this, Jesus told them to feed the girl and left.

But of course the story flew around the countryside. Who could resist passing on such a tale, and even if the parents kept silence, no one could miss the little girl who was once dead prancing around her family home, no doubt joyous at having received her life back.

Jairus came to Jesus with faith. But when he heard of his daughter's death, how grieved and hopeless he must have felt. Yet Jesus, honoring that first bit of faith, told him not to worry. "Hold on to your faith," was His message in this father's darkest hour.

That's the message Jesus gives to us, too. Nothing is too impossible for Him, no situation too bleak for us to trust that His help will not change our lives. Let's hold on, no matter what lies before us.

ADMIT IT

Just then a woman who had suffered for twelve years
with constant bleeding came up behind him.
She touched the fringe of his robe, for she thought,
"If I can just touch his robe, I will be healed."
Jesus turned around, and when he saw her he said,
"Daughter, be encouraged! Your faith has made you well."
And the woman was healed at that moment.
MATTHEW 9:20–22 NLT

As Jairus called Jesus away to heal his daughter, a poor woman got up some courage. *If I can just touch his clothing, I will be healed,* she thought. She wasn't looking for attention, just an end to the bleeding that had made her ritually impure and destroyed her life. Though she had sought out many doctors, spending all her money, no healing resulted.

As her fingers reached out and touched the fabric, she felt the bleeding stop. But instead of being a quiet testimony to Jesus' power, her miracle was about to go public. For the Lord turned around and asked who had touched Him. His disciples made light of it, since a crowd pressed around Him, but Jesus knew power had gone from Him. When the trembling woman admitted what had happened, He confirmed her healing with His words.

Sometimes we'd prefer a quiet testimony, perhaps only to our friends. But Jesus wants the Good News spread. Are we willing, like this woman, to admit to our healing?

SHRIVELED HEARTS

Then He said to the man, "Stretch out your hand."
And he stretched it out, and it was restored as whole as the other.
MATTHEW 12:13 NKJV

As we read this single verse, we're likely to write it off as merely another minor miracle. But reading the context of this verse, we may come to another conclusion.

This was a confrontation between Jesus and the Pharisees, a small group of men who seemed to have godly devotion but had gotten caught up in traditions and formal observances rather than heartfelt faith. The Pharisees, who only numbered about six thousand in Jesus' day, had influence in the religious community. Some were even part of the Sanhedrin, the Jewish ruling body.

Doctrinally, Jesus usually agreed with the Pharisees, but here He takes them on. They wanted Him to wait until the end of the Sabbath to heal, but He pointed out their inconsistency of thought: they allowed an animal to be rescued on the Sabbath but committed a man to suffering. Then, right in their faces, He healed the man with a shriveled hand.

The Pharisees didn't have a theology problem: they had a heart problem. Can we take them as an example of what not to do and instead love others as Jesus calls us to? Then neither our hearts nor spirits will be shriveled.

OUT OF LITTLE, MUCH

"Bring them here to me," [Jesus] said. And he directed the people to sit down on the grass. Taking the five loaves and the two fish and looking up to heaven, he gave thanks and broke the loaves. Then he gave them to the disciples, and the disciples gave them to the people. They all ate and were satisfied, and the disciples picked up twelve basketfuls of broken pieces that were left over. The number of those who ate was about five thousand men, besides women and children.
MATTHEW 14:18–21

After hearing that His cousin, John the Baptist, had been beheaded, Jesus withdrew by boat to Bethsaida. But the crowds hounded Him, following on foot. Putting aside His own desires, the Master began healing the sick. Then, feeling compassion for all the people, He taught them until evening.

As the shadows lengthened, Jesus' disciples came to Him, suggesting that He send the people out to pick up some fast food before night came. In this out-of-the-way place, they reminded Him, there were few spots where His listeners could find any food at all, much less enough for such a crowd. Knowing full well what He planned to do, Jesus told them the people did not need to leave and asked the disciples to feed them.

Surprise must have filled their faces at that request, but Andrew offered the best he had: he'd met a boy who had brought along five small barley loaves and a couple of fish. But how could so little feed so many? this faithful follower wondered. Despite the many healings they'd witnessed, the disciples seemingly had no clue what was about to occur.

Jesus commanded all the people to sit down, and the disciples passed on the message to the crowd. Five thousand men, not counting the women and children, plunked down in the dirt.

Jesus took the boy's pitifully small amount of food. After giving thanks, He broke the loaves and passed them to the disciples, who handed them out. How amazed everyone must have been when five loaves turned into well over five thousand, and two fish fed all the thousands sitting in the grass around Jesus.

Everyone had a full meal out of one boy's small dinner.

Jesus told His disciples to gather the uneaten pieces. The Jews of that era saw bread as a gift from God that should not be wasted—its scraps were always gathered at the end of a meal. The twelve each filled a small basket with bread and fish leftovers.

The meal had not started with the most impressive of ingredients. This would have been a poor boy's dinner, not the finer bread that the wealthy consumed. But even if the food was not gourmet quality, the miracle the spectators saw performed was more than worth their time. As they ate, astonished friends must have chattered about the day's healings and about the multiplication of the bare essentials of a meal into catering for the whole crowd. It had been an eventful day, and what a joyous one for those who had been healed.

Out of such a meager meal, Jesus fed many, to the surprise of His disciples. Do we, too, expect so little from our Lord that we doubt His ability to solve our crises? Though we bring our needs before Him, do we feel we also need to describe the solution to Him? Like the disciples, we need to ask ourselves whom we address here: Is He Lord, or simply a person? Does He rule the universe, or everything but the universe of our hearts?

He brings much out of little. He can do that with our hearts, too, if we are willing.

WALK ON WATER

Immediately he made the disciples get into the boat and go before him to the other side, while he dismissed the crowds. And after he had dismissed the crowds, he went up on the mountain by himself to pray. When evening came, he was there alone, but the boat by this time was a long way from the land, beaten by the waves, for the wind was against them. And in the fourth watch of the night he came to them, walking on the sea. But when the disciples saw him walking on the sea, they were terrified, and said, "It is a ghost!" and they cried out in fear. But immediately Jesus spoke to them, saying, "Take heart; it is I. Do not be afraid."
MATTHEW 14:22–27 ESV

Right after feeding more than five thousand, Jesus dispatched the disciples off in their boat and sent the crowds home. Then He continued what was probably His original purpose in going off alone: He went to pray.

As dusk settled over the sky, Jesus stood alone on the shore. His disciples were having a rough time sailing. The wind was coming pretty much from the direction in which they were headed, so they had to tack back and forth, moving a little at a time toward their goal. In addition, the waves worked against them. Between three and six in the morning, the tired and wet disciples saw Jesus coming toward them, walking on the water.

Water isn't exactly the sidewalk anyone would expect a person to walk on. Terrified at the sight of Jesus on the water, the disciples came to a quick and somewhat logical solution: They were looking at a ghost. After all, a ghost would be lightweight enough to appear above the water. they cried out in fear.

Jesus soothed them, assuring them He was no ghost and telling them not to fear.

Practical Peter wanted proof. "Lord, if it is you, command me to come to you on the water," he demanded (Matthew 14:28 ESV).

Jesus called him to Himself, and courageous Peter stepped out of the boat onto the water. Watching Jesus, the disciple walked toward Him. His trust lay fully in the Lord, and as much as it was a miracle that Jesus walked on water, it was even more so that Peter could do so through His power. But as he got out into the whipping wind, Peter began to fear and started to sink into the water. "Lord, save me," he cried out (14:30 ESV).

Jesus immediately grabbed hold of the sinking disciple. Chastising Peter for his doubts, He saved him from a watery death. As soon as the two men got in the boat, the wind stopped roaring in their ears and the water was calm.

All twelve disciples, understanding what this meant, worshipped Him. For there remained no doubt in their minds that one who could do these things was God.

When we read this story, whom do we see ourselves as? Is it the eleven disciples huddling in the boat, afraid of the man who walks on the sea? Could he be Jesus or an evil being? Or do we see ourselves as foolhardy Peter, who gathers up his courage, steps out of the boat, but is distracted by the sights around him and begins to sink?

The truth of the matter is that whichever disciple we are, we're prone to failure. Under our own power, we can never effectively live the Christian life. But when Jesus fills our hearts and spirits with His Spirit and we look steadily at Him, we too can walk on water. We may never set foot on a sea, but spiritually we can do things we'd never done before.

Ready to look Jesus straight in the eye and step out of the boat?

DOING LAPS

Then Jesus called his disciples to him and said, "I have compassion on the crowd
because they have been with me now three days and have nothing to eat.
And I am unwilling to send them away hungry, lest they faint on the way."
And the disciples said to him, "Where are we to get enough bread in
such a desolate place to feed so great a crowd?" And Jesus said to them,
"How many loaves do you have?" They said, "Seven, and a few small fish."
And directing the crowd to sit down on the ground,
he took the seven loaves and the fish, and having given thanks
he broke them and gave them to the disciples,
and the disciples gave them to the crowds.
And they all ate and were satisfied.
And they took up seven baskets full of the broken pieces left over.
MATTHEW 15:32–37 ESV

Sometimes we may feel as if God has us doing laps: just when we think we have
a faith concept down pat, it returns to our lives. Perhaps that's the way at least
one of the disciples felt when compassionate Jesus asked how they should feed
the four thousand folks who'd come to Him for healing. He'd healed many bodies, and now, after three days, even those who had brought food along were out
of it. So Jesus planned to feed the whole crowd before Him.

Haven't we already done this for a larger group? the more alert of the Twelve
must have been thinking. Someone asked where they could get a truckload
of bread anyway. Yet when Jesus requested them, the disciples immediately
directed Jesus to a smaller quantity of loaves and fish. Again Jesus gave thanks
and started to distribute the food. A second time, everyone ate and was satisfied.
The disciples picked up the leftovers.

This time, the surprise must not have been so great. Jesus had done it
before, and doubtless word of the previous miracle had spread. But surely the
recipients were thankful they'd go home with full stomachs.

The disciples probably never forgot Jesus' compassionate lesson. A second
time they'd seen Him care for those who needed food. Though the crowd was
sometimes irritating and certainly interfered with His plans, Jesus did not hold
it against them. Instead He gave them all they required.

Have we done laps lately? Is God trying to impress something on our
hearts? Let's not become resentful. Instead let's benefit from it by taking the
message to heart and making it a permanent part of our spiritual lives.

RECOGNITION

"Nevertheless, lest we offend them, go to the sea,
cast in a hook, and take the fish that comes up first.
And when you have opened its mouth,
you will find a piece of money; take that
and give it to them for Me and you."
MATTHEW 17:27 NKJV

When we read this story of Peter's faux pas, we feel for him. After all, he meant well enough, trying to make it clear to the Pharisees that Jesus was a faithful Jew. Perhaps it never entered Peter's mind that Jesus wouldn't pay the temple tax established by Moses and repeated throughout Israel's history.

Jesus points out to His disciple that as the Son of David and the Son of God, it is not for Him to have to pay a tax. How foolish Peter must have felt when the Lord reminded him He was the honored, not just another worshipper. Yet Jesus will not unnecessarily offend the Pharisees, so He provides the money for both Himself and Peter in a miraculous way—that had to be the most unusual catch Peter ever had, and he'd certainly never forget it.

Do we recognize Jesus as the powerful Lord He is, or when we witness, do we bend the truth a bit so people will think kindly of Him? If so, in the end, we may do more damage to His reputation than we expected.

DOUBT OR BELIEF?

In the morning, as [Jesus] was returning to the city, he became hungry.
And seeing a fig tree by the wayside, he went to it and found nothing on it
but only leaves. And he said to it, "May no fruit ever come from you again!"
And the fig tree withered at once.
MATTHEW 21:18–19 ESV

On the day following His triumphal entry into Jerusalem, Jesus headed from Bethany, where He'd spent the night, to Jerusalem. Hungry, when He saw a fig tree heavy with leaves, it seemed that though it was early for fruit, since it had the leaves that indicated so, it should be bearing. But when He neared the tree, it was barren.

In an unusual event, Jesus cursed the tree. None would eat from it again. When He and His disciples passed that way the next day, the tree was withered (see Mark 11:20).

Some scholars assume the fig tree is a symbol of Israel and that this is a curse upon that nation, but in the text that directly follows, Jesus speaks instead of faith rather than doubt and the power of believing prayer.

The first application may not closely touch our lives. The second will. Do we have faith that God's works will come to pass, or do we doubt? How will that affect our prayers?

MERCIFUL DARKNESS

Now from the sixth hour there was darkness over all the land until the ninth hour.
And about the ninth hour Jesus cried out with a loud voice, saying,
"Eli, Eli, lema sabachthani?" that is,
"My God, my God, why have you forsaken me?"
MATTHEW 27:45–46 ESV

Following a kangaroo court trial, Jesus had been forced to march from Pilate's residence in Jerusalem to Golgotha. Mocking voices followed Him onto the cross. Scripture provides all the details of the people around Him, and every event is laid out. As if on a stage, the entire history of the morning plays out before our eyes. But around noon, a mysterious event occurs when a strange darkness covers the land.

The brief description of the event in scripture gives us few clues about how the miraculous darkness happened. "The sun stopped shining," Luke simply reports (23:45). Many assume this was an eclipse of the sun, but if so, surely the timing of it was still perfectly miraculous, for it began at the perfect moment and lasted only three hours, the time during which Jesus was on the cross. God's Son was mercifully hidden from the light of day as He suffered for humanity's sin.

The darkness that covered the earth as Jesus suffered certainly symbolizes sin and the removal of light from the Jews who did not accept this permanent sacrifice for their sin. But did the people who observed it pass it off as a "business as usual" eclipse, or did they recognize the connection between the Crucifixion and the sky's darkening? Scripture does not tell us that as He died any Jews turned with fear or recognition of their own unbelief. But some time after all the events were ended, a large number of priests came to the faith (see Acts 6:7). Perhaps they remembered Amos 8:9–10 NIV: "'In that day,' declares the Sovereign LORD, 'I will make the sun go down at noon and darken the earth in broad daylight. . . . I will make that time like mourning for an only son and the end of it like a bitter day.'"

Perhaps the mercy of darkness that covered the Lord's suffering is also shown to us today. For who among us can really stand a clear view of what our sin cost God's Son? When we think of it, even at Easter, don't our eyes turn down in shame, our spirits seek to escape the enormity of our own failings? Some sin we can admit, but the whole of it would topple our spirits in a moment. Can we bear the full knowledge that is was for our every wrong that He cried out in pain, "My God, my God, why have you forsaken me?"

Our merciful God confronts us with just enough knowledge of our sin to bring us to Himself. The pain we feel when we recognize our own wrongs or the emptiness that draws us to Him may wrench our lives, but they do not destroy us. In His grace, He will not give us more than we can bear.

But we do need to recognize that our sins were paid for on the cross. For us Jesus suffered and died. And we must acknowledge the grace that paid for it all and demands every bit of our lives in return. As we understand that, the darkness is no longer dark, for we live in the brightness of eternity with Jesus, our Lord and Savior.

THE HOLIEST PLACE

And when Jesus had cried out again in a loud voice, he gave up his spirit.
At that moment the curtain of the temple was torn in two from top to bottom.
MATTHEW 27:50–51

At the moment Jesus died, the world changed forever. Believers no longer needed to make animal sacrifices for their sins. The final sacrifice had been made, and through Jesus, people now had direct access to God.

In the Jewish temple, a curtain separated the Holy of Holies, the holiest part of the temple, from the rest of the worship center. Only the high priest could go there, and then only once yearly, with a blood sacrifice. The Holy of Holies was an awesome place containing, among other things, the ark of the covenant, which held the tablets of the Law, and Aaron's rod, which had budded in the wilderness when the Israelites questioned Moses' authority. When the Jews thought of the Holy of Holies, they understood how far they were from God's perfection. And they feared God because they understood that He could not tolerate their sin.

God opened this holiest place to all His people through the sacrifice of Jesus. That wasn't because God had changed. He was still as holy as ever, as awesome as He'd been before. But now humanity's sins had been permanently forgiven through His Son, and people could approach Him with confidence. They no longer needed to walk into the holy of holies with fear. The blood of the Son had been shed to bring before God's throne those who believe in Him.

The temple curtain that tore from top to bottom was no flimsy bit of chiffon, but a thick, durable linen, in which the threads had been doubled over numerous times. No stray wind flew through the temple and caused this. No priest accidentally caused any rent in the fabric. God was intentionally and personally ending the separation between His people and Himself. After all, who else could rip forty cubits of fabric from the top?

Did the priests wonder how and why this happened? Is that one reason why, in the book of Acts, so many of them came to faith in Jesus as the Messiah? Perhaps, like the centurion, they saw proof that this was surely God's Son.

Through Jesus' sacrifice, we have direct access to God, the Holy One. But do we sufficiently recognize His holiness, or are we quick to treat Him as a heavenly Santa who should bow to our wishes? If so, we are not worshipping the Lord of the Bible. Though He gives us direct access to His throne room, He is not pleased if we treat Him lightly.

The Lord we serve is as awesome as His holiest of places showed Him to be. Do we treat Him with great respect? Let's not forget who He really is, for though He loves us deeply, He is still the Lord of all.

NEED PROOF?

The earth shook and the rocks split. The tombs broke open and the bodies of many holy people who had died were raised to life. They came out of the tombs, and after Jesus' resurrection they went into the holy city and appeared to many people.
MATTHEW 27:51–53

Just as the temple curtain tore from top to bottom, the earth convulsed, breaking open tombs. This was not simply a geological coincidence. Rocks split, and the heavy stones that barred the way into first-century Jewish tombs may have rolled away. This heaving of the ground occurred just at the end of Jesus' earthly life, along with another, more stunning event. According to the book of Matthew, the only Gospel to record this, after Jesus' resurrection many believers were also resurrected. Were they given life for a few minutes, a few hours, a few days, or much longer? We don't know. But imagine the shock it must have been for loving relatives to suddenly see Uncle Samuel or Aunt Rebekah alive again! What were they to make of it?

In case the questioning relatives had doubts of their own sanity, many others saw the resurrected ones, too. But the event meant more than a return to friends and family. With Jesus' resurrection, death ended not only for Himself, but for all who trust in Him. The risen believers picture the work His resurrection accomplishes.

No one in Jerusalem that week could have ignored the events that took place when Jesus died. Those who came up with an explanation for the temple curtain ripping so unexpectedly might also have discounted the earthquake but would have been hard pressed to explain this resurrection reported by multiple witnesses. Only a determined but illogical decision to suppress the truth would have covered it over. And that's what many people in Jerusalem must have chosen.

God probably has not brought a loved one to life to get our attention, but He has placed many indicators in our paths that show us the truth about Jesus and His resurrection. Will we deny them? Then our hearts are as stubbornly against Him as were some of those first-century Jews'.

EMPTY TOMB!

Toward the dawn of the first day of the week,
Mary Magdalene and the other Mary went to see the tomb.
And behold, there was a great earthquake,
for an angel of the Lord descended from heaven
and came and rolled back the stone and sat on it.
His appearance was like lightning, and his clothing white as snow.
And for fear of him the guards trembled and became like dead men.
But the angel said to the women, "Do not be afraid, for I know that you seek Jesus
who was crucified. He is not here, for he has risen, as he said. Come, see the place
where he lay. Then go quickly and tell his disciples that he has risen from the dead,
and behold, he is going before you to Galilee; there you will see him."
MATTHEW 28:1–7 ESV

Another earthquake heralded what may have been the greatest surprise for both the nearest disciples and the occasional followers of Jesus. Though He'd warned about His death and spoken of His resurrection, clearly they had not quite understood what to expect. The women who went to His tomb the day after the Sabbath, though faithful followers, were probably fairly clueless about what the future held. But it was to the women that news of the greatest event in church history was given.

The two Marys came to the tomb with some other women, according to the other Gospels (see Mark 16:1; Luke 24:10). As they neared the grave, the earth moved as an angel of the Lord came down (Luke and John report there were two angels). At least the angel solved one problem the women had discussed: How would they open the tomb? For the angel sat on the stone that should have barred their way but had been moved aside by his power. How they'd have access to the body was the least important issue now, for they received perplexing news from the terrifying messenger: Jesus was no longer there.

The guards who had been placed on tomb duty to make sure no believers took Jesus' body trembled at the sight of an angelic presence and "became like dead men." Once the guards were peacefully out of the way, the angel gave his message. And he sent the women to the eleven, to tell them about the Resurrection and send them to Galilee.

Fear and joy filled the women's hearts as they headed off to tell the disciples. On their way to see Peter, John, and the others, Jesus met them, told them not to fear, and repeated the angel's message for the eleven.

Not surprisingly, when Jesus' closest disciples heard the story, they had their doubts. They hadn't expected this, despite what Jesus had told them before His death. But Peter and John went to check out the story anyway. Thunderstruck by the physical proof there, they believed.

Faithful Mary Magdalene stayed behind, weeping at the loss of her Lord. Because she remained, she had the first opportunity to see the risen Christ, though it took her awhile to recognize Him.

Those who witnessed the truth of the Resurrection could hardly believe their eyes. The events that followed proved that in reality seeing is not always believing. But we can be sympathetic to their plight. The news they received was unlike anything that had happened before. Even the return to life they'd seen with Lazarus could not have prepared them for a crucified man being resurrected. They'd seen Jesus' corpse, and unlike some modern skeptics, they knew that He could not spring to life simply because He'd been left in a cool place.

To us today, the news of the Resurrection can seem beyond belief. But it is the one great proof that Jesus was who He said He was and that He does what He claimed He could. The evidence is aimed at faith, not scientific proof, but God has given us all we need to know. Will we believe, or will we stand with the skeptical first-century Jews who never looked inside the empty tomb?

SHOUTING SPIRIT

And immediately there was in their synagogue a man with an unclean spirit.
And he cried out, "What have you to do with us, Jesus of Nazareth?
Have you come to destroy us? I know who you are—the Holy One of God."
But Jesus rebuked him, saying, "Be silent, and come out of him!"
And the unclean spirit, convulsing him and crying out
with a loud voice, came out of him.
MARK 1:23–26 ESV

No sooner had Jesus begun His teaching ministry in Capernaum than the voice of a man with an evil spirit interrupted Him. Though his words seem to praise Jesus, they are merely an identification of His power and authority—something to be feared by evil spirits, as this one rightly assesses. In agony, the spirit cries out against the Holy One.

Jesus immediately quelled the interruption. The words politely translated "be silent" literally mean "be muzzled." Then he freed the man from the demonic being. In a noisy manner, the demon left the man's body.

Jesus' audience had been marveling at His authority in teaching; now they were amazed. A man with little formal education, who could teach this way and free men from demons! Their gossip filled Galilee in short order.

Do we recognize Jesus' authority over the spirit, as they did? Or do our spirits shout against Him? If so, we need to come to Him for cleansing so we can walk in His ways.

PARDON ME!

"But that you may know that the Son of Man has authority
on earth to forgive sins. . . ." He said to the paralytic,
"I tell you, get up, take your mat and go home." He got up, took his mat
and walked out in full view of them all. This amazed everyone
and they praised God, saying, "We have never seen anything like this!"
MARK 2:10–12

Though the paralyzed man lay on a mat, unable to help himself, he had four good friends or family members who went to great lengths to help him. For when they discovered the way to Jesus was blocked by a crowd, they climbed on the roof and dug through it so they could lower the man down to Jesus for healing.

What a shock it must have been for the people in the room with Jesus to hear the noise of the roof removal, then see the man lowered down on his mat. Perhaps willing arms reached up to grab the one who could do nothing but hope nobody dropped him.

The faith of his friends encouraged Jesus to heal the man. "Son, your sins are forgiven," He declared (2:5).

While the hurting man looked on in horror, the teachers of the law started a debate with Jesus on whether or not He could forgive sins. Here this helpless fellow lay, and the religious men wanted to start an argument! The man on the mat probably wanted to break in, "Pardon me, but could you let Him heal me first!"

Not losing sight of the importance of this healing, Jesus quickly asked which was easier, to tell someone his sins were forgiven, or to heal him? But to prove His point, He declared the man healed, then told him to take up his mat and go home.

While the crowd was praising God, how much more loudly the four friends must have extolled Him. The one whom they'd lowered on a mat could walk freely and strongly and live in a body that was no longer sin-damaged.

Who are we? The paralyzed man, who had lost his life to sin? The loving friends, who worked hard to see him healed? Or the litigious teachers, nailing down the theology of the issue before the man can be helped?

What will most glorify God today? Our personally turning from sin? Helping others come to faith and turn from wrongdoing? Or discussing the theological implications? Having good theology is important. But it does not substitute for the other two. Loving action that recognizes the claims of Jesus is more critical than senseless debates. When we know His power, we live in it.

A LEGION OF DEMONS

And Jesus asked him, "What is your name?" He replied,
"My name is Legion, for we are many." And he begged him earnestly
not to send them out of the country. Now a great herd of pigs was feeding there on
the hillside, and they begged him, saying, "Send us to the pigs; let us enter them."
So he gave them permission. And the unclean spirits came out,
and entered the pigs, and the herd, numbering about two thousand,
rushed down the steep bank into the sea and were drowned in the sea.
MARK 5:9–13 ESV

Had the media existed then, this story could have made headlines around the world. Even without them, you can bet descriptions flew around the Gerasene region for weeks. Gossip and storytelling took the place of media in that age.

Jesus and His disciples had crossed to this Gentile area, and no sooner had Jesus debarked than a man with an evil spirit emerged from the cavern tomb where he lived. His friends and neighbors had tried to chain him, perhaps for their protection and his own, but he had broken the bonds. No one could control him, and according to the book of Luke, he did not even wear clothes (see 8:27). As he lived among the tombs, he cut himself and cried out day and night.

This miserable man ran to Jesus and fell on his knees. The demon within him shouted at the top of his voice, "What have you to do with me, Jesus, Son of the Most High God? I adjure you by God, do not torment me" (Mark 5:7 ESV). How ironic that a demon would claim the name of God, whom he had refused to serve. But though humans could deny Jesus was Messiah, no demon could ignore His real identity.

The demon spoke these words because Jesus had already been commanding him to leave the man, and he didn't like it. Calmly, Jesus asked his name. "Legion," he replied, for the man had many demons controlling him. This was the beginning of a spiritual battle, for in the first century, knowing a name was believed to mean one had power over the named one.

Recognizing the inevitable, the demons asked Jesus not to send them back to hell, but to allow them to stay in the pagan country they now inhabited and to let them enter a herd of pigs feeding on a nearby hillside.

Jesus allowed them to enter the pigs, and they immediately took them over as they had overtaken the man. The troublesome demons caused the two thousand unclean beasts to rush down the steep bank and drown in the sea.

The herdsmen ran to tell the news to all they met, and soon Jesus had a crowd around Him. When they saw the once demon-possessed man sitting there clothed and in his right mind, they became so fearful they begged Jesus to leave.

The man who had been healed wanted to go back into Israel with Jesus, but He left him in his hometown as a testimony to God. The excited man must have immediately started to tell his neighbors, who had already heard all the gossip. His experience would have been hard to hide, anyway.

There are always at least two ways of thinking about spiritual things. The demon-possessed man's neighbors could have looked at his healing and thought, *How wonderful! A man who can do that is certainly worth following.* But they didn't. Perhaps because of the loss of the pigs—was their owner a big man in town?—they worried about what might happen. They couldn't wait to get this "troublemaker" away. How many other healings did they miss because they were unwilling hosts?

Jesus has power over all spirits. But the heart that resists Him may well miss out on the good He wants to perform in that life. God will woo the sinner, but He will not bash down doors. He calls us with His grace, but some still remain on their sinful path.

God is calling you, wooing you with His grace. Will you fall on your knees and worship Him, like the healed man who had nothing to lose, or will you cling to your pigs and lose what is to gain?

UNSTOPPED

Then they brought to Him one who was deaf and had an impediment
in his speech, and they begged Him to put His hand on him. And He took him
aside from the multitude, and put His fingers in his ears, and He spat and touched
his tongue. Then, looking up to heaven, He sighed, and said to him, "Ephphatha,"
that is, "Be opened." Immediately his ears were opened, and the impediment
of his tongue was loosed, and he spoke plainly.
MARK 7:32–35 NKJV

The man brought before Jesus this day had double trouble: deafness and a speech impediment. How limited his life was. He was trapped inside himself, with few ways of communicating with the world.

Then someone brought him to Jesus and begged the Master to heal him. Jesus took the man aside, perhaps so that he'd not be overwhelmed by the noise of the crowds about him.

Jesus put his fingers in the man's ears, spit and touched the man's tongue, and looked up into heaven. He commanded the ears to open, and the man's ears began to function and his voice spoke out plainly. In a few moments he'd been perfectly healed and Jesus had fulfilled Isaiah's prophecy that the ears of the deaf would be unstopped and the tongue of the dumb would sing (see Isaiah 35:5–6).

We who have our voices and the ability to hear, are our faculties open to God? Are we praising Him with all He's given us?

MARVELOUS THINGS

And some people brought to him a blind man and begged him to touch him.
And he took the blind man by the hand and led him out of the village,
and when he had spit on his eyes and laid his hands on him, he asked him,
"Do you see anything?" And he looked up and said,
"I see men, but they look like trees, walking."
Then Jesus laid his hands on his eyes again; and
he opened his eyes, his sight was restored,
and he saw everything clearly.
MARK 8:22–25 ESV

Again desperate friends or family members brought a blind man to Jesus. The Master took him by the hand and led him apart from his friends. He spit on the man's eyes—for what reason no one knows—and laid hands on him. When He asked the man if he saw, he indicated partial vision—the only case in scripture in which Jesus did not heal someone immediately and fully. Scripture does not give us a reason for this gradual improvement.

But when Jesus touched him again, the healing was complete.

Do we doubt that Jesus can help us? Perhaps that's why we receive less than we expect from Him. Let's trust in Him and see marvelous things in our spiritual lives.

BOLD FAITH

When he heard that it was Jesus of Nazareth, he began to shout,
"Jesus, Son of David, have mercy on me!"
Many rebuked him and told him to be quiet, but he shouted all the more,
"Son of David, have mercy on me!" . . .
"What do you want me to do for you?" Jesus asked him.
The blind man said, "Rabbi, I want to see."
"Go," said Jesus, "your faith has healed you."
Immediately he received his sight and followed Jesus along the road.
MARK 10:47–48, 51–52

Bartimaeus, a blind beggar, sat by the side of the road. Being unable to ply a trade, he made his living asking others for charity, a humiliating situation for anyone of this man's spirit.

Though he couldn't see, one day Bartimaeus heard a commotion going on and asked what it was. The people around him, probably the start of quite a crowd, answered that Jesus was coming by. The blind man immediately began shouting at the top of his lungs, "Jesus, Son of David, have mercy on me!" (10:47).

Those around the blind man began to take him to task. "Be quiet!" was probably the nicest rebuke he heard that day. But their discouragement just made the desperate man shout louder. Doubtless he wasn't at the front of the crowd, and he wanted Jesus to know he was there.

Jesus heard the hoopla and ordered His disciples to bring the man to Him. "Cheer up! On your feet! He's calling you," they told Bartimaeus (verse 49). The fearless man threw off his cloak, jumped to his feet, and came to Jesus.

When the Master asked what he wanted, Bartimaeus decisively told Him he wanted to see. No doubts in this man's mind or heart. He knew what he needed and had no qualms about asking for it. Jesus told him his faith had healed him.

The once-blind man immediately followed Jesus, praising God as he went. His joy was contagious, and others joined his praise party. Unlike some of those He healed, the Master did not tell him to stay at his home in Jericho. Can we doubt that He had a mission for Bartimaeus in the larger world?

Are we like blind Bartimaeus, sitting by the side of a spiritual road? If so, do we know what we want from Jesus, and are we unafraid to ask? The blind man's boldness brought him just the miracle he needed: his faith made him whole.

RECOGNIZING THE LORD

And Simon answered, "Master, we toiled all night and took nothing!
But at your word I will let down the nets."
And when they had done this, they enclosed a large number of fish,
and their nets were breaking.
LUKE 5:5–6 ESV

Pressured by the crowds surrounding Him, Jesus asked some fishermen for help. Peter and at least one more man (perhaps his brother, Andrew), who had probably been listening in on the Master's sermon, left their net washing to take Jesus on board. On the edge of the Sea of Galilee, their vessel became a temporary pulpit.

When Jesus finished teaching, He told Peter to go fishing. Though the fisherman had his doubts—he hadn't caught anything in a hard night's work—he headed for the deep water.

Peter caught so many fish his nets began to break. So he signaled his partners, James and John, to come help. As the second vessel came alongside, they tossed fish into that boat, too. And soon the two boats were all but overflowing.

Astonished at their catch, the fishermen knew what to make of it. Peter fell at the miracle-worker's feet and declared Him Lord.

We, too, see Jesus do astonishing things. How do we react? Will we call Him Lord, too?

A WONDROUS WORK

As he approached the town gate, a dead person was being carried out—the only
son of his mother, and she was a widow. And a large crowd from the town was
with her. When the Lord saw her, his heart went out to her and he said, "Don't
cry." Then he went up and touched the coffin, and those carrying it stood still.
He said, "Young man, I say to you, get up!" The dead man sat up
and began to talk, and Jesus gave him back to his mother.
LUKE 7:12–15

At Nain's gate, Jesus and the crowd around Him were met by a funeral cortege. The dead young man's mother, a widow, led the way to the burial place, with the men carrying her son's bier behind her, surrounded by all her friends, family, and neighbors. She wept at the loss of her only son—the one she depended on for her support. For though a large crowd followed her today, where would they be for the rest of her life? At that moment, the widow's future looked rather grim.

Touched by her situation, the Lord approached and gently told her not to cry. She must have looked up at Him in shock. Her only son had died, and this stranger told her not to cry? If she shouldn't cry at this, what should she cry about?

But unlike some men, the Lord was not simply objecting because her tears made Him uncomfortable—He spoke the words from compassion. Jesus walked over to the bier her son lay on and touched it. Then He called the young man to arise.

Had the people of Nain heard of Jesus? Almost undoubtedly, since the city was in Galilee. Could they have known what to expect? No. This was the first of three resurrections Jesus performed during His ministry. Not since the days of the prophets Elijah and Elisha had men returned from death at the touch of another man.

When the young man sat up, talking, Jesus returned him to his mother. Fear filled her eyes as she saw what Jesus had done, and the crowd about her feared, too. But their emotions turned to joy as they recognized the wondrous work of God among them.

Who could resist sharing this story? News of the event spread through the countryside. How many more people glorified God as they learned of this work?

When we hear of God's surprising work in another place, do we rejoice with those who have been blessed, or are we too busy gossiping about the story to recognize its importance? When one is healed, can we thankfully recognize the Great Physician's work in response to faithful prayer?

IN HIS NAME

After this the Lord chose seventy others. He sent them out two together to every city and place where He would be going later. . . . The seventy came back full of joy. They said, "Lord, even the demons obeyed us when we used Your name."
LUKE 10:1, 17 NLV

To further spread the ministry, Jesus sent about seventy men (some ancient manuscripts say seventy, some seventy-two) on a road trip. They went ahead of Him, in pairs, to prepare the way. If a town accepted them, they were to heal the ill there; if not, they were simply to leave.

This must have been an extraordinarily successful mission, since they reported that even those controlled by demons were cured when they healed in Jesus' name. Should the seventy have been surprised? They'd seen Jesus perform numerous healings. But perhaps their amazement came because God had used them. Through their imperfect hands, Jesus had healed many more people than He could have personally touched in a day.

Like the seventy-odd, we are sinful humans to whom God has entrusted ministry. Despite our weaknesses, He works through our hands. Do we engage in that ministry reverently, aware of our own failings and humbled that God lets us work in His name?

FAITHFUL SAMARITAN, UNFAITHFUL JEWS

And as he entered a village, he was met by ten lepers,
who stood at a distance and lifted up their voices, saying,
"Jesus, Master, have mercy on us." When he saw them he said to them,
"Go and show yourselves to the priests." And as they went they were cleansed.
LUKE 17:12–14 ESV

"Jesus, Master, have mercy on us." Jesus heard the cry as He entered the village, and off to one side stood ten lepers. Certainly they stood apart so as not to spread infection, but in that day they also would have been viewed as spiritually diseased. For in a day of limited medical knowledge, Jews saw this disease as a sign of God's displeasure. Their lives must have been a misery alleviated only by companionship with those who shared their impurity.

So when they heard Jesus was coming to town, they banded together to seek healing. All He required of them was that they show themselves to the priests, whose job it was to check on such skin diseases and declare when a person was healed.

As the ten traveled to the priests, they received their healing, so they must have believed in Jesus and His powers. But we have to wonder just how grateful nine of them were for the healing. For only one of the ten returned to Jesus to report and appreciate. As he walked down the road toward Jesus, the former leper praised God loudly. When he reached the Master, he fell at His feet and thanked Him.

Ironically, the single man who returned was a Samaritan, a race hated by the Jews because they had fallen into paganism. Yet the "good Jews" had not bothered to return to the One who healed them.

Jesus was not pleased at seeing only the one man. Though he who came could not be called an unbeliever now, he had not been born a Jew. Did Jesus' own people not appreciate what He had done?

We hear no more about the ungrateful nine. Perhaps they were still somewhat spiritually diseased, since praise and thankfulness did not return them to Jesus. But the single grateful man pierces our hearts as we read the story. Have we been guilty, like the missing nine, of ungratefulness? Are we faithful Samaritans or unfaithful Jews? Our level of thankfulness tells that to the Lord.

MERCY UNDER PRESSURE

When Jesus' disciples saw what was about to happen, they asked,
"Lord, should we attack them with a sword?"
One of the disciples even struck at the high priest's servant with his sword
and cut off the servant's right ear. "Enough of that!" Jesus said.
Then he touched the servant's ear and healed it.
LUKE 22:49–51 CEV

Judas led a crowd of Jesus' enemies, armed with swords and clubs, to the Garden of Gethsemane. There he betrayed the Master with a kiss. Though Jesus instantly recognized his intention, He did not fight back. He only tried to protect His disciples, asking that they be let go.

John tells us Peter was the one who tried to defend the Master by grabbing a sword and hacking off the ear of the high priest's servant, Malchus. Jesus rebuked Peter, pointing out that He could have called on the Father for protection, but scripture must be fulfilled (see Matthew 26:53). Then the Savior healed Malchus and demanded of His would-be attackers why they needed such force and stealth against someone who had been preaching publicly.

Even when Jesus was under the most pressure He'd confront in His earthly life, His forgiving nature demanded that He heal His enemy. How Malchus responded, we do not know. But this story encourages us to forgive when we are oppressed. Will we offer healing to our enemies or begin a feud that can never end in peace?

WATER TO WINE

Jesus said to the servants, "Fill the jars with water." And they filled them up to the brim. And he said to them, "Now draw some out and take it to the master of the feast." So they took it. When the master of the feast tasted the water now become wine, and did not know where it came from (though the servants who had drawn the water knew), the master of the feast called the bridegroom and said to him, "Everyone serves the good wine first, and when people have drunk freely, then the poor wine. But you have kept the good wine until now."
JOHN 2:7–10 ESV

Jesus' first miracle, described only in John's Gospel, took place at a wedding, quite possibly the wedding of one of His relatives. Along with His first-called disciples and His mother, He was invited. Legally, in that day, ten men were required to be at a wedding, and perhaps they invited Jesus and His disciples to make up six of that number.

This may not have been a very wealthy family, and though the guests may not have been numerous, the family was not too well prepared and ran out of wine. Weddings often went on for as much as a week. A poorer family might not celebrate all day long but would invite guests in for an evening meal each night. So running out of wine was a serious problem. Those who had enjoyed their friends' and neighbors' hospitality at their weddings committed a serious social faux pas by not returning their generosity—especially if those friends and neighbors were not well-to-do, either.

She's not in charge of the feast, but Mary comes to her son for a solution to the problem. Though she indirectly approaches the issue, not actually asking Him to perform a miracle, she earns a mild rebuke, indicating she is not in charge of His messianic ministry. "Woman," He replies, using a term that was more respectful than it appears in English, "what does this have to do with me? My hour has not yet come" (2:4 ESV). Jesus indicates He is no longer under her authority, as He had been as a child. The ministry will be God directed, not ordered by His mama.

Mary simply left things to Jesus, ordering the servants to follow His direction. Doubtless, along with the rebuke was much affection. She must have understood this was not a firm dismissal of the need.

Six stone water jars, used for the Jewish purification rituals, stood nearby. Each held somewhere between twenty and thirty gallons. Jesus told the servants to fill each with water, and they filled them to the brim, losing no opportunity to be generous with the guests (and maybe to taste a little for themselves).

When they had hauled enough water to fill the jars, Jesus told them to give a cup to the banquet master. The master tasted it, unaware of where it had come from. Then he took the bridegroom aside and commended him on the wine. He simply wondered why they'd held on to the really good stuff until the end of the feast.

The water that became wine is symbolic on a number of levels. First it represents the difference between the old and new covenants. But it also stands for the change in a new believer. The old spirit is gone, and the new one that replaces it has an unusual power, directly from God. A formerly sinful existence, once so dull and unimportant, takes on a new life, verve, and significance.

What of our lives? Are they water or wine? Has God's Spirit filled us with the new life that enlivens like wine, or are we dull, ordinary water that lacks joy?

Even if we've come to know Jesus, if sin obstructs the Spirit's work in our lives, we may feel more like water than wine. Even the most faithful of us have dull days that are filled with obedience, but if every day seems dull, perhaps we need a little more of the Spirit's wine in our lives. If we cast aside anger, resentment, and bitterness, confessing our failures, the sparkle may come back. We don't have to live on a constant high, but the idea that God will use us for His purposes should cause within us a burst of joy, not a sigh of despair.

Today, are we water or wine?

WHOLE FAITH?

The man said to Him, "Sir, come with me before my son dies."
Jesus said to him, "Go your way. Your son will live."
The man put his trust in what Jesus said and left.
As he was on his way home, his servants met him.
They said to him, "Your son is living!"
JOHN 4:49–51 NLV

Sometime later, when Jesus returned to Cana, where he'd provided wine for the wedding feast, He was well received. But it wasn't because the Galileans believed in Him. Though He came from that part of Israel, they did not respect Him. They simply wanted to see more miracles.

When he heard that Jesus was nearby, a royal official came, asking Him to heal his son, who was dying of a fever. How desperate this man must have felt, yet Jesus did not jump up to follow him to his son's bedside. Instead, the Master confronted this "important" man with his need for signs and wonders.

The official persisted, asking Him to heal his son. So Jesus, probably tired of being appreciated only for entertainment value, compromised and healed the son without going to him.

The man proved he was not like the others, for he believed Jesus' promise of healing. While he was traveling home, his servants met him with joyous news: the boy lived. "When did he get better?" the official questioned his servants. They explained that the boy's fever left him at the seventh hour (one o'clock our time).

The trusting father realized that was just the time at which Jesus had spoken the words "Your son will live." As they learned this, the official and his entire household believed.

Jesus was a man of His word. When He told a grieving father his child was healed, there was no question it had happened. But people are slow to realize that He is truthful above all men. The grieving father did well to trust as he walked home, but it was not until he learned the reality of his son's healing that the whole truth became apparent: not only had his son been healed, but the man who healed him was the Messiah.

Will we believe wholeheartedly, or is our faith all too partial? Jesus alone can be trusted to be all truth. Whom else could we turn to?

RULE FOLLOWER

The sick man answered Him, "Sir, I have no man to put me into the pool when
the water is stirred up; but while I am coming, another steps down before me."
Jesus said to him, "Rise, take up your bed and walk."
And immediately the man was made well,
took up his bed, and walked.
JOHN 5:7–9 NKJV

On the Saturday Jesus visited the pool of Bethesda, many blind, lame, and paralyzed men, women, and children lay near the water, hoping for a miraculous cure. Jesus saw one man who probably looked as if he'd been around Bethesda's colonnaded porch a long time and asked about him. His was not some passing illness; he was an invalid. Someone reported he'd been so for thirty-eight years. Had he been lying near the pool every day for that time? Scripture never tells us. But we can be certain doubt and depression had often filled his heart.

This day, Jesus asked if he wanted to be healed. Did the man jump at the chance? No. He carefully listed all the reasons why he couldn't be healed. Jesus did not rebuke his doubt; instead He told him to get up, take his mat, and walk. And the man did just that. But as he walked away, some "holy" people asked what he was doing carrying a mat on the Sabbath. He explained but could not name his healer. Later Jesus went to him and warned him to avoid sin, or worse would come upon him. Then the former invalid let the censorious Jews know His name.

This man was probably someone who played by the rules. He followed the healing rules, and he willingly informed on Jesus to the supposedly holy Jews who followed all the human laws Judaism had added to scripture. But these would-be holy ones missed out on the compassion that should have been part of their faith, and the healed man missed understanding that following all the rules had brought nothing; only when Jesus miraculously broke the laws of science could he walk.

Are we so busy following human rules that we miss out on understanding the Savior? Or are we taking scripture at its word and following closely in Jesus' steps?

OPEN THE TOMB

So they took away the stone. And Jesus lifted up his eyes and said,
"Father, I thank you that you have heard me.
I knew that you always hear me, but I said this on account
of the people standing around, that they may believe that you sent me."
When he had said these things, he cried out with a loud voice,
"Lazarus, come out." The man who had died came out,
his hands and feet bound with linen strips, and his face wrapped with a cloth.
Jesus said to them, "Unbind him, and let him go."
JOHN 11:41–44 ESV

At first, when Lazarus got ill, no one may have thought it was a big deal. He'd get over it, with the best medical care available. Since he and his family were obviously well-to-do, getting good care would have been no problem. A visit to an apothecary would have provided medications. When things became more dire, a doctor would have been called in. This healer may even have gone to one of the best medical schools of his day. But obviously all the doctor's and apothecary's best efforts didn't work. Lazarus became weaker.

His sisters, Mary and Martha, knew how much Jesus loved their brother. They sent to Him, knowing He could heal Lazarus in a moment. But time went on, and the Master didn't come. Lazarus became even weaker and eventually died. His sisters, who loved him deeply, became distraught. Not only had they lost their brother; they could not understand why Jesus had failed them.

The grieving sisters buried their brother. Friends and neighbors surrounded them, but Jesus and His disciples remained absent. Several days after Lazarus's death, they still hadn't seen Him. Maybe a few wondered if the danger He was in from Jerusalem's religious leaders had kept Him far away. Since Bethany was a short trip into the capital city, had it been too close to those who hated Jesus?

Four days after the burial, five days from Lazarus's death, Jesus came. Somewhat gloomily, Martha told Him she knew that if He'd been there, her brother would not have died. Brightening a bit, she told Him of her trust that even now, God would do whatever He asked. Obviously she was hoping to see her brother again.

Jesus replied that her brother would rise again. Martha admitted she would see him in the resurrection on the last day, but she didn't admit she was hoping for something sooner than that.

"I am the resurrection and the life," Jesus reminded her (11:25 ESV). Death was not the end of the road for Lazarus, who had trusted in Him. The loving sister confessed Him as the Messiah and went to call her sister.

Mary came quickly to Jesus and repeated Martha's first words to Him, "Lord, if you had been here, my brother would not have died" (11:32 ESV).

From neither sister did the Savior take offense. The two women did not lack faith, and perhaps they were stating fact, not rebuking Him. Their grief made them tenderly aware of Jesus' healing powers. Oh, that He had been there when Lazarus was so ill! Mary wept at the thought.

Jesus gently asked to see where Lazarus was laid—a normal request for a grieving friend. He wept on His way to His friend's resting place. The Jews (John only uses that term about Jesus' enemies) who had come to share the women's grief were amazed at Jesus' love for Lazarus, but some began to question why He hadn't healed one He loved so deeply.

When He came to the grave, Jesus asked that the stone be rolled away. Faithful Martha painfully reminded Him that by now her brother's body would be decomposing. "Did I not tell you that if you believed you would see the glory of God?" Jesus responded (11:40 ESV). Perhaps with a bit of hope, Martha commanded some men to move the stone.

Lifting His eyes to heaven, Jesus prayed, then commanded Lazarus to come forth from the tomb. He came out, the burial wrappings still surrounding his resurrected body. Jesus commanded his friends to unbind him, and what a celebration must have followed!

As a result of the miracle, many "Jews" believed in Jesus. But others reported the miracle to the Pharisees, who plotted to kill both Jesus and His resurrected friend.

We believe. Have we also seen the glory of God? Or do our own low expectations seem to limit the effectiveness of God's work in our lives? As He worked the most astounding miracle for the faithful sisters, Jesus will do so for us. He may not bring the physically dead back to life, but He'll work in our lives, if only we'll open the tomb door.

DOUBTLESS

On the evening of that day, the first day of the week,
the doors being locked where the disciples were for fear of the Jews,
Jesus came and stood among them and said to them, "Peace be with you."
When he had said this, he showed them his hands and his side.
Then the disciples were glad when they saw the Lord.
Jesus said to them again, "Peace be with you.
As the Father has sent me, even so I am sending you."
JOHN 20:19–21 ESV

Following Jesus' death and even His resurrection, the disciples were holed up, trying to avoid His enemies. No question but that those unbelieving men would be angry at the news that all their efforts at ridding themselves of Jesus had been unsuccessful. But how long could the disciples remain in one place, keeping their heads low?

The evening of the day when Mary Magdalene and the other women had seen the resurrected Jesus, Jesus also appeared to ten of the eleven. He didn't knock on their locked door, just appeared unexpectedly in the room they'd been sharing in their fear.

"Peace be with you," He greeted them. Then He proved He was no ghost, but the man they'd seen crucified, for He showed them all the signs of crucifixion upon Him—the marks of the nails in His hands and feet and the sword cut in His side. How delighted the disciples must have been to see Jesus. Perhaps they'd been wondering when He'd appear to them. After all, hadn't the women seen Him?

As the Father had sent Him, Jesus now sent the disciples to the world. He breathed on them, and they received the Holy Spirit. With His commission and the Spirit, they were ready to take on the world.

One of the eleven was not with them—Thomas. When the others told him they'd seen the Lord, he would not believe. He wanted to see and judge for himself. Eight days later, Jesus reappeared in the same way. He encouraged Thomas to experience for himself the wounds that proved His had been a real resurrection. Jesus encouraged him, not in doubt but faith. Immediately Thomas recognized Him as Lord.

"Blessed," Jesus replied, "are those who have not seen and yet have believed" (20:29 ESV).

We, too, have been confronted with the Lord's resurrection. Have we believed? If He has breathed His Spirit upon us, we are ready for ministry. Will doubt delay us? We have no reason to wait.

GONE FISHING

Early in the morning Jesus stood on the shore of the lake.
The followers did not know it was Jesus. Then Jesus said to them,
"Children, do you have any fish?" They said, "No." He said to them,
"Put your net over the right side of the boat. Then you will catch some fish."
They put out the net. They were not able to pull it in because it was so full of fish.
JOHN 21:4–6 NLV

Perhaps feeling a little bit at a loss after the Resurrection, Peter decided to go night fishing. Thomas, Nathanael, James, and John joined him; arduous work was better than idle waiting. All night the men floated on the Sea of Galilee, working hard but catching nothing.

About the time tempers were probably getting short, early the next morning they saw a figure on the shore. "Children, do you have any fish?" the man asked (21:5 NLV). When they replied in the negative, He told them to put their net over on the right side of their vessel and promised they'd make a catch.

Fishermen of that day often used spotters, who stood on the shore and directed the men in the boat to the schools of fish. But what a catch they hauled in this time—they couldn't pull the net in because it was so full. Muscles aching, John finally realized who that spotter had been. "It is the Lord!" he cried (21:7 NLV).

Enthusiastic Peter leapt into the water and headed for the shore, with the other disciples following in the boat. When they got to shore, they found a fire, ready to cook a fish breakfast. Though they'd caught 153 fish, their nets were undamaged.

None of us enjoy waiting for God. We want to be on the move with ministry, making ourselves worthwhile. But sometimes we run headlong into God's plan, which requires us to wait patiently while other things resolve themselves. As we wait, we too may go fishing, returning to ordinary tasks. Though God abundantly blesses these, we need to stand ready for His call to return to our work for Him. Are we ready to drop our nets and take up His work today?

MORE THAN WIND

When the day of Pentecost arrived, they were all together in one place.
And suddenly there came from heaven a sound like a mighty rushing wind,
and it filled the entire house where they were sitting.
And divided tongues as of fire appeared to them and rested on each one of them.
And they were all filled with the Holy Spirit and began to speak
in other tongues as the Spirit gave them utterance.
ACTS 2:1–4 ESV

Fifty days after Passover, the eleven and probably 120 other Christians (see verse 5) gathered for the Jewish feast of Pentecost. It may have seemed an ordinary feast day, but suddenly, a rushing wind filled the house and tongues of fire rested on every person present. All were filled with the Holy Spirit and began speaking in foreign tongues, whether or not they had ever known how to speak them before!

Hearing these Christians, devout Jews came to see what was going on and heard them speaking their own languages—for many foreign-language speakers either lived in the capital city or had gathered from other parts of the world to celebrate Pentecost. They all marveled at the event. Yet a few unbelievers tried to blame it on too much wine.

Peter preached a sermon, explaining that Old Testament prophecies had been fulfilled, and God's Spirit now indwelled those who believed in Jesus. That day, about three thousand more believed in Him anew.

The Holy Spirit may not come to us in a whoosh of wind, and we may never wear a tongue of fire, but He works within our hearts when we accept His power and trust in Jesus. He is more than wind in our lives—He fills our spirits and leads us in God's truth, if only we open ourselves to Him.

POINTING TO JESUS

But Peter said, "I have no silver and gold,
but what I do have I give to you.
In the name of Jesus Christ of Nazareth, rise up and walk!"
And he took him by the right hand and raised him up,
and immediately his feet and ankles were made strong.
And leaping up he stood and began to walk, and entered the
temple with them, walking and leaping and praising God.
ACTS 3:6–8 ESV

Peter and John were headed for the temple one afternoon for prayer when some men carried a crippled man to the most popular gate of the worship center. There he earned a living by begging for alms from worshippers.

As he did with everyone else, the man begged for some of the apostles' loose change. But Peter was about to give him something much, much better. He engaged the man's attention and told him he had no gold. Then he commanded the man to walk in the name of Jesus. Taking the beggar by one hand, the apostle lifted him to his feet. In an instant, the man's feet and ankles became strong. He jumped up and walked, following the apostles into the temple courts.

When worshippers recognized the healed man, they were amazed. Peter, ever the preacher, took the opportunity to point them to Jesus.

Do we take every opportunity to point people to Jesus? Let's not ignore His Spirit's call.

RECONSIDER

But Peter said, "Ananias, why has Satan filled your heart to lie
to the Holy Spirit and keep back part of the price of the land for yourself? . . .
You have not lied to men but to God." Then Ananias,
hearing these words, fell down and breathed his last. . . .
"Look, the feet of those who have buried your husband are at the door,
and they will carry you out." Then immediately [Sapphira] fell down at his feet
and breathed her last. And the young men came in and found her dead,
and carrying her out, buried her by her husband.

ACTS 5:3–5, 9–10 NKJV

Generosity filled the young church when Barnabas sold some land so that he could offer the money to the apostles. But one couple didn't quite get the point of this kind of giving. They saw Barnabas give so unreservedly and heard other church members sing his praises. Together they decided they'd like that kind of recognition, but not at the price Barnabas had paid. The couple decided to sell a spare piece of property and give money to the church. But why should they lose everything? They'd give Peter only part of the cash.

If they'd stopped there, it would have been fine. But the couple led everyone to believe they'd given the whole price of the land.

When they brought the offering before Peter, he was incensed. He didn't care if they'd only given a certain amount to the church—but to claim one thing and do another was another matter. He indicted Ananias with his words, indicating he knew what they'd done. He informed them that the couple had lied to God, not man.

Ananias fell down and died when he heard the apostle's words. Men came forward and buried him immediately.

Later, Ananias's wife, Sapphira, came in. Peter asked her about the price they'd paid for the land, and she too lied. She quickly followed her husband to the grave. Fear filled the church when folks found out about these events.

Do we lie to God? Let's remember the ending of this story and reconsider all we say and do.

SIGNS AND WONDERS

And through the hands of the apostles many signs and wonders were done among
the people. . . . They brought the sick out into the streets and laid them on beds
and couches, that at least the shadow of Peter passing by might fall on some of them.
Also a multitude gathered from the surrounding cities to Jerusalem, bringing sick
people and those who were tormented by unclean spirits, and they were all healed.

ACTS 5:12, 15–16 NKJV

The Jewish people might have gotten somewhat used to Jesus' miracles, but their astonishment peaked again, after His death, when they discovered the miracles had not ended. Though Jesus no longer walked among them, the apostles did. And from them proceeded amazing signs and wonders.

Is it any wonder that the people thought well of the eleven? Even the religious authorities did not keep them from meeting in the temple.

When they saw the miracles, many came to believe in Jesus, and others, even those from outside Jerusalem, brought the sick and those afflicted with evil spirits. They placed them on the cots and mats in the street, hoping Peter's shadow would fall over them and they would be healed. In His mercy, God caused them all to return to health.

God is more willing to do miracles in our lives than we might expect. Are we in a humble, spiritual state in which He can bless us?

PUBLIC ENEMY NUMBER ONE

But Saul, still breathing threats and murder against the disciples of the Lord,
went to the high priest and asked him for letters to the synagogues at Damascus,
so that if he found any belonging to the Way, men or women, he might bring them
bound to Jerusalem. Now as he went on his way, he approached Damascus,
and suddenly a light from heaven flashed around him. And falling to the ground
he heard a voice saying to him, "Saul, Saul, why are you persecuting me?"
And he said, "Who are you, Lord?" And he said, "I am Jesus,
whom you are persecuting. But rise and enter the city, and you will be told what
you are to do.". . . Saul rose from the ground, and although his eyes were opened,
he saw nothing. So they led him by the hand and brought him into Damascus.
And for three days he was without sight, and neither ate nor drank.

ACTS 9:1–6, 8–9 ESV

Public Enemy Number One: that's what the Pharisee Saul started out being to first-century Christians. He had approved of and even taken part in Stephen's stoning. Then he'd persecuted Christians, sending them to prison. As a result, many believers left Jerusalem to settle elsewhere.

One day, on his way to Damascus to expand his persecution of Christians, Saul was traveling unconcernedly when a heavenly light flashed around him. He fell to the ground and heard a voice asking, "Saul, Saul, why are you persecuting me?" (Acts 9:4 ESV). Because he couldn't see anything, Saul asked who was speaking to him. That's when he learned it was Jesus—a shocking discovery indeed.

The voice told him to rise and enter Damascus. Saul started to obey, but he could not move ahead on his own: he was completely blind. The men who traveled with him had heard the mysterious voice but could not understand it (see 22:9). They stood speechless, seeing no one. But when Saul rose, they took him by the hand and brought him into the city.

For three days, the sightless Saul fasted and prayed. This sudden, enforced retreat was designed to make him rethink his opinion of Jesus and His people. During those days, a Christian named Ananias (obviously not Sapphira's husband but a man of Damascus) had a vision. God told him to go to Straight Street and look for Saul of Tarsus (see 9:11).

This was not news Ananias wanted to hear. He quickly recognized the name of the man he was to visit. His response was something like, "Lord, are You kidding? Do You remember how dangerous this guy is? He might decide he wants to throw me in prison, like a lot of the other Christians he's run into. And the chief priests think he's the greatest thing since challah bread!"

But the Lord repeated His command to go. He shared that He was about to turn Saul so far around that he'd become a missionary to the Gentiles.

Comforted, Ananias went to Straight Street. He laid hands on the former Public Enemy Number One and told him Jesus had sent him. Saul was to receive his sight back and be filled with the Holy Spirit (9:17).

Something like scales fell from Saul's eyes, and he could see again. He arose, received baptism, and ate again (9:18–19). Then he set off on his mission, first meeting with the disciples in the city, then preaching in the Damascene synagogues. Everyone there was amazed at Saul's change of heart, and his powerful preaching turned hearts toward Jesus (9:20–22).

When we speak of conversions, we often think of Saul's dramatic experience. And for many of us, that seems to be the way that leads to Christ. Suddenly, we recognize our own sin and fall on the tarmac before Him. But other Christians have a quiet or slowly increasing conviction that He is Lord. However we come to Jesus, He transforms our lives, if we are willing to make them a mission for Him. Whether we fall down on the road to Damascus or simply feel the still, small voice that leads us into faith, we will never be the same. New life is a sign of new faith.

TESTIMONY

Now as Peter went here and there among them all,
he came down also to the saints who lived at Lydda.
There he found a man named Aeneas, bedridden for eight years,
who was paralyzed. And Peter said to him, "Aeneas,
Jesus Christ heals you; rise and make your bed." And immediately he rose.
And all the residents of Lydda and Sharon saw him, and they turned to the Lord.
ACTS 9:32–35 ESV

Aeneas had lain in bed for eight years, paralyzed. As the apostle Peter went about his work for the Lord, overseeing church growth, he came into Aeneas's hometown of Lydda. Perhaps the town gossips had told Aeneas about the healings that had taken place in Jerusalem. Or maybe a relative or friend went to Peter to call him to the paralyzed man's bedside. Whatever caused the apostle to come there, it was a wonderful time for Aeneas. No doctor could help him. This was his only hope.

Of course, Peter did not take the credit for himself. He healed the man in the name of Jesus and told him to rise and make his bed. Aeneas couldn't jump up fast enough! The healed man must have spread his joy not only through his community but to those all around, because the residents of both Lydda and the Plain of Sharon saw him walking and turned to his Lord.

We, too, have a testimony. Will our energy for Jesus draw others to Him?

SHINE BRIGHTLY

Peter sent them all out of the room; then he got down on his knees and prayed.
Turning toward the dead woman, he said, "Tabitha, get up."
She opened her eyes, and seeing Peter she sat up.
He took her by the hand and helped her to her feet.
Then he called the believers and the widows and presented her to them alive.
This became known all over Joppa, and many people believed in the Lord.
ACTS 9:40–42

Farther along the Plain of Sharon lay Joppa. When word came that Peter was in nearby Lydda, the Christians of this seaport town sent to ask him to come. One of their members, Tabitha (her name in Aramaic) or Dorcas (a Greek translation of her name), who delighted in doing good works for the church, had died. Her body had been washed for burial, but before they went further, the Christians sent two men to Lydda to ask the apostle to come to her aid. Peter accompanied these messengers back to their city.

In an upper room, the other widows showed him all the garments she had made for them. But Peter wasn't interested in a fashion show. He put them gently out of the room, prayed, and called Tabitha's name, telling her to arise. Opening her eyes and sitting up, she looked at the apostle. He took her hand, raised her out of the bed, and called in the other Christians, who were probably waiting anxiously on the lower floor.

The story of her return to life must have flown around the town, and surely people came to see her with their own eyes. When they saw what had happened and heard her testimony, it certainly caused them to think. Since the apostle stayed for some time in the city, they must also have heard his preaching. As a result of this miracle, many came to know the Lord.

Tabitha's good works did not end with making clothes, a time-consuming effort in the days before sewing machines. Obviously she allowed her new life, following her death, to shine as brightly as her good works had before Peter came to raise her. Because she had a consistent Christian walk, people could believe in her resurrection and the Lord who had been behind the miracle.

Will our lives show forth God's truth this clearly? All we do out of love for Him can serve to make His name known. When we need to shine out brightly for Him, will we be ready to do so?

WITNESSING WELL

In Lystra there sat a man crippled in his feet, who was lame from birth and had never walked. He listened to Paul as he was speaking. Paul looked directly at him, saw that he had faith to be healed and called out, "Stand up on your feet!" At that, the man jumped up and began to walk.
ACTS 14:8–10

This unnamed man of Lystra, a Galatian city, had never effectively set foot on earth. With no wheelchairs available, moving him from one place to another must have been a chore. Yet when Paul and Barnabas spoke in his city, he was there, ears and heart wide open.

Paul noticed the man and studied him for a bit before he spoke out, calling the cripple to stand. The man energetically sprang up and began walking.

The watching crowd immediately came to the wrong conclusion: they decided Barnabas and Paul were gods and started to call for sacrifices to be made to them. The anguished apostles spoke out, witnessing about the Lord, and just barely stopped the sacrifices from taking place.

Sometimes we witness and people come to the wrong conclusion. Like Paul and Barnabas, we need to make efforts to redirect their thinking into a better way. Can we explain Christ to people in a number of ways so they can clearly understand who He is?

DEMONIC AFFLICTION

As we were going to the place of prayer, we were met by a slave girl
who had a spirit of divination and brought her owners much gain
by fortune-telling. She followed Paul and us, crying out,
"These men are servants of the Most High God, who proclaim to you
the way of salvation." And this she kept doing for many days.
Paul, having become greatly annoyed, turned and said to the spirit,
"I command you in the name of Jesus Christ to come out of her."
And it came out that very hour.

ACTS 16:16–18 ESV

In Acts, Luke tells this story that took place in the Macedonian city of Philippi, as a slave girl filled with a demonic spirit spoke out occult oracles.

Paul and his companions, including Luke, may have met for prayer outside the city because their religion was considered a strange cult by the Philippians and therefore could not be practiced inside the municipality. On their way to the prayer place near the river, they met this slave girl, who was filled with an irritating spirit that pestered Paul by declaring that he and his friends served the Most High God. A Jew might properly have understood that description, but there were few Jews in the city, which numbered many former Roman soldiers in its population. Most of the people in Philippi held to some sort of pagan belief and probably would have thought the phrase referred to the god Zeus. Then as now, Satan could mislead with crafty words; even when he spoke the truth, it could lead people in the wrong direction.

Greek religion had a mishmash of influences. Cults from all over the Near East had influenced this pagan faith. Magic and sorcery were popular methods people tried to use to understand an often confusing world. The kind of spirit this girl was afflicted with is described as a *python,* the same kind of spirit that supposedly gave visions to the Greek oracle at Delphi. This pagan priestess was consulted by Greek rulers and common people alike and responded to them in riddles. (That way the recipient could always assume, *The oracle was right. I just didn't understand what she said.*)

Naturally, Paul did not appreciate the slave girl's running commentary, especially when it led people away from Christ. After many days of patiently putting up with her, Paul had had enough. He commanded the spirit to come out of her.

Though that cleansing freed the servant girl from the demon, it brought the wrath of her owners down on Paul's head. No longer could she earn plenty of money by telling people's fortunes—her owners had lost a valuable commodity. And someone was going to pay. The owners dragged Paul and Silas in front of the authorities.

"They advocate customs that are not lawful for us as Romans to accept or practice," the irate owners claimed about Paul and his disciples (16:21 ESV). Philippi was a Roman colony and proud of its connection with the Italian city. It didn't hurt their case to claim that these outlanders were running counter to the Roman way of life and were a danger to the city. But in reality, they wanted their oracle back.

As a result, Paul and Silas spent an eventful night in jail. First they were beaten. Then at midnight the foundations of their place of incarceration were shattered by an earthquake. Their testimony converted the jailer, and in the end, at Paul's insistence, the city magistrates led them honorably out of the jail.

Do we recognize the joys of knowing Jesus? Let's think what it would be like to live a pagan lifestyle. The slave girl didn't experience joy as a demon directed all she did. Even those who did not have a demon within lived without security, seeing themselves as being at the whim of gods whose minds changed constantly.

Maybe their lives aren't so different from today's unbelievers who suffer the same doubts and troubles. Can we have compassion on them and seek to separate them from their demonic afflictions?

AN EXTRAORDINARY PATH

God did extraordinary miracles through Paul,
so that even handkerchiefs and aprons
that had touched him were taken to the sick,
and their illnesses were cured and the evil spirits left them.
ACTS 19:11–12

The apostle Peter's shadow was sought for its healing properties (see Acts 5:12, 15–16), but with Paul, people looked to fabric that had touched him to heal their bodies and souls.

While he preached in Corinth with Priscilla and Aquila, Paul had returned to his trade as a tentmaker. He must have continued his trade, for somehow, when he moved on to Ephesus, the items he used as protection or for personal comfort as he worked began to be valued by those seeking healing.

These were not ordinary miracles, and they certainly did not follow any previous pattern, but God graciously used even these common items to bring healing to those who sought Paul out.

Ephesus was the most important city in Asia Minor, both politically and commercially. Worship of the fertility goddess Artemis made the local idol makers successful. So it's not surprising that the outcome of the healings associated with Paul stirred up dissatisfaction in that quarter. A riot resulted, which caused Paul to move on to Macedonia.

Are we willing to give our lives to Jesus and let Him do as He wills with them? Maybe He will send us down an extraordinary path. Are we willing to go wherever He calls us?

DEVOTED TO THE WORD

Seated in a window was a young man named Eutychus,
who was sinking into a deep sleep as Paul talked on and on.
When he was sound asleep, he fell to the ground from the third story and was
picked up dead. Paul went down, threw himself on the young man and put his
arms around him. "Don't be alarmed," he said. "He's alive!"
Then he went upstairs again and broke bread and ate.
After talking until daylight, he left.
ACTS 20:9–11

Paul came to the city of Troas for a brief visit. No doubt the believers there were well aware they needed to make the most of the time they had with him. On his last night there, a crowd of folks must have been ready to hear his preaching, because young Eutychus ended up sitting in a window. Or perhaps the air was cooler there, so he chose the precarious place. Though the sill may have been broad and seemed safe enough, perhaps the young freedman had had a long day and underestimated how tired he'd feel after Paul had talked for a while. Unwilling to miss anything, the young Christian remained, growing ever sleepier.

Though Paul was planning to travel the next day, he was anxious to share as much as possible with the fledgling congregation. He kept preaching late into the night, by lamplight. Around midnight, it all became too much for Eutychus. He fell sound asleep. Since the Christians were meeting in a third-floor room, the sleeping man fell headlong to the ground and was killed.

The believers of Troas, seeing and hearing him fall, hurried to help their brother. Quickly Paul appeared beside them. The apostle threw himself on Eutychus and took him in his arms. "Don't be alarmed," he comforted the grieving Christians, "he's alive."

Obviously, the Christians of Troas had had time enough to check things out and know Eutychus had not been living when they first came to him. A rare kind of miracle had occurred right before their eyes.

Paul returned to the room and began to serve the Lord's Supper to the no-doubt-excited congregation. Then he ate a late dinner and talked with the congregation until daybreak.

We've all listened to long, and possibly even dull, sermons. We can feel for this young man as his head nods. But have we been so devoted to hearing the Word that we were willing to stay under less than comfortable circumstances? Let's avoid his foolhardiness even as we share Eutychus's devotion to God's Word.

SNAKE ESCAPE

Paul gathered a pile of brushwood and, as he put it on the fire,
a viper, driven out by the heat, fastened itself on his hand.
When the islanders saw the snake hanging from his hand,
they said to each other, "This man must be a murderer;
for though he escaped from the sea, Justice has not allowed him to live."
But Paul shook the snake off into the fire and suffered no ill effects.
The people expected him to swell up or suddenly fall dead, but after
waiting a long time and seeing nothing unusual happen to him,
they changed their minds and said he was a god.
ACTS 28:3–6

Paul and his companions were sailing to Rome when their vessel was shipwrecked; after an eventful night on the sea, they landed on the Isle of Malta. The people of the island, having seen the wreck, came to their aid, building a fire to warm the survivors. Ever helpful, the apostle set himself to gathering wood to feed the fire. But when he put the sticks on it, a viper, attempting to escape the flames, grabbed on to Paul's hand.

The snake must have been a poisonous one, for as soon as they saw this, the islanders assumed Paul was a dead man. Knowing he was a Roman prisoner, they assumed he was a murderer and that though he'd escaped drowning, he would now receive his just reward.

Imagine their shock when Paul shook off the snake and went on as before. Instead of falling dead, he remained perfectly healthy. They decided he must be a god.

Maybe we'd better not fool with poisonous snakes and assume God will keep us alive. But we can praise Him that He gave everyone this impressive sign of His power.

WELCOME GUESTS

There was an estate nearby that belonged to Publius,
the chief official of the island. He welcomed us to his home
and for three days entertained us hospitably.
His father was sick in bed, suffering from fever and dysentery.
Paul went in to see him and, after prayer, placed his hands
on him and healed him. When this had happened,
the rest of the sick on the island came and were cured.
They honored us in many ways and when we were ready to sail,
they furnished us with the supplies we needed.

ACTS 28:7–10

After Paul proved he was no murderer, the chief official on Malta, Publius, invited Paul and his companion Luke into his home. Perhaps others joined them, too. But Paul must have made the greatest impression on the official, because when he discovered that Publius's father was suffering from fever and dysentery, the apostle went to see what he could do. He came to the man, prayed, and placed his hands on him to heal him.

When the people of the island saw what Paul had done, they brought the sick to him, and they also were cured. As Paul and his companion left, the island dwellers honored them greatly and gave them all the supplies they'd need for their travel. Their original fear, that Paul was a dangerous murderer, had disappeared.

Paul made himself and Luke very welcome guests, for they did what they could to help their host. We may not be able to heal the ill, but we can defy Benjamin Franklin's idea that after three days, fish and guests stink. May we serve, not expect to be served, wherever we go.

LOOK FOR HIM

These men have power to shut up the sky so that it will not rain
during the time they are prophesying; and they have power to turn
the waters into blood and to strike the earth with every kind of plague
as often as they want. Now when they have finished their testimony,
the beast that comes up from the Abyss will attack them, and overpower
and kill them. Their bodies will lie in the street of the great city. . . .
For three and a half days men from every people, tribe, language
and nation will gaze on their bodies and refuse them burial.
The inhabitants of the earth will gloat over them and will celebrate
by sending each other gifts, because these two prophets
had tormented those who live on the earth. But after the three
and a half days a breath of life from God entered them,
and they stood on their feet, and terror struck those who saw them.
Then they heard a loud voice from heaven saying to them, "Come up here."
And they went up to heaven in a cloud, while their enemies looked on.
REVELATION 11:6–12

In the book of Revelation, God gave the apostle John a prophetic vision concerning two miraculous witnesses who, at the end time, will prophesy for 1,260 days.

John's description of these future events reminds us of numerous Old Testament passages. He describes the two men as olive trees and lamp stands. Though scholars disagree about whether these are two actual people or symbolic figures who stand for the church, and though they debate when these two will appear, there is no question that when we see miraculous events that remind us of Elijah and Moses, we'll know the events John prophesied are taking place. Under the prophets' command rain will stop and the waters turn to blood. Through them, people will be struck with plagues.

Once their testimony is done, the demonic beast will attack and destroy them, but only in a temporary, earthly sense. Their bodies will remain unburied—a great insult in the first-century world and a horror to us today—and many of their enemies come to gawk. Though victory holds off, three days later, as with Jesus, God will raise them back to life. Then He'll call His faithful witnesses to Himself in eternity, and they'll rise up into heaven in a cloud. When the prophets' enemies see what happens, terror will strike them.

As the prophets leave earth, the city (variously described by scholars as Jerusalem, Rome, or another evil city) will experience an earthquake that will kill seven thousand people and terrify the rest into worshiping the Lord.

What do these prophecies symbolize? It isn't the most detailed description, and as we read, it leaves us with many unanswered questions. Let's take comfort in the fact that we have plenty of company—both scholars and lay Christians have doubts about what the Revelation means. We all read it carefully, but none of us understand it completely.

When we read the book of Revelation, we are in the same position Old Testament believers who studied the Messianic prophecies were in: We can't clearly see what God's Word means, and we cannot accurately predict how it will work out. Just as the ancient Israelites read the prophets and trusted that Jesus would come, we need to keep our minds open to see God's outworking of His prophecy. Jesus did not come exactly the way people in the first century expected, and it's likely God will have a few surprises for us, too. But as we look ahead to the fulfillment of New Testament prophecy, we know that God will fulfill His will. All we need to do is continue to seek Him.

In the meantime, let's not become too certain we know just what God plans as He begins to close out this earthly life, or we might be looking in the wrong direction when He comes.

HIS ETERNALLY

Then I saw a new heaven and a new earth, for the first heaven
and the first earth had passed away, and there was no longer any sea.
I saw the Holy City, the new Jerusalem, coming down out of heaven from God,
prepared as a bride beautifully dressed for her husband.
And I heard a loud voice from the throne saying,
"Now the dwelling of God is with men, and he will live with them.
They will be his people, and God himself will be with them and be their God.
He will wipe every tear from their eyes.
There will be no more death or mourning or crying or pain,
for the old order of things has passed away."
REVELATION 21:1–4

While many prophetic passages in Revelation cause us to question, this one simply brings us much courage and hope. As we look at the Bible's final miracle, our hearts lift up. For the sins and hardships of this world will not last forever. Everything we know now will be erased, and God will provide a beautiful Jerusalem without sin or stain. There He will live with us, and no one will cry over death or anything else. We will endlessly know the joy of living with Jesus forever.

Today, when life is hard or we don't see the purpose in our Christian lives, we can look forward to the last miracle God will perform on earth. It's a miracle that renews the earth—and renews us, too. For we will be without sin, living with Him eternally.

THE TOP
100
NAMES
OF GOD

INTRODUCTION

Who is God? Likely, you've listened to many sermons on this topic. You've probably seen artists' representations of a benevolent father figure in the heavens or of a haloed Jesus tending a flock of sheep. And chances are you've watched the fabled Hollywood versions of Bible stories, those epics that feature an unapproachable, omnipotent Spirit as God.

But one of the easiest and most fulfilling ways to know God is to consider His names and what each one tells you about Him.

In this book, *The Top 100 Names of God*, you'll find names for God that describe:

- Who He is—Holy, Almighty, Righteous, the Author of Our Faith, the Beginning, and Alpha and Omega.
- What He's like—Everlasting Father, Prince of Peace, Light of the World, Bread of Life, the Way, the Truth, the Life, the Word, and the Rock.
- Why He or Jesus came to earth (and why Jesus is coming again!)— Anointed One, Messiah, Salvation, King of Kings, Sun of Righteousness, Bridegroom, and the Resurrection and the Life.
- What He does for you—Comforter, Counselor, Mediator, Physician, Shepherd, Guide, Friend, and Savior.

When you consider each name and then delve into the many scripture references provided, your spiritual life is sure to be enriched and your relationship with God deepened. You'll find that each name is a window, shining a light on the timelessness of our Lord.

Within the pages of this book, you'll find the treasured names of God, passed down from the ancients to you.

ADONAI

But Abram said, "O Sovereign LORD,
what can you give me since I remain childless
and the one who will inherit my estate is Eliezer of Damascus?"

GENESIS 15:2

When Abram uttered these words, his relationship with God, as recorded in the Bible, was relatively new. Yet based on the evidence so far in his own life—God's leading his family from Ur to Canaan, the rescue of his nephew Lot from the four kings, and the promise by God that Abram would be the father of a great people—Abram knew there was only one God, the Lord, Adonai.

The name Adonai is actually the plural of *Adon*, which means "Lord" or "Majesty." By addressing God as Adonai, Abram was emphatically praising the One who has no equal, the Lord of lords and the Lord of all the earth. In early texts, Adonai was used in place of the sacred "YHWH," or Yahweh, since no Jew was allowed to say that most reverent word. Adonai in all its variations is used hundreds of times throughout the Bible.

Despite Abram's appreciation of the divine, the next words out of his mouth were pathetically human: "What can you give me?" Even though God had told him, "I will make your offspring like the dust of the earth" (Genesis 13:16), Abram obviously wanted concrete results, not just poetic promises. Abram would have to wait many years to hold baby Isaac in his arms, the beginning of the fulfillment of God's covenant.

To call God "Adonai" implies a personal relationship with our Lord. We can call God "my Lord" or "our Lord," but how do we know He is Adonai if we haven't called out to Him in the middle of the night, perhaps to plead for a wayward child or a more hopeful diagnosis? How do we know He is Adonai if we haven't trusted Him to lead us to the right spouse, to the right job, to the right church? Only by seeing the Lord of lords work in our lives, whether by providing concrete answers or a magnificent sense of inner peace, can we voice the word first used by this Old Testament patriarch.

God wants you to acknowledge Him as Adonai. . .but more than that, He wants to have a personal relationship with you. He wants to work in your life. He wants to be your Lord. When that happens, you will echo the psalmist: "O God, You are my God; early will I seek You; my soul thirsts for You; my flesh longs for You in a dry and thirsty land where there is no water" (Psalm 63:1 NKJV).

ADVOCATE

My little children, these things I write to you,
so that you may not sin. And if anyone sins,
we have an Advocate with the Father,
Jesus Christ the righteous.

1 JOHN 2:1 NKJV

Just before He rose into heaven forty days after the Resurrection, Jesus told His disciples, "I am with you always, even to the end of the age" (Matthew 28:20 NKJV). Likely, at that moment, the eleven men left gazing into the clouds were somewhat confused. What did that mean? Writing years later, and divinely inspired, the apostle John provided the answer. Jesus is now our Advocate in heaven, interceding for us when we fail to follow His will.

Even if you have never entered a real courtroom, you know from countless television dramas the meaning of the word *advocate*—the legal representative presenting your case before a judge and jury. By interviewing witnesses and presenting various exhibits, an attorney or advocate tries to make a case why his or her client is not guilty. When it's time for the verdict to be read, typically the judge asks the one on trial to stand beside his or her advocate.

In the same way, Jesus is our Advocate, pleading the "cases" of His followers to His Father, standing beside us in spirit. In the original New Testament Greek text, the word *parakletos* means "intercessor."

John's interpretation was substantiated by the writer of Hebrews: "For Christ has not entered the holy places made with hands, which are copies of the true, but into heaven itself, now to appear in the presence of God for us" (Hebrews 9:24 NKJV). Paul, writing to the Romans, put it this way: "It is Christ who died, and furthermore is also risen, who is even at the right hand of God, who also makes intercession for us" (Romans 8:34 NKJV).

What John isn't saying here in 1 John 2:1 is implied nonetheless: for Jesus to be our Advocate, we have to so appoint Him first. In other words, we have to ask Him to be Savior of our lives. We have to acknowledge that He is the Son of God, who came to earth to save us from our sins.

Unlike those courtroom dramas, there are no lost cases or mistrials in heaven once you've accepted Jesus as your Savior. There is no threat of punishment, civil or criminal, and no fear that your "record" will come back to haunt you. Once you've asked Jesus to forgive you, your record is clean. When you have Jesus as your Advocate, you have the ultimate counsel.

ALMIGHTY

I am Alpha and Omega, the beginning and the ending, saith the Lord,
which is, and which was, and which is to come, the Almighty.
REVELATION 1:8 KJV

When the apostle John heard a voice one very special Lord's Day, there was no mistaking whose it was. Loud and clear as a trumpet's blast, yet more intimate. Alone in exile, John suddenly found Jesus with him. Jesus, the One John loved more than any other. . .Jesus, whom John described just moments before hearing His voice as the Almighty.

Considering where John found himself, such a description is a powerful testimony. In AD 95, the Roman emperor Domitian had exiled the apostle to the then remote Aegean island of Patmos, a place of banishment for criminals and dissidents. For a reason that would soon be revealed, John had sidestepped martyrdom, a fate that had claimed so many other disciples. God was about to use John to pen the events of the end times, events both amazing and horrifying, which would someday be preserved as the book of Revelation.

John's description of Jesus as Almighty would surely have rankled the religious Jews of Jerusalem, whose actions he had described in his Gospel account. " 'We are not stoning you for any of these [Jesus' miracles],' replied the Jews, 'but for blasphemy, because you, a mere man, claim to be God' " (John 10:33). Countering that, Paul wrote to the Colossians, "For in Christ all the fullness of the Deity lives in bodily form" (Colossians 2:9).

To John, the attributes of the Almighty were threefold: Jesus lives, He has always lived, and He will live for all eternity. In fact, the first verse of John's Gospel confirmed this: "In the beginning was the Word, and the Word was with God, and the Word was God" (John 1:1 KJV). John recorded later the power of life through Jesus: "I am the living bread which came down from heaven: if any man eat of this bread, he shall live for ever" (John 6:51 KJV); "Because I live, ye shall live also" (John 14:19 KJV). Jesus as an eternal presence is described by John as One who sits on His throne, living "for ever and ever" (Revelation 4:9 KJV).

The Old Testament writers commonly addressed the "Lord God Almighty," or simply the "Almighty," or recorded proclamations by Him. It was to the Lord God Almighty that sacrifices were made; His strength in battle was praised; complaints about one's state in life were moaned to the Lord God Almighty; hopes for retribution were expressed to Him; and it is He whom we are to praise for everything in creation. Amos the prophet declared, "He who forms the mountains, creates the wind, and reveals his thoughts to man, he who turns dawn to darkness, and treads the high places of the earth—the LORD God Almighty is his name" (Amos 4:13).

The Almighty promises deliverance for His people, if they will return to Him; revenge for Israel's enemies; and hope of eternal life. Job, in particular, rarely failed to acknowledge God as Almighty—and never did he despise the "discipline" received from Him (Job 5:17). Much as John described the greatness of the Almighty, the writer of Job penned these words: "Can you fathom the mysteries of God? Can you probe the limits of the Almighty?" (Job 11:7).

Such reverence for the Almighty God is sorely lacking in the twenty-first century. We often hear God's or Jesus' name bandied about casually, His name used as a substitute for "Wow!" or an outburst of anger. Yet how often do we take the time to defend the name of Jesus? We feel embarrassed. We don't want to appear "holier than thou," or we're simply too harried to care.

Take a minute to reflect on John's reaction to Jesus when he saw Him. John wrote, "And when I saw him, I fell at his feet as dead" (Revelation 1:17 KJV). God has said, "Before me every knee will bow; by me every tongue will swear" (Isaiah 45:23).

One day we, too, will be able to meet the Almighty, our God who has always been and always will be—our God who is greater than human understanding.

ALPHA AND OMEGA

I am Alpha and Omega, the beginning and the end.
I will give unto him that is athirst of the fountain of the water of life freely.
REVELATION 21:6 KJV

Jesus described Himself as Alpha and Omega—the first and last letters of the Greek alphabet—three times in the Bible, and all of them occur in the book of Revelation. All of them were recorded by His beloved disciple, John. Because John's "assignment" on Patmos was to write about the events of the end times of this world, perhaps Jesus wanted to stress that He would always be with us. The world as we know it will end someday, but there will be another world, an eternal world that awaits believers, one that is dominated by our Lord Jesus Christ, the Alpha and Omega, the One who has no end.

Even from Old Testament times, Bible writers recorded the timelessness of God. "See now that I myself am He! There is no god besides me. I put to death and I bring to life, I have wounded and I will heal, and no one can deliver out of my hand. I lift my hand to heaven and declare: As surely as I live forever, when I sharpen my flashing sword and my hand grasps it in judgment, I will take vengeance on my adversaries and repay those who hate me" (Deuteronomy 32:39–41).

Just as the God of the Old Testament lifted His "flashing sword" against the enemies of Israel, so Jesus, according to the book of Revelation, at the end of time will destroy those who do not acknowledge Him as Lord.

He has always been Alpha and Omega. Just as you cannot distinguish the beginning or end of a circle, so it is with God. The writer of Hebrews tells us that over the course of thousands of years, "Jesus Christ is the same yesterday and today and forever" (Hebrews 13:8).

After John recorded the destruction of the world and the judgment of those whose names were not found written in "the book of life" (Revelation 20:15), he described a new city, a New Jerusalem, coming down from heaven, "prepared as a bride beautifully dressed for her husband" (21:2). In the New Jerusalem, God or Jesus will live with His people and there will be no death, no crying, and no pain. After giving John this vision, Jesus said, "It is done. I am the Alpha and the Omega, the Beginning and the End. To him who is thirsty I will give to drink without cost from the spring of the water of life. He who overcomes will inherit all this, and I will be his God and he will be my son" (21:6–7).

As God created the Garden of Eden for the first man and woman as a perfect place, so He is creating another perfect place for those who declare Him Lord of their lives. Sin had no place in Eden, and it has no place in the New Jerusalem. Once we accept Jesus as our Savior—a gift without cost—we earn the right to live with Him.

In the final chapter of Revelation, Jesus impressed upon John the immediacy of these events. Three times in this chapter Jesus said that He is coming soon. So profoundly does Jesus want each person to declare Him Lord, and enjoy eternity with Him, that He's saying there's no time to waste. "Behold, I am coming soon! . . . I am the Alpha and the Omega, the First and the Last, the Beginning and the End" (22:12–13).

When you stop for your morning coffee at your favorite hangout, have you ever wondered about those workers who open and close the shop every day? As the "first" on the job, they make the coffee and set out fresh pastries. As the "last" to leave, they clean up the shop, restock the shelves, and make sure everything is ready to go the next morning.

There's a parallel here with Jesus as the Alpha and Omega. Every day, Jesus offers Himself to us—He's the same every day—and every day we have the opportunity to taste and see that He is good. At the end of each day, He prepares again to meet us the next morning, bright and early. Don't let another day go by without Jesus in your life. He wants to spend eternity with you.

AMEN

"To the angel of the church in Laodicea write:
These are the words of the Amen, the faithful and true witness,
the ruler of God's creation."
REVELATION 3:14

The word *amen*, usually translated as "so be it," typically signifies the end of a prayer or a declaration. But as part of Jesus' dictation to the apostle John, the word takes on another meaning. From the tradition of Judaism, "Amen" was used to describe "God, the Trustworthy King." Jesus, "the way and the truth and the life" (John 14:6), embraced that definition as well.

John was instructed by Jesus to write letters to seven churches, with Laodicea being the final one. As the "faithful and true witness," Jesus can only tell it like it was: Laodicea was suffering from lukewarm faith. Laodicea, a thriving metropolis in Asia Minor, a cultural and educational center, was not suffering from plague or drought. No, its condition was much more serious.

Turning the mirror onto this twenty-first century, the parallels between Laodicea and our society are obvious. Most of us lead fairly comfortable lives, barely aware of societal influences that lead us away from the Bible. What Jesus said to the Laodiceans stands today: the Amen (our trustworthy God) is waiting for you to answer His call.

ANCIENT OF DAYS

As I looked, thrones were set in place, and the Ancient of Days took his seat.
His clothing was as white as snow; the hair of his head was white like wool.
His throne was flaming with fire, and its wheels were all ablaze.
DANIEL 7:9

Like John, the Old Testament prophet Daniel was given a vision by God of the end times. He wasn't exiled on a lonely island, but he had been taken away from his homeland to the courts of Babylon as part of the legendary Babylonian captivity. There he spent his entire adult life, interpreting dreams and becoming a trusted advisor to kings, all the while maintaining his steadfast faith in God. As a very old man, he had been thrown into a lions' den because he refused to stop praying to his God—and survived.

Daniel's description of God as the Ancient of Days may have been culled from the prophet Isaiah's writings years earlier: " 'You are my witnesses,' declares the LORD, 'that I am God. Yes, and from ancient days I am he' " (Isaiah 43:12–13). Knowing that God would be on His throne during the final judgment and beyond—and that He had been ruling the world since the beginning—Daniel's divinely appropriated choice of words was apt indeed. God is the Ancient of Days—He is eternal.

In Daniel's vision, despite the onslaught of four earthly kingdoms, described as beasts, the Ancient of Days remains on His throne. After the beasts have been vanquished, one called the "son of man," or Jesus, approaches the throne. "He approached the Ancient of Days and was led into his presence. He was given authority, glory, and sovereign power; all peoples, nations and men of every language worshiped him. His dominion is an everlasting dominion that will not pass away, and his kingdom is one that will never be destroyed" (Daniel 7:13–14).

Our culture has been called a "throwaway society"—we don't expect many of our consumer goods, our technologies, even our personal relationships, to last forever. Yet we know one thing for sure: the Ancient of Days is forever. If Jesus is Lord of our lives, one day, we'll spend forever with Him.

ANOINTED ONE

The kings of the earth take their stand and the rulers gather together against the LORD and against his Anointed One.
PSALM 2:2

In the Old Testament, the Lord's anointed would have been the king of Israel. Consider Samuel's anointing of David: "Then Samuel took the horn of oil, and anointed him. . .and the Spirit of the LORD came upon David" (1 Samuel 16:13 KJV).

This verse, however, from one of the prophetic psalms, can only be describing Jesus either at His crucifixion or in the end times. While Jesus was not anointed with oil by a prophet, He was baptized, or anointed, by the Holy Spirit. John the Baptist described this scene in the Jordan River: "I saw the Spirit descending from heaven like a dove, and it abode upon him [Jesus]" (John 1:32 KJV).

Later, in a synagogue in Nazareth, Jesus preached from the book of Isaiah, reading, "The Spirit of the Lord is upon me, because he hath anointed me to preach the gospel to the poor; he hath sent me to heal the brokenhearted, to preach deliverance to the captives, and recovering of sight to the blind, to set at liberty them that are bruised" (Luke 4:18 KJV). Speaking at Cornelius's house, the apostle Peter said, "God anointed Jesus of Nazareth with the Holy Ghost and with power" (Acts 10:38 KJV).

To be anointed means to have God's presence upon you. We couldn't be any closer to Him unless we were face-to-face with Jesus.

AUTHOR AND PERFECTER OF OUR FAITH

Let us fix our eyes on Jesus, the author and perfecter of our faith,
who for the joy set before him endured the cross, scorning its shame,
and sat down at the right hand of the throne of God.

HEBREWS 12:2

Because of Jesus Christ, we call ourselves Christians—that is, because He is the author of our faith. Without Jesus, there would be no Christian faith. And so it makes sense that He is also the perfecter, or finisher or completer, of our faith, depending on the Bible translation you use. What Jesus has started, He will certainly see through to perfection. As Paul writes, "He who began a good work in you will carry it on to completion until the day of Christ Jesus" (Philippians 1:6).

The word *author* was used about Jesus one other time in the Bible when Peter addressed the onlookers after he and John had healed a crippled beggar in Jesus' name: "You killed the author of life, but God raised him from the dead. We are witnesses of this. By faith in the name of Jesus, this man whom you see and know was made strong" (Acts 3:15–16).

What is this faith that we attribute to Jesus? It sent Him to the cross; it heals bodies and souls; and it will one day be our passport to heaven. The writer of Hebrews explained, "Now faith is being sure of what we hope for and certain of what we do not see. . . . By faith we understand that the universe was formed at God's command, so that what is seen was not made out of what was visible" (Hebrews 11:1, 3).

And the way to obtain such faith? Paul said we need to respond to the Author's work: "Faith comes from hearing the message, and the message is heard through the word of Christ" (Romans 10:17).

Some of the rewards of such faith are peace—"You will keep in perfect peace him [who]. . .trusts in you" (Isaiah 26:3)—and confidence—"The effect of righteousness will be quietness and confidence forever" (Isaiah 32:17), with the ultimate reward being eternal life.

As the author of the Bible, Jesus wants us to read His Book. He wants us to be knowledgeable about our faith. And He wants us to ask questions—so He can provide the answers. Most of all, He wants us to acknowledge Him as Author and Savior. Once we are His, we are His forever.

BEGINNING

He said to me: "It is done.
I am the Alpha and the Omega, the Beginning and the End."
REVELATION 21:6

From the first chapter of the first book of the Bible to the final chapter of the last book, we are told God has always existed. He was there at the beginning of the world—"In the beginning God created the heavens and the earth" (Genesis 1:1)—and He will be there in the New Jerusalem (Revelation 21–22).

This sense of equating beginning with creating can be almost overwhelming, as it was to King Solomon when he penned these words: "He [God] has made everything beautiful in its time. He has also set eternity in the hearts of men; yet they cannot fathom what God has done from beginning to end" (Ecclesiastes 3:11).

When the apostle John wrote, "That which was from the beginning, which we have heard, which we have seen with our eyes, which we have looked at and our hands have touched" (1 John 1:1), he was writing as an eyewitness to Jesus. In any court of law, that's powerful testimony. For us, that's a good reason to read more.

Do you know the One who was from the beginning? When you do, you will feel the sense of eternity in your heart, the knowledge that you have been saved and will spend eternity with Him.

BRANCH

Hear now, O Joshua the high priest, thou, and thy fellows that sit
before thee: for they are men wondered at: for, behold,
I will bring forth my servant the BRANCH.
ZECHARIAH 3:8 KJV

The Babylonian captivity, having just ended a decade or so earlier, was fresh in the minds of Zechariah's listeners. God knew the people needed encouragement, a reason to look to the future. And so He gave Zechariah a vision of the One to come, the Messiah, the Branch.

Years earlier, the prophet Isaiah had been the first to use this name of Jesus: "In that day the Branch of the LORD will be beautiful and glorious, and the fruit of the land will be the pride and glory of the survivors in Israel" (Isaiah 4:2). Isaiah also described the Branch as coming from "the stump of Jesse," a reference to Jesus tracing His lineage to Jesse's son David: "From his roots a Branch will bear fruit. The Spirit of the LORD will rest on him" (Isaiah 11:1–2). Later, Jesus would describe Himself as the vine, with His followers as the branches, saying: "If a man remains in me and I in him, he will bear much fruit; apart from me you can do nothing" (John 15:5).

Seeing a relative suffer from a debilitating disease has led many a researcher to develop ideas that become successful experiments, which then become drugs that save lives. Yes, when ideas bear fruit, good things happen. The same is true if we follow Jesus. When we hear and accept the Word, we can then plant the seeds of salvation in the hearts of many others. The fruit never stops ripening on the Branch!

BREAD OF LIFE

Then Jesus declared, "I am the bread of life.
He who comes to me will never go hungry,
and he who believes in me will never be thirsty. . . .
I am the bread of life."
JOHN 6:35, 48

To "break bread" with someone usually means more than sharing a simple meal. This quaint concept implies that you have begun a relationship based on trust with another.

Jesus, as the master teacher, understood the importance of breaking bread. The day before He offered Himself as the spiritual antidote for hunger in the sixth chapter of John's Gospel, He provided a feast for thousands. By this time in His earthly ministry, Jesus had already performed several miracles and word of His powers had spread. No sooner did He sit down to rest on a mountainside than a crowd of five thousand appeared!

While His disciples despaired at their predicament—it would take eight months' wages to feed this mob—Jesus had the situation in hand. With five small barley loaves and two small fish provided by a boy, Jesus blessed the food and fed the hungry throng. When appetites had been sated, there were enough leftovers to fill twelve baskets.

The next day, Jesus followed up this miracle with the spiritual interpretation: He is the Bread of Life. He was like the manna God provided for the wandering Hebrews, but He was much more. Unlike that bread—which would spoil after a day—Jesus' gift, His bread, to believers is eternal life: "Just as the living Father sent me and I live because of the Father, so the one who feeds on me will live because of me. This is the bread that came down from heaven. Your forefathers ate manna and died, but he who feeds on this bread will live forever" (John 6:57–58). Moses only led the Hebrews to the brink of the Promised Land. When we trust in Jesus, we will live forever with Him in heaven.

For this to happen—eternal life based simply on belief in Jesus—Jesus first had to pay the price of our sin on the cross. "I am the living bread that came down from heaven. If anyone eats of this bread, he will live forever. This bread is my flesh, which I will give for the life of the world" (John 6:51). Jesus knew that His disciples would have preferred seeing Him miraculously "ascend to where he was before" (John 6:62), but that was not God's plan.

The concept of Jesus as the Bread of Life was hard to swallow, both for the crowds that followed Him and His disciples. You can almost hear their murmurings: Isn't this the son of Joseph and Mary? Didn't He come from Nazareth? Likely they wondered what He meant when He said, "Whoever eats my flesh and drinks my blood remains in me, and I in him" (John 6:56). Many "disciples," but not any of the Twelve, no longer followed Him. Jesus knew their hearts had not been prepared by God to receive Him.

Only Peter's staunch statement of faith was recorded by John: "Lord, to whom shall we go? You have the words of eternal life. We believe and know that you are the Holy One of God" (John 6:68–69). Peter had broken bread with the Savior, he had witnessed His miracles, and he accepted Him as the Bread of Life. Peter was no longer searching for answers; he had found the One who would reserve his place in heaven.

Many of us live day-to-day, paycheck-to-paycheck. We need our daily fix of caffeine, our bagel or hard roll, and then we're "good to go"—for a while. We try to pay the bills and maybe put a little aside, all the while hoping we won't be "downsized." But life doesn't have to be that depressing. We need to seek after that which is everlasting. We need to be saved by Jesus, the Bread of Life: "Salvation is found in no one else, for there is no other name under heaven given to men by which we must be saved" (Acts 4:12).

BRIDEGROOM

Jesus answered, "How can the guests of the bridegroom mourn while he is with them? The time will come when the bridegroom will be taken from them; then they will fast."
MATTHEW 9:15

Married or single, all Christians one day will meet their Bridegroom, Jesus. As part of Jesus' church, also known as the bride, a great ceremony awaits us in heaven where we will worship God with acclaim and jubilation (Revelation 19:6–8).

But that's getting ahead of the love story. Way back in the book of Isaiah, Jesus was introduced as the Bridegroom: "As a bridegroom rejoices over his bride, so will your God rejoice over you" (Isaiah 62:5). During Jesus' earthly ministry, He used the image of Himself as Bridegroom in parables. In the Matthew 9 passage, Jesus is foretelling His crucifixion; in the parable of the ten virgins (Matthew 25:1–13), He is cautioning believers, or His church, to be alert for His second coming. After Jesus began preaching, John the Baptist used the imagery, too, to deflect interest away from himself: "The bride belongs to the bridegroom. The friend who attends the bridegroom waits and listens for him, and is full of joy when he hears the bridegroom's voice. That joy is mine, and it is now complete" (John 3:29).

Jesus' courtship of His church has followed traditional guidelines. He chose us to be His own (John 15:16), professing His deep and abiding love: "Greater love has no one than this, that he lay down his life for his friends" (John 15:13). As all worthy ancient bridegrooms, He paid a "bride price." Instead of money or property, most significantly, He shed His blood on the cross for us. As Paul wrote, "You are not your own; you were bought at a price" (1 Corinthians 6:19–20). At the Last Supper, Jesus declared, "This cup is the new covenant in my blood, which is poured out for you" (Luke 22:20). Now Jesus awaits the arrival of His bride in heaven: "In my Father's house are many rooms; if it were not so, I would have told you. I am going there to prepare a place for you" (John 14:2).

The only step that awaits is our heartfelt consent to be His.

Think about someone you love so much you can't imagine your life without them. Every time you think of them in this way, your eyes tear up and you can barely talk. Now, if possible, multiply this feeling by several times. . .and you may begin to realize how much Jesus, the Bridegroom, loves you.

CARPENTER

"Isn't this the carpenter? Isn't this Mary's son
and the brother of James, Joseph, Judas, and Simon?
Aren't his sisters here with us?"
And they took offense at him.
MARK 6:3

Jesus' ministry on earth lasted around three and one-half years, beginning when He was about thirty (Luke 3:23). Growing up in the first century in the small town of Nazareth as the "stepson" of Joseph, who was a carpenter (Matthew 13:55), Jesus, as the firstborn, would naturally have gravitated to Joseph's profession. That means that Jesus spent more years on earth being a carpenter than preaching! Is it any wonder that the townspeople of Nazareth were amazed? They knew Him only as a lowly tradesman.

Yes, Jesus, who was fully divine and fully human (Philippians 2:6), knew what it was like to work hard for little pay. He also knew how to appeal to the common man and woman, by using references to everyday life in His sermons. He refers to the "narrow road" (Matthew 7:14), the man who built his house upon the rock (Matthew 7:25), and His yoke, which He said is easy (Matthew 11:30). He also described Himself as "the stone the builders rejected" (Matthew 21:42).

Every job involves some element of drudgery. When you've made too many copies, wiped up too many spills, gone to too many meetings, and done too many loads of laundry, think about Jesus the Carpenter. He knows what you're going through, and He wants your "burden" to be His.

CHIEF SHEPHERD

And when the Chief Shepherd appears,
you will receive the crown of glory that will never fade away.
1 PETER 5:4

Peter was writing to encourage the elders of a congregation in northern Asia Minor, people persecuted harshly for their faith. The Greek word *poimen*, which has been translated "shepherd," can also mean "pastor." Although this church was struggling, they could rest assured that they were being fed by Jesus Himself and would one day be rewarded by Him.

Because raising sheep was a main source of livelihood for ancient peoples, shepherds are mentioned frequently in the Bible. Kings received instruction to "shepherd" God's people, and one king in particular, David, was a shepherd. But even shepherds need leading, as evidenced when David wrote, "The LORD is my shepherd, I shall not be in want" (Psalm 23:1). Centuries later, Jesus said, "I am the good shepherd. The good shepherd lays down his life for the sheep" (John 10:11).

Yet Peter's divinely penned description has a deeper meaning. By calling Jesus the Chief Shepherd, he is saying He is shepherd over all other shepherds, pastor over all other pastors. Just as Jesus was sent by His Father, pastors are to be called by God. They are then to follow God's leading to wherever He sends them and lead their flocks to true knowledge of Jesus' saving grace. They are to be fed on God's Word and to feed their flocks accordingly.

Peter, as a pastor himself, knew what it was like to be fed by the Chief Shepherd. At Jesus' arrest in Gethsemane, the impetuous but achingly loyal Peter had cut off the ear of the high priest's servant. A short time later, though, this once boastful disciple denied three times that he was Jesus' disciple, an act foretold by Jesus. Ashamed by his own cowardice, Peter would nonetheless be reinstated by Jesus. Following His resurrection, Jesus asked the disciple if he loved Him and three times Peter responded emphatically. In response to Peter, Jesus said, "Feed my lambs," "Take care of my sheep," and "Feed my sheep." (See John 21:15–17.) Peter eventually died a martyr's death after leading many to Jesus.

When we make the decision to follow Jesus, there's no fine print to decipher, no rebate instructions to follow meticulously, no additional hoops to jump through. When we trust in the Chief Shepherd, we are simply, blessedly, His for life. Jesus said, "My sheep listen to my voice; I know them, and they follow me. I give them eternal life, and they shall never perish; no one can snatch them out of my hand" (John 10:27–28).

THE CHRIST

And Jacob the father of Joseph, the husband of Mary,
of whom was born Jesus, who is called Christ.
MATTHEW 1:16

What's the purpose of having the genealogy of Jesus besides making our eyes get blurry? There are several reasons, but the most important may be that Jesus' lineage proves, in part, that He is the Christ. To be called the Christ, from the Greek *Christos*, meaning "the Anointed One," was another way of saying that Jesus was the long-awaited Messiah.

First, the Messiah was to come from the tribe of Judah, a prophecy described in the book of Genesis: "The scepter will not depart from Judah, nor the ruler's staff from between his feet, until he comes to whom it belongs and the obedience of the nations is his" (Genesis 49:10). Matthew 1:2–3 and Luke 3:29 confirm that Jesus was of the tribe of Judah.

The prophet Jeremiah foretold that the Messiah would be directly related to David: " 'The days are coming,' declares the LORD, 'when I will raise up to David a righteous Branch, a King who will reign wisely. . . . This is the name by which he will be called: The LORD Our Righteousness' " (Jeremiah 23:5–6). A quick glance at Matthew 1:6 and Luke 3:31 confirm that Jesus as a man had descended from King David.

Still, those two pieces of evidence are not enough to erase doubt. Jesus Himself said others would present themselves as "the Christ," but that we, as true believers, are not to be deceived (Matthew 24:23). So what else was prophesied that confirms Jesus as the Christ?

For starters, the prophet Micah described the site of Jesus' birth: "But you, Bethlehem Ephrathah, though you are small among the clans of Judah, out of you will come for me one who will be ruler over Israel, whose origins are from of old, from ancient times" (Micah 5:2).

Another prophet, Zechariah, described Jesus' triumphal entry into Jerusalem on what is now known as Palm Sunday: "See, your king comes to you, righteous and having salvation, gentle and riding on a donkey" (Zechariah 9:9).

In one of his psalms, David described intimate details of what would be

Jesus' crucifixion: water would pour out from Jesus; His feet and hands would be pierced; none of Jesus' bones would be broken; and lots would be cast for His clothing (Psalm 22:14–18).

The prophet Isaiah is probably the best known of the Old Testament prophets who foretold the Messiah or the Christ. While Israel was undoubtedly expecting a handsome man to come from God, the prophet dispelled those notions: "He had no beauty or majesty to attract us to him, nothing in his appearance that we should desire him" (Isaiah 53:2). Although no accurate paintings of Jesus exist, there is evidence from early writers that substantiates Isaiah's claim.

Isaiah went on to describe the healing power of the Messiah: "Surely he took up our infirmities and carried our sorrows" (Isaiah 53:4). Matthew was the first to confirm Isaiah's prophecy, even citing it in his Gospel (Matthew 8:16–17).

Isaiah also described the Crucifixion: "But he was pierced for our transgressions, he was crushed for our iniquities; the punishment that brought us peace was upon him, and by his wounds we are healed" (Isaiah 53:5). All of the Gospel writers described Jesus' death in detail, precisely the way the Christ's death had been foretold centuries before.

We are so conditioned to use the title "Jesus Christ" that we don't realize what we're really saying. Jesus was not just a poor Jewish man who preached about love and forgiveness in the first century. He was not simply a holy man unjustly accused and forced to die a horrible death. His birth, life, and death were all foretold by ancient prophets, as well as His second coming. He was the true Anointed One, the Messiah, the Christ. One day all believers will have the privilege of echoing Peter's words: "You are the Christ, the Son of the living God" (Matthew 16:16).

COMFORTER

And I will pray the Father, and he shall give you another Comforter,
that he may abide with you for ever.
JOHN 14:16 KJV

Jesus and His disciples were passing through the city of Nain when they encountered a first-century traffic jam. A funeral procession was attracting more than the usual crowd, and Jesus and His friends were swept into the melee. A young man had died, not an unusual occurrence. But this man was the only son of his widowed mother, and now she was left desolate. Luke wrote, "And when the Lord saw her, he had compassion on her, and said unto her, Weep not. And he came and touched the bier: and they that bare him stood still. And he said, Young man, I say unto thee, Arise" (Luke 7:13–14 KJV).

During Jesus' ministry on earth, the picture of Jesus as Comforter was presented many times. But Jesus' ministry was to be brief. What John was describing in John 14:16 was not another preacher who would come after Jesus but the Holy Spirit. This Holy Spirit, or Comforter, from the Greek *parakletos*, would comfort the disciples—and all believers—when Jesus returned to heaven.

Jesus shared this news at what has come to be called the Last Supper, the last Passover He would share with His closest associates on earth. Jesus had already told them He was going away to a place they knew, where He would prepare "mansions" for them. The Comforter He was sending was Himself—in Spirit form and invisible to human eyes, but living inside each of them (John 14:17), a Spirit that could not come to them until Jesus had departed (John 16:7). Jesus continued: "But the Comforter. . .whom the Father will send in my name, he shall teach you all things, and bring all things to your remembrance, whatsoever I have said unto you" (John 14:26 KJV). After Peter, along with the others gathered "in one place," received the Holy Spirit on the day of Pentecost (Acts 2), Peter was able to preach so effectively that three thousand came to faith in Jesus that day.

Because Jesus has not yet returned, the Holy Spirit, or the Comforter, continues to reside in all who believe on the name of Jesus. As Peter exhorted the crowds in Jerusalem on Pentecost, "Repent, and be baptized every one of you in the name of Jesus Christ for the remission of sins, and ye shall receive the gift of the Holy Ghost. For the promise is unto you, and to your children" (Acts 2:38–39 KJV).

CONSOLATION OF ISRAEL

Behold, there was a man in Jerusalem, whose name was Simeon;
and the same man was just and devout, waiting for the consolation of Israel:
and the Holy Ghost was upon him.
LUKE 2:25 KJV

We often say that people "know" their Bible. That could be said of Simeon, who could probably recite Isaiah 49:13: "Sing, O heavens; and be joyful, O earth; and break forth into singing, O mountains: for the LORD hath comforted his people, and will have mercy upon his afflicted" (KJV). And without doubt, he knew Isaiah 9:6: "For unto us a child is born, unto us a son is given. . .and his name shall be. . .The mighty God, The everlasting Father, The Prince of Peace" (KJV). The Holy Spirit had told Simeon that he would not die before he had seen this very child (Luke 2:26).

When the Spirit led him to the temple in Jerusalem on this particular day, he saw Mary and Joseph with baby in tow, who had come to give an offering of two pigeons, the amount due for their firstborn. Simeon went up to them, took Jesus in his arms, and praised God, saying, "Lord, now lettest thou thy servant depart in peace. . .for mine eyes have seen thy salvation, which thou has prepared before the face of all people: a light to lighten the Gentiles, and the glory of thy people Israel" (Luke 2:29–32 KJV).

The word *consolation* comes from the Greek *paraklesis*, which means "help, encouragement, and refreshment." That definition is especially apt considering Israel's tumultuous history. Isaiah recorded the Assyrian conflict and the approaching Babylonian captivity. Following that, while a remnant of Jews returned to Jerusalem, most were scattered in the Persian Empire. As the time for Jesus' birth neared, Jews in Jerusalem were suffering under the Roman Empire and, in particular, under Herod, who had been appointed "king of the Jews."

To Simeon, under the guidance of the Holy Spirit, the child he beheld was God, come to heal, revive, and console the troubled land.

Like Simeon, we, too, have the opportunity to see Jesus, the Consolation of Israel—because He is coming again! The writer of Hebrews says, "He will appear a second time, not to bear sin, but to bring salvation to those who are waiting for him" (Hebrews 9:28). Peter says we are "to prepare [our] minds for action" (1 Peter 1:13), and Paul says those who long for His appearing will receive a crown of righteousness (2 Timothy 4:8). He's coming soon. . .are you watching and waiting?

CORNERSTONE

Consequently, you are. . .fellow citizens with God's people and members of God's household, built on the foundation of the apostles and prophets, with Christ Jesus himself as the chief cornerstone.
EPHESIANS 2:19–20

Cornerstones on modern buildings are largely ceremonial, with civic leaders' names proudly chiseled next to the foundation date carved in Roman numerals. In ancient times, though, the stones were anything but trivial. Usually laid in the northeast corner, the cornerstone was the largest, most expensive rock that united two walls of the foundation. Great care went into picking just the right stone. The cornerstone had to be laid before the building could be built; without the cornerstone there would be no building.

Likewise, Jesus is the Cornerstone of the Christian church, for without His ministry on earth, His death on the cross, and His resurrection, there would be no church. Jesus' role as Cornerstone was proclaimed first by the psalmist, who also alluded to Jesus' rejection as the Messiah: "The stone which the builders refused is become the head stone of the corner" (Psalm 118:22 KJV).

God said to the prophet Isaiah, "Behold, I lay in Zion for a foundation a stone, a tried stone, a precious corner stone, a sure foundation" (Isaiah 28:16 KJV). And the prophet Zechariah wrote, "From Judah will come the cornerstone" (Zechariah 10:4).

While the concept of Jesus as the foundation for the entire church all over the world may be a little overwhelming, Jesus can also be the cornerstone of our lives. To illustrate this, Jesus told a parable about the wise and foolish builders (Matthew 7:24–27). When we read the Bible or hear God's Word and then live the way Jesus wants, we're like the man who built his house on the rock. Come what may—rain, wind, and life in general—our foundation is secure. Those who don't put into practice Jesus' words are like the man who built his house on sand. When the rains and the wind came, that house fell "with a great crash." In other words, without Jesus, to use modern parlance, we self-destruct.

When was the last time you read the Bible? As King Solomon wrote, "There is nothing new under the sun" (Ecclesiastes 1:9). Any trial you're going through probably occurred somewhere in the pages of God's Book. God has the answer for every situation. . .if you first cling to the rock, Jesus, the Cornerstone of the Christian faith.

COUNSELOR

"Unless I go away, the Counselor will not come to you;
but if I go, I will send him to you."
JOHN 16:7

Under cover of night, Nicodemus made his way to where Jesus was staying. A Pharisee and member of the Sanhedrin, the Jewish ruling council, Nicodemus was making what we would call an unsanctioned visit. As a group, the Pharisees questioned everything about Jesus. Nicodemus wanted to know more, and Jesus, as Counselor, did not disappoint.

First, Jesus told Nicodemus that he must be born again, the second time of the Spirit. When this concept proved difficult for Nicodemus to understand, Jesus shared the crux of the Christian faith in one sentence: "For God so loved the world that he gave his one and only Son, that whoever believes in him shall not perish but have eternal life" (John 3:16). Jesus' final recorded words to Nicodemus that evening are especially telling when considering Jesus as Counselor: "But whoever lives by the truth comes into the light, so that it may be seen plainly that what he has done has been done through God" (John 3:21).

Later, when Jesus encountered the Samaritan woman at the well at Sychar,

He astounded her with a detailed description of her marital history, including knowledge of her present illicit relationship. To her He said, "God is spirit, and his worshipers must worship in spirit and in truth" (John 4:24).

This Spirit of truth is Jesus as Counselor. At what has come to be called the Last Supper, Jesus said to His disciples, "And I will ask the Father, and he will give you another Counselor to be with you forever—the Spirit of truth" (John 14:16–17). Jesus did not want to leave His followers without a moral compass or, more important, a guide to living the Christian life. To all who believe in Him, as He told Nicodemus, He promises the Holy Spirit will reside in them, to lead them in a closer walk with Him.

And why should we trust Jesus? John gives the answer early in his Gospel account: because Jesus came from God. "We have seen his glory, the glory of the One and Only, who came from the Father, full of grace and truth" (John 1:14).

This Spirit of truth, however, is not a voice of condemnation. We are not going to be berated by the Counselor, but rather, we will be encouraged to do what is right.

Jesus demonstrated this during His encounter with an adulterous woman who was being held by the Pharisees. When a large crowd had gathered in the temple courts in Jerusalem to hear Jesus teach, the Pharisees hustled the woman into His presence, trying to bait Him in front of His listeners (John 8:2–11).

"Teacher," they said, "the Law of Moses commanded us to stone such women. Now what do you say?"

Instead of accusing her, Jesus bent down and started to write in the dirt with His finger. As the Pharisees continued to needle Him, Jesus stood and said, "If any one of you is without sin, let him be the first to throw a stone at her."

One by one, the Pharisees left the temple courts, leaving only Jesus and the woman standing there.

Still, Jesus did not condemn her even though they were alone. "Woman, where are they?" He asked. "Has no one condemned you?"

She answered, "No one."

The wisest Counselor then declared, "Then neither do I condemn you. Go now and leave your life of sin."

Because Jesus has given us this Spirit of truth, He wants us not only to lead a better life, but also to be a witness. Because the Spirit of truth testifies to us about Jesus, we must testify about Jesus to others.

We don't know much about Nicodemus, but we do know that he continued to love Jesus. He accompanied Joseph of Arimathea to collect Jesus' body after the Crucifixion, bringing with him about 75 pounds of spices, as was the burial custom (see John 19:38–40). Together Nicodemus and Joseph laid Jesus' body in the garden tomb. Years later, Nicodemus is said to have died a martyr's death for his faith.

If, like Nicodemus, you have had to go against the religious traditions of your family or culture to follow where God is leading, you know the struggles he experienced. But likely, you have also experienced the rewards. Have you heard the Counselor's voice? Believe, and you will.

DAYSPRING

Through the tender mercy of our God;
whereby the dayspring from on high hath visited us.
To give light to them that sit in darkness and in the shadow of death,
to guide our feet into the way of peace.
LUKE 1:78–79 KJV

The Babylonian captivity had ended and God's people had returned to Jerusalem to rebuild the temple and restore the city gates. Like other prophets writing in this postexilic period, Malachi brought a painful message from God—but this time the focus was different. This time, instead of chastising the people for their failure to rebuild, God focused on how they were worshipping Him. The lazy priests were offering unworthy sacrifices and the men were divorcing their wives to marry younger, pagan women. Tithes and offerings were being kept for themselves and not offered to God.

Still, the Lord offered a glimmer of hope to the faithful few: "But for you who revere my name, the sun of righteousness will rise with healing in its wings" (Malachi 4:2). Four hundred years passed before that prophecy would be fulfilled, before the Dayspring first rose over the earth—at the birth of God's Son, Jesus.

A dayspring is a place of rising or the dawn. Because of God's great gift to us, the gift of His Son, we have hope and a future. Because of Jesus the Dayspring, the greatest question of life—where we will rise to spend eternity—has been answered.

DAY STAR

We have also a more sure word of prophecy; whereunto ye do well
that ye take heed, as unto a light that shineth in a dark place,
until the day dawn, and the day star arise in your hearts.
2 PETER 1:19 KJV

Mornings are times of promise. After nights of inky blackness, uncertainty, and fear, that shaft of light warming your face as you awake signals a new opportunity. King David understood this when he wrote, "Weeping may remain for a night, but rejoicing comes in the morning" (Psalm 30:5). Mornings are also times of prayer and praise, as we thank God for the gift of another day. Again, David wrote, "Let the morning bring me word of your unfailing love, for I have put my trust in you" (Psalm 143:8).

As the Day Star, Jesus is the bringer or bearer of light. Jesus said, "I am the light of the world. Whoever follows me will never walk in darkness, but will have the light of life" (John 8:12). When we live without Jesus, we are figuratively wandering in the dark, without purpose and without promise. But those who know Him as Savior experience the gift of morning all day, every day.

Without knowing exactly what or whom they would find, the Magi followed the star to Bethlehem, seeking to worship a newborn king. Unlike those learned men of old, we know whom we are following and we know the ending of our life journey. But what about the stops along the way? Let's wait for the Day Star to guide us.

DELIVERER

And so all Israel will be saved, as it is written:
"The deliverer will come from Zion;
he will turn godlessness away from Jacob."
ROMANS 11:26

One Sabbath in Capernaum, Jesus was teaching in the synagogue when a man possessed by an evil spirit confronted Him. Speaking through the man, the spirit said, "I know who you are—the Holy One of God!" (Mark 1:24). With great authority, Jesus commanded the spirit to come out of the man and the spirit obeyed. The people who witnessed this were amazed: Who was this Jesus, whom even the evil spirits obeyed?

This Jesus is the Deliverer, the One who has power to keep us from evil and save us from eternal damnation. As Paul wrote, "For he has rescued us from the dominion of darkness and brought us into the kingdom of the Son he loves, in whom we have redemption, the forgiveness of sins" (Colossians 1:13–14). Writing to the Ephesians, Paul reminds us that our struggle is not against "flesh and blood" but rather against the "spiritual forces of evil," Satan's domain (Ephesians 6:12).

Choices come our way every day and the wrong ones may lead us down a slippery slope to more compromising situations. Our Deliverer, Jesus, is more than up to the challenge of dark forces. "In this world you will have trouble," Jesus said. "But take heart! I have overcome the world" (John 16:33).

DESIRE OF NATIONS

And I will shake all nations, and the desire of all nations shall come:
and I will fill this house with glory,
saith the LORD of hosts.
HAGGAI 2:7 KJV

The rebuilding of the temple in Jerusalem had halted ten years earlier and the people were despondent. How could they equal the glory of Solomon's first temple—built with the finest materials—when they had few resources? God's message through the prophet Haggai was this: What is lacking on the outside will be more than made up for by what is inside.

Five hundred years later, into this second temple came the Desire of Nations, God's Son, Jesus. While God first brought this message to Israel, His chosen nation, the prophet Isaiah made it clear that salvation was for all peoples: "Turn to me and be saved, all you ends of the earth; for I am God, and there is no other" (Isaiah 45:22).

Today, with the click of a mouse, information can be shared around the world. Yet in this globally driven culture, Jesus is still the Desire of Nations. Instead of acknowledging our differences—as Paul wrote, "there is no Greek or Jew, circumcised or uncircumcised. . .slave or free" (Colossians 3:11)—He unites us in Him. Jesus still fills houses of worship with His glory when people, all peoples, profess His holy name.

EL-ELYON

The LORD thundered from heaven; the voice of the Most High resounded.
PSALM 18:13

The Most High God, the God surpassing all others, is El-Elyon. Considering that many of the psalms are songs of praise, it's not surprising that the name El-Elyon is used almost twenty times in that one book of the Bible. The psalmist extolled, "There is a river whose streams make glad the city of God, the holy place where the Most High dwells" (Psalm 46:4), and at another time declared, "Let them know that you, whose name is the LORD—that you alone are the Most High over all the earth" (Psalm 83:18).

The first mention of God as El-Elyon occurs in the first book of the Bible, after the patriarch Abram defeated the four kings who had kidnapped his nephew Lot. Abram was greeted by Melchizedek, the king of Salem (or Jerusalem), who said to him, "Blessed be Abram by God Most High. . .who delivered your enemies into your hand" (Genesis 14:19–20).

Such sovereign power was acknowledged later by the prophet Daniel, who, after informing King Nebuchadnezzar that his royal power had been taken away, told the king, "Seven times will pass by for you until you acknowledge that the Most High is sovereign over the kingdoms of men and gives them to anyone he wishes" (Daniel 4:32).

A few verses later, Nebuchadnezzar praised El-Elyon himself, declaring, "His dominion is an eternal dominion; his kingdom endures from generation to generation. . . . No one can hold back his hand or say to him: 'What have you done?'"(Daniel 4:34–35).

As a young girl growing up in Nazareth, an insignificant village in Galilee, Mary might have questioned El-Elyon's plans for her. But when the angel Gabriel advised her, "The Holy Spirit will come upon you, and the power of the Most High will overshadow you" (Luke 1:35), Mary responded, "I am the Lord's servant. . . . May it be to me as you have said" (Luke 1:38).

And instead of railing against God for striking him dumb during the months of his wife's pregnancy, Zechariah, with his speech restored, praised El-Elyon at the birth of his son, John the Baptist: "And you, my child, will be called a prophet of the Most High; for you will go on before the Lord to prepare the way for him. . .because of the tender mercy of our God, by which the rising sun will come to us from heaven to shine on those living in darkness and in the shadow of death, to guide our feet into the path of peace" (Luke 1:76, 78–79).

There are times when we surely have doubted God's plans for our lives. When the "perfect" job is given to another, when the child who always listened and obeyed now makes poor choices, or when a close relative or friend dies "too soon"—the list is practically endless—we may question what God is doing. At those times, and all others, too, we need to trust in the God who surpasses all others. As El-Elyon, He has revealed Himself throughout the ages to all who trust in Him, and He will continue to do so.

EMMANUEL

Behold, a virgin shall be with child, and shall bring forth a son,
and they shall call his name Emmanuel, which being interpreted is, God with us.
Matthew 1:23 kjv

The angel of the Lord appeared to Joseph in a dream, and not a moment too soon. Joseph was on the verge of divorcing Mary and he needed some convincing to do otherwise. First, the angel told Joseph to take Mary as his wife because her baby was conceived by God. Second, the angel commanded that he, Joseph, was to name the child Jesus. And thirdly, the angel brought news: The birth of Mary's child would fulfill ancient prophecy. Seven hundred years earlier, the prophet

Isaiah had written, "The virgin will be with child and will give birth to a son, and will call him Immanuel" (Isaiah 7:14).

Immanuel, the name in Hebrew, means "God with us." The name was never meant to be Jesus' first name and in fact is used only twice in the Bible. Rather, Immanuel is a description of Jesus.

To the ancients, a name meaning "God with us" would have conjured images of Old Testament Bible heroes who knew God was with them and accomplished great things because of His guiding hand. To Abram, God said, "I will make you into a great nation" (Genesis 12:2), and indeed did just that, leading him to Canaan, the future home of the nation of Israel. God assured Abram, "I am your shield, your very great reward" (Genesis 15:1).

To Moses, God said, "I will be with you" (Exodus 3:12), and used him as the facilitator to lead His people out of Egypt. On the long journey across the Sinai, God's presence was felt by the pillar of cloud by day and the pillar of fire by night (Exodus 13:21).

To Joshua, God said, "As I was with Moses, so I will be with you; I will never leave you nor forsake you" (Joshua 1:5), before guiding him and the Israelites into the Promised Land.

To King David, God said, "I have been with you wherever you have gone, and I have cut off all your enemies from before you" (2 Samuel 7:9). And indeed under his reign, the conquest of Canaan was completed. But David would be blessed like no other: "I will raise up your offspring to succeed you, who will come from your own body, and I will establish his kingdom. He is the one who will build a house for my Name, and I will establish the throne of his kingdom forever" (2 Samuel 7:12–13).

Although Solomon, David's son, was granted the privilege of building a temple for God, the house God was speaking of is the Church and the One whose kingdom will last forever is Jesus, our Emmanuel, our "God with us." (Jesus' earthly stepfather, Joseph, and His mother, Mary, were direct descendants of King David. See Matthew 1:1–16 for Joseph's lineage and Luke 3:23–37 for Mary's—note that Heli is thought to be Mary's father.)

As Emmanuel, Jesus brings certain credentials that none of the Old Testament heroes could claim. "He is the image of the invisible God, the firstborn over all creation," Paul writes (Colossians 1:15). When He was born in the manger in Bethlehem, it was the first time God was truly among us, walking on the earth as a fully human, fully divine being. His purpose in coming was made clear by His name, Jesus: He came to save His people from their sins (Matthew 1:21).

Lastly, He will be with us not just during our lifetime but forever, once we accept Him as our Savior. Paul writes, "For I am convinced that neither death nor life, neither angels nor demons, neither the present nor the future, nor any powers, neither height nor depth, nor anything else in all creation, will be able to separate us from the love of God that is in Christ Jesus our Lord" (Romans 8:38–39).

Do you remember the first time your parents left you alone? Maybe you made the mistake of watching a scary movie on television and then were kept awake by various noises, not to mention a very active imagination. As our Emmanuel, Jesus has promised never to leave us—ever. As He said to the disciples before He ascended into heaven, "Surely I am with you always, to the very end of the age" (Matthew 28:20).

EVERLASTING FATHER

For unto us a child is born, unto us a son is given:
and the government shall be upon his shoulder:
and his name shall be called. . .The everlasting Father.
ISAIAH 9:6 KJV

Glimpses from the Gospels show how much Jesus loved children. Mark recorded Jesus holding a child in His arms, saying, "Whoever welcomes one of these little children in my name welcomes me" (Mark 9:37). Luke witnessed Jesus saying that the truths of the Bible were more readily accepted by children than "the wise and learned" (Luke 10:21). Jesus was also a fierce defender of children, giving one of His most savage rebukes to anyone who would lead them astray (Mark 9:42).

While we think of God as the Father, Isaiah's inspired prophecy of Jesus describes an attribute of the Messiah, one evident from His caring attitude toward children. Yet He is the Everlasting Father—His kingdom is eternal and He is the sole giver of eternal life. Speaking to John on the island of Patmos, Jesus declared Himself Alpha and Omega, "who is, and who was, and who is to come" (Revelation 1:8). To Mary, Jesus' mother, the angel Gabriel described Jesus' kingdom as one that would never end (Luke 1:33).

As a father is a creator of life, so Jesus has given us spiritual life. "He that hath the Son hath life," writes the apostle John (1 John 5:12 KJV). Indeed, when we accept Jesus as our Savior, we are born a second time. As Paul writes, "Therefore, if anyone is in Christ, he is a new creation; the old has gone, the new has come!" (2 Corinthians 5:17). Jesus Himself declares in the final book of the Bible, "Behold, I make all things new" (Revelation 21:5 KJV). All who have accepted Him as Savior can attest to the amazing transformations in their lives, not just at the moment of acceptance but from that moment onward until departing this life.

Finally, while any father is a giver of life, the best fathers are those who love their children unconditionally. "We love him, because he first loved us," John writes (1 John 4:19 KJV). Bearing the burden of the sins of humanity, Jesus gave His life on the cross so that we could be saved and live eternally with Him. We cannot (and did not) do anything to make Him love us; He simply loves us because He created us. And when we accept His gift of salvation, He loves us because we are His.

Maybe the earthly father you cherish isn't your biological one or even a relative. No matter if you call him Daddy, Uncle, Grandpa, or by his first name, the qualities this person embodies are surely those seen in Jesus. To His disciples, Jesus said, "I will not leave you as orphans; I will come to you" (John 14:18). Jesus, the Everlasting Father, is coming again to gather into His arms all who love Him back—who have accepted His gift of salvation.

FAITHFUL AND TRUE WITNESS

"To the angel of the church in Laodicea write:
These are the words of the Amen,
the faithful and true witness,
the ruler of God's creation."
REVELATION 3:14

Writing to a group of persecuted Christians in Asia Minor, Peter wrote encouraging words. But he also filled his two epistles with warnings, among them one concerning "false teachers," saying, "They will secretly introduce destructive heresies, even denying the sovereign Lord who bought them. . . . Many will follow their shameful ways and will bring the way of truth into disrepute" (2 Peter 2:1–2). While false teachers occupy pulpits, the airwaves, and blogs, there is still one Faithful and True Witness: Jesus.

As Jesus said when the Pharisees challenged Him: "I am one who testifies for myself; my other witness is the Father, who sent me" (John 8:18). And what is Jesus' testimony? John wrote, "And this is the testimony: God has given us eternal life, and this life is in his Son" (1 John 5:11). A few verses later, John said, "We know also that the Son of God has come and has given us understanding, so that we may know him who is true" (1 John 5:20).

King Solomon once lamented, "A faithful man who can find?" (Proverbs 20:6). We who know Jesus have found the Faithful and True Witness—and much more. Because of Jesus, we have also found the source of truth and salvation.

FIRSTFRUITS

For as in Adam all die, so in Christ all will be made alive.
But each in his own turn: Christ, the firstfruits;
then, when he comes, those who belong to him.
1 CORINTHIANS 15:22–23

To honor God after He led them out of bondage in Egypt, ancient Israelites were required to make certain offerings to Him. Among these offerings were the "firstfruits" of their soil, the best of the first crops to ripen each season (Exodus 23:19). Such offerings were part of the Feast of the Firstfruits that began the day following the Sabbath during Passover (Leviticus 23:9–14).

Now fast-forward to the New Testament. Not coincidentally, Jesus was crucified during Passover and He arose from the dead three days later. On "the first day of the week," the day following the Sabbath, the Feast of the Firstfruits, the women discovered His empty tomb (Mark 16:1–6).

Jesus was the best offering; He was the Firstfruits. He was the firstborn son of God, the first son of Mary, and "the firstborn over all creation" (Colossians 1:15). And, as Paul wrote in 1 Corinthians 15, He was also the first to be raised from the dead and ascend into heaven—and will at some future time return to earth to raise His followers.

Parents often say to children, "Just do your best," as if that's not an outstanding effort but an acceptable one. But to God, best is best. . .and the best is the firstfruits of our income, our talents, and our time.

FOUNDATION

Therefore thus saith the Lord GOD, Behold, I lay in Zion for a foundation
a stone, a tried stone, a precious corner stone, a sure foundation:
he that believeth shall not make haste.
ISAIAH 28:16 KJV

Writing to the church at Corinth, Paul said that as Christians we are "God's building" (1 Corinthians 3:9). But every building needs a foundation, in effect, a prepared base on which the construction rests, and for the church of God and all believers, that foundation is Jesus Christ. Paul went on to say, "For no one can lay any foundation other than the one already laid, which is Jesus Christ" (verse 11). Centuries earlier, a psalmist wrote: "Unless the LORD builds the house, its builders labor in vain" (Psalm 127:1).

Jesus Christ provides a foundation that is of lasting and eternal value. When we profess faith in Him, He, in turn, assures us of an eternal future. Jesus said, "The words I have spoken to you are spirit and they are life" (John 6:63). With Jesus as our foundation and with the Bible as our guide, we can build meaningful lives.

The old hymn "Standing on the Promises" contains this verse:

Standing on the promises that cannot fail,
When the howling storms of doubt and fear assail,
By the living Word of God I shall prevail,
Standing on the promises of God.

With Jesus as our Foundation, we will not be immune from trouble—but we've got a future that's unbeatable.

FOUNTAIN

On that day a fountain will be opened to the house
of David and the inhabitants of Jerusalem,
to cleanse them from sin and impurity.
ZECHARIAH 13:1

At a time in the future, the exact date of which is unknown except to God, Jesus will return and establish His perfect kingdom, the New Jerusalem (Revelation 21). The prophet Joel describes mountains dripping with new wine, hills flowing with milk, and ravines running with water (Joel 3:18). And, in the same vein as Zechariah, Joel wrote, "A fountain will flow out of the LORD's house and will water the valley of acacias."

Throughout the Bible, the precious commodity water and a source of it, the fountain, are associated with the quenching of thirst, both physically and spiritually, and forgiveness (the cleansing of sin). Jesus as the Fountain is the source of "living water," a gift He pours out in the form of His Holy Spirit on all who believe. As Jesus told the Samaritan woman at the well: "The water I give. . .will become. . .a spring of water welling up to eternal life" (John 4:14).

In what we used to call "westerns," those action-filled dramas on television and in the movies, there was often a stranded cowboy staggering across an unforgiving desert with his empty canteen. That's a good picture of what we're really like without Jesus—thirsty for spiritual enlightenment and in need of salvation. Come to Jesus today and be refreshed and renewed.

FRIEND OF SINNERS

The Son of Man came eating and drinking, and they say,
"Here is a glutton and a drunkard, a friend of tax collectors and 'sinners.'"
MATTHEW 11:19

To the Jews living under the thumb of the Roman Empire, tax collectors were pawns of their oppressors—they called them "licensed robbers." They were daily reminders that God had truly forsaken them. So great was ancient Jewry's disdain for these men that they were denied fellowship in the temple and their money was considered tainted.

In this contentious milieu, Jesus befriended two tax collectors. One, Levi (also known as Matthew), even became one of His twelve disciples. Upon calling Matthew to follow Him, Jesus said, "I have not come to call the righteous, but sinners to repentance" (Luke 5:32). Witnesses commented that Jesus was the "guest of a sinner" when He visited the home of the tax collector Zacchaeus (Luke 19:7). Later, after Zacchaeus pledged to return ill-gotten gains, Jesus offered Him salvation.

As the Friend of Sinners, though, Jesus did not come just to redeem tax collectors. When Jesus walked the earth, He befriended the physically handicapped (Matthew 11:1–5), the sick (Matthew 14:14), the demon-possessed (Luke 4:35), and the immoral (John 4:18). He made no distinction between classes or races. In fact, in His final words to His disciples, He told them to "go and make disciples of all nations, baptizing them in the name of the Father and of the Son and of the Holy Spirit" (Matthew 28:19).

Who, then, is a sinner? Paul wrote, "There is no one righteous, not even one" (Romans 3:10). A few verses later, he stated, "Righteousness from God comes through faith in Jesus Christ to all who believe. There is no difference, for all have sinned and fall short of the glory of God" (verses 22–23). No matter our occupation or our social status, our education or our background, or the condition of our health, we are all sinners in need of a Friend—a Friend who can save us from our sins.

Such a Friend can only be one without sin Himself. "For we do not have a high priest who is unable to sympathize with our weaknesses," said the writer of Hebrews, "but we have one who has been tempted in every way, just as we are—yet was without sin" (Hebrews 4:15).

Jesus understands how and why we make poor choices. That's why He offered Himself as the ultimate sacrifice for our sinful nature. Jesus said, "Love each other as I have loved you. Greater love has no one than this, that he lay down his life for his friends" (John 15:12–13). By following Jesus, we are not called to be martyrs, but we are commanded to love those in need. In other words, we are commanded to seek out modern-day tax collectors—and all who need the Friend of Sinners.

GATE FOR THE SHEEP

Therefore Jesus said again,
"I tell you the truth, I am the gate for the sheep."
JOHN 10:7

Jesus' first-century audience would have perfectly understood this metaphorical description. Shepherds in the fields routinely built crude enclosures for their sheep out of branches and stones, leaving space for a single entrance or a gate. At night, after all the sheep were safely inside the enclosure, the shepherd would sleep across the gateway, thus making sure that no wild animals or bandits entered the pen.

Jesus is the Gate for His sheep: we enter into Christian fellowship only by believing in Him. And once we cross that threshold and experience salvation, we are always His and our salvation will never be stolen or lost. Jesus said, "I am the gate; whoever enters through me will be saved. He will come in and go out, and find pasture" (John 10:9).

As the Gate to the pasture, once we belong to Jesus, we experience peace as well as receive sustenance. We want to learn more about our Shepherd, knowledge that can be gleaned by reading God's Word. And the peace we so crave is readily available by seeking Him in earnest prayer.

From the moment we enter this world, we have a need to be protected. Babies cling to favorite blankets or stuffed toys; young children hold on to a parent's hand; teenagers often travel in groups; and adults have wills and insurance. What's missing? Go through the Gate for the Sheep to find the protection that transcends human understanding, as well as deep fulfillment and peace and eternal life.

GIFT OF GOD

Thanks be to God for his indescribable gift!
2 CORINTHIANS 9:15

Jesus is God's gift to the world. John wrote, "And we have seen and do testify that the Father sent the Son to be the Saviour of the world" (1 John 4:14 KJV). Jesus was God's own presence in a human body—as Jesus said, "I and the Father are one" (John 10:30)—come to earth to show us how to live abundantly and eternally.

Jesus, the Gift of God, gave us, in turn, the gift of salvation. As Paul wrote to the church in Rome, "The wages of sin is death; but the gift of God is eternal life through Jesus Christ our Lord" (Romans 6:23 KJV). We can ask for this gift by inviting Jesus into our lives, but we can do nothing to earn this reward. "For by grace are ye saved through faith; and that not of yourselves; it is the gift of God," Paul stated unequivocally (Ephesians 2:8 KJV). Jesus is simply a gift of love from the Father ("For God so loved the world" [John 3:16]), who wants to have a never-ending relationship with us.

There are many adages that speak to procrastinators. "The early bird catches the worm" and "Don't put off until tomorrow what you can do today" are two examples. The Bible says, "Behold, now is the accepted time; behold, now is the day of salvation" (2 Corinthians 6:2 KJV). If you have never done so, today is the day to accept Jesus, the Gift of God.

GLORY OF THE LORD

Arise, shine; for thy light is come,
and the glory of the LORD is risen upon thee.
ISAIAH 60:1 KJV

Isaiah didn't have much good news for the Israelites. In fact, the first thirty-nine chapters of his book are filled with gloom and doom. Based on the way the Israelites were living—perverting God's justice and turning to pagan gods— God was clearly displeased with them. But God had not forgotten His people. Salvation was coming! The glory of the Lord that Isaiah described would be Jesus, God's Son, come to earth in the image of God (Colossians 1:15).

Prior to Isaiah, Old Testament writers wrote of the glory of the Lord, or God's presence, in the tabernacle (Exodus 40:34) and the temple (1 Kings 8:11). When a cloud filled the structure, God's glory was there and no one could enter or perform any official duties. Likely, Isaiah's audience was astounded when the prophet relayed these words: "And the glory of the LORD will be revealed, and all mankind together will see it" (Isaiah 40:5).

From the beginning of Jesus' life on earth, an event heralded by angels displaying the glory of the Lord to terrified shepherds, to His resurrection and ascension to heaven, God's glory was continually on display.

When you love and admire someone, you try to be like them. Paul wrote, "We. . .all reflect the Lord's glory. . .being transformed into his likeness with ever-increasing glory" (2 Corinthians 3:18). Once covered by a cloud, the glory of the Lord now transforms the faces of all who love God's Son.

GOD

In the beginning was the Word, and the Word was with God,
and the Word was God.
JOHN 1:1 KJV

One Bible verse that almost everyone knows also happens to be a good introduction to God: "In the beginning God created the heaven and the earth" (Genesis 1:1 KJV). From that verse alone, God, the creator of the universe, can be seen as timeless, all-knowing, and all-powerful.

The word *God*, which does not appear in the original Hebrew or Greek manuscripts of the Bible, comes from an Old English word meaning "that which is invoked." *God* is a translation of the Hebrew *El* and *Elohim*, meaning "to be strong," words used when describing the creator of the universe and the judge of the world.

God once said to Moses, "I AM WHO I AM" (Exodus 3:14 NKJV). The Bible makes clear that God is not a man (Numbers 23:19) but rather the Spirit (John 3:5–8) that is invisible (1 Timothy 1:17) and is everywhere (Psalm 139:7–12). No man has ever seen God. In fact, when Moses went up Mount Sinai to receive the Ten Commandments from God, the mountain was covered in clouds and a murky darkness, masking God's presence (Exodus 19:16–18). The point is that God simply is who He is and He has always been the same. He had no beginning because He has always existed: "Before the mountains were brought forth, or ever thou hadst formed the earth and the world, even from everlasting to everlasting, thou art God" (Psalm 90:2 KJV). God is truly without beginning or end.

What is God like? Back we go to Genesis 1:1. As the Creator, His knowledge is so vast that it defies description, yet His attention to detail is truly staggering. As John writes, "God is greater than our heart, and knoweth all things" (1 John 3:20 KJV). So great is God's wisdom that He knows our very thoughts: "For my thoughts are not your thoughts" (Isaiah 55:8 KJV). And He knows that His words will have an effect on us. He has said that "my word. . .shall not return unto me void, but it shall accomplish that which I please" (Isaiah 55:11 KJV).

As Creator, God is all-powerful. Throughout the Old Testament, "the hand of God" was seen guiding the Israelites as they vanquished their enemies. It also punished those who defied the Almighty. Jeremiah writes, "Ah, Lord GOD! behold, thou hast made the heaven and the earth by thy great power and stretched out arm, and there is nothing too hard for thee" (Jeremiah 32:17 KJV).

God embodies holiness and goodness, patience, justice, mercy, and love. In a vision given him by God, Isaiah describes seeing the throne of God, surrounded by seraphim who cried, "Holy, holy, holy, is the LORD of hosts: the whole earth is full of his glory" (Isaiah 6:3 KJV).

Yet His lofty status in no way prevents Him from exuding compassion and goodness. David wrote, "The LORD is good to all; he has compassion on all he has made" (Psalm 145:9). All good gifts we receive are from God. James wrote, "The Father. . .does not change like shifting shadows" (James 1:17). Because He is so compassionate, He is slow to anger, wanting to show mercy to all (Exodus 34:6).

For that reason—wanting everyone to come to knowledge of the truth in Him (1 Timothy 2:4)—God demonstrated His overwhelming love by sending His Son, Jesus, to die on the cross for the sins of humanity. By accepting Jesus as Savior, we are guaranteed eternal life and thus escape eternal punishment, which is God's justice, for our sins (1 John 4:8–10). Ultimately, God is the fullest expression of love and the reason we are capable of love: "We love because he first loved us" (1 John 4:19).

There's an expression that's become a favorite of life coaches and personal trainers: "Life is not a dress rehearsal." God has given you this one opportunity to "act on life's stage"—and this one opportunity to know Him. "If. . .you seek the LORD your God, you will find him if you look for him with all your heart and with all your soul" (Deuteronomy 4:29). Make the most of your life by seeking Him today.

GOOD SHEPHERD

"I am the good shepherd.
The good shepherd lays down his life for the sheep."
JOHN 10:11

Shepherding is a lonely, lowly profession. Yet those who do it must be physically and emotionally resilient, patient, strong, and brave. Sheep require constant care to do the simplest things, and the shepherd must also be ever vigilant against threats to their safety. He usually carries a rod with a crook to pull in wayward sheep and also to defend against predators.

With this job description in mind, it's not surprising that God called several men of the Bible who were shepherds and also gave Himself that name. Moses was tending the flocks of Jethro, his father-in-law, when God called him from the burning bush; David was watching his father, Jesse's, sheep when summoned to eventually defeat Goliath; and Amos was a shepherd in Tekoa when God gave him a message of coming destruction to take to Israel.

Contained in the psalms are well-known descriptions of God as our shepherd: "The LORD is my shepherd, I shall not be in want. He makes me lie down in green pastures, he leads me beside quiet waters, he restores my soul. . . . Even though I walk through the valley of the shadow of death, I will fear no evil, for you are with me; your rod and your staff, they comfort me" (Psalm 23:1–4); "Know that the LORD is God. It is he who made us, and we are his; we are his people, the sheep of his pasture" (Psalm 100:3).

Just before Jesus revealed Himself as the Good Shepherd, the Pharisees had been questioning Him about a miracle He performed on the Sabbath, the healing of a man born blind. First, though, they had grilled the former blind man, who stated simply, "I was blind but now I see!" (John 9:25).

Jesus answered the Pharisees, "I have come into this world, so that the blind will see and those who see will become blind" (John 9:39). Jesus knew that these Jewish religious leaders would not accept Him, but there were many, such as the blind man, hungry to know Him and believe. To them, Jesus said, "I am the good shepherd."

Hundreds of years before, Isaiah had prophesied this of Jesus: "He tends his flock like a shepherd: He gathers the lambs in his arms and carries them close to his heart; he gently leads those that have young" (Isaiah 40:11).

Note that Jesus isn't just any shepherd: He is the Good Shepherd. Unlike the "hired hand" who sees the wolf coming and runs away, Jesus willingly lays down His life for the sheep (John 10:15). The hired help cares nothing for the sheep and leaves the flock defenseless in the face of danger (John 10:12–13).

Further, as the Good Shepherd, Jesus knows His sheep and they know Him, yet there are other sheep to be added to His fold. One day there will be one flock of sheep with Jesus as its one shepherd (John 10:14, 16).

Jesus' parable isn't hard to understand. When we believe in Jesus, we follow Him, much like sheep follow a shepherd. Yet like sheep, we need constant care and guidance, and often, very often, we go astray and sin. At the same time, there are those more than willing to lead us astray, the "hired hands," false teachers and other professionals, who claim to have life's answers (or tell us the answers are inside of us) and yet really don't care what happens to us. Only Jesus dealt with sin; only Jesus, who had no sin, willingly gave His life to redeem us. One day, all believers will be reunited with Jesus, our Good Shepherd, and live forever with Him.

Talk shows dominate the television listings—they're on all day. And on almost any given day, you can tune in and hear some new catchphrase that's "guaranteed" to change your life. Who's telling you the truth and who's selling you a bill of goods? Know that there are many hired hands but only one Good Shepherd. There are many guides to living but only one Bible. Take the time to read God's Word and trust Him to lead you to greener pastures.

GREAT SHEPHERD

May the God of peace, who through the blood of the eternal covenant brought
back from the dead our Lord Jesus, that great Shepherd of the sheep,
equip you with everything good for doing his will.
HEBREWS 13:20–21

For centuries, the Jewish people had been entrenched in one form of worship, a worship that emphasized sacrificial offerings, strict adherence to rituals, and limited access to God. Now, through the book of Hebrews, they were being asked to consider a better way to worship with Jesus at the center, no rituals or sacrifices, and unlimited access to God.

To help the Jewish people better connect with Jesus, the writer of Hebrews attached several titles to Him. He is one of Abraham's descendants (chapter 2); greater than Moses (chapter 3); a great high priest (chapter 5), one of the order of Melchizedek (chapter 7); mediator of a new covenant (chapter 8); and the Great Shepherd (chapter 13). Jesus, like the Old Testament shepherds Moses and David, would be their leader.

Jesus' role as shepherd had been foretold by the prophet Ezekiel: "For this is what the Sovereign LORD says: I myself will search for my sheep and look after them. As a shepherd looks after his scattered flock when he is with them, so will I look after my sheep" (Ezekiel 34:11–12).

Ezekiel then relayed these words from God: "I will place over them one shepherd, my servant David, and he will tend them; he will tend them and be their shepherd" (Ezekiel 34:23). The prophet wasn't referring to David, who had already died, but to David's descendant, Jesus the Messiah.

Why does the writer call Jesus the "great" shepherd? Surely His Old Testament counterparts were great shepherds, too. Yet Jesus was distinguished by two phenomenal events that changed humanity forever: His sacrifice on the cross and His resurrection from the dead.

That sacrifice, the essence of the new and eternal covenant, would erase the burning of countless offerings and the minutiae of rituals. As God said to Ezekiel: "I will make a covenant of peace with them" (Ezekiel 34:25). It is a covenant that would give peace to our souls.

It's amazing that children develop from totally dependent babies into toddlers who declare, "I can do it myself!" The Jews of the Old Testament had to depend on the high priests to make their offerings to God and on prophets to speak God's words to them. Jesus' sacrifice and resurrection changed all that. We can now speak directly to Jesus, our Great Shepherd, anytime we want. Most importantly, we—and not through a third party—can have a relationship with Him.

GUIDE

For this God is our God for ever and ever; he will be our guide even to the end.
PSALM 48:14

Jesus said, "I am the way and the truth and the life. No one comes to the Father except through me" (John 14:6). Jesus as our Guide was sent to earth to provide the way to salvation and eternal life. And there is only one way to salvation, as Luke recorded, quoting Paul and Silas: "Believe in the Lord Jesus, and you will be saved" (Acts 16:31).

As anyone who's ever been on a tour will tell you, the best guides are those who take care of every detail. No sacrifice is too great for them; no request is too outlandish for them to accommodate. With Jesus as our Guide—Jesus, the beginning and the end—all we have to do is trust in Him.

When we walk with Jesus as our Guide, He takes care of the details. He leads us in the light, never allowing us to stumble in the dark. Jesus said, "Whoever follows me will never walk in darkness, but will have the light of life" (John 8:12).

No sin—no wrongdoing or evil thought—of ours was too great to prevent Him from dying on the cross and then rising from the dead three days later. No request that we make prayerfully in His name, believing in Him, is too great: "Ask and you will receive, and your joy will be complete" (John 16:24).

HEAD OF THE CHURCH

And he is the head of the body, the church; he is the beginning and the firstborn
from among the dead, so that in everything he might have the supremacy.
COLOSSIANS 1:18

Paul speaks of the church as one body (see also Ephesians 4:4), so it makes sense that there is only one head—and that is Jesus. Only Jesus has been given the authority by God to have preeminence over His Church. God raised Jesus from the dead, seated Him at His right hand in heaven, put Him above every title that can be given, and, as Paul expressed it, "God placed all things under his feet and appointed him to be head over everything for the church, which is his body, the fullness of him who fills everything in every way" (Ephesians 1:22–23).

Much like the head of a company, Jesus, as the head of the Church, has delegated responsibility to those in leadership positions—to elders and deacons, men who "keep hold of the deep truths of the faith with a clear conscience" (1 Timothy 3:9). Every person who professes faith in Jesus Christ is a member of the body of the Church, and his or her gifts are appointed by God (1 Corinthians 12:27–31).

Announcements from the pulpit during a worship service often contain requests for help. There are the easy, onetime pleas: "We need someone to bring paper cups for the children's summer program." Then there is the more challenging variety: "We still need a Sunday school teacher for seventh grade."

Every believer has been gifted to serve in the local church in some way. As a member of His body, how can you best serve the Head of the Church?

HIGH PRIEST

Wherefore, holy brethren, partakers of the heavenly calling,
consider the Apostle and High Priest of our profession, Christ Jesus.
HEBREWS 3:1 KJV

The Hebrew Christians to whom this letter was addressed might have read this sentence again and again. Likely, they were willing to accept Jesus as the long-awaited Messiah, but Jesus as High Priest? That notion was problematic.

After the Hebrews, led by Moses and his brother, Aaron, escaped the tyranny of Pharaoh in Egypt, God gave them the Ten Commandments, the laws by which they were to live. Those laws were followed by more detailed instructions for harmonious living and for the tabernacle, feasts, and sacrifices.

Some of those instructions had to do with establishing a priesthood to offer the various sacrifices, observe the rituals, and be the liaison between the Hebrew people and God. Aaron, who was Moses' brother and of the tribe of Levi, and his sons were anointed as the first priests—and God directed that this "lasting ordinance" (Exodus 29:9) of the priesthood would be for Aaron and his descendants (Exodus 29:29). From that time on, through the first and second temples in Jerusalem (until AD 70), high priests were only from the tribe of Levi.

Well aware of Jesus' lineage, the Hebrew Christians knew that He wasn't from the tribe of Levi. Jesus' earthly stepfather, Joseph, was a descendant of the tribe of Judah (see Matthew 1:3), and His mother, Mary, was as well (see Luke 3:29). How could He then be the high priest?

Like Aaron, the writer of Hebrews said, Jesus was called by God. But there the similarities end: Jesus "was designated by God to be high priest in the order of Melchizedek" (Hebrews 5:10).

Going all the way back to the book of Genesis, after Abram defeated the four kings, he gave the high priest Melchizedek, whose name means "king of righteousness," one-tenth of everything he had acquired in the war (Genesis 14:18–20). At the time of Melchizedek, there was no tribe of Levi—Isaac, the grandfather of Levi, had yet to be born!

Since Abram, the patriarch of the Hebrews, paid tribute to this high priest, it follows that Melchizedek should be considered a higher priest than Aaron.

Therefore, if Jesus is a high priest in the order of Melchizedek, He is a greater high priest than Aaron.

Jesus is a greater high priest for other reasons as well. Unlike Aaron, Jesus lived a perfect life on earth—He was sinless. For that reason He was the perfect sacrifice, dying on the cross for all of our sins. And because Jesus rose from the dead and now resides in heaven, His priesthood is eternal. "Therefore he is able to save completely those who come to God through him, because he always lives to intercede for them" (Hebrews 7:25).

"I've got your back" has become a popular expression, meaning, "Don't worry, I'll take care of you." That's what Jesus as High Priest says to us when we commit our lives to Him. He is the eternal High Priest, always there to present our case to the Father in heaven.

HOLY ONE OF ISRAEL

"Do not be afraid, O worm Jacob, O little Israel, for I myself will help you,"
declares the LORD, your Redeemer, the Holy One of Israel.
ISAIAH 41:14

King Sennacherib of Assyria had already captured all the fortified cities of Judah. Now he set his sights on the grand prize—Jerusalem.

There was just one problem: Hezekiah, the king of Judah, trusted in the Lord. After the Assyrian king's field commander shouted blasphemous insults outside the palace wall in Jerusalem, Hezekiah tore his clothes and went to the temple to pray.

Soon Judah's king received a message from the prophet Isaiah, a message directed at Sennacherib: "Who is it you have insulted and blasphemed? Against whom have you raised your voice and lifted your eyes in pride? Against the Holy One of Israel!" (2 Kings 19:22).

That night an angel of the Lord put to death the Assyrian forces camped outside Jerusalem, and soon after Sennacherib was killed by his own sons in the temple of his pagan god.

The Holy One of Israel, K'dosh Israel, is an exalted God who cannot sin and who does not tolerate sin. Not coincidentally, the name appears more times in the book of Isaiah than any other book in the Bible. When Isaiah was commissioned, he was given a vision of heaven with God on His throne and seraphim singing, "Holy, holy, holy is the LORD Almighty" (Isaiah 6:3). Isaiah knew he was in the presence of the Holy One of Israel.

Clearly, Sennacherib didn't know with whom he was dealing, and at first, Isaiah didn't either. But seeing the resplendent holiness of God caused the would-be prophet to recognize his own sinful state—and then to repent. Only then was Isaiah able to recognize God's call and say, "Here am I. Send me!" (Isaiah 6:8). You, too, serve an exalted, holy God!

HOLY SPIRIT

For prophecy never had its origin in the will of man,
but men spoke from God as they were carried along by the Holy Spirit.
2 PETER 1:21

After He had been tempted in the wilderness by Satan, Jesus returned to Nazareth, His boyhood home, to preach in the synagogue on the Sabbath. The scroll containing the book of Isaiah was handed to Him and He began to read: "The Spirit of the Lord is on me. . ." (Luke 4:18). Previously, when John the Baptist had baptized Jesus in the Jordan River, the Holy Spirit had descended on Jesus from heaven in the form of a dove (Luke 3:22). Now the Holy Spirit was on Him again.

Was the Spirit a ghost, as translated by the King James Version of the Bible, or perhaps an angel, or maybe even another heavenly being?

The Holy Spirit is a person of the Trinity and was recognized by Jesus as such. When Jesus gave His disciples "the Great Commission" after being resurrected, He said to "go and make disciples of all nations, baptizing them in the name of the Father and of the Son and of the Holy Spirit" (Matthew 28:19). Much like someone can say they are a mother and a daughter, the Holy Spirit can also be considered a "role" of God and Jesus. Paul wrote that "the Lord is the Spirit, and where the Spirit of the Lord is, there is freedom" (2 Corinthians 3:17). Jesus told His disciples that He would not leave them but would come to them, that He would ask the Father to send them the Holy Spirit (John 14:16–18). The Holy Spirit is also called Comforter, Counselor, Helper, the Spirit of truth, and a Gift.

Many traits are embodied in the Holy Spirit. The Spirit is all-wise, possessing understanding well beyond our mortal grasp. As Paul wrote, "No one knows the thoughts of God except the Spirit of God" (1 Corinthians 2:11). Through the Holy Spirit, prophets in scripture were given the words of God to speak (2 Peter 1:20–21).

The Spirit embodies many gifts, which He gives "for the common good" (1 Corinthians 12:7). Among these are the gifts of wisdom, knowledge, healing, miraculous powers, and prophecy. Although the Spirit can be "grieved" by our actions, He is also known for His love (Romans 15:30). When we are bitter and angry and hurt each other with our words and actions, we also hurt the Holy Spirit (Ephesians 4:30–31). Paul advised us to be kind and compassionate, "forgiving each other, just as in Christ God forgave you" (Ephesians 4:32).

Since the day of Pentecost—fifty days after Jesus' resurrection and ten days after His ascension—all believers of Jesus have been filled with the Holy Spirit. Jesus foretold this event during His forty days on earth following the resurrection: "But you will receive power when the Holy Spirit comes on you" (Acts 1:8). Such power enabled the disciples to speak in different languages so they could travel "to the ends of the earth" spreading the words of Jesus.

From that moment until the present, the Holy Spirit has drawn believers closer to Jesus. As Jesus said, "But the. . .Holy Spirit, whom the Father will send in my name, will teach you all things and will remind you of everything I have said to you" (John 14:26). Bearing witness for Jesus, the Holy Spirit speaks only the truth, relaying the words of Jesus so that believers can bring greater glory to Him.

But how do we know what the Holy Spirit wants us to do, or where He wants us to go? As we spend time in prayer and the Word before acting, we will realize God's will for us; only then will we be able to distinguish what is true and what is fleeting—because the Holy Spirit will give us discernment. And only then will the Holy Spirit be able to lead us, as He did Barnabas and Paul (Acts 13:2), to the work for which He has called us.

HORN OF SALVATION

"He has raised up a horn of salvation for us in the house of his servant David."
Luke 1:69

It began as just another day at the temple for the priest Zechariah. When he began to burn incense at the altar, though, he found himself alone, all the worshippers having gone outside. Suddenly, the angel Gabriel appeared out of nowhere and began to speak. Zechariah couldn't stop trembling. . .what had he done to deserve this? He and his wife, Elizabeth, both along in years, had lived righteous lives. The only "hiccup" had been Elizabeth's inability to have children.

Gabriel informed Zechariah that he and Elizabeth would have a son, whom they would name John, a son who would "make ready a people prepared for the Lord" (Luke 1:17). When Zechariah doubted the angel, Gabriel took away his power of speech until John was born. At baby John's circumcision, Zechariah recovered his speech and began to prophesy, praising God for redeeming His people—and for sending a horn of salvation.

This horn of salvation was not Zechariah's son, because as a priest, Zechariah was of the tribe of Levi. This redeemer was to be a descendant of David, from the tribe of Judah. Zechariah's son, who would be known as John the Baptist, would prepare the way for the long-awaited Messiah.

Animal horns connote power, and indeed Jesus brought His message of salvation with a fierce passion—and with power. Jesus as the horn of salvation had been foretold in the Old Testament: "Here I will make a horn grow for David," God says (Psalm 132:17). And the psalmist also wrote, "You have exalted my horn like that of a wild ox" (Psalm 92:10). When Jesus returns to establish His kingdom, this power will be on display for all to see.

At some point we've found ourselves hitting a brick wall or getting stuck between a rock and a hard place. Whatever the euphemism for our condition, only Jesus has the strength to save us. Only He is, as David writes, "my shield and the horn of my salvation, my stronghold" (Psalm 18:2).

I AM

And God said unto Moses, I AM THAT I AM: and he said,
Thus shalt thou say unto the children of Israel, I AM hath sent me unto you.
EXODUS 3:14 KJV

For four hundred years, the children of Israel had been living in Egypt. At first, when the patriarch Jacob's son Joseph was a high-ranking official in Pharaoh's palace, they enjoyed respect and prosperity. Later, though, under a different pharaoh, they were reduced to being slaves. They had come to Egypt as a people who worshipped one God, and He had not forgotten them. God heard their cries for help and He chose Moses, a child of Israel raised by the daughter of Pharaoh, to lead them out of slavery.

Speaking to Moses from a burning bush, God told him, "I am the God of your father, the God of Abraham, the God of Isaac and the God of Jacob" (Exodus 3:6). Despite that description, Moses needed further clarification before declaring himself as the leader of the Israelites. "Suppose I go to the Israelites and say to them, 'The God of your fathers has sent me to you,' and they ask me, 'What is his name?' Then what shall I tell them?" (Exodus 3:13).

Moses knew the Egyptians worshipped many gods, and he also knew that his people had been living in this culture for many generations. Would they remember God's covenant with Abram, the covenant that gave his descendants the land "from the river of Egypt to the great river, the Euphrates" (Genesis 15:18)?

And then God said that His name was "I AM." He was stating unequivocally that He was the God of Abraham, Isaac, and Jacob and that He would be their God "from generation to generation" (Exodus 3:15). God was stating that He never changes. Indeed, the name I AM is a translation of the Hebrew *Ehyeh asher ehyeh or Hayah*, meaning, "I am that I am" or "I will be that I will be."

Like His Father, Jesus also never changes. The writer of the book of Hebrews declared, "Jesus Christ is the same yesterday and today and forever" (Hebrews 13:8). Jesus, who has been with God since the beginning of time, will one day return to rule over His new kingdom. As God was creating Adam, He said, "Let us make man in *our* image, in *our* likeness" (Genesis 1:26, emphasis added), meaning that we are made in Jesus' image as well. And from the last book in the Bible, Jesus called Himself "the Alpha and the Omega, the First and the Last, the Beginning and the End" (Revelation 22:13).

To the Jews who questioned Jesus' assertion that He had seen Abraham, Jesus said, "I tell you the truth. . .before Abraham was born, I am!" (John 8:58). Throughout John's Gospel, Jesus made several statements that started with "I am." Among other things, He said He is the bread of life, the light of the world, the door, the good shepherd, the resurrection and the life, the way and the truth and the life, and the true vine.

Traveling to ancient cultures is a mind-blowing experience. How amazing it is to walk on roads trod by Roman soldiers, to stand in the same room where Christopher Columbus received his commission to sail to the New World from Isabella and Ferdinand, or to climb up the Areopagus, or Mars Hill, in Athens, where Paul preached to the Greeks.

Yet before all cultures existed, before the earth was formed, God was and Jesus was. And Father and Son are still here, and will be forever. "I AM THAT I AM" has no beginning and no end.

JEHOVAH

That men may know that thou, whose name alone is JEHOVAH,
art the most high over all the earth.
PSALM 83:18 KJV

When Moses first asked God for His name, God gave him the name "I AM." And then God gave the newly appointed shepherd of His people another name. "Say to the Israelites, 'The LORD, the God of your fathers—the God of Abraham, the God of Isaac and the God of Jacob—has sent me to you.' This is my name forever, the name by which I am to be remembered from generation to generation" (Exodus 3:15).

That name, Jehovah, was a name no religious Jew living in Bible times would have dared to speak. The sacred name was never spoken aloud for fear of taking the Lord's name in vain. The English translation of the Hebrew *Yahweh*, the name Jehovah, which means "to be," would have appeared in the earliest manuscripts of the Bible as "YHWH" because ancient Hebrew contained no vowels. The exact pronunciation of YHWH, also called the Tetragrammaton, is unknown.

Empowered by Jehovah, Moses and his brother, Aaron, approached Pharaoh with their famous request to "let my people go." When Pharaoh answered, "Who is the LORD, that I should obey his voice. . . ?" (Exodus 5:2 KJV), Jehovah responded with a vengeance. While the patriarchs had known Him as "God Almighty," He was now known as Jehovah: He would honor the covenant He made with Abraham to deliver His people to the land of Canaan, and He would do so with a "stretched out arm and with great judgments" (Exodus 6:6 KJV). These judgments—ten "plagues" that began with rivers turning to blood and ended with the death of all firstborn—were followed by Jehovah's dramatic escape route for His beleaguered people, the parting of the Red Sea.

That Jehovah is strong to save is a theme recorded in the book of Isaiah as well. "Behold, God is my salvation; I will trust, and not be afraid: for the LORD JEHOVAH is my strength and my song; he also is become my salvation" (Isaiah 12:2 KJV). Later, the prophet wrote, "Trust ye in the LORD for ever; for in the Lord JEHOVAH is everlasting strength" (Isaiah 26:4 KJV).

There is no record of Jesus ever using the name Jehovah—and for good reason. Scholars have suggested that had He uttered that name in the presence of other Jews, especially the Pharisees and Sadducees, He would have been subjected to extreme punishment. As God's Son, Jesus knew when He would be arrested and He chose His words carefully. Instead of Jehovah, Jesus emphasized God the Father. As John wrote, "But as many as received him [Jesus], to them gave he power to become the sons of God [the Father] even to them that believe on his name" (John 1:12 KJV).

Have you ever been introduced to someone and two seconds later forgotten his name? Or someone talks to you and later you have trouble remembering the gist of the conversation. God, the great Jehovah, isn't like that. He heard every cry of His oppressed people in Egypt. He hears, and remembers, every word of every prayer we utter—and then He responds as only an eternal, compassionate God can. Jehovah's arm is still stretched out to save us.

JEHOVAH-JIREH

And Abraham called the name of that place Jehovahjireh:
as it is said to this day, In the mount of the LORD it shall be seen.
GENESIS 22:14 KJV

The day before, the Lord had given Abraham a command, and now the aged patriarch arose early in the morning to obey. Accompanied by two of his servants, one donkey, and his son Isaac, Abraham set out for one of the mountains in the region of Moriah. Before leaving, he cut enough wood to make a burnt offering. When he saw Moriah in the distance, Abraham took the wood and his son and told his servants to stay with the donkey and wait. He said, "We will worship and then we will come back to you" (Genesis 22:5).

Abraham was on his way to sacrifice his beloved son, the only child of his wife, Sarah. God had asked him to kill Isaac as a burnt offering.

As father and son continued their journey alone, Isaac's curiosity could not be contained. "Where is the lamb for the burnt offering?" he asked. And Abraham answered, "God himself will provide the lamb" (Genesis 22:7–8). The explanation satisfied the boy and they strode on.

When they reached the place God had chosen, Abraham built an altar, placed the wood he had carried upon it, and bound his son, as he would a lamb, and placed him on the altar. As he raised his knife to slay his son, he heard the voice of the angel of God and he stopped. The angel—some scholars say this was Jesus' voice—told him not to lay a hand on the boy, that he had proven his faith in God. And when Abraham looked up, away from his son, he saw a ram caught by its horns in a thicket. That was the sacrifice the Lord had provided instead of Isaac. That was why Abraham called the place of the altar Jehovah-jireh: the Lord will provide.

The name Jehovah-jireh means not only "The Lord will provide" but has also been translated "The Lord will see" and "The Lord shall be seen." Indeed, the Lord saw that Abraham would obey, that his love for God was greater than it was for any thing or person, and He provided the ram caught in the thicket. Because of Abraham's unswerving devotion, the Lord shall be seen. As God told Abraham, "Through your offspring all nations on earth will be blessed, because you have obeyed me" (Genesis 22:18).

God was speaking of His own Son, Jesus. Just as God provided a ram in place of Isaac, so God provided Jesus as the sacrifice in place of all humanity. "For God did not send his Son into the world to condemn the world," John wrote, "but to save the world through him" (John 3:17). As Paul wrote, "But God demonstrates his own love for us in this: While we were still sinners, Christ died for us" (Romans 5:8). Jesus as the Lamb of God died on the cross so that we—all believers—could live eternally. For all who trust in Him, He, Jehovah-jireh, will provide.

Frequently on the news we see a political leader make an announcement, followed by the ubiquitous Q-and-A session, often cut short by a press secretary. Yet, reflecting on God's request of Abraham and Abraham's obedience, it is significant that Abraham asked no questions. All we read is Abraham's unquestioning trust in God, from the beginning of the journey to Moriah to the provision of the ram, the intended sacrifice. Abraham believed that Jehovah-jireh would provide—and He did. As Solomon wrote, "Trust in the LORD with all your heart and lean not on your own understanding; in all your ways acknowledge him, and he will make your paths straight" (Proverbs 3:5–6). Are you trusting God wholeheartedly?

JEHOVAH-ROPHE

For I will restore health unto thee,
and I will heal thee of thy wounds, saith the LORD.
JEREMIAH 30:17 KJV

Jeremiah's role as a prophet ends with the start of the Babylonian captivity, a time of tribulation he foretold throughout his book. But he had good tidings, too, words of restoration from the Lord, whom the people of Judah had forsaken. The "wounds" he was speaking of were not physical but spiritual in nature, brought on by "many sins." One day the people would be restored to their homeland and healed by the Lord, whom the prophet called Jehovah-rophe, a name that means "The Lord heals."

The name Jehovah-rophe was first used when the Israelites, just three days into their journey after crossing the Red Sea, came to the bitter, undrinkable waters of Marah. The people were thirsty and complaining, so Moses called upon the Lord. When God told Moses to throw a piece of wood into the waters, the springs became potable. And then Jehovah-rophe made a pact with the people: If you listen to Me and do what is right, I will not afflict you with any of the diseases I rained down on the Egyptians, for I am the Lord who heals you (Exodus 15:26). For the next forty years of wandering, God kept His promise.

When we're worried about our physical health, we often turn to God in prayer. Seldom are we as concerned about the state of our spiritual health. For a promising spiritual prognosis, the prescription is simple: Trust in Jesus. His healing powers, foretold by Isaiah—"By his wounds we are healed" (Isaiah 53:5)—are there for the asking. Jesus, our Jehovah-rophe, restores our spiritual health and ensures life for eternity.

JEHOVAHSHALOM

Then Gideon built an altar there unto the LORD, and called it Jehovahshalom.
JUDGES 6:24 KJV

For seven years, the Israelites had been at the mercy of the Midianites, a people so ruthless and ravenous, scripture compares them to locusts. When they descended on the Israelites' land, they ruined all their crops "and did not spare a living thing" (Judges 6:4). Consequently, the Israelites had taken to hiding in mountain caves, out of sight of these predators. In desperation, this wayward people cried out to God, and once again, He was prepared to deliver them.

To do so, God chose an unlikely candidate. By his own reckoning, Gideon came from the "weakest" clan of the tribe of Manasseh and was considered "the least" of his family. Cowed as well by the Midianites, Gideon was threshing wheat in a winepress, out of sight of the enemy, when the angel of the Lord approached him. Responding to the angel's words, "Peace! Do not be afraid" (Judges 6:23), Gideon built an altar on the very spot, calling it Jehovah-shalom.

Jehovah-shalom means "The Lord is peace" or "The Lord our peace." Through Gideon, God delivered peace to His people; through His Son, Jesus, and His Word, He continues to offer a balm for human souls.

"For he himself is our peace," wrote Paul (Ephesians 2:14), providing access to the Father. Because of Jesus' sacrifice on the cross and His position at God's right hand, He is able to serve as mediator for all who come to Him.

Paul also wrote of the peace Jesus brings to our hearts and minds, the peace of God "which transcends all understanding" (Philippians 4:7). Despite the troubles of the world, John told us, we still can have peace for one reason: Jesus has "overcome the world" (John 16:33).

A quick perusal of the headlines or five minutes' worth of the evening news is enough to make a person fearful. And then there are those worries closer to home, the kind that keep us up at night. At times like these, it's comforting to remember Jesus' words. "Don't be afraid," Jehovah-shalom says. "My peace I give you."

JEHOVAH-SHAMMAH

It was round about eighteen thousand measures:
and the name of the city from that day shall be, The LORD is there.
EZEKIEL 48:35 KJV

Ezekiel was a young man when he was taken to Babylon in 597 BC, as part of the second wave of the captivity. A few years later, he received a call from God to hit the streets of Babylon, prophesying and preaching. God had prepared him for the stubborn attitudes of the Israelites, and Ezekiel was not to be deterred. Among his messages was that Jerusalem would be destroyed by Babylon and also that God would bring His people back to Israel.

After Jerusalem fell, Ezekiel was directed by God to talk about the far-distant future. The city he described, which has a circumference of "eighteen thousand measures," is the same one referred to by John in the book of Revelation. This New Jerusalem "shone with the glory of God, and its brilliance was like that of a very precious jewel" (Revelation 21:11). The glory of God was evident because, as Ezekiel stated, the name of the city was Jehovah-shammah, meaning "The Lord is there."

Possessions come and go and friends may drift apart or move away—that's the nature of modern life. As believers, though, we're blessed to have "God with us" all the time. That's because as Emmanuel, Jesus has promised never to leave us, giving us His Holy Spirit as our comforter and guide. Jesus, our Jehovah-shammah, is always there.

JEHOVAH-TSIDKENU

Behold, the days come, saith the LORD, that I will raise unto David a righteous Branch, and a King shall reign and prosper, and shall execute judgment and justice in the earth. In his days Judah shall be saved, and Israel shall dwell safely: and this is his name whereby he shall be called,
THE LORD OUR RIGHTEOUSNESS.
JEREMIAH 23:5–6 KJV

Jeremiah prophesied during the reigns of Judah's last five kings before the start of the Babylonian captivity. With the exception of Josiah, like most of the kings before them, they were an evil bunch, denounced by scripture as having "done evil in the sight of the LORD." Now God was promising a just ruler who was a descendant of David. The word *oxymoron* wasn't part of Jeremiah's vocabulary, but he probably wondered: Is there such a thing as a righteous king?

Jesus is Jehovah-tsidkenu, a name that means "The Lord our righteousness." Only Jesus, in whom there is no sin (1 John 3:5), can stand before God the Father and say that we are His. If left on our own, without a Savior, we would struggle hopelessly to follow God's laws established in the Old Testament. As Paul wrote, "No one will be declared righteous in his sight by observing the law" (Romans 3:20). Jesus is "our righteousness, holiness and redemption" (1 Corinthians 1:30).

We like to pat ourselves on the back when we "do the right thing"—almost as if it's out of character. Unlike our feeble selves, Jesus is right and righteous all the time. As our Jehovah-tsidkenu, we owe our lives to Him.

JESUS

And she shall bring forth a son, and thou shalt call his name Jesus:
for he shall save his people from their sins.
MATTHEW 1:21 KJV

Joseph woke up and knew what he had to do. Suffice it to say, he'd never had a dream like this before. In his dream, an angel of the Lord had told him to take Mary as his wife. That took care of one of his problems, in a way. Joseph was on the verge of divorcing Mary because she was expecting a baby—and it wasn't his. But then the angel told Joseph that this baby had been conceived by the Holy Spirit and that he, Joseph, was to name the baby Jesus.

This child of the virgin birth would be the long-awaited Emmanuel, "God with us," and now declared by an angel, "God has saved us."

Jesus, a name that means "salvation," is the Anglicized form of the Latin *Iesu*, which was derived from the Greek *Iesous*. The Greek form was coined from the Aramaic name *Yeshua* and the Hebrew *Yehoshua*. As the One who came to "save his people from their sins," Jesus' arrival had been foretold for hundreds of years.

Although the name Jesus is never mentioned in the Old Testament, Jesus as the salvation, Yehoshua, is invoked several times. The psalmist writes, "The LORD has made his salvation known and revealed his righteousness to the nations. . .all the ends of the earth have seen the salvation of our God" (Psalm 98:2–3). And Isaiah prophesied, "Behold, the LORD hath proclaimed unto the end of the world, Say ye to the daughter of Zion, Behold, thy salvation cometh" (Isaiah 62:11 KJV).

When the devout Simeon, who had been awaiting "the consolation of Israel," is led by the Holy Spirit to the temple in Jerusalem on the very day that Mary and Joseph and the baby Jesus come to give the required offering, he also acknowledges Yehoshua. "For mine eyes have seen thy salvation," Simeon declares, "which thou hast prepared before the face of all people" (Luke 2:30–31 KJV).

The very name of Jesus is saving, and it is powerful. Jesus said, "Whatsoever ye shall ask the Father in my name, he will give it you" (John 16:23 KJV). Peter said, "There is none other name under heaven given among men, whereby we must be saved" (Acts 4:12 KJV).

In the days of the early church, the apostles healed the sick and lame, exorcised demons, baptized, and taught and preached fearlessly—all in the name of Jesus. They knew firsthand that Jesus was no ordinary teacher; they knew that He, Yehoshua, was the Son of God. God gave Jesus a name "which is above every name," wrote Paul, "that at the name of Jesus every knee should bow" (Philippians 2:9–10 KJV).

When he awoke the next morning, scripture says that Joseph "did what the angel of the Lord had commanded him" (Matthew 1:24). He agreed to let salvation come into his house. Have you made a similar decision? Has your heart been touched by God's Word in such a way that you want to know more? Are you searching for meaning in life and getting more frustrated day after day? Jesus wants to come and live with you, too.

KING OF ISRAEL

He saved others; himself he cannot save.
If he be the King of Israel, let him now come down from the cross,
and we will believe him.

MATTHEW 27:42 KJV

The chief priests, the teachers of the law, and the elders should have known better. Yet looking up at Jesus, dying a thief's death on a wooden cross, they led the other passersby in mocking Him. But what they regarded as sarcasm was the Gospel truth: Jesus is the King of Israel, and His kingdom will never end.

When the angel Gabriel gave Mary the news that she would bear God's Son, he said, "The Lord God will give him the throne of his father David, and he will reign over the house of Jacob forever; his kingdom will never end" (Luke 1:32–33). That throne of David's was the throne of Israel, and Jesus was a direct descendant of David through Mary (see Luke 3:23; Heli is thought to be Mary's father). Almost two years after Jesus' birth, the Magi confirmed His royal status, asking, "Where is the one who has been born king of the Jews?" (Matthew 2:2).

During Jesus' earthly ministry, He was acknowledged by His disciple Nathanael as the Son of God and the King of Israel (John 1:49). As He entered Jerusalem on a donkey during His last week on earth, the great crowd acknowledged His kingship, crying, "Blessed is the King of Israel!" (John 12:13). And when the Roman governor Pontius Pilate questioned Jesus before handing Him over to be crucified, Jesus admitted that He indeed was a king but that His kingdom was not of this world (John 18:36).

Jesus has promised one day to return to establish His kingdom, a kingdom in which He will reign "for ever and ever" (Revelation 11:15). Of that kingdom, the prophet Zephaniah wrote, hundreds of years before Jesus was born to Mary, "The LORD, the King of Israel, is with you; never again will you fear any harm" (Zephaniah 3:15).

Those mockers of Jesus had, in a biblical way of speaking, hardened their hearts to His message. Sometimes we do that, too. Rather than concentrate on a daily devotional reading, we're thinking about our to-do list. Or while we're supposedly listening to a Sunday sermon, we're thinking about whom we need to talk to after church. The King of Israel wants to command our entire attention.

KING OF KINGS

Who is the blessed and only Potentate, the King of kings, and Lord of lords.
1 TIMOTHY 6:15 KJV

And he hath on his vesture and on his thigh a name written,
KING OF KINGS AND LORD OF LORDS.
REVELATION 19:16 KJV

To the mob of angry Jews awaiting his verdict, Pontius Pilate merely said, "Here is your king" (John 19:14). The Roman governor had questioned Jesus and found no fault in Him—but he had been intrigued by the notion of Jesus as king.

Although Pilate acquiesced to the crowd's demand that Jesus be crucified, he refused to be cowed completely by the religious leaders. Pilate's gesture was significant: attached to Jesus' cross was a sign that read, "Jesus of Nazareth, The King of the Jews." When the chief priests protested the wording, Pilate remained firm. "What I have written, I have written," he said (John 19:22).

For whatever reason he attached the sign—to rankle the religious Jews or to insert an ironic touch—little did Pilate realize the profound truth of his action. Yes, Jesus is the King of the Jews, but He is also the King of all kings.

To call someone a king in Bible times was to make a grand statement. Kings held supreme power over their subjects and were regarded with awe. They held the power of life and death and controlled the fate of thousands. The course of world history was affected by their decisions.

As the long-awaited Messiah or Christ, Jesus was recognized as the "Anointed One," the precursor to kingship. Writing to Timothy, Paul recognized Jesus' royal stature for all time: "Now to the King eternal, immortal, invisible, the only God, be honor and glory for ever and ever" (1 Timothy 1:17).

By defeating death and sin by His sacrifice on the cross, Jesus now reigns in heaven, awaiting the day when He will return to establish His new kingdom. At that time in the future, described by the apostle John, during the greatest confrontation in the history of the world, Jesus will defeat Satan, sending him to a fiery lake of burning sulfur. And on Jesus' robe and His thigh will not be Pilate's appellation but the name that belongs to Jesus and only Jesus: King of kings (Revelation 19:16).

Today, members of royal families are treated with equal parts respect and ridicule. It's hard to imagine falling on our faces in the presence of a modern-day king. Yet one day, our King of kings will return to vanquish evil for all time—and to claim us as His. Awed by His majesty and glory, we will bow before Him. "Who is he, this King of glory?" David once asked rhetorically. In the next breath, he gives the answer: "The LORD Almighty—he is the King of glory" (Psalm 24:10).

LAMB OF GOD

The next day John saw Jesus coming toward him and said,
"Look, the Lamb of God, who takes away the sin of the world!"
JOHN 1:29

He had been born to prepare the way for Jesus' ministry on earth. And now, at last, John the Baptist was meeting Jesus face-to-face. In salutation, John addressed Jesus as the "Lamb of God," a role that was foretold in the first book of the Bible and ordained since the beginning of time.

When God asked Abraham to take Isaac, his beloved son, and sacrifice him on Moriah, God was painting a picture of the future sacrifice of His own Son, Jesus. Abraham himself said that God will provide the sacrifice (Genesis 22:8) and later named the site of the sacrifice of the ram "The Lord Will Provide."

But perhaps nowhere in the Bible is the parallel with Jesus' sacrifice seen more clearly than during the Israelites' final days in Egypt. When, after nine plagues sent by God, Pharaoh still refused to release the Israelites from bondage, God delivered the ultimate blow. The Israelites were instructed to slaughter one lamb per household. The lamb was to be without defect and they were to take some of its blood and put it on the sides and tops of their doorframes. The cooked lamb would then be consumed by each family as part of a feast known as the Lord's Passover. That night, all Egyptian families, whose houses did not have blood on the doors, suffered an incalculable loss: the death of all firstborn men and animals (see Exodus 12:12). For the Israelites, the years of bondage in Egypt were over.

Like the Passover lamb, Jesus is without defect or sin. And like that lamb's blood, Jesus' blood on the cross was shed to save God's people. As further confirmation of God's divine plan, the Passover feast—celebrated by Jesus and His disciples—occurred the night before Jesus was crucified.

During the Israelites' exodus toward the Promised Land, as part of God's laws for Israel, two lambs were to be slaughtered every day, one in the morning and one at twilight, on the altar in the Tent of Meeting, and later, in the temple (see Exodus 29:38–41). When John addressed Jesus as the Lamb of God, religious Jews understood that He was being compared to the daily offerings. Not coincidentally, Jesus' death on the cross occurred around the time of the twilight sacrifice.

Lambs are known as submissive creatures, willing to be led. The same was true for Jesus, as described by the prophet Isaiah hundreds of years earlier: "He was led like a lamb to the slaughter, and as a sheep before her shearers is silent, so he did not open his mouth" (Isaiah 53:7). Jesus willingly laid down His life for the sins of humanity so that believers could have eternal life. Isaiah continued, "Yet it was the LORD's will to crush him and cause him to suffer, and though the

LORD makes his life a guilt offering, he will see his offspring and prolong his days, and the will of the LORD will prosper in his hand" (Isaiah 53:10).

Jesus' sacrifice once and for all eliminated all other sacrifices, which were unable to take away sin. Because of the precious blood of the Lamb of God, redemption is possible. Because of Jesus' resurrection, faith and hope are possible, too (see 1 Peter 1:18–21).

Peter admonished us to live our lives on earth "as strangers. . .in reverent fear" (1 Peter 1:17). Yet how often do we consider the price paid by Jesus for our salvation? We were saved not by a written contract, a hefty down payment, or a handshake, but by the spilled blood of the Lamb of God. Jesus gave His life for us.

LAST ADAM

So it is written: "The first man Adam became a living being";
the last Adam, a life-giving spirit.
1 CORINTHIANS 15:45

The story of the creation of Adam, the first man, is well known. He was created in the image of God by God and given dominion over all the earth. Initially, he was destined to live forever, at peace with God and the natural world. But soon Adam and the first woman, Eve, succumbed to temptation, defied God, and were banished by God from the Garden of Eden, a perfect place. Adam was "sentenced" to a life of hard work, a life that would one day end in death.

Like the first man, Jesus, who is called the Last Adam, was also created in the image of God. Yet Jesus, who existed before Adam and before the creation of the world, is called the firstborn (see Colossians 1:15) and He has dominion over not only the earth but heaven as well. And while He, like the first Adam, was tempted by Satan, Jesus overcame evil. Jesus, as God in the flesh, was fully human and fully divine, and as such, was incapable of sin. As the first Adam was a life-giver, beginning the human race, so the Last Adam gives life, eternal life, to those who trust in Him (see John 3:16).

Finally, the first Adam died because of his sin, but the Last Adam died to conquer sin—and then arose three days later to overcome death as well. As Paul wrote, "For if, by the trespass of the one man, death reigned through that one man, how much more will those who receive God's abundant provision of grace and of the gift of righteousness reign in life through the one man, Jesus Christ" (Romans 5:17).

It's hard to wrap your mind around the notion that all human beings, throughout all the centuries, are descended from one man. Yet, as believers, we're all children of God, too. Our past may be connected genetically to the first Adam, but our present and future are connected spiritually, physically, and emotionally to the Last Adam, our Savior, Jesus Christ.

LIGHT OF THE WORLD

Then spake Jesus again unto them, saying, I am the light of the world:
he that followeth me shall not walk in darkness, but shall have the light of life.
JOHN 8:12 KJV

As long as I am in the world, I am the light of the world.
JOHN 9:5 KJV

In the Tent of Meeting, used during the journeys of Israel after they left Egypt, there was a magnificent golden lampstand. In the richly appointed temple built by King Solomon, there were ten candlesticks of gold. And in John's Gospel, Jesus is probably standing in the courtyard of the temple rebuilt after the Babylonian captivity, where He declares Himself to be the light of the world.

Undoubtedly, the candles in the temple were glowing brilliantly, but their light dimmed beside Jesus. Much as the candles in the temple illuminated the table on which the showbread—a symbol of Jesus as the bread of life—was displayed, the glory of God shone on Jesus all the days He walked on earth.

The name "Light of the World" is used only three times in the New Testament—and all by Jesus. Jesus proclaimed Himself the source of life (and light) and all good things, a stance underscored by John: "In him was life; and the life was the light of men" (John 1:4 KJV). Jesus Himself said, "I am come a light into the world, that whosoever believeth on me should not abide in darkness" (John 12:46 KJV).

Jesus was also foretelling the future, a time when He would no longer be in the flesh with His disciples and others. After He had made His triumphal entry into Jerusalem, just days before His crucifixion, He said, "Yet a little while is the light with you. Walk while ye have the light, lest darkness come upon you: for he that walketh in darkness knoweth not whither he goeth" (John 12:35 KJV).

That darkness is considered the domain of Satan and the "rulers of the darkness of this world" (see Ephesians 6:12 KJV). As the light of the world, Jesus is the antithesis and antidote to such darkness.

Finally, Jesus said that His followers are the light of the world. "A city on a hill cannot be hidden," He said. To give light to everyone, His followers need to let their light "shine before men, that they may see your good deeds and praise your Father in heaven" (Matthew 5:14–16).

As you get to know people, you often discover some interesting facts about their lives. Sometimes those tidbits are surprising. They may not look like former gymnasts or beauty queens, and some of the things you learn about their high school years would not make them ideal candidates to be teachers or doctors. Then consider yourself: Would people be surprised to learn that you are a Christian? When you let the goodness of God shine through your actions, no one will doubt the integrity of your faith.

LION OF THE TRIBE OF JUDAH

Then one of the elders said to me,
"Do not weep! See, the Lion of the tribe of Judah,
the Root of David, has triumphed.
He is able to open the scroll and its seven seals."
REVELATION 5:5

The scroll the apostle John was describing is thought to be the "deed" to the earth. By opening the scroll and its seven seals, the Lion of Judah is unleashing the final assaults on the world before conquering sin and Satan and becoming the undisputed ruler.

The Lion of the tribe of Judah, the Root of David, is Jesus. A descendant of David (Matthew 1:1), Jesus could also trace His ancestry to Judah (Matthew 1:3; Luke 3:34), one of the twelve sons of Jacob. In a final blessing to his sons before he died, in which he foretold their future roles, Jacob said to Judah, "You are a lion's cub" (Genesis 49:9). That image of Jesus as the Lion was repeated by Amos, when he said, "The lion has roared—who will not fear? The Sovereign LORD has spoken—who can but prophesy?" (Amos 3:8).

While on earth, Jesus certainly offered glimpses of the Lion He is. He cleared the temple of money changers, calling His house "a house of prayer" (see Matthew 21:13); He also escaped an angry mob in His hometown of Nazareth that was determined to throw Him off a cliff (see Luke 4:28–30). Yet these previews pale in comparison with what is to come: Jesus on a white horse, His eyes blazing like fire, the name "KING OF KINGS AND LORD OF LORDS" written on His robe (see Revelation 19:11–21).

Like a lion's roar, which can be heard for miles, Jesus' words have spread far and wide. As the Lion of the tribe of Judah, He continues to empower His followers to fearlessly go to the ends of the earth—and just around the corner, too. If you're lacking the courage to share your faith, remember you serve a Lion. Jesus will give you strength.

LORD OF HOSTS

And Elisha said, As the LORD of hosts liveth, before whom I stand, surely,
were it not that I regard the presence of Jehoshaphat the king of Judah,
I would not look toward thee, nor see thee.

2 KINGS 3:14 KJV

Three kings had formed an unlikely alliance. Now marching to battle against Moab, they were stopped in their tracks by a common dilemma in their part of the world: no more water for themselves or their animals. Desperate, they asked where a prophet of the Lord might be, and they were directed to Elisha. When the prophet saw King Jehoshaphat of Judah among the group—the only righteous king of the three—he agreed to inquire of the Lord for them.

Proclaiming the Lord of hosts, Elisha felt the hand of the Lord come upon him—and then delivered the solution to the kings' quandary. After digging ditches in the valley, as the Lord directed, the kings' troops were rewarded the next morning with a landscape filled with water. No rain had fallen; water had simply flowed from the direction of Edom. "This is an easy thing in the eyes of the LORD; he will also hand Moab over to you," said the prophet (2 Kings 3:18).

The Lord of hosts, or Jehovah-sabaoth, is a name used hundreds of times in the Old Testament. The name extols God's sovereignty, His omnipotence, and His transcendence. Familiar to many are the heavenly cries recorded by Isaiah: "Holy, holy, holy, is the LORD of hosts: the whole earth is full of his glory" (Isaiah 6:3 KJV).

The word *sabaoth*, from the Hebrew *tsaba*, is used in connection with warfare and control of armies. Jehovah-sabaoth is thus interpreted as "Yahweh the warrior" or "Yahweh the divine king." Who else would David invoke when confronting the giant Goliath but the Lord of hosts? "Thou comest to me with a sword, and with a spear, and with a shield: but I come to thee in the name of the LORD of hosts, the God of the armies of Israel, whom thou hast defied" (1 Samuel 17:45 KJV).

But the Lord of hosts oversees more than mortal armies. He is also Lord over heavenly hosts, such as angels, and the host of heaven, or the physical stars in the sky, as well as the creator of the world. The psalmist says that God directs His angels to guard us (see Psalm 91:11), and in the Bible, angels were often the bearers of God's messages to men and women.

Perhaps the prophet Amos most eloquently described this name of the Lord: "For, lo, he that formeth the mountains, and createth the wind, and declareth unto man what is his thought, that maketh the morning darkness, and treadeth upon the high places of the earth, The LORD, The God of hosts, is his name" (Amos 4:13 KJV).

Time and again, we read in the Bible of battle lines drawn and armies facing off, with God directing the endgame for Israel or Judah. But what about the private battles we wage, the ones confined to the four walls of our lives? As believers, we're privileged to have God, the Lord of hosts, on our side. Through the Holy Spirit, He can give us the words to say to assuage a heated or sticky situation. And when the time for words is over, He can nudge us to wrap our arms around a child, spouse, or friend and give us peace.

LORD OF LORDS

God, the blessed and only Ruler, the King of kings and Lord of lords.
1 TIMOTHY 6:15

On his robe and on his thigh he has this name written:
KING OF KINGS AND LORD OF LORDS.
REVELATION 19:16

After the day of Pentecost, Jesus' disciples, who had been given the Holy Spirit as well as other spiritual gifts, began to preach, leading many to accept Jesus. As recorded by Luke in the book of Acts, these disciples then baptized new believers "into the name of the Lord Jesus" (see Acts 19:5). They acknowledged Jesus' sovereignty and power to save—and they knew Him as the Lord of lords.

The English word *Lord* had its roots in the original Hebrew Tetragrammaton YHWH, or Yahweh, which was then translated into the Greek *Kyrios*, meaning "power" or "powerful master." Jesus embodies such a description, as revealed in His words when He departed from His disciples: "All authority in heaven and on earth has been given to me" (Matthew 28:18). When He died on the cross and was resurrected, overcoming death, He assumed lordship of both the dead and the living (see Romans 14:9).

There is one God and one Lord, one Creator and omnipotent and omniscient ruler of the universe. All other gods and lords, those conceived of or given these earthly titles by mortal minds, are subservient to the Lord Jesus. As Paul wrote, "Yet for us there is but one God, the Father, from whom all things came and for whom we live; and there is but one Lord, Jesus Christ, through whom all things came and through whom we live" (1 Corinthians 8:6).

Jesus wanted His disciples to know Him as Lord of lords, but He also wanted them to recognize His servant's heart. At the Last Supper, when Jesus began to wash the disciples' feet, Peter immediately objected, thinking it beneath his Lord. But Jesus said, "Now that I, your Lord and Teacher, have washed your feet, you also should wash one another's feet" (John 13:14). The lesson was well learned: through their selfless lives and extraordinary commitment to Jesus, the disciples surely demonstrated that Jesus' lordship is one of power and love that knows no bounds.

The initials WWJD—"What would Jesus do?"—were seen everywhere for a while, most especially on plastic wristbands and other accessories. The gist of WWJD is really acknowledging Jesus' lordship and denying the supremacy of other "gods." When we think about what Jesus would do, we're steered in the right direction, away from corrupting influences, and we're also led to worship and acknowledge Him as Savior and Lord.

MASTER

But be not ye called Rabbi: for one is your Master,
even Christ; and all ye are brethren.
MATTHEW 23:8 KJV

Once again, Jesus took on the Pharisees as examples of what not to do. Much to His disgust, these supposed religious men loved to sit in positions of honor, being feted by the masses of those less rigorously schooled than they. And they loved to have men call them "Rabbi." To Jesus, though, greatness comes by serving others, not by having others serve you.

Before the fall of the second temple (AD 70), the title of Rabbi was one used for a respected teacher, a synonym for Master. The title *Rabboni*, used by Mary Magdalene when she saw Jesus alive after His crucifixion (see John 20:16), is an Aramaic word that means "my master."

As the Master, Jesus focused intently for three years on training the twelve men He selected as His disciples. They watched Him preach the message of salvation; they observed Him teaching by using parables. And as evidence of His divinity, they saw Him perform a myriad of miracles, including restoring life to His friend Lazarus. At the end of His ministry on earth, Jesus prayed, "As you sent me into the world, I have sent them into the world" (John 17:18).

While we can't sit at the knee of the Master as the disciples did, drinking in His words, we can open our Bibles and hear His voice. As Paul wrote, "All Scripture is God-breathed and is useful for teaching" (2 Timothy 3:16). We don't have to be in His "classroom" because we have Jesus' "lectures" right in God's Word. All we have to do is read—and believe.

MEDIATOR

For there is one God and one mediator between God and men,
the man Christ Jesus.
1 TIMOTHY 2:5

Before Jesus came on the scene, the high priest in the temple had the role of mediator. Once a year, the high priest entered the Holy of Holies to make an animal sacrifice for the atonement of the sins of Israel (see Leviticus 16). Since Jesus' death on the cross and resurrection, which served as the atonement for our sins, such a ritual is no longer necessary. God has "reconciled" the world to Himself through Jesus (see 2 Corinthians 5:19). Jesus is now our Mediator.

From a legal standpoint, a mediator is a go-between, someone who stands between two parties in a dispute to reach a common goal. In his or her role, the mediator must have a complete understanding of both parties and their wishes and the nature of the dispute itself.

From a spiritual standpoint, the two parties, God and humanity, are separated by sin. The common goal is salvation, because God wants everyone to believe in Him. To achieve that goal, we must ask Jesus to forgive our wrongdoings and we must accept Jesus as Lord and Savior.

Jesus, fully man and fully divine, understands the human condition. As the author of Hebrews wrote: "We do not have a high priest who is unable to sympathize with our weaknesses, but we have one who has been tempted in every way, just as we are—yet was without sin" (Hebrews 4:15). Jesus is also aware of the human craving for peace. As "our peace," Jesus has destroyed the barrier that separated men and women from God (see Ephesians 2:14–16).

Jesus, who is superior to the high priests of old, is the only one qualified to be Mediator. As He said, "I am the way and the truth and the life. No one comes to the Father except through me" (John 14:6).

How many people know the real you? We all have our long-hidden secrets and most of us allow precious few, if any, to know them. To Jesus, our Mediator, our lives are an open book. He knows the hurt that won't go away, the love we can't profess, the guilt that still consumes us—and the sin we don't confess. When we accept Him as Savior, He immediately becomes our go-between to the Father, ready to defend us, ready to plead our case, ready to love us.

MESSIAH

He first found his own brother Simon, and said to him,
"We have found the Messiah" (which is translated, the Christ).
JOHN 1:41 NKJV

Andrew and most probably John, the writer of this Gospel account, were initially followers of John the Baptist. But John the Baptist's role was to point the way to Jesus by telling people about Jesus, baptizing Jesus, and then directing his own disciples to seek Jesus themselves.

After spending just one day with Jesus, Andrew couldn't wait to tell his brother Simon Peter the most remarkable news. He, a common fisherman, had found the long-awaited Messiah! In short order, Simon, soon to be known simply as Peter, became one of Jesus' disciples himself.

Andrew's announcement of the Messiah, or "Anointed One," was the climax of thousands of years of waiting and hundreds of Old Testament prophecies. To his son Judah, the patriarch Jacob had declared, "The scepter shall not depart from Judah, nor a lawgiver from between his feet, until Shiloh comes; and to Him shall be the obedience of the people" (Genesis 49:10 NKJV). Shiloh, which means "The Peaceful One," was another name for the Messiah. Such a prophecy had to be fulfilled before AD 70 when Jerusalem and much of Judah were destroyed by Rome.

Many prophecies of the Messiah concern His relationship to David. As God told David, "I will set up your seed after you, who will come from your body, and I will establish his kingdom. He shall build a house for My name, and I will establish the throne of his kingdom forever. I will be his Father, and he shall be My son" (2 Samuel 7:12–14 NKJV). Jesus' mother, Mary, was a direct descendant of David, as was His stepfather, Joseph.

The prophet Daniel foretold not only the arrival of the Messiah but also His death and the subsequent destruction of Jerusalem. Daniel was divinely inspired to predict that sixty-nine "Sabbaths" (or 483 sabbatical years) would pass between the decree to rebuild Jerusalem after the Babylonian captivity and the arrival of the Anointed One (see Daniel 9:24–27).

To Moses, God said that He would "raise up" a prophet like him, from among his own brothers (see Deuteronomy 18:15). While many religious Jews believed that God was speaking of Joshua, who led the Israelites into the Promised Land, two prominent early Christians were directed by God to believe otherwise. Shortly before he was stoned to death, the apostle Stephen quoted this scripture (see Acts 7:37), as did Peter while he was preaching at the temple (see Acts 3:22). Peter was trying to convince the Jews that this long-awaited Messiah, Jesus, had come to preach to them first—but sadly, they had rejected Him.

Still, the spark igniting the Christian faith had been lit among a small group of Jewish men, the disciples, who would testify far and wide that they had seen the Messiah.

Do you remember when you first accepted Jesus as Savior? Likely, you couldn't wait to tell someone close to you what had happened—just like Andrew. Andrew didn't need to find confirmation in the scriptures and he didn't need to consult with the religious leaders in the temple. He simply felt the truth of the Messiah in his heart. Finding Jesus isn't a laborious process. . . it's a beautiful step of faith.

MIGHTY GOD

For to us a child is born, to us a son is given. . . .
And he will be called. . .Mighty God.
ISAIAH 9:6

The prophet Isaiah was really going out on a limb: Whoever heard of a baby being called the Mighty God? But such a statement wasn't coming from the prophet's imagination. Isaiah had been given this message from God. And it was God who was coming to earth, in the flesh, Emmanuel (God with us), to establish His kingdom "with justice and righteousness from that time on and forever" (Isaiah 9:7).

Jesus was heralded as the Mighty God, the Hebrew *El Gibbor*, at His birth. Witness the angels proclaiming to the shepherds that their Savior, who was Christ the Lord, had been born (see Luke 2:8–12). Witness the Magi inquiring in Jerusalem where the one "who has been born king of the Jews" might be found (see Matthew 2:2), and upon finding Him, bowing down and worshipping Him.

At the age of twelve, Jesus stunned the learned men in Jerusalem's temple with His uncanny command of scripture. Because He was without sin, as a grown man, He resisted Satan's offers of power and grandeur and began His humble ministry on earth. His might, while reflected in numerous miracles, was most clearly demonstrated on the cross and beyond. For hours, He endured the shame and pain of the cross—and then arose from the tomb three days later, the wounds still visible but His flesh uncorrupted. Only the Mighty God could overcome the grave and then ascend forty days later to sit at the right hand of God the Father in heaven.

Jesus, Mighty God, was given power over creation (see John 1:3) and heaven, with "angels, authorities and powers in submission to him" (1 Peter 3:22). One day, when He returns to earth, His might will be displayed for all to see. The prophet Daniel described seeing the Son of man, or Jesus, "coming with the clouds of heaven." His dominion, Daniel wrote, "will not pass away, and his kingdom is one that will never be destroyed" (Daniel 7:13–14).

Do you prefer giving gifts or receiving them? Many people have trouble being on the receiving end. They're uncomfortable being acknowledged or they're hard to buy for, or they're afraid they'll respond inappropriately to the gift. If you're like this, here's something that will change your mind: As Isaiah wrote, Jesus, the Mighty God, is a gift to us. He satisfies the needs of everyone— and He keeps on giving until you respond to Him.

MORNING STAR

I am the root and the offspring of David, and the bright and morning star.
REVELATION 22:16 KJV

John had been given an amazing vision of events to come—startling, jaw-dropping, awe-inspiring occurrences—and now he fell to the ground at the feet of an angel. Immediately, though, the angel admonished him, "Worship God!" (see Revelation 22:8–9). And as the apostle did so, Jesus spoke again, departing words, words that filled John with hope.

Jesus calls Himself the Morning Star, the beacon heralding the end of the night. He is the light of salvation to all who call upon His name, "the sun of righteousness. . .with healing in its wings" (Malachi 4:2). He is a bright star of great beauty, "the radiance of God's glory and the exact representation of his being" (Hebrews 1:3). Much as the morning star remains the same, guiding sailors and seekers, Jesus told His followers that He would be with them always, "to the very end of the age" (Matthew 28:20). As Jesus said, "I have come into the world as a light, so that no one who believes in me should stay in darkness" (John 12:46).

The current events in the Middle East have led many Bible scholars to speculate that John's vision may be about to unfold in real time. While such discussions can be upsetting, as believers we have nothing to fear. Our salvation is secure, and our hope is placed on that great dawning day when Jesus, our Morning Star, vanquishes darkness once and for all.

NAZARENE

And he came and dwelt in a city called Nazareth:
that it might be fulfilled which was spoken by the prophets,
He shall be called a Nazarene.
MATTHEW 2:23 KJV

To escape the murderous rampage of King Herod, who had ordered all baby boys two years and younger to be killed, Joseph and Mary had fled to Egypt with Jesus. Now that Herod was dead, Joseph returned to Israel, but he had his qualms about settling in Judea. Instead, he took his family to the district of Galilee, and to the town of Nazareth. Jesus would thus be called a Nazarene, a name meaning a resident of the vicinity of Nazareth.

Although no Old Testament prophets foretold that Jesus would be raised in Nazareth, the one most cited, Isaiah, referred to Jesus as the Branch, which in Hebrew is *nacar* or *necer*, a word similar to *Nazarene* (see Isaiah 11:1). In general, Nazarenes were a despised people, perhaps because of the region's history of pagan influences. Recall Jesus' disciple Nathanael's comment—"Nazareth! Can anything good come from there?" (John 1:46). Accordingly, Isaiah alluded to Jesus as despised and rejected (see Isaiah 53:3) and David foretold "a worm and not a man, scorned by men and despised by the people" (Psalm 22:6).

Dealing with rejection is one of the hardest life lessons to learn. Yet as the Nazarene, Jesus suffered rejection early and often, even being rejected by His fellow Nazarenes when He began His ministry. And that was only the beginning—Calvary's cross awaited Him. When you're rejected and dejected, remember the Nazarene and pour out your heart to Him.

PASSOVER LAMB

Get rid of the old yeast that you may be a new batch without yeast—
as you really are. For Christ, our Passover lamb, has been sacrificed.
1 CORINTHIANS 5:7

Ever since the Israelites were delivered out of Egypt by God, Jewish people have celebrated the yearly Passover feast. In ancient times, the feast consisted of bitter herbs, unleavened bread, and lamb. The herbs represented repentance and confession of sin; the unleavened bread was a symbol of purity; and the lamb was to remember the blood sacrifices of the first Passover and God's deliverance of His people from Pharaoh.

God gave the Israelites particular instructions as to the Passover lamb: The animal had to be a male lamb without defect, roasted whole with none of its bones broken. No meat was to be left until the following morning (see Numbers 9:1–14).

When Jesus celebrated His last Passover on earth with His disciples, just hours before He would be betrayed, arrested, and crucified, He described Himself as the feast. After He gave thanks for the bread, Jesus said, "Take and eat; this is my body." And after He gave thanks for the wine, He said, "This is my blood of the covenant, which is poured out for many for the forgiveness of sins" (see Matthew 26:26–28).

Jesus is the Passover Lamb: He was a sinless man who was killed on the cross (or roasted over the fire), a sacrifice that was made without any of His bones being broken (see John 19:33). Before the following morning, His body was removed from the cross and placed in the tomb.

The covenant Jesus spoke of, the one in which God's law would be in the minds of the people, written on their hearts (see Jeremiah 31:33), would be fulfilled by His sacrifice on the cross. As the Passover Lamb, His blood was the ultimate atonement for sin, a onetime sacrifice negating the ritual temple sacrifices. As Peter wrote, we were redeemed "from the empty way of life handed down to you from your forefathers. . .with the precious blood of Christ, a lamb without blemish or defect" (1 Peter 1:18–19).

Baker's yeast, a type of fermented fungi used in baking, was as essential in ancient Egypt as it is today. When the Israelites hurriedly pulled up stakes in Egypt, though, they had no time to produce yeast and had to bake unleavened bread. As part of God's plan, they were symbolically leaving behind the old on their journey to the new. When we ask Jesus into our hearts, we need to do the same. Whatever may lead us back to a sinful lifestyle or bad habits, we need to avoid, discard, or leave behind.

PHYSICIAN

But when Jesus heard that, he said unto them,
They that be whole need not a physician, but they that are sick.
MATTHEW 9:12 KJV

Jesus was having dinner with a new disciple—but once again, He was being critically observed by the Pharisees. The Pharisees, who were not invited to dine with Jesus, nonetheless made sure He could hear what they were saying. "Why does your teacher eat with tax collectors and 'sinners'?" they asked the other disciples (verse 11).

Jesus the Physician came to heal sinners and to give men and women the opportunity for life after death. He healed many who had physical ailments or disabilities, and the Bible only describes a fraction of those healed by His touch, His words, or His actions. A woman who had been bleeding for years merely had to touch His cloak (see Mark 5:25–34); a Roman centurion returned home to find his servant healed by Jesus' command (see Matthew 8:5–13); and Jairus' daughter was restored to life when Jesus took her hand (see Mark 5:35–43).

Many of us dread going to the doctor. We rationalize that we know as much as the doctor or that we'll be back on our feet in no time. Those excuses don't work when the diagnosis is sin and the physician is Jesus. As sinners, we are all destined to die one day (see Romans 6:23). But when we believe in Jesus, after we die we will live again with Him in heaven.

POTENTATE

Which in his times he shall shew,
who is the blessed and only Potentate,
the King of kings, and Lord of lords.
1 TIMOTHY 6:15 KJV

The apostle Paul knew that his days were numbered. It was only a matter of time before Emperor Nero would set about to eliminate the "scourge" of Christianity from the Roman Empire—and execute one of its leading proponents, the fearless Paul. So Paul put pen to paper, or quill to papyrus, and wrote to his beloved protégé, the young minister Timothy. Above all, he wanted Timothy to "fight the good fight of the faith" (1 Timothy 6:12) because he served a true Potentate.

Jesus is the blessed and only Potentate, from the Latin *potens*, meaning "powerful," by definition a ruler who is above the law.

When He came to earth, He was born under the Mosaic law and grew up abiding by its severe regulations. Yet He came to abolish the law and to redeem those who were under the law (see Galatians 4:4–5). As Paul wrote, "Christ is the end of the law so that there may be righteousness for everyone who believes" (Romans 10:4). Because Jesus sacrificed Himself on the cross, we are saved by His blood—not by slavish compliance with the law.

All Americans are governed by federal, state, and municipal statutes. Yet the complexity of our justice system pales when compared to the Mosaic code. Imagine not wearing clothes made of two different kinds of material or not planting two different kinds of seeds in your garden (see Leviticus 19:19)! Praise God, we serve a Potentate who is above the law, who has saved us by His grace.

PRINCE OF PEACE

For unto us a child is born, unto us a son is given. . .and
his name shall be called. . .The Prince of Peace.
ISAIAH 9:6 KJV

For hundreds of years, Isaiah's words had rung out from synagogues and been passed from parent to child in hopeful expectation. In the first century AD, though, the scripture had taken on particular importance. Since AD 6, the province of Judea had been under Roman occupation—which meant a constant military presence even in Jerusalem's outer temple court, plus heavy taxation. If the Prince of Peace came, He would surely rescue His people from such tyranny!

Jesus the Prince of Peace did come, but, to the consternation of many, the peace He brought did not vanquish Rome. Instead He brought *shalom*, the Hebrew word for "peace," which has been translated "completeness" and "contentment." Jesus' sacrifice would signal the beginning of the new covenant, completing Jeremiah's prophecy (see Jeremiah 31:33). Those who accept Him as Savior are rewarded with contentment of the soul and peace with God through the new covenant relationship.

Before the advent of the Prince of Peace, peace with God meant obeying His commands. As God told Isaiah, "If only you had paid attention to my commands, your peace would have been like a river, your righteousness like the waves of the sea" (Isaiah 48:18). When the people trusted in Him, they would realize God's plans to prosper them, plans to give them hope and a future (see Jeremiah 29:11).

Jesus' mission of peace was heralded by angels, who proclaimed to the shepherds in Bethlehem's fields, "Glory to God in the highest, and on earth peace to men on whom his favor rests" (Luke 2:14). For His disciples, Jesus calmed the sea (see Matthew 8:23–27); for all people for all time, Jesus overcame the world (see John 16:33).

As the prophesied arbiter of peace, Jesus declared Himself openly and on several occasions. "Peace I leave with you; my peace I give you," He said. "I do not give to you as the world gives. Do not let your hearts be troubled and do not be afraid" (John 14:27).

Waiting is hard to do, and it's especially trying to wait for something wonderful. A child can't wait to open gifts on Christmas, a bride and groom can't wait to take their wedding vows, and an expectant couple (and yes, those future grandparents) can't wait to hold their baby in their arms. Just like those early Judeans, we're also waiting for something wonderful—for Jesus, the Prince of Peace, to come. When He returns the second time, He will usher in His eternal kingdom, a kingdom of shalom.

PROPITIATION

And he is the propitiation for our sins: and not for ours only,
but also for the sins of the whole world.
1 JOHN 2:2 KJV

Every year on the Day of Atonement, the high priest would enter the Most Holy Place, the holiest place of the tabernacle or temple, and sprinkle blood on the mercy seat. The mercy seat was the gold-covered lid of the ark of the covenant, the sacred vessel that held the golden pot of manna and the tablets on which the

Ten Commandments were written. When the priest did this, he was offering a propitiation, or an appeasement, for the sins of the people. In other words, he was making peace with God.

Such an offering of blood was required every year because men and women are habitually sinful (see Romans 3:23) and no one offering made by a mortal high priest was capable of satisfying God's sense of justice because God is completely holy.

So God in His infinite wisdom provided His own solution: He sent His only Son, Jesus, to spill His blood and die on the cross. Jesus became the propitiation for the sins of humanity for all time, and in so doing, reconciled humankind to God. As John the Baptist declared, "Look, the Lamb of God, who takes away the sin of the world!" (John 1:29).

Some of us always see things in terms of "black and white," while others tend to consider "gray" areas. In terms of our salvation, though, there is only one way of looking at it, one way of achieving it—and that is through Jesus. "I am the way and the truth and the life. No one comes to the Father except through me," He said (John 14:6). Only Jesus, as the propitiation for our sins, could save us by His blood and lead us to the Father in heaven.

RABBI

Nathanael answered and saith unto him, Rabbi,
thou art the Son of God; thou art the King of Israel.
JOHN 1:49 KJV

What had happened to turn this skeptic into a believer? Moments earlier, Nathanael had mocked Jesus' hometown. But that was before Jesus declared what He knew about His future disciple. Amazed, Nathanael acknowledged that he was in the presence of not only a great teacher but the Messiah.

Jesus was accorded the title of Rabbi by many, including common people and religious leaders. It is a name that means "teacher," "great one," and "my master." In the early first century, "Rabbi" was more a title of respect than an occupation, though rabbis were learned men familiar with the ancient scriptures.

As Rabbi, Jesus traveled from town to town, visiting synagogues and reading from scripture. He taught using parables, or stories incorporating scenes from daily life, a familiar technique employed by other first-century teachers. But clearly, Jesus was no ordinary teacher. Following one particular sermon, Matthew recorded, "the people were astonished at his doctrine: For he taught them as one having authority" (Matthew 7:28–29 KJV). As Nathanael declared, the Rabbi Jesus was also the Son of God.

The exchange between Nathanael and Jesus was brief but telling. In two sentences, Jesus conveyed to Nathanael a simple truth: I know you. Jesus didn't give His life to save strangers but to save those He knows and loves.

RANSOM

Who gave himself a ransom for all, to be testified in due time.
1 TIMOTHY 2:6 KJV

The prophet Hosea foretold the result of Jesus as Ransom: "I will ransom them from the power of the grave; I will redeem them from death" (Hosea 13:14). Indeed, Jesus' sacrifice of Himself on the cross freed those who believe in Him from eternal damnation.

In the New Testament the word "ransom" comes from the Greek *lutron*, signifying a payment made to liberate captives or slaves. Because "everyone who sins is a slave to sin" (John 8:34), Jesus acted as our ransom, "paying" for our freedom with His life, a payment made by the shedding of His blood.

But the sacrifice of Jesus is something more: His ransom is an act of love. As Paul wrote, "But God demonstrates his own love for us in this: While we were still sinners, Christ died for us" (Romans 5:8). By Jesus' wounds—His pierced hands and feet—we have been healed of sin and given new life (see 1 Peter 2:24).

Although we prize our freedoms and are quick to decry oppressive regimes, we ourselves were slaves to sin before we accepted Jesus' gift of salvation. Even after salvation, we can allow sin to have power over us. It's easy to see how one compromise leads to another, or how moral precedents collapse under the weight of peer pressure, greed, or lust (or name your poison). Praise God that Jesus was our Ransom, and that in Him is forgiveness and a future.

REDEEMER

Fear not, thou worm Jacob, and ye men of Israel;
I will help thee, saith the LORD, and thy redeemer,
the Holy One of Israel.
ISAIAH 41:14 KJV

To the ancients, the idea of a redeemer coming to the aid of Israel was a familiar one. Such a person was known as a kinsman-redeemer, and his role was well established in Mosaic law.

In the book of Ruth, the destitute Naomi, a widow, discovered that Boaz, a wealthy landowner, was a close relative of her dead husband and a kinsman-redeemer. As such, he was able to marry Naomi's widowed daughter-in-law Ruth, thereby redeeming them both from a life of poverty. Kinsman-redeemers could also purchase relatives who had been sold into slavery (see Leviticus 25:47–49). The redeemer had to be a kinsman who was able and willing to pay the price.

As our Redeemer, Jesus satisfies those requirements of old. By becoming part of the human race, He became our kinsman, but one who is without sin. From the beginning of time, it was God's plan that Jesus would come to earth to offer Himself as the redeeming sacrifice for our sins. Jesus thus willingly and ably redeemed humankind from a life of slavery to sin.

Why do we need redemption? Plain and simple, because we sin. Thus, our redemption by Jesus was supremely an act of mercy. As Paul wrote, "For God has bound all men over to disobedience so that he may have mercy on them all" (Romans 11:32). Without redemption, humankind would be condemned to hell—that would be the only recourse for a disobedient life. Because Jesus is the Redeemer, there is the possibility of forgiveness for sin. And because Jesus is the Redeemer, there is the possibility of life after physical death if one professes faith in Him.

To forgive and forget is a nice platitude that is harder to do than it sounds. If we feel we've been wronged by the same person time and again, that laundry list of bad deeds seems to resurface without prompting. Thankfully, God is not like us. Because Jesus is our Redeemer, we can go directly to the Father for forgiveness—and He will forgive and forget. "I, even I, am he who blots out your transgressions, for my own sake, and remembers your sins no more" (Isaiah 43:25).

REFINER

But who can endure the day of his coming?
Who can stand when he appears? For he will be like a refiner's fire.
MALACHI 3:2

To Malachi, God gave a prophecy of two messengers. The first, whom God said "will prepare the way before me" (3:1), is understood to be John the Baptist, who declared those same intentions himself (see John 1:23). The second, God said, was "the messenger of the covenant, whom you desire" (3:1). That messenger, who has been called the Refiner, can only be Jesus. He was sent by God to establish a new covenant of grace, which was accomplished by His sacrifice on the cross.

When we ask Jesus into our hearts, we also desire to be like Him. To that end, Jesus, the Refiner, purifies our souls much like metals were purified in ancient times. In those days, silver and gold were melted down in the refiner's fire, a process that separated the impurities from the metals, leaving the gold and silver intact.

Likewise, when we are tested by Jesus, though the process may be painful, the result will be a more joyful life (see James 1:2–4). We will be able to "stand when he appears"—a reference to the final judgment (see Revelation 20:11–15)—because we belong to Him.

No one relishes the bad times. But if we think of them as opportunities to develop perseverance, as James did, there's reason for hope. When a new day dawns, and it will by God's perfect timing, you will like what you see in the mirror: someone mature and complete, someone refined by Jesus.

REFUGE

You have been a refuge for the poor,
a refuge for the needy in his distress.
ISAIAH 25:4

Much like Noah's ark was the only place of refuge to survive the great flood, and much like the cities of refuge of the Old Testament were the only places to escape punishment and death, Jesus is our refuge.

Because Noah "found favor in the eyes of the LORD" (Genesis 6:8), he and his family, and the pairs of all creatures, were offered refuge in the ark—but all others perished. When Joshua and the people of Israel settled into the land, they were to establish cities of refuge to protect those who killed unintentionally and without malice from the "avengers of blood" (see Joshua 20:1–6). Such cities offered easy access, provided sustenance to the escapees, and were open to all who needed protection.

When we ask Jesus to be our Savior, we find favor in His eyes and He becomes our refuge. Only Jesus can save us from eternal death; there is no other way to salvation (see Acts 4:12). And once we are His, we are saved from the clutches of that perennial avenger of blood known as Satan. Jesus will never turn away anyone who comes to Him (see John 6:37).

When the sky gets dark and the wind picks up, that's the time to seek shelter from the elements. Likewise, when problems begin to multiply and you can't see a way out, turn to Jesus as your Refuge. "Come to me," Jesus said, "all you who are weary and burdened, and I will give you rest" (Matthew 11:28).

THE RESURRECTION AND THE LIFE

Jesus said unto her, I am the resurrection, and the life:
he that believeth in me, though he were dead,
yet shall he live.

JOHN 11:25 KJV

In the Gospel accounts, Jesus was depicted as the son of Mary and Joseph; the teacher and mentor of the twelve disciples; and the Son of God. But He was also described as a friend to Lazarus and his sisters, Martha and Mary. Curiously, though, in John 11, when word reached Jesus that Lazarus was sick, Jesus did nothing. In fact, He stayed where He was for two more days before traveling with His disciples to Lazarus's home in Bethany.

When Jesus arrived, Lazarus was dead and had been buried for four days. Confronting Him, Martha and Mary had one big question practically written on their faces: "Where were You?" If He had been there, they knew He would have saved their brother. They knew that because they believed that Jesus was the Son of God and because He had already healed many.

Instead of answering Martha directly, Jesus told her He was the Resurrection and the Life. Instead of offering His friend's grieving sister comfort, Jesus offered eternal hope.

And then, guided by Mary, He went to the tomb and wept. Moments later, after praying to God the Father, Jesus commanded Lazarus to walk out of the tomb. Suddenly Lazarus appeared, his body still shrouded in the linen burial garments.

Before He and the disciples returned to Bethany, Jesus foretold what would happen. He said that the purpose of Lazarus's sickness, which wouldn't end in death, was to glorify God's Son (see verse 4). By bringing Lazarus back from the dead, Jesus was showing Himself as the Resurrection. By Lazarus's faith, and that of his sisters, Jesus was showing that He is Life. Whoever believes in Jesus will never die; eternal life is a reality.

Lazarus's death and resurrection were also foreshadowing the events about to unfold in Jesus' life. Very soon, Jesus would be handed over to the Jewish and Roman authorities to be crucified on a wooden cross and then buried in a tomb sealed with a giant stone and guarded by Roman soldiers. At Lazarus's tomb, Jesus had demonstrated He already had power over death. When He arose from the dead after three days in His own tomb, He underscored His power for all time. "Death has been swallowed up in victory," Paul wrote (1 Corinthians 15:54). Because Jesus is the Resurrection and the Life, all Christians can claim victory as well.

Like Martha and Mary, at times we all question Jesus. We may not have lost someone we love, but we wonder why things turned out the way they did. And "wonder" may be putting it gently: we cry, stomp our feet, wring our hands, and lose sleep. When we've had our say, it's best to consider Martha's reaction. No matter what happened or why, she said, "I believe that you are the Christ, the Son of God" (verse 27). Jesus, the Resurrection and the Life, came to earth and died for us so that we might have life with Him. One day we'll have answers to our questions, but for the moment, we need to keep strong in the faith.

RIGHTEOUSNESS

In his days Judah shall be saved, and Israel shall dwell safely:
and this is his name whereby he shall be called,
THE LORD OUR RIGHTEOUSNESS.
JEREMIAH 23:6 KJV

The prophet Jeremiah wrote and spoke out during the reigns of the last five kings of Judah—before Jerusalem would be conquered by Babylon in 586 BC. Despite what was about to happen to Judah, God had not forgotten His people. One day God would "raise up to David a righteous Branch" (verse 5), a king who would be called our Righteousness, His Son, Jesus.

Paul wrote that Jesus is our righteousness, holiness, and redemption (see 1 Corinthians 1:30). As sinners, we need the righteousness of Jesus in order to be saved. By God's grace we have been acquitted for Jesus' sake (because of His death on the cross and resurrection) to receive the free gift of salvation—if we but believe. Once we profess belief, we, too, become righteous in the eyes of God and are thus entitled to the reward of righteousness, which is eternal life.

Yes, once we are His, we are His forever. King Solomon wrote that "the righteous cannot be uprooted" (Proverbs 12:3). He goes on to say that "the root of the righteous flourishes" (Proverbs 12:12). That's because the "root" is Jesus.

Eventually most people like to "put down roots" somewhere. Usually such longings occur when you get a "real" job or get married or can't think about packing one more time. God wants your faith to develop deep roots in Him, too. When our faith grows and flourishes, our Righteousness touches others.

ROCK

He is the Rock, his works are perfect,
and all his ways are just.
DEUTERONOMY 32:4

In a song to the Israelites shortly before he died, Moses gave his people a brief history lesson. His song reminded them that throughout all the generations, though the people had turned to other gods, their Rock had not forsaken them. Their Rock was a Savior; He was not like any other gods.

Recalling the Israelites' exodus from Egypt to the Promised Land, Paul wrote, "They all ate the same spiritual food and drank the same spiritual drink; for they drank from the spiritual rock that accompanied them, and that rock was Christ" (1 Corinthians 10:3–4). Jesus, who is the same yesterday and today, and who has been since before the beginning of time, is the Rock.

As the spiritual rock of the Christian faith, Jesus is the foundation and chief cornerstone of His Church (see 1 Corinthians 3:11 and Ephesians 2:19–22). There have been and will be many "rocks" embedded in its structure, but there is only one Head, and that is Jesus. As David wrote, "And who is the Rock except our God?" (Psalm 18:31).

One of the greatest blessings is to have been raised in a Christian home. What a thrill to hold a family Bible and know that previous generations have read and cherished God's Word! If that doesn't describe your family, imagine the legacy you can leave. How has Jesus been your Rock?

ROOT OF DAVID

I am the root and the offspring of David,
and the bright and morning star.
REVELATION 22:16 KJV

Many prophecies speak of the Messiah being the descendant of King David— and two genealogies in the New Testament provide the necessary evidence. But as John records, Jesus acknowledged Himself as the Root of David, too. How can Jesus be the root and the offspring of the legendary king? To use Jesus' own names, how can the Branch be the Root?

The genealogies again supply the answers. Matthew's genealogy traces Jesus' lineage from the patriarch Abraham to His stepfather, Joseph (see Matthew 1:1–16). From this record, Jesus can clearly be seen as the offspring of David. Luke's record (see Luke 3:23–37), however, gives a different result. Luke traces Jesus' ancestry from Mary's father, Heli, all the way back to Adam, who was "the son of God." Because Jesus is acknowledged as the Creator—"All things were created by him and for him" (Colossians 1:16)—Jesus must also be the Root of David. Paul continues by stating, "He is before all things, and in him all things hold together" (Colossians 1:17).

Some pictures defy description. Consider an ocean beach at sunrise; springtime in an alpine meadow; evergreen trees blanketed in snow; pristine, undulating sand dunes. Such beauty, like its Creator, is beyond comprehension. Jesus, the Root of David, is too wonderful for words.

ROSE OF SHARON

I am the rose of Sharon, and the lily of the valleys.
SONG OF SOLOMON 2:1 KJV

Because the Song of Solomon is a wedding song, many Bible scholars have interpreted the book as an allegory about the Bridegroom Jesus' love for His Church. However one wishes to read the book, as an allegory or as simply a dialogue of love between King Solomon and his bride, the image of Jesus as the rose of Sharon is vivid and real.

At the time of Solomon, Sharon was a vast plain, extending from the Mediterranean Sea to the hill country west of Jerusalem, and was known for its beautiful flowers. To compare Jesus to a rose is to say that He is the most beautiful flower, a bloom without imperfection. As a plain or meadow is a serene place, so to be with Jesus is to be at peace. As David wrote, "The LORD is my shepherd, I shall not be in want. He makes me lie down in green pastures" (Psalm 23:1–2).

If it's been one of those days, all you want is a moment's peace. But if you manage this feat, you still have to face the music sometime. Jesus, the Rose of Sharon, gives a different kind of peace—the kind that lasts, if we truly trust in Him. "Do not let your hearts be troubled and do not be afraid," He said (John 14:27).

SACRIFICE

Live a life of love, just as Christ loved us and gave himself up
for us as a fragrant offering and sacrifice to God.
EPHESIANS 5:2

At the moment of Jesus' death, the curtain separating the Most Holy Place from the Holy Place in Jerusalem's temple was torn in two, from top to bottom (see

Matthew 27:51). That act was symbolic evidence that the necessary sacrifice had been made. No longer would the high priest have to enter the Most Holy Place once a year and make atonement for sin. No longer would any blood sacrifice have to be made.

By His sacrifice, Jesus brought down all barriers separating man and God. Only Jesus was worthy to be the single sacrifice for all time for all human beings.

Like the spotless, flawless lambs offered as sacrifices, Jesus was without blemish or sin because He is holy. As the writer of Hebrews penned, "You have loved righteousness and hated wickedness; therefore God, your God, has set you above your companions by anointing you with the oil of joy" (Hebrews 1:9). But because it was impossible for the blood of animals to take away sin, Jesus became incarnate, being born on earth, with the sole purpose of being that sacrifice and thereby offering salvation to all who believe in Him (see Hebrews 9:26–28).

Guilt is one of the evil one's favorite tools. Satan knows just how to make us feel worthless and unworthy of receiving forgiveness. But no one is beyond the saving grasp of Jesus—and no one was left out of the saving grace of His sacrifice. Jesus died for you!

SAVIOR

The LORD lives! Praise be to my Rock!
Exalted be God, the Rock, my Savior!
2 SAMUEL 22:47

"My soul glorifies the Lord and my spirit rejoices in God my Savior."
LUKE 1:46–47

Mary already knew something exceedingly special had happened to her. After all, how many teenaged girls in Galilee were visited by angels? And not only that. . .how many teenaged girls in Galilee had been chosen by God to be the mother of His Son? But when she went to visit her relative Elizabeth, who was also expecting a baby, Mary must have been astounded at Elizabeth's welcome. Filled by the Holy Spirit, Elizabeth exclaimed, "Blessed are you among women!" And then she said, "Blessed is she who has believed that what the Lord has said to her will be accomplished!" (see Luke 1:39–45).

Mary is to be commended. Instead of expressing doubt or asking questions of the angel, Mary accepted her situation dutifully—and with reverent awe. Further, she acknowledged God as her Savior.

The son Mary would bear would be named Jesus, which is from the Hebrew *Yehoshua*, meaning "Jehovah saves." That name and its meaning would become the foundation of Christianity. Only Jesus could be the Savior; only Jesus could save us from our sins. As Luke wrote, "Salvation is found in no one else, for there is no other name under heaven given to men by which we must be saved" (Acts 4:12).

As Savior, Jesus has counted all believers as righteous—even though they are sinners—in a process known as justification. He did this by His sacrifice on the cross and the shedding of His blood.

As Savior, Jesus has made all believers holy, a process known as sanctification. John wrote that the blood of Jesus has purified us from all sin (see 1 John 1:7).

Finally, Jesus has redeemed us from a future of eternal damnation, or hell. He purchased our redemption with His blood sacrifice: "You were bought at a price" (1 Corinthians 6:20). By believing in Jesus, we are guaranteed an eternal future in heaven.

Different religions have different means of salvation. Are they all valid in their own way, or is there just one Savior and just one path to salvation? The words of Acts 4:12 brook no argument: Jesus is the Savior. We need to know God's Word so we won't be misled. And we need to know Jesus to be saved.

SECOND ADAM

The first man is of the earth, earthy;
the second man is the Lord from heaven.
1 CORINTHIANS 15:47 KJV

The beginning of the downfall of humankind can be traced to Adam and to his single desire: he wanted to be like God. It didn't take much tempting from the evil one, disguised as a serpent, to get the first man to eat from the forbidden tree so that he could supposedly "be like God" (see Genesis 3:1–6).

Like Adam, Jesus—who has been called the Second Adam—was a living being. But Jesus was also what Adam was not and could never be: He was God in the flesh. Jesus, Paul wrote, "being in very nature God, did not consider equality with God something to be grasped" (Philippians 2:6).

Because of Adam's fall, sin entered the world, resulting in death for all who chronologically followed him. Because of the Second Adam's resurrection, death is not the final chapter for believers: "For as in Adam all die, so in Christ all will be made alive" (1 Corinthians 15:22).

It's a bit of an understatement, but Adam made a poor choice in the Garden of Eden. When you think about it, though, his choice is like many we face. Will we honor God or won't we? Will we follow Jesus, the Second Adam? We are responsible for the choices we make.

SEED OF ABRAHAM

The promises were spoken to Abraham and to his seed.
The Scripture does not say "and to seeds," meaning many people,
but "and to your seed," meaning one person, who is Christ.
GALATIANS 3:16

The Galatians, formerly a pagan people—and like many new Christians—were eager to learn but not always so discerning. Since the time when Paul had led them to Christ, they had been influenced by other interpreters of the faith and now Paul needed to set the record straight.

Some of these interpreters were known as "Judaizers," or Jewish Christians who believed that in order to be saved, certain aspects of Mosaic law had to be followed as well as Jesus' teachings. To counter such theories, Paul went to the heart of the matter: Who is Jesus, and who are Jesus' followers?

First, he said, Jesus is the natural descendant, or seed, of Abraham (see Matthew 1). But Paul went further: Jesus, as the seed of Abraham, is the fulfillment of God's covenant. That meant that all people of all nations, including the Galatians, would be blessed through Jesus (see Genesis 12:3). If you have faith in Jesus, Paul said, you are Abraham's seed, too (see Galatians 3:29), and have been freed from having to follow the rituals of the law.

Jesus doesn't care where or if we went to college, and He isn't fazed by our club memberships, stock portfolio, or familial pedigree. Moreover, He is blind to the color of our skin and our ethnic and religious background. To Him, the Seed of Abraham, we are all precious in His sight.

SEED OF THE WOMAN

"And I will put enmity between you and the woman, and between your offspring
and hers; he will crush your head, and you will strike his heel."
GENESIS 3:15

Before issuing His punishment of Adam and Eve, who had just eaten the forbidden fruit, God delivered a stinging, prophetic rebuke to the serpent. God sentenced the creature to a future of crawling on its belly and eating dust. And God sentenced Satan, who inhabited the creature, to a future of struggle, ending with his ultimate defeat (crushed) by the seed of the woman.

Jesus would be the offspring or seed of the woman, born on earth to a virgin and to a Father who was God. During Jesus' time on earth, Satan would repeatedly "strike his heel," or attempt to hurt Him, but he would not succeed. When Jesus rose from the dead after three days in the tomb, He effectively "crushed the head" of Satan by defeating death and overcoming the power of sin. (Scholars have noted that while striking someone's heel is painful, it is not a life-threatening injury. On the other hand, crushing someone's head is usually fatal.) When Jesus returns a second time to establish His kingdom, He will vanquish Satan forever (see Revelation 20:1–10). As Paul wrote, "The God of peace will soon crush Satan under your feet" (Romans 16:20).

Evil forces continue to surround and torment us, and Christians especially are under attack around the world. Remember the missionaries and Christians who live where Christianity is not tolerated in your prayers, and take heart from Paul's words in Romans 8:31: "If God is for us, who can be against us?"

SERVANT

Behold my servant, whom I uphold;
mine elect, in whom my soul delighteth;
I have put my spirit upon him:
he shall bring forth judgment to the Gentiles.
ISAIAH 42:1 KJV

Not only did Isaiah predict the eventual result of Jesus' servant ministry—that the Gentiles would be reached—but he also described His servant attitude. Isaiah wrote that Jesus would be "led like a lamb to the slaughter" (Isaiah 53:7), a reference to His obedience to His Father by submitting to a most brutal and painful death. Mark, the Gospel writer, also commented on this: "For even the Son of Man did not come to be served, but to serve, and to give his life as a ransom for many" (Mark 10:45).

Jesus as Servant may be most clearly seen when He washed the feet of His disciples during the serving of the Last Supper (see John 13:1–20). When Peter told Him that He would never wash his feet, Jesus replied, "Unless I wash you, you have no part with me" (verse 8). When He finished washing their feet, Jesus told His disciples that He had done it so that they could go and do likewise.

The idea of being a servant, or displaying such servantlike qualities as meekness and humility, was also threaded throughout Jesus' sermons. Jesus praised the "poor in spirit" and the "meek" (see Matthew 5:3–5), advocated loving and praying for your enemy (5:44), and extolled giving anonymously to the needy (6:3).

We're expected to follow Jesus' example—but how exactly do we serve God? There is nothing we can give or do for God because He created everything. Peter, having learned the hard way about obedience, supplied the answer: "If anyone serves, he should do it with the strength God provides, so that in all things God may be praised through Jesus Christ" (1 Peter 4:11). We serve God by praising Jesus. . .servants praising the Servant.

SHEPHERD

For you were like sheep going astray, but now you have returned
to the Shepherd and Overseer of your souls.
1 PETER 2:25

Jesus had once told Peter to "feed my sheep" (see John 21:17)—and now the disciple was doing just that. Writing to Jewish Christians who had fled Jerusalem because of intense persecution, Peter encouraged them about how to live during difficult times. Perhaps because Jesus had often referred to Himself as a Shepherd, Peter also described his Lord as such, as the One who would lead His people to greener pastures and still waters.

In this passage, the words "Shepherd and Overseer" come from the Greek *poimen kai episkopos*, which can be translated "Guardian Shepherd." Not only does Jesus as Shepherd care for and feed His sheep; He also protects them.

Jesus showed His compassion time and again, whether by healing and restoring to life or by His words. His parable of the Good Samaritan who goes out of his way to show abundant mercy is an illustration of Jesus Himself (see Luke 10:25–37). When Jesus saw the five thousand gathered to see Him, "he had compassion on them, because they were like sheep without a shepherd" (Mark 6:34). To those people, and to all who read His Word, Jesus feeds His flock with living water and the bread of life (see John 4).

When He walked the earth, Jesus demonstrated His desire to protect His followers. Praying to God the Father shortly before His arrest, Jesus said of His disciples, "While I was with them, I protected them and kept them safe by that name you gave me" (John 17:12). And speaking of the Jewish people whom He had come to save and who rejected Him, Jesus said, "How often I have longed to gather your children together, as a hen gathers her chicks under her wings, but you were not willing!" (Luke 13:34).

Having ascended to heaven, Jesus is now the ultimate Shepherd, not allowing anything—"neither death nor life, neither angels nor demons, neither the present nor the future, nor any powers, neither height nor depth, nor anything else in all creation" (Romans 8:38–39)—to separate His believers from His love.

Most of us are not being persecuted for our faith. But that doesn't mean we don't need a Shepherd. While not often life-threatening, what's going on in our daily existence can be unsettling to say the least. Seek Jesus' plan for your life and ask Him to protect your paths—and then wait and listen.

SHILOH

The sceptre shall not depart from Judah, nor a lawgiver from between his feet,
until Shiloh come; and unto him shall the gathering of the people be.
GENESIS 49:10 KJV

Jacob's final prophetic blessing to his sons, whose names became those of the twelve tribes of Israel, contains many enigmatic passages. The most detailed blessing was bestowed on Judah, from which tribe Jesus' earthly parents were descended.

Shiloh, which has been translated as "to whom dominion belongs" or "resting place," or as a derivative of Shalom ("Peaceful One"), is the Messiah or Jesus. When Jesus began His ministry on earth, He declared Himself the Son of God and acknowledged His authority as such (John 5:16–27). At the end of His earthly ministry, He declared, "All authority in heaven and on earth has been given to me" (Matthew 28:18).

The scepter of Judah, recognized by scholars as the tribal identity, and in particular, the right of the tribe to impose capital punishment, did not depart from Judah until the first century AD, corresponding with the arrival of Jesus.

While crowds in Galilee gathered to hear Jesus wherever He went, one day, when He returns, He will rule an eternal kingdom and be lauded as the King of kings (see Revelation 21). In the resting place of Shiloh, the New Jerusalem, peace will reign at last.

Jacob could not have known the exact meaning of his farewell messages to his sons. The words he spoke were divinely inspired by God so that seeds would be planted and hopes would be raised of the Messiah to come. God wanted there to be no doubt that when Jesus did come, He alone fulfilled every ancient prophecy. Rest assured that Shiloh is Jesus, and that Jesus is the Son of God.

SON OF DAVID

And, behold, a woman of Canaan. . .cried unto him, saying,
Have mercy on me, O Lord, thou son of David.
MATTHEW 15:22 KJV

The woman had been pestering the disciples and they wanted to be rid of her. But she wouldn't stop crying out for Jesus. She wouldn't stop because she had been pushed to the edge, having to deal with a daughter suffering from demon possession. Her faith had led her to Jesus, and because of her deep convictions, she addressed Him as the Son of David.

More than a thousand years earlier, the prophet Nathan had told King

David that God would establish the eternal throne of one of his offspring (see 2 Samuel 7:13). God had said of this king, "I will be his father, and he will be my son" (verse 14). The prophet Jeremiah had also foretold that this Son of David would be a "righteous Branch sprout[ed] from David's line" (Jeremiah 33:15). Such prophecies, fulfilled upon Jesus' birth, were confirmed in the genealogies found in the Gospels of Matthew and Luke.

Jesus didn't go to the Canaanite woman's house and lay His hands on her daughter. He merely praised the woman's great faith and said that her request was granted. From that very hour, her daughter was healed. Have you exercised your faith today? Jesus, the Son of David, wants us to trust in Him.

SON OF GOD

The angel answered, "The Holy Spirit will come upon you,
and the power of the Most High will overshadow you.
So the holy one to be born will be called the Son of God."
LUKE 1:35

Even though Jesus was born of Mary, who received this pronouncement from the angel, He was conceived by the Holy Spirit. In other words, Jesus is God in human form. And because He was from God and of God, He was heralded as the Son of God.

While righteous followers of Jesus have been described as sons of God (see Matthew 5:9), and believers have been designated as children of God (see John 1:12), there is only one unique Son of God. The words "only begotten" from John 3:16 (KJV)—"For God so loved the world, that he gave his only begotten Son"—come from the Greek *monogenes*, which means "one of a kind." Only the Son of God could have the same nature as God, could demonstrate unearthly power, and could have been resurrected from the dead.

Jesus has been described as "the radiance of God's glory and the exact representation of his being" (Hebrews 1:3). So it follows that Jesus, as the Son, has seen God. John wrote, "No one has ever seen God, but God the One and Only, who is at the Father's side, has made him known" (John 1:18). Only Jesus, the Son of God, is seated at the right hand of God (see Colossians 3:1).

Because God put all things under His power (see John 13:3), Jesus was able to perform feats never before witnessed on earth: He stilled the wind and the waves; He walked on water; He turned water into wine; He fed thousands with a few loaves and fish (and had leftovers!); He healed the lame, blind, demon-possessed, and ill; and He raised people from the dead.

More than those extraordinary acts, though, Jesus proved that He was the Son of God by being resurrected from the dead (see Romans 1:4). By taking all of humankind's wrongdoing with Him to the cross, dying for the sins of the world, and then overcoming the power of sin by rising from the dead, He saved His believers from God's judgment and eternal damnation.

Why did Jesus come to earth as the Son of God? The story of His disciple Thomas provides some insight. While some of the other disciples had encountered Jesus after the Resurrection, Thomas hadn't actually seen the Lord for himself. Stubbornly, he declared that unless he saw the nail marks in Jesus' hands and side, he wouldn't believe that Jesus had risen from the dead. A week later, Jesus faced him in person and said, "Stop doubting and believe" (John 20:27).

Because of the miracle of the Resurrection, and because of all that Jesus said and did, we can have faith that He is who He says He is. By coming to earth, Jesus proved that God exists and that He is the Son of God. Stop doubting and believe.

SON OF MAN

For the Son of man is come to save that which was lost.
MATTHEW 18:11 KJV

In the Bible, the name "Son of Man" is used to describe Jesus around eighty times. In Matthew 18, Jesus was teaching because the disciples had asked Him who would be the greatest in heaven. Jesus said that those who possess a childlike faith will enter the kingdom of heaven and those who humble themselves will be the greatest. Jesus referred to Himself as the Son of Man because He, too, was human (the Son of Man is, after all, a man) and He understood them. Moreover, He was the perfect representation of humility. (This name was also used by God when addressing the prophet Ezekiel.)

"Son of Man" was also used to proclaim Jesus as Messiah. In one of the visions given him by God of the end times, the prophet Daniel described "one like a son of man, coming with the clouds of heaven. . . . He was given authority, glory and sovereign power; all peoples, nations and men of every language worshiped him" (Daniel 7:13–14). As the Son of Man, Jesus also evoked these images (see Matthew 24:27–44) while describing how He would have to suffer, die, and be resurrected to fulfill prophecies made only of the Messiah.

Anyone who's lived with a teenager has probably heard these words: "You just don't understand me!" That excuse won't work with Jesus. As the Son of Man and the Son of God, Jesus knows inside and out the trials of the human condition. He's been there and done that. When we follow Him, He wants to help us lead the best life that's humanly possible.

SON OF MARY

Is not this the carpenter, the son of Mary. . . ?
And they were offended at him.
MARK 6:3 KJV

The people of Nazareth certainly weren't looking at the larger picture. They couldn't separate their idea of who Jesus was—local carpenter and son of Mary—from the man He had become. How could a boy raised in a dusty village possess such knowledge? How could He perform miracles?

Little is known of Mary, save her role as the vessel for the birth of God's Son, Jesus. She was of the tribe of Judah and a relative of Elizabeth, the mother of John the Baptist. Mary was the only person to have been with Jesus from His birth to His death on earth.

By the time Jesus came to Nazareth's synagogue, Mary was probably a widow since there is no mention of Jesus being Joseph's son. She was blessed to have a large family, giving birth to four more sons and some daughters after Jesus. She was at the cross when Jesus was crucified and then afterward went to live with the disciple John.

Who is Jesus to you? Like the people of Nazareth in Jesus' day, we sometimes assign Jesus a role and refuse to see Him as He really is. Yes, He was the Son of Mary, but more importantly, He is the Son of God, the Creator of the earth, and the King of kings and Lord of lords. He is worthy of our highest praise, our utmost reverence, and our undying devotion.

SON OF THE MOST HIGH

"He will be great and will be called the Son of the Most High."
LUKE 1:32

Hearing those words, Mary must have trembled. Of all the women in the world, God, the Most High, had chosen her to bear His Son. This precious baby, who would grow in her womb and to whom she would give birth, would be called the Son of the Most High.

In the Old Testament, God the Father is frequently referred to as the Most High. The psalmist wrote, "For you, O LORD, are the Most High over all the earth; you are exalted far above all gods" (Psalm 97:9). In the New Testament, Jesus is acknowledged as the Son of the Most High only twice: by the angel Gabriel and by a demon-possessed man who lived in the tombs near the Sea of Galilee (see Luke 8:26–39). Seeing Jesus, the man cried out, "What do you want with me, Jesus, Son of the Most High God?" Jesus proceeded to send the demons out of the man and into a herd of pigs, which then ran off a cliff and drowned.

Proudly announced by an angel and fearfully declared by a legion of demons, Jesus is truly the Son of the Most High.

Every believer has a role to play in God's kingdom. We may not be missionary material or pulpit prospects, but Jesus has chosen us to serve Him, the Son of the Most High, in some way. Pray to be led. . .and then be prepared to follow.

SPIRIT OF TRUTH

"But when he, the Spirit of truth, comes, he will guide you into all truth."
JOHN 16:13

The disciples were understandably depressed. For more than three years they had followed Jesus faithfully, trying (often unsuccessfully) to grasp His concepts, and now He was telling them that He was leaving. Why was He going when there was so much more to do in Galilee? And how could they carry on without Him?

Recognizing that the disciples had enough to deal with at present—they didn't need to know the details of His departure—Jesus offered these words of comfort. Yes, He was going away, but the Spirit of Truth, which is really Jesus' Spirit, would come to them and live inside of them. He would never leave them "as orphans" because He would always be with them (see John 14:15–19).

The truth of Jesus' words wouldn't become clear until after His death, resurrection, and ascension. On the day of Pentecost, ten days after Jesus' ascension, the disciples were filled with the Holy Spirit, the Spirit of Truth. They were then able, because of the guiding of the Spirit of Truth, to spread the Gospel, perform miracles in Jesus' name, and write their accounts of Jesus' ministry (see Ephesians 3:5).

In Old Testament times, the Spirit of Truth also guided the words of the prophets: "No prophecy of Scripture came about by the prophet's own interpretation. For prophecy never had its origin in the will of man, but men spoke from God as they were carried along by the Holy Spirit" (2 Peter 1:20–21).

Because of Jesus' promise to the disciples, all believers in Him continue to receive the gift of the Spirit of Truth. How do we know that we are being guided by the Holy Spirit? Only the Spirit of Truth acknowledges that Jesus came to earth; the others are from the evil one (see 1 John 4:1–6). The power to overcome evil comes only from the Spirit of Truth: "The one who is in you is greater than the one who is in the world" (1 John 4:4).

The self-help section in bookstores is overflowing with books designed to help you love yourself—and then go on to amazing personal relationships and careers. But instead of turning to ourselves for help, why not seek the source of all truth and strength? When you follow Jesus, only then can you look inside yourself and find help—because the Spirit of Truth is there.

SUN OF RIGHTEOUSNESS

But unto you that fear my name shall the Sun of righteousness
arise with healing in his wings; and ye shall go forth,
and grow up as calves of the stall.
MALACHI 4:2 KJV

Jesus said that He is the light of the world—and many of His names attest to this. From the days of the early church, the name "Sun of Righteousness" referred to Jesus, a name that had been prophesied four hundred years before Jesus' birth in Bethlehem.

When John the Baptist was born, his father, Zechariah, filled with the Holy Spirit, praised "the tender mercy of our God, by which the rising sun will come to us from heaven to shine on those living in darkness" (Luke 1:78–79). He was speaking of Jesus, whose ministry would be preceded by that of John the Baptist.

Since Jesus came to earth, the Sun of Righteousness has risen and has been shining continuously. Like the rays emanating from the sun, Jesus' healing powers have touched countless souls, making them whole. The light that He radiates is greater than any darkness: when we are in His presence, He shows the way to go. That way is the way to freedom from the oppressive realm of sin.

At times, the forces of evil surrounding us are almost palpable. When those feelings arise, call upon the name of Jesus. Say His name until His peace surrounds you. Say His name until you feel the Sun of Righteousness shine down on you.

TEACHER

He replied, "Go into the city to a certain man and tell him,
'The Teacher says: My appointed time is near.
I am going to celebrate the Passover with my disciples at your house.' "
MATTHEW 26:18

There was no need for further clarification. For the last three years—in the temple in Jerusalem, in the synagogues of Galilee, and from hillsides and in boats—one Teacher, Jesus, had astounded the people with His message. He taught in parables, and His words often confused and confounded His listeners. And all along the way, He was preparing His disciples to continue His ministry.

The prophet Isaiah had foretold Jesus' great skills as the Teacher: "The Spirit of the LORD will rest on him—the Spirit of wisdom and of understanding, the Spirit of counsel and of power, the Spirit of knowledge and of the fear of the *Lord*—and he will delight in the fear of the *Lord*" (Isaiah 11:2–3).When He taught, the people were amazed because He taught them from a position of authority—not like the teachers of the law (see Mark 1:22). They wondered where He got His wisdom (see Mark 6:2), and they wondered at His message. Who before Jesus had said "The first shall be last" or that the meek would inherit the earth? Who before Jesus had said that, upon believing in Him, thieves, prostitutes, and sinners of all kinds would be welcomed in heaven? Only God's Son, Jesus, the Teacher, could impart such wisdom.

We can't join the crowds on a Galilean hillside to hear Jesus—but that doesn't mean He's not still teaching us. He still instructs us through His Word, the Bible. And every day, He still sends people and opportunities into our lives to guide us and, in the process, draw us closer to Himself. We just have to be paying attention.

VINE

I am the true vine, and my Father is the husbandman.
JOHN 15:1 KJV

Jesus probably spoke these words while He and the disciples were still sitting at the table of the Last Supper, the goblets that held wine in full view. Jesus knew the analogy was particularly apt. In ancient Israel, winemaking was one of the pillars of the economy. Healthy vines were much prized, and able husbandmen, or vinedressers, were in demand.

Jesus was going away—to be crucified and then to return to heaven—and the disciples needed something to cling to. They needed to know that Jesus was the Vine and God was the Husbandman. They needed to know that they were branches of that vine and that only as they stayed closely connected to Him (like a branch to a vine) would His life flow through them and bear fruit by bringing others to know Him.

How were they to abide in the Vine? Jesus told them to abide in His words, to remember what He taught them; to abide in His love and to love others as He loved them; and to obey His teaching. Later, the disciples would realize the heartbreaking reality of His words: "Greater love has no one than this, that he lay down his life for his friends" (John 15:13).

Sports enthusiasts talk about "getting in the game"—playing the sport, knowing the rules and the teams, being part of the action. How about "getting in the Vine"? You can't be an effective Sunday school teacher, Bible study leader, or witness unless that's where you are. . .learning from, loving, and obeying Jesus.

THE WAY, THE TRUTH, AND THE LIFE

Jesus saith unto him, I am the way, the truth, and the life:
no man cometh unto the Father, but by me.
JOHN 14:6 KJV

Time was running out for Jesus' ministry on earth and also for Jesus to make sure the disciples really knew who He was. While they were sharing the Last Supper, which would be their final meal together before Jesus' crucifixion, Jesus told the disciples again that He was going away and that He would prepare a place for them to join Him. Thomas responded by saying the disciples didn't know where He was going, and besides, how could they join Him since they don't know the way?

In response, Jesus made things simple. He told them that He was the Way, the Truth, and the Life.

Jesus had taught earlier about the way to heaven. "For wide is the gate and broad is the road that leads to destruction, and many enter through it. But small is the gate and narrow the road that leads to life, and only a few find it" (Matthew 7:13–14). There are two roads (ways) to travel in life, but only one leads to heaven. That way is marked by sacrifice, commitment, and belief in Jesus (see Luke 9:23). That Way is Jesus.

While talking to some Jewish people who believed in Him, Jesus said that if they held to His teachings, they would know the truth and that truth would set them free (see John 8:32). Later, when He prayed to the Father for His disciples, Jesus said, "Sanctify them by the truth; your word is truth" (John 17:17). As John declared early in his Gospel account, Jesus is the Word (see John 1:1); therefore, Jesus is the Truth.

Jesus was not only offering eternal life to His disciples; He was declaring Himself as the source of life. Indeed, John described Jesus as the Creator, saying, "Through him all things were made; without him nothing was made that has been made. In Him was life, and that life was the light of men" (John 1:3–4). Paul wrote that Jesus "is before all things, and in him all things hold together" (Colossians 1:17).

Because Jesus is the Way, the Truth, and the Life, He is the Savior. Only He has the power to offer salvation for sin; only He has the power to give eternal life. As Jesus said, "I have come that they may have life, and have it to the full" (John 10:10).

Some choices in life you make without thinking—or, rather, without thinking of the consequences. Those are the kinds of choices littered alongside the broad road, the road Jesus spoke of that doesn't lead to life. On that road, travelers simply satisfy their senses for immediate gratification. To travel on the other road, one must understand, accept, and believe, and then live by faith. Life isn't easy, but it is fulfilling when you follow Jesus. Just as He wanted the disciples to know, Jesus wants you to know who He is—and why you believe what you do.

WONDERFUL COUNSELOR

For to us a child is born, to us a son is given,
and the government will be on his shoulders.
And he will be called Wonderful Counselor.
ISAIAH 9:6

Isaiah had tried to get King Ahaz to listen to him. With Assyria threatening Judah, the king was in a dire situation and he desperately needed God's wisdom and counsel. But unlike his predecessor, King Uzziah, King Ahaz was an evil ruler who ultimately went his own way—with predictably disastrous results. Even though Judah formed a coalition with Assyria, in short order, Assyria conquered them, taking their people captive. Isaiah described Judah's people then as "distressed and hungry. . .[who] looking upward, will curse their king and their God" (Isaiah 8:21).

Suddenly, into this dark and murky milieu came a ray of inexplicable, incomprehensible brightness. Despite Ahaz's obstinance, and that of generations of kings before him, God had not forgotten His people. A child was to be born. . .a child who would rescue God's people. The word that was translated as "wonderful" also means "beyond understanding." And the word "counselor" doesn't mean a lawyer, psychologist, or therapist. Rather, the word was initially used to describe a military strategist.

Still, as Jesus began His ministry, He quickly gained a reputation as a man of compassion and someone who keenly understood the human condition. John wrote, "He did not need man's testimony about man, for he knew what was in a man" (John 2:25). He suffered humiliation and pain; He experienced joy and peace. Indeed, His purpose in becoming a man was so He could help those "who are being tempted" (Hebrews 2:18). Jesus knew that the world is overwhelming at times and that, because of sin, we all need to have a relationship with Him.

And how does Jesus serve as the Wonderful Counselor? By asking us to trust in Him. Only Jesus has overcome the world; only Jesus has power over sin and death. He has never turned away those who earnestly seek Him. When we love Jesus, we obey His teachings (see John 14:24)—and in turn, we begin to lead a better life.

Like King Ahaz, we often want to do things our own way. After covering all the bases and considering all the outcomes, we usually come to one conclusion—our own. But we all need a Wonderful Counselor, and we all need His guidance. To exclude God from our decisions is to deny Him lordship of our lives. Remember: Nothing is too hard for Jesus.

WORD

In the beginning was the Word, and the Word was with God,
and the Word was God.
JOHN 1:1 KJV

Bible scholars have said that Matthew's Gospel shows that Jesus is the Messiah, Mark's account points to Jesus as the Servant, and Luke reveals Jesus as a man. John, though, describes Jesus as God—and he gets to the point right away.

Jesus is the Word, which is translated from the Greek word *logos*, a word that can also mean "wisdom." To the ancients, words were the personification of their speakers, being considered almost living beings. They had no trouble believing that God is the Word, and several verses from the Old Testament attest to this: "By the word of the LORD were the heavens made; their starry host by the breath of his mouth" (Psalm 33:6); "He sent forth his word and healed them" (Psalm 107:20); "So is my word that goes out from my mouth: It will not return to me empty" (Isaiah 55:11); and "Is not my word like fire. . .and like a hammer that breaks a rock in pieces?" (Jeremiah 23:29).

The New Testament Greeks believed that Jesus as *logos* was a bridge between God and His creation. In other words, Jesus was the mediator between heaven and earth. The New Testament Hebrews, on the other hand, believed that Jesus as *logos* was the thinker and the eternal Creator. John incorporated both of these viewpoints into his Gospel.

John's Gospel account shows that because Jesus is the Word, and the Word has always been God, then Jesus is God. Thus, every characteristic of Jesus is a reflection of God, and every word that He spoke came from God. Hear the power of the Word in these verses spoken by Jesus: "For God so loved the world that he gave his one and only Son, that whoever believes in him shall not perish but have eternal life" (John 3:16); and "I tell you the truth, whoever hears my word and believes him who sent me has eternal life and will not be condemned; he has crossed over from death to life" (John 5:24).

The Word has the power of life, eternal life, but the Word is also spirit. Jesus said, "The Spirit gives life; the flesh counts for nothing. The words I have spoken to you are spirit and they are life" (John 6:63). The Word was not revealed by the wisdom of men and women but only by the Holy Spirit, who is Jesus. Without the Word, there would be no Christian faith, no Holy Spirit, and no eternal life.

The Word is also the essence of truth—and there is only one standard for truth. Scholars point to the Greek letter *omicron* preceding the word logos as evidence that the writer meant the Word (as opposed to a Word). When Jesus prayed for His disciples, He said, "Sanctify them by the truth; your word is truth" (John 17:17). And when Jesus testified in front of Pontius Pilate, He said, "For this reason I was born, and for this I came into the world, to testify to the truth" (John 18:37). Every word spoken by Jesus, by God, is true and can be trusted.

It's fitting that "the Word" be the last name of God in this book, because that name is truly the summation of everything He is. In the beginning was the Word. . .and, when the world as we know it no longer exists, the Word will rule when Jesus reigns over the New Jerusalem. The Word announced His birth; was the witness of His ministry; and brought the message of salvation to a world covered in darkness. The Word is comfort and consolation, gift, guide, and refuge. The Word is a rock, the foundation of our faith, and through its teaching, the path to the Way, the Truth, and the Life. The Word is God speaking to you.

THE TOP
100
WOMEN OF
THE CHRISTIAN FAITH

INTRODUCTION

"We are surrounded by such a great cloud of witnesses," the writer of Hebrews tells us (Hebrews 12:1 NIV). Included in this crowd are the Christian women whose names fill the pages of this book: missionaries, songwriters, pastors' wives, preachers, evangelists, housewives, and businesswomen. Some of their beliefs and activities were controversial in their time—and could still be today. But each has a message for us. What they did and how they lived their lives speaks to us today.

Some of these women have passed on. Others remain. These hundred women did a variety of work as they labored for good causes. Although some died young, such as Mary Ann Paton who died at nineteen, each was productive in her own way.

One message that will come to you as you read is that God has given each of us gifts. These vary and are unique, so there is no need to be discontent with yours or envy another woman's gift. And this world desperately needs our gifts. As you read each woman's story, you will be reminded of the apostle Paul's admonition to Timothy regarding his ministry; "Keep that ablaze!"(2 Timothy 1:6 THE MESSAGE).

But the main truth these women's lives impart to us is to be faithful—to our families, churches, nation, and God. In spite of health problems, as in the case of Mary Lyon; in spite of the deaths of children, as Hannah Whitall Smith experienced; and even in the face of grave disappointment in ministry, as happened to Mary McLeod Bethune when she was refused a missionary appointment to Africa twice, these women were faithful to overcome every obstacle to use their gifts.

We don't struggle alone—others have run the race before us. They patiently endured suffering, overcame temptations, and, using their gifts, completed the work assigned to them. They won! And you and I will, too, as we "fix our eyes on Jesus."

Take a few moments each day to ponder the scripture verse that introduces each woman's story. Listen to what each faithful woman says. Pray about the messages you hear. And ask God to help you also be a faithful witness.

ANN HASSELTINE JUDSON

Missionary (1789–1826)

"I am the Lord's servant,
and I am willing to accept whatever he wants."
LUKE 1:38 NLT

At age sixteen, Ann Hasseltine wrote in her journal, "Only let me know Thy will, and I will readily comply." Five years later, she met Adoniram Judson. The two fell in love, and a day after their wedding in 1812, the couple sailed for missionary service in India.

The Judsons were not allowed to enter India, however, and instead went to Burma. Ann learned the language, translated the book of Jonah into Burmese, and opened a school for girls. During that time, she gave birth to a son who, at eight months, died of jungle fever.

When a war broke out, Adoniram was arrested and tortured. Ann, pregnant with their second child, brought her husband food and pled for his release. During his almost two-year imprisonment, she gave birth to the child and endured horrendous conditions to minister to her husband. Soon after Adoniram's release, Ann died of spotted fever.

Did Ann's earlier commitment bear any fruit? Her short life inspired others to accept the challenges of difficult mission fields—and sixty years after her death, Burma had sixty-three churches served by 163 workers.

God's work advances through the dedicated lives of His people—people who place no restrictions on God, who rather say, "I am willing to accept whatever You want."

MARY MCLEOD BETHUNE

Christian Educator (1875–1955)

Do not be anxious about anything, but in everything, by prayer and petition,
with thanksgiving, present your requests to God.
PHILIPPIANS 4:6 NIV

Mary McLeod, one of seventeen children born to ex-slaves, became a Christian and learned to pray at a young age. When she asked her father if she could attend school, he said there were no schools for black children. But one day a missionary teacher appeared at the McLeod cabin and announced she was starting a school. Mary's father gave his permission for her to attend.

After each school day, the family gathered as Mary told them what she had learned. She also began helping neighbors with reading and arithmetic. Mary graduated from the mission school at age twelve, yet her heart yearned for more education. The family had no money—and when their mule dropped dead, Mary, with other family members, took turns pulling a plow.

Then a miracle happened. A Quaker woman donated money to allow a black child to attend a school in North Carolina. Mary was chosen for the scholarship and attended seven years. Later she went to Moody Bible Institute, the only black student on campus. Upon graduation, Mary felt called to take the Gospel to Africa. But when she applied to a mission board, they rejected her—not once, but twice. She said, "It was the greatest disappointment of my life."

Consumed with a desire to help black women have a better life, Mary began a school in her home for five girls. The school grew, and Mary founded Daytona Normal and Industrial School for Girls. Money was scarce, and Mary went from house to house begging for funds. Using her fine singing voice, she also held concerts.

The Ku Klux Klan didn't like Mary's bold stand for blacks voting in public elections—and one night, eighty hooded men rode up to the school carrying torches, threatening to burn the buildings. Mary told them, "If you burn my buildings, I'll build them again. If you burn them a second time, I'll build them again." Then she and the students sang, "Be not dismayed whate'er betide; God will take care of you." The white hoods slipped away.

Mary was appointed to various government posts during the terms of Presidents Calvin Coolidge, Herbert Hoover, and Franklin Roosevelt. From 1936 to 1944, she served as director of the Division of Negro Affairs of the National Youth Administration, the first black woman to head a federal agency.

At an early age, Mary learned to trust God—and her faith, coupled with prayer, sustained her for a lifetime. God promises to do the same for anyone who believes, prays, and trusts Him to provide.

ELIZABETH KA'AHUMANU

Hawaiian Queen (1768–1832)

Those who become Christians become new persons. . .
the old life is gone. A new life has begun!
2 CORINTHIANS 5:17 NLT

After Ka'ahumanu became a Christian, her subjects referred to her as the "new Ka'ahumanu." But their queen's conversion did not come without a struggle.

When missionaries first came to Hawaii around 1820, Ka'ahumanu listened to their message. She attended their schools. But abandon her idols and accept their God? She hesitated.

Ka'ahumanu had married at age thirteen and became one of the many wives of King Kamehameha. Soon after their marriage, the king died and Ka'ahumanu married his son. He also died, leaving Ka'ahumanu queen regnant of the Hawaiian Islands.

For four years, Ka'ahumanu carefully weighed her decision. When she converted to Christianity in 1824, the change was drastic. She publicly embraced Christianity and encouraged her subjects to do the same. Before she was baptized, she instituted new laws based on the Ten Commandments. She also ordered the pagan idols to be torn down and destroyed the sugar cane fields to stop the production of rum. No wonder citizens of Hawaii called her the "new Ka'ahumanu"!

Salvation is not a reformation or a rehabilitation program. When we believe in Jesus, we receive a new heart. Hawaiians noted the Gospel's power to change their queen, and a watching world also notices when we find a brand new life in Christ.

FRANCES RIDLEY HAVERGAL

Hymn Writer, Author (1836–79)

" 'Love the Lord your God with all your heart and with all your soul and with all your mind.' This is the first and greatest commandment."
MATTHEW 22:37–38 NIV

Frances Havergal read French, Greek, and Hebrew. She was an accomplished pianist and had a well-trained voice. Frances was also a vibrant Christian, possessing a simple faith and unwavering joy.

Frances was born in England. Her father, a Church of England minister, was

usician as well who wrote over one hundred hymns. A bright child, Frances
s educated at home and could read by age three. She developed a love for the
criptures as a youngster, possibly because her father held her on his lap each
day as he read from the Bible. At age four she began memorizing Bible verses,
and was soon writing poetry.

Frances's happy home life was disrupted when her mother became
seriously sick. After a long illness, she died, leaving Frances, her four sisters,
and a brother. Frances said of that time, "A mother's death must be childhood's
greatest grief."

As a child, Frances was especially intrigued by the communion service.
Because children were not allowed at the Lord's Supper, she would listen
through the vestry door, counting the years until she could at last take part in
the sacrament.

Her conversion experience began with a deep sense of sinfulness. Frances
would lie in bed and cry, pondering how wicked she was. At that time she
attended a private school. Mrs. Teed, a godly teacher, told the girls both in class
and privately of their need for the Savior. As a result, several girls were saved.
When a fellow student testified of her great joy, Frances experienced what she
called a "revival"—she was genuinely converted to Jesus.

Thus Frances entered into a life of deep dedication to Christ. She maintained
a disciplined devotional life, praying three times a day, taking a topic such as
forgiveness or watchfulness for each prayer time.

After her father remarried, Frances accompanied him and his new wife to
Germany in 1852. There she saw a painting of Christ's crucifixion and read the
words engraved beneath: "This I have done for thee; what hast thou done for
Me?" Moved by the words and the painting, she wrote the poem, "I Gave My
Life for Thee." Later she read the verses and, in disgust, decided they did not
convey what her heart felt. She crumpled the paper and threw it in the fire, only
to have it leap from the flames to the floor. Frances showed the verses to her
father, who wrote a melody for the words.

> I gave My life for thee; My precious blood I shed,
> That thou might ransomed be, And quickened from the dead.
> I gave, I gave My life for thee, What hast thou giv'n for Me?

Another of Frances's hymns, "Take My Life," came about when she spent
five days visiting a friend's house. Ten other people were also guests in the home,
and Frances, at the onset of the visit, prayed, "Lord, give me all in this house!"
Before the guests left, each person had received a blessing in answer to her
prayer. On the last night of the visit, Frances, too excited to sleep, praised God
and renewed her consecration. Soon words came to her and she wrote, "Take
my life and let it be, consecrated, Lord, to Thee."

Always frail in health, in 1879 Frances caught a cold that escalated into a lung infection. When she was told her life was in danger, she said, "That's too good to be true." Her sister, Maria, writing of her sister's last moments, said Frances began to sing "Golden Harps Are Sounding," a song she had written. "There was a radiance on her face," Maria said. "It was as though she had already seen the Lord."

Through Frances Havergal's life and the verses she wrote, we catch a glimpse into the heart of a deeply spiritual person. Today her hymns call us to live fervently for Jesus so our deaths will also be a simple transition into the presence of our best Friend.

HANNAH MORE

Author, Teacher (1745–1833)

I have become all things to all men so that
by all possible means I might save some.
I do all this for the sake of the gospel,
that I may share in its blessings.
1 CORINTHIANS 9:22–23 NIV

As a young adult, Hannah More wrote plays for the theater and mingled with England's elite. But at age thirty-five, her attention shifted, and she became friends with hymn writer John Newton and Christian statesman William Wilberforce.

One day Hannah accompanied Wilberforce to a mining district. After seeing the needs of the poverty-stricken families, she established a Sunday school for the children and gave them Bibles and clothing. With her sister, she organized Sunday schools that eventually instructed as many as twenty thousand children.

Not willing to leave one stone unturned to reach people for Christ, Hannah created a pamphlet, called a tract, in which she did battle with the promoters of atheism and the political radicals of the day. In 1795, she published three tracts a month. In one year, she reported selling over two million tracts.

How will the people of our communities be won for Christ? As members of Christ's body, when we use our talents to do what we can, every person around us will feel God's love and be challenged to serve the Savior.

GRACIA BURNHAM

Missionary (1959–)

Even though I walk through the valley of the shadow of death,
I will fear no evil, for you are with me.
PSALM 23:4 NIV

Gracia and Martin Burnham, missionaries in the Philippines, were celebrating their eighteenth wedding anniversary at an island resort when, early one morning, they were awakened by a banging on their door. Before Martin could open the door, three men with M16 rifles charged into the room yelling, "Go! Go!" The Burnhams, with other resort guests, were herded onto a speedboat, hostages of an Islamic group called Abu Sayyaf. With only the few clothes she was wearing, Gracia did not dream their captivity would stretch into a year, ending with her husband's death.

Gracia and Martin met at Calvary Bible College in Kansas City. After their marriage in 1983, the couple applied for missionary service—and when the New Tribes Mission needed a pilot in the Philippines, the Burnhams were appointed.

They lived on the northern island of Luzon where Martin flew supplies to missionary families. Gracia kept in contact with him and the missionaries by radio. Soon three children joined their family.

That day in May 2001, Gracia and Martin's captors demanded large sums of money for their safe return—but in the meantime they hid them at gunpoint in the jungle. As the hostages were moved to avoid contact with Filipino military forces, food and water were often scarce. On one occasion the Burnhams went nine days without a meal, eating only leaves. With poor food and water sources, Gracia and Martin struggled with intestinal problems. The jungle marches were often at night. When they slept, it was on the ground with Martin chained to a tree.

Besides the physical suffering, the Burnhams endured intense mental agony. Occasionally packages arrived from family members, but the food was taken by their captors. Although Gracia and Martin were frequently promised a release, the promises never materialized. As the captivity continued, Gracia experienced depression and Martin's weight dropped drastically.

Gracia didn't always feel God near during her captivity, but she and Martin never doubted His presence. Although they had no Bible, they encouraged each other with scripture verses and prayed together daily.

On June 7, 2002, the Filipino military closed in around the Abu Sayyaf and their hostages. A gun battle ensued. As Gracia and Martin ran, she was shot in the leg and he in the chest. Gracia was rescued, but Martin died.

While we may not be held hostage by enemy forces, we all have experiences in which we feel estranged from God. The Bible assures us that God does not leave us in our valleys. That is our comfort as we face perilous times.

MORROW GRAHAM

Housewife, Mother (1892–1981)

*Let the word of Christ dwell in you richly
as you teach and admonish one another with all wisdom.*
COLOSSIANS 3:16 NIV

"There's only one right way to live," Morrow Graham said, "and it's all laid out in the Bible." She also believed the prayers of a mother greatly influence her children's choices.

Morrow's prayers evidently made a difference in the life of her oldest son, Billy Graham, who has preached in more than 185 countries; reached millions through radio, television, and film; and counseled heads of governments.

When Morrow married Frank Graham in 1916, they moved to a North Carolina farm. On the first day of their marriage, they established a family altar—a time of Bible reading and prayer. The Grahams ran a dairy farm, rising at 2:30 in the morning to milk as many as seventy-five cows. In spite of a hectic schedule, before they ate, Frank prayed a blessing on the food—and at breakfast, Morrow read a verse from a scripture calendar. As she packed the children's lunches, her husband helped them memorize Bible verses. In the evening, the family gathered to read the Bible and pray.

Morrow, a busy housewife, gave priority to the basics, and it paid big dividends for her family and the world. When we make eternal matters the priority, our families will also reap a spiritual harvest for generations to come.

HANNAH WHITALL SMITH

Author, Bible Teacher (1832–1911)

*"You will seek me and find me when
you seek me with all your heart."*
JEREMIAH 29:13 NIV

Hannah Whitall Smith wasn't afraid to ask God difficult questions. As she searched, she found answers and shared them in her book *The Christian's Secret of a Happy Life*.

When the book appeared in print in 1875, it immediately became a bestseller and was translated into every European language and a number of Asian languages. The book remains popular today.

Hannah was born into a Quaker family in Philadelphia. Her father, a wealthy glass manufacturer, provided his daughter with a happy childhood. As a young adult, Hannah studied the scriptures and made an astounding discovery: Christ was her salvation. No amount of good works placed her in right standing with God. He didn't love her more because she wore plain clothes or refrained from wearing jewelry. With this discovery, the Bible became a new book to Hannah—and she declared Christ's salvation should not make one miserable, but rather happy.

Hannah married Robert Smith, also a Quaker, and together they preached and led Bible studies. When they moved to Millville, New Jersey, the couple caused a stir in their families when they abandoned the Quaker persuasion for the holiness movement. Hannah's father, usually good-natured, commanded the couple to leave his house. She wrote of that time, ". . .like an outcast from my earthly father's house. But not from my heavenly Father's house."

Early in her Christian life, Hannah became extremely concerned for people who did not know Christ as their Savior. One day while riding a streetcar, she became burdened for two passengers. Hannah pulled her veil tightly around her face to hide her anguish. A Voice assured her, "It is not My will that any should perish." The burden lifted and a relieved Hannah stepped off the streetcar.

When Hannah and Robert moved to Millville, Hannah missed her friends in the Bible study she had attended in Pennsylvania. Her pastor suggested she befriend the poor people in her neighborhood. She accepted an invitation from her dressmaker to attend a testimony meeting. Hannah, feeling her grasp of Bible knowledge superior to that of factory workers, wondered what the congregation could teach her. A woman with a shawl on her head rose and confessed that her life used to be filled with "this big me." But after receiving a vision of her humble Savior, "this big me melted to nothing." Humbled by the words, and aware of a prideful heart, Hannah concluded that "this was real Christianity, the kind I long for."

Hannah and Robert had five children. When their five-year-old daughter died from a bronchial condition, Hannah could not be consoled. That summer, the family spent their vacation at a beach, and Hannah took only one book with her—the Bible. Day after day she read, searching for comfort. One day it happened. She rose from her chair and shouted, "I believe. Oh, Lord, I believe!" As a result of this experience, Hannah wrote the book *The God of All Comfort*.

While the couple preached in England, Hannah was plunged into despair upon learning that Robert had an extramarital affair. Rejection and shame threatened her peace of mind. Again she sought God's answers in the Bible. She came to the conclusion that God was enough for her lonely heart. Not His gifts or blessings, but God Himself was enough for life at its best and at its lowest points. She told a friend, dejected because she was not married, "Thy loneliness is the loneliness of a heart made for God. I am determined I will be satisfied with God alone."

Questions! Life is full of them. Hannah found answers in the Bible, and Christian believers also know where to go when facing life's complex, seemingly unanswerable questions. As we pray and search His Word, God may give us insight into the "whys." However, sometimes the answer will not be revealed to us. In these instances, we rest in His peace, knowing the answers are not as important as having a faith that remains steady when facing life's storms.

CHARLOTTE ELLIOTT

Hymn Writer (1789–1871)

For Christ's sake, I delight in weaknesses, in insults,
in hardships, in persecutions, in difficulties.
For when I am weak, then I am strong.
2 CORINTHIANS 12:10 NIV

One day a minister asked Charlotte Elliot if she was a Christian. Depressed because of ill health, she informed him she did not want to discuss religion. A few days later, Charlotte thought about the minister's question. She went to him and said, "I want to be saved, but I don't know how."

"Come to Him just as you are," he replied. That day Charlotte received Jesus into her heart. Fourteen years later, as she thought about those words, she wrote the now-popular invitation hymn "Just as I Am."

Charlotte's health did not improve, yet she continued to write hymns. She compiled *The Invalid's Hymn Book*—and after several editions, the hymnbook eventually contained one hundred of Charlotte's songs.

The last fifty years of her life, Charlotte was confined to her home. Her brother, a pastor, said he had some results from his ministry, but Charlotte's one hymn saw more fruit than all his sermons.

God didn't remove Charlotte's physical afflictions; rather, He used her in her weakness. We, too, may face obstacles that attempt to deter us from doing a work for God, but in our weakness—relying on His strength—we can bless others.

CORETTA SCOTT KING

Author, Activist, Civil Rights Leader (1927–2006)

Live in harmony with one another; be sympathetic, love as brothers. . . .
Do not repay evil with evil or insult with insult,
but with blessing.
1 PETER 3:8–9 NIV

Martin Luther King Jr. was killed in April 1968, near the anniversary of Jesus' death and resurrection. Remembering her Savior's death, Coretta King was comforted. Dare she hope her husband's death would also bring comfort to the world's downtrodden?

Coretta Scott grew up in Marian, Alabama. Early in life, she noticed white children rode buses to school while she and other black children walked. She and her friends attended school seven months of the year. The white children attended nine months.

Coretta's sister attended Antioch College in Ohio—and when Coretta applied for a scholarship, she was accepted. Life was different for her in the North. She noticed there were no Whites Only and Colored Only signs on public buildings. She could eat in local restaurants and walk in any city park.

At Antioch, Coretta began giving concerts in churches and decided to further her musical studies. She was accepted at the New England Conservatory of Music in Boston. There she met Martin Luther King Jr. who was working on a theology degree at Boston University. They married in 1953, and Martin became a pastor in Montgomery, Alabama.

Coretta and Martin were familiar with Southern segregation laws and had reluctantly accepted the unfair treatment of their race. That changed in 1955 when a black woman, Rosa Parks, refused to give up her seat on a Montgomery bus and was arrested. Local black leaders decided to boycott the bus company, and Martin was chosen as the leader of the Montgomery Improvement Association.

Coretta and Martin agreed they would fight injustice as Jesus did: with love and compassion. When the four King children asked why they couldn't play in parks marked Whites Only, Coretta told them their daddy was trying to change the unfair rules.

Not everyone believed nonviolence was the way to deal with segregation. The Kings were bombarded daily with hate mail. In 1956, Coretta heard a thud on the porch. She grabbed the baby and ran to the rear of the home as an explosion shook the building. When her husband led peaceful demonstrations, he was repeatedly arrested and jailed.

Coretta did not seek revenge for her husband's senseless murder. Rather, following Jesus' words to love her enemies, she spent her entire life working for equality for all people. Our natural response to injustice is to lash out. Coretta proved how much more effective it is to pray for those who spitefully use us, conquering hatred with Christ's love.

MARY DYER

Martyr (1611?–60)

Don't condemn each other anymore.
Decide instead to. . .not put an obstacle in another Christian's path.
ROMANS 14:13 NLT

In 1635, Puritans Mary and William Dyer immigrated to Boston where Mary gave birth to a deformed stillborn child. When other Puritans learned Mary had "birthed a monster," they believed this was evidence of God's displeasure. As a result, Mary and her family were banished from Massachusetts Bay.

The Dyers then made a trip to England where they came in contact with George Fox, the founder of the Quakers. Mary accepted the teaching, knowing his followers were suffering persecution for their faith.

Returning to America, Mary ignored a law that banned Quakers from Boston and was arrested. She escaped death when her husband intervened. Defying the laws again, Mary returned to Boston—and when she refused to stop preaching, Governor John Endicott demanded her death. Again her husband came to her rescue. In May 1660, Mary appeared in Boston a third time, and authorities condemned her to death by hanging.

Was Mary Dyer overstepping her boundaries by defying Puritan authority? Were the Puritans—who enjoyed religious freedom in America—unwilling to grant the same privilege to others? Whatever the case, Mary's death calls attention to the evils of religious intolerance. We do well to pattern our lives after Jesus, the Prince of Peace, and leave the judging to God.

GRACE LIVINGSTON HILL

Author (1865–1947)

God has given each of us the ability to do certain things well.
So if God has given you the ability to prophesy, speak out
when you have faith that God is speaking through you.
ROMANS 12:6 NLT

Her daughters saw her as a woman of great strength. Her readers knew her as the "Queen of the Christian Romance," the writer who single-handedly laid the foundation for the now-popular Christian romance genre.

In 1892, Grace Livingston married Frank Hill, a pastor. Within a few days of their marriage, Grace noticed Frank experienced frequent mood swings. One Sunday, while he led the church service, he suddenly left the platform. Grace followed him and saw him swallow two pills. When she questioned him, he admitted to an addiction that had begun years earlier. Treatment for addictions and rehabilitation centers were unknown in 1892.

A shadow had entered their marriage, yet Grace told no one. Seven years later, Frank died of a ruptured appendix, and Grace became the sole support of their two daughters.

A short time later, Grace's father also died, and her mother came to live with her. Now Grace was responsible to support a family of four. She assessed her skills and decided she would meet the crisis using her talent for writing.

Writing for publication was not new to Grace. Years earlier when her family was unable to afford a vacation, she had an idea for a novel. A contract came, Grace wrote *A Chautauqua Idyl*, and the family took the vacation.

As Grace seriously pursued a writing career, there was no doubt what type of novel she would write. She determined her books would carry a clear Gospel message. But when she submitted a book to an editor, he rejected her manuscript, telling her to "take out the gospel. This sort of thing won't sell." Grace refused. She managed to write eight novels in the next six years. Each book depicted the struggle of good against evil and concluded with the theme of God's ability to change and restore.

People evidently needed the messages of Grace's books. She wrote over one hundred romance novels, which sold approximately one million copies in her lifetime. In addition, Grace, with Evangeline Booth, wrote a history of the Salvation Army during World War I.

"God gave me gifts," Grace said. "I will do all I can to show Him how grateful I am to Him. I'm going to spend more of my time and effort spreading Christ's gospel."

We can use our talents in selfish pursuits—or, like Grace Livingston Hill, we can find creative ways to spread the light of Christ's glorious salvation using the gifts He's given to us.

BLANDINA

Christian Martyr (?–177)

*Many were amazed when they saw him—beaten and bloodied,
so disfigured one would scarcely know he was a person.*
ISAIAH 52:14 NLT

To honor Rome and the emperor, the governor of Lyons (now France) decided to entertain his citizens by torturing Christians.

Christianity had come to the city twenty-five years earlier—and as the church grew, Christians were shut out of businesses, robbed, and beaten. When believers continued to testify, they were thrown into prison.

Blandina, a slave girl, was also in prison—and that day, she watched as hot irons were pressed on fellow Christians and they were torn apart by wild animals. When it was her turn, she was tied to a stake and wild beasts were released to torment her. To the spectators' surprise, none of the beasts touched her.

On the final day of "entertainment," Blandina was beaten from morning until evening. Then she was thrown to a wild bull and placed on the roasting seat until her body was one gaping wound. In the midst of her pain, she cried out, "I am a Christian, and there is nothing vile done by us."

The treatment Blandina received reminds us of Christ's sufferings. Her reaction to her persecutors was similar to the Savior's. Both endured. And we take notice, ponder, and know we, too, will receive strength should such persecution be our fate.

HARRIET TUBMAN

Emancipator (1820?–1913)

"Be strong and courageous,
because you will lead these people to inherit the land
I swore to their forefathers to give them.
Be strong and very courageous."
JOSHUA 1:6–7 NIV

Harriet Tubman was born into slavery on a plantation in Maryland. One day after six-year-old Harriet had worked all day, her owner's wife told her to care for a sick child through the night. She fell asleep, the baby cried—and for the remainder of her life, Harriet bore scars from the whipping she received.

By the time she was eleven, she worked in the field like a man. On one occasion, an overseer threw a metal weight at another slave and hit Harriet, causing a head injury. For days she hovered between life and death. When she recovered, she suffered from headaches, seizures, and periods of uncontrollable sleepiness. After the injury, she also experienced visions and dreams that she believed came from God.

Although her parents could not read or write, Harriet's mother told her children Bible stories and raised them to fear God. When Harriet told her father she yearned for freedom, he told her to trust God. She prayed that her harsh master would become a Christian, but when that prayer wasn't answered, Harriet asked God to take him out of the way. She became terrified when the man died.

Harriet lived in constant fear of white people: fear of punishment and fear of being sold into the Deep South, which had been the fate of her three sisters. When Harriet married, she shared with her husband, John, her desire for freedom—but he discouraged such talk.

In 1849, unknown to Harriet, her owner planned to sell her. Before this happened, by mysterious means, Harriet was warned to flee. Aided by a Quaker woman, Harriet and two of her brothers began the dangerous journey north. Soon the frightened brothers turned back.

Harriet traveled by night, her eye on the North Star. During the day, she hid in swamps or burrowed in holes in fields. Along the way, she stopped for food and directions at Underground Railroad homes. Slave catchers, with their vicious dogs, were a constant threat—yet Harriet vowed she would not be taken alive.

At last Harriet reached Pennsylvania, a free state. But without her family she was lonely. For a year Harriet worked and saved her money. When she received word that a niece and her young children were to be sold, Harriet did the unthinkable: she traveled south and safely guided the family to freedom. The next year, Harriet rescued her three brothers and other slaves. Later she freed her parents. Once a person agreed to escape with Harriet, there was no turning around. If a slave threatened to go back, Harriet would pull out a revolver and tell the frightened black, "You go on or die."

As a "conductor" on the Underground Railroad for eight years, Harriet experienced many narrow escapes, yet the five-foot-tall woman gave Jesus credit for each successful rescue. She boasted that she "never lost a passenger."

Slaves loved her and called her "Moses" after Israel's deliverer from Egyptian bondage. John Brown consulted with Harriet about recruiting soldiers to help him in the raid on Harper's Ferry. Slaveholders feared Harriet and offered a reward for her dead or alive, yet she was not captured. In 1860, Harriet made her nineteenth and last trip south. She had rescued more than three hundred slaves from bondage.

During the Civil War, Harriet served in the Union Army as a cook, spy, scout, and nurse. In 1863, she led the Union Army in an armed assault along the Combahee River that liberated more than seven hundred slaves. Harriet never was paid for her services. After the war, she established homes for orphans, the aged, and the homeless.

Harriet received courage to perform dangerous exploits. While most believers aren't called to such heroism, we all face tasks that require more courage than we ordinarily possess. At these times, we can rely on God. Just at the right moment, when we need it the most, He has promised to give us all the courage we need.

DOROTHY CAREY

Missionary Wife (1755–1807)

Who then is willing to consecrate his service this day unto the LORD?
1 CHRONICLES 29:5 KJV

She had willingly served with her husband in small Baptist churches in England—but when William announced his plans to go as a missionary to India, Dorothy Carey refused to go. Though uneducated, she was aware of the dangers she'd face in a foreign country. And there were her children to consider. She had three young sons to raise, a fourth child on the way, and she had recently buried a two-year-old.

William, with the couple's oldest son, left England without Dorothy. But while he was delayed at the Isle of Wight trying to find a ship to take him to India, she delivered her child and had a change of heart. She would go with her husband, provided her sister accompany the party.

The dangers Dorothy and her family faced in India were monumental. The heat was oppressive, and she and the children were frequently ill with fevers and dysentery. Daily they encountered wild animals and poisonous snakes. The worst trial occurred in 1794 when their five-year-old son died. Soon Dorothy became mentally unstable—and for the last twenty years of her life, she was confined with the diagnosis of insanity.

Although Dorothy was little help to her husband in missionary work, she went—she was willing. Was Dorothy a failure as a missionary wife? No! She answered yes and obeyed. That's all God asks of anyone.

ANGELINA GRIMKÉ

Author, Abolitionist (1805–79)

"Now, Lord, consider their threats and enable your servants
to speak your word with great boldness."
ACTS 4:29 NIV

Angelina Grimké was raised on a South Carolina plantation by an aristocratic, slaveholding family. A devout Christian, she accepted slavery as the norm until Sarah, her sister, traveled to Philadelphia with their father and heard abolitionists speak against slavery. When Sarah returned, Angelina became convinced the slave system was wrong, and she began a Sunday school class for slaves. She also taught them to read, although it was against the state's law. When she openly voiced her views of slavery, she was ostracized from family and neighbors. Eventually, she was forced to join her sister in the North.

In Philadelphia, Angelina made another choice: she aligned herself with Quaker abolitionists and the Female Anti-Slavery Society. In 1836, she wrote a pamphlet to Christian Southern women, calling for them to "overturn a system of complicated crime." Her writings were publicly burned in South Carolina, and authorities threatened to arrest her if she returned to the state.

Angelina spoke to Northern audiences, giving eyewitness details of slavery, asking women to actively stand against the system. Many people thought she disobeyed New Testament rules for female behavior by speaking and preaching to mixed crowds. Because a female speaker was a rarity, large crowds gathered to hear her, but the meetings were often interrupted by mobs throwing rocks and shattering windows. In 1837, she became the first woman to speak before the Massachusetts State Legislature.

When Angelina married abolitionist Theodore Weld, together they became more aggressive in their fight against the slave system. They wrote *American*

Slavery as It Is: Testimony of a Thousand Voices, a story of the horrors slaves faced daily.

After her father's death, Angelina was given her share of the family estate, and she immediately freed the slaves she had inherited. When she discovered her brother had fathered two sons by a slave, she took the boys into her home and sponsored their education.

When confronted with truth, Angelina made biblically based choices, although it meant alienation from family and friends. When she had to choose whether to be quiet or speak against an evil, she spoke boldly. When she had to choose between her Christian convictions or popular opinion, Angelina followed her convictions. Were the choices easy? No, it is never easy to stand with the minority.

Today we face evil in many forms: abortion, child abuse, prostitution, alcoholism, and human trafficking to name a few. We can allow these free rein—or we, like Angelina Grimké, can boldly speak against wrong, choosing what is right and godly.

VONETTE BRIGHT

Founder of the National Day of Prayer (1926–)

Pray at all times and on every occasion in the power of the Holy Spirit.
Stay alert and be persistent in your prayers for all Christians everywhere.
EPHESIANS 6:18 NLT

Vonette Zachery was a freshman at Texas Women's University when she received a letter from a hometown acquaintance, Bill Bright. Flowers and candy followed—and soon, romance blossomed. Bill attended college in California, and when Vonette visited him, he realized she was not a Christian. He asked his friend Henrietta Mears to talk to her, and that day, Vonette became a believer. In 1948, she and Bill were married.

The Brights saw the need for Christian ministries on college campuses, and Campus Crusade for Christ was born. The couple organized a twenty-four-hour prayer chain at their headquarters near the UCLA campus, and the ministry grew. Vonette said, "We surrounded everything we did with constant prayer."

Convinced that prayer is America's greatest resource, Vonette founded the National Day of Prayer Task Force and served as the chairwoman for nine years. In 1988, she introduced legislation to establish a day of nationwide prayer. When President Ronald Reagan signed the bill, the first Thursday of May became America's National Day of Prayer.

Prayer! A few simple words. God changes hearts and nations when we call on Him in prayer.

CORRIE TEN BOOM

Author, Evangelist (1892–1983)

You have been a refuge for the poor, a refuge for the needy in his distress,
a shelter from the storm and a shade from the heat.
Isaiah 25:4 NIV

Corrie ten Boom possibly thought she would live out her days peacefully as a watchmaker in Holland as her father before her. It was not to be. In 1939, as Hitler's armies swept across Europe, he targeted certain people for annihilation, among them the Jews. Corrie's father believed God's people should be protected, and the ten Boom family began hiding the threatened people in their home.

One day in 1944, a man secretly working for the Nazis came to Corrie asking help for his wife, whom he claimed had been arrested for aiding Jews. Corrie quickly gathered the money needed to pay the bribe for the woman's release. In a few minutes, Gestapo agents stormed into the clock shop, arresting Corrie, her father, and thirty-five others.

Within ten days of his arrest, Corrie's eighty-four-year-old father died. Soon she, with her sister Betsie, was imprisoned in a concentration camp. As Allied troops came closer to Holland in 1944, Corrie, with others, was herded into a boxcar, bound for Germany and the dreaded women's extermination camp, Ravensbrück.

One of the first indignities at Ravensbrück was an inspection that required the women to walk naked before the male guards. Before Corrie stripped off her clothes, she reached into her pillowcase and pulled out a small Bible, which she hid behind a pile of benches. After she showered, Corrie was issued a thin dress and a pair of shoes. She found the Bible and quickly put it in a bag with a cord around her neck. The officers searched the woman ahead of Corrie. Behind her Betsie was searched. No one touched Corrie. As she and Betsie read the Bible to the women in Barracks 8, their building became known as "the crazy place where they have hope."

Food was scarce at Ravensbrück, and treatment was unbelievably cruel with roll call at 4:30 a.m. Yet as Corrie read the Bible, new revelations leaped from the pages. One morning, as the women stood at attention, Corrie leaned ahead and whispered to Betsie, "They took Jesus' clothes, too, and I've never thanked Him for it."

When the prisoners were moved to new barracks, the place swarmed with fleas. There were no individual cots, only huge platforms where the women slept nine across on filthy straw. Betsie reminded her of a scripture they had read that morning: "Giving thanks always for all things" (Ephesians 5:20 KJV). The two thanked God that because the women were closer together, more could hear the scripture readings. They also thanked God for the fleas. Because of them, the guards stayed away from Barracks 28.

During the day, Corrie pushed heavy handcarts to a railroad siding. And each evening women listened as Corrie read from the little Bible. Soon the crowds increased, and they had a second service.

With little food and hard work, Betsie became ill. As she weakened, she saw in a vision a rehabilitation home where those ravaged by war would come to heal. "Corrie, you must tell them," Betsie said. "Your whole life has been training for the work you are doing in prison—and for the work you will do afterwards."

Ninety-six thousand women perished in Ravensbrück. Betsie was one of them. At roll call four days after Betsie's death, Corrie's name was called. *Does this mean the gas chamber?* she wondered. Instead, Corrie was released. A week later, all women her age died in the gas chambers.

Doors opened for Corrie to share her experiences—and over the next thirty years, she preached in sixty-one countries. Everywhere her message was the same: No pit can be so deep that Jesus is not deeper still. No wonder the words "Jesus is Victor" are engraved on her tombstone.

Through God's Word, Corrie tapped into a well of strength that prison, cruelty, hunger, and death could not conquer. Whatever tragedy we are now experiencing or will in the future, we are not defeated. Jesus is our victory!

CARRIE NATION

Activist, Preacher, Author (1846–1911)

Do not join those who drink too much wine or gorge themselves on meat,
for drunkards and gluttons become poor,
and drowsiness clothes them in rags.
PROVERBS 23:20–21 NIV

As a young woman, Carrie became acquainted with the evils of demon rum when she married a man who became an alcoholic. After his death, she married David Nation, a minister and a lawyer. The couple moved to Medicine Lodge, Kansas, where Carrie again saw the ravages of liquor as she worked as a jail evangelist and led a temperance group.

Carrie and the temperance women took their campaign against alcohol to a new level when they asked saloon keepers if they could hold Gospel services on the premises. With Bibles in hand, the women sang and preached to the patrons. Later they grew more aggressive as they broke saloon windows and smashed liquor bottles. In a ten-year span, Carrie was arrested thirty times for disturbing the peace. Yet her efforts proved successful when the saloons in Medicine Lodge closed for a time.

While Carrie Nation's methods were extreme, we admire her courage and sincerity. Her efforts brought to light the problems associated with alcohol. There are many things that bring sorrow and strife, impair judgment, and lead to poverty. A wise person will take the advice of scripture and follow a path of sober reflection and wholesome living.

DALE EVANS ROGERS

Actress, Singer, Author (1912–2001)

*"Here on earth you will have many trials and sorrows.
But take heart, because I have overcome the world."*
JOHN 16:33 NLT

In 1947, when Dale Evans, the Queen of the West, married Roy Rogers, the King of the Cowboys, she wondered if their marriage would stand the pressures of a Hollywood lifestyle.

Dale, a native of Texas, had asked Jesus into her life at age ten. She married at fourteen and had a son by age fifteen. The couple soon divorced. Dale's second marriage also failed.

She moved to California, did a screen test, and met Roy Rogers. When his wife died, leaving him with three small children, Roy asked Dale to marry him. Dale worried that his children would not accept her as a new mother. But Dale's son, Tom, suggested the solution might be as close as the nearest church.

She took her son's advice—and the first Sunday Dale walked into a church, the pastor's sermon title was "The House That Is Built on the Rock." Soon the Rogers children were attending Sunday school, saying grace before meals, having family devotions, and memorizing Bible verses.

In 1950, the world rejoiced when Dale announced she was pregnant. When Robin Elizabeth was born, she was diagnosed with Down syndrome. In the next years, the family grew closer as they coped with Robin's numerous health problems. At age two, Robin died. Dale wrote her story, *Angel Unaware*, to encourage parents who had lost a child.

Two years later, Dale and Roy adopted baby Dodie and six-year-old Sandy, an abused child. Soon Mimi, a child from Scotland, and Debbie Lee, a part–Korean, part–Puerto Rican girl, joined the family.

Yet sorrow was never far from Dale and Roy. When Debbie Lee was twelve, she went on a church trip. A tire on the bus blew, the driver lost control, and

Debbie Lee was thrown through a window and died. Dale wrote *Dearest Debbie* in her memory.

It had been Sandy's dream to join the army—and, in spite of handicaps, he passed the physical examination. Stationed in Germany, Sandy was encouraged by fellow soldiers to drink liquor. One night, he overdosed. Again Dale, with her family, made the sad trip to Forest Lawn Cemetery. Dale wrote a tribute to their son, *Salute to Sandy*. To further honor his memory, Dale and Roy traveled to Vietnam to entertain servicemen.

With her faith firm in Christ, Dale Evans triumphed over the almost insurmountable sorrow of losing three children. Because Jesus overcame death, those who trust in Him will also find strength to rise from sorrow's ashes to His peace and hope.

BETTY ANN OLSON

Missionary Martyr (1934–67)

My help comes from the LORD,
who made the heavens and the earth!
PSALM 121:2 NLT

When Betty Ann Olson was seventeen, her missionary mother died—and the once-loving child turned into a defiant young woman. After training as a nurse, Betty wanted to use her skills on the foreign field, but no mission board would accept her. She went to Africa to help her missionary father and stepmother, but she caused so many problems, they asked her to leave.

Betty returned to the United States, and after receiving Christian counseling, she turned her life around and was accepted for mission work in Vietnam. In 1968, the Viet Cong attacked the mission, taking Betty and fellow missionary Henry Blood hostage. Also captured was Mike Benge, an American journalist.

Chained together, the three were marched through the jungle. Food was scarce and mistreatment was common. Betty, weakened by dysentery and fevers, was kicked and dragged by the Viet Cong soldiers to make her move. She died on September 28, 1967. Mike survived and said, "She never showed any bitterness or resentment. To the end, she loved the ones who mistreated her."

Beset by anger and rebellion as a young person, when Betty sought help, her life changed. No one is too far gone. No one is beyond God's help. There is always hope and help for every person in God.

ELIZABETH BLACKWELL

First Female Physician in the United States (1821–1910)

"I command you—be strong and courageous!
Do not be afraid or discouraged.
For the LORD your God is with you wherever you go."
JOSHUA 1:9 NLT

Imagine the stir at Geneva (New York) College of Medicine in 1847 when Elizabeth Blackwell appeared in class one day. At that time, it was considered improper for women to study the human body, the medical profession being for men only.

Elizabeth was born in England and came to America with her family in 1832. Her father, a businessman and staunch abolitionist, was also a lay minister. The family read the Bible, prayed together, and faithfully attended church.

When Elizabeth's father died, leaving the family penniless, she became a teacher. But she didn't like teaching and considered other ways to make a living. Yet there were few career options for women in that era. An ill friend suggested Elizabeth consider the medical field. After much thought, Elizabeth said, "I have made up my mind to devote myself to the study of medicine." She planned to become a surgeon.

Elizabeth applied to twenty-eight medical schools. School administrators ridiculed her application. Others laughed at the idea of a woman becoming a doctor. Each school informed her they did not admit women.

Because Elizabeth had no income, she also faced the problem of tuition. She taught school and saved her money. When she was not teaching, she studied medical books. Eventually Elizabeth moved to Philadelphia where she hoped to attend one of the city's four medical schools. Finally, she asked a famous doctor, Joseph Warrington, to use his influence to help. He wrote a letter to Geneva Medical College, and they decided to admit her if the 129 male students agreed. Thinking it was a joke, the men voted in favor.

Elizabeth braved prejudice from professors and students. She once told an instructor that if her presence was upsetting, she'd be happy to remove her bonnet and sit in the rear of the classroom. When a professor was to lecture on male anatomy, he asked her not to attend class. Elizabeth told him the human body was holy, and she would not miss the lecture. When she walked into class the next day, the students cheered. In time, teachers and male students began treating her like a sister.

In January of 1849, Elizabeth graduated with honors to become the first woman in the United States to earn a medical degree.

Because she was banned from practicing in most American hospitals, friends advised her to go to Paris. Even in Europe, however, she met with opposition to female physicians—and one doctor suggested she disguise herself as a man. While in France, Elizabeth trained to treat women in childbirth. There she contracted an eye infection that resulted in the removal of one eye, which forced her to give up her dream of becoming a surgeon. During a visit to England, she became friends with young Florence Nightingale, whom Elizabeth encouraged to pursue a career in nursing.

She returned to America and planned to open an office in New York, but no one would rent her space. Elizabeth finally obtained a room in a church basement where she lectured on health and sanitation. Eventually, she obtained a small office in the slums and treated poor women and children.

Emily, her sister, had also graduated from medical school—and, together with another female doctor, they founded New York Infirmary, a small hospital for women and children.

During the Civil War, Elizabeth recruited and trained nurses for the Union Army. In 1868, she established Women's Medical College where she trained other women to become doctors.

Elizabeth Blackwell bravely walked where no woman had ever walked, paving the way for women to become physicians. No doubt it was a painful, lonely path. When we stand for what is right, we may also meet with scorn and rejection. However, when our cause is just, God will help us—and we will reach our goals using our God-given talents.

LADY JANE GREY

English Queen, Martyr (1537–54)

We are therefore Christ's ambassadors,
as though God were making his appeal through us.
2 CORINTHIANS 5:20 NIV

Under the tutelage of Mr. Aylmer, English aristocrat Lady Jane Grey became proficient in Latin, Greek, Italian, and French. She was also a strong Christian, speaking boldly for Christ.

When King Edward VI was near death, he gave Lady Jane the right to succeed him as England's ruler. However, the throne rightfully belonged to his sister, Mary, a Catholic. Lady Jane, too, recognized Mary as the heir—but being young, she had little to say in the decision. Nine days after Lady Jane was crowned, Mary proclaimed herself queen.

Lady Jane was charged with treason—and she, her husband, and her parents were imprisoned and condemned to die. When Lady Jane was taken to her execution, she gave a bold testimony for Christ that moved onlookers to tears. Before she was beheaded, she recited Psalm 51. As her head lay on the chopping block, she said, "Lord, into Thy hand I commend my spirit."

It is not difficult to speak for Jesus when conditions are ideal. It is quite another matter when our lives are in danger. Lady Jane calmly, consistently gave her testimony up to the end of her short life. May we also be so convinced of our Savior's cause that we speak boldly as His ambassadors in life and in death.

GERTRUDE CHAMBERS

Author (1883–1966)

Your attitude should be the same as that of Christ Jesus. . .
he humbled himself and became obedient to death—even death on a cross!
PHILIPPIANS 2:5–8 NIV

Oswald Chambers would have been known as a great Bible teacher—however, without his wife, his writings could have been forever lost to succeeding generations. Because of Biddy, as Oswald called her, the devotional book *My Utmost for His Highest* has been in print continuously since 1935, and currently is available in forty languages. It remains in the top ten titles of religious book bestsellers with millions of copies in print. Next to the Bible, it is the most used devotional book and is considered a Christian classic.

Gertrude Hobbs was sickly as a child, suffering from chronic bouts of bronchitis. So her older brother and sister could continue their education, Gertrude left school to help their mother at home. Eventually, she learned Pitman shorthand, studying and practicing so that by the time she was old enough to work full-time, she could take dictation at a rate of 250 words per minute.

In 1908, Gertrude sailed to the United States where she met Oswald Chambers, a Scottish Bible scholar, who traveled the world conducting Bible conferences. They married in 1910. Oswald had founded the Bible Training College in London, and this became the couple's first home. There Biddy began taking shorthand notes of her husband's lectures, as well as opening their home to missionaries and others who needed a place to rest and recuperate.

With the onset of World War I, Oswald offered his services as a YMCA chaplain to the troops. In 1915, the couple and their young daughter sailed to Egypt to minister to British, Australian, and New Zealand soldiers. While Oswald taught the Bible to the men, Biddy busily recorded his sermon notes in shorthand and once again offered the hospitality of their home to those who needed it.

In 1917, Oswald became ill with appendicitis and underwent surgery. He developed complications and died at age forty-three. He and Biddy had been married only seven years.

Biddy, a destitute thirty-four-year-old widow with a small child, returned to London where she operated a busy boardinghouse. Would her husband's voice be forever silenced? Biddy determined this would not happen. She contacted an editor who showed an interest in her notes of Oswald's teachings.

Biddy, although busy with duties as a landlady and mother, undertook the tremendous task of transcribing hundreds of shorthand notes of his sermons into a 365-day devotional book, each with one theme. After three years of work, *My Utmost for His Highest* appeared in print. Nowhere in the book does Biddy mention her part in the publication. In the book's foreword, the letters "B.C." appear.

Oswald Chambers wrote only one book—but today, because of Biddy's untiring efforts, more than thirty titles bear his name. Biddy Chambers well deserves the title of humble servant of God.

Our human nature craves recognition, but Jesus taught that His disciples willingly, humbly serve unnoticed behind the scenes. This was the attitude of the lowly carpenter from Nazareth, and He desires the same of His followers.

ANNE BRADSTREET

First Notable American Female Poet (1612–72)

Let us encourage one another—
and all the more as you see the Day approaching.
HEBREWS 10:25 NIV

Life was hard for the Puritans who came to the Massachusetts Bay Colony in 1630. It had been especially difficult for Anne Bradstreet to leave England, where her father had worked for a nobleman. There, she had lived in a manor house in which she had access to a vast library and neatly manicured gardens. Now she and her family were thrust into a raw, harsh world.

In America, Anne birthed eight children, and with other colonists, struggled to survive. But in the midst of child-rearing problems and household chores, Anne stole away to write poetry. In 1647, her brother-in-law sailed for England and, unknown to Anne, took her writings with him and had them published. Her book of poems *The Tenth Muse Lately Sprung Up in America*, recording the struggles of a Christian, was well received in England. A second book, *Religious Experiences*, was read by people on both sides of the Atlantic and encouraged those who, like Anne, questioned the meaning of life.

As we come closer to Christ's return, we will face difficult days. Even now, people around us are suffering various degrees of discouragement. Cultivate the habit of speaking encouraging words to everyone. It may be the only glimmer of light on some friend's pathway.

RUTH BELL GRAHAM

Housewife, Mother, Author (1920–2007)

"My thoughts are completely different
from yours," says the LORD.
"And my ways are far beyond anything you could imagine."
ISAIAH 55:8 NLT

As a young person, Ruth Bell thought she knew God's plan for her life: she would be a single missionary to Tibet. Born in China to missionary parents, her father was a doctor, her mother a nurse. Although it was a time of political unrest in the country, Ruth never remembers her parents being afraid.

At that time, missionary parents sent their children to boarding schools—and the Bells sent thirteen-year-old Ruth and her older sister to a school in North Korea. When Ruth became homesick, she turned to the Bible for comfort.

While her parents remained in China, Ruth—at eighteen—came to the United States to attend Wheaton College. Her focus for the future was Tibet.

Ruth accepted the Christian faith as passed to her from loving parents, but at college, for the first time she had doubts about God and the Bible. *Who is Jesus?* she asked herself. She finally came to the realization that some questions of faith cannot be answered. Believers simply accept God and His Word. With that knowledge, she experienced a deepening of her faith.

At college Ruth met Billy Graham. He, too, knew his life work: he would be a preacher. Ruth's first contact with Billy was when she heard him pray. She had never heard anyone pray that way, and she sensed that here was a man who had a special relationship with God.

On the couple's first date, they attended a performance of Handel's *Messiah*. When Ruth returned to her room that night, she fell to her knees and prayed, "If you let me serve You with that man, I would consider it the greatest privilege of my life."

Ruth felt drawn to the young man from North Carolina—and because she was going to Tibet, she encouraged Billy to also consider a missionary calling. About that time, Tibet closed to missionary efforts and Billy Graham proposed to Ruth. They married in 1943.

For a year, Billy served as a pastor in a church in Illinois—but soon an opportunity came for him to work with Youth for Christ. This led to evangelistic meetings, which meant the couple would be separated for weeks.

At first Ruth became ill when her husband left home. But as it became evident Billy's calling was evangelism, Ruth came to grips with the separations. Soul-winning—Billy's passion—now was also hers.

With the arrival of children—five in all—Ruth kept busy with their care. She had her own revival at home as she spent hours studying the Bible and paged through magazines and books looking for sermon illustrations for Billy. She also worked in her local Presbyterian church where she had a ministry to college students.

During the Los Angeles tent crusade in 1949, Ruth left the children with family members to attend the meetings. A notorious criminal, Jim Vaus, was converted in the crusade, along with radio star Stuart Hamblen. When their conversion stories were reported in newspapers across America, Billy Graham became nationally known. Now Ruth was even more convinced that evangelism was her husband's calling—hers was to stay home and care for their children.

As Billy would be away from home for up to six months at a time, Ruth learned that the call to motherhood was hard work. If an appliance needed repairs, she took care of it. When child-rearing problems arose, she dealt with the situation. While her job wasn't as glamorous as that of a missionary, or being at the side of a successful evangelist, Ruth was happy in her calling as mother and wife.

While she worried the children would suffer from their father's absence, she had confidence that God would make up the slack. For several years, Ruth's parents lived nearby and Dr. Bell was a father figure to the Graham children.

Ruth Graham's mission field was not Tibet. Through her husband—and eventually their children—it became the world. When we pray for God's will, we should not be surprised when some doors close while others swing open.

ELIZABETH PAYSON PRENTISS

Hymn Writer, Author (1818–78)

In thy presence is fulness of joy;
at thy right hand there are pleasures for evermore.
PSALM 16:11 KJV

In spite of personal tragedy and poor health most of her life, Elizabeth Prentiss found great joy in her Christian walk. She wrote: "You can't think how sweet it is to be a pastor's wife. . .to sympathize with those who mourn. . .to keep testifying to them what Christ can and will become to them."

Elizabeth experienced painful losses when her four-year-old child and a newborn died within three months. She eventually had three healthy children and went on to write the Little Suzy series for children. Her most famous book is a Christian novel, *Stepping Heavenward*.

Elizabeth is most remembered for her hymn "More Love to Thee, O Christ," which opens a window into a heart of deep devotion to Jesus.

More love to Thee, O Christ, more love to Thee!
Hear Thou the prayer I make on bended knee.
This is my earnest plea: More love, O Christ to Thee,
More love to Thee, more love to Thee!

Jesus intends for believers to find great joy in serving Him—but often, present heartaches cloud our happiness. Yet, as for Elizabeth Prentiss, it is possible for us to look higher than the immediate into the face of our loving Savior—and rejoice!

FRANCES WILLARD

Reformer, Teacher, Author (1839–98)

"Choose today whom you will serve. Would you prefer
the gods your ancestors served beyond the Euphrates? . . .
But as for me and my family, we will serve the LORD."
JOSHUA 24:15 NLT

While twenty to thirty women knelt in the snow in front of a Chicago saloon, the barkeeper stood nearby wringing his hands. The praying, hymn-singing women had already closed fifteen saloons that week by their aggressive actions.

A crowd gathered, and a woman began to pray for the men whose lives "demon liquor" had ruined. The woman was Frances Willard.

Alcohol consumption was a serious problem in the United States following the Civil War. Money that should have been used to feed and clothe children went to saloon keepers. As mothers saw their families suffer, they demanded the sale of liquor be prohibited. In 1873, they banded together to pray and formed the Women's Christian Temperance Union. Frances Willard became president of the national WCTU in 1879.

Frances was born on a farm in Wisconsin. Although her parents were Christians, as a young person, she questioned if the Bible was true. She doubted the existence of God. When Frances attended Northwestern Female College in Illinois, she voiced her radical views, and the college president called for special prayer for the student whom he labeled an "infidel."

That summer, Frances became sick with typhoid fever. As she struggled with the disease, she said two voices spoke to her. One encouraged her to commit her life to Christ. The other told her not to give in to such weakness. She obeyed the first voice.

Frances taught school for fifteen years. She spent two years in Europe. In 1871, she became president of Evanston College for Ladies. For a time, she worked with evangelist D. L. Moody.

When Frances was offered the position of national president of the WCTU, she was uncertain as to God's will. After praying about her decision, she opened her Bible to Psalm 37:3 (KJV): "Trust in the LORD, and do good; so shalt thou dwell in the land, and verily thou shalt be fed." She accepted the position without pay.

Under her leadership, the membership of the WCTU reached half a million and became the largest nineteenth-century women's organization in the United States. Soon Frances Willard was a recognized name across America.

As a young woman, Frances chose to follow Christ—and all her future activities were filtered through her deep religious faith. Our choices are important. As we choose the good and right, these choices will also have a positive influence on our families, churches, communities, even the entire world.

CECIL FRANCES ALEXANDER

Hymn Writer (1818–96)

"I tell you the truth, anyone who will not receive the kingdom
of God like a little child will never enter it."
And he took the children in his arms,
put his hands on them and blessed them.
MARK 10:15–16 NIV

Although Cecil Alexander was a busy pastor's wife in Ireland, she took time for children and taught them about God through her poems and songs. When she published a hymnbook, she gave the profits to help handicapped children. Her hymn "There Is a Green Hill Far Away" has been described as a near-perfect hymn and was intended to teach children God's plan of salvation. Cecil wrote more than four hundred songs and poems in which she explained Jesus' love to children.

Cecil began writing poetry at age nine. Fearing her father would not approve, she hid her writings under a bedroom rug. When her father found the poems, he gave Cecil a box to store them in—and on Saturday evenings, he read his daughter's poems to the family.

Children believe what they are told. They realize their helplessness and readily turn to another for help. Adults would do well to come to God in the same way. In fact, possessing the faith of a child is our entrance into His kingdom.

FLORENCE NIGHTINGALE

Nurse, Social Reformer (1820–1910)

A vast crowd was there as he stepped from the boat,
and he had compassion on them and healed their sick.
MATTHEW 14:14 NLT

Florence Nightingale's father, a banker, taught her Latin, German, French, and Italian. He also instructed her in Greek so she could read the New Testament in the original language. Florence's mother, a socialite, favored elegant parties, travel, and being waited on by servants. From this aristocratic union emerged a daughter who, at an early age, rejected an affluent lifestyle, showing compassion for sick people and animals.

At age seventeen, Florence said God spoke to her and called her into His service. When she announced to her family her intention to train as a nurse, they reacted with horror. Nursing at that time was an occupation reserved for drunkards and prostitutes. To be admitted to a hospital in that era was a death sentence.

Traveling in Europe with her parents and sister, young Florence said, "I craved some occupation, for something worth doing, instead of frittering time away on useless trifles." At age thirty-two, she persuaded her parents to allow her to attend the Institute of Protestant Deaconesses at Kaiserswerth in Germany where she observed the compassionate care of former female convicts and the insane. She compared the happy lives of the deaconesses to those of her wealthy friends, who complained they "go mad for want of something to do."

Florence returned to England and again begged her family to allow her to follow her calling. When they gave their assent, she became superintendent of a women's hospital and took steps to change the dismal conditions of England's hospitals.

In 1854, Florence heard of the appalling conditions of wounded soldiers in the Crimea during England's war with Russia. Forty-one percent of the men died from wounds and diseases. Thirty-eight nurses volunteered to accompany Florence to the war zone. Upon entering the massive gates of the hospital in Scutari, Florence said, "Abandon hope, all ye who enter here." The hospital was overrun by rats and fleas. Cholera and dysentery killed more men than the enemy. The food was not edible. The wounded lay on the floor without water, bandages, or medicine.

Florence, a brilliant administrator, set up a nursing schedule. She opened kitchens that offered special diets. She wrote countless letters begging for supplies.

Upon the nurses' arrival, there were six hundred wounded at the hospital—but as the war continued, the census rose to three thousand. As Florence and the nurses worked to change conditions for the wounded, they were opposed by officers and doctors who didn't want a female dictating to them. When the British press reported the changes brought by the nurses, opposition subsided.

With kindness and respect, Florence cared for the wounded, and the men saw compassion in action. They called it "Nightingale power." No job was beneath her. Besides her administrative duties, she scrubbed floors, and at night she could be seen passing between the cots with a light in her hand. One observer said, "I much admired her manner. . . . It was so tender and kind." Soldiers compared the hospital to a church, and Florence, the minister. With improved conditions, the hospital death rate dropped to less than three percent.

Single-handedly, Florence Nightingale transformed public opinion of two professions. Before the Crimean War, British army officers regarded their men as no better than animals. Because of her compassionate treatment of soldiers, officers began treating their men with respect. Florence said of nursing, "Christ is the author of our profession." And nursing, too, became an honorable profession.

Florence arrived home from the Crimea a national hero. Gifts flowed in, which she used to found the Nightingale Home for Nurses at St. Thomas's Hospital. Queen Victoria honored her with a cross of diamonds.

Florence continued to work for army reform and improved hospital care. In 1859, she wrote *Notes on Nursing*, a classic book of the profession.

Filled with Christ's compassion, Florence Nightingale gave herself to her calling. Whatever our profession, as we allow Christ's love to fill our hearts, respect, kindness, and blessings will flow from our lives to all we attempt to help. The Christ of Calvary has an abundance of compassion to share with us.

PHOEBE PALMER

Evangelist, Author (1807–74)

Let us purify ourselves from everything
that contaminates body and spirit,
perfecting holiness out of reverence for God.
2 CORINTHIANS 7:1 NIV

Early in her life, Phoebe Palmer became convinced that a holy God desires His people to live holy lives. In 1837, she laid claim to an experience of holiness. To help other women reach this goal, she began meetings called the Tuesday Meeting for the Promotion of Holiness. This was the beginning of the "holiness movement" in America and Britain when Christians of every denomination were stirred to seek God to become more like Christ.

Besides raising a family, Phoebe distributed tracts in New York City slums, did prison visitation, and founded Five Points Mission. Later, as her husband traveled in evangelistic meetings, Phoebe served as the "exhorter." Soon, great crowds in America and England came to hear the eloquent female preacher proclaim the message of holiness. Phoebe's books, *The Way of Holiness* and *Guide to Holiness*, were read widely, and from these roots emerged several holiness denominations.

This "Mother of the Holiness Movement" never sought to be ordained as a minister, yet it is estimated that twenty-five thousand people came to Christ through her preaching.

One day when we see Jesus, we will be like Him (see 1 John 3:2). But until that time, we are admonished to pursue holiness, becoming more like the holy Son of God.

MARIAN ANDERSON

Musician (1897–1993)

The Lord's servant must not quarrel; instead,
he must be kind to everyone,
able to teach, not resentful.
Those who oppose him he must gently instruct.
2 TIMOTHY 2:24–25 NIV

When the prestigious conductor Arturo Toscanni heard Marian Anderson sing, he said, "Yours is a voice such as one hears once in a hundred years." But Marian, a black woman, had much to overcome to use her talent.

Marian was born into a poor but loving family in Philadelphia. At age six she began singing in her church choir. Other churches heard of her talent and invited her to sing in their churches. When her father died, money was scarce, and her choir raised money for her first voice lessons. Later, when Marian attempted to enroll at a music academy, she was turned away because of her race. Her mother didn't make a fuss of the incident and assured Marian, "Something will work out."

Marian continued to study voice and perform. But when she gave a recital in New York's Town Hall, the attendance was poor and critics had little good to say about her voice. Discouraged, Marian wondered if she should continue to sing.

Her career again gained momentum when she entered a voice contest and won over more than three hundred rivals. Marian continued to hold concerts in the United States. In 1933 and 1934, she performed 142 concerts in Scandinavia and received rave reviews.

Returning to the United States, she again confronted racism. She received the key to Atlantic City, New Jersey, but was refused a hotel room. She was barred from eating in "whites only" restaurants. In 1939, her manager attempted to rent Constitutional Hall in Washington, D.C., for a concert. "No Negro will ever appear in this hall!" he was told. Many people became outraged, including First Lady Eleanor Roosevelt. Instead, a concert was held on the steps of the Lincoln Memorial on Easter Sunday. That day Marian sang Negro spirituals and operatic arias to seventy-five thousand people while millions more listened by radio.

Marian sang at Dwight Eisenhower's and John F. Kennedy's presidential inaugurations. President Ronald Reagan presented her with the National Medal of Arts. Quietly, Marian faced intolerance and prejudice. She said, "If I were inclined to be combative, I suppose I might insist on making an issue of these things. But. . .my mission is to leave behind me the kind of impression that will make it easier for those who follow." Following her mother's advice and the admonition of scripture, Marian fought prejudice with gentleness.

Little is accomplished when we attack prejudice with angry words. We fight intolerance more effectively by following our Lord's example—with quietness and kindness.

JANET PARSHALL

Broadcaster, Author (1950–)

I heard the Lord asking,
"Whom should I send as a messenger to my people?
Who will go for us?" And I said,
"Lord, I'll go! Send me."
ISAIAH 6:8 NLT

As a young Christian, Janet Parshall thought God wanted her to serve on the foreign mission field. She received a degree in music, married, and had four children. As a stay-at-home mother, Janet was aware of world events that threatened her children's future.

She wanted to hide from the threats, yet she realized Christians do not run from problems; they confront them. With missionary zeal, using a microphone, Janet did just that. She took a job at a local radio station as a talk show host, commenting on world issues, interviewing guests, and taking listeners' comments. *Janet Parshall's America* is now heard on eighty stations. She discusses issues affecting the family, such as homosexuality, pornography, abortion, and civil rights.

A concern close to Janet's heart is biblical illiteracy. She believes the American family will only be strong as they know what God says on issues and strive to implement His Word into their lives.

Janet Parshall answered God's plea to "go"—she is involved. The next move is up to each believer. Will we only talk about what's wrong with the world? Or, like Janet, will we go and be salt and light in our homes, churches, and communities?

FANNY CROSBY

Hymn Writer (1820–1915)

*Out of the most severe trial, their overflowing joy
and their extreme poverty welled up in rich generosity.*
2 Corinthians 8:2 niv

At six months of age, Fanny Crosby contracted a purulent eye infection. When a doctor treated the condition with hot poultices, the result was total blindness. The same year, Fanny's father died and her mother was forced to work outside the home.

In spite of a distressing disability, young Fanny possessed a cheerful disposition and accepted her blindness. At age eight she wrote:

*Oh, what a happy child I am,
Although I cannot see!
I am resolved that in this world
Contented I will be!*

Fanny's grandmother, Eunice, became the little girl's eyes. The older woman described to Fanny the world around her until she recognized the call of birds and knew the color of flowers and the beauty of a sunset. The grandmother and Mrs. Hawley, a landlady, taught Fanny the Bible until she could recite from memory the Pentateuch, the Gospels, Proverbs, the Song of Solomon, and many psalms. Later she would use this knowledge when she wrote hymns.

Fanny received a good education at the New York Institute for the Blind, and later she taught at the school. She married a blind musician, Alexander van Alstine.

At age thirty, Fanny attended a revival meeting and felt God tug at her heart. She prayed, "Include me! Do not pass me by, Lord." That day she dedicated her life to God and from the experience wrote the invitation hymn "Pass Me Not, O Gentle Savior." Shortly afterward, in a vision, God told her He had a work for her. In 1864, she met William B. Bradbury, a Christian music publisher. When he shared a melody with her, Fanny wrote words for the tune, and from then on her verses took on spiritual meaning.

In the 1860s, Fanny contracted with a publishing company to write three hymns a week, but more often she wrote seven songs a day. For these, she was paid one or two dollars apiece—and the composer of the music usually kept the rights for the hymns. In spite of her success as a hymn writer, Fanny had her critics. One evaluator claimed her poems did not possess high poetic quality.

Fanny agreed with them. She said she wanted common, ordinary people to understand her hymns.

One day Fanny needed a specific amount of money and asked God to supply the need. Soon the doorbell rang and a stranger greeted Fanny. As the person left, Fanny felt a bill slip into her hand. It was the exact amount of money she had prayed for. From this experience, she wrote the hymn "All the Way My Savior Leads Me."

Most of Fanny's hymns were written in the first ten years of her hymn-writing ministry. When she was over sixty, she began spending several days a week speaking and counseling at New York City missions. She said of the alcoholics, prostitutes, and jobless she encountered, "You can't save a man by telling him of his sins. Tell him there is pardon and love awaiting him." She wrote the hymn "Rescue the Perishing" to encourage believers to reach out in love to destitute people.

Fanny never wasted time feeling sorry for herself. When evangelist D. L. Moody asked her if she had one wish, what it would be, he thought she'd ask for her sight. Instead, Fanny said, "I'd wish that I might continue blind the rest of my life."

In her nineties, Fanny, described as extremely thin and bent over nearly double, said of her life, "I am so busy I hardly know my name." This blind woman seemed destined for obscurity. Yet during her lifetime, she became acquainted with four United States presidents; addressed the U.S. Congress on the needs of the blind; wrote more than seven thousand hymns; and, at age ninety-three, spoke in Carnegie Hall. By her life and with her hymns, she has blessed people in all walks of life.

Our human nature is prone to dwell on what we lack. As we follow Fanny Crosby's spirited example, we will take the jewel of joyfulness and move on to the wonders of God's plans for our lives.

BETH MOORE

Bible Teacher, Author (1957–)

For the word of God is full of living power.
It is sharper than the sharpest knife,
cutting deep into our innermost thoughts and desires.
HEBREWS 4:12 NLT

As a child growing up in Arkansas, Beth Moore loved listening to the stories she heard about Jesus in her church. In her teen years, Beth sensed God had a work for her to do; and although she didn't know what it would be, she said yes.

After college, marriage, and the birth of two daughters, Beth began teaching a Sunday school class. As she studied the scriptures, she felt her lack of biblical knowledge. In a Bible doctrine class, she developed a love for the Word of God—and soon Beth was teaching a women's Bible class that grew to include two thousand women.

In 1994, Beth founded Living Proof Ministries, an organization to teach women to love and live by God's Word. The organization expanded, and now Beth's Bible study books are distributed worldwide. Living Proof Live conferences give Beth the opportunity to encourage women of every race and country to diligently study the Word of God.

As we pick up our Bible, search its pages, and read it prayerfully, we hold in our hands all we need to solve our problems, heal our hurts, and bring peace to our often confused lives.

KATHRYN KUHLMAN

Evangelist, Author (1907–76)

God chose the foolish things of the world to shame the wise. . .
so that no one may boast before him.
1 CORINTHIANS 1:27, 29 NIV

Skeptics came with their doubts. Scoffers came to ridicule. The sick came in wheelchairs and on stretchers expecting healing, and loyal followers came to be blessed. Throngs of people came to hear "faith healer" Kathryn Kuhlman. And her audiences were not disappointed as the tall, red-haired woman in a flowing white dress stood behind the pulpit and declared, "I believe in miracles!"

One Sunday, as fourteen-year-old Kathryn stood in the morning service at the Methodist church in her hometown of Concordia, Missouri, she began trembling until she could no longer hold the hymnbook. She slipped to the front pew and, weeping, acknowledged she was a sinner. Later she said of that time, "In that moment, the blood of Jesus Christ, God's Son, cleansed me from all sin." God's Holy Spirit had touched Kathryn, and her life was never the same.

Kathryn quit high school before her junior year to travel with an evangelistic team. Then at twenty-one, without formal training, she went on her own, holding services in tents and small churches in Idaho. An unlikely candidate for a speaking ministry, Kathryn had stuttered as a child. Her mother had encouraged her to talk slowly, and Kathryn developed the habit of speaking very distinctly. Yet she didn't want to be known as a preacher or evangelist. All her life she said, "I can't preach." Rather, she claimed to simply "carry a water bucket for the Lord."

In 1933, Kathryn began a church and a radio ministry in Denver. Because of personal problems, this was a difficult time that led her to make a fresh surrender of her life to God. With Kathryn's new dedication, the miracles began.

Later she moved to Franklin, Pennsylvania. One day, while Kathryn was speaking on the resurrection power of Christ, a woman in the audience was healed and a doctor later confirmed the healing. Next, a man blind for twenty-two years received his sight, and the word spread.

Kathryn wrote the book *I Believe in Miracles*, yet she denied being a faith healer. She explained the healing miracles as "just the mercy of God." With the advent of a weekly television program, her followers numbered in the thousands.

Kathryn's faith was simple. She said, "God said it, I believe it, that settles it." She acknowledged God as her source—she was only carrying the "bucket" from which He dispensed His blessings. As we accomplish feats large or small for our Lord, we do well to also humbly give Him all the glory.

TWILA PARIS

Composer, Vocalist, Author (1958–)

Worship the LORD with gladness;
come before him with joyful songs.
PSALM 100:2 NIV

Twila Paris believes a Christian's high calling is to worship God, and she writes music such as "We Bow Down" and "He Is Exalted" to assist believers in doing this. She has released twenty-two albums. Three times, she was named Gospel Music Association Female Vocalist of the Year. Called a modern-day psalmist, Twila's songs can be found in numerous church hymnals. She also coauthored the book *In This Sanctuary*, in which she explains the importance of worship.

Raised in a Christian family, Twila's parents gathered daily their four children for family worship. They were also a musical family who loved the hymns of the church. Twila displayed an interest in music at a young age and began piano lessons when she was six. Her career as a singer-songwriter began in 1981 with the release of her first full-length album, *Knowin' You're Around*.

Where does Twila find inspiration for her music? She says, "God raises the window a crack and slips in a song every now and then. I find worship rises in such a natural way."

Worship to God may be expressed by a simple "thank you" or in a song of joy. Either way, we do well to follow the psalmist's admonition to worship the Lord with a glad heart.

JONI EARECKSON TADA

Advocate for the Disabled, Author (1949–)

"Here on earth you will have many trials and sorrows.
But take heart, because I have overcome the world."
JOHN 16:33 NLT

At seventeen, Joni Eareckson enjoyed riding horses, swimming, and playing lacrosse. One July day in 1967, she dove into a shallow spot in Chesapeake Bay and pounded her head into the bay bottom. She would have drowned except for her sister, who pulled Joni out of the water. At the hospital the doctor told her family the grim news: Joni's spinal cord was permanently damaged. She was paralyzed from the shoulders down.

For the next two years, Joni was in and out of hospitals and rehabilitation centers. Friends came to encourage and pray for her. She questioned, *Why did this happen? How could God allow this?* Joni pled with God to heal her—and when it didn't happen, she became severely depressed. She begged friends to slit her wrists or give her pills to kill her.

Raised in a Christian home, Joni had accepted Jesus during her sophomore year of high school. Slowly, ever so slowly, after her accident, it dawned on her that God possibly had a reason for her injury.

When Joni expressed her frustrations to Steve, another teenager, he had no answers. Instead, he opened his Bible and read to her of Jesus' suffering. Steve said she would find the answers to her questions in Christ. Joni began studying the Bible with Steve, and he asked her to speak to his youth group. Joni felt she spoke poorly, so she took a class in public speaking.

Joni learned to write and draw holding a brush or pen in her mouth. One day a family friend visited the Eareckson home and saw her drawings. He organized an exhibit of her work at a Baltimore restaurant. As Joni mingled with the crowd that day, she was approached by a young fireman who had lost both hands in a fire. Bitter and angry, the man told his story to Joni. For a half hour, she shared with him what she had learned through her disability.

In the next years, Joni faced the challenges of plugged catheters and pressure sores that required weeks of bed rest. Aided by friends, Joni learned to deal with the hurdles.

In 1974, Joni appeared with Barbara Walters on the *Today Show*. This led to invitations to speak to churches and clubs. When she wrote *Joni*, the story of her life, letters flooded her Baltimore home. The book has been translated into thirty languages. She wrote a sequel, *A Step Further*, in which she addressed the problems of the disabled. A film was made of her life in which she played herself. She also created a line of greeting cards.

When Joni expressed a desire to drive a car, a doctor told her she would never drive. Yet when she moved to Los Angeles, another doctor encouraged her to drive, and soon she was maneuvering her car on crowded freeways.

In California, Joni met Ken Tada, a teacher and coach. Romance blossomed, and Joni and Ken married in 1982. Ken now serves with his wife in ministry.

Joni began helping other disabled people—and because she understood the problems they faced, in 1979 she created Joni and Friends International Disability Center, a Christian organization to minister to the disabled and their families. The work is now active in twenty European countries. Her ministry Wheels for the World has distributed thousands of wheelchairs to needy disabled people in more than fifty countries. She is the author of thirty books.

Suffering is a mystery not easily fixed. Joni calls her disability "a severe mercy." Through it, she found a deeper meaning for her life: She is to help others who, like herself, struggle to make sense of suffering.

Trials and sorrows come in many shapes. For Joni, it was the loss of mobility. For others, it may be a seemingly hopeless situation. The scriptures assure us suffering is part of the fabric of life. However, when Christ died on the cross, He overcame every trial and sorrow. As God helped Joni, so He will help all who call on Him in the midst of the tumult.

AUDREY WETHERELL JOHNSON

Bible Study Organizer (1907–84)

Trust in the LORD with all your heart; do not depend on your own understanding. Seek his will in all you do, and he will direct your paths.
PROVERBS 3:5–6 NLT

When China closed to missionary efforts in 1950, forty-three-year-old Audrey Wetherell Johnson, a British citizen, reluctantly left the land of her calling and came to America. *What ministry does God have for me now?* she wondered. God reminded her of His past faithfulness, and her heart filled with peace.

While Audrey rested at a friend's home in California, five women asked her to begin a Bible study on the book of Colossians. Audrey hesitated. Weren't there plenty of churches in America to teach the Bible? After praying about the request, she prepared a lesson and taught the women. They invited their friends and the group grew.

Bible Study Fellowship—a nonprofit, international, interdenominational organization—mushroomed across America. Within twenty years of its inception, one hundred thousand people had taken Audrey's five-year course. Mothers requested a children's program, and Children's Christian Training Program was born.

It all happened as one displaced missionary rested in God's faithfulness. When our plans fall apart, we need not panic. As God had a plan for Audrey, we can also trust Him to open new paths for us.

LISA BEAMER

Wife of 9/11 Hero Todd Beamer (1969–)

May the God of hope fill you with all joy and peace. . .
so that you may overflow with hope
by the power of the Holy Spirit.
ROMANS 15:13 NIV

"Let's roll!" were the last words Lisa heard her husband say on a cell phone before his death on September 11, 2001. Because she hoped in God, Lisa received courage to go on without him, raise their two young sons, and—four months after Todd's death—give birth to their daughter.

Lisa was no stranger to tragedy. When she was fifteen, her faith was shaken when her father died unexpectedly. A scripture—Jeremiah 29:11—served to comfort her through the family's sadness. " 'I know the plans I have for you,' declares the LORD, 'plans to prosper you. . .to give you hope and a future' " (NIV).

Lisa met Todd Beamer at Wheaton College in Chicago. On May 14, 1994, they married. Soon Todd accepted a position with a software company in New Jersey. The couple planned to build a home and live the American dream.

Both Christians, Lisa and Todd served in their church, becoming part of a young couples' group that met to discuss issues of faith and the home. Soon the Beamers had a son, David. Two years later, Drew joined the family. Lisa was five months pregnant on September 11.

On September 10, the couple returned from a business trip to Rome. Todd had a flight to catch the next day and rose early. Lisa was getting ready to run errands when her phone rang and a friend asked, "Do you have your television on?"

As she watched the World Trade Center events unfold, Lisa wondered why Todd didn't call. Then the television flashed news of another crash. This one, Flight 93, was bound for San Francisco, Todd's destination. Lisa knew immediately her husband was on that flight. She cried out to God and felt His peace envelop her. *Todd is in heaven*, she thought.

In the aftermath of her husband's death, Lisa attended a memorial service in Pennsylvania, the site of the crash. She was honored by the United States Congress and appeared on numerous television shows. In an interview with Larry King, he said, "You've given a lot of people a lot of hope."

Hope was what Lisa Beamer held on to after her husband's death: hope for her children's future and hope of heaven where she and the children will again be united with Todd.

We don't know what tomorrow will bring. But even when dark clouds of tragedy arise on our horizon, as Christians, our hearts overflow with hope—imparted by the God of hope.

JOY RIDDERHOF

Founder of Gospel Recordings (1903–84)

Be joyful always; pray continually; give thanks in all circumstances,
for this is God's will for you in Christ Jesus.
1 THESSALONIANS 5:16–18 NIV

While a student at Columbia Bible School, Joy Ridderhof heard a message on "rejoicing evermore"—and she began the practice of giving thanks in every situation. This principle would serve her well in the years ahead.

In 1930, Joy went as a missionary to Honduras. Soon she found herself struggling with malaria, flu, and smallpox. Yet she continued to rejoice. Broken in health, in 1936, she was forced to leave the mission field.

As she lay in her parents' attic bedroom in Los Angeles, Joy pondered her future. The prospect of returning to Honduras was gone. She had no financial support. As she attempted to rejoice, Joy remembered the gramophone machines that had blared out popular tunes in Honduras. She made a three-and-a-half-minute Gospel recording in the Spanish language and sent it to the village she had left.

Other missionaries heard of Joy's recording, and they wanted tapes to share with unreached groups. By 1984, Gospel Recordings had provided a tool whereby people in four thousand languages had heard of Jesus' love.

Loss and illness need not lead to despair. God has provided an open door to escape that fate. Rejoice evermore! It's more than good advice—it is God's command to His people.

EDITH SCHAEFFER

Author, Cofounder of L'Abri (1914–2013)

Continue to love each other with true Christian love.
Don't forget to show hospitality to strangers,
for some who have done this have entertained
angels without realizing it!
HEBREWS 13:1–2 NLT

Can a housewife help bring change to a world indifferent to Christ and the Bible? More important, will the little she does make a difference? With a teapot in one hand and a platter of cakes in the other, a smiling Edith Schaeffer did make a difference and helped influence countless people to follow Christ.

Edith Seville was born in China to missionary parents. She attended Beaver College in Pennsylvania where she met ministerial student Francis Schaeffer. They married in 1935.

In 1947, when Europe was recovering from the devastation of World War II, Francis was commissioned by his denomination to visit Europe to assess the spiritual health of the churches. He discovered that European churches and pastors lacked spiritual vitality. Children were being raised without a knowledge of the Bible. The mission board asked Edith and Francis to consider moving to the Continent to strengthen what remained. The Schaeffers moved to Switzerland in 1948—and while Francis led children and young people in informal Bible studies, Edith entertained their guests in a relaxed atmosphere. Soon people of all ages were being counseled, taught, and fed around Edith's table.

After a furlough in 1954, the Schaeffers experienced a series of difficulties when Frankie, their three-year-old son, became ill with polio. Then the mission board cut the family's salary. Next Susan, their daughter, was diagnosed with rheumatic fever and ordered on bed rest. With every setback, Edith went to God in prayer.

But the trials didn't end. The local Swiss authorities, unfriendly to the Schaeffers' religious influence, ordered them to leave town. *Is our time in Europe over?* Edith wondered as she prayed. While Francis packed for the move, Edith went to neighboring villages looking for a house to rent.

A real estate agent showed her a home near a bus stop that would be ideal for their ministry, but the property was not for rent—it was for sale. Should they buy the house? The Schaeffers needed to know, and Edith again prayed. If God wanted them to have the property, a thousand dollars needed to come in the mail the next day. The following day at ten in the morning, the postman arrived with a letter in his hand. It contained the money.

The new location—called L'Abri, meaning "shelter" in French—became a sanctuary for people of all races, ages, and backgrounds. Often as many as one hundred people would crowd under the Schaeffers' roof. Famous musicians came with questions. Alcoholics came for counseling. Students came to debate Christianity. For some, L'Abri was their last hope. All came searching for truth—and no subject was off limits as the guests discussed music, art, medicine, and the Bible. Some stayed for a day. Others spent weeks and even months.

During the day, Edith supervised the guests as they helped with meal preparation, gardening, canning, cleaning, and laundry. In the evening, after Edith's sumptuous dinner, the people gathered around the fireplace or stayed by the table to talk. Edith said, "Life at L'Abri was never, ever easy, but it was always rewarding." As guests sipped tea and munched on Edith's homemade goodies, her hospitality became legendary.

Besides the comfort of her guests, Edith also had other issues to deal with. Three of the Schaeffers' four children suffered from chronic diseases. Then Edith's mother-in-law, a stroke victim, moved in with the family.

L'Abri went on to expand to other locations. When her husband was diagnosed with cancer and received treatment at Mayo Clinic in Rochester, Minnesota, Edith established a center there. The purpose of each location was to communicate Christianity in a relaxed, homelike atmosphere.

While Francis's books deal with theological subjects, some of Edith's book titles are *What Is a Family?* and *The Hidden Art of Homemaking*. In all, she published seventeen books.

Some preach or sing of Jesus' love. Others, like Edith Schaeffer, touch lives by cooking, cleaning, and serving meals. Like Edith Schaeffer, try to find simple acts of hospitality to do every day to show others Jesus' love.

AMANDA SMITH

Evangelist (1837–1915)

God chose things despised by the world,
things counted as nothing at all,
and used them. . .so that no one can ever
boast in the presence of God.
1 Corinthians 1:28–29 nlt

While attending a revival meeting in 1868, Amanda Smith saw in a vision the fiery word "Go!" and heard a voice say, "Go, preach." She said God touched her "from the crown of my head to the soles of my feet." In spite of long days at a washtub, she began holding revival meetings.

There was not a more unlikely person to preach the Gospel than Amanda Smith, a former slave with only three and a half months of education. As a young woman, she had worked as a maid in Pennsylvania, where she was converted in a revival service. When she married, her husband—a soldier in the Union army—never returned from war.

Amanda became an effective evangelist. In 1876, an opportunity came for her to preach in England. Later she was invited to conduct meetings in Scotland, India, and Africa. Besides preaching and singing, she organized women's and men's groups and temperance societies.

Whom does God choose to preach His glorious salvation message? Regardless of race, education, status, or background, God calls those who willingly say yes and reserve for Him any glory that results.

PHILLIS WHEATLEY

African-American Poet (1753–84)

*"Don't rejoice just because evil spirits obey you;
rejoice because your names are registered as citizens of heaven."*
LUKE 10:20 NLT

Imagine being kidnapped at age seven and thrust into the hold of a dirty slave ship. After spending several months at sea, you stand on the auction block dressed only in a piece of filthy carpet.

That day in 1761, John and Suzanna Wheatley were looking for a servant to help in their Boston house. Pity flooded Suzanna's heart as she saw the dirty child, and she begged John to buy her. Noticing the child's frail condition, he shook his head. Suzanna persisted.

The Wheatleys brought the sickly child home and named her Phillis. Reluctant to place her in the cold slave quarters, Suzanna made a bed for Phillis in a room with the Wheatleys' daughter, Mary.

Mary showed her new friend around their home, which included an extensive library. Although most people of the time believed slaves weren't capable of being educated, when Phillis showed an interest in learning, Mary taught her to read and write. Phillis attended church with the family—and instead of sitting in the gallery with other slaves, the Wheatleys had her sit with them. Through the influence of this pious family, Phillis became a devout Christian. She studied the Bible. Soon she read Latin and the classics. Around age thirteen, she began writing verse of literary quality.

In 1765, all Boston was in an uproar when the British government passed the Stamp Act, which levied a heavy tax on the colonists. Phillis also felt the tax was unfair and, without the Wheatleys' knowledge, wrote and sent a poem to King George III in England. In a few months a delegation appeared at the Wheatley home. The men marveled that a slave could write a letter like the one the king had received.

Phillis accompanied the Wheatleys to England in 1773. Unknown to her, a Christian woman had thirty-nine of Phillis's poems published in a book. The black slave became popular in London and was known as the "Sable Muse." She was possibly the first black American to have a book published.

While slavery was a serious evil, Phillis's poems do not question the slave system. Rather, her writings thank God for Christian people who brought her the Gospel. Phillis's capture made it possible for her to hear of God's wonderful salvation and prepare for a glorious future in eternity beyond.

While many things of life give us great joy, the greatest is knowing we've accepted Jesus, God's provision for our eternal redemption. How glorious to know our names are recorded on heaven's roster!

LILIAS TROTTER

Missionary to North Africa (1853–1928)

Wait patiently for the LORD. Be brave and courageous.
Yes, wait patiently for the LORD.
PSALM 27:14 NLT

As a child in a wealthy English family, Lilias Trotter studied art with the goal of becoming an artist. However, this objective became secondary after she trusted in Christ as her Savior.

Young Lilias shared in the religious fervor that swept across England in the 1870s. When she heard Hannah Whitall Smith preach, the Bible teacher became Lilias's role model. Evangelist D. L. Moody held meetings in London, and as Lilias helped counsel converts, she received a passion to lead people to Christ.

Lilias felt called to bring the Gospel to the Muslims, and in 1888 she went to North Africa. Knowing Muslims could not be reached by conventional missionary methods, she used her artistic talents to design attractive tracts for distribution. Beginning with three workers, soon thirty missionaries worked full-time in Gospel distribution. Her greatest achievement was the translation of the New Testament into the Algerian dialect. Although there were few converts, Lilias plodded on for thirty-eight years. In letters she often wrote, "Blessed are all they that wait for Him."

Sometimes, no matter how hard we work doing good, we see little progress. In those times, we can prayerfully and patiently wait on God. Who is more trustworthy to wait upon?

KATHARINA LUTHER

Wife of the Reformer (1499–1552)

A worthy wife is her husband's joy and crown.
PROVERBS 12:4 NLT

Who would have thought romance could flourish during the dark days of the Protestant Reformation? Affairs of the heart were possibly the last thing on Martin Luther's mind when he nailed his Ninety-Five Theses to the door of the Wittenberg church.

On April 4, 1523, under cover of darkness, twelve nuns from the Nimbschen nunnery climbed out of a window and crept into the back of Leonard Koppe's wagon bound for Wittenberg. One of the nuns—feisty, redheaded Katharina von

Bora—had entered a convent school at age five when her mother died. At age sixteen, she took vows of chastity, poverty, and obedience.

A few years earlier, Katharina and the other sisters had heard of the radical teacher Martin Luther. While they continued to chant prayers and embroider, their whispered conversations centered on the monk's audacity to refute the church's sale of indulgences as a means of receiving forgiveness of sins.

One of the women, Magdalena von Staupitz, wrote Luther, saying that some of the nuns wanted out of the nunnery and asking for his help. Luther responded that if the elders in Torgau would plan the escape, he would find homes and husbands for the women.

In the next two years, Luther helped eleven of the women find husbands. For the twelfth escapee, Katharina von Bora, he was unsuccessful. While working for a wealthy family, she fell in love with Jerome Baumgartner, a student. But he left Wittenberg; and when word reached Katharina that he was engaged, she was heartbroken. Another suitor, Dr. Glatz, showed an interest in the ex-nun, but she spurned his attention. Secretly, she had set her sights on Luther. While Luther encouraged other ex-monks to marry, he never planned to himself. As a hunted heretic, his life was often threatened and could end at any moment.

No one is sure what changed Luther's mind—but on June 13, 1525, Katharina, age twenty-six, and Luther, forty-two, married in a quiet ceremony. News of their marriage rocked the Western world. Hadn't the ex-nun and monk taken irrevocable vows? Many openly opposed the union, predicting the marriage would produce the Antichrist. Luther explained that he married to "please his father, tease the pope, and spite the devil."

The Luthers' first home was a forsaken monastery. In spite of critics, Katharina proved capable of handling the problems that beset their marriage. She managed their finances, freeing her husband to teach, preach, and write. Luther suffered from various diseases, and Katharina treated him with herbs, poultices, and massages. She operated a brewery, bought cattle, drove a wagon, and maintained a garden and an orchard. Humorously, Luther said she also sometimes found time to read the Bible.

Often, as many as twenty-five guests gathered around Katharina's table as she took in student boarders, refugees fleeing persecution, four orphans of relatives, and the many guests who came to consult with her famous husband. Luther recognized his wife's able management and said he wouldn't trade his Katie for France and Venice.

Katharina and Luther had six children. But diseases dealt harshly with the young during the Middle Ages, and the couple was saddened when a daughter died at eight months and another girl at age fourteen.

In 1546, Luther became ill while away from home and died without his beloved Katie at his side. War raged in Germany at that time—and a year after her husband's death, Katharina, with the children, was forced to flee their home. They came back in 1547 to find the farm in ruins. For a time, the penniless widow took in boarders. Then a plague hit Wittenberg, and again Katharina and her family fled. While en route, the horses bolted and Katharina fell from the wagon and received severe bruises. She died three months later.

With industry and love, Katharina Luther enriched her husband's life. God has a plan and role for every woman to fill. We each are called to become all God intended us to be, in our homes, our workplaces, our churches, and our communities.

WILHELMINA

Queen of the Netherlands (1880–1962)

The LORD will guide you continually,
watering your life when you are dry
and keeping you healthy, too.
ISAIAH 58:11 NLT

God guides the affairs of individual lives and nations. No one was more aware of this than Wilhelmina, queen of the Netherlands. When her father, King William III, died, ten-year-old Wilhelmina became queen. Encouraged by a devout mother, the princess trusted in Christ. During her formative years, Wilhelmina sought God's guidance for her life and her nation.

When bombs fell and German tanks rolled across the Netherlands in 1940, Queen Wilhelmina determined to stay with her people. But when the situation threatened her life, the queen escaped to England where she directed Dutch forces in Germany and Japan. During World War II, more than 270,000 of her subjects were killed or died from starvation. Wilhelmina broadcast weekly messages to comfort the survivors and encourage them to resist the German occupation. After the war, Wilhelmina abdicated the throne to Juliana, her daughter.

What does a queen do upon retirement? Wilhelmina felt directed to "bring all men to Christ." She did this through radio broadcasts, personal correspondence, and her book *Lonely, but Not Alone*.

How comforting to know God has a plan for every life! Each day we, like Wilhelmina, can live securely, our lives guided by the hand of a loving Father.

SHIRLEY DOBSON

Author, Chairwoman of National Day
of Prayer Task Force (1937–)

"If my people, who are called by my name,
will humble themselves and pray
and seek my face and turn from their wicked ways,
then will I hear from heaven
and will forgive their sin and will heal their land."

2 CHRONICLES 7:14 NIV

Shirley Dobson didn't wake up one morning and suddenly believe God answers prayer. Rather, her journey to be chairwoman of America's National Day of Prayer began in childhood.

When Shirley was a little girl, a Sunday school teacher told the students that God loved them and knew each one by name. Shirley believed the teacher and gave her heart to Jesus. The teacher also taught the children how to pray—and when Shirley's parents divorced, she asked God to give her a new father. Within a year her mother married a Christian man, and Shirley realized God had heard and answered her prayer.

Several years later, Shirley asked God to give her a Christian husband. On the campus of Pasadena State College, where she was pursuing a degree in education, she met James Dobson, captain of the tennis team, and was impressed by his stand for Christian principles. The couple dated for three years and married in 1960. Again God had answered Shirley's prayer.

When their home was blessed with children, Shirley and her husband taught their daughter and son the importance of prayer through times of family devotions.

In the years to come, Shirley and James were alarmed when they saw many American families being ravaged by divorce and other evils. To counteract society's destructive forces, they established Focus on the Family, an organization to help families fight the pressures of a worldly culture.

Every year since 1950, the United States president and all fifty governors have signed a proclamation encouraging Americans to pray for their nation on the first Thursday in May. Vonette Bright had been chairwoman of this effort, and upon her retirement, she urged Shirley to take the post. At the onset, Shirley refused, but after praying about it, she accepted the position of chairwoman of the National Day of Prayer.

Shirley has received many honorary awards and degrees. In 1996, she was designated the Church Woman of the Year. Besides leading America in the annual Day of Prayer, she authored two books with Gloria Gaither on strengthening family ties by creating and observing family traditions.

Prayer was never an afterthought in Shirley Dobson's Christian walk, and neither should it be for any believer. Fervent, sincere prayer is the very foundation for our lives. God promises to bless the person, the family, and the nation that prays.

HANNAH ADAMS

Author (1755–1831)

These also are sayings of the wise:
To show partiality in judging is not good.
PROVERBS 24:23 NIV

Hannah Adams became interested in writing when one of her father's students gave her a dictionary of all the religions from the beginning of time. She noticed the author treated most religious faiths with prejudice and even hostility.

In 1778, Hannah began to compile her own reference book of religions, based not on opinions or biases, but on factual information. This wasn't her only reason for attempting to publish a book, however—her family also needed the money.

In 1784, Hannah published *An Alphabetical Compendium of the Various Sects Which Have Appeared from the Beginning of the Christian Era*. The first edition sold out, but because of an unscrupulous agent, Hannah received little pay for her book.

While Hannah taught school to supplement the family income, she published a history of New England. She went on to author *History of the Jews, Letters on the Gospels,* and *A Dictionary of All Religions and Religious Denominations.* Hannah Adams was the first American woman to make a living as an author. In all her writings, she did extensive research and attempted to write truthfully.

It is difficult to be free of biased opinions when people's views differ from yours. We don't do this by compromising our beliefs, but by respecting what others believe. Our only debt to others—whether or not their opinions agree with ours—is to love them.

VICTORIA

English Queen (1819–1901)

"Because of me, kings reign, and rulers make just laws.
Rulers lead with my help,
and nobles make righteous judgments."
PROVERBS 8:15–16 NLT

When thirteen-year-old Victoria visited industrial towns in Wales, she was horrified to see ragged, hungry children living in wretched huts black with coal dust. The trip marked the beginning of a social conscience for the young woman destined to become queen of the British Empire.

Upon the death of her uncle, King William IV, eighteen-year-old Victoria was informed she was queen. Before her coronation in Westminster Abbey in 1838, she requested two hours of solitude to pray for divine wisdom.

Two years later she fell in love with Prince Albert, her cousin. Because Victoria was the queen, she had to propose marriage to Albert. He accepted, and the royal couple enjoyed a happily married life for twenty-one years.

A well-educated man, Albert encouraged his wife to engage in worthwhile activities—and together they crusaded against slavery, child labor, and dueling. The couple eventually had nine children and, as they devoted themselves to their family, they became role models for other British families.

Although the monarchy had little power at this time, the queen was consulted on world and domestic affairs. Appalled by the living conditions of England's poor, she supported the Mines Act of 1842, which banned women and children from working underground. By 1870, education was compulsory for all British children. Students not belonging to the Church of England had been banned from attending Oxford and Cambridge Universities, but through Victoria's influence the schools were opened to all.

Victoria's reign was a time of great expansion for the empire. Britain was at the height of the Industrial Revolution and became the foremost world power. Her navy ruled the seas. A missionary fervor also swept the nation during this era. David Livingstone and others left Britain's shores, taking the Gospel to far-off places. Great religious groups like the Salvation Army were founded to help the poor.

One Sunday, after hearing a sermon at St. Paul's Cathedral, Victoria asked the chaplain if a person could be absolutely sure of his eternal safety. "No one can be absolutely sure," she was told. John Townsend, a Christian, heard of the queen's question and wrote her a letter in which he quoted John 3:16 and Romans 10:9–10. Soon thereafter, Mr. Townsend received a letter from Victoria. She had read the verses and wrote, "I believe in the finished work of

Christ for me and trust by God's grace to meet you in that home of which He said, 'I go to prepare a place for you.' "

Seven assassination attempts were made on the queen's life during her reign. Yet she did not appear moved by the narrow escapes. Her courageous spirit only made her more popular with her subjects.

Victoria and Albert's fourth son, Leopold, was a hemophiliac. The queen anguished over her son's condition but was comforted when, at Albert's suggestion, she spoke openly to her subjects of Leopold's malady.

In 1861, at age forty-two, Prince Albert became ill with typhoid fever. In a few days he died. Victoria could not be consoled—and for two years, she refused to appear in public. She dressed in black for the remainder of her life.

Before Victoria's reign, English people had little respect for the throne. By her decency, honesty, dignity, and sense of duty, Victoria made the monarchy respectable and created standards for future royal conduct. At her Diamond Jubilee in 1897, it was said no one in the empire was more admired than Queen Victoria. The entire time period was named after her: the Victorian Era.

Although she had worn black since the death of her husband, Victoria requested the dark color not be used at her burial. Instead, her body was dressed in white and she wore her wedding veil.

One good woman doing what was right—promoting and demonstrating a wholesome, godly lifestyle—influenced an entire nation to pursue righteousness. We, too, have a sphere of influence. As we stand on the side of good, many will be persuaded to follow in our steps.

LILLIAN TRASHER

Founder of Assiout Orphanage in Egypt (1887–1961)

He took the children in his arms,
put his hands on them and blessed them.
MARK 10:16 NIV

As a young girl growing up in Florida, Lillian Trasher wanted to marry and have children. When she became engaged to a young preacher, it seemed her dream would become a reality. Ten days before their wedding, however, Lillian attended a missionary service and received a call to missionary work.

Without a sponsoring mission board, Lillian sailed for Egypt in 1910. One day a dying mother gave Lillian her three-month-old infant. When Lillian brought the baby home, fellow missionaries told her to take the child back. She informed them the mother was dead. Lillian managed to rent a house and began gathering in homeless children. That was the beginning of Assiout Orphanage.

Although Lillian did not marry or have children, fifty years after coming to Egypt, she could look out the orphanage window and see hundreds of "her" children being fed, educated, and taught the Bible. During her lifetime, Assiout Orphanage cared for more than twenty-five thousand Egyptian children.

Children are often the object of neglect and abuse. They need to feel the strong arms of Jesus encircling them. As we pray for children, teach them God's Word, and tenderly care for them, we become His arms of blessing.

BEVERLY LAHAYE

Founder of Concerned Women for America, Author (1929–)

"You will receive power when the Holy Spirit comes on you;
and you will be my witnesses in Jerusalem,
and in all Judea and Samaria,
and to the ends of the earth."
ACTS 1:8 NIV

One day in 1979, Beverly LaHaye listened to a television interview featuring a feminist who promoted anti-God and anti-family views. The speaker claimed to speak for America's women. Beverly knew the woman did not speak for all the nation's women, and certainly not for her. *Who will speak for America's Christian women?* Beverly asked. She decided that she would be their voice.

Beverly organized Concerned Women for America in 1979. The mission of the organization is to promote biblical principles through prayer and education. Members seek to influence society and reverse the decline of moral values in the nation. They promote sexual abstinence and support crisis pregnancy centers. The women also educate people in their communities concerning the harmful effects of drugs, pornography, and a homosexual lifestyle.

The organization has more than five hundred thousand members and includes women in all fifty states and every religious denomination. Their headquarters are in Washington, D.C., where leaders often testify before the U.S. Congress on issues such as the sanctity of human life, education, pornography, and religious freedom.

As a young woman, Beverly had attended a Christian college where she met and married Tim LaHaye, who planned to be a minister. While the couple served a church in California, Beverly heard a teacher speak about the abundant Christian life and being filled with God's Holy Spirit. She asked God to fill her, and her life changed dramatically. Once plagued with low self-esteem, Beverly believed God had equipped her to do a work through the Holy Spirit's power.

Soon she would need that power as she organized women to combat the forces of evil threatening America.

Beverly believes that whatever a woman's calling is, she needs the Holy Spirit's help. She says, "The missing dimension in the feminist movement is the Holy Spirit. . . . I know how this changed my life and what the Holy Spirit will do for others." She explained her experiences in the book *The Spirit-Controlled Woman*. Beverly also coauthored a fiction series with Terri Blackstock, the Seasons series. The books blend Christian values with real-life situations.

Child-rearing challenges, caring for older parents, stretching the budget, and being a single parent are only a few problems women face today. As Beverly LaHaye asked the third person of the Trinity to indwell and help her, so we can also ask the Holy Spirit to fill us so we can positively and powerfully influence those in our communities, schools, and churches to remain true to biblical principles.

MARJORIE SAINT VANDERPUY

Missionary (1923–2004)

Even when I walk through the dark valley of death,
I will not be afraid, for you are close beside me.
PSALM 23:4 NLT

On January 8, 1956, Marjorie Saint sat by the two-way radio waiting for the signal that let her know her husband and four other young missionaries were safe. The contact never came. The five men had been murdered by the Auca Indians in the Amazon jungle while attempting to bring them the Gospel. In spite of the intense sorrow she felt, Marj knew God had a plan.

Marj was a student nurse when she met Nate Saint, who planned to be a missionary pilot. After she and Nate married, they moved to Ecuador—and while her husband delivered supplies to jungle locations, Marj charted his course on the radio.

After Nate's death, Marj and her three young children moved to Quito, Ecuador, where she worked as a nurse in the World Radio Missionary Fellowship hospital. In Quito she also met and married missionary Abe VanDerPuy.

From the ashes of tragedy, Marj rebuilt her life. She counseled others who had experienced losses and reared her children so they loved those who had killed their father.

We never know when tragedy may strike our lives. Yet we need not fear the unknown future—Christ promises to walk close beside us through life's dark valleys.

HENRIETTA MEARS

Christian Educator, Author (1890–1963)

"Go and make disciples of all the nations. . . .
Teach these new disciples to obey all the commands I have given you."
MATTHEW 28:19–20 NLT

When Henrietta Mears was born, the doctor told her mother the child had extremely poor eyesight and would be blind by age thirty. Yet the child went on to become one of the greatest Christian educators of the twentieth century, influencing many young people to become active in Christian ministries.

Henrietta was greatly influenced by her mother, who taught a Bible class and was reported to spend one or two hours a day in prayer. In spite of poor eyesight, Henrietta graduated from the University of Minnesota and took a job teaching high school chemistry. During this time, she also took on the task of teaching a Sunday school class of eighteen-year-old girls who called themselves "the Snobs." Under Henrietta's teaching, the class grew to more than five hundred members.

While spending time in California in 1928, Henrietta had lunch with a pastor who invited her to become the director of education at his church. As the two talked, it became evident to Henrietta that God was opening a new door of service for her.

At that time the Sunday school attendance at Hollywood Presbyterian Church was about four hundred. In two and a half years, that number soared to more than four thousand—and the congregation needed more rooms for classes. This was not a problem for Henrietta, who slated classes to meet in homes and nearby schools. Clearly, Sunday school in America was entering a new and exciting era.

One day, as Henrietta looked over the Sunday school material for the primary department, she noticed it had no pictures and was not closely graded, nor was it Christ-centered. She wrote a few lessons and mimeographed them for the next Sunday. Soon she was writing lessons for other classes. Churches in the area heard of her lessons and wanted copies. Eventually she founded Gospel Light Press, which produced Bible-based, Christ-centered, child-focused, closely graded lessons.

As the Sunday school grew, Henrietta was faced with the dilemma of obtaining trained teachers. She told those she trained, "The key is in one word—*work*. . . . Wishful thinking will never take the place of hard work." No matter how gifted a person claimed to be, Henrietta insisted potential teachers have a relationship with Christ. She further urged the teachers to completely surrender to the Holy Spirit. Henrietta told her workers, "The building of a

Sunday school is a long road, and there are many climbs and turns, but the rewards are worth the effort."

In the 1930s and '40s, Henrietta could be seen riding in the back of a cattle truck taking a load of young people to the beach or mountains as she began camping programs. Her goals for her camps were the salvation and Christian growth of each camper, as well as development of vision for the world. At camp, she addressed subjects such as evolution, miracles, prophecy, and the deity of Christ. In the early days, the camps were held at various sites, but later a resort— Forest Home Christian Conference Center—was purchased.

Perhaps Henrietta's greatest impact worldwide was through the college students she instructed. She told them, "What does God want you to do? Meet Him face-to-face and you will find out." While Henrietta served at the Hollywood church, more than four hundred young men who attended her classes answered the call to serve churches. Others went as missionaries. Bill and Vonette Bright, who founded Campus Crusade for Christ, lived with Henrietta for ten years while they began their ministry. She also counseled evangelist Billy Graham during a difficult time in his ministry.

Henrietta was not an ordained minister, nor did she have a theology degree—but she did have a heart brimming with love for God's Word and the desire to share it with every person. All believers should seriously consider their part in instructing the next generation in the truths that will transform their lives and, in the end, bring them into Christ's glorious eternity.

EVELYN LETOURNEAU

Wife and Mother (1900–1987)

*She extends a helping hand to the poor
and opens her arms to the needy.*
PROVERBS 31:20 NLT

While R.G. LeTourneau moved mountains with the giant earthmoving machines he invented, his wife, Evelyn, moved mountains of loneliness and poverty by the love that flowed from her heart and hands.

As a young couple, Evelyn and R.G. were indifferent to God and faith. But when their son died from influenza in 1918, they gave their lives to Christ and changed their priority from "things" to God.

The LeTourneaus began working in a church, and R.G. built a twenty-four-foot trailer so Evelyn could transport children to Sunday school and summer camps. During World War II, her home became a "home away from home" for servicemen.

When R.G. invited thirty homeless boys to work for him, Evelyn made room for them in her three-story home. Through the fifty-two years of their marriage, she housed and cared for many young men attending LeTourneau College, the school R.G. founded. While under her roof, she encouraged them to go to church and live for God. Because of her practical, hands-on work, Evelyn LeTourneau was chosen American National Mother of the Year in 1969.

When we ask God to use us, He often directs us to help, feed, house, and clothe the needy. Thus we become Christ's extended hands.

ROSA PARKS

Mother of the Civil Rights Movement (1913–2005)

"For the time is coming," says the LORD,
"when I will place a righteous Branch
on King David's throne. . . .
He will do what is just and right throughout the land."
JEREMIAH 23:5 NLT

One courageous act by one courageous woman—that's all it took. But it was enough to begin a movement that created a more just life for thousands of African-Americans living in America's South.

On December 1, 1955, Rosa Parks left her job as a seamstress in Montgomery, Alabama, and boarded a city bus. She dropped into a seat in the back reserved for black people like herself. When a white man came on the bus, there was no place for him, and the driver asked black passengers to give their seat to him. Rosa didn't move and was arrested. She said at that time, "I was tired of giving in to white people." As word of Rosa's courageous stand for justice spread throughout Montgomery, black leaders decided to boycott the bus system.

December 5 was chosen as the day no black person would ride the buses. The effort was successful and led the city's black leaders to work for desegregation of the bus system, allowing them to sit wherever they desired. For over a year, no black person rode the buses. Because they comprised 66 percent of the buses' customers, the company was forced to cease operations.

During this time, Rosa received threatening phone calls. She feared for her life and her family's lives. She and her husband lost their jobs. Yet as news of the Montgomery boycott spread around the world, Rosa received letters of support from as far away as Ghana and France. On November 13, 1956, justice prevailed when the United States Supreme Court declared bus segregation unconstitutional.

Injustice had always been part of Rosa's life. As a child growing up in Alabama, she had noticed black children walked to school while white children rode buses. Rosa's school had been a one-room building without glass in the windows, while the school for white students was a sturdy brick structure. Yet Rosa was happy living on a small farm with her mother and grandparents. Before going into the cotton fields, her grandmother read the Bible. They attended nearby Mount Zion African Methodist Episcopal Church. Her grandfather took her fishing. He also taught her to stand up for her rights. Although she had little to do with white people during her childhood, she did not grow up hating them.

When Rosa completed sixth grade, her mother sent her to live with relatives in Montgomery where she attended Alice White's school for girls. The school, taught by white teachers, instilled in Rosa a sense of dignity and self-respect. Yet outside the school, Rosa saw injustice in action. Black citizens drank from separate public water fountains and were not allowed to eat in restaurants marked with Whites Only signs.

At nineteen, she married Raymond Parks, who worked as a barber while Rosa took a job as a seamstress. She also joined the National Association for the Advancement of Colored People, an organization of black people that sought equality for their race. Rosa was appointed the organization's secretary.

After the bus incident, Rosa continued to get threatening phone calls, and she doubted if she could get work in Montgomery. In 1957, she, with her husband and mother, moved to Detroit, Michigan, where they found work.

In 1996, Rosa was awarded the Presidential Medal of Freedom by President Bill Clinton. She was also honored when Cleveland Avenue in Montgomery was renamed Rosa Parks Boulevard.

As a result of Rosa's brave act, justice for African-Americans has improved. They vote in elections without harassment and are elected to public office. There are no Colored signs on water fountains or Whites Only postings in restaurants in Southern states. And in 2008, Americans elected the first African-American to the presidency.

However, in the hearts of some people, prejudice and hatred for other races still exist. That, too, can change as they allow Christ, the Just One, to live within. And someday when He appears, perfect justice, love, and equality will prevail for all peoples. Even so, come, Lord Jesus!

MARJORIE HOLMES

Author (1910–2002)

Elijah was as human as we are, and yet when he prayed earnestly
that no rain would fall, none fell for the next three and a half years!
Then he prayed for rain, and down it poured.

JAMES 5:17–18 NLT

Marjorie Holmes's purpose for writing *Two from Galilee*, a fictionalized account of the lives of Mary and Joseph, was to make the Holy Family as real to readers as the folks next door. With her thirty books and numerous magazine articles, Marjorie attempted to clear away the mystery surrounding Jesus, the Bible, and spiritual concepts, making God accessible and alive to the average person.

Marjorie was born in Iowa and graduated from Cornell College. In the 1940s, she published her first novel, *World by the Tail*. She also wrote a column, "Love and Laughter," for a Washington, D.C., newspaper, which especially appealed to homemakers.

Marjorie is best known for her trilogy, *Two from Galilee*, *Three from Galilee*, and *The Messiah*—all written in the 1980s. After the death of her husband, she wrote books about grief and healing. She also taught classes on writing and received numerous awards for her works.

With her books, Marjorie Holmes took Bible characters off their pedestals so readers could see them as real people. They overcame daily struggles using the same weapons available to us: prayer, God's Word, and faith in a caring heavenly Father.

KAY ARTHUR

Bible Study Leader and Author (1933–)

"My thoughts are completely different from yours," says the LORD.
"And my ways are far beyond anything you could imagine."

ISAIAH 55:8 NLT

After Kay Arthur became a Christian, her dream was to become a missionary. She achieved this goal in 1965 when she and her husband, Jack, and sons went as missionaries to Mexico. But after three years, Kay developed an infection in the lining of her heart, and the family was forced to return to Tennessee.

Kay grieved, prayed, and wept. "I mourned the fact I had taken a much-needed man off the mission field." Jack had worked with the Pocket Testament

League in Africa and South America. Now the couple was on the shelf.

Back in the United States, Jack became the manager for a Christian radio station, and Kay started a Bible study for teens in her living room. The study group grew, and the Arthurs purchased a chicken farm where the young people studied the Bible in a barn.

Then Kay began a women's Bible study. Seeing their wives' enthusiasm, husbands asked to attend. The studies grew, and it was necessary to train others to lead classes. From this, Kay developed a method of inductive Bible study known as Precept upon Precept.

Churches and groups in the United States began using her studies. Next the lessons were sent to Korea, Mexico, and Romania. Before long, Kay's Bible study method had reached 114 countries and was published in sixty languages.

Kay's early adult life wasn't so glorious. As an attention-starved young woman, she sought love in the wrong places and ended up miserable. A friend told her she needed Jesus, and Kay finally told God, "I don't care what You do to me. . .if You'll just give me peace." Kay said she went down on her knees a harlot and came up a saint. At that moment, God set her apart for Himself.

Kay received an intense hunger for the scriptures. She would prop her Bible up on the car's steering wheel and attempt to read it as she drove to work. She said, "When the Holy Spirit comes inside you, He takes the veil off the Word of God."

Kay Arthur has published thirty-six books in forty-eight languages. More than four million copies of her Bible study courses are in print. A radio broadcast, *Precept with Kay Arthur*, is heard on as many as two hundred stations. She also has a weekly call-in program, *Precept Line with Kay and Jan*.

Kay thought she knew God's purpose for her life, but He had a better idea. As we keep our hearts open to the bigger picture—God's will—His plans may also be a delightful surprise to us.

HELEN BARRETT MONTGOMERY

Author, Church Leader (1861–1934)

*"He is Lord over all lords. . .and his people
are the called and chosen and faithful ones."*
REVELATION 17:14 NLT

Which is more important: faithfulness to God's work or success in the work? Helen Montgomery achieved both. She has been described as "a woman of ten talents who used them all."

In 1924, Helen translated the Greek New Testament into English, the only woman to publish such a work. She was also licensed by her church to preach—and, at age forty-nine, she became the president of the Northern Baptist Convention, another first for a woman.

An ardent supporter of missions, Helen raised large sums of money for mission causes and traveled the world to observe the work of missionaries. For one project, Seven Colleges for Women in Asia, Helen solicited funds from American women and built Christian colleges in Japan, China, and India.

Perhaps the greatest demonstration of Helen's faithfulness was seen in her service to her church in Rochester, New York, where for forty-four years, she taught a women's Bible class that numbered more than two hundred attendees each Sunday.

No doubt Helen Montgomery heard Christ's "Well done" when she entered heaven. As we strive to faithfully do God's work, we will also hear those words when we bow before His glorious presence.

GLADYS AYLWARD

Missionary (1902–70)

In your strength I can crush an army; with my God I can scale any wall.
PSALM 18:29 NLT

Gladys Aylward stood on the platform of the Liverpool Street Station in London, an old fur rug draped over her arm. Beside her was a suitcase filled with crackers and tins of corned beef, baked beans, and fish. Her clothes, bedding, and cooking utensils were wrapped in a blanket.

It was October 18, 1930—and the tiny, twenty-eight-year-old woman was leaving England for China. Rather than take a ship, she chose the cheaper route overland by rail through Europe and Russia.

Two years earlier when Gladys had applied to a mission society for an appointment to China, she was told, "Your qualifications are too slight, your education limited. The Chinese language would be far too difficult for you to learn."

While those words sounded in her ears, another voice said, "Gladys, millions of Chinese have never heard of Jesus Christ."

Convinced that God had called her, Gladys worked as a maid and saved her money for the fare. After traveling by train, boat, and mule, Gladys arrived at the home of Jeannie Lawson, a seventy-four-year-old missionary living in Yangcheng, a city in northern China.

"How shall we live with no money?" Gladys asked the older missionary one day. While Mrs. Lawson received a small amount of support, Gladys had no income. Mrs. Lawson, who had recently purchased an old house, suggested they turn it into an inn. The mule trains would stop there, and after the men were fed, she would tell them Bible stories.

At first Gladys fed the mules while Jeannie Lawson told the stories. In a year's time, Gladys began telling the muleteers about Jesus—and one of the men became her first convert.

A year after Gladys's arrival, Mrs. Lawson died. Gladys managed to keep the inn going, but without the second income, there wasn't enough money to buy food.

One morning, Gladys heard a commotion at the gate of the inn, and the mandarin—the highest-ranking official in the district—entered the courtyard. He had received a letter from the Central Government demanding the custom of binding women's feet to cease. He asked Gladys to find a woman to do the inspections.

In a month's time, Gladys had not found a foot inspector, and when the mandarin returned, he told her to take the job. "If I inspect feet, I will also tell the people about God," she said. Because the mandarin believed a man's gods were his own affair, Gladys was hired. Her salary was one measure of millet a day and a farthing.

With soldiers to protect her from robbers, Gladys went from village to village. During the day, she inspected feet—and in the evening, people gathered as she told them about Jesus. With the salary she received, she was able to stay in Yangcheng and keep the inn operating.

One morning, Gladys was summoned to the men's prison. A riot had broken out, and the governor of the prison asked Gladys to stop the fighting. When she voiced her fears to the governor, he reminded her that she had told everyone, "The living God protects me."

What Gladys saw in the prison courtyard horrified her. Bodies of the dead and wounded lay on the flagstones. A convict, flashing a bloodstained chopper, stopped a few feet from Gladys. When she demanded the weapon, he took two steps closer and meekly held out the ax. Not only was the riot stopped, but Gladys was able to bring reform to the badly managed prison. Soon the prisoners were weaving and tending gardens.

When Japanese planes dropped bombs on Yangcheng in 1938, Gladys guided nearly one hundred children on a twenty-eight-day march over the mountains before the advancing Japanese army. Later she went to Taiwan to work with refugees and orphans.

The woman who was told she could not learn the Chinese language mastered six Chinese dialects. You may have others around you saying you are unqualified for the job God has asked you to do. However, whether you are called to be a more effective parent, begin a new ministry, or share Christ with a neighbor, God is your source. With His help, you can scale any wall.

DOROTHEA DIX

Humanitarian, Teacher, Nurse (1802–87)

Dear children, let us not love with words
or tongue but with actions and in truth.
I JOHN 3:18 NIV

In 1841, Dorothea Dix volunteered to teach a women's Sunday school class at the East Cambridge, Massachusetts, House of Correction. What she saw disturbed her. The women—many mentally ill—were confined in unheated smelly cages, closets, cellars, stalls, and pens. They were chained, naked, beaten with rods, and lashed into obedience. Dorothea brought the abuses to the attention of the state's court—and in time, they were corrected.

In the next four years she visited jails and almshouses in every state east of the Mississippi River and took detailed notes. Everywhere Dorothea traveled, it was the same: prisoners, the mentally ill, and disabled people were treated harshly. She pled before state legislatures, and as a result, she helped establish thirty-two mental hospitals and fifteen schools for the mentally disabled. When she was commended for her efforts, she said, "I am merely acting in obedience to the voice of God."

Dorothea Dix believed every person has value, and she worked to see that those unable to speak for themselves received fair treatment. Certain groups of people in our communities may also be neglected. We can do something. We may call their need to the attention of those who can help. And we can show God's love to them by becoming actively involved in their lives.

MAHALIA JACKSON

Gospel Singer (1911–72)

Commit everything you do to the LORD.
Trust him, and he will help you.
PSALM 37:5 NLT

She was called "Queen of Gospel Music," recording thirty albums during her career—including a dozen that sold over a million copies. Some regard her as the greatest Gospel singer in history. Yet Mahalia Jackson did not have a great beginning.

Besides her mother and preacher father, several aunts and cousins lived with the Jacksons in a three-room house in a poor neighborhood of New

Orleans. Mahalia sang in a children's choir in her church—and even then, she was greatly influenced by the popular jazz music of the city. When her mother died, five-year-old Mahalia and her brother went to live with their Aunt Duke, who did not allow secular music to be played in her home. There Mahalia made a commitment to sing only Gospel music.

At age sixteen, Mahalia moved to Chicago where she worked as a laundress for a dollar a day. She became involved in a church choir and was soon singing in storefront churches and tent revivals. In 1948, Mahalia recorded "Move On Up a Little Higher." The record sold a million copies, and Mahalia rocketed to fame. She toured the United States and Europe, singing in concert halls. Her rendition of "Silent Night" became one of the bestselling singles in the history of Norway.

Mahalia had her critics, however. More formal congregations disapproved of her exuberant singing, a combination of Gospel and jazz. The remarks didn't change her clapping, swaying, shouting performances. She said, "I want my hands, my feet, my whole body to praise God." Jazz recording companies tried to lure her with lucrative contracts, and family members urged her to try other types of music, but she refused. Neither would she sing the popular blues music of the time. She said, "Gospel songs are songs of hope. When you sing them, you are delivered from your burden."

Mahalia became the first Gospel singer to perform in Carnegie Hall. In 1961, she sang at President John F. Kennedy's inauguration. Before Dr. Martin Luther King gave his "I Have a Dream" speech, Mahalia sang a Negro spiritual. At his funeral five years later, she sang her signature song, "Precious Lord, Take My Hand."

Early in her career, Mahalia Jackson made a commitment to sing only Gospel music. She never compromised this vow to her "precious Lord," and God honored her with success. The Lord takes our commitments to Him seriously. When we make and keep promises that honor God, He will also crown our efforts with success.

MARY BUNYAN

Wife and Mother (1625–56?)

*"You are the light of the world—like a city on a mountain,
glowing in the night for all to see."*
MATTHEW 5:14 NLT

Mary could not read or write. A poor woman, she did not have a dowry when she married John Bunyan, the rowdy, blaspheming tinker (maker and mender of utensils). But she was a godly woman, and she brought two books to their marriage: *The Practice of Piety* and *The Plain Man's Pathway to Heaven*. As John read them to her, he became interested in his wife's faith.

Mary attended church and continued to live by biblical principles in her home, which eventually led to her husband's conversion. However, Mary's life did not become easier with John's change of heart. Now he began to preach— and because this was illegal for those not ordained by the Church of England, John was often in jail. There he wrote *Pilgrim's Progress*, a book destined to become a classic Christian work.

Mary managed the household and cared for the couple's four children, including a blind child, while John spent most of twelve years in prison.

Mary Bunyan's life is an example of faith in action. How can we more effectively influence others for God? The same way Mary did. Our godly lives will serve as a light, pointing them to Jesus, the Light of the world.

SUSANNA WESLEY

Teacher, Author, Mother (1669–1742)

*Teach your children to choose the right path,
and when they are older, they will remain upon it.*
PROVERBS 22:6 NLT

Susanna Wesley was beset by many problems while raising her family. Nine of her nineteen children died soon after birth. One infant was accidently smothered by a servant. Her oldest son didn't talk as a child. After Susanna "prayed day and night," at age five he said his first words. When troubles increased, this mother spent more time in prayer.

Described as a beautiful young lady, Susanna Annesley was the twenty-fifth child born into a pastor's family in England. Susanna's home was filled with good books, and she learned to read Hebrew, Greek, and Latin. She could also discuss theology with any preacher.

At thirteen, Susanna met Samuel Wesley, who became a minister in the Church of England. They married when she was nineteen.

The couple's first pastorate was a rural church in South Ormsby, where the manse was a one-room mud hut with a loft. Lack of money was always a problem for the Wesleys. Once, when Samuel was put in prison because he could not pay his debts, Susanna sent him her wedding ring so he'd have something to barter for food. After eight years in South Ormsby, Samuel accepted a church in Epsworth, where an increase in salary helped meet the needs of the growing family.

Susanna was the primary source of her children's education and taught them Latin, Greek, French, logic, the Bible, and Christian conduct. Classes were held six hours daily, six days a week. She wrote three textbooks: commentaries on the Apostles' Creed, the Lord's Prayer, and the Ten Commandments. Susanna said the purpose of her children's education was the saving of their souls.

A devoted mother, Susanna spent time alone with each child during the week. Monday was given to John, Tuesday to Hetty, and so on until each child had one-on-one time with his or her mother. The large household also had strict rules of discipline. The children were taught to cry softly and to eat whatever was set before them. No child got his or her way by whining.

Susanna gave two hours each day to private devotions. With the children's education, household duties, and tending to the cows, pigs, and hens, how did she find time for personal meditation? She would throw a large apron over her head, and in the midst of the noisy household, she prayed.

Trouble was never far from Susanna. On two occasions, the Wesleys' home burned to the ground. During one fire, a six-year-old son narrowly escaped death when he was rescued through an upstairs window. After the incident, Susanna gave special attention to this child so divinely protected. John Wesley went on to become the founder of the Methodist Church.

Susanna and Samuel had strong opinions—and when they disagreed about a particular political matter, Samuel left his wife and family for one year, vowing never to return until Susanna changed her views.

During her husband's absence, Susanna began a Sunday afternoon religious service in her home for the family. The small congregation sang a psalm, prayed, and listened while Susanna read a sermon. Soon neighbors asked to join the group. Eventually, more than two hundred people gathered while Susanna shared the Gospel with them. When England's political situation changed, Samuel returned home.

After her husband's death, Susanna lived with various children. She stood in fields and listened to her sons John and Charles preach to thousands of England's poor. She sang the songs Charles wrote to instruct converts in worship. As she lay dying, she told her children, "As soon as I am released, sing a psalm of praise to God."

Initially, Susanna's godly influence was confined to her family. Soon her faith impacted her neighbors. However, because of her well-taught children, the whole world eventually felt God's love through Susanna Wesley, a preacher of righteousness.

Most mothers can't hope to accomplish all Susanna did. Yet as we teach our children by word and example, the Bible promises they will remain on the right path and, by their righteous lives, positively influence others.

LETTIE COWMAN

Author, Missionary, Evangelist (1870–1960)

"There's a young boy here with five barley loaves and two fish.
But what good is that with this huge crowd?"
JOHN 6:9 NLT

When Charles Cowman became seriously ill, his wife, Lettie, gathered short inspirational writings to read to him. From that small beginning, her collection of poems and prose became the book *Streams in the Desert*. Lettie's book has been published in more than one hundred English printings and is translated into fifteen languages. Chinese leader Chiang Kai-shek requested her book be buried with him.

Lettie and Charles Cowman went as missionaries to Japan in 1900 and founded the Oriental Missionary Society. Their goal was to place a scripture portion in every home in the empire. When Charles died, Lettie became president of the society. She befriended national leaders, preached around the world, and wrote Christian books. Today the mission society she and her husband founded is one of the major missions.

Small things! A boy gave his lunch to Jesus. We share a few dollars with a missionary or a homeless person. We discount little kindnesses, thinking they don't matter. Though Lettie Cowman had no thought of sharing her writings with the world, God had other plans, and her books have blessed generations. Our kind deeds, too, have that potential.

FLANNERY O'CONNOR

Author (1925–64)

Where sin abounded, grace did much more abound. . . .
Even so might grace reign through righteousness
unto eternal life by Jesus Christ our Lord.
ROMANS 5:20–21 KJV

The *New York Times* said of Flannery O'Connor, "Her talent for fiction is so great as to be overwhelming." Flannery received a passion for writing while attending Georgia State College for Women where she was part of the yearbook staff and editor of a literary magazine. After graduation, she attended the famous writers' school at the University of Iowa, where she began her first novel, Wise Blood, which was published in 1952.

Often violent, Flannery's novels showed flawed, ignorant, religious characters transformed by pain and conflict. As a Catholic living in the Protestant South, her stories deal with racial issues, poverty, religion, and the Holocaust. She said, "My subject in fiction is the action of grace in territory held largely by the devil." Through foreshadowing and the use of suspense, Flannery's books keep the reader turning pages.

A student of the Bible, Flannery wrote slowly and prayerfully, listening to the inner voice. She believed that her talent was God-given and that she was responsible to develop and use it to honor God. She painstakingly edited and rewrote her works until a perfect story with believable characters emerged. Through fiction, she showed readers the struggles of life and ultimate triumph of those who trust God.

In many ways, Flannery's stories are a reflection of her life. She was devastated when her father died from lupus when she was fifteen. At age twenty-six, she was diagnosed with the same disease. Upon receiving the news, she moved back to her ancestral farm in Georgia, where she wrote and also raised various kinds of fowl. Fascinated by birds, Flannery incorporated them into her stories. Though often weak during the course of the disease, she was able to write two to three hours a day and completed two novels and thirty-two short stories. Flannery also wrote numerous letters that give insight into her deep Christian beliefs. At the onset of lupus, she was told she had five years to live—yet she lived several years beyond that prediction.

Flannery died at age thirty-nine. While her writings received little recognition during her lifetime, she is now considered one of the most important American writers of the twentieth century.

Flannery wrote in a letter, "Grace changes us and change is painful." Through trouble and conflict we often feel the "grace of God" working in our lives. We can thank God for these difficulties. They are evidence of His powerful efforts to transform us to be like Christ and, at life's end, take us to be forever in His presence.

JOSEPHINE BUTLER

Crusader for Women (1828–1906)

"For I, the LORD, love justice.
I hate robbery and wrongdoing."
ISAIAH 61:8 NLT

Injustice in any form made Josephine Butler's blood boil! Even as a child, she wanted everyone treated fairly. After the tragic death of her six-year-old daughter, Josephine began a campaign against an injustice prevalent in the world: prostitution.

Josephine longed to "rescue fallen women for Jesus," but her friends were shocked when she took the unfortunate women into her home. Later she founded House of Rest, a home for girls in danger of falling into prostitution.

Her greatest fight was against the Contagious Disease Act, an effort to legalize prostitution in cities occupied by military troops. While people of the time often called prostitutes "the sewers of society," Josephine knew women entered this lifestyle because of poverty, force, or lack of education.

Josephine's crusade spread to Europe, and she helped establish the first international movement to aid prostitutes. She dared speak against an evil and addressed large audiences at a time when prostitution was considered a shameful topic to discuss and women were expected to remain silent on public issues.

Because many people find it convenient to ignore evil, it will never be easy to confront injustice. Yet the downtrodden often lack a voice. Perhaps you and I can speak for them in our communities.

SOJOURNER TRUTH

Evangelist, Abolitionist (1797?–1883)

"Love one another. As I have loved you,
so you must love one another.
By this all men will know that you are my disciples,
if you love one another."
JOHN 13:34–35 NIV

Mau Mau Bett, a slave mother, couldn't give her thirteen children much—but she loved Jesus and passed His love on to them.

Often her child Isabella would slip away to an alcove of willows to pray. She would soon need the strength of those prayers when, at about age nine, she was sold for one hundred dollars and a flock of sheep. In the new place, Isabella was whipped regularly—and for the remainder of her life bore the scars.

When the treatment became unbearable, she prayed for deliverance. Her owner eventually died, and she was sold to a tavern owner. When this man fell on hard times, Isabella was again sold. Her treatment at the hands of John Dumont and his wife was harsh and, besides daily humiliations, may have included sexual abuse.

As a young woman, Isabella fell in love with Robert, a slave on a neighboring farm. Dumont forbade the relationship, and after Robert visited Isabella one night, his owner beat him savagely in the face and sent him away. From this relationship, Isabella had a daughter. In 1817, she was forced to marry an older slave named Thomas, and the couple had four children. Isabella became heartbroken when her owner illegally sold Peter, her five-year-old son.

John Dumont had promised to free Isabella—but when the time came, he refused. Bitter, filled with raging hatred, Isabella decided to escape with her infant. As she fled, she prayed and eventually stumbled onto the home of Isaac and Marie Van Wagenen. When Dumont demanded the return of his slave, the Van Wagenens paid him twenty dollars for her services for a year. The couple insisted Isabella call them by their first names rather than master and mistress—and for the first time, she received kind treatment from white people.

While living with the Van Wagenens, Isabella attended the Methodist Episcopal Church and experienced a life-changing conversion. During this time, she also appealed to the Quakers, who helped her seek the return of Peter. After months of legal proceedings, a scarred and battered son returned to his mother. In 1827, New York emancipated all slaves, and Isabella, now free, took a job as a servant.

In 1843, she received a call from God to preach the Gospel. Isabella changed her name to Sojourner Truth and began traveling throughout New England on foot, preaching in camp meetings and churches. A tall woman with a deep voice, she included in her preaching stories from her slave days—and in spite of the harsh treatment she'd received most of her life, she spoke of "God's mystical love." As she preached, she would often break into song, singing of her freedom in Jesus.

During her travels, Sojourner met prominent abolitionist Frederick Douglass, who asked her to appear with him in abolition rallies. Although Sojourner couldn't read or write, she began dictating her memoirs. In 1850, her story, *The Narrative of Sojourner Truth*, was published. The book provided her with an income and opened the door for Sojourner to preach, recount stories of her slave days, and sell her books.

During the Civil War, Sojourner gathered supplies for black soldiers. One day, while working with refugees in Washington, D.C., she visited President Lincoln and had her picture taken with him. He showed her a Bible he had received from the black people in Baltimore, and she had him sign her autograph book. He wrote, "For Aunty Sojourner Truth. October 29, 1864. A. Lincoln." After the war, Sojourner helped ex-slaves find jobs, and she worked for temperance causes and women's rights.

Most of her life, Sojourner received cruel treatment, which resulted in a fiercely bitter woman. That changed when she was touched by God. From then on, His love flowed through her, even to those who had treated her harshly. If we find it difficult to forgive people for past wrongs, we, like Sojourner Truth, can go to Calvary. Jesus has plenty of love to share with us—at His cross.

SARAH ADAMS

Hymn Writer (1805–48)

Come near to God and he will come near to you.
JAMES 4:8 NIV

Was it a spiritual experience that prompted Sarah Adams to write the powerful hymn "Nearer, My God, to Thee," or did a scripture one day suddenly jump off the page and speak to her? No one knows for sure—but looking into her life, we find clues to her inspiration.

Young Sarah believed God's truth could effectively be conveyed on the stage, and she aspired to be an actress. Ill health prevented her from reaching this goal, and she turned to writing to express her faith. Yet sickness and discouragements were never far away. The English poet Robert Browning was greatly used to encourage her, and it is believed she received the inspiration for her famous hymn through his influence.

The hymn has blessed many, including England's Queen Victoria and King Edward VII. When United States president William McKinley lay dying from an assassin's bullet, he quoted Sarah's hymn and told the doctor, "This has been my constant prayer."

You can draw near to God. Say the name of Jesus. Whisper a prayer or quote a verse of Sarah Adams's hymn:

Nearer, my God, to Thee,
Nearer to Thee,
E'en though it be a cross
That raiseth me!
Still all my song shall be:
Nearer, my God, to Thee;
Nearer, my God, to Thee,
Nearer to Thee.

BETTY STAM

Missionary Martyr (1906–34)

You will keep in perfect peace all who trust in you,
whose thoughts are fixed on you!
Isaiah 26:3 NLT

When missionary John Stam inquired whether it was safe to take his wife and child into Tsingteh, a Chinese village, he was assured Communist activity was not a threat. Yet while Betty and John passed out tracts and held meetings in the small city, rumors of nearby rebel activity persisted. On December 6, 1934, a frightening message reached them: Enemy soldiers were approaching. When the Stams realized it was too late to flee, they calmly knelt in prayer and committed their lives to God.

Betty Scott met John Stam at Moody Bible Institute. Her parents were missionaries to China, and Betty also felt called to missions. She and John fell in love—but because the call was their priority, marriage was not in the near future. Betty went to China, and John followed in a year. They met in Shanghai and were married. A year later, their child, Helen Priscilla, was born.

That day in December, Communist soldiers burst into the Stams' home, bound John, and took him away. Later they came for Betty and the baby. While John and Betty's fate was sealed, the soldiers questioned what they should do with the baby. When a soldier suggested killing her, a bystander offered to die in her place. Soon the man was dead.

While held hostage in an abandoned mansion during the night, Betty managed to feed her daughter and wrap her securely. The next morning, the couple was ordered to leave the baby. They were stripped of outer clothing and marched through the village to the taunts of onlookers. At a spot outside town, while a crowd looked on, an acquaintance of the Stams pled for their lives. The man admitted he was a Christian and was swiftly killed. When the sword struck John, Betty fell over his body. Then it was her turn.

Upon hearing of John and Betty's deaths, Mr. Lo, an evangelist, was told the location of their child. Although she'd gone two days without food, little Helen Priscilla was well. Mr. Lo quickly transported the baby to missionaries a hundred miles from Tsingteh. Then he faced the grim task of burying the bodies of Betty and John Stam.

How did Betty Stam maintain peace of mind when she, her husband, and their child were almost certain to perish? No doubt, she fixed her mind on God. Could we be as courageous under the same circumstances? God's strength does not come before it is needed. At the exact moment, we, too, will have strength to face severe adversity should that be our fate.

ELIZABETH FRY

Prison Reformer (1780–1845)

"Whatever you did for one of the least of these brothers of mine, you did for me."
MATTHEW 25:40 NIV

When Elizabeth Gurney was eighteen years old, a Quaker friend told her, "You are born to be a light to the blind, speech to the dumb, and feet to the lame." This prediction saw fulfillment one day in 1817 when Elizabeth visited the women in London's Newgate prison. Three hundred women and their children were crowded into four small rooms. They slept on straw. The smells were unbearable, the language foul. The women and children existed on a pitifully small amount of food.

That day Elizabeth, in her plain Quaker dress, opened her Bible and read to the women. On her next visit, she was accompanied by her Quaker friends who brought clothes and supplies to teach the women to sew.

At that time, selected women criminals were transported to a penal colony in Australia. Elizabeth and her friends visited the ships before they sailed and gave the women cloth and thread so they could make items to sell once they reached their destination.

Other countries heard of Elizabeth's reform efforts and sought her advice to assess their prison systems.

Christ commands His followers to help the outcasts. Unbelievable as it seems, when we visit, clothe, and feed them, we actually do the kind deeds to Jesus.

MADAME JEANNE-MARIE GUYON

French Mystic, Author, Hymn Writer (1648–1717)

You should be known for the beauty that comes from within,
the unfading beauty of a gentle and quiet spirit,
which is so precious to God.

1 PETER 3:4 NLT

At age ten, Jeanne-Marie Bouvier de la Motte's aristocratic, well-to-do French family placed her in a convent, where she spent time studying the Bible and memorizing scripture verses. During this time, she also vowed to do the will of God in everything. She wanted to become a nun. But when Jeanne was sixteen, her mother arranged for Jeanne's marriage to a wealthy, older, handicapped man, and she became Madame Guyon. Because of a cruel, domineering mother-in-law, it was not a happy situation—yet Jeanne learned to submit to keep the peace. In the early years of marriage, she contracted smallpox, which left her face permanently scarred.

After twelve years of marriage, Madame Guyon, at age twenty-eight, was left a widow with three small children. Concerned for her spiritual welfare, she counseled with a Franciscan priest who advised her to "do what our Lord has made you know He desired of you." Her heart was changed, and she turned her back on Paris's social life, refused offers of marriage, and spent her time studying devotional books and caring for her children.

At age thirty-four, she began what she called "an apostolic life." In the next eight years, Madame Guyon traveled through villages in France and Switzerland teaching rich and poor alike how to pray and encouraging them to live holy lives. Often, her life was in danger as she traveled, and on one occasion, her carriage was stopped by robbers. When the men opened the carriage door, they fled when they saw a woman in black smiling at them.

Madame Guyon found a great spiritual hunger for her teaching of Quietism, which renounced creeds and works, emphasizing passive contemplation, meekness, and contentment in all circumstances. She gave out food, took the sick and dying into her home, and eventually founded two hospitals.

Madame Guyon's activities soon caught the attention of the church. The authorities—jealous of her popularity—said she was out of order to pray and preach. Didn't she know only priests were to pray, not women?

During this time, monasteries were off-limits for women—yet Madame Guyon gained entrance and proclaimed her faith to the monks. She also preached in nunneries. A nun, contemplating suicide because she felt she couldn't be reconciled to God, consulted with Madame Guyon, who assured her she could rely on Christ's righteousness. Healing miracles often accompanied Madame

Guyon's ministry, and she claimed to have visions. While she remained faithful to the Catholic Church, officials continued condemning her actions and placed her in a prison cell in the Bastille—an imprisonment that continued for seven years. The last two years were spent in solitary confinement. Yet she didn't complain and spent her time singing, praying, and writing. She believed Christians should pray at all times, and she wrote *The Method of Prayer*, based on 1 Thessalonians 5:17, "Pray without ceasing" (KJV). Most of her writing was done at night, and she claimed God wrote the books through her. From a cell, she eventually wrote forty books. The church condemned these books and publicly burned some copies.

While in prison, Madame Guyon also wrote hundreds of hymns. Her best-known hymn, "O Lord, How Full of Sweet Content," written in 1681, was translated into English by William Cowper. She said of her time in prison, "There is nothing for me to do but adore Thee and carry my cross." Because she had learned to quiet her inner self, she calmly bore her imprisonment.

Later John Wesley studied Madame Guyon's twenty-volume commentary on the Bible and said she was an example of true holiness. Adoniram Judson, missionary to Burma, also read her books and imitated her meek acceptance during his two years in prison.

Though her face was scarred by smallpox and lined from multiple trials, Jeanne Guyon exuded an inner beauty. As we spend time in Christ's presence, as we absorb the truths of His Word and pray for a calm spirit, we, too, will show forth the glory of a Christlike countenance and life.

IDA SCUDDER

Medical Missionary (1870–1960)

*The Holy Spirit said,
"Dedicate Barnabas and Saul
for the special work I have for them."*
ACTS 13:2 NLT

Young Ida Scudder had no intention of becoming a missionary to India as three generations of Scudders had done. She'd rather do "something exciting." But while helping her mother in India, a Brahmin man came to Ida asking help for his fourteen-year-old wife, who was having a difficult labor. Ida explained she had no training, but her father, a doctor, would help. The man shook his head. His religion prohibited a man from attending a woman. That evening, two more men came to the mission with the same request. Each time, Ida sadly refused. In the morning the tom-toms tolled the deaths of the three women. As

Ida searched her soul, she realized God wanted her to put aside her plans and follow His will.

Ida went to America and enrolled in medical school. She returned to India in 1900 and founded a hospital and sponsored roadside clinics, branch hospitals, training courses for girls, and a medical school.

What is God's highest design for our lives? As we pray and see world needs, we, too, will "hear" His voice telling us to put aside our petty plans for His better plan—one that will benefit many and give us a more purposeful life.

RUTH STAFFORD PEALE

Author, Wife (1906–2008)

The LORD God said, "It is not good for the man to be alone.
I will make a companion who will help him."
GENESIS 2:18 NLT

When Ruth Stafford was a senior at Syracuse University, friends told her about a young minister whom they said was "the most eligible bachelor." Ruth met Norman Vincent Peale at a party, and when they were introduced, it seemed he held her hand longer than necessary. After college, Ruth took a job teaching mathematics in high school and began dating the minister. Two years later, they married.

The Great Depression was heavy upon the nation, and the pews were mostly empty when the young couple moved to New York City to pastor the Marble Collegiate Church. In an effort to increase their congregation, Ruth suggested that Norman become more visible in the community. When he accepted speaking engagements at area clubs and organizations, the church gradually filled.

While Norman was a great preacher, he was not a good organizer, nor did he enjoy business meetings. Early in their marriage, Ruth determined to be interested in what concerned her husband. She attended committee meetings and reported back to Norman, freeing him to write, counsel, and prepare sermons.

Once, when Norman voiced discouragement because of problems in the church, Ruth startled him by telling him he needed to become converted. He assured her he was converted. Yet his wife's remark led Norman to rethink his level of trust in God. After earnest prayer, he plunged into his work convinced that, with God's help, nothing was impossible.

When Norman submitted his book *The Power of Positive Thinking* to publishers, it was rejected numerous times. Finally, in disgust, he threw it aside. Ruth retrieved the manuscript and submitted it again. The book appeared in print in 1952 and sold twenty million copies.

Then trouble began. Prominent ministers said Norman's book did not express Christian values. When the scathing remarks became known to Norman, he was deeply hurt. Ruth advised her husband to counter with Christ's love. With her encouragement, Norman "outloved" his critics. Ruth shared her experiences in her books *The Secrets of Staying in Love* and *The Adventure of Being a Wife*.

In 1944, a group of people gathered around Ruth's kitchen table and planned a new magazine. The publication would relate true stories of how faith helped people in everyday life. With Ruth as executive vice president, *Guideposts* hit the newsstands in 1948. The magazine eventually became the most widely read religious inspirational magazine in the world.

When a wife actively supports her husband, she is also realizing her God-appointed destiny—to be a helper to the man she loves.

MARY LYON

Christian Educator (1797–1849)

Fear of the LORD is the beginning of wisdom.
Knowledge of the Holy One results in understanding.
PROVERBS 9:10 NLT

In 1834, Mary Lyon began an arduous journey: she would go to New England villagers and farmers and solicit funds to begin a women's college. Whoever heard of women attending college? many asked. Most people of the time thought women needed only basic reading, writing, and arithmetic skills, if even that.

In spite of poor health, for three years Mary persisted—and Mount Holyoke Female Seminary opened its doors in 1837. Mary's initial order of business for the eighty young women in the first class was to challenge them to become Christians. Besides a rigorous curriculum in languages, science, and literature, the students were instructed in the benefits of a balanced diet and exercise. Mary's educational purposes were clear: the women were to be educated so they could evangelize the world.

Her efforts were effective. By the time of her death, seventy graduates had gone to foreign mission fields, and many more were missionaries to the American Indians.

Mary Lyon recognized that true knowledge begins with recognizing God and knowing Christ as our Savior. From that point on, all knowledge we acquire is filtered through God's powerful book of wisdom—the Bible.

MARY SMITH MOFFAT

Missionary (1795–1870)

What is faith? It is the confident assurance that
what we hope for is going to happen.
It is the evidence of things we cannot yet see.
HEBREWS 11:1 NLT

As apprehensive parents waved good-bye, an excited young woman, Mary Smith, boarded a ship in London bound for South Africa. *Will we ever see our daughter alive again?* the Smiths wondered. Probably not. Most white people didn't live long on the Dark Continent. Their daughter did not entertain such dismal thoughts. Mary only knew that after a three-month voyage to Cape Town, she would be with her beloved Robert.

The couple had met in Scotland when Robert Moffat worked as a gardener for Mary's father. Both were dedicated Christians. Both felt called to mission work. When he proposed marriage, Mary's parents said no. In 1816, Robert sailed for Africa alone. Later Mary's parents changed their minds—and in 1819, she followed Robert.

The romance of missions quickly faded as Mary and Robert set out by oxcart on a six-hundred-mile journey inland. After crossing raging rivers and evading giant anthills, Mary found herself living on the edge of a parched desert in Kuruman with a totally degraded people. When she went to church, she carried her pots and pans with her lest the natives steal them. The garden Robert so proudly cultivated was also subject to thievery. Yet she wrote, "When I sit in the house of God surrounded by the natives. . .I feel that an honor has been conferred upon me which the kings of the earth could never have done for me."

In Kuruman, Mary washed clothes in a river and made soap from sheep fat. She ground wheat for the bread she baked in an outdoor oven. As she worked to transform their one-room mud hut into a home, she cleaned her floor with cow dung to kill the fleas. Mary gave birth to ten children and raised them in the most primitive conditions. She also taught native children about Jesus.

Perhaps the most painful problem the Moffats faced in the early days of the mission was the lack of converts. After working for ten years without one conversion, the mission society considered abandoning the work. Again Mary's faith was evident as she wrote a friend: "Send us a communion service; we shall want it someday." When Robert, busy with translation work, became discouraged, she reminded him, "We walk by faith, not by sight." Always confident, she said, "We may not live to see it, but the awakening will come as sure as the sun will rise tomorrow."

The awakening came in 1828. Heathen songs and dances stopped. Long before the meetings began on Sunday, the church crowded with singing Christians.

Prayers were heard, and the conduct of the natives improved.

As the church grew, so did Mary's family. Besides raising ten children of her own, Mary took in three native children who, according to custom, would have been buried alive with their dead mother.

Yet death and tragedy were never far from Mary. After twenty years without a furlough, the Moffats embarked for Scotland. On board ship, her six-year-old died and was buried at sea. During the Moffats' time on the British Isles, Mary rarely saw her husband as he traveled, promoting mission causes. She gave birth to another child while on furlough.

While Robert was in London, a young man, David Livingstone, heard him preach and felt called to Africa. Livingstone later married the Moffats' oldest daughter, Mary. At age forty, Mary Livingstone died. One of the Moffats' sons, Robert, also died young, as did a missionary daughter, Elizabeth. Four of the surviving Moffat children became missionaries.

After fifty years in South Africa, the Moffats, weak and sickly, retired to England where Mary died four years later.

Mary Moffat believed in the sun when the sky was the blackest. She learned to smile while her heart brimmed with sorrow. She lived contently in the most uncomfortable situations. By her faith, she overcame the obstacles. Mary's brand of faith is available to anyone willing to endure the rigors that allow this quality of faith to grow.

HELENA OF CONSTANTINOPLE

Mother of the First Christian Emperor (250?–330?)

I have been reminded of your sincere faith,
which first lived in your grandmother Lois
and in your mother Eunice and,
I am persuaded, now lives in you also.
2 TIMOTHY 1:5 NIV

The first three centuries were a time of intense persecution for Christians as they faced the terrors of the pagan Roman Empire. But all that changed in 312 when Emperor Constantine became a Christian. Credit for his conversion goes largely to Helena, his mother.

As a young woman, Helena converted to Christianity. She married Constantius Chlorus, who later divorced her for political reasons. After Helena's son became emperor, he restored her to court where she attempted to persuade him of the truths of Christianity.

Although not a Christian, when Constantine prayed before a critical battle, he saw a cross in the sky. Above it were the words, "By this thou shalt conquer." When the battle ended in victory for Constantine, he became a Christian and declared religious freedom for the followers of Christ.

Helena influenced her son for Christ and helped change history. We, too, have a sphere of influence. As we live our lives by Christian principles and speak of the change Jesus has brought to us, we will also affect people for Christ and His cross.

CASSIE BERNALL

Student (1981–99)

Everyone born of God overcomes the world.
This is the victory that has overcome the world, even our faith.
I JOHN 5:4 NIV

After her death, musicians wrote songs about her; yet on the day seventeen-year-old Cassie Bernall died, she was only thinking about studying *Macbeth* for an English class. When two gunmen walked into the library, she said, "Dear God, what is happening? I just want to go home." A gunman slammed his hand on the table and yelled, "Peekaboo!" Although reports vary, witnesses say the gunmen asked several students if they believed in God. Cassie was one of the students killed in the massacre.

A casual reader of the Columbine High School massacre may not realize that Cassie was headed on the same road as her killers—but for a series of choices she had made earlier.

In her teens, Cassie turned from being a happy child into a sulking stranger. Her parents thought this was normal teenage behavior until one day her mother found letters Cassie had written to friends. The letters spoke of killing her parents and drinking blood. Sketches of vampire teeth and axes decorated the pages.

When Cassie's mother confronted her daughter, Cassie went into a screaming rage and vowed to kill herself. Her parents, Misty and Bert, broke off their daughter's friendships with occult-practicing friends. The only activity they allowed Cassie outside school was attending a church youth group.

Every effort the parents made to control Cassie met with resistance. When she erupted in fits of anger, her mother or father would sit with their hand on her knee, praying aloud, telling her they loved her.

The Bernalls enrolled their two children in a private school. To escape Cassie's friends, the family moved to a new neighborhood.

One weekend, the Bernalls allowed Cassie to attend a church youth retreat. The theme for the retreat was overcoming temptations. As Cassie watched young people lay drug paraphernalia and occult materials at an altar, the walls surrounding her began to fall. When she arrived home, she told her mother, "I've totally changed."

Dressed in baggy jeans and wearing ball-and-chain necklaces, an insecure Cassie became part of a youth group. In her junior year, she transferred to Columbine High School. Friends remember seeing her reading her Bible in class. Instead of talking about vampires and death rock, she became interested in photography.

On April 21, Cassie said good-bye to her mother and went to school. She didn't return home. Two years earlier, Cassie had made the choice to overcome evil. That choice ended with her victorious home-going.

When we choose to place our faith in Christ, we, too, are promised an overcoming life—and death.

ELIZABETH HOOTEN

First Female Preacher (1598–1672)

Don't be surprised at the fiery trials you are going through. . . .
Instead, be very glad—because these trials
will make you partners with Christ.
1 PETER 4:12–13 NLT

George Fox, founder of the Quakers, believed women should share equally in ministry with men. His first convert, fifty-year-old Elizabeth Hooten, felt called to preach and traveled across England boldly urging people to repent.

When Elizabeth's cattle were stolen, she appealed to King Charles II. Believing all people were equal, she refused to bow to the king—a serious crime. Rather, she used the opportunity to preach repentance to him. The king promised Elizabeth she could settle anywhere in the American colonies, but when Elizabeth arrived in New England, authorities scorned the king's letter. She received whippings in three Massachusetts towns. At one location they led her into the wilderness in the middle of winter and left her there. Elizabeth found her way back to civilization and sailed for England.

Beatings, time in prison, and abandonment in dense forest did not discourage Elizabeth. Her courage remained unshakable, and her message of repentance was given with zeal.

We can stay in our comfort zones and not voice our convictions. Yet there are times when we, like Elizabeth Hooten, need to honestly tell people the truth about God and their eternal destiny. Be prepared: your actions may bring you persecution.

CATHERINE MARSHALL

Author (1914–83)

Surely your goodness and unfailing love
will pursue me all the days of my life,
and I will live in the house of the LORD forever.
PSALM 23:6 NLT

Through life's varied experiences, Catherine Marshall learned that God makes the difference in every situation. With Him, the word *impossible* flees. Defeat turns to victory, and what looks like a dark future becomes bright—with God.

Catherine Wood was raised in a pastor's home in the South during the Depression. There was never enough money for the needs of the family of five—but because there was plenty of love, Catherine did not know her family was poor. As a teen, Catherine had three passions: She dreamed of becoming an author; she wanted to attend Agnes Scott College in Decatur, Georgia; and she aspired to marry a "wonderful man." But how could she go to college when her family couldn't even afford a car? Mother and daughter knelt and asked God's help. A few months later, Catherine's mother received a letter from the federal government asking her to write a history of the county. Catherine felt God's goodness and mercy as her mother's project covered college expenses.

At Agnes Scott College, Catherine developed her love for writing. During her freshman year, she heard about Peter Marshall, the handsome bachelor preacher with the delightful Scottish accent. On Sundays, she often took the long streetcar ride to the Westminster Presbyterian Church in Atlanta to hear him. Catherine was smitten by the silver-tongued preacher, but so were other girls. Rationalizing her attraction was only a schoolgirl's crush, she tried to stay away from the church but was always drawn back.

Was it her imagination that the young pastor's eyes seemed to seek her out during his sermon? Soon he asked to drive her back to college—and in her senior year, he proposed. With marriage and the arrival of a son, Peter John, Catherine realized more of God's goodness and mercy.

When Peter John was three, Catherine was diagnosed with tuberculosis and ordered to stay in bed. She asked God to heal her, but her health did not improve. As she studied her Bible one night, Christ's presence filled her bedroom and He assured her, "There is nothing wrong with you that I can't take care of." After three years, her health improved.

But a greater challenge followed when her husband, Peter, died of a heart attack at age forty-six. As Catherine pondered how a thirty-four-year-old widow with a nine-year-old son could make a living, a verse from Psalm 23 came to mind. *Goodness and mercy from Peter's death?* she wondered. When a publishing house asked her to compile a book of Peter's sermons, *Mr. Jones, Meet the Master* soon appeared in bookstores. Then Catherine wrote *A Man Called Peter*, the story of her husband's life. The book remained on the *New York Times* bestseller list for more than fifty consecutive weeks.

As a young woman, Catherine's mother had taught school in the Great Smoky Mountains of eastern Tennessee. Her experiences became the basis for Catherine's book *Christy*, which sold more than eight million copies. Other books followed.

In spite of success and the busyness of raising her son, Catherine was lonely. Suitors pursued the eligible young widow, but it was Len LeSourd, a *Guideposts* editor with three young children, who captured her heart.

As Catherine tackled the job of blending two families into one, rejection by Len's children was just one problem she faced. Seeking solutions, Catherine and Len agreed to attack their difficulties using God's weapon of prayer. All their prayers weren't answered as they desired, yet answers eventually came. Again, Catherine experienced goodness and mercy.

When two grandchildren—Peter John's children—died shortly after birth, Catherine asked, "Is God in everything?" When she looked for answers in the long shadows of life, she found comfort.

With her faith firmly in God, Catherine Marshall trusted Him in life's good times and the difficult places. In every instance, she experienced goodness and mercy. We, too, will sense the Lord beside us at every bend in the road if we keep our faith anchored firmly in Christ.

DOROTHY SAYERS

Novelist, Playwright (1893–1957)

"Love the Lord with all your heart and with all your soul and with all your strength and with all your mind."
LUKE 10:27 NIV

Dorothy Sayers felt a responsibility to use her talents to influence as many people for Christ as she could. Witty and outspoken, she did this in a variety of ways.

Her father, a minister, surrounded his daughter with good books—and in a loving home, Dorothy became a Christian. Later she declared it made more sense to be a believer in Christ than a heretic.

After graduating from Oxford University, Dorothy became friends with C. S. Lewis, J. R. R. Tolkien, and other Christian writers. When she wrote and published sixteen detective novels, she achieved celebrity status in England.

She did a series of radio plays of the life of Christ entitled *The Man Born to Be King*. Her book *The Mind of the Maker* is considered her best work and expresses biblical truth in a unique way. Dorothy also made a translation of Dante's *Divine Comedy*.

Working passionately, Dorothy used her talents to their full potential to allow the light of Christ to shine in a dark world. Our passion determines what we do and how we do it. As we are passionate for Christ, we'll use our gifts, laboring for His cause and for others who do not know Him.

LAURA INGALLS WILDER

Author (1867–1957)

For the word of God is full of living power.
It is sharper than the sharpest knife,
cutting deep into our innermost thoughts and desires.
It exposes us for what we really are.
HEBREWS 4:12 NLT

The winter of 1880–81 was severe for the community of De Smet in Dakota Territory. The little town experienced a blizzard almost every day until snow reached the roofs of the houses, and food and fuel supplies ran dangerously low. As the winds raged, thirteen-year-old Laura Ingalls read her Bible and memorized scripture verses. This was not a new activity for Laura. When the family lived in Minnesota, she had memorized one hundred verses to win a competition in a Methodist church. These verses became the sustaining force for Laura as she faced other "storms" of life.

The Ingalls family had experienced troubles of all kinds during Laura's growing-up years. In Minnesota, a plague of grasshoppers came through and devoured their crops. It was repeated the next year. To supplement the family income, Laura, at age twelve, took a job caring for an ill neighbor. Away from home, she became homesick. As she prayed, she felt a "hovering Presence, a Power comforting and sustaining."

Laura's sister Mary became blind as a result of scarlet fever. To help pay Mary's tuition to an Iowa school for the blind, Laura, at fifteen, took a job teaching school.

Even after Laura married Almanzo Wilder, the couple's life was a round of disappointments. Their second child died soon after birth. The house Almanzo had built burned to the ground. Hard times struck again when Laura and her husband became ill with diphtheria, from which Almanzo never regained his strength.

When the family moved to the milder climate of Missouri for Almanzo's health, money was scarce. Laura raised chickens and wrote a column for the local newspaper to make ends meet.

Laura never intended to become a noted author. She was concerned that the way of life she had known on the American frontier would be forgotten, and in an effort to preserve it, she began writing stories of her youth. When Laura was sixty-five years old, her first book, *Little House in the Big Woods*, was published.

Where did Laura receive strength to overcome the years of adversity? How do we survive the cruel twists of fate that often come our way? The Bible verses Laura had learned as a child gave her courage and strength during the hard times. God's Word is full of living power! As we read its promises and trust in God, we, too, will come through on the other side of adversity into overcoming victory.

MARY ANN PATON

Missionary (1840–59)

"Blessed are the dead who die in the Lord. . . .
They will rest from their labor, for their deeds will follow them."
REVELATION 14:13 NIV

Some people are highly influential during their lifetimes. Others wield the greatest influence after their death. This is the case with Mary Ann Paton, who died at age nineteen.

Fourteen days after their wedding in 1858, Mary Ann and John Paton sailed from Scotland for missionary work in the South Pacific. What they found on the island of Tanna shocked them. The "painted savages," most of them nude, were untouched by civilization. Fierce tribes struggled for control of the island. After killing their victims, they cooked their bodies and ate them. In this harsh land, Mary Ann gathered eight women to instruct in Christian teaching. Three months after arriving, Mary Ann gave birth to a son. She then contracted a tropical fever and soon died.

After Mary Ann's death, missionaries on the island passed a resolution that read: "Her earnest Christian character, her devoted missionary spirit, her excellent education. . .excited expectation of great future usefulness."

Mary Ann Paton's brief life echoes down through the eons of time, reminding us that it is not so important how long we live, but that in the time we are given, by faithfulness, goodness, and love, our lives produce fruit that lasts forever.

ELISABETH ELLIOT

Missionary, Author (1926–)

*"You will receive power when the Holy Spirit comes on you;
and you will be my witnesses in Jerusalem, and in all Judea
and Samaria, and to the ends of the earth."*
ACTS 1:8 NIV

In January 1956, Elisabeth Elliot's husband, with four other missionaries, was speared to death in the Amazon jungle. The killers, from a tribe deep in the rain forest of Ecuador, were the Auca Indians, who avoided contact with white men and other Indian tribes.

Elisabeth Howard had grown up in a mission-minded family. She read missionary biographies and attended services in which missionaries showed slides of their work. From these mission workers, Elisabeth learned of the hardships of their work. She also had a good ear for languages—and when she heard there were more than two thousand language groups in the world without the Bible in their tongue, she thought she might help decrease that number.

While at Wheaton College, Elisabeth felt a definite call to Bible translation work. Jim Elliot, a fellow student, also felt called to the mission field.

After graduation, Elisabeth attended the Summer Institute of Linguistics under Wycliffe Bible Translators. She continued to correspond with Jim after they both went to work in different areas as translators to Ecuador's Quichua Indians. In January 1953, they married. Their daughter, Valarie, was born in 1955.

While working with the Quichuas, Jim—with Nate Saint, Pete Fleming, Roger Youderian, and Edward McCully—attempted to make contact with the Auca Indians. Flying over the jungle settlements, the men dropped gifts from the plane as a show of friendliness. On January 8, they landed their Piper by the Curarey River and met two Auca men and a woman. The missionaries were promptly speared to death.

Shock waves rippled around the world when the deaths were reported. Elisabeth and the other wives clung to each other for comfort. For Elisabeth, this was not a tragedy. She said, "God has a plan and purpose in all things." Jim had loved the Aucas, and Elisabeth's love for them intensified after her husband's death. There was no doubt in her mind what she would do: she was called to be a witness.

Shortly after the spearing, Elisabeth, her three-year-old daughter, Valarie, and Rachel Saint, the sister of Nate Saint, who also was killed, made plans to go to the Aucas—now known as Huaorani. They lived with them and attempted to reduce their language to writing in order to translate the Bible into their language.

If a language is to be reduced to writing, the translator must first find an informant—someone who knows the language and is willing to help. As Elisabeth prayed for such a person, two Auca women appeared at the mission station. They invited Elisabeth and Rachel Saint to live with them.

Moving deep into the Amazon jungle, the women went to a remote Auca village with no modern conveniences. They lived in a hut with only a roof to protect them from torrential tropical rains and, for the most part, ate what the villagers ate. They swam and fished with the Aucas. Elisabeth struggled to reach across the communication barrier, while Valarie quickly learned the language.

Elisabeth lived with the Aucas for two years, perfecting her language skills. Wycliffe Bible Translators then became involved, and nine years after the slaying of the five missionaries, the Gospel of Mark was printed in the Auca language.

Elisabeth and Valarie returned to the Quichua work and remained there until 1963, when they came to the United States. In the ensuing years, Elisabeth wrote more than twenty books. She also served as a stylist consultant for the New International Version of the Bible committee, and today she is in demand as a speaker.

Power to go, power to tell. For more than fifty years Elisabeth received power to go and tell. She told the most primitive Indian tribes of the Amazon jungle. With her superb writing skills, she told the world's enlightened population. The command to "go" is to all believers, even you and me. Changing lives is also our goal.

MONICA

Mother of Augustine (331–87)

Pray at all times and on every occasion in the power of the Holy Spirit.
Stay alert and be persistent in your prayers
for all Christians everywhere.
EPHESIANS 6:18 NLT

Is prayer an effective way to change a wayward heart? Monica, a Christian mother, prayed year after year for her prodigal son—and her prayers were eventually answered when God touched Augustine's heart and, through him, the entire world.

Before her son was born, Monica consecrated him to God's work. She warned young Augustine of the evils of the age, but he paid no attention. At sixteen, he was a thief and deceiver. In his teens, he took a mistress and had a child with her. Augustine later wrote he "walked the streets of Babylon in moral filth." Monica consulted with a bishop who advised her to "only pray God for him."

One day, Augustine heard a voice repeatedly say, "Take it, read it!" He took this to mean the book of Romans. When he read Paul's admonition to make no provision for the flesh, Augustine believed. A changed man, he became a leader in the church, and his writings profoundly influenced later Protestant reformers.

Persistent, continued prayer is a tool every believer can use to change the heart of one person, a family, a community—the entire world. Pray on!

GLORIA GAITHER

Musician, Songwriter, Author (1942–)

Worship the LORD with gladness;
come before him with joyful songs.
PSALM 100:2 NIV

Gloria Gaither has written lyrics for more than six hundred songs, many of which have become Gospel classics. With the Gaither Trio, she has recorded more than sixty albums. She is the lyricist of twenty songs that received the Gospel Music Association's Dove Award, and the author of twelve books and a dozen musicals. Six universities have awarded her honorary doctorate degrees. Yet Gloria and her husband, Bill, claim to be "just plain folks."

As a preacher's daughter growing up in Michigan, Gloria Sickal wanted to be involved in Christian ministry. She attended Anderson College in Indiana and majored in French and sociology with plans to go to Africa as a missionary.

When Gloria was a junior in college, she met Bill Gaither, an English teacher. As they dated, he talked about the Gospel songs he'd written, and she showed him her poetry. After their marriage, they became soul mates, working together to compose songs. Soon their music opened doors for concerts and recordings. Much credit for the popularity of Gospel music today goes to Gloria and Bill as a result of their Homecoming concerts and videos.

Where does Gloria get the ideas for her songs? Many come from life experiences. In the 1960s, with two young children, Gloria became pregnant with a third child. The "God is dead" theory was rampant at that time, and she wondered if it was wise to bring children into such a world. Noting their doubts and problems, a friend prayed with Gloria and Bill, and hope revived. After the birth of a healthy child, the lyrics to "Because He Lives" flowed from Gloria's grateful heart.

A student of literature and a lover of words, ideas for songs come to Gloria from a phrase of a sermon, a line in a prayer, or a thought in a scripture verse. Her book *We Have This Moment* is based on years of personal journaling.

In the 1980s, the Gaithers began a television show—*The Gaither Gospel*

Hour—which includes a touring schedule. Sometime later came *Homecoming*, a magazine that includes information about concerts and videos and stories about the musicians.

In spite of success in Gospel music, Gloria believes relationships with family, friends, and her Lord are more important than fame. She freely gives her time, love, and attention to their three children, six grandchildren, and Jesus, her Savior, through prayer and Bible reading.

The psalms encourage us to sing joyful songs. Gloria Gaither's lyrics help us to do just that, and future generations will be inspired to sing joyfully because she poured out her soul in heartfelt, inspiring verses.

EVANGELINE BOOTH

First Female General of the Salvation Army
(1865–1950)

Whatever your hand finds to do, do it with all your might.
ECCLESIASTES 9:10 NIV

From childhood, Evangeline Booth's parents taught her to serve God and others fervently. As a young woman, she worked in the slums of London. A many-talented person, she played the harp and wrote hymns. At age thirty-one, she became commander of the Salvation Army in Canada and Newfoundland. She led the United States Salvation Army for thirty years, and in 1934 she became the Army's first female general. Her father, William Booth, rightfully described his daughter when he said, "The best men in the Army are the women."

During World War I, the public's respect for the Army soared when Evangeline sent officers to France to support the troops. Her "Doughnut Girls" brought the Salvation Army worldwide fame as female officers fried and served doughnuts to soldiers close to the front. Returning veterans praised their efforts. When disasters, earthquakes, famines, and fires occurred, Evangeline quickly sent food and relief. Because of her humanitarian efforts, President Woodrow Wilson bestowed upon her the Distinguished Service Medal.

Evangeline burned brightly for others, making a difference in the world. Like her, we can develop and use our talents for the good of humankind. The world will be a better place when we do.

HARRIET BEECHER STOWE

Author, Hymn Writer (1811–96)

Righteousness exalts a nation, but sin is a disgrace to any people.
PROVERBS 14:34 NIV

In 1793, the American Congress passed the Fugitive Slave Act, which said fugitive slaves had to be returned to their owners. As slavery issues became heated in the mid-1800s, the Fugitive Slave Law of 1850 was passed, and anyone feeding or sheltering a slave was fined a thousand dollars. All over the North, law officers looked for and were paid bonuses for finding runaways—sometimes based only on unsubstantiated claims of ownership. As a result, even free black people living in the North were sometimes captured by slave hunters and shipped south in chains.

The law infuriated many Northern people, especially those who wanted slavery abolished. The most unlikely person to do anything about the unfair law was a woman. Yet that is exactly whom God chose to call attention to the sordid injustices of slavery.

In 1850, Harriet received a letter from her sister-in-law Isabella, who told Harriet she should write something to call attention to the law. That day, the mother of six vowed, "I will write something. I will—if I live." Yet for months Harriet's mind was blank. One day while sitting in church, a vision formed in her mind. She saw an old slave named Tom asking God to forgive his tormentors as he was being whipped. Harriet accepted the vision as from God. She hurried home and scribbled words on scraps of paper. She later said the Lord wrote the book and she merely transcribed His words. *Uncle Tom's Cabin*, a novel uncovering the horrors of slavery, first appeared as a magazine serial. In 1852, it was published as a novel—and in one week, the book sold ten thousand copies. It was later translated into seventeen languages.

Harriet Beecher was one of nine children born into a distinguished clergyman's family in Connecticut. When she was four, her mother died and Catherine, an older sister, took over the household. At an early age, Harriet memorized more than twenty-five hymns and long passages from the Bible. When she was twelve, she committed her life to Christ during a church service.

As a young woman, Harriet taught in a seminary for females operated by Catherine. When her father became president of a theological seminary, Harriet and her family moved to Cincinnati, Ohio. Across the river in Kentucky, slavery was legal—and for the first time, Harriet saw the effects of the slave system. There she married Calvin Stowe, a professor in the school and an outspoken opponent of slavery.

As the seminary enrollment decreased, Calvin was paid little and the family was besieged by poverty. To supplement their pitiful income, Harriet took in boarders and, at one time, started a small school. Harriet also wrote and sold her work to help support her family, which, by 1847, included five children with another child on the way. Later she wrote dramatic serials for a magazine.

Uncle Tom's Cabin gained Harriet fame and provided opportunities for her and Calvin to speak at antislavery rallies. Harriet prayed her book would also heal the differences of America's North and South. Instead, it helped fan the strife between the two sections and culminated in the Civil War. When President Abraham Lincoln met Harriet in 1862, he said, "So this is the little lady who made this big war."

The Civil War touched Harriet deeply when her son, Fred, was wounded. He also suffered from alcoholism and later moved west. His family never heard from him again.

God is concerned that all people are treated justly. Harriet Beecher Stowe's book, America's first protest novel, called attention to the horrible injustice of one man owning another and helped abolish slavery from America's soil. Other unjust practices continue in our world. These, too, need to be highlighted. We can do this in a variety of ways: by voting for fair laws, speaking out against society's evil practices, and even with our pens. Like Harriet Beecher Stowe, we can do our part to see that all men and women are treated with dignity and fairness.

CATHERINE OF SIENA

Reformer (1347–80)

"Love the Lord your God with all your heart
and with all your soul and with all your mind."
MATTHEW 22:37 NIV

Catherine was the twenty-fifth child born into a Christian family in Italy. As her family gathered every evening for prayer, she developed an intense love for Jesus. At age six, she received a vision of Christ.

When she told her parents she must spend time alone with God, they made a small room for her where she fasted and prayed. During her teen years, her parents encouraged her to marry, but she vowed to dedicate her life to God. She spent three years in seclusion, and at age sixteen, she was ready to begin her mission to serve people.

Catherine visited prisons and comforted criminals at their executions. When the Black Death swept through Siena, killing hundreds, she nursed the sick.

This was a time of unparalleled corruption in the church, and Catherine dared to confront queens, kings, and popes with the truth of God. Her message: There are two realms—one of darkness, the other of light. She urged leaders to choose light. Yet Catherine's call to purity was for the most part ignored.

As we read the Bible, one command stands out: Love God with your entire being. Catherine heeded this admonition. We also do well to make love for God our aim.

HELEN STEINER RICE

Poet (1900–81)

"Don't be afraid of what you are about to suffer. . . .
Remain faithful even when facing death,
and I will give you the crown of life."
REVELATION 2:10 NLT

Helen Steiner Rice believed much of life consists in carrying crosses, and she had many to bear. She also asserted a Christian's cross eventually leads to a crown.

When Helen Steiner was sixteen, her father, whom she adored, died in the 1918 flu epidemic. With this loss, Helen's plans to attend college were dashed. To help support her family, she took a job making lampshades. This led to work as an advertising manager for a company where Helen met Franklin Rice, a wealthy banker. In 1929, they married, and the couple enjoyed lavish homes, luxury cars, and servants. This ended with the stock market crash later that year when Franklin lost his money—and in 1932, he took his life. After Helen paid the family's debts, she had little left.

Helen took a job writing greeting cards for Gibson Art Company. She soon became the editor of the company and stayed at this post for forty-two years. During this time she wrote thousands of poems. Her books of poetry eventually sold nearly seven million copies.

When Helen wrote a line of Christmas cards that expressed deep spiritual insights, her fame as a greeting card writer soared. And when she combined her poem "The Praying Hands" with Albrecht Dürer's drawing *Praying Hands*, it became the most popular greeting card ever issued.

In 1960, Helen's poem "The Priceless Gift of Christmas" was read on a national television show, and her dream to share the true message of Christ's birth was realized when thousands of listeners wrote asking for a copy of the poem.

Helen's first book, *Just for You*, published in 1967, launched her to international fame. Other books followed. All her books express Helen's deep devotion to Christ. She said, "I believe in miracles. I believe in prayer. I know God is the answer to everything."

As Helen's greeting cards and books became popular, letters came to her from all parts of the world, and the writers often shared their problems. Helen advised one depressed person to read the Twenty-Third Psalm very slowly with deep meditation. Helen said, "You can heal your body and mind and heart with this psalm."

Crosses too heavy to bear. Most people experience heartbreaking crosses during their lifetimes. A verse from Helen's poem "Let Not Your Heart Be Troubled" gives "cross bearers" good advice.

> *Whenever I am troubled*
> *And lost in deep despair,*
> *I bundle all my troubles up*
> *And go to God in prayer.*

With prayer and faith in God, our crosses lead to crowns.

CHRISTINA GEORGINA ROSSETTI

Poet, Hymn Writer (1830–94)

> *There is only one God and one Mediator*
> *who can reconcile God and people.*
> *He is the man Christ Jesus.*
> 1 TIMOTHY 2:5 NLT

Christina Rossetti wrote more than nine hundred poems in English and six hundred in Italian, as well as three books of poetry, four books of devotions, and six hymns. She has been called one of the greatest English female poets of all time. Also a devout Christian, Christina poured her deep faith into her writings.

Christina was raised by godly parents. Her mother read to the children from the Bible and *Pilgrim's Progress*. Her father, a poet and university professor, died suddenly—and the family was stricken with sorrow and, eventually, poverty. At age fourteen, Christina's faith was further tested when she suffered a nervous breakdown.

She was engaged to marry on two occasions, but Christina didn't go through with either wedding for what she called "religious reasons." Instead, she focused on writing devotional material and children's poetry. Christina's devotion to Christ is reflected in her poem "None Other Lamb":

None other Lamb, none other name,
None other hope in heaven or earth or sea,
None other hiding-place from guilt and shame,
None beside Thee.

Christina's poem assures us that there is only one bridge across life's inevitable heartaches. There is only one way to God's peace—through Jesus, the Lamb of God.

AMY CARMICHAEL

Missionary, Author (1867–1951)

Jesus said, "Let the children come to me. Don't stop them!
For the Kingdom of Heaven belongs to such as these."
And he put his hands on their heads and blessed them.
MATTHEW 19:14–15 NLT

As Amy Carmichael grew up in Ireland, she enjoyed a loving relationship with her Christian mother. From her, Amy also learned effective mothering skills, which she would use when she became a "mother" to India's children.

One cold day as young Amy and her brother walked home from church, they noticed an outcast woman shuffling along the road carrying a heavy burden. The two siblings rushed to aid the woman. As the wind blew the woman's rags, the three passed a stone fountain and a voice spoke to Amy. "Gold, silver, precious stones, wood, hay, stubble. . .fire shall try every man's work of what sort it is."

Amy turned to see who had spoken. No one was there, but the incident spoke to her: she was to turn from worthless things—wood, hay, and stubble— and minister God's love to outcasts.

As a young woman, Amy taught Bible studies for "shawlies"—women working in factories who wore shawls because they couldn't afford hats. Energetic and well organized, Amy's studies eventually attracted hundreds of women.

It was a time of intense missionary fervor in Great Britain. Missionary David Livingstone's exploits in Africa were recounted in churches. Amy became acquainted with notable Christians, including missionary Hudson Taylor. When she asked God what she should do, she again heard a voice. This time it said, "Go ye."

A mission society accepted Amy, and she sailed for Japan. After a year, she became ill and transferred to Ceylon where the climate better suited her. Within a year, Amy, sick with a serious fever, returned to Ireland.

In 1895, she went as a missionary to South India. Immediately she contracted dengue fever. Amy wrote home asking for prayer as she struggled to learn the Tamil language. When her health improved and she could converse in Tamil, she, with others, traveled for seven years to small villages evangelizing women. Her motto: "Love through me, Love of God."

Hinduism, the religion of much of India, practiced temple slavery of children. Poor parents sold their boys and girls to priests for prostitution. When a slave girl named Preena fled the temple, her hands branded as punishment from previous escapes, she came to Amy. Three months after Preena's arrival, four more children appeared at Amy's door. Gradually, she realized her mission was to rescue India's children and provide a Christian home for them. Using the skills she had learned from her mother, Amy began Dohnavur Fellowship. She said of the Fellowship, "We are not an institution. We are a family."

Not everyone was happy with her rescue efforts. Her supporters said she wasn't a real missionary, only a babysitter. Others said Amy could not hope to change a centuries-old tradition such as temple prostitution. Indian authorities accused her of kidnapping, and her life was threatened. Yet to save the children became a "fire in her bones."

As Dohnavur grew, there was not enough money to provide for the children, but Amy refused to beg for funds. She simply presented the needs to God. Workers, too, were scarce—and in 1904, Amy's mother came to help her daughter.

When cholera struck a nearby village, Amy and others helped nurse the village people; yet the plague did not touch the children at Dohnavur. Other times, epidemics raged through the cottages and Amy kissed the children as they died in her arms.

A mission society asked Amy to write a book about her experiences in India. But when she wrote *Things as They Are*, the society rejected the manuscript, saying it was too dismal. Amy's friends learned of the book and had it published. In all, she authored forty books.

At age sixty-four, Amy experienced a fall and remained disabled the rest of her life. During her fifty-five years in India, she never took a furlough.

While child prostitution is now illegal in India, the world's children continue to be targeted by evil people. In some way, reach out to a child. Pray for children. Place your hands on them.

EUGENIA PRICE

Author (1916–96)

"My sheep recognize my voice;
I know them, and they follow me."
JOHN 10:27 NLT

Eugenia Price didn't become a Christian to escape hell or to assure herself a place in heaven. She said, "I was captivated by the One who holds 'captivity captive.' " After her conversion, she confessed, "I am His and He is mine! That is my theology. It is very simple and I have discovered. . .that it works."

Eugenia was born into a privileged family in West Virginia. In college, she studied journalism and soon was writing scripts for radio. She moved to Chicago and, from a childhood friend, Eugenia heard about being born again. Captivated by cigarettes, drugs, and drink, she resisted the salvation message. In 1949, she gave heed to Christ's voice, became a believer, and began writing scripts for *Unshackled*, a Christian radio program.

Later God led Eugenia to move to Georgia, where she wrote Christian historical novels of the area. She eventually wrote fourteen novels and twenty-six nonfiction titles. Her books repeatedly made the *New York Times* bestseller lists and sold more than fifty million copies in eighteen languages. It happened as she listened to the voice of her Shepherd.

Jesus compares His relationship to the believer as that of a shepherd to his sheep. The Shepherd calls to His sheep. Our challenge is to listen, obey, and follow our Lord.

MARY KAY ASH

Christian Businesswoman, Author (1918–2001)

"Well done, my good and faithful servant.
You have been faithful in handling this small amount,
so now I will give you many more responsibilities.
Let's celebrate together!"
MATTHEW 25:21 NLT

She has been called one of the greatest female entrepreneurs in American history, but Mary Kay didn't set out to be the "greatest." She wanted to help women like herself succeed in the business world, and she accomplished her goal by employing the Golden Rule—"Do unto others as you would have them do unto you."

She said, "I can say unequivocally that every decision we make at Mary Kay is based on the Golden Rule."

While growing up in Texas during the Great Depression, her mother often told her, "Mary Kay, you can do it!" This "can-do" attitude stuck. In spite of a failed marriage and having three children to support, Mary Kay made plans to become a doctor. Taking an aptitude test, she learned she had a gift for sales. In 1963, after a successful career in direct sales, Mary Kay decided to write a book to help other women in business. She compiled a list of positive points she had observed in companies and another list featuring ways to improve these businesses. When she read the list, Mary Kay realized she had created her own marketing plan. With her savings of five thousand dollars and the help of her son Richard, she created Mary Kay Cosmetics. Her philosophy for the new company was God first, family second, and career third.

After achieving success, Mary Kay was often asked to autograph dollar bills. Beside her name, she'd write Matthew 25:14–30, the parable of the talents. She said, "I really believe that we are meant to use and increase whatever God has given us. The scripture tells us that when we do, we shall be given more."

Mary Kay received the Horatio Alger Distinguished American Citizen Award in 1978—and in 1985, she was named one of "America's 25 Most Influential Women" in *The World Almanac and Book of Facts*. In 1996, Mary Kay Cosmetics was highlighted in the book *Forbes Greatest Business Stories of All Times*.

As great as Mary Kay's achievements were, perhaps her greatest achievement was encouraging women to believe in themselves and use their talents to improve their lives. A dynamic Christian, she praised her employees and inspired them with these words: "Expect great things and great things will happen. . . . Expect a miracle every day."

God has given every person talents, and He challenges us to invest them wisely. When we use what we have, as Mary Kay did, God can then bless us with much more.

ANNA BARTLETT WARNER

Hymn Writer, Author (1827–1915)

"If anyone gives even a cup of cold water to one of these little ones because he is my disciple. . .he will certainly not lose his reward."
MATTHEW 10:42 NIV

A boy gave his lunch to Jesus, and that simple act fed five thousand people (see John 6:9). Anna Warner took a simple, well-known Bible truth and wrote the poem "Jesus Loves Me." The verses, when combined with music, have touched children and adults in every country of the world for 150 years and remain the most popular hymn of all time.

Anna and her sister lived near West Point Military Academy; and for more than fifty years, they conducted a Sunday Bible class for cadets. Both sisters became successful novelists. However, Anna preferred writing hymns. In 1858, she wrote her famous song.

When China was closed under Communism, the world heard little from Chinese Christians. In 1972, a letter came through with this line: "The 'this I know' people are well." The message passed through censors, but Christians understood the meaning.

Most of us pass through life doing simple things. We teach a child, feed a hungry person, or care for an ill family member. These deeds done as unto Christ are promised a rich reward. And God may use our kindness, as He did Anna Warner's song, to feed a multitude.

CATHERINE BOOTH

Cofounder of the Salvation Army, Author, Evangelist (1829–90)

In all these things we are more than conquerors through him who loved us.
ROMANS 8:37 NIV

In Victorian England women rarely raised their voices in public and almost never preached in churches, but Catherine Booth changed that custom. Her fame as an evangelist endured for thirty years and forever altered women's roles in ministry.

Because she was a sickly child, most of Catherine Mumford's early education was done at home. Her mother, fearing worldly influences, considered the Bible and *Pilgrim's Progress* the only acceptable reading for her daughter. By the time

Catherine was twelve, she had read the Bible through several times.

She said her "heart always yearned after God." However, at sixteen, Catherine experienced "a great controversy of soul" and subsequently received assurance of her salvation after reading Charles Wesley's hymn "My God, I Am Thine."

Because her father was an alcoholic, Catherine took a firm stand against alcohol. At a temperance meeting, she met young evangelist William Booth—and he made the mistake of saying he didn't believe in total abstinence from alcohol. Catherine politely attacked that idea. Later, through her influence, the Salvation Army took a firm stand against alcohol consumption.

The Booths married in 1855. In the early years of their marriage, Catherine occasionally filled the pulpit. But on Pentecost Sunday in 1860, she rose from her seat in London's crowded Bethesda Chapel and joined her husband on the platform, telling him she wanted to say a word. A surprised William Booth turned the pulpit over to his wife, and Catherine confessed that, while she proclaimed a woman's right to preach, she had never been willing to preach the Gospel. Now she was willing to be "a fool for Christ."

Five years after the birth of their fourth child, she began preaching revival meetings. With the establishment of the Salvation Army, women shared equally with men as preachers and leaders.

Catherine's appearance in the pulpit was described by an observer: "Nothing could be neater, a plain black straw bonnet. . .a black loose jacket. . .and a black silk dress." Her preaching style was said to be a "calm and precise delivery."

As Catherine's family grew, so did her popularity as an evangelist. She soon filled large halls and made converts wherever she preached. A month after recovering from the birth of her sixth child, she was preaching again. In some places, there were not halls large enough to hold the crowds, and dozens of people stood outside.

Clergymen of the day regularly attacked "female ranting" in the pulpit. In reply, Catherine wrote *Female Ministry: Woman's Right to Preach the Gospel*, a pamphlet denying the charge that female ministry was forbidden in the Bible.

When Catherine and William established the Salvation Army in 1878, she designed the army flag, inscribed with the words "Blood and Fire." She also fashioned the "Hallelujah" bonnet for female soldiers.

It was a time of high infant mortality when Catherine had her family. In Britain, one child in three died at or soon after birth. Yet Catherine did not bury one of her eight children. She told them at a young age, "You are not in this world for yourself. You have been sent for others." Seven of her eight children became active in the Army.

Catherine was between meetings when she confessed she had a painful lump on her breast. The diagnosis was cancer. She preached her last sermon on June 21, 1888.

Catherine Booth triumphed over childhood illnesses, helped her husband establish the Salvation Army, bore eight children in eleven years, and faced the "female ministry" dispute of the day. She became a successful evangelist, paving the way for women in the Salvation Army to serve equally with men.

This Army "lassie" never received a rank in the organization. She was simply known as "Mother to an Army." The brass plaque on Catherine Booth's coffin rightfully described her: MORE THAN CONQUEROR.

What an example this heroine of the faith provides for us! As believers in Christ, we will also face persecutions, illnesses, and death. The Bible assures us, however, that like Catherine Booth, we will overcome. Surrounded by Jesus' love and with His courage, we are more than conquerors.

TERESA OF AVILA

Reformer, Mystic (1515–82)

I want to know Christ and the power of his resurrection
and the fellowship of sharing his sufferings,
becoming like him in his death.
PHILIPPIANS 3:10 NIV

As Teresa, a sixteenth-century Carmelite nun, sought God in prayer, she became more aware of errors in the church—and starting with her order, she sought to bring reform to the entire Christian world of that time.

Teresa was raised in a Christian home in Spain. Influenced by her father, who studied religious books, she became interested in spiritual matters. When her mother died, Teresa's father placed her in a convent. At age twenty, she took vows as a nun. A short time later, she became seriously ill. When restored to health, Teresa said her healing was miraculous.

Teresa lived an austere life, sleeping on straw, eating no meat, and wearing coarse garments. She held herself to a strict standard for Christian conduct and was known to punish herself for small infractions. This changed when she read Augustine's *Confessions*, and as he had heard God's voice, Teresa claimed the Lord also spoke to her.

While Teresa didn't seek ecstatic experiences as she sought God in prayer, she received visions and raptures, which she recorded in a journal. When she shared the mystical happenings with friends, they criticized and shunned her, claiming she was demon possessed.

Teresa wrote five books. In *Interior Castle*, she described the progress of a soul toward union with God. She said prayer is "a friendly conversation with One who loves us," and stated there are four stages of spiritual meditation.

First, one must quiet the inner self. Second, a seeker becomes one with God by concentrating on His will. Third comes the repose or joy of the soul. Fourth, Teresa claimed the person experiences his soul's union with God, which she called a spiritual marriage. She wrote much on "mental prayer," which she described as taking time to frequently commune with God.

When Teresa was in her forties, she received a vision of the crucified Christ and became concerned for the spiritual state of the nuns in the Carmelite order, encouraging them to put God first and depend on Him for all their needs. She acknowledged abuses and coldness in the church, and she was a leader in the Counter-Reformation. Church authorities, threatened by her ministry, strongly opposed Teresa and called her a restless gadabout. When the pope investigated Teresa's activities, he ruled in her favor.

Through prayer and study, Teresa enjoyed an intimate relationship with God—and He revealed His glory to her. We can know God and enjoy His presence. This deep friendship comes as we commune with Him day after day.

MARY SLESSOR

Missionary (1848–1915)

Pray about everything.
Tell God what you need, and thank him for all he has done.
If you do this, you will experience God's peace.
PHILIPPIANS 4:6–7 NLT

Most Europeans who stepped foot on Calabar's soil quickly died from disease or violence. Yet for thirty-eight years, missionary Mary Slessor shared the Gospel with the people in this African country. She attributed her survival to prayer— prayer for strength to live with chronic malaria day after day while confronting the spiritual darkness in a land where the Gospel had never before penetrated.

Mary was born in Scotland. As a child, she often cowered in fear when her father returned home in a drunken rage. Her mother, a Christian, worked in a textile mill. At age eleven, Mary began working part-time while attending school. Four years later, she worked ten hours a day at a loom.

Through the efforts of an elderly widow, Mary accepted Christ at a young age. Another bright spot in her life was her church, where she taught a Sunday school class, worked at a mission, and helped in street services where she was exposed to rough street gangs. Although Mary didn't know it, these experiences were preparing her for life in Calabar.

With the death of missionary David Livingstone, waves of missionary fervor swept across Great Britain—and in 1876, with no formal training, twenty-eight-year-old Mary sailed for Africa.

Calabar's swamps, infested with poisonous snakes and alligators, were the breeding ground for deadly fevers. The natives practiced human sacrifice. Twins were considered a curse and swiftly murdered or buried alive. Neighboring tribes often fought and made slaves of their captives or ate them. For centuries, white men had not traveled more than a few miles inland.

Mary was assigned to Duke Town, where she quickly learned the Efik language. She taught, preached, and nursed the sick. Yet she longed to push inland. The mission board, however, thought the move too dangerous for a single woman. Finally, in 1886, she established a mission in Old Town and "went native." She ate what the natives ate and lived in a mud hut infested with roaches, rats, and snakes.

Mary preached, established schools, and acted as a circuit preacher, traveling to remote villages to share the Gospel. Rum was king in Old Town. It was used in trade and given to babies. Often Mary was the only sober person for miles around. When she heard of the birth of twins, she'd walk hours in torrential rains through dense jungles to find the abandoned babies. Soon several children lived under her roof.

In 1888, Mary again pushed inland. At Okoyong, the British government recognized her influence and appointed her vice counsel of the territory. In this capacity, "White Ma," as she was called, acted as a judge in the many disputes between tribes. It was a ludicrous sight: Mary, barefoot, wearing a loose dress, her short red hair flaming, calmly holding court to determine the fate of a native. When the decision was left up to Mary, the person survived. But before she came to this part of Africa, many innocent natives were buried alive or suffered death by flogging for minor crimes.

During one of Mary's furloughs to the coast, she met and fell in love with missionary Charles Morrison. She accepted his proposal of marriage on the condition that he would work with her in Okoyong. When his health failed, making it impossible for him to move inland, Mary broke their engagement. Her call to the work was her priority.

Mary saw little progress in establishing a church and viewed her efforts as preparation for future missionary work. In 1903, she conducted her first baptismal service when she baptized eleven people. Seven were her adopted children.

How did Mary survive the years in Calabar? She later testified that her life was "one daily, hourly record of answered prayer, for physical health, guidance, for errors, dangers, food, and total peace."

How do we survive the rigors of our godless society? Prayer. As prayer was the answer for Mary Slessor, so prayer will help us overcome physical weaknesses, temptations, fears, and evil, all the while keeping us in God's perfect peace.

THEODORA

Christian Empress (508–48)

By me kings reign and rulers make laws that are just;
by me princes govern, and all nobles who rule on earth.
PROVERBS 8:15–16 NIV

Theodora was born in Cyprus. Encouraged by her family, she became an actress, although it was considered an immoral occupation at that time. After she was mistreated and abandoned by the man she lived with, she converted to Christianity. In 525, she married Justinian I. Two years later, he became emperor of the Byzantine Empire.

Theodora successfully reigned with her husband for thirty-eight years. During this time the couple worked to restore Constantinople to its former glory. They rebuilt bridges and aqueducts and erected twenty-five churches. When a rebellion arose to overthrow the empire, Theodora persuaded her husband to defend the city rather than flee. Justinian, filled with new courage, soon crushed the enemy and restored order.

Concerned for women's causes, Theodora instituted the death penalty for rape. She forbade the killing of a wife who had committed adultery and passed laws to outlaw prostitution. With the closing of brothels, she founded a convent where the ex-prostitutes could live.

Because Theodora, a sixth-century empress, knew God, she made laws based on biblical truth. We are commanded to pray for our leaders so they, too, will make laws that uphold God's standard of righteousness and justice.

LOTTIE MOON

Missionary (1840–1912)

I plead with you to give your bodies to God.
Let them be a living and holy sacrifice. . . .
When you think of what he has done for you,
is this too much to ask?
ROMANS 12:1 NLT

As a young girl, Charlotte Digges Moon's interest in missions was stirred as her mother read missionary stories to her. Lottie attended a women's seminary and became one of the first Southern women to obtain a master's degree. When she heard a sermon on the text "Lift up your eyes, and look on the fields; for they are white already to harvest" (John 4:35 KJV), she determined to become a missionary.

In 1873, at age thirty-three, Lottie left plantation life in post–Civil War Virginia bound for China. She quickly learned the language and adopted Chinese dress. After accompanying fellow missionaries to outlying villages, she felt called as an evangelist. Instead, she was assigned to teach in a girls' school, which she considered "a folly and a waste."

Lottie was lonely in China. A Civil War chaplain had proposed marriage, but because he accepted the evolutionary theory of creation, she refused his offer.

A prolific letter writer, Lottie frequently wrote to American church women asking for help. When her pleas were not realized, Lottie purchased books and supplies with her own meager salary. Discouraged because of lack of funds and workers, on one occasion she wrote to the mission board, "I wonder how these things look in heaven. They certainly look very queer in China."

When she first began teaching Chinese women and children, they called her "the Old Devil Woman." As she nursed them through smallpox plagues and protected them in times of revolution, they changed her name to "the Heavenly Book Visitor."

In 1885, Lottie made a treacherous journey to an area where no female missionary had ever been. Alone at Pingtu, she evangelized the area, and soon converts numbered in the hundreds. Four years later, she established a church.

Lottie wrote a letter in 1888 that changed the course of Southern Baptist missions: She asked the women of America to give a special Christmas offering to mission efforts. Thus began the now-famous Lottie Moon Christmas Offering.

Because of a revolution in 1912, the American council advised all missionaries to leave; yet Lottie stayed at her mission. As food became scarce, she gave all she had to Chinese believers. Weak, malnourished, and aided by a nurse, Lottie sailed for America. En route, she died in Japan.

Lottie once said, "I would that I had a thousand lives that I might give them to the women of China." As we ponder Christ's sacrifice on Calvary, total dedication to His cause is also the acceptable response for us to make.

BIBLE TRANSLATION CREDITS

The Top 100 Women of the Bible

The Top 100 Men of the Bible

The Top 100 Miracles of the Bible

The Top 100 Miracles of God

The Top 100 Women of the Christian Faith

NOTES

NOTES

NOTES

NOTES

NOTES

NOTES